A Commentary on
THE GOSPEL OF JOHN

# A Commentary on
# The Gospel of John

Johannes Beutler, SJ

*Translated by*
Michael Tait

WILLIAM B. EERDMANS PUBLISHING COMPANY
GRAND RAPIDS, MICHIGAN

Wm. B. Eerdmans Publishing Co.
4035 Park East Court SE, Grand Rapids, MI 49546
www.eerdmans.com

Originally published in German as *Das Johannesevangelium: Kommentar*
2013 © Verlag Herder GmbH, Freiburg im Breisgau, Germany
English translation © 2017 William B. Eerdmans Publishing Co.
All rights reserved.

Hardcover edition 2017
Paperback edition 2024

ISBN 978-0-8028-8482-4

**Library of Congress Cataloging-in-Publication Data**

Names: Beutler, Johannes, author.
Title: A commentary on the Gospel of John / Johannes Beutler, SJ ; translated by Michael Tait.
Other titles: Johannesevangelium. English
Description: Grand Rapids : Eerdmans Publishing Co., 2017. | Includes bibliographical
    references and index.
Identifiers: LCCN 2017014825 | ISBN 9780802884824 (pbk. : alk. paper)
Subjects: LCSH: Bible. John—Commentaries.
Classification: LCC BS2615.53 .B4813 2017 | DDC 226.5/077—dc23
    LC record available at https://lccn.loc.gov/2017014825

# Contents

*Foreword*, by Francis J. Moloney … ix
*Preface* … xiii
*Abbreviations* … xv

## INTRODUCTION … 1

1. Character … 1
2. Structure … 4
3. Aim … 9
4. Unity and Sources … 13
5. History of Religions Background … 17
6. Author, Time, Place … 21
7. Text … 24
8. Canonicity … 25
9. Contemporary Significance … 26
10. The Present Exegesis … 29

## THE DIVINE WORD ENTERS THE WORLD (1:1–4:54) … 30

1. Prologue (1:1–18) … 31

CONTENTS

  2. The Testimony of the Baptist (1:19–34) .......... 52

  3. The Call of the First Disciples (1:35–51) .......... 62

  4. The First Sign of Jesus in Cana (2:1–12) .......... 74

  5. The First Passover: Cleansing of the Temple (2:13–25) .......... 83

  6. The Dialogue with Nicodemus in Jerusalem (3:1–21) .......... 89

  7. Jesus in Judaea: Further Testimony of the Baptist (3:22–36) .......... 100

  8. Jesus in Samaria (4:1–42) .......... 109

  9. Jesus in Galilee (4:43–45) .......... 128

10. Jesus's Second Sign in Cana of Galilee (4:46–54) .......... 132

## JESUS REVEALS HIMSELF TO HIS PEOPLE (5:1–10:42) .......... 139

  1. Jesus at the Feast of Weeks (5:1–47) .......... 140

  2. The Passover in Galilee (6:1–71) .......... 164

  3. Jesus at the Feast of Tabernacles (7:1–10:21) .......... 198

  4. Jesus at the Feast of the Dedication of the Temple. His Withdrawal over the Jordan (10:22–39, 40–42) .......... 280

## JESUS ON THE WAY TO HIS PASSION (11:1–12:50) .......... 289

  1. The Raising of Lazarus (11:1–46) .......... 290

  2. The Decision to Kill Jesus (11:47–54) .......... 309

  3. The Last Passover (11:55–57) .......... 315

  4. The Anointing of Jesus in Bethany (12:1–11) .......... 316

  5. Jesus's Entry into Jerusalem (12:12–19) .......... 323

  6. The Coming of the Greeks (12:20–36) .......... 328

  7. Look Back on the Activity of Jesus and Final Summons to Faith (12:37–50) .......... 339

## Jesus Bids Farewell (13:1–17:26) — 347

1. The Footwashing (13:1–20) — 349
2. The Identification of Judas and His Exit (13:21–30) — 358
3. Transition to the Farewell Discourses (13:31–38) — 362
4. The First Farewell Discourse (14:1–31) — 368
5. The Second Farewell Discourse (15:1–16:4d) — 392
6. The Third Farewell Discourse (16:4e–33) — 412
7. The Prayer of the Departing Jesus (17:1–26) — 424

## Jesus's "Hour": Passion, Death, and Resurrection (18:1–20:31) — 441

1. The Arrest of Jesus and the Jewish Trial (18:1–27) — 449
2. The Roman Trial of Jesus (18:28–19:16b) — 464
3. Crucifixion, Death, and Burial of Jesus (19:16c–42) — 479
4. The Easter Narrative: Jesus's Appearances to the Disciples (20:1–31) — 496

## Epilogue: Jesus, Peter, and the Beloved Disciple (21:1–25) — 520

*Bibliography* — 547

*Index of Names* — 589

*Index of Primary Sources* — 596

# Foreword

Johannes Beutler has been an important contributor to Johannine studies for almost fifty years. Equally important, he has become a friend and guide to many contemporary European scholars. From Frankfurt am Main and Rome, an impressive *Beutler-Schule* has emerged. Anyone familiar with the past fifty years of Johannine scholarship knows the significant changes in approach that have shaped the interpretation of the Fourth Gospel. Beutler has been a major player in these developments.

Johannine scholars now look back at proposals for radical restructuring and reordering of the text itself, the development of extensive source theories, explorations of influence in the History of Religions, and the application of more literary and reader-response focus upon the drama of the narrative. This commentary presents contemporary interpreters of the Gospel of John a respectful and accurate distillation of all that has emerged across these exciting years. Such contributions are rare. It is not only a quality introduction and commentary to the Gospel of John. A careful reader—devoting attention to the discussions Beutler introduces into his analysis of the text, and the brief and informative accompanying footnotes—will discover a first-hand witness to fifty years of Johannine scholarship.

The concise introductory chapter sets the agenda for the commentary. Beutler devotes most of his attention to matters that impact the interpretation of the text. He also gives attention to the stability of the Johannine text and its acceptance in Scripture. After an overview of speculation about the author, Beutler plausibly suggests that "[f]rom the perspective of a literary-critical treatment of John's Gospel the question of the message is more important than that of its author." Yet, such questions are dealt with adequately, even if summarily, as they should be in a commentary of this nature.

A similar balance can be found in his discussions of the literary structure of the document and its aim. His breadth of awareness of the many possibilities is impressive. Beutler suggests that narrative is structured around a number of journeys, an exegetical decision that situates him with other significant contemporary interpreters in Europe and the USA. Reading the verb "to believe" in John 20:31 as a present subjunctive, he stresses the importance of the narrative as an account of the life of Jesus that calls already believing Christians to greater faith.

He accepts the canonical text as the object of his analysis. Beutler presents the case for such an interpretation, with respectful recognition of other approaches. For example, he fairly presents the conclusions reached by the History of Religions and speculation about Gnostic background, the possibility of tracing other identifiable Christian and Johannine sources, the identification of a number of editorial activities that eventually produced the Gospel in its current form, and the role of the Synoptic tradition in the formation of the Fourth Gospel. Contemporary English-speaking interpreters of John will be grateful for this even-handed treatment of largely European approaches that have dominated the field.

Beutler's analysis of the Johannine text is committed to a reading of the Gospel as a whole, largely structured around the theme of journeys. In 1:1–4:54, the divine Word enters the world. Jesus reveals himself to his people in 5:1–10:42, depending upon the use of the Jewish feasts of Pentecost (5:1 [Beutler's suggestion, as the feast is not named]), Passover (6:4), Tabernacles (7:2), and Dedication (10:22). In 11:1–12:50 Jesus is on the way to his Passion. He bids farewell to his own in 13:1–17:26. In 18:1–20:31 John tells the story of Jesus's "hour": passion, death and resurrection. The original Gospel closed with a statement of its purpose in 20:30–31. John 21:1–25 is regarded as an epilogue, a *relecture* of earlier texts. In John 21 the "Gospel is being updated."

Each section is subdivided into identifiable subunits, an English text is provided, and the commentary follows. The English text claims to be a revision based on the RSV and the NRSV translations. This is an admirable approach. There are many places where important exegetical issues are handled (e.g., singular verbs are rendered plural to be "inclusive," and some Christological possibilities are flattened [e.g., "the Son of Man" sometimes becomes "the human one," and "I am He" becomes "It is I"]).

*Foreword*

One respects the worthy desire of the editors of the NRSV to produce an inclusive text, but the RSV remains more faithful to the original Greek.

The exegesis first situates the passage under consideration within its context and its literary genre is determined, in so far as this is possible. The step-by-step exegesis begins with a synchronic analysis, a reading of the passage without any search for possible sources. Once that is in place, Beutler asks questions about the traditions that have been used to generate the text: Jewish, Christian, or pre-Christian. This approach is especially satisfying. Many significant commentary series (e.g., Word Bible Commentary, Anchor Bible Commentary, and Sacra Pagina) ask the reader to wade through pages of historical-critical "notes" before arriving at any assessment of what the passage means in its Johannine setting. The final step asks questions about the contemporary relevance of texts. Here, Beutler issues a challenge to believe more deeply.

European, and especially German, Johannine scholarship will always dedicate some attention to "sources." Beutler is no exception to that rule. Yet, he is unique in the way he envisions and uses them. Looking back a generation, he accepts the claims of Frans Neirynck and the so-called Leuven school that the Gospel of John manifests a level of dependence upon the Synoptic tradition. There are a number of places where this is important, none more so than his exegesis of John 6:1–71. Beutler regards this as a late addition to the Johannine Gospel, inserted under the influence of Mark 6:33–8:33. The fact that the Passover episode is the only report of a Jewish feast not located in Jerusalem indicates the originality of this later addition.

Beutler's other major interest is to trace passages that can be regarded as a *relecture*, a practice widely used in contemporary German Johannine scholarship (and significantly by Jean Zumstein). He claims that some passages can be seen as a *rereading* of passages that had been formed earlier in the tradition. This is an important element in today's interpretation of the Gospel of John. An older school of thought regarded many similar texts as coming from different traditions. What may have happened, as the story was told and retold, was that earlier texts were reread and rewritten. *Relecture* is not tradition-focused, but text-focused. There are many examples of this: the first discourse of Jesus in 14:1–31 may reappear in 16:4–33 where it repeats while deepening and developing 14:1–31. Beutler joins Zumstein in regarding John 21:1–25 as a *relecture* of earlier passages in the Johannine tradition.

No single voice can offer the final solution to every issue. I wonder

## FOREWORD

about the association of John 1:1–18 with 1:19–4:54 as part of the first "journey." Whatever the history of the traditions (and the practice of *relecture*) that formed 13:1–17:26, this long section of the Gospel (one quarter of its length) deserves close attention as a self-contained unit, with an overall unified literary and theological agenda. Not all "confessions of faith"—so important for Beutler's reading of the Fourth Gospel as a challenge for the reader of today—can be read on their face value. Context determines meaning. For example, Martha's words in John 11:27 do not respond to Jesus's self-revelation in 11:25–26. A few verses later, Martha is complaining that the tomb will have a bad odor, earning herself a rebuke (11:39–40). This needs to be compared with Jesus's response to Mary's subsequent actions and the beautiful odor that flows from them in 12:1–8. I like Beutler's reading of 21:1–25 as an Epilogue (not an "addendum"), perhaps the result of *relecture*. However, there is much in the Gospel of John in need of a narrative resolution that can (at least in part) be found in 21:1–25. I like to regard the final chapter as "a necessary Epilogue." It is more than an "update."

Everyone interested in the Gospel of John—from the student to the pastor to the professional biblical scholar and theologian—has been rendered a great service by the publication of this translation. Uncomplicated, excellently documented, and written with a lightness of touch, Johannes Beutler's commentary on the Gospel of John will provide a wonderful window for all English-only readers. They can now gaze through it into the exciting world of the best of European Johannine scholarship.

FRANCIS J. MOLONEY, SDB, AM, FAHA
*Catholic Theological College*
*University of Divinity*
*Melbourne, Victoria,*
*Australia*

# *Preface*

This commentary goes back to my lectures on John's Gospel at the Pontifical Biblical Institute in Rome in the years 2000 to 2007 before my return to Germany in the same year. These Rome lectures had their predecessors in various teaching sessions in Frankfurt am Main from 1971 on. Thus, here, my life's work on John's Gospel has come together although some of it has already been given expression in various publications. My interest in this Gospel was aroused through my dissertation on the testimony theme in John at the Pontifical Gregorian University in 1972. This appeared in the same year under the title *Martyria*. At that time, I was supposed to be lecturing on Fundamental Theology with the emphasis on the New Testament. The testimony theme in John seemed a suitable way of answering the question about the grounds for faith in Jesus according to the New Testament. Naturally, my work on John's Gospel has subsequently come to stand on its own and to be parted from issues of Fundamental Theology.

Characteristic of the work of the following years and also of the present commentary is the effort to understand John against his Old Testament–Jewish background. I have gradually disengaged myself from hypotheses about the sources for the Fourth Gospel. They have come to be replaced by an interest in the Synoptic Gospels whose importance for John's Gospel I have come to recognize more and more, not least under the influence of the Louvain school of Frans Neirynck. To that should be added what I gained from conversations with Swiss and German colleagues who reckoned the later strata in John's Gospel to be *relecture* of the earlier text. This insight led, among other things, to my suggestion that John 6 should be regarded as just such a *relecture* of its context. Here, among predecessors, we must acknowledge Barnabas Lindars and René Kieffer.

PREFACE

All in all, my work owes a lot to international dialogue, above all in the context of the Studiorum Novi Testamenti Societas (SNTS) to which I have belonged since 1975. I have drawn much profit from its seminars and not only in the academic sense.

My thanks goes first and foremost to Herder Publications for accepting my manuscript and looking after it carefully, closely followed by all those who have accompanied me on my academic journey, from my teachers to my colleagues and pupils but also my family, my order, and my personal friends. To them this volume is dedicated with gratitude.

JOHANNES BEUTLER, SJ
*Frankfurt am Main, June 5, 2013*

*Abbrevations*

Abbreviations of biblical and extrabiblical Jewish-Christian sources, series, periodicals, and standard works follow *The SBL Handbook of Style: For Biblical Studies and Related Disciplines*, 2nd ed. (Atlanta: SBL Press, 2014).

Commentaries on John's Gospel are cited with the names of the authors and page numbers.

# Introduction

## 1. Character

The readers of the Gospel of John enter a new world. From the beginning, they hear a new language. Jesus's announcement of the Kingdom of God gives way to a new conceptual world. The prologue of the Fourth Gospel (John 1:1–18) is already characterized by this change of paradigm. There is talk of the divine Logos that brings light and life, but also of the forces of darkness. There is talk about the truth that Jesus both brings and is, and about the lie that opposes him. In particular, the extended discourses of Jesus in the first half of the Gospel and his controversies with the "Jews" are characterized by this language. So too are the farewell discourses before his passion thus characterized. Even as late as the dialogue with Pilate, Jesus will confess himself as the king who came to bear witness to the truth. This is a tone previously unheard in the Gospels.

Characteristic of John's Gospel is, then, its dualistic language and conceptual world. In contrast to the Synoptic Gospels, this dualism is not temporal but spatial. Jesus comes "from above," his opponents "from below." They are "of this world," he is "not of this world." Jesus brings life and even is the life. Whoever opposes him walks in the darkness. Jesus brings the truth and even is the truth, and his adversary is the "father of lies." The "world" can be the arena for the mission of the Son, but also the symbol of everything that opposes Jesus and his message. The representatives of this "world" appear in John's Gospel as the "Jews" in a particular sense (specifically, indeed, the Jewish authorities in Jerusalem, but, in a larger sense as well, all adherents of the Jewish religion in so far as they refuse to believe in Jesus).

The multiplicity of Jewish groups we encounter in the Synoptic Gospels has given way to a single group—the Pharisees. This may be due to the relatively late date of the Fourth Gospel's composition. After the destruction of Jerusalem and the temple in 70 CE, the Sadducees, the Zealots, and the Essenes lost their importance. The only remaining significant group was that of the Pharisees. It is they who are identified in John's Gospel with the "Jews."

The impression that the Fourth Gospel is for this reason anti-Jewish is, nonetheless, mistaken. Hardly any Gospel has been influenced as strongly by Judaism and its institutions as this one. This is already attested by the very structure of the Gospel. As will be shown later on, the Jewish Feasts of Pilgrimage are structurally important. Between the first Passover of John 2:13 and the last of 11:55, there are: the unnamed feast of 5:1, which can probably be interpreted as Pentecost, Tabernacles of 7:2, and the Feast of Dedication in 10:22. Disregarding for the moment the Passover of 6:4, we can see the whole of Jesus's public life according to John integrated into one annual cycle of Jewish Feasts. Jerusalem and the Temple are the privileged places of Jesus's teaching and activity. Individual places like the Pools of Siloam or Bethesda are named explicitly.

In John, the sequence of events in the life of Jesus does not always correspond to that in the Synoptic Gospels. The Purification of the Temple takes place already on the occasion of Jesus's first visit to Jerusalem on the Feast of the Passover (John 2:13–22). In this way, a dramatic tension is created since, from this moment on, there is a dangerous conflict between Jesus and the Jewish authorities (with a certain parallel in Mark 3:6 where we find the Pharisees and Herodians planning to eliminate Jesus after a healing on the Sabbath).

If Mark deliberately selects from the miraculous deeds of Jesus, this tendency is reinforced in John. The fourth evangelist does not report any exorcism or healing of a leper, and the number of Jesus's miracles is strikingly reduced. The healings that remain are those of the royal officer's son (John 4:46–54), the paralytic (John 5), a man born blind (John 9), and the raising of Lazarus (John 11:1–44). Moreover, these miracles are refracted through a theological lens as "Signs" of Jesus's authority, in part by the extended dialogue scenes and discourses of Jesus that follow the miracle or accompany it. This is also the case in the narrative of the multiplication of the loaves in John 6. The account of the changing of water into wine at the wedding of Cana, which is attested only by John, again calls this miracle a "sign" (John 2:11), even though an interpretive discourse or dialogue is missing. The miraculous catch of fish in John 21:1–14 does not follow this scheme but is, in turn, characterized by symbolic elements.

The Parables of the Kingdom, so characteristic of the Synoptic Gospels, are missing in John, but the author certainly likes metaphorical language. This language serves to illustrate the identity of Jesus, in particular in the so-called "I Am Sayings" typical of John, in which Jesus expresses his significance for the believer ("I am the bread of life," John 6:35; "I am the light of the world," John 8:12). In two passages, we encounter in John a literary genre similar to that of the parable or similitude, the so-called "*Bildrede*" or extended metaphor: the *Bildrede* of the Good Shepherd in John 10:1–5 and that of the True Vine in John 15:1–8. In this figure of speech, which is related to allegory, the metaphorical level and the real level penetrate each other.

Mark begins his Gospel with the activity of John the Baptist. Matthew and Luke begin their accounts much earlier and integrate an account of Jesus's infancy into their Gospels. The fourth evangelist goes a step further and, in his prologue (John 1:1–18), traces Jesus's origin back to his eternal provenance from the Father. Who Jesus is and where he comes from is illustrated not biographically but theologically, and in the form of a hymn at that.

Already in the prologue, we find the characteristic theology of the fourth evangelist as well as its unique expression. The divine Word, Jesus, not only comes from God but is God; that is to say, he is of divine essence. This affirmation frames the prologue of John (John 1:1, 18). Thomas will resume this statement at the end of the Gospel before the additional ch. 21, and will make it his confession of faith and that of John's reading community (John 20:28): "My Lord and my God." In this way, the confession of Jesus's divinity also frames the whole of John's Gospel in its original extent. That Jesus is the Son of God is a key issue in Mark (cf. Mark 1:11; 9:7; 14:61; 15:39), but becomes the leading christological title in John. In addition, Jesus is called "the Son," but also the "Son of Man," the latter again in harmony with the Synoptic Gospels. The attributes of this Johannine "Son of Man" correspond to those of the Isaian Servant of God: he will be "lifted up and glorified" (cf. Isa 52:13 LXX), once his "hour" has come.

With this, Johannine eschatology comes to the fore. In John, there is no discourse on the coming end of the world and the destruction of Jerusalem as in Mark 13 par. For John the end of time will not come at a given moment or even soon but has begun already (perhaps with a view to Synoptic texts such as Matt 12:28; Luke 11:20). In John, this can mean: "The hour is coming and now is," i.e., the hour of the true worshipers in the

Spirit in the end time (John 4:23) and, at the same time, the hour in which the dead will hear the voice of the Son of Man and rise for judgement or salvation (John 5:25). In particular, by locating the final judgement and eternal life in the present, John goes beyond the Synoptics. The passion, death, and resurrection of Jesus are the turning point in history. In Johannine language this is formulated as the "hour" of his "lifting up" on the cross and to the Father. It is from this perspective that the words of Jesus must be understood. In particular, in the Farewell Discourses of Jesus in John 13–17, we hear the voice of the one who has been lifted up. He is no longer visibly present among his own, but will send his representative, the Paraclete, who will lead his disciples into all truth (John 16:13). Thus, after Easter, the community of the disciples lives in the end time and shares in God's eschatological promises.

## 2. Structure

Right up to the present there are varied opinions about the structure of John's Gospel. Indeed, there has been a doubt, particularly in German-speaking research, whether it would ever be possible to find a convincing structure for this Gospel. This skepticism can be observed in Rudolf Schnackenburg's voluminous commentary, among other contributions. The reason for this cautious attitude lies, in part, in the fact that authors like him consider John's Gospel to be the product of a long process of redaction on the basis of various sources, with the consequence that its original shape can hardly be reconstructed any longer.

The great twentieth-century interpreters of John's Gospel structure the work predominantly from a *thematic* point of view. Thus, in his commentary, Rudolf Bultmann divides it into two main parts: "The revelation of the δόξα to the world" (John 2–12) and "The revelation of the δόξα to the community" (John 13–20). Chapter 1, with the prologue, serves as an introduction, while ch. 21 constitutes an epilogue or supplement. Similarly, C. H. Dodd divides the Gospel into chs. 2–12 "The Book of Signs" and chs. 13–20 "The Book of the Passion." In his commentary, Raymond E. Brown modifies Dodd's proposal and calls the second part "The Book of Glory," which is certainly more appropriate. Brown divides the first half of the Gospel into four sections: "The Opening Days of the Revelation of Jesus" (John 1:19–51), "From Cana to Cana" (chs. 2–4), "Jesus and the Principal Feasts of the Jews" (chs. 5–10) and the section in chs. 11–12 that he recognizes as "Jesus moves towards the Hour of Death and Glory." Alongside thematic criteria, topographical, chronological, and liturgical ones are utilized as well.[1]

Other authors see a division of the Gospel according to *dramatic* criteria. For J. Louis Martyn,[2] the "drama" of the conflict between Jesus and those Jews who refuse to believe in him determines the narrative of the Fourth Gospel. Since this conflict pervades the whole of the text, this point of view is of limited use for discovering its structure. Dramatic elements are also important for Mark W. G. Stibbe in his various publications[3] and for Ludger Schenke in his commentary on John. The latter divides the Gospel after the prologue into two main sections: "The activity of Jesus before the disciples as 'descent from heaven'" (John 1:19–12:36) in eight scenes with a first epilogue in John 12:37–50, and: "The activity of Jesus before the disciples as 'ascent/lifting up to heaven'" in John 13:1–20:29 in three scenes with a second epilogue in John 20:30–31, an appendix in John 21:1–24, and the conclusion in John 21:25.[4] Here, the influence of Bultmann can still be observed. However, Schenke complements this point of view with the idea that John's Gospel follows the technique of ancient dramas by being divided into five acts with exposition, repetition and consolidation, climax, peripeteia, and solution.[5] Like Schenke, Hartwig Thyen also structures John's Gospel as a kind of drama, following, to a large extent, his Danish predecessor, Gunnar Østenstad.[6] His proposal to structure the Gospel around acts and scenes appears so strongly influenced by the literary genre of drama that the multiplicity of criteria relevant for the structure of John can no longer be taken into account here. Michael Theobald sees the Fourth Gospel as a "dramatic narrative,"[7] even if he also denies that the drama can be "retrieved from the plan of the book."[8]

George L. Parsenios, whose study represents a considerable body of more recent literature from the United States,[9] is equally interested in

---

1. This approach was taken up and further developed by Moloney in his commentary.
2. Martyn, *History*.
3. Cf. his commentary as also his monograph *John as Storyteller*.
4. Schenke, 17.
5. Schenke, 16; likewise Schenke, *Das Johannesevangelium, Einführung–Text–Dramatische Gestalt*, 219.
6. Østenstad, "Structure."
7. Theobald, 1:14.
8. Theobald, 1:29.
9. Parsenios, *Rhetoric and Drama*; cf. here especially the reference to Brant, *Dialogue and Drama*.

drama as the design element in the Fourth Gospel. According to Parsenios, it is not ancient drama as such that is helpful for a better understanding of John's Gospel but the development of drama in the rhetoric of the Roman Empire.[10]

Proposals to see the structure of John as determined by *chronological* and *liturgical* criteria come closer to the structural signals of the text. Thus, after an "inaugural week" (John 1:19–2:12), Donatien Mollat recognizes, in his commentary in the Jerusalem Bible, the Jewish Principal and Pilgrimage Feasts as key structural components: the first Passover in Jerusalem that Jesus attends (2:13), the unnamed feast of 5:1 (possibly Pentecost), the Passover in Galilee (6:4), Tabernacles (7:2) with the following feast of the Dedication of the Temple (10:22) and the last Passover (11:55; 12:1; 13:1 to 19:42).[11] This proposal is appealing because of its combination of thematic, spatial, and temporal structural elements. We shall return to it later on.

More recently, *topographical* elements have claimed stronger attention in the search for the structure of John. Mathias Rissi distinguishes three journeys of Jesus before his last journey to Jerusalem.[12] These journeys begin in non-Jewish or pagan territory, pass through Galilee, and finally lead to Jerusalem: 1:19–3:36; 4:1–5:47; 6:1–10:39. Jesus's final departure for Jerusalem starts at this point (10:40–12:41), followed by Jesus's farewell 13:1–14:31 (chs. 15–17 have been added) and the Return of the Son to his Father 18:1–20:31 (ch. 21 has been added). At the beginning stands the prologue. This produces a division of John into seven sections, with two three-part sections after the prologue, and the turning point in 10:40.

Jeff Staley takes over from Rissi in particular the proposal that John 10:40 constitutes a turning point (an idea with which Thyen[13] also agrees), only with the modification that, for him, a new section begins in John 11:1 (so too Thyen).[14] Staley sees the idea of the "journey" already forecast in the prologue when it describes the descent and ascent of the Logos. We

---

10. Cf. Brant, *Dialogue and Drama*, 12: "The following monograph argues that the Gospel of John also resonates with the echoes of Athenian tragedy in the Roman Empire. And a key note in the harmony that links John to ancient tragedy is the legal emphasis of both."

11. Mollat, 32–36, 90.

12. Rissi, "Aufbau."

13. Thyen, "Johannes 10," and his commentary; similarly, Labahn, "Bedeutung und Frucht des Todes Jesu," 435, sees John 11–12 as a kind of "lens with a focusing and interpretative tendency."

14. Staley, "Structure."

*Introduction*

are thus able to observe a structure of four journeys: 1:19–3:36; 4:1–6:71; 7:1–10:42 and 11:1–21:25. Jesus's journey in the first half of the Gospel (1:19–10:42) brings him from Bethany (on the Jordan) to Bethany (near Jerusalem) (1:28; 11:1, 18). His most important companion is John the Baptist, first named as such in John 1:28 and last mentioned in 10:41. In what follows, he will be "replaced" by Lazarus whom Jesus "loved" (11:5) and then by the "disciple whom Jesus loved" (for Luc Devillers,[15] the "three witnesses" of Jesus).

Kieffer divides up our Gospel according to Jesus's four journeys, all of which have a common point of departure, namely the region beside or on the other side of the Jordan (or of the Sea of Gennesareth): John 1:19–51; 3:22–36; 6:1–16 and 10:40–42.[16]

In his two contributions, Fernando F. Segovia sees more clearly that Jesus's journeys lead regularly to Jerusalem.[17] Like Rissi, he recognizes three journeys of Jesus (John 1:19–3:36; 4:1–5:47; 6:1–10:42) before the last and decisive one in 11:1. These journeys allow the reader to share in the hero's adventures. In the process, however, the importance of the Jewish feasts for Jesus's journeys and for the structure of John seems to be overlooked.

In recent years, it has become more common to *combine* various formal and thematic criteria in trying to discover the structure of John. This procedure can be observed in the work of George Mlakuzhyil,[18] who belongs to the school of Ignace de la Potterie of the Pontifical Biblical Institute. According to him, Christology is decisively important for the understanding of John's Gospel and its structure. After a christological introduction (John 1:1–2:11), the author of the Gospel distinguishes the "Book of the Signs of Jesus" (2:1–12:50) with the account of the wedding at Cana as a transitional passage, and the "Book of the Hour of Jesus" (11:1–20:29), with John 11:1–12:50 as another transition (as above for Thyen and others). There follows the "christological conclusion" in 20:30–31 and an epilogue in 21:1–25. In this proposal, the classification of John 2:1–11 and 11:1–12:50 as transitional passages is attractive. Less convincing is the restriction of the cycle of Jewish feasts to the great controversies of Jesus with the "Jews" in Jerusalem in John 5:1–10:42.

---

15. Devillers, "Témoins."
16. Cf. Kieffer, *Johannesevangeliet* 2.500.
17. Segovia, "Journeys of the Word"; Segovia, "Journeys of Jesus."
18. Mlakuzhyil, *Structure*.

The proposal of Charles H. Giblin combines formal and thematic criteria for the division of John.[19] The author takes his starting point from spatial and temporal indications in the text as well as from dramatic ones. In John 1:19–4:54, the universal mission of Jesus is described; in 5:1–10:42, one finds hostility against Jesus in the great controversies; from 11:1 until the end, Jesus's love for his own is of primary importance. The formal transition to the second part comes only in 13:1, so that the classical division of John into two retains its value. Again, the question is whether the spatial and temporal indications in John have received the attention they deserve.

The *present exegesis* attempts to combine the structural criteria of division that have been tried and tested so far. We shall pay attention, therefore, to topographical, chronological, liturgical, formal and thematic aspects. From Mollat we are adopting the role of the Jewish feasts for the structure of John;[20] from Rissi, Staley, Kieffer. and Segovia, the importance of the journeys up to Jesus's last journey to Jerusalem. Jesus's journeys to Jerusalem should be taken as pilgrimages to the principal Jewish feasts. A one-year cycle of Jewish feasts probably forms the framework for the narrative part of the Gospel between John 2:13 and 11:55. Jesus sets out for Jerusalem four times: for the first Passover in 2:13, for the unnamed feast of 5:1 (presumably Pentecost), for Tabernacles in 7:2, and for the last Passover in 11:1 (mentioned in 11:55; 12:1; 13:1). For the Passover feast of John 6:4, Jesus does not go to Jerusalem. The whole of ch. 6 could have been added to the text of John under the influence of the Synoptic Gospels.[21] The Feast of Dedication in John 10:22 fits into this framework and does not require a new pilgrimage to Jerusalem since Jesus is already in the city. From the theological point of view, Jesus is bringing to perfection the sacred times and sacred places of Israel (the temple stands at the beginning and at the end). With good reason, exegetes see at the beginning an "Inaugural Week" leading into the public life of Jesus in John 1:19–2:12 with its seven-day pattern, and, at the end, the week of Jesus's departure to the Father that starts with his anointing "six days before the Passover" in 12:1. The six days of the Lazarus story in John 11 also fit into this scheme.

---

19. Giblin, "Structure."
20. Their Jewish background has now been investigated by Felsch, *Feste*.
21. Cf. Beutler, "Joh 6," and the exegesis of John 6 below.

*Introduction*

## 3. Aim

The question as to the aim or purpose of the composition of the Fourth Gospel has been answered by the majority of scholars until now with reference to the first ending of the Gospel in John 20:30-31: "Now Jesus did many other signs in the presence of his disciples, which are not written in this book. But these are written so that you may believe that Jesus is the Messiah, the Son of God, and that through believing you may have life in his name." For the phrase "that you may believe," there are two variants in the original Greek text. One, attested by P$^{66vid}$ ℵ* B Q 892$^s$ *l* 2211—thus by the oldest Egyptian tradition—reads the present subjunctive ἵνα πιστεύητε; the other is attested by ℵ$^2$ A C D K L N W Γ Δ Ψ *f*$^{1.13}$ 33 and others. M reads the aorist subjunctive ἵνα πιστεύσητε. In the first case, the Gospel's aim is to strengthen belief in Jesus; in the second, to lead to faith in Jesus. On the basis of external attestation, it seems reasonable to prefer the first variant, the predominant view in the more recent commentaries.

Older research was interested in the question of the addressees of the Fourth Gospel and, not infrequently, the starting point was the second textual variant just mentioned. A survey of models like this can be found, among others, in the great Johannine commentaries of Schnackenburg[22] and Brown.[23] There has also been subsequent development along these lines.[24] According to an opinion that is expressed occasionally, John's Gospel serves the purpose of stirring disciples of John the Baptist to faith in Jesus. Reference is then made to the prologue that expressly records that John the Baptist was not the light but only came to bear witness to the light (John 1:8).[25] This then remains the Baptist's role according to the fourth evangelist (cf. John 1:19, 32, 34; 3:26; 5:33-34). In John 1:20, the Baptist stresses explicitly that he is not the Messiah. This is a plausible scenario, for in Acts 18:24-19:7 in Ephesus, Paul came across some disciples of Jesus who knew only of the baptism of John.

According to another idea, advocated by Karl Bornhäuser, John's Gospel is "a mission document for Israel."[26] Alongside the already mentioned first ending of the Gospel, the starting point here is the great con-

---

22. Schnackenburg, 1:146-53.
23. Brown, 1:lxvii-lxxix.
24. Cf. Beutler, *Martyria*, 340-51.
25. Cf. Baldensperger, *Prolog*.
26. Bornhäuser, *Johannesevangelium*.

troversies between Jesus and the "Jews" over Jesus's claim to be the Christ and the Son of God.

As an alternative to this idea, it has been suggested that the Fourth Gospel should be seen as addressed to the Greeks. With Johannine irony, Jesus's Jewish audience in John 7:35 ask whether Jesus perhaps intends to go to the Greek diaspora to preach. It is Greeks like this who come to see Jesus according to John 12:20. Is the Fourth Gospel out to win to belief Greeks such as these? Or is it rather Jews of the Diaspora who are meant here?[27]

According to other authors, the Fourth Gospel displays a special interest in the Samaritans.[28] Especially relevant here is Jesus's journey through Samaria with the dialogues and encounters that take place there according to John 4:1–42. The Gospel's critical standpoint towards the temple, something shared with the Qumran movement and also with the Hellenists in the Acts of the Apostles, could point in this direction.

However, Gnostics and Docetics should also be considered as possible addressees for the Fourth Gospel. This would explain the emphasis on the "flesh" of Jesus (cf. John 1:14; 6:51–56) and his bloody death on the cross, followed by the piercing of his side from which blood and water flowed (John 19:34).[29]

Scholars have increasingly come to believe that John's Gospel is intended first and foremost as a reinforcement of the faith of its Christian readers. This is not just because of the probable preferred reading of John 20:31, but also because of the very construction of the Fourth Gospel. At key moments in the text, prominent disciples formulate the confession to which the whole Gospel leads in John 20:30–31. Thus, after the first falling away of some of Jesus's disciples in John 6:66, Peter, as spokesman for the Twelve, makes the confession: "Lord, to whom should we go? You have the words of eternal life. We have come to believe and know: You are the Holy One of God." Later, in John 11:27, Martha will express the confession of the Johannine community: "Yes, Lord, I believe that you are the Messiah, the Son of God, the one who is to come into the world." Confessions like this have been prepared for from the first chapter of the Gospel (cf. Andrew in John 1:41 and Nathanael in John 1:49).

---

27. So Robinson, "Destination." Kossen, "Greeks," reckons with non-Jewish Greeks at least for John 12:20.

28. Cf., already in this connection, Bowman, *Probleme*, especially 53–76: "Die Samaritaner und das Evangelium," particularly 55–61 on John.

29. Cf. Bornkamm, "Interpretation," contra Käsemann, *Jesu letzter Wille*, who sees a "naive Docetism" in John. Further, Schnelle, *Christologie*.

*Introduction*

John's Gospel intends, then, to lead to faith in Jesus, the Messiah and Son of God, and to strengthen those who have already come to this faith. According to widespread consensus, especially in German-speaking scholarship, this is also its only aim. The influence of the Reformation could be playing a role here for, according to it, everything culminates with Christ and faith in him. Recently in Anglophone circles it has increasingly been perceived that part of faith in Jesus is confession of that faith.[30] Two reasons may be working together here: greater independence from the confessional perspectives of Middle Europe, and the paradigm shift from an author- to a reader-oriented exegesis of the text of the New Testament. In the United States particularly, a more intense text-pragmatic exegesis of the New Testament, working alongside the methods of rhetorical criticism and reader response criticism, has been establishing itself for some time.

An indication of the need to remain in the faith and allow it to be strengthened is found already in the text of John 20:31 itself. The present subjunctive of πιστεύητε means exactly this: "that you may persevere in faith." Such faithfulness may be impeded by the situation of the Gospel's readers. If they want to live an authentic faith, they must also confess it outwardly. Evidently, however, this too is difficult for them. That is why, from its beginning, the Fourth Gospel lays great weight on confessing Jesus, directly or indirectly.[31] When the Baptist is asked if he is the Messiah, the text says: "And he confessed and did not deny it; he confessed: I am not the Messiah" (John 1:20). This confession is clear in its emphasis. As John's Gospel progresses, men come on the scene who seem to want to come to faith in Jesus but do not confess him openly for fear of the Pharisees who had decided to exclude from the synagogue those who confessed Jesus openly (John 12:42). For these disciples of Jesus, the praise of men was more important than the praise of God (cf. John 5:41–44).[32] Joseph of Arimathea was another such disciple who nevertheless had the courage later to go with Nicodemus to Pilate to beg the body of Jesus (John 19:38–40).

We come now to those exemplary figures who, in John's Gospel, set an example of fearless confession. We can mention Nicodemus again here. Being a member of the Jewish Council, in his first appearance he comes to Jesus by night, probably out of fear of being spotted. Nicodemus's noc-

---

30. Cf. among others, Brown, 1:lxxvii–lxxix; Painter, *John: Witness*, 12–15; du Rand, *Perspectives*, 1.55; Kysar, 14–15, 310; Kysar, *Fourth Evangelist*, 147–65; Kysar, *Maverick Gospel*, 18–26.

31. Cf. for the following, Beutler, "Faith and Confession."

32. Cf. Beutler, "Ehre Gottes."

turnal visit is not quickly forgotten, since there is an allusion to it in John 19:39. The outcome of his first conversation with Jesus in John 3:1–21 is unknown. He simply disappears from the scene, and the reader does not learn what he took away from this dialogue. When Jesus is later the subject of allegations in the Sanhedrin, it is the same Nicodemus who takes his side and asks that the accused be heard according to the Law (John 7:50–51). By doing this, Nicodemus takes the social risk of being considered "one of them" (v. 50). At the close of the Gospel, Nicodemus along with Joseph of Arimathea begs Pilate for the body of Jesus. This time it is with the Roman authority that he risks his life.[33] It can be assumed that, with this biography, the fourth evangelist wanted to show his readers how one should confess Jesus without caring for life or position. Like Joseph of Arimathea, Nicodemus was probably one of Jesus's disciples "in secret" (John 19:39), but, when the time came, found the courage to stand up for his faith. This is something the readers too have to learn.

Perhaps the most important role model for the Johannine reader is the man born blind in John 9. He not only obtains his eyesight from Jesus; he also comes gradually to faith in him. By contrast with his parents, he dares to make an open confession of his faith despite the decree of the "Jews" (i.e., the Jewish authorities in Jerusalem) to expel from the synagogue anyone confessing faith in Jesus (John 9:22). Indeed, a little later his confession leads to his being cast out (9:34). Similar expulsions are mentioned also in John 12:42 and 16:2. According to Martyn,[34] this is a reflection of the relationships of the time after the destruction of the temple, specifically the decree of the so-called "Synod of Jamnia" adopting a cursing of heretics in the prayer of the Eighteen Benedictions. Contemporary exegetes think rather of an expulsion of Christians from the synagogue at the local level as the background for these Johannine texts. In any case, the man born blind remains the classic example of those who come to faith in Jesus and confess it without care for the social consequences.[35]

Further examples of this reader orientation can be cited. For instance there is Thomas who, when Jesus sets out on his last journey to Jerusalem, fully aware of the risk to the other disciples says: "Let us go with him, that

---

33. Cassidy, *John's Gospel*, sees the aim of the evangelist precisely in the encouragement of the reader to stand firm under Roman persecution since conflicts with the Jewish authorities can scarcely have been dangerous for Christians any longer.

34. Martyn, *History*.

35. Cf. also, in this connection, Labahn, "Der Weg eines Namenlosen."

*Introduction*

we may die with him" (John 11:16).[36] There is Peter, who first denies Jesus three times but then renews his love for him and then hears from Jesus that he will be led where he does not want to go (John 21:18). There is the beloved disciple who, like Jesus's mother, follows his master as far as the cross (John 19:25–27). There are the women, above all Mary Magdalene, who come to look for and bury the body of Jesus as his true disciples (John 20:1–2). There are also Lazarus and his sisters who continue to entertain Jesus even at the moment of greatest threat (John 12:1–11). The list could be enlarged.

Jesus himself demands from his disciples the readiness to follow him wherever he goes. Where he is, there his disciples are to be also. Like him, they are to be ready to fall into the earth like a grain of wheat and so bring forth fruit (John 12:24–26). Such texts belong to the heart of John's Gospel, not its periphery.[37] They show the reader what he should be prepared for in extreme circumstances.

## 4. Unity and Sources

Before Johannine research saw the rise of text-linguistic methods, which spring from the text as it stands in its final form, it was the literary-critical model of Bultmann that dominated the discussion, at least in German-speaking study. Bultmann's model does not emerge directly from his commentary, however, and so D. Moody Smith[38] has undertaken the task of presenting it in a systematic way. According to Bultmann, the evangelist draws on three different sources, each of a different kind. Most of the prologue and the bulk of Jesus's speeches in the Fourth Gospel are ascribed by Bultmann to a sayings source from Gnostic Baptist circles. The Mandean and Manichean texts, which were newly or more easily available from the beginning of the twentieth century, formed the history of religions background together with the *Odes of Solomon*.[39] The evangelist would have reinterpreted this source in the sense of a "paradox" between the heavenly

---

36. Cf. Beutler, "Lasst uns mit ihm gehen."
37. This is to be held contra Becker, 2:448f, who, with Langbrandtner, *Gott*, regards John 12:24–26 as a secondary interpolation by the ecclesiastical redactor, not least because of the orientation of the verse towards the fellowship of the disciples, not only of their faith. In this sense, cf., also, Dietzfelbinger, 398.
38. Smith, *Composition*; more recently, cf. Labahn, "Bultmanns Konzeption."
39. Bultmann, "Bedeutung."

origin of the Logos and his incarnation and inserted it into his Gospel. In addition, he would have had at his disposal a source of the "signs" of Jesus and another one with an account of his passion, death, and resurrection. For Bultmann, the distinction between the "signs source" and the evangelist is particularly important. The former regards Jesus as a "divine man" on the Hellenistic pattern who leads men to faith in his prophetic and messianic word on the basis of his signs. If the original Gospel was focused wholly on this faith in Jesus and the salvation mediated by him in the present, a later "ecclesiastical redaction" put greater emphasis on the still pending fulfillment in resurrection and judgement, and the necessity of the sacraments of Baptism and the Lord's Supper as well as the importance of ministry in the church. Thus this Gospel was able to become acceptable to the great Church and form part of the canon of the Gospels.

According to Bultmann, some of the narrative sections, like that of the call of the first disciples in John 1:35–51, belongs to the "signs source." This assumption was then later expanded into a hypothetical "*Grundschrift*"[40] or a "signs Gospel"[41] together with the theory of an ever increasing amount of Johannine redaction. To this redaction, for example, belong all the parts of the later Gospel that deal with the "beloved disciple." At the end of this development, there remained scarcely anything of Bultmann's "evangelist." It was precisely this view that led Thyen to be the spokesman of a new way of looking at things, namely, to first describe the final redactor as the "evangelist"[42] and then to give up the entire source and strata model completely and come away with the Fourth Gospel as a unitary text that is coherent in itself.[43] Since the adoption of text-linguistic methods in Johannine research, this tendency has increasingly become the norm. At the same time, of course, we must distinguish between abstaining from identifying sources and strata and denying their existence. The latter needs its own form of argument, perhaps something like Eugen Ruckstuhl and Peter Dschulnigg have propounded for the area of style criticism.[44]

It still remains disputed how far and in what form John depends on the Synoptic Gospels. Against P. Gardner-Smith's thesis[45] that the

---

40. Cf. the commentaries of Becker and Haenchen as well as Richter, *Studien*.
41. Cf. Fortna, *Gospel of Signs*; Fortna, *Predecessor*.
42. Cf. Thyen, "Entwicklungen."
43. This is the foundation of Thyen's commentary on John as well as his final position in *Studien*.
44. Ruckstuhl, *Einheit*; Ruckstuhl and Dschulnigg, *Stilkritik*.
45. Gardner-Smith, *Saint John*.

## Introduction

Fourth Gospel does not directly presume knowledge of the first three, German-speaking scholars since the 1970s have increasingly tended to go for the thesis of the so-called Louvain school of Neirynck, his colleagues and pupils, according to whom John would have known and used the Synoptic Gospels. Certainly, it is not to be imagined that John used the other evangelists in such a way that he becomes a kind of "fourth Synoptic." According to the Louvain school, he makes very free use of the Synoptics, and not always to the same extent. John's points of contact with the first three evangelists occur especially in the Baptist tradition, in some miracles (such as the healing of the son of the royal official in John 4:46-54), in John 6 (with the multiplication of the loaves, the walking on the water, the demand for a sign, the bread discourse, and the split among the disciples before Peter's confession) and in the account of the passion, death, and resurrection of Jesus. In this commentary, we shall advocate the dependence of the Fourth Gospel on the other three despite the occasional more recent challenging of this opinion especially among Anglo-Saxon scholars.[46] The assumption of other sources will be rejected in the present work all the more so as, in the Johannine account of the passion, death, and resurrection, it can be shown how even in the details John has creatively developed the Synoptic tradition just as he had done in his reception of the Baptist tradition.

A good introduction to recent discussion on John's relationship to the Synoptics is given by Michael Labahn and Manfred Lang in their detailed article.[47] On the one hand, they observe increasing agreement as to the dependence of the Fourth Gospel on the other three; on the other hand, however, they note caution over this among an array of authors, not only those who regard John as early. It remains difficult to explain the relative gap between John and his three predecessors. On the one hand, we have to take account of his literary and theological creativity, which will also be championed in the present commentary; on the other hand, it is possible that the Synoptic tradition reached our evangelist through a process of "secondary orality," that is, through a subsequent re-oralizing of the Synoptics. This model is especially advocated by Labahn. However, it is also conceivable that John is quoting the Synoptics

---

46. Use of the Synoptics is ignored in Fortna and Thatcher, eds., *Jesus*, 113-88; it is examined critically in Lozada and Thatcher, eds., *New Currents*. A dating of John earlier than the Synoptics (advocated, among others, by Berger) is discussed in the volume by Hofrichter, *Priorität*.

47. Cf. Labahn and Lang, "Johannes und die Synoptiker."

from memory very freely. Then one would also have to dispense with the medium of the "Johannine community" transmitting tradition. One of the strongest arguments for Synoptic influence on John remains the "Gospel" genre itself that could scarcely have been created in two places at the same time.[48]

There remains the striking similarity between John 6 and the section Mark 6:32–8:33. In addition to this, we can observe some peculiarities in John 6. Thus, Jesus appears not to go to Jerusalem to the Passover feast mentioned in John 6:4. It appears to have been relocated to Galilee. At the same time the only instance in John of the theme of the Eucharist comes up (John 6:27, 51c–58). Additionally, there is mention of a "resurrection on the last day" (John 6:39–40, 44, 54). Moreover, only here in John do we come across "Jews" as opponents of Jesus who, at the same time, do not appear to come from Judaea (from v. 41). In this commentary, we shall argue that this chapter comes from a secondary source.[49] Furthermore, there are other texts that could have been added to the kernel of the Fourth Gospel. In the case of John 21 this is still the view of the majority of scholars, even those who otherwise prefer to read the Fourth Gospel in a synchronic manner.[50] Similarly, John 15–17 seem to be secondary. The "signal for departure" in John 14:31 is actually taken up only in 18:1.[51] Finally, there are also reasons to understand the prologue as a kind of foreword that was composed later as a briefing for the reader.[52] Neither the personal Logos-concept, understood christologically, nor the idea of creation, nor still the incarnation will be taken up again in the course of the Gospel. In the present commentary, the additions to the traditional text of the Fourth Gospel will be understood, in connection with Jean Zumstein, Andreas Dettwiler, and Klaus Scholtissek, as a *"relecture"* of the earlier text, that is, a new reading in the light of new situations among the readers. By contrast with classical literary criticism, it is a matter not of a series of authors but of texts. The present commentary thus represents a synthesis of synchronic and diachronic readings of the Fourth Gospel. This commentary also takes into account the Old and New Testament tradition in its exegesis.

---

48. Cf. Labahn and Lang, "Johannes und die Synoptiker," 504f., the reference to Thyen.
49. Cf. Beutler, "Joh 6."
50. Cf. the commentary of Schnelle.
51. Cf. Beutler, "Steht auf."
52. Cf. Beutler, "Johannes-Prolog."

## 5. History of Religions Background

The question as to the history of religions background for John's Gospel cannot be answered for the Gospel as a whole, for the content and forms taken over are too different. It is a good idea, therefore, to distinguish the most important literary genres within John's Gospel and to pose the question of the history of religions background for the individual genres separately.[53] At a basic level we can distinguish between narrative and speech sections in John. To this should be added the prologue as a separate genre with its own history of religions background.

The narrative material exhibits strong links with biblical texts and traditions throughout. This goes both for the Johannine calling and healing stories as well as for the Johannine account of the passion, death, and resurrection of Jesus. Of especial interest as far as the history of religions is concerned are the Johannine miracle stories. For their part, as interpreted "signs," they display a number of connections with the speech material. In particular, the Johannine miracle healings show a strong relationship with the corresponding Synoptic narratives. One of these stories, that of the healing of the son of the royal officer (John 4:46-54), finds its direct parallel in the corresponding account in Matthew that we generally ascribe to the "Q source" (Matt 8:5-13; Luke 7:1-10). Two further healing miracles in John illustrate that the "blind see, the lame walk" (Matt 11:5; Luke 7:22), namely, the healing of the lame man in John 5:1-9b and that of the man born blind in John 9:1-7. Accounts like these are probably intended to show that the eschatological promises of Isa 35:5-6; 29:18 have been fulfilled in Jesus. Here too, the Synoptic tradition's corresponding healings (Mark 8:22-26 par., 10:46-52 par., 2:1-12 par.) stand between John and the prophetic texts. For the form of such miracles stories, scholars for a long time used to point to Hellenistic and Jewish texts.[54] In fact, the story of the raising of Lazarus has no direct Synoptic parallel. However, it is in the form of stories of the raising of the dead used by the Synoptics (cf. Mark 5:21-24, 35-43 par.; Luke 7:11-17). Here too, there are Old Testament examples in stories about the prophets of the northern kingdom raising the dead (cf. 1 Kgs 17:17-24 [Elijah]; 2 Kgs 4:18-37 [Elisha]). The sequence

---

53. Cf. Beutler, "Literarische Gattungen."
54. Cf. Fiebig, *Antike Wundergeschichten*; Fiebig, *Rabbinische Wundergeschichten*; Fiebig, *Jüdische Wundergeschichten*; Weinreich, *Antike Heilungswunder*, evaluated in Bultmann, *Geschichte*, 223-60; Dibelius, *Formgeschichte*, 26-56.

of Jesus's miraculous feeding of the multitude and then walking on water before the disciples has its precedent in the tradition of Mark (cf. Mark 6:30–52 par.) and recalls a similar sequence in the Exodus tradition with Israel's passage through the Red Sea (Exod 14), the feeding of the people in the desert (Exod 16) and the theophany at Sinai (Exod 19). The feeding miracle in John 6 reminds us of the gift miracles of Elijah (1 Kgs 17:7–16) and Elisha (2 Kgs 4:42–44) in the miracle cycles of the great prophets of the northern kingdom. Here too, mediation through the Synoptic tradition may be taking place.

The account of the changing of water into wine by Jesus at the wedding of Cana in John 2:1–11 may have had its own tradition history. For a long time, scholars were unable to find convincing biblical parallels for this text. Probably, there is influence here of the ancient Dionysius legend,[55] something made more likely by the fact that this legend appears to have Oriental roots. Dionysius was the son of Semele, a daughter of the king's son Cadmus, who came to Greece from Tyre or Sidon. Thus, Greek coins from Syria-Palestine contain Dionysian motifs. According to Pliny (*Nat.* 2.18.74), the city of Skythopolis (today Bet-Shean in Lower Galilee) prided itself on being the birthplace of Dionysius. Because of this and other information collected by Martin Hengel,[56] an influence of the Dionysius legend on the text of Jesus's changing the water into wine in John 2:1–11 seems reasonable. Naturally, biblical images of wine as God's gift and marriage as the symbol of the covenant relationship between God and his people also contribute to this text (cf. for the wine, Gen 49:10–12; Mark 14:25; for the wedding and for the feast as images of eschatological joy, Isa 25:6; Matt 8:11; Luke 13:29; Matt 22:1–10; Luke 14:16–24; Rev 19:9).

The description of Jesus's miracles as "signs" (σημεῖα) is one of the characteristic features of John's Gospel. It might have a Hellenistic-Jewish origin; at the very least, it goes back to the Septuagint text of the book of Exodus. This is especially true of the "signs" (σημεῖα) that Moses works before Pharaoh and that legitimate him as the leader of God's people (cf. Exod 4:8–9, 28, 30; 7:9; also 10:1–2; 11:9–10) and are meant to lead to "faith" in his prophetic mission (Exod 4:5, 8–9, 31). This connection between seeing "signs" and "faith" appears in John 2:11, 23; 12:37; 20:30–31 (ascribed by some to a pre-Johannine "sign source"). Moreover, the connection between Jesus's signs and the manifesting

---

55. Cf. Lütgehetmann, *Hochzeit.*
56. Hengel, "Messias."

of his "glory" (δόξα, cf. John 11:4, 40) seems to be prepared for in the Septuagint. Of course, what is happening there (Num 14:10–11, 21–22) has nothing to do with the shining of the glory of the wonder worker (as John 2:11; cf. 11:4).

Characteristic of John's Gospel is the connection between the miracles of Jesus as "signs" and his revelation of himself in the revelation discourses and dialogue scenes in the Fourth Gospel. Thus, the bread discourse of John 6 with Jesus's description of himself as the "bread of life" (John 6:35, 48, 51) interprets the sign of the miraculous multiplication of the loaves (John 6:1–15). Similarly, Jesus's saying that he is the "light of the world" (John 9:5) interprets the sign of the healing of the man born blind (John 9:1–7), and the description of himself as "the Resurrection and the Life" (John 11:25) interprets the last public sign, that of the raising of Lazarus from the dead (John 11:1–44). This theological evaluation of the Johannine "signs" may probably be attributed to the evangelist himself.[57]

In the twentieth century, the origin of the *speech material* in John's Gospel was readily assumed to be in Gnostic texts or circles. Bultmann reconstructed long, thematically unified revelation speeches as *Vorlage* of the Fourth Gospel. He then interpreted them in his commentary in the form in which they had been revised by the evangelist. Followed by his pupil Heinz Becker,[58] Bultmann saw the origin of these speeches in Gnostic circles as they appear to be attested in the texts of the Mandeans and Manicheans, but also in the *Odes of Solomon* and in the *Corpus Hermeticum*. A difficulty in this hypothesis lies in the fact that it makes it necessary to split up the Johannine speeches. Moreover, since the basic texts prove to be clearly more recent than John's Gospel, John's dependence on them turns out to be difficult. Furthermore, the hypothesis of a Gnostic "*Urmensch*" myth cannot actually be substantiated.[59]

Still influential was the attempt that had already been made by Becker to discover a basic form of the Johannine revelation discourses that the fourth evangelist had already encountered in their Gnostic *Vorlage* and adopted. In this form, there stood at the beginning of a shorter revelation discourse, a self-description of the revealer that was then developed in what followed. On the basis of this hypothesis, Eduard Schweizer in his

---

57. Cf. Lütgehetmann, *Hochzeit*, 216–61.
58. Becker, *Reden*.
59. Cf. Colpe, *Schule*.

dissertation *Ego eimi*,[60] completed under the supervision of Bultmann, developed briefer Johannine revelation sayings introduced by "I am" with a basic form characteristic of and borrowed from the gnosis tradition, particularly the Mandean variety. Siegfried Schulz took up this proposal and presented an expanded model of the Johannine revelation discourses.[61] According to his proposal, these sayings begin with the "self-presentation" of the revealer ("I am . . ."). This is then followed by an invitation and also a promise or a threat respectively. An example would be John 6:35: "I am the bread of life" (self-presentation). "Whoever comes to me" (invitation) "shall never hunger, and whoever believes in me, shall never thirst" (promise). Already, Schweizer had assumed Old Testament and Jewish precedents for the images of self-description that are used. This conjecture was confirmed by Schulz, who also included the Qumran texts in his research. Furthermore, Schulz sees the form of the revelation discourses set out in Gnostic texts, especially those of the Mandeans. Reference has also been made recently to other texts that were found in Nag Hammadi.[62] Thus, for example, in the Bronte manuscript (Thunder: Perfect Mind: NHC VI 2), there is the sequence of the self-presentation of the revealer, invitation and, occasionally, promise. Of course, this manuscript is not itself directly Gnostic. Further evidence is found in the conclusion of the longer version of the Secret Book of John (NHC II 1 and IV 1) as well as in the Three Forms of First Thought (NHC XIII 1). These texts are not part of the documents of the so-called Valentinian Gnosis, and so their dependence on Christian texts is less probable. Of course, they are reckoned to be so late that they cannot be considered as *Vorlage* of the Johannine discourses. Obvious too is that the fourth evangelist might still have borrowed his images out of his early Jewish and Christian environment.[63]

It still remains to explain the insertion of the shorter revelation sayings into the larger Johannine discourse and dialogue compositions.[64] Here we can suppose Platonic influence. In any case, the Johannine dialogues and controversies exhibit few common features with the Synoptic school and conflict dialogues. As for the genre of farewell sayings in John there are Hellenistic and especially Jewish precedents.[65]

60. Schweizer, *Ego eimi*, 114–24.
61. Schulz, *Komposition*, 85–90.
62. Cf. MacRae, "Nag Hammadi," 156f.
63. Cf. Schweizer in the second edition of *Ego eimi*.
64. Cf. Beutler, "Literarische Gattungen," 2551f.
65. Cf., among others, Cortès, *Discursos*; Nordheim, *Die Lehre der Alten* I.

*Introduction*

Alongside these non-Christian precedents and examples, we should naturally not forget the Christians. Above all, Barnabas Lindars, in his commentary on John, in line with Brown,[66] supposes that homilies from the Johannine community have influenced the Fourth Gospel. This approach has proved to be fruitful and has been adopted by Jörg Frey,[67] among others, for the eschatological tradition in John.

For the history of religions background of the *prologue*, the reader is directed to exegesis of the prologue below. Here too, hypotheses of a Gnostic source have been superseded by derivation from biblical, Jewish and, above all, Hellenistic-Jewish tradition. Along with the wisdom literature of the Old Testament, Philo of Alexandria is the influence most frequently adduced.

### 6. Author, Time, Place

The question as to the author of the Fourth Gospel is easier posed than answered. We must distinguish between the information in the Gospel itself and the later testimonies regarding its origins. According to the testimony of the Gospel itself (John 21:24), it was composed by the "disciple whom Jesus loved" (cf. John 13:23; 19:26; 20:2; 21:7, 20). Since the late second century, this has been identified with John the apostle and "disciple of the Lord" (cf. Irenaeus, *Haer.* 2.22.5; Muratorian Canon 9; Clement of Alexandria in Eusebius, *Hist. Eccl.* 6.14.7; Polycrates of Ephesus in Eusebius, *Hist. Eccl.* 3.31.3).[68] At the same time, it is not easy to decide whether the tradition since Irenaeus has developed the identification of the Gospel's author with the beloved disciple from the text of the Gospel itself or whether it is based on historical information. It is striking that in the Fourth Gospel, when "John" is mentioned, it is always in the sense of the Baptist or the father of Simon (John 1:42; 21:15-17), and John, the son of Zebedee, is missing from the call of the first disciples in John 1:35-42. Was he one of the unnamed disciples mentioned in John 1:35 and 40?

A John of some kind is already recognized as author of the Fourth Gospel in the second century. Hengel points out, correctly, that the Fourth Gospel was transmitted under the name of John from the begin-

---

66. Brown, 1:c–ci.
67. Cf. Frey, *Eschatologie*, 3:369–91, on John 5:24–29.
68. All this and other evidence is to be found in Aland, *Synopsis*, 533–39.

ning.[69] Perhaps the most important witness to the origin of our Gospel is the second-century Bishop of Hierapolis, Papias. His five-volume "Interpretation of the Words of the Lord" is now lost, but fragments are preserved. In an Armenian fragment,[70] he claims to know and have used the Fourth Gospel (John 19:39). In another fragment that is preserved by, among others, Eusebius (*Hist. Eccl.* 3.39.3f.), Papias evidently distinguishes between the apostle and an Elder John whose graves, according to Eusebius, are now to be seen in Ephesus. This information from Papias forms the cornerstone for Hengel's great and detailed study *Die johanneische Frage*.[71] Hengel presses the suggestive conclusion of identifying the "Elder" John, the author of the Second and Third Letters of John, with the author of the First Letter of John, and this one, in turn, with Papias's "Elder." On the grounds of the stylistic and theological closeness of the Letters of John to the Fourth Gospel, Hengel then reaches the conclusion that the whole Johannine corpus probably goes back to John the Elder of Ephesus. That means that the assumption of Eusebius that the Fourth Gospel goes back to the Apostle John and the Apocalypse to the Elder of Ephesus remains unverified.

Further on in the second century, Justin knows and uses John's Gospel. In *Dial.* 106:1, he ascribes information from John 20:17, 19 and other places to the "Memoirs of the Apostles."[72] Tatian's Diatessaron begins and ends with John's Gospel, which also appears to be presupposed in the secondary ending to Mark. In Bishop Theophilus of Antioch, we find the Johannine prologue (John 1:1, 3) cited as of equal value with the "holy Scriptures" and attributed to John (*Autol.* 2.22). Among the Gnostics, John 1:9 is cited among the "Gospels" by Basilides (in Hippolytus, *Haer.* 7.22.4f.) and John 2:4 as the word of the "Savior" (in Hippolytus, *Haer.* 7.27.5). In Ptolemaeus (cited by Epiphanius, *Pan.* 33.6), John 1:3f. appears as the word of the "Apostle." The first commentary on John's Gospel stems from the quill of the Gnostic, Herakleon. Papyrus 66 (second-third centuries) and papyrus 75 (third century) contain in their super- or subscription to the text of the Gospel the words "according to John."

The identification of the author with the "disciple whom Jesus loved,"

---

69. Cf. Hengel, *Evangelienüberschriften*, 3.

70. Cf. Siegert, "Papiaszitate," 607-9.

71. The text of the Papias fragment is to be found in Aland, *Synopsis*, 531 with further evidence there and on the following page.

72. See for this extract, Beutler and Meredith, "Johannesevangelium (und -Briefe)," 646f. Justin's text is quoted in Aland, *Synopsis*, 532.

*Introduction*

goes back to the text of the Gospel itself (John 21:24). For his identification with the son of Zebedee, there is no clear witness before Irenaeus. The chief difficulty for this must surely be that it presents a Galilean as the author of a Gospel strongly influenced by the Jewish Diaspora. Some authors, therefore, think rather of a disciple of Jesus who came from Jerusalem, and they go on from this to think of the "other disciple" who went in with Peter into the courtyard of the high priest because he was known to the latter (John 18:15-16). One could also imagine that the redactor of the Fourth Gospel laid clues that led, on the one hand to John, the son of Zebedee, and, on the other, to a Jerusalem disciple who came from priestly circles.[73]

A radical alternative to such hypotheses would be the supposition that the whole figure of the beloved disciple is a fiction or, at least, his connection with the origin of the Gospel is a literary fiction. This idea was already put forward by Franz Overbeck a century ago. Recently, it has been followed by Thyen in his commentary. Discussion on these introductory questions will continue. From the perspective of a literary-critical treatment of John's Gospel the question of its message is more important than that of its author.

The question of the Fourth Gospel's relationship to the Synoptic Gospels is important for establishing the date of its emergence. If John presupposes the Synoptics, and a fortiori all three of them, then an estimate before 90 CE is scarcely possible.[74] On the other hand, it is likely that John's Gospel, at least in its basic form, should be reckoned before the Letters of Ignatius that are dated to the later years of the Emperor Trajan (98-117 CE).[75] The parts that we have labeled *"relecture"* could also be reckoned after the turn of the century, but reliable information for this is lacking. Certainly Docetic tendencies appear at this time that, among other things, lead to the counteremphasis on Jesus's "flesh" as important for salvation (John 1:14; 6:51-56). An extended study of the Johannine letters leads to the result that these (beginning with 1 John 1:1-4) presuppose John's Gospel rather than vice versa.[76]

The place of composition of John's Gospel remains debated. On account of the testimony of Irenaeus (*Haer.* 3.1.2), from the second century until the present day Ephesus has been frequently named. However, this

---

73. Thus, among others, Hengel, *Frage*, 313-20. For such a "priestly" author, cf. Rigato, "L' 'apostolo.'"
74. This is also the view of Barrett, 142. The reader is referred to the Introduction to his commentary, 138-49.
75. Cf. Fischer, *Die Apostolischen Väter*, 114.
76. Cf. Beutler, *Johannesbriefe*.

testimony is undermined by the doubt that it presupposes the identity of the beloved disciple and the author of the Fourth Gospel with the apostle John. C. K. Barrett invokes further evidence for this locale such as that of Polycrates and the closeness of John to Melito of Sardis and to the Acts of John.[77] However, there could also be grounds to name Alexandria or Antioch as the place of origin for John's Gospel.[78] For the time being, any certainty must be eschewed.

## 7. Text

In the earliest manuscript tradition, no New Testament writing is better attested than the Gospel of John.[79] At least two papyri reach back to the second century.[80] At the same time, their precise dating still remains disputed. For a long time, $P^{52}$ with the text of John 18:31-33, 37-38 has enjoyed the status of being the oldest New Testament text fragment. It was thereby reckoned, often with the citation of Kurt Aland, to about the year 125. In recent times, however, this dating has been called into question, and a reckoning sometime in the second century seems more reasonable.[81] To the same time belongs $P^{90}$ with the text of John 18:36-19:1; 19:2-7. Around 200 is the assessment for $P^{66}$ (Bodmer II); it contains the majority of the Gospel. The spread of this Gospel in Egypt in the second century is also evidenced by Papyrus Egerton 2, which combines extracts from John's Gospel with fragments of the text of the Synoptics.

Seven papyrus fragments are assigned to the third century:[82] $P^5$ with fragments from John 1, 16, and 20; $P^{28}$ with the text of John 6:8-12, 17-22; $P^{39}$ with the text of John 8:14-22; $P^{45}$ with extracts from chs. 4-5 and 10-11; $P^{75}$ (Bodmer XV) with the text of John 1:1-11:45, 48-57; 12:3-13:10; 14:8-15:10; $P^{80}$ with the text of John 3:3; and $P^{95}$ with the text of John 5:26-29, 36-38.

The quality of $P^{75}$ (Bodmer XIV for Luke and Bodmer XV for John) is supported especially by Codex Vaticanus (B). As already shown earlier

---

77. Cf. Barrett, 143.
78. Cf. Barrett, 143-46.
79. Cf. Aland and Aland, *Der Text des Neuen Testaments*, 97.
80. Cf. Aland and Aland, *Der Text des Neuen Testaments*, 97. See also Aland, "Der Text des Johannesevangeliums."
81. Thus, now, Nongbri, "Use and Abuse."
82. The survey draws on Nestle-Aland[27], 684-89; cf. Nestle-Aland[28], 792-97; cf., further, Aland and Aland, *Der Text des Neuen Testaments*, 106-11.

by Carlo M. Martini for Luke[83] and Calvin L. Porter for John,[84] this text contains an old Egyptian text tradition of considerable reliability. $P^{66}$ coincides with this text form, but in a freer type of text that is also represented by the Chester Beatty Papyri $P^{45}$, $P^{46}$, and $P^{47}$. The pericope of Jesus and the woman taken in adultery presents its own problems that will be tackled in the appropriate part of the following commentary.[85]

## 8. Canonicity

Since the beginning of its tradition history, John has enjoyed the status of a sacred text. The earliest stages of its attestation are treated above (under 6., Author). Since there have been lists of Gospels, John's Gospel has been included in them. Perhaps the oldest text of this kind is the so-called Muratorian Canon that is dated around the year 200 CE. The Muratorian Canon records: "Quartum evangeliorum Johannis ex discipulis."[86] Similarly early are the ancient Gospel prologues that are preserved for Mark, Luke, and John. They testify to the authenticity of the Gospel by appealing to Papias, a disciple of the evangelist, and emphasize the contrast with Marcion from whom John is said to have expressly distanced himself.[87]

In the first more extensive lists of the New Testament writings, John has his place taken for granted from the beginning. Here belongs the so-called *Decretum Damasi* that was handed down in connection with a council held at Rome under Pope Damasus in 382 (DS 180). Even if other parts of this decree belong to a later time perhaps, this part is considered substantially authentic.

For its part, a Council of Carthage from the year 397 compiled a canon of the sacred books and numbered among these four Gospels, undoubtedly those that until then had generally been listed (DS 186). All that remains is for the later councils to draw on this tradition: the Council of Florence in its Decree for the Jacobites (DS 1335) and the Council of Trent in its fourth session (DS 1503).

83. Martini, *Codice B*.
84. Porter, "Papyrus Bodmer XV."
85. Cf. Aland and Aland, *Der Text des Neuen Testaments*, 97, 103, 105, 109. We now have documentation and evaluation of the situation with the Uncials and Papyri in Schmid, *The New Testament in Greek* IV (cf. the bibliography).
86. Text in Aland, *Synopsis*, 538.
87. Text in Aland, *Synopsis*, 533.

## 9. Contemporary Significance

Throughout history, John's Gospel has inspired a special fascination. In the early church, it served as the basis of the great christological and trinitarian controversies. At the beginning of the modern age, Martin Luther saw it as "the unique, beautiful, proper, chief Gospel."[88] His reason was that faith in Jesus appears to be its central theme. In the last century, Bultmann took up this perspective and made it the key point of his exegesis. Naturally, he was able to free the Fourth Gospel thereby from myth and to interpret it in an existential manner.

The debate over demythologizing has faded away, but its concerns remain worth considering. The present age is marked by a rapid waning of plausibility where the Christian message is concerned, particularly in the industrial West. Whoever is looking for a new or deeper way of faith would rather not have it as a system of sweeping, isolated theories but instead experience it as a simple message able to be summarized in a single statement, accepted and translated into action. The Fourth Gospel responds to this need in a big way. In this connection, it is sufficient to remember the sentence that probably stood at its original conclusion: "Now Jesus did many other signs in the presence of his disciples, which are not written in this book. But these are written so that you may believe that Jesus is the Messiah, the Son of God, and that through believing you may have life in his name" (John 20:30–31).

It is part of the special character and merit of John that it displays what is perhaps the most strongly developed and thought-through Christology in the New Testament. Jesus appears throughout as the "Son of God" or, simply, "the Son," and this is also the sense in which his role as Messiah is understood. He is one with the Father (John 10:30) and the basis of the union of his disciples with him, with the Father, and with one another (John 17:21). As divine Logos, Jesus existed from eternity before he became flesh (John 1:1–18). Such a declaration of pre-existence is found rarely in the New Testament. There are parallels only in the pre-Pauline hymns or fragments (Gal 4:4; Phil 2:2–11; Col 1:15–18) or in the Epistle to the Hebrews (1:3). Faith in him is decisive for salvation and damnation.

According to the Fourth Gospel, Jesus developed and justified his claim to be the Messiah sent by God and Son of God especially in the

---

88. Luther, "Vorrede zum Neuen Testament."

course of the great controversies with the representatives of the Jewish people and its religion, the so-called "Jews." Particularly since the systematic annihilation of the Jews in central Europe during Hitler's dictatorship, it has been suggested over and over again that the forms of expression in John's Gospel could lend support to anti-Semitic prejudice, and indeed have done so. It is not sufficient to point out that, with the "Jews," John probably meant the leaders of the Jewish people in Jerusalem during the time of Jesus. Very early on, the readers of this Gospel, who read it along with the other writings of the New Testament, must have gained the impression that "the Jews," in the sense of the Jewish people and the Jewish religious community, had persecuted Jesus and finally handed him over for execution.[89] From then on, Christian and post-Christian anti-Semitism was not only possible but also took place. The medieval pogroms, in connection with the Good Friday Liturgy and its reading aloud of the St. John Passion, are a sure witness of this.

Among the more recent commentaries, great credit is due to that of Klaus Wengst, who makes the basis of his exegesis John's polemic against the "Jews," which finds its harshest expression in John 8:44 (the "Jews" as children of the devil). Without whitewashing this tendency of the Fourth Gospel, Wengst works out how strongly rooted the Fourth Gospel is in Judaism. In this connection, he resorts especially to the rabbinic tradition. This has the advantage that Wengst can thereby demonstrate the relationship of the Fourth Gospel with contemporary Judaism that has in turn been shaped by the rabbis. A disadvantage of this procedure may lie in the fact that John's Gospel came into being and was written down just as the normative rabbinic tradition began to be formed after the destruction of Jerusalem. Wengst perceives this difficulty but meets it with the justification that the rabbinic tradition grew up over a long period of time and was thus broadly stable.[90]

However, there is yet another possibility for demonstrating John's rootedness in Judaism. It lies in showing that the great themes of Johannine theology are anchored in the Old Testament and in Second Temple Judaism. We shall adopt this approach in the present exegesis. While Bultmann and the Johannine research influenced by him painted Gnosticism as the decisive factor in the history of religions background of the Fourth Gospel, the picture changed after the Second World War. Apart from this recent

---

89. Cf. Beutler, "Identity."
90. Cf. Wengst, 1:32.

need to observe more carefully that John's Gospel is anchored in Judaism, other factors come into play as a result of the change of perspective marked by the end of the war. On the one hand, the discovery of the Gnostic library at Nag Hammadi in 1945 has permitted a more exact dating of the Gnostic texts, the main conclusion being that these generally presuppose Christianity and not vice versa. On the other hand, the texts discovered from near the Dead Sea in 1947 provide evidence for the existence of a dualistically conceived Judaism in Palestine before the Jewish War (66–70 CE) with strong parallels to the dualistic texts of the New Testament and especially to the Johannine literature. Since that time, therefore, above all in English and French-speaking literature, there has been a greater emphasis on the relationship of John's Gospel to the Old Testament and to Judaism in place of the Gnostic paradigm. As two examples among many, it suffices to mention the great commentaries of Schnackenburg (1965–1984) and Brown (1966–1970).

So, then, the present exegesis will be especially concerned to demonstrate the roots of Johannine thought and Johannine theology in the Old Testament and in Second Temple Judaism. It thus forms a kind of complement to the commentary of Klaus Wengst. In both cases, care is given to display John's Gospel in its closeness to Judaism and not only the critical aspects of the text itself.[91]

There is yet another reason why John's Gospel appears to possess relevance for today. It requires of its readers a fearless confession of their faith, a very serious concern at present in many parts of the world. For a long time, the dominant opinion was that the aim of John's Gospel was outlined sufficiently in its first conclusion, namely, to arouse faith in Jesus, the Messiah and Son of God (John 20:30–31). However, it can be shown that another concern is present, namely, to encourage the fearless confession of Christ. This purpose emerges especially from the narrative strategy of the Fourth Gospel and the exemplary figures who model this fearless confession, such as the man born blind in John 9, Nicodemus in his development to the point of his taking part in the burial of Jesus under the eyes of the occupying power, or Thomas who declares: "Let us go with him, that we may die with him" (John 11:16).[92]

---

91. Cf. Beutler, *Judaism*; Beutler, *L'Ebraismo*.

92. Cf., for this view, above, section 3, as well as Beutler, "Faith and Confession"; Beutler, "Lasst uns mit ihm gehen."

*Introduction*

## 10. The Present Exegesis

The present exegesis is set out according to the pattern chosen by the author for his commentary on the Johannine letters in the series "Regensburger Neues Testament."[93] At the beginning of each pericope, there is a translation of the relevant passage. It consists of a revision of the RSV and the NRSV. Disputed areas will be identified as such.

The first step of the exegesis will deal with the introductory questions. First, the textual unit will be delineated and set in its context. I shall then try to determine the structure of the unit and, on this basis, so far as possible, the literary genre of the text itself or of its *Vorlagen*. A complete assignment of sections of the text to written sources is avoided. At best, some sections will be assigned to a Johannine revision. Naturally, this judgement takes account of the individual exegesis.

The second step consists of the step-by-step exegesis. In each instance, the relevant text is introduced and analyzed with the methods of synchronic exegesis. There will thus be questions on its grammar, semantics, and pragmatic aspects. Then, in connection with this, the diachronic treatment will be factored in. Thus, the text is also read in the light of the traditions that it employs, be they Jewish, pre-Christian, or early Christian.

In a third step, we shall seek to situate the passage in terms of its current significance. Here, therefore, we are concerned with the message of the text, not only in the sense of a timeless *Textpragmatik*, but also with a glance at contemporary readers. Certainly, this is where the perspective of the exegete comes into play in a special way. In the present commentary, I have tried to focus on those readers who are conscious of being confronted with the tensions of the present in the social, cultural, religious, and political spheres. Such a reading can also be "spiritual": "When he comes, the Spirit of truth, he will lead you into the complete truth. For he will not speak on his own authority, but, whatever he hears, he will speak, and he will declare to you the things that are to come" (John 16:13)

---

93. Cf. Beutler, *Johannesbriefe*.

# The Divine Word Enters the World (1:1–4:54)

John's Gospel begins solemnly with a prologue (1:1–18) that celebrates the incarnation of the eternal Word. In his Word, God enters into and takes part in human history. This prologue is often prefixed to the rest of the Gospel as a separate text. There is something to be said, however, for treating it with the following chapters. The testimony of the Baptist (1:19–34) has already been prepared for in the prologue (1:6–8, 15). Jesus Christ, who is already expressly named in the prologue (1:17), is now proclaimed by John. The latter introduces the first disciples to Jesus (1:35–51), who then become witnesses of his first sign in Cana of Galilee (2:1–12). The first Passover takes Jesus to Jerusalem, where he cleanses the temple (2:13–25) and conducts a dialogue with Nicodemus, a member of the Council (3:1–21). Thereafter, we see Jesus in concentric circles on his way to new areas: from Judaea (3:22–36) via Samaria (4:1–42) as far as Galilee (4:43–45), where he then works his second sign in Cana (4:46–54). Distance from Jerusalem involves opening up to new groups of people such as the Samaritans, who are not fully united in faith with Judah, and the Galileans whose region is called by Isaiah "land of Zebulun and land of Naphtali, the area of the Gentiles" (Isa 9:1, taken up in Matt 4:14–16). Thus, subsequent to his first pilgrim journey to the Passover in Jerusalem, Jesus begins a journey that leads him to people who are ever more distant from Jerusalem, its cult, and its faith. This will change beginning in 5:1 when Jesus uses the pilgrimage feasts to reveal himself to his people and their leaders (with the exception of the Passover feast of John 6 in Galilee). It is better, therefore, not to see in John 2–12 (with Bultmann) "the revelation of δόξα before the world" or in John 5–12 (with the *Einheitsübersetzung* of 1980) "the self-revelation of Jesus before the world," but to distinguish between Jesus's revelation

*The Divine Word Enters the World (1:1–4:54)*

before the world in John 1–4 and his revelation before his people in John 5–10, with a look back in John 12:37–43 and a final summons to belief in John 12:44–50.

## 1. The Prologue (1:1–18)

¹ In the beginning was the Word, and the Word was with God, and the Word was God. ² He was in the beginning with God. ³ All things came into being through him, and without him nothing came into being. What came into being through him ⁴ was life, and the life was the light of men. ⁵ And the light is shining in the darkness, and the darkness has not grasped it.

⁶ There appeared a man, sent from God; his name was John. ⁷ He came as a witness, to testify for the light, so that all through him might come to faith. ⁸ He himself was not the light, he had only to testify for the light. ⁹ The true light, which gives light to every man, came into the world. ¹⁰ He was in the world, and the world came into being through him, but the world did not recognize him. ¹¹ He came to his own, but his own did not receive him. ¹² But to all who did receive him, he gave the power to become the children of God – all who believe in his name, ¹³ who were born not from blood, nor from the will of the flesh, nor from the will of man but from God.

¹⁴ And the Word became flesh and lived among us, and we saw his glory, the glory of the only Son of the Father, full of grace and truth. ¹⁵ John testifies for him and cries: This was the one I was speaking of: The one who comes after me is before me, because he was before me. ¹⁶ Of his fullness we have all received, grace upon grace. ¹⁷ For the Law was given through Moses; grace and truth came through Jesus Christ. ¹⁸ No one has ever seen God. The Only One, who is God and rests in the Father's heart, has brought the message.

### I

The fourth evangelist begins his account of Jesus, not with a separate historical scene like the appearance of John the Baptist in Mark or with a story about the earthly origin of Jesus such as we find in Matthew and Luke. Rather, he takes us right back to the very beginning, as is shown by the allusion to Gen 1:1 (LXX) in John 1:1, and, indeed, further back still, before all time in God's eternity. It is from there that the Logos originates and came into the world in order to become flesh.

John's prologue forms a literary unit, markedly separate from the following text. While the prologue's verses acknowledging the testimony of John are integrated into its language and train of thought, the section concerning the Baptist's witness in John 1:19–34 leads clearly into the narrative part of the Fourth Gospel. The μαρτυρία of John that is heralded in John 1:6–8, 15 is now defined in content in a more detailed way and located in history.

Research today treats John's prologue as a literary unit that can be explained as making sense in itself. Previously, there was almost a century of literary-critical hypotheses about the formation of the prologue. Here, the controlling factor was mainly the stylistic difference between the verses that sounded like parts of a hymn and those of a more prosaic character. Thus, in 1908 Julius Wellhausen wondered how "the Baptist sneaked into eternity" in v. 6.[1] Twentieth-century research was strongly marked by the hypothesis that a pre-Johannine hymn lay behind John 1:1–18. Sometimes, even two hymns were postulated, since verses 14 and 16 are stylistically separate from the opening verses. From the history of religions point of view, instead of the assumption of a Gnostic hymn from Baptist circles, as Bultmann had suggested, the place was soon taken by a Christian hymn (or two Christian hymns). These hypotheses do not stand given recent evidence, and today preference is increasingly being given to a synchronic reading.[2]

Three models have been suggested for the structure of the prologue. Numerous authors go for a *linear structure*. Heinrich Julius Holtzmann recalls examples among the Fathers of the Church of a threefold division of the prologue: vv. 1–5, the pre-existence of the Logos and his role in creation; vv. 6–13, the preparation for the incarnation; and vv. 14–18, the incarnation.[3] In recent times, the identity of the Logos with Jesus Christ (first named in v. 17) has been recognized more clearly. A similar threefold division of the prologue is often found in the commentaries. Heinrich Lausberg provides a linguistic reason for this threefold structure.[4] He proceeds from the occurrence of the title "Logos" in verses 1 and 14. In verses 1–5, the theme is developed with recourse to the Old Testament

---

1. Wellhausen, *Evangelium*, 8.

2. A good survey of the literary criticism of John's prologue is found in Hofrichter, *Im Anfang*, 13–82. Cf., also, Beutler, "Johannes-Prolog," 78–84. For more recent contributions since 1988, cf. Theobald, "Der älteste Kommentar."

3. Holtzmann, 26.

4. Lausberg, *Johannes-Prolog*.

tradition, in verses 6–13 with recourse to that of the New Testament. In verses 14 and 16–18 Lausberg sees, above all, the use of the Exodus traditions. According to Lausberg the author of the prologue made use of an older "exordium" to the Gospel (vv. 6–7) in order to create a new one that summarizes the Gospel and prepares the readers for its main themes. In verses 1–5, Schenke sees a "myth"; in verses 6–13, "history"; and, in verses 14–18, the "confession" of the community.[5]

A string of authors see a *concentric* structure in the prologue. An influential suggestion was made by Marie-Émile Boismard,[6] who views the prologue as structured concentrically around v. 13. Boismard reads the singular here, "who . . . was born of God," for which reading, however, he cannot call on any ancient Greek manuscripts. Accordingly, it would no longer be the statement about the incarnation that would stand in the center of the prologue but the confession of God's Son born of a virgin. With good reason, de la Potterie criticizes Boismard's suggestion on four grounds: the model is static, not dynamic; the incarnation does not stand in the center; the two sections on the Baptist (vv. 6–8 and 15) are not identical, since the second is in the present; similarly, verses 1 and 18 do not correspond to each other (the latter verse assumes that the Word has become incarnate).[7] To avoid these difficulties, some authors like de la Potterie have suggested a spiral structure for the prologue.[8] Themes are taken up again and developed further on a higher level. The Belgian author's proposal for dividing the text remains disputed since he relies chiefly on semantic and theological rather than linguistic criteria.

In retrospect, it appears reasonable to start off from a *linear* structure for John's prologue. Here, it is the proposal of Lausberg that has won the most recognition and agreement.[9] It is related to that of Zumstein,[10] although Zumstein does not expressly presuppose Lausberg's contribution. According to this proposal, we can recognize in the prologue three main sections that build on one another: the origin of the divine Word (vv. 1–5); his destiny in history (vv. 6–13); and, finally, his incarnation and his reception in the community (vv. 14–18).

The basic starting point for the exegesis is the text of the prologue

5. Schenke, *Johannes. Kommentar*, 22–36.
6. Boismard, *Prologue*.
7. de la Potterie, "Structure."
8. de la Potterie, "Structure."
9. Cf. n. 4 above.
10. Zumstein, "Prolog."

that has been transmitted to us. Thus, we first abandon the hypothesis of the pre-existing hymnic parts of the prologue, although these are probable both in verses 1–5 as well as in 10–12 and 14, 16. As soon as the internal form of the text has been reliably secured, our exegesis follows the methodological steps of exegesis with a linguistic-syntactic, semantic, and pragmatic analysis of the text. The influence of the literary environment of the prologue should similarly be considered. With Lausberg, among others, we see behind vv. 1–5 the beginning of Genesis as well as the wisdom traditions that speak of the entry of Wisdom into the human world; behind vv. 6–8 and 15 we see the influence of the New Testament traditions of John the Baptist; and, behind vv. 14–18, we see Moses traditions that go back to the book of Exodus.[11]

In what follows, we see John's prologue as a homogeneous and linear text. The distinction between a first part in vv. 1–13, which is supposed to speak of the Logos before the incarnation, and a second part, which speaks of the incarnate Logos in vv. 14–18,[12] seems to us not to be justified by the text. Rather, it is apparent that, from v. 4, the text speaks of the coming of Christ as the divine Word among men. Verses 4–5, 9–10, and 11 resemble one another to a large extent. Inspired by the myth of the coming of the divine Wisdom, they speak of the destiny of the divine Word among men without mentioning his coming in the flesh explicitly. This is not mentioned expressly until vv. 14–18. Only here, in v. 17, is Jesus Christ named as such for the first time. Thus, the observation of the homogeneous and linear structure of the prologue is confirmed: the movement is one from veiled and implicit language to unveiled and explicit language. The one in whom the divine Word has come and found his dwelling among men is Jesus Christ.

In recent times, instead of the question of the prehistory of John's prologue, it is that of its function that is discussed. This is in keeping with the paradigm shift from the historical-critical to the literary treatment of New Testament texts. Now, the relationship of the prologue to the rest of John's Gospel stands at the center of interest. This relationship can be better described as literary or theological. Mostly, both perspectives are linked together.

According to a more recent suggestion, we should see in the pro-

---

11. For Jewish tradition behind John's prologue, cf. Markstahler, *Prolog*.

12. Cf., still, for this distinction going back to the fathers between the λόγος ἄσαρκος and the λόγος ἔνσαρκος, Léon-Dufour, *Lecture*, 1:48–50. However, the author sees the movement rather as one on the part of the reader than on that of the Logos.

logue a text that is meant to legitimate the theological position of the Gospel.[13] The Christology of John is anchored in the sending of the divine Word from eternity. Thus, it can also be helpful in disputes with groups that represent a dissenting confession within the religious environment of the fourth evangelist.

Since his *Habilitationsschrift*,[14] Theobald has worked on the relationship of the prologue to the rest of John's Gospel. For Theobald, the prologue is a prelude to the Fourth Gospel as a whole, written with the aim of introducing the readers to its great themes. Thus, it follows that this introduction was composed—as usual—after the work was finished. This makes it understandable why some of the prologue's concepts (such as the personal Logos and "grace") do not feature any more in the rest of the Gospel.

Another recent study examines John's prologue precisely as that—a prologue.[15] This literary genre was known in ancient times. Already in the sixth century BCE, we find an example by the Greek author Thespis, who uses this genre to introduce the plot to the audience of a play. Subsequently, prologues were also used to introduce speeches alongside dramas and dramatic narratives. Apparently, John—the only one among the evangelists—used this genre to introduce his readers to the message of his Gospel and present its main characters: Jesus Christ, the eternal Logos, Moses, and John the Baptist.

Zumstein reads John's prologue in the sense of his model of "*relecture*."[16] These "*relectures*" ("re-readings") occur in the Bible in various guises: as title, as intertextuality or intratextuality (back references to different texts or within the same text), and as paratext. Zumstein finds this last form in John's prologue and in the epilogue of John 21. A paratext has the function of looking back on a finished work or preparing the readers for reading it. Such a text protects the reader from misunderstandings, provides the code for deciphering the literary work, and guides the reader during the reading. Zumstein finds the justification for regarding the prologue as paratext above all from Aristotle (*Rhet*. 3.1414b). With this tool we can better understand the function of John's prologue within the Gospel.

If we can assume that the prologue was inserted only in the last phase

---

13. Cf. McGrath, *Prologue*.
14. Theobald, *Fleischwerdung*, and, since then, Theobald, "Geist- und Inkarnationschristologie," the author's Commentary as well as "Der älteste Kommentar."
15. Cf. Harris, *Prologue*.
16. Zumstein, "Prolog."

of the redaction of the Fourth Gospel, it is easier to explain why central concepts and themes of the prologue are not found again explicitly in the Gospel. We are referencing here the personal Logos and his part in the work of creation, but also the concept of "grace." However, the "word" of Jesus belongs to the fundamental notions of the Gospel. Already in the prologue itself, there is a movement from the divine existence of the Logos to his mission to men. He is "light" and "life" for men. John testifies to him. All should come to faith in him (1:7; cf. 1:12). The exegesis of the prologue will show how the coming of the divine Logos into the world is proclaimed in the prologue.

## II

### *The Origin of the Divine Word (1:1–5)*

The first five verses of John's prologue concern the origin of the divine Word. In form and content, they turn out to be a coherent textual unit distinct from the following context. Characteristic of this group of verses is its stepped structure. One concept is situated at the end of a statement and then taken up again at the beginning of the next line. That concept is explained by means of a further concept that then, for its part, appears at the beginning of the third line (a–b, b–c, c–d). In the first three lines, the concept of the Logos leads to the catchword "God" at the beginning of the second line. This is developed by the catchword "Logos," which recurs from the first line onward. The result is an inclusio in v. 1 between the first and the second lines. Verse 2 takes up the first catchword from the first line and the second catchword from the second line. In this way, they are each duplicated. In terms of content, these verses are concerned with the existence of the divine Logos with God and his divine being. Verse 3 portrays the role of the divine Logos at the creation. The tense changes from the imperfect to the aorist. We thus link the phrase "what came into being" at the end of v. 3 to what follows, as is explained in the detailed exegesis: "What came into being with him was (the) life." We see here already the passage from the creation to the economy of salvation. "Life" and "light," which are counterposed to the "darkness," are gifts of salvation. Their relation to the divine Word is everlasting (imperfect), the offer of them is a mark of the present (the light "shines" in the darkness, present), but has already been rejected in history (aorist). Thus, the opening section of the prologue leads into the fate of the Word in the world. The stepped form continues to mark the construction of verses 3c–5: The catchword "came into being" leads to the benefit of "life," this, in turn, leads to "light," this leads in turn to "darkness," and this to the rejection of the Logos. Thus, the whole of the first section of the prologue appears to be a stylistically coherent unit.

The construction of this small unit is thus:

- The Word with the Father from the very beginning (vv. 1–2)
- The collaboration of the Word in the creation (v. 3a–b)
- The significance of the Word for men and their destiny (vv. 3c–5)

**1:1–2** The opening of John's prologue goes back to the very beginning. "In the beginning" points forward to creation and history. There is a biblical allusion here to Gen 1:1: "In the beginning, God created." In John's prologue, the subject is, above all, God's activity in his being. To be more precise, the main subject is God's activity in the being of the divine Logos, his existence with God, and his divine nature. The Logos is from eternity. One can understand, therefore, that he is with God and equal to him (expressed by the Greek πρός), and he is of divine substance. θεός is thus to be understood as a noun predicate: he is God. Precisely this Word who was from the beginning, who was with God and who is of divine substance, was in the beginning with God, as v. 2 declares again.

**1:3a–b** After describing the eternal presence of the divine Word with God, the text passes on to the role of the Word in the creation of the world. The emphasis here is striking. The statement of the text in v. 3 is repeated in synonymous parallelism with a double negative. Thus, in every aspect, the whole world goes back to the divine Word as the mediator of creation. The passage from the imperfect to the aorist is already preparing for the transition to history.

**1:3c–4** With Nestle-Aland[28] and the GNT[4], we are linking the ὃ γέγονεν at the end of v. 3 with the following sentence. Aland himself has given decisive reasons for this in a detailed article.[17] The proposed reading is *difficilior* and for this reason to be preferred. Among the ancient versions, the Sahidic and Syro-Curetonian prefer the Aland reading, just as the majority of the Old Latin textual witnesses as well as Tatian's *Diatessaron*. The

---

17. Aland, "Eine Untersuchung zu Joh 1,3.4"; cf., further, Metzger, *Textual Commentary*; Miller, *Salvation-History*.

majority of the Old Greek witnesses from a later time prefer the version with "what came into being" as the conclusion of the statement in v. 3, but the other version is supported in a number of manuscripts. Ancient manuscripts are without punctuation marks, but occasionally there appears a gap between words. This is the case with our verse (codices C and D, also P[75]). The fathers of the second century, together with those of the first half of the third from Gaul, Africa, Egypt, and Palestine, know only the version preferred by Aland. The Gnostic and anti-Gnostic texts of this period presuppose it. It is the fourth century when the linking of the text "what came into being" with the previous context begins to gain prominence. This could go back to the polemics of the Greek Church against the Arians (who regarded the Logos as having come into being), although our preferred reading also appears infrequently before the Arian controversy. In the West, this tendency in the texts is not yet in evidence. From the point of view of content, this version, which links "what came into being" with what goes before, seems out of place in the Fourth Gospel since it constitutes pure repetition. On such and similar grounds, multiple editions of the NT[18] as well as commentaries and translations opt for the Aland-preferred reading.[19]

There then arises the question of its meaning. Clearly, the expression ὃ γέγονεν is linked to the ἐγένετο from v. 3a and 3b. The change of tense from aorist to perfect is already a warning not to equate the two expressions without further ado. It is now a matter of what came into being permanently through the Word and operates in the present. Thus the present tense of φαίνει in v. 5 is already being forecast. Clearly, at the end of v. 3, we are dealing with another kind of coming into being than the creation in v. 3a and 3b. The text is concerned much more with the economy of salvation. The difficulty of the sentence beginning with ὃ γέγονεν lies in the ἐν αὐτῷ. Exegetes have mainly chosen between three models. One possibility is that "what came into being" is to be understood as a *casus pendens* and the sentence translated thus: "What came into being, in it he was the life." "He" would then be understood christologically as the Logos (thus Bultmann, Jürgen Becker, G. R. Beasley-Murray, Theobald,[20] the Jerusalem Bible). Without this christological understanding, one could also

---

18. Cf. Tischendorf (8th ed.; 1969), Westcott-Hort (1881), v. Soden (1913), and Vogels (3rd ed.; 1949).

19. Cf. the commentaries of Bultmann (1941), Brown (1966), Becker (1978), Moloney (1998), Beasley-Murray (2nd ed.; 1999), and Keener (2005) as well as the commented translation in the Jerusalem Bible. The traditional view is still maintained by Thyen, "ὃ γέγονεν."

20. Theobald, "Der älteste Kommentar," 58f.

say: "What came into being, in it was life." The meaning would be approximately the same since the "life" is to be understood theologically from the following context. The best possible meaning is represented by Eddie L. Miller and is to be found also in Brown. "What came into being" is, in that case, not a *casus pendens*, but the subject of a nominal statement and to be linked with "in him": "What came into being in him, was (the) life." The christological reference to the Logos is thus preserved. The linguistically difficult *casus pendens* is avoided. In this case, the prologue would already be passing over to the mission of the Logos in the world, from creation to salvation history. This meaning is also suggested by the rhythm of the wording. It remains true to the step pattern of the first three verses that then also regulates the following statements to the end of v. 5. From the ἐγένετο of v. 3b to the ὃ γέγονεν of the end of v. 3, the semantic result is an adjournment of the creation theme in favor of life and light in history. It is precisely this adjournment that can easily be overlooked, leading to the misunderstandings that have been noted and have induced so eminent an author as C. K. Barrett to abandon his preference for one of the above possible meanings. The transition from the creation "through" (διά) the Logos in v. 3a to the γέγονεν ἐν at the beginning of v. 4, over which Bultmann stumbled, can be explained through the indication that v. 4 is precisely not dealing with the creation any longer but with salvation "in" the Logos. A mediating position between the two expressions is adopted in Col 1:16, where it says: ὅτι ἐν αὐτῷ ἐκτίσθη τὰ πάντα (Brown).

With "light" and "life," two central catchwords of Johannine theology are introduced. Just as Jesus gives life (cf. 3:16, 36), and indeed is life (14:6), so he is also the light of the world (9:5; 8:12; 12:46). The incarnation of the divine Word is not directly expressed yet, but nonetheless appears to be presupposed here.

**1:5** The light shines in the darkness. This statement too refers to the fate of the divine Word in the world. John expresses it with the dualism of "light" and "darkness." According to him, the sending of the light into the world is such that it shines into the darkness and delivers from it (cf. 8:12; 12:35, 46).

There is dispute as to the meaning of the statement at the end of the first section of the prologue: καὶ ἡ σκοτία αὐτὸ οὐ κατέλαβεν.[21] For the translation "And the darkness has not overcome it,"[22] John 12:35 is often

---

21. Cf. also now, Beutler, "Und die Finsternis hat es nicht ergriffen."
22. Recently, in Thyen; Theobald, "Der älteste Kommentar," 50 n. 9; Theobald, "'Welt' bei Paulus und Johannes," 423.

mustered in support. However, this proof is confined to John. The Greek dictionary of Walter Bauer knows of a root meaning "seize, grasp, capture," which also extends into "understand." Where the meaning of "seize" is evidenced, there enters an element of surprise that, in the light of φαίνει in John 1:5, is excluded (cf. 1 Thess 5:4; Mark 9:18). It is a question of the fundamental relationship of light and darkness. When, above all, Anglo-Saxon translations (like the RSV and NRSV) and commentaries choose to render αὐτὸ οὐ κατέλαβεν with "has not overcome it," then this is not least because of the appeal to the majority of the Greek fathers since Origen. Here, in fact, no attention was paid as to how Origen reached his meaning. The Alexandrian had, above all, a theological interest in his text. According to him, the darkness is fundamentally unable to overpower the divine light in the Logos. Thus, he introduces an additional notion, namely that of pursuing. The darkness pursues the light and tries to overcome it but is not able to do so.[23] This notion of the "pursuit" is, of course, not in the text of John's prologue. The Latin tradition is unaware of it and so stays with the sense of "grasp." Above all, the context of John 1:5 supports this meaning. In verses 10 and 11, it says: "He was in the world, and the world came into being through him, but the world did not recognize him. He came to his own, but his own did not receive him." It is precisely this sense that appears to be present in verse 5 and across vv. 6–8, which deal with the Baptist.

The flashback of the first verse of John's prologue to the first verses of the Bible, Gen 1:1–2:4a, is clear. Both texts open with "in the beginning." They counterpose "light" and "darkness." To the phrase "God spoke" of Genesis corresponds the "Word" of the prologue. Both texts speak of "coming into being" (ἐγένετο is the most frequent verb form in the first creation account). Both also speak of "life" as the work of God (in Genesis, applied to the creatures, Gen 1:20–30).

On the other hand, it is evident that Old Testament texts about Wisdom and her mission to men have had an impact on John's prologue. Some of these appear to assume the pre-existence of Wisdom (Prov 8:22–36; Wisd 9:9–10; Sir 24:1–22), whereas others do not (Wisd 6:12–16; 7:22–8:1).[24] Of course, it is also necessary to bear in mind the differences between these texts and our prologue.[25] The Old Testament texts speak of

---

23. Cf. Origen, *Comm. Jo.* 17.167, 168–70.

24. Cf. Beutler and Meredith, "Johannes-Evangelium (u. –Briefe)," 657; Beutler, "Johannesevangelium, Johannesbriefe," 34; Beutler, "Der Johannes-Prolog," 88; Sticher, "Frau Weisheit"; Gordley, "Prologue."

25. Cf. Tobin, "The Prologue of John."

*The Divine Word Enters the World (1:1–4:54)*

"Wisdom," not of the "Logos."[26] Moreover, the functions of Wisdom and the Logos are different. The wisdom texts lack the creation of the world "through" (διά) the Logos, the dualistic opposition between "light" and "darkness" (which is encountered rather in the creation account), and the connection of the gift of "life" with the reception of Wisdom or the Logos.

For this complex of ideas, Philo of Alexandria offers the closest parallels.[27] The great philosophical traditions of his time flow into Philo's teaching about the Logos: the Stoic notion of the Logos as a rational principle pervading the world, and the Platonic teaching of the Logos as the World Soul in the sense of the *Timaeus*. Naturally, the Genesis account of creation also influences Philo, something that leads to characteristic shifts in his thought. The concept of a collaboration of the Logos in the creation of the world in Philo could stem from Middle Platonism. The instrumental collaboration of the Logos in creation thus goes beyond the wisdom tradition's notions of the role of Wisdom in creation (cf. *Leg.* 3.96; *Cher.* 127; *Migr.* 6; *Spec.* 1.81; cf. the rabbinic 'Abot 3.15 for the creation of the world through the Torah; cf. the early Christian 1 Cor 8:6, Jesus Christ as the one "through whom" all exists; Col 1:16 as he in whom all things were created and have their existence). Together with John's prologue, Philo also has the opposition between light and darkness, the assignment of the Logos to the sphere of light, as well as his role in the emergence of "life."[28] This complex of ideas is at its clearest in *Opif.* 29–35.

To what extent Gnostic texts like the Three Forms of First Thought (NHC XIII 1) can be compared appropriately with John's prologue remains controversial. In any case, the aforementioned text from Nag Hammadi presupposes Christianity.

*The Destiny of the Divine Word in History (1:6–13)*

The transition to the verses about the Baptist has been perceived not infrequently as a stylistic and theological rupture within John's prologue. We recall that it was Wellhausen who already wondered why the Baptist "sneaked into eternity" in v. 6. This rupture is regarded as still greater if, along with

---

26. However, cf. the reference to Wis 9:1f in Nicacci, "Logos e Sapienza," 79.

27. Cf., again, Tobin, "The Prologue of John"; Beutler, "Johannes-Evangelium (u. -Briefe)," 657f.; Beutler, "Johannesevangelium, Johannesbriefe," 34–36.

28. Cf. Tobin, "The Prologue," 262–65.

numerous authors, one proceeds from the notion of a pre-Johannine hymn behind the prologue. Of course, this hypothesis also carries with it an explanation of the rupture at v. 6. At this place in the text, the evangelist would have inserted a tradition about the Baptist or else used these verses to comment on the pre-existing hymn with the material about the Baptist.

At this point, we refrain from discussing each and every literary hypothesis and observe within the prologue itself a stylistic transition from a hymnic to a more strictly narrative style. This transition is apparent also in the change from the present, imperfect, and perfect tenses of the first four verses to the narrative aorist in v. 6. This aorist has already occurred twice: in the ἐγένετο of the creation in v. 3 and in the κατέλαβεν of the reaction to the revelation of the Logos in v. 5.

As we noticed already in the previous section, in the transition from the first five verses of the prologue to verses 6–13, we do not see a movement away from eternity or from prehistory to history. Such a view is already excluded by our understanding of verses 4 and 5: the divine Logos, the light for men, is shining into the world until the present moment except that the world has not wanted to be open to this light. We are thus already located in history here and not in some kind of misty prehistory. From this perspective, the introduction of the Baptist also cannot have the sense of introducing a new phase of salvation history. It serves only to make the reading community aware of an important antithesis. It was not John who was and is the light of the world but the divine Logos who will be known very soon by his name: Jesus Christ (v. 17).

It is appropriate to regard verses 6–13 as a separate section within the prologue, especially when the plural is read in v. 13. Only those authors who read the singular ("who . . . was born from God") in v. 13 take this verse in close connection with v. 14. As mentioned, there are, above all, those authors who see a concentric construction in the prologue with its center in verses 13–14. However, de la Potterie, who reads the singular here, has registered his reservations about this structure.[29]

The whole section is clearly arranged in two parts. At the beginning, verses 6–8 get things going. They introduce John the Baptist, speak of his mission, and contrast him with the "light." He was not the light but only had to bear witness to the light. While the first pair of statements employ the aorist, the third (v. 8) speaks of the light in the imperfect. The change of subject prepares the passage to the following verse.

29. Cf. de la Potterie, "Structure."

*The Divine Word Enters the World (1:1–4:54)*

Verses 9–13 can be seen as a separate subunit, as in the Nestle-Aland edition of the text.[28] Here, once again, we can distinguish two halves. First comes the statement of the failure of the sending of the "light" into the world and to his own in vv. 9–11. Then the subject changes to those who received him (vv. 12–13). The linguistic transition comes about through the verb παρέλαβον at the end of v. 11 and the ἔλαβον at the beginning of v. 12 (cf. the κατέλαβεν in v. 5, which through this twofold usage is confirmed in its meaning of "receive").

Thus, the following construction appears for verses 6–13:

- The sending of John (vv. 6–8)
- The coming of the "light" and its rejection (vv. 9–11)
- The receiving of the "light" by those who believe (vv. 12–13)

**1:6–8** The prologue has already used the verb γίνεσθαι three times. In v. 3, it is said, twice, that all things "came into being" through the divine Word. In v. 4, we understood ὃ γέγονεν in such a way that what "came into being" through him was life. In this way, the expression already has an orientation towards history. With the Ἐγένετο ἄνθρωπος of v. 6, known history has finally been reached. The sense of the expression is conveyed by "appeared" or "came." This also becomes clear from the context: John was sent from God and "came," to bear witness (v. 7). Here, we become aware of the increasing concretization that we have recognized as a fundamental feature of the prologue—from the creation to human history in general up to the historical moment of John's appearance.

It is striking that the fourth evangelist withholds the title of "Baptist" from the figure of John. He gives no account of the baptism of Jesus by John such as we find in the other Gospels. The reason for this omission lies in Johannine theology, which looks on John exclusively as the witness to Jesus. The whole section John 1:19–34 serves as a demonstration of this. To this, we can add John 3:26 and 5:33. Here, in the prologue, John's significance seems to be at the same time diminished and enhanced: he is none other than the witness to Jesus Christ, the light and redeemer of the world. Exegetes like to refer to a possible cult of John the Baptist on the part of Jewish and, perhaps also, Christian circles (cf. Acts 19:3–4). Alongside such an apologetic objective that aims to emphasize the uniqueness of Christ, however, the role of John also fits in with the Johannine theology of witness. According to it, it is not only John who bears witness to Jesus, but the Father himself, Israel's Scriptures, Jesus's works, the Spirit, and Jesus's disciples are also witnesses for Jesus in his "great trial" with the world (cf. John 5:31-40; 8:12-20; 10:25; 15:26-27).[30] The linking of μαρτυρέω with the preposition περί in the sense of witness to a person, in this case Jesus, is characteristic of the fourth evangelist and apart from John is rarely found in the NT. As a rule, in John, testimony "on behalf of" Jesus is meant. Our text speaks of witness to "the light," and so makes use of the expression that, at the beginning of the prologue, describes the function of the divine Word at his entry into the world.

Invariably, witness in John is intended to arouse faith in Jesus. We see this in John 3 with its reference to the witness of the Baptist (3:26), with the promise of life for those who receive Jesus in faith (3:36). The whole section of John 5:31-40 serves the purpose of leading to faith in Jesus on account of the manifold testimony to him (cf. v. 38). The same goes for John 8:12-20, even if the verb πιστεύειν is missing. The concepts used are "knowing" and "judging."

The influence on John 1:6-8 of the Synoptic tradition about the beginning of the public activity of John the Baptist is obvious. In Mark 1:4, it says: ἐγένετο Ἰωάννης ὁ βαπτίζων ἐν τῇ ἐρήμῳ (cf. Matt 3:1; Luke 3:2). Perhaps the original opening of John's Gospel was something similar.[31]

**1:9-11** After the "digression" concerning John in verses 6-8, the text returns to the opening verses, especially v. 5. There is an element of continuity in the concept of the "light" that was made use of in connection with the sending of the Baptist in verses 7-8. Perhaps v. 5 was originally continued in v. 10.[32] It is also possible that an original hymn contained verses 5 and 9 after each other.[33] According to Schnackenburg, the hymn began with verses 1-4 and continued in v. 9.[34]

The beginning of v. 9 poses a problem of translation. The words ἐρχόμενον εἰς τὸν κόσμον can be taken either with Ἦν τὸ φῶς τὸ ἀληθινόν or with πάντα ἄνθρωπον. Exegetes' views differ, but the majority prefer the link with Ἦν τὸ φῶς τὸ ἀληθινόν. The notion of the coming of a hu-

---

30. Cf. Beutler, *Martyria*, 209-306; Beutler, "μαρτυρέω" and "μαρτυρία" in *EWNT* 2:958-73; *EDNT* 2:389-93.

31. Thus, already, Brown, 1:27f. with Boismard; recently, Theobald, "Der älteste Kommentar," 49f. According to him, the Baptist verses would not have been inserted into a pre-existing hymn, but, vice versa, the hymn attached to a beginning of John's Gospel corresponding to John 1:6f.

32. Cf. the reference in Dettwiler, "Le prologue johannique," 188 with n. 16.

33. Thus Dettwiler himself.

34. Cf. Schnackenburg, 1:221.

man being into the world is rather strange both to biblical and Johannine thought, whereas the coming of Christ into the world is a rather common concept in John. For the "coming" of the Christ from God, the *EWNT* cites the following texts: John 5:43; 7:28; 8:14, 21; 9:39; 10:10; 12:47; 13:3; 16:28; 18:37.[35] Especially close to what we have here are the verses John 9:39 and 12:47, since here "coming" is connected with the "light" (cf., also, John 8:14). Thus, John 1:9 is rendered either with a periphrastic construction: "The true light, which enlightens every man, came into the world" or with an identifying statement: "(The Word) was the true light, which enlightens every man; he came into the world." Most of the more recent translations understand the ἐρχόμενον εἰς τὸν κόσμον in this way.[36]

As regards content, in v. 9 the coming of the light into the world is picked up again from v. 5. The notion that the light enlightens every man is taken up again from v. 4. According to v. 9, it comes not just to the enlightened ones but to the "whole world." This universalism is maintained in v. 10. Just as the whole world was created through the divine Word, so it ought to receive him. It is possible tha the words καὶ ὁ κόσμος δι' αὐτοῦ ἐγένετο were inserted to strengthen the statement and to emphasize the link with v. 3. Incidentally, the rejection of the divine Word by the "world" seems to be unlimited. The Word has not been recognized by this world. In a matching statement, it goes on in v. 11: "He came to his own, but his own did not receive him." Who are "his own"? The Jews are a possibility, but the universal perspective of the context does not lend itself to this. "His own" are the men created by God through the Word, the "all" of v. 7, "every man" of v. 9, and "the world" of v. 10. The destiny of the divine Wisdom comes into mind as it is described in the books of Proverbs, Wisdom, or Sirach.[37] According to these hymns, Wisdom takes part in the work of creation. According to Prov 8:31, it was her "joy to be among men." The hymn in Sir 24 praises the sending of Wisdom into the world and her reception in Israel and on Zion. To identify "his own" in John 1:11 with Israel would contradict this sapiential notion.

**1:12-13** Many authors think that v. 12a-b still belongs to the pre-Johannine hymn that was adopted.[38] The following lines (vv. 12c-13) would

---

35. Schramm, "ἔρχομαι," *EWNT* 2:143; *EDNT* 2:57.

36. Cf. the Jerusalem Bible, the RSV and NRSV, and the *Einheitsübersersetzung* deviating here from Luther's text.

37. See above under v. 5.

38. Cf. Dettwiler, "Le prologue," and the survey in Theobald, "Der älteste Kommentar," 57.

then have been inserted by the evangelist. This hypothesis would clear up a logical difficulty. On the one hand, v. 12a–b promises believers adoption as God's children; on the other hand, according to vv. 12c–13, one can only come to faith if one is born from God and not just from human parents. To "receive" the light/Word (v. 12a) is tantamount to "believing" in the light (v. 12c). This faith appears as a divine gift, the fruit of being born from God. In v. 13, therefore, every human cooperation in the birth, physical (ἐξ αἱμάτων) or psychological (ἐκ θελήματος σαρκὸς . . . ἀνδρός), of those who are born from God is ruled out. The idea of such a birth or begetting from God is quite foreign to the Bible. However, it finds its parallels in Oriental and Graeco-Roman mythology (one thinks of names such as "Diogenes" or "Hermogenes"). Viewed theologically, the apparent contradiction between divine adoption as the prerequisite or the consequence of faith is resolved into a complementary perspective: on the one hand, faith presupposes divine grace, yet, on the other hand, also leads to divine adoption. The fourth evangelist does not have at his command a system by which he could reconcile both aspects and so he places them side by side. Thus, the correct viewpoint is achieved by treating them concurrently.

There is still no agreement as to the text of v. 13. Since early on, instead of the plural "who . . . were born/begotten of God,"[39] there has also, if rarely, been the singular ("who . . . was born/begotten"). The plural is represented in Nestle-Aland[28] and GNT[4], where it obtains the highest level of certainty (A = without doubt). It is found in all the Greek manuscripts of the NT. Since the second century, the singular is occasionally attested and is found probably for the first time in Tertullian, possibly in Justin and Hippolytus, certainly in Irenaeus, in the *Epistula Apostolorum*, in Codex "b" of the Vetus Latina (Codex Veronensis), in the so-called *Liber Comicus* (Lectionary of Toledo), and in some manuscripts of the Syrian tradition.[40] Reference is made to such evidence in detail by de la Potterie[41] and Jean Galot.[42] However, the external attestation of the singular reading remains weak, especially given its absence from every Greek manuscript of the NT. This is the basis of the judgement of the editors of Nestle-Aland[28] and GNT[4]. The external attestation of the plural reading is supported by the papyri of the second and third centu-

---

39. The translation "begotten" is advocated throughout by Menken, "'Born of God.'" As a result, the difficulty of the imagery of John 3:3–8 remains.
   40. Schnackenburg, 1:240f.
   41. de la Potterie, *La conception*.
   42. Galot, *Être né de Dieu*.

ries (P⁶⁶ and P⁷⁵) and by Tertullian himself in his polemical controversy regarding this plural reading.[43]

It remains to consider the internal witness of the text. According to Tertullian, the plural was inserted by the Gnostics in order to gain scriptural support for the divine origin of their spiritual men. This argument is certainly not convincing, as Bruce M. Metzger has already noted.[44] The Gnostics distinguish between men of the spirit, the pneumatics, and other men, the men of the flesh. To state that all men stem from God and not from woman would contradict the Gnostics' convictions. On the other hand, the origin of the singular reading can be understood as the effort of the old church authors to find in John evidence for the virginal origin of Jesus that is attested by Matthew and Luke. The αὐτοῦ at the end of v. 12 could have played its part in this.[45] More recent contributions that prefer the singular reading no longer ascribe it to the canonical text of John's Gospel.[46]

### The Incarnation of the Word and His Reception in the Community (1:14–18)

The majority of exegetes regard the last five verses of the prologue as the climax of this foundational Johannine text. Now, at last, in these verses, the name of Jesus Christ appears (v. 17). Only in these verses are the concepts "λόγος" and "θεός" taken up again from the opening verses and applied to Jesus. The impression of an inclusio between v. 1 and vv. 14–18 is confirmed in the fact that the confession of Jesus as "God" occurs only once more in the Gospel, and that in the confession of Thomas shortly before the end of

---

43. Metzger, *Textual Commentary*.
44. Metzger, *Textual Commentary*.
45. Metzger, *Textual Commentary*.
46. According to Theobald, "Le prologue," the singular reading is a late gloss to the canonical text. If he nonetheless preferred this text in this earlier publication, then this was probably under the influence of Francophone Catholic exegesis. However, see now his commentary. The original edition of the Jerusalem Bible of 1955 reads the singular, followed by the German edition (Freiburg 1968), and the English (1966). However, the New Jerusalem Bible (London 1985) decided for the plural. Hofrichter earlier preferred the singular reading but then turned back to the plural for the canonical text: cf. Hofrichter, *Im Anfang*. According to him, the singular was to be found in a hypothetical original prologue that was an independent song behind both the Gnostic texts and the Gospel of John. This hypothesis has not been widely accepted.

the Johannine Gospel account in John 20 (v. 28), before the supplementary chapter, John 21. This would then produce a further inclusio that would have embraced the whole of the Fourth Gospel in its original form. The incarnation of the Logos has no echo in John's Gospel. From the theological point of view, it certainly forms the climax of the prologue. The further course of the Gospel will describe the path of this incarnate Word.

Looking at the structure of John 1:14–18, one is struck especially by the difference in style and content between v. 15 and its context. Verses 14 and 16 exhibit a hymnic style, connect well with each other, and praise the incarnation of the Word and its impact on the community. Verse 15 again takes up the mention of the Baptist from vv. 6–8 and does not share the meter of the surrounding verses. Verses 17 and 18 resonate more strongly with v. 15 and also turn out to be related to each other.

**1:14** The central verse is divided into five lines. The first two speak of the incarnation of the Word and his living "among us" whereby the community of readers comes into the picture. That community is also the subject of the third line: it has seen the glory of the incarnate Word. The two last lines unfold the meaning of this "glory," with reference to the one bearing it and to its impact on the community.

The first line is marked by Johannine language and concepts. The following lines draw more strongly on the vocabulary and concepts of Israel's Scripture. As mentioned briefly above,[47] behind the first five verses of the prologue stands the creation account of Genesis; behind the following verses, the Gospel tradition of John the Baptist; and, behind John 1:14, 16–18, the Exodus tradition. This thesis is shared by many exegetes. The figure of Moses appears first in v. 17, but the theophany on Sinai stands behind the whole section. In the priestly tradition, the creation found its fulfillment in the erection of the "tabernacle" among the children of Israel (Exod 40). In this tent, God lived among his people and rested from his work.[48] In the Targum tradition, "shekinah" ("tenting") of God, "Word" of God, and "glory" of God all stand for God himself so that mention of his name may be avoided. All these expressions appear in John's prologue and, in fact, in our verse. The double expression "grace and truth" originates from the words heard by Moses at the theophany in Exod 34: "The Lord, the Lord, a merciful and gracious God, long-suffering and of great grace and faithfulness," in the Greek of the Septuagint: πολυέλεος καὶ ἀληθινός.

---

47. See section 1 above.
48. Cf. Wengst; Böhler, "Abraham," 32.

## The Divine Word Enters the World (1:1–4:54)

The only thing that is new in our verse is that this God has revealed himself in Jesus Christ, the incarnate Logos. For this, both Jewish and Christian parallels are lacking. He is the "only" Son as Gen 22:2 leads us to suppose of Isaac. Why does the prologue say that the Word became "flesh" and not "man"? The reason could be that, at the time of the composition of the prologue, the true manhood of Jesus, his existence in flesh and blood, and his birth and his death had already become the object of controversy and dispute in early Gnostic circles. This is how the emphasis on the flesh of Jesus in the later Johannine texts—in the Gospel (John 6:51) and in the letters of John (1 John 4:2–3; 2 John 7)—is understood. Conversely, this leads to the conclusion that the prologue (at least this section of the prologue) belongs to the last phase of the Gospel's redaction (as "*relecture*"), even if a post-Johannine origin of this verse does not follow from this observation.[49]

**1:15** Verse 15 sees the re-emergence of John the Baptist, who was already mentioned in verses 6–8. His mention there marked the introduction of the divine Word into human history, and the mention of him here as a witness for Jesus marks the beginning of the "great trial" between Jesus and the world. As de la Potterie observes,[50] there is a grammatical difference between verses 6–8 and v. 15. In verses 6–8, John's testimony appears as something that happened in the past. John appeared and bore witness to the light, to Jesus, to the Logos. According to v. 15, John's testimony is something that is happening in the present: "John testifies for him and cries." The perfect κέκραγεν may have a present tense nuance here on account of its parallelism with μαρτυρεῖ.[51] The content of the testimony takes up John 1:30 in advance. By contrast with what is said there, our verse turns the precedence of Jesus over the Baptist into the main statement. Physically, Jesus is behind John and also comes among the Israelites after him; but he is older and goes further back in time. Thus John the Baptist becomes a witness to Jesus's pre-existence that, for the reader, stretches back into eternity (cf. vv. 1–2). For the ancient reader, greater age was worthy of greater respect. The reader of John's Gospel knew in addition that Jesus was not only older than John but that he lay beyond all reckoning of time.

**1:16** In v. 16, several aspects of v. 14 are taken up again. Thus, the first person plural, already found in v. 14, returns: the "we" of the praising com-

---

49. Thus in Richter, "Fleischwerdung."
50. See above in section 1.
51. Cf. Bauer, *Wörterbuch*.

munity. The talk is once again of "grace." In v. 14, this was still clearly from the Exodus tradition. In v. 16, the mention of "grace" has a more strongly Christian sense. The expression χάριν ἀντὶ χάριτος can be variously understood: as "grace upon grace," as "ever more grace," or as "one grace instead of another." The first possibility appears to be the most probable,[52] also because of its connection with the accompanying expression "fullness" (πλήρωμα). Outside the present case, it occurs in the NT only with Paul and his school, and stands for the fullness of the eschatological salvation in Christ (esp. Col 1:19; Eph 1:10, 23).

**1:17-18** In the last two verses, the text returns to the third person singular with two antitheses as their content: the gift of the Law through the mediation of Moses and the coming of grace and truth in Jesus Christ in v. 17, as well as the invisibility of God and his revelation through Jesus Christ, the Father's "Exegete" in v. 18. The gift of the Law through Moses and the coming of grace and truth through Jesus Christ can be variously understood. According to some authors, this would be a case of antithetical parallelism, and as such an antithesis. This interpretation is already found in P[66] and in some other ancient textual witnesses. Contemporary exegetes usually prefer climactic parallelism: the grace and truth that come in Jesus Christ surpass the gift of the Law through the mediation of Moses. For the reader, this is thus a question not only of a quantitative but a qualitative difference. A certain irony lies in the fact that Jesus's gift of "grace and truth" stems, of all things, from God's second revelation to Moses at Sinai according to Exod 34:6 LXX (cf. v. 14).

The antithesis in v. 18 is inspired by the book of Exodus. After the incident with the golden calf, Moses asks God for a new meeting. God partly hears this request but adds: "You cannot see my face; for no man can see me and live" (Exod 33:20). Moses will see only the Lord's back when he passes by him; he will not be able to see his face (Exod 33:23). That no man has seen God is something that John repeats (cf. John 5:37; 6:46; also 14:9). Only Jesus has seen him; he is the one who "rests in the Father's heart," by contrast with Moses who saw God only from behind. The reason for this is that Jesus is "the Only One,"[53] from the likeness and being of the Father, i.e., "God."[54] Only he can bring messages from the Father and be

---

52. Cf. Thyen, "Erwägungen," with Schnackenburg, Brown, Lindars, and even Luther.

53. Cf., for this term, Morgen, "Le (Fils) monogène."

54. In v. 18, numerous manuscripts read υἱός instead of θεός. For this, see the detailed discussion in Metzger, *Textual Commentary*. The reading θεός is now found also in

his "Exegete."⁵⁵ (For his place "in the heart" of the Father, cf. the beloved disciple who, according to John 13:23, had a similar place "in the heart of Jesus" at the Last Supper and who will bring news of him.)

## III

What has this text to say to contemporary readers?⁵⁶ The answer to this question has to take into account both the narrative strategy of the text and, additionally, the expectations and understanding of modern readers.

As has become apparent, John's prologue leads its readership step by step to the recognition of the divine Word in the historical figure of Jesus Christ. Only in v. 17 is the veil lifted, but the incarnation of the Word in human history has been proclaimed since the end of v. 3. "Light" and "life" are bestowed on men in the historical appearance of the divine Word. The Baptist has testified to this, and the mention of the incarnation of the Word in v. 14 is only making explicit what was said previously.

The appropriate answer to the news of the coming of the divine Word into history is faith. This is especially the subject of the middle of the prologue, in verses 6–13. The testimony of the Baptist is intended to lead to faith. Whoever finds this faith will become the child of God and at the same time manifests himself as the child of God.

The Synoptic Gospels begin with an account of the appearance of Jesus (Mark) or his origin (Matt, Luke). By contrast, at the beginning of his Gospel, John the Evangelist has a hymn that sings the divine origin of the Word. The singers of this hymn come forward expressly in v. 14 as "we." The readers are thereby brought into the account of the eternal beginning.

---

P⁶⁶ and P⁷⁵ from the second and third centuries. There is support (in P⁷⁵ with the article as in other manuscripts) also, among others, in Sinaiticus *prima manu*, in Codex Vaticanus, and in Codex C *prima manu*. The reading υἱός is less well attested (A C³ K Γ Δ Θ Ψ ƒ¹·¹³, some minuscules, M lat sy^{c.h}) and could be influenced from similar texts such as John 3:16, 18; 1 John 4:9. For its part, the article could be influenced from the title of "the Son" (Metzger).

55. Devillers, "Le sein du Père," 70, thinks otherwise of the closing verse of the prologue: "Le Fils unique, Dieu, Celui qui Est (cf. Ex 3,14 et egō eimi de Jean), dans le sein du Père, lui, a conduit." This suggestion remains highly hypothetical and may fail owing to the fact that in the previous and following context, the talk is of the communication of the Word or the knowledge of God and not of the access to him.

56. For the reception history of John's prologue, cf. Enders and Kühn, "*Im Anfang war der Logos.*"

They sing of it together with the author and his circle. So it is not just a question of hearing a report but also of adopting a confession and bringing it to expression in worship. It will appear that this way of speaking about the incarnation of God is appropriate to its subject. In the final analysis, God's coming to men cannot be spoken of in the objective language of a report but only in the form of a proclamation to which the response of faith of the community of believers corresponds. Thus, John's prologue is at once the expression of its time and also "God-talk" in the sense of contemporary theological thinking.[57]

## 2. The Testimony of the Baptist (1:19–34)

[19] And this is the testimony of John, when the Jews sent priests and levites from Jerusalem with the question: Who are you? [20] And he confessed and did not deny; he confessed: I am not the Messiah. [21] They asked him: What are you then? Are you Elijah? And he said: I am not. Are you the prophet? And he answered: No. [22] Then they said to him: Who are you? We have to give an answer to those who sent us. What do you say about yourself? [23] He said: I am the voice of the one who cries in the wilderness: Prepare the way of the Lord!, as the prophet Isaiah said. [24] Now they had been sent by the Pharisees. [25] They asked John and said to him: Why are you baptizing then if you are not the Messiah or Elijah and not the prophet? [26] John answered them: I baptize with water. Among you there stands one whom you do not know [27] and who is coming after me; I am not worthy to untie his shoes. [28] This took place in Bethany, on the other side of the Jordan, where John was baptizing.

[29] The next day, he saw Jesus coming to him and said: Behold, the Lamb of God, that takes away the sins of the world. [30] He is the one of whom I have spoken: After me comes one who is before me because he was before me. [31] Even I did not know him; but I have come and am baptizing with water so that he may be revealed to Israel. [32] And John bore testimony: I saw that the Spirit came from heaven like a dove and remained on him. [33] Even I did not know him; but the one who sent me to baptize with water said to me: The one on whom you see the Spirit come and remain, he it is who baptizes with the Holy Spirit. [34] And I have seen it and borne witness: This is the Son of God.

---

57. Cf. Beutler, "Und das Wort ist Fleisch geworden."

*The Divine Word Enters the World (1:1–4:54)*

*I*

With John 1:19, the narrative of John's Gospel opens after the prologue. At the beginning, John 1:19–51 has four scenes that are linked by location, date, and the characters involved. An additional indication of time in John 2:1 rounds off the succession of scenes from an "opening week," of which there is occasional mention. It ends with the account of the marriage at Cana. The first four scenes are separated from one another with the information "on the following day" in John 1:29, 35, 43. They all take place at the Jordan. The first two scenes show themselves to belong together, as do the third and fourth scenes. The two scenes John 1:19–28 and 1:29–34 are held together by the common theme of "testimony," which was already introduced in 1:6–8 and 1:15. Verse 1:19 serves as a "title" for the whole section John 1:19–34; the twofold occurrence of "testimony/witness" in 1:32–34 rounds off the section.

The section can be subdivided according to the stage directions and the content. The date "on the following day" in 1:29 causes a division of the group of verses into two, something suggested also by the content. In John 1:19–28, John speaks of himself and his deeds, and only indirectly about Jesus; in 1:29–34, he then speaks directly about Jesus as the one who is to come. Thus, we can entitle 1:19–28 "The Indirect Testimony of John to Jesus" and 1:29–34 "The Direct Testimony of John to Jesus."

In the narrative part of John's Gospel, the Baptist's witness in John 1:19–34 forms a bracket with John 10:40–42. This is the last mention of John. Again, it is the Jordan that provides the background. John had not performed any signs, but everything that he had said about Jesus had shown itself to be true. From this, many came to faith in Jesus. Thus John finally exits the stage and leaves the place at Jesus's side to his friend Lazarus (John 11–12), before he too is replaced by the beloved disciple (John 13–21). These are also the principal divisions of John's Gospel.

*II*

*The Indirect Testimony of John to Jesus (1:19–28)*

This section can be divided into two according to the criteria of form and content. In the middle stands the information (v. 24) that the priests and levites who had been sent to Jesus were sent by the Pharisees. Verses 19–23 answer the question "Who are you?," addressed to John, verses 25–28 the question why he is baptizing.

**1:19-23** Vv. 19–23 concern the person of John, vv. 25–28 his activity, the baptizing. At the beginning, v. 19 contains a title, worded in typical Johannine style (with a demonstrative pronoun at the beginning of a statement of definition, cf. John 15:12; 17:3; 1 John 3:11 etc.). The extent of this section thus introduced is not quite clear. According to many exegetes, it extends as far as John 1:34. However, the Baptist's testimony also points beyond this verse. Thus, it is taken up again in John's indication in 1:36: "Behold, the Lamb of God." There are further sections on the Baptist in John 3:22-30; 5:33-35 and 10:40-42, as already mentioned. Thus one could also see John 1:19 as the title for the whole of the first part of the Gospel. Also, in this verse, the remaining actors in the first section of the narrative part of the Gospel are introduced: priests and levites who were sent from Jerusalem to obtain information about the person and activity of John. The Jerusalem group doing the sending are the "Jews," understood as those responsible for the Jewish people in Jerusalem.

From the end of v. 19 to the end of the section in v. 23, the group of verses is characterized by nominal statements in the present tense. The figure of the Baptist stands at the center of the account. His answer to the Jerusalem delegation is introduced with a solemn formula: "He confessed and did not deny; he confessed." Here appears for the first time the meaning of "confessing" for the Gospel's reading community to which there has already been a preliminary reference.[58]

John's answer can be divided into a negative and positive part. The beginning of the first, negative part consists of John's most important declaration for the readers: the Baptist is not the Christ. This statement takes up what was said of the Baptist in the prologue (John 1:6-8): John is "not the light," the Logos incarnate in Jesus Christ. Furthermore, John denies that he is Elijah, whose second coming was expected for the end time, or the promised prophet to come in the sense of Deut 18:18. The reason for this denial lies chiefly in the fact that the concept of the "forerunner" was connected with the figure of Elijah and this was a role that is steadily denied to John in the Fourth Gospel. Jesus's origin is of a different nature, and so, from the point of view of the fourth evangelist, he cannot have any kind of "forerunner."[59]

---

58. Cf. the introduction above; Beutler, "Faith and Confession."
59. Cf. Koch, "Der Täufer," 1970f.

*The Divine Word Enters the World (1:1–4:54)*

The Baptist's positive answer in vv. 22–23 makes use of Isa 40:3 LXX, a text already employed by the Synoptics in this connection. The Baptist (though this epithet is continually avoided in John) is none other than the voice of one who cries in the wilderness inviting people to prepare the way for the Lord. The text of the quotation agrees broadly with the Septuagint, with a deviation in the second line (εὐθύνατε) that, today, is ascribed to the evangelist rather than to a pre-Johannine source. Certainly, the initial ἐγώ goes back to the pen of the evangelist. For a Christian writer like John, it is unquestionable that Christ is meant with the κύριος of Isa 40:3, the Lord of the Christian community in whom God has come to visit his people. John appears not as his forerunner, but rather as the one who proclaims his coming.

Behind this section, John 1:19–23, as also behind the following verses as far as v. 34, we can discern the Synoptic tradition. First, the scene of the appearance of the Baptist in Mark 1:2–11 is recognizable here. From the fact that John has no description of the Baptist and his preaching of repentance we can conclude that he is chiefly dependent on Mark here and not on the parallel Q tradition from Matthew and Luke. Deviations from Mark can be traced back to the redactional work of John.[60]

Right at the beginning of the section in v. 19, the influence of the Johannine perspective is visible. The fundamental Johannine theme of testimony is introduced here. The mission from Jerusalem opens a first and critical phase of the relationship between Jesus or the Baptist and the Jewish authorities in Jerusalem. John speaks of "priests and levites," probably to lend this mission from Jerusalem a negative profile, a choice of words that points to no independent, pre-Johannine source.

The fact that, from the beginning, the dialogue is focused on the person of the Baptist can, again, be explained with an eye to John's literary and theological interests. Since the prologue, the relationship between Jesus and the Baptist has been a central theme for him. The fact that John has not taken up the quotation from Malachi (3:1), which is found in the Synoptics, is explained from the evangelist's aim not to allow John the Baptist to appear as Jesus's forerunner. When the Isaiah quotation appears in John in the Baptist's mouth, it takes on more weight. The introduction to the Baptist's answer through the expression "and he confessed and did not deny, he confessed" is explained

---

60. Cf. Koch, "Der Täufer"; also, Trocmé, "Jean et les Synoptiques," and Freed, "Jn 1,19-27."

by the meaning of confessing in John, something that has already been emphasized.[61]

Why do those sent from Jerusalem ask John the Baptist whether he is the Christ, Elijah, or one of the prophets? According to Becker, these titles are lacking in the Synoptic tradition concerning the Baptist. This argument is only partly valid. U. Busse[62] and Dietrich-Alex Koch[63] have noticed how this series of titles could have originated from Mark 8:27–30. We could also add Mark 6:14–16 par.[64] In the text from Mark 8, the disciples answer Jesus's question as to who the people hold him to be with the information: some John the Baptist, others Elijah, still others another prophet. On behalf of the disciple, Peter gives the right answer: You are the Messiah. The Fourth Gospel places this title at the beginning of this section, naturally excludes the Baptist, and continues with the titles of Elijah and the prophet, understood as "the prophet" in the sense of Deut 18:18.

Other elements from Mark's opening are absent from John such as the mention of the "wilderness" as the scene of John's activity since this would underline John's role as prophet too strongly, as well as the description of his clothing and his diet that would have the same effect. For the fourth evangelist, John is Jesus's witness, no more and no less.

**1:24–28** The second subdivision begins with more exact information about the group of people mentioned at the beginning (v. 19). Verse 24 can be understood in different ways. It is often translated: "And those who were sent came from the Pharisees." In that case, of course, one would expect the article οἱ before ἀπεσταλμένοι. However, this is absent from the most ancient manuscripts and has only been added in corrections to some manuscripts (a² Aᶜ C³ Wˢ), otherwise attested weakly and late (Κ Ν Γ Δ Θ 0234 $f^{1.13}$ 33 u. a. M boᵐˢ). Thus, we shall translate: "and they had been sent by the Pharisees" (with Luther and the new Zürcher Bibel among others). In that case, ἐκ appears to stand for ἀπό. Elsewhere, the Pharisees constitute for John the leading Jewish group in Jerusalem, probably under the influence of the time when the Fourth Gospel was composed when, after 70 CE, the Pharisees represented the only surviving authoritative group in Judaism. Since they were more of a lay group, it is not easy to imagine the priests and levites of v. 19 belonging to them.

---

61. Cf. v. 20 above.
62. Busse, "Das Eröffnungszeugnis," 39.
63. Koch, "Der Täufer," 1972.
64. Cf. Freed, "Jn 1,19–27," 1947f.

*The Divine Word Enters the World (1:1–4:54)*

John's answer to the question of why he is baptizing does not explain his activity directly but sets it in relation to Christ. While he, the Baptist, baptizes with water, there stands among the Jews at the Jordan one who comes after him and whose shoes he is not worthy to unloose. Here, one expects a word about the baptism with the Holy Spirit that Jesus would administer, but this is not introduced until the next scene in v. 33. Here, in the episode in vv. 1:24–28, the only subject is that of Jesus's dignity in comparison with the Baptist. The fact that the Jews do not know him is interpreted as belonging to the motif of the unknown Messiah (v. 26). At the end of the section, there is information about the location (v. 28). It appears to have been added, but it belongs to the Johannine style and should not be denied to the evangelist.[65] With the later mention of Bethany near Jerusalem (John 11:1), the account of the public life of Jesus forms an inclusio, just as the expression "on the other side of the Jordan" points forward to John 10:40–42.[66]

The quest for the origin of John 1:24–28 leads to the conclusion that the section is strongly marked by the hand of the fourth evangelist. The terminological difference between the "Jews" in v. 19 and the "Pharisees" does not necessarily point to different sources but can be explained from Johannine usage, for, in other places, the fourth evangelist seems to employ both expressions as synonyms.[67] The Baptist's answer in v. 26 corresponds to Mark 1:8. However, the fourth evangelist has left out the Baptist's preaching that after him will come one who is stronger than he since this would involve only a quantitative difference between himself and Jesus. Such a notion would be unacceptable to the fourth evangelist. Here, there is also lacking the second half of the Baptist's words about the one who will baptize with the Holy Spirit. The fourth evangelist reports this saying of the Baptist only in v. 33 in connection with the descent of the Holy Spirit on Jesus. In verses 24–28, he has the figure of the Baptist standing in the foreground. Jesus comes after the Baptist but is superior to him in dignity. This is expressed in a saying taken over from Mark: the Baptist is not worthy to unloose the straps of Jesus's shoes. This corresponds to Mark 1:7 par. and is found also in Acts 13:25, as Étienne Trocmé indicates.[68] This could

---

65. Cf. van Belle, *Les parenthèses*; Bjerkelund, *Tauta egeneto*.

66. Attempts to locate the Bethany of John 1:28 have thus far failed. Since the time of Origen, there occurs the competing reading "Bethabara," not to mention "Betharaba." Cf. Earl, "(Bethany) Beyond the Jordan"; Hutton, "Bethany Beyond the Jordan."

67. Cf. the reference to John 9 in Koch, "Der Täufer," 1972f.

68. Cf. Trocmé, "Jean et les Synoptiques." According to him, the adjective ἄξιος for

be significant for the tradition-historical origin of this theme in John. The theme of the unknown Messiah is similarly traditional and Johannine: the world and all those belonging to it do not know Jesus, the true light (cf., already, John 1:10-11).

### *The Direct Testimony of John to Jesus (1:29-34)*

One could entitle the following verses: "The Testimony of John to Jesus." However, this is less suitable in that, as we have seen, verses 19-28 have already dealt with a testimony of John to Jesus, albeit indirectly. The Baptist has denied being the Messiah or any kind of messianic "forerunner." The new scene in v. 29 begins with an indication of time. It takes place on the following day. It ends in v. 34, before the new indication of time in v. 35. In vv. 29-34, the Baptist sees Jesus approaching him and points him out with the words: "Behold, the Lamb of God." In connection with this, the Baptist testifies to a spiritual experience that he has had in which he saw the Holy Spirit descend on Jesus and remain on him. The scene concludes with a testimony to Jesus that corresponds entirely to the credo of the Johannine community.

According to criteria of language and content, the scene in vv. 29-34 can once again be divided into two subunits, as is the case also in Nestle-Aland. The second subsection, vv. 32-34, appears to be framed by the theme of "testifying" in v. 32 and v. 34 (μαρτυρεῖν). John the Baptist testifies to a vision and an audition that took place on the occasion of his first encounter with Jesus. This first meeting is described in verses 29-31. At the end or in the middle of the declarations of John the Baptist in verses 29-31 and 32-34, stand, respectively, statements of identification: "οὗτός ἐστιν" (v. 30 and v. 34): "He is the one of whom I have spoken," "This is the Son of God."

**1:29-31** Verses 29-31 can be entitled: "The Lamb of God." The section begins in v. 29 with the date "on the next day" with which a new scene opens. It is possible that John's hearers are no longer the Jerusalem delegation but the crowds of people who were flocking to the Jordan to hear John and be baptized by him. "He saw and said: Behold..." is a biblical formula as Brown shows (cf. John 1:47). The "coming" of Jesus could have a deeper

---

"worthy" is found only in John 1:27 and Acts 13:25, as opposed to ἱκανός in Mark 1:7, par. Matt 3:11; Luke 3:16.

## The Divine Word Enters the World (1:1–4:54)

sense (as the "coming" of the one who is to come; cf. 1:9; 4:25–26). But what is the meaning of John's saying: "Behold, the Lamb of God"? With Brown, we can distinguish three principal meanings:

- an apocalyptic lamb, as mentioned in contemporary apocalyptic texts (Testament of Joseph 19.8; 1 Enoch 90.38), an eschatological and messianic figure; this solution is preferred mainly by those authors who wish to rescue the saying about the lamb for the historic Baptist;
- the Passover lamb because of the significance of the feast of the Passover during the life and passion of Jesus in John (so C. K. Barrett);
- the lamb mentioned in the Fourth Servant Song (Isa 53:7), which does not open its mouth before the shearers and symbolizes God's servant himself. This meaning commends itself because of the significance of the servant in John, especially in John 12:20–43.[69] The theme of the taking away of sins suits this meaning well for, according to the Fourth Servant Song, the servant takes the sins of many on himself (a suggestion already in Brown who also adopts it for his own). If this meaning is accepted, the reading "This is the chosen One of God" in v. 34 becomes easier to understand.

By contrast with the text of Isaiah, Jesus, the true lamb, bears not sins but the sin of the world. The singular chosen by the evangelist corresponds to the singular in Paul. The fourth evangelist prefers this type of expression since, for him, there is, in the final analysis, only one sin, unbelief, which, concretely speaking, consists in not believing in Jesus and his mission (cf. John 16:9). This is the sin of "the world."[70]

Verse 30 is linked with the previous v. 29 by the catchword "coming." According to v. 29, John saw Jesus "coming" and testified to his work of redemption. Now the "coming" of Jesus is interpreted in the sense of his pre-existence before the Baptist. The verse resembles John 1:15. In v. 15, our verse 30 seems to be presupposed, and in v. 30, a reference to a previous testimony of the Baptist to Jesus concerning Jesus's temporal priority over the Baptist. The solution of the puzzle lies in the assumption that the

---

69. Cf. Beutler, "Griechen."

70. The connection with the Servant is seen by Rusam, "Das 'Lamm Gottes,'" and Schwindt, "Seht das Lamm Gottes." According to both authors, the Servant bears the sin of the world (away) in that he sends the Spirit. The "Lamb of God" saying is thus to be read in its Johannine context in John 1:29–34.

Baptist tradition already belonged to the oral tradition of the Johannine community.[71]

When, in v. 31, the Baptist declares that he did not know Jesus before their meeting, he is taking up the motif of the hidden Messiah from v. 26. John's peculiar mission is to make Jesus known. Even his activity as Baptist has no other aim than to make Jesus known to the people of Israel. There was a similar perspective in verses 24–27: upon being asked why he baptized, the Baptist answered with a saying about Jesus who was to come and whose shoes he was not worthy to unloose. The motif of baptizing "with water" is also a linguistic element linking the two sections.

**1:32–34** The last three verses of the section could be entitled: "The (Chosen) Son of God." We shall postpone for the moment the related text-critical problem of which christological title to read. In comparison with the previous verses, John's testimony has become more concrete. In the process, the saying about the twofold baptism is taken up again: the Baptist's baptism with water and the baptism with the Holy Spirit that Jesus would bestow. The premise for this latter baptism was the descent of the Spirit on Jesus. John had taken part in this event and could bear witness to it. The image of the dove as a symbol of the Holy Spirit is traditional and demonstrates again the dependence of the evangelist on these kinds of traditions.

According to v. 33, John did not know Jesus before their meeting, a repetition from v. 31. His knowledge of Jesus was bestowed on him by God, and thus revealed by the one who had commissioned him to baptize with water. Now he has to announce to the people a new baptism bestowed by Jesus, a baptism with the Holy Spirit. The premise for this, as is emphasized once again, is that the Spirit descended on Jesus and remained on him. It is striking that in the whole of the first chapter of this Gospel, there is never any question of John's having baptized Jesus. The hearing of the heavenly voice is also not connected with the baptism scene as in the Synoptics. The fourth evangelist limits the role of John "the Baptist" to that of being the witness to Jesus even at the price of not being able to name him as "the Baptist." For him, it would have been preferable to speak of "John the Witness."

If the Holy Spirit descended on Jesus and remained on him, then it follows from that that Jesus must be the Son of God. Even if the title was affected by the tradition, it also appears as a faith experience of the Baptist:

---

71. Cf. Trocmé, "Jean et les Synoptiques."

*The Divine Word Enters the World (1:1–4:54)*

he has "seen" with the eyes of faith that Jesus is the Son of God and can bear witness to this.

At the end of v. 34, there is a text-critical problem. With the majority of ancient manuscripts and modern versions of the Bible, translations, and exegetes, Nestle-Aland²⁸ reads ὁ υἱὸς τοῦ θεοῦ, though there is also, beside it, the competing reading ὁ ἐκλεκτὸς τοῦ θεοῦ (א* b e ff²* sy^(s.c)). It is less well attested but deserves consideration.⁷² In terms of their sense, there is little difference. Both titles appear to point to the servant, at least if, behind the Johannine text (Mark 1:11 par.), one conjectures the Synoptics' baptism scene where, corresponding to Isa 42:1, it says: σὺ εἶ ὁ υἱός μου ὁ ἀγαπητός, ἐν σοὶ εὐδόκησα. Cf. Isa 42:1 LXX: Ιακωβ ὁ παῖς μου, ἀντιλήμψομαι αὐτοῦ· Ισραηλ ὁ ἐκλεκτός μου, προσεδέξατο αὐτὸν ἡ ψυχή μου. Precisely because of this closeness to this passage in Isaiah, it is possible that ἐκλεκτός could have been inserted into the text if it is not in fact original. What is important is that, in any case, the Baptist's christological confession seems to have been influenced here by the image of the servant. We shall come across this Christology again in the course of John's Gospel.⁷³

## III

The opening section of the Gospel after the prologue is devoted to the theme of "testimony." For contemporary readers some important perspectives emerge here.

First and foremost, the readers are reminded that their faith rests on a firm foundation. For the fourth evangelist, John the Baptist is a witness for Jesus, for his divine origin and mission. In this way, John represents further witness for Jesus, as becomes apparent as the Gospel progresses. The chain stretches from the beloved disciple and author of the Gospel (John 21:24) as far as the whole circle of the disciples (John 15:26–27). Thus, the message of the Gospel is reliable.

In so far as the readers consciously live out their discipleship, they themselves are taken up into this series of witnesses. They will not only be

---

72. This reading has recently been favored by Quek, "A Text-Critical Study"; cf. Morris, 134. The similarly poorly attested reading (P⁷⁵* [a] ff²ᶜ sa) ἐκλεκτός υἱός is adovcated in Flink, "Son and Chosen."

73. Cf. Beutler, "Griechen."

able and ready to speak of their faith but also to witness to it. That means to speak of it in such a way that they themselves stand up for it.

That then leads to confessing. Thus, just as the text says of John: "He confessed and did not deny; he confessed." (v. 20), so will they also see themselves called to confessing. Just as John the Baptist had to do this before a critical delegation, so also will the readers of today confess their faith in a forum that is not always friendly and open to the Christian faith. The relevance of this section could lie precisely here.

## 3. The Call of the First Disciples (1:35–51)

[35] The next day, John was standing there again, and two of his disciples were standing with him. [36] As Jesus was passing by, John looked at him and said: Behold, the Lamb of God! [37] The two disciples heard what he said and followed Jesus. [38] Jesus turned and, when he saw that they were following him, said to them: What do you want? They said to him: Rabbi — that means "Master" — where do you live? [39] He said to them: Come and see! They went with him and saw where he lived, and remained with him that day; it was about the tenth hour. [40] Andrew, the brother of Simon Peter, was one of the two who heard what John said and followed Jesus. [41] He first found his brother Simon and said to him: We have found the Messiah, that means Christ. [42] He brought him to Jesus. Jesus looked at him and said: You are Simon, the son of John: you are to be called Cephas, that means Peter, rock.

[43] The next day, Jesus wanted to set out for Galilee and met Philip. And Jesus said to him: Follow me! [44] Philip was from Bethsaida, the town of Andrew and Peter. [45] Philip met Nathanael and said to him: We have found the one whom Moses in the Law and also the prophets have written about: Jesus, the son of Joseph, from Nazareth. [46] Then Nathanael said to him: Can anything good come from Nazareth? Philip said to him: Come and see! [47] Jesus saw Nathanael coming to him and said of him: Behold, a true Israelite in whom there is nothing false. [48] Nathanael said to him: How do you know me? Jesus replied: Before Philip called you, I saw you under the fig tree. [49] Nathanael answered him: Rabbi, you are the son of God, you are the King of Israel! [50] Jesus replied: Do you believe because I said to you that I saw you under the fig tree? You will see something still greater. [51] And he said to him: Amen, amen, I say to you: you will see heaven opened, and the angels of God ascending and descending over the Son of Man.

*The Divine Word Enters the World (1:1–4:54)*

*I*

Following the section on John's testimony to Jesus (John 1:19–34), there comes another in which Jesus himself now appears as the chief agent. It records the call of the first disciples (John 1:35–51). We still encounter the figure of John in the first three verses, but then he retreats into the background. Insofar as John has delivered his testimony and introduced the first disciples to Jesus, his commission is fulfilled for the time being. Like the previous section, so too this one is divided into two by the chronological indication "on the following day" (John 1:35, 43, cf. 1:29). This separates two scenes: the call of the first three disciples (1:35–42) and then of a further two (1:43–51).

*II*

*The Call of the First Three Disciples (1:35–42)*

On further consideration, our section can be divided into two scenes: vv. 35–39 and 40–42. The first scene is framed by two chronological indications: "the next day" (v. 35) and "about the tenth hour" (v. 39). The *dramatis personae* are John, two not yet named disciples, and Jesus. The second scene begins with information as to the identity of one of the two disciples who had found Jesus: Andrew. He finds his brother, Simon Peter, and brings him to Jesus, whom he describes as Messiah. Jesus turns to Peter and gives him a new name.

The development of both scenes (vv. 35–42 and 43–51) displays similarities: a person meets Jesus and introduces him to another or to two other people. Thus, John the Baptist points two of his disciples in the direction of Jesus, whom he had previously encountered. One of these two, Andrew, meets his brother, and introduces Jesus to him as Messiah. Subsequently, the one who has met Jesus brings another or several others to Jesus. Jesus sees the person or people being brought to him and addresses them with a question and an invitation or prediction that concerns that person ("you are to be called Cephas").

Already in this section, we find verbs that will be characteristic of the whole text as far as v. 51: "see" or "look, behold" (vv. 36, 38, 39 [2x], 42), "find" (v. 41, cf. 43, 45 [2x]) and "stay" (vv. 38, 39).

Older literary-critical analysis liked to distinguish in the whole section John 1:35–51 between the "signs source" and its redaction by the evangelist to whom, perhaps, go back the differing form of the call in v. 43 as well as parts of vv. 35-36 and v. 51.[74] Today, such attempts have largely been abandoned. Instead, the possible dependence of John on the Synoptic Gospels receives consideration.[75] Relevant here are the call scenes of the first three evangelists (Mark 1:16–20 par.; 3:13–19 par.; Luke 5:1–11; cf. Matt 16:16–19). The influence of these scenes on our text is undoubted despite their clear differences. To them belongs the distinctive structure of the calling (with the exception of that of Philip in v. 43 and the fact that, in the Synoptics, Peter receives his new name only at the climax of Jesus's public ministry).

More recently, this section has been examined more from the narrative and theological points of view. Thus, among others, Scholtissek sees in the succession of christological titles in John 1:35–51 a mystagogic introduction to the mystery of Jesus for believers and catechumens.[76] There is a gradual deepening of faith in Jesus that begins with "Lamb of God" (v. 36), leads to "Rabbi" and "Master" (v. 38) and then to the "Messiah" (v. 41), "whom Moses in the Law and also the prophets have written about" (v. 45), and on to "Son of God, King of Israel" (v. 49) and "Son of Man" (v. 51). Step by step, along with the disciples, the readers are led into the mystery of Jesus.

From the point of view of narrative criticism, we can recognize an invitation to discipleship in this section.[77] The initiative starts with John the Baptist, who introduces Jesus to the two disciples with the words: "Behold, the Lamb of God." Thereupon, the disciples, for their part, take the initiative and bring other people to Jesus: Andrew, his brother Simon Peter, Philip, and his friend Nathanael. Philip's case remains the exception, with Jesus approaching him without any intermediary (v. 43). However, it is not a good idea to separate this verse from its context on account of its use of a different form for the call. Two reasons can be invoked for this variation: recourse to a tradition that is closer to the Synoptics (with

---

74. Thus, in development of Bultmann's model, see the commentary of Becker; similarly, Kuhn, *Christologie und Wunder*. The latter distinguishes in John 1:35–51 a view of Jesus as wonder worker and prophet who has the gift of reading hearts (vv. 47-48), and as Messiah, as he is proclaimed in verses 41 and 49. Theobald, 50, also advocates further the sign source behind John 1:19–28, 35–50.

75. This is also seen by Kuhn, *Christologie und Wunder*.

76. Scholtissek, "Rabbi"; similarly too, Meyer, *Kommt und seht*.

77. In this sense, Fischer and Hasitschka, *Sulla tua parola*.

the sequence "saw/met," "said/follow me"), or the agenda of the fourth evangelist to emphasize the position of Philip as an apostle who enjoyed a special reputation in the Johannine community (cf. 6:5, 7; 12:22; 14:8–9).

**1:35–37** Till now, John the Baptist has witnessed to Jesus only in a general sense. Now we have an account of how he "looked" at Jesus, who was passing by and pointed him out to two of his own disciples with the words: "Behold, the Lamb of God." The meaning of this description has already been outlined (cf. v. 29). Instead of ascribing it a historical explanation (perhaps as a mistranslation of the Aramaic word *taliah* that can have the double meaning "Lamb" and "Servant"), it is preferable to see in this expression a summary of Johannine theology. The Baptist does not introduce Jesus to his disciples in the first place as Messiah but as a redeemer who will redeem the world through his mission to the point of his death on the cross. The two disciples hear this message and take it on board: they "follow" Jesus. The general view here is that the verb is still to be understood literally as "to go behind someone," in this case, probably, in order to get to know him.

**1:38–39** This interpretation is also suggested by v. 38: Jesus turns around, sees the two disciples of John following him, and asks them: "What do you want?" The "seeing" corresponds to the Synoptic account of the call of the disciples (cf. Mark 1:16, 19 par.; 2:14). Admittedly, the question "What do you want?" is not found in these texts. In this question of Jesus, a whole theology of calling to faith can be glimpsed: the meeting with Jesus leads, not to the accepting of a message strange to men and imposed from outside, but the fulfilling of their innermost desires.[78] The answer of both disciples to Jesus's question is also typically Johannine. The word "remain" (μένειν) is a favorite word of John. We have come across it already in the scene of the vision and audition of the Baptist at the Jordan: he "sees" the Spirit descend on Jesus and "remain" (John 1:32–33). In 1:38, the word has the meaning "live." It reminds us of the prologue: "and the Word became flesh and lived among us" (John 1:14). Jesus answers the disciples' question not simply with information but with an invitation: "Come and see." The narrator takes up both these verbs to describe the disciples' reaction: "They went with him and saw." The narrator takes up the motif of "living" in what follows: they saw "where he lived, and remained with him that day." The narrative flow goes from Jesus's "living" to the disciples "remaining." In looking at Jesus, the disciples take part in the experience

---

78. Cf., in the next section, the reference to Painter, *The Quest*.

of John's Christian community: "he lived among us, and we saw his glory, the glory of the only Son of the Father, full of grace and truth" (John 1:14). The indication of time, "it was about the tenth hour," points in more than one direction. In John's Gospel, important moments in the life and passion of Jesus will be recorded hour by hour. For the disciples, this tenth hour is the decisive turning point in their lives.

**1:40–42** The call accounts in John 1:35–51 are like an avalanche that tears up ever greater amounts of snow as it progresses. They also resemble a relay race in which each runner hands on the baton to the next one. Thus, Andrew, one of those called first, meets his brother, Simon, says to him, "We have found the Messiah, that means Christ," and brings him to Jesus.

This scene raises many questions. A first question, regarding which a great deal has been written, concerns the "other disciple" who, according to John 1:40, was called by Jesus. Church tradition holds that this was John, the brother of James. The main reason for this lies in the parallel tradition in the Synoptics (Mark 1:16–20 par.), according to which John was among the first four disciples called by Jesus, along with his brother James (who is not mentioned in John 1) and the two brothers, Andrew and Peter. Since the church tradition identifies the apostle John with Jesus's beloved disciple, his identification with the "other disciple" is a natural step. More recently, this identification has been called into question. It appears to be questionable on methodological grounds to interpret John through Mark. Linguistically, there is a distinction between "a disciple" and "the disciple." This is especially true for the disciple mentioned in the passion narrative (John 18:15), whom many regard as Jesus's beloved disciple. In John 1:40, the identity of the "other disciple" seems to have no special significance.[79]

A further theme of contemporary interest is the fact that the first disciples called by Jesus were a pair of brothers. In John especially, there is a distinct connection between kinship, friendship, and discipleship.[80]

Verses 1:40–42 speak of a twofold identification: Andrew calls Jesus "the Messiah, the Christ," Jesus calls Simon "Cephas, Peter." The former identification is astonishing at this stage in the narrative. The reader asks himself how Andrew, after a first meeting of a few hours, is supposed to come to the conclusion that Jesus is the Messiah when Jesus has not yet performed any "signs." The solution to this problem lies in John's post-Easter perspective that condenses and leaps over a long development to

---

79. Cf. Neirynck, "The Anonymous Disciple."
80. Cf. Destro and Pesce, "Kinship, Discipleship, and Movement."

the confession of faith formulated by Andrew. In this respect, the Fourth Gospel is significantly different from the first three. According to them, Peter comes to his confession of Jesus as Messiah only at the end of Jesus's public ministry (Mark 8:27–30). According to Matthew, it is on this occasion that he receives his new name (cf. Matt 16:17–19). In Mark, however, Peter's sobriquet appears first in the account of the calling of the Twelve (Mark 3:16). Influence of the Synoptic tradition on John 1:42 can certainly be supposed.

There remains a remarkable difference between the scene in John 1:40–42 and the Synoptic parallels. In the latter, Simon's new name is connected with a new role (cf., especially, Matt 16:17–19; Luke 5:1–11, where the new name is connected explicitly with Peter's new task to be a fisher of men; cf., also, John 21:1–17). In John 1:40–42, the designation of Simon as "Cephas," "Peter" corresponds to his acknowledgment of Jesus as Messiah. Both cases are to do with the person, not the work. Because Peter has come up with a declaration as to who Jesus is, he, for his part, receives a new identity. This perspective corresponds to that of John 1:35–39: to be with Jesus and to see where he lives precede every assignment to his service. There is already a parallel to this point of view in Mark 3:14–15: "And he appointed twelve, to be with him and to be sent out to preach and have power to cast out demons." We cannot exclude the possibility of a literary connection between these two texts.

### The Call of Two More Disciples (1:43–51)

The following section is separated from the previous one by the opening phrase: "The next day." There is a similar chronological indication ("on the third day") in 2:1. It is right, therefore, to regard John 1:43–51 as an independent unit. This impression is confirmed by the persons involved in the action (new disciples, Jesus) and the story line: it concerns new first meetings of future disciples with Jesus.

The groups of verses vv. 43–44 and 45–51 may be distinguished by content and form (the "finding" of another disciple): Jesus comes across Philip who, in turn, finds Nathanael, whom he then brings to Jesus. The final words of Jesus in v. 51 burst the boundaries of a dialogue scene and open the horizon to a further circle of listeners (ultimately, the community of readers) with the use of the plural: "You (pl.) will see."

The call of Philip in v. 43 contrasts with the form of the other first encounters of disciples with Jesus in John 1:35–51. It is not a disciple (cf. vv. 41. 45), but Jesus himself who "finds" the new disciple. There is no further identification of Jesus. He speaks with full authority and calls Philip to follow him. At the same time, it is not specifically reported how Philip reacts to this call. This has to be deduced instead from his behavior. He announces to Nathanael that he has come across the one about whom Moses and the prophets wrote (v. 45). Nathanael's first meeting with Jesus follows the pattern that is also to be observed in verses 35–42: one of the first two disciples "finds" his brother, Simon, tells him that he has found the Messiah, and brings him to Jesus. Correspondingly, after his call from Jesus, Philip tells Nathanael that he has "encountered" the one about whom Moses and the prophets wrote and brings him to Jesus after he has overcome Nathanael's skepticism.

In order to explain the difference between these two forms of call or "first encounter with Jesus," scholars have basically suggested two models. According to Martyn,[81] John would have edited v. 43 and the original composition would have had the form "one disciple finds another." When it says in v. 41, Andrew "first" found his brother Simon, it is expected that he, in his turn, will then find someone else. Instead of that, the evangelist has Jesus finding Philip. Martyn sees this hypothesis confirmed by the fact that Andrew's return to Galilee would be easier to explain as a departure by Jesus into this part of the land of Israel.

With the majority of authors, John Painter prefers the alternative: in v. 43, we would have a form of "call story" that is close to those in the Synoptics (Mark 1:16–20 par.; 2:14; 3:13–19 par.; Luke 5:1–11).[82] Under the influence of the Louvain school, an increasing number of students today suppose a direct influence of the Synoptic evangelists on John's Gospel. Accordingly, John would have re-edited Mark 1:16–20 par. and given these "call stories" a new character as "quest stories." These stories follow a pattern: a person seeks someone or something and "finds" him or it whereupon there can follow a concluding saying by the protagonist.

**1:43-44** The short account of the call of Philip appears to be separated from the following context in that it says at the beginning: "He found a named disciple and said to him." This pattern already attracted our attention in v. 41. In v. 43, it is preceded by an indication of time that separates the

---

81. Martyn, *The Gospel of John in Christian History*, 29–54, elaborated in detail in Painter, *Quest*, 145–48.

82. Painter, *Quest*, 145–48.

*The Divine Word Enters the World (1:1–4:54)*

previous two call stories from the present one, possibly in aid of a seven-day scenario that lasts until John 2:1. Jesus's intention to set out for Galilee and his summons to Philip mark him out as the protagonist. Thus, his authority stands out so greatly in the foreground that an account of Philip's reaction to Jesus's call is eschewed. It can be deduced from the following verses.

In an aside, the narrator explains that Philip hailed from Bethsaida, the town of Andrew and Peter. This reference to Philip's place of origin is repeated in John 12:21. There, the subject is the coming to Jesus of the Greeks for whom Philip acts as intermediary. This detail could have been significant for John. After all, Bethsaida lay east of the entry of the Jordan into the Sea of Gennesareth as part of the dominion of the tetrarch Philip and probably as a small town with stronger Hellenistic influence than elsewhere. This was certainly significant for the readers of the Fourth Gospel. Moreover, Peter and Andrew were disciples of Jesus with Greek names. Andrew takes part in the scene in John 12:21–36. In the Synoptics, Bethsaida appears in Mark 6:45; 8:22; Luke 9:10; 10:13 par. Matt 11:21 without reference to the disciples called by Jesus.

**1:45–46** The closing verses of the chapter report the call of Nathanael to faith. They may be divided into the dialogue between Philip and Nathanael (vv. 45–46) and the dialogue between Jesus and Nathanael (vv. 47–51). The latter can be further divided into Nathanael's way to faith after his initial hesitations (vv. 47–49) and Jesus's concluding saying in v. 51, which is prepared for in v. 50. We thus find in this section a series of christological statements that build on one another and end up with their climax in the saying about the Son of Man in v. 51. Jesus is "the one whom Moses in the Law and also the prophets have written about" (v. 45); he is called "Rabbi," but then recognized as "the Son of God and the King of Israel" (v. 49). The conclusion and climax is formed out of the self-description of Jesus as "Son of Man" in v. 51.

First of all, the encounter of Nathanael with Jesus is prepared for by what precedes. It follows the pattern of v. 41 that was modified in v. 43: Philip "finds" Nathanael and announces to him that he and his companions have "found" the one of whom Moses wrote in the Law and the Prophets. Here we have a basic Johannine perspective according to which not only this or that piece of Scripture points to Jesus, but the whole Scripture of Israel bears witness to him when properly read and understood (cf. John 5:39).[83] Moses wrote of him (John 5:46). If the two disciples at the tomb

---

83. Cf. Beutler, "Der Gebrauch von 'Schrift'"; Menken, *Old Testament Quotations*;

had understood the Scriptures, then they would not have been seeking the living among the dead (John 20:9).

Nathanael's astonishment lies in the fact that Israel's expected eschatological savior is to supposed to have come from the biblically insignificant Nazareth. Clearly, the place suffered from a poor reputation, for Nathanael asks: "From Nazareth? Can anything good come from Nazareth?" Against such a sentiment, the only sufficient response is a personal encounter that could banish prejudice: "Come and see!" Thus, the author echoes the "Come and see!" of verse 39.

**1:47–49** Vv. 47–51 consist of a dialogue between Jesus and Nathanael in which Nathanael twice replies to sayings of Jesus before Jesus closes the conversation. On account of their content, vv. 50–51 can be understood as a small subsection.

Philip had said to Nathanael: "Come and see!" (v. 46). Nathanael now actually comes to Jesus, but before he "sees" Jesus, Jesus "sees" him coming. The scene recalls the meeting of the first disciples with Jesus according to vv. 35–36 where John the Baptist sees Jesus coming and points him out. The same invitation: "Behold (see)," (ἴδε) recurs here. Jesus has, in fact, a definite view of Nathanael and communicates it. Nathanael is "a true Israelite in whom there is nothing false." Jesus's statement belongs to a series of texts in John in which there appears a positive assessment of Israel. To this too belong the ensuing words of Nathanael: "You are the King of Israel" (v. 49). This title is repeated in John 12:13; similar texts with the name "Israel" are to be found in John 1:31 and 3:10. They help to better put into context John's often critical expression "the Jews." These, then, are the faith-denying members of the Jewish people and its leadership, but precisely not "Israel."[84]

Just as Nathanael had answered Philip's piece of information with a skeptical question, so now he reacts skeptically to Jesus's words of praise (v. 48). That the narrator rates this critical disposition positively is shown by Jesus's words of commendation. Nathanael could not know that Jesus possessed knowledge of his heart. However, Jesus had seen him under the fig tree before Philip called him. He showed thereby a power that was superhuman, ultimately given by God. This prompts Nathanael to the declaration: "Rabbi, you are the Son of God, you are the King of Israel." The appellation "Rabbi" enrolls Jesus among the teachers of Israel; the twofold

---

Pontifical Biblical Commission, *Israel and Its Sacred Scriptures*; Labahn, "Jesus und die Autorität der Schrift."

84. Cf. Beutler, "The Identity."

title goes much further, of course, and corresponds to the creed of the Johannine community. Already, at the first encounter, Nathanael comes to the insight of faith that the reader of John's Gospel will have to reach at the end of the work (cf. John 20:31). More clearly than before, the account of the call of the disciples in John 1 appears to have been written from a post-Easter perspective.

The title "Son of God" has its ancient roots in Greco-Roman and Oriental religion (cf. above on God's children in John 1:12). Even so, a Jewish tradition is not lacking where this theme is concerned. Illuminating here is Jesus's own recourse in John 10:34–36 to the "Law" (meant here is Ps 82:6) in justification of his claim to be "Son of God," even God himself. According to more recent research, there is a Jewish tradition according to which, at Sinai, the Israelites received the privilege to be sons of God and immortal, a privilege they lost only through their subsequent fall into sin. If this was in view, Jesus would have been claiming this privilege of Israel for himself.[85]

In the New Testament, the confession of Jesus as "King of Israel" is restricted to John's Gospel. According to the Synoptic passion narratives (Mark 15:32 par. Matt 27:42), the chief priests, scribes, and elders (Matt) mock the crucified Jesus with this title and demand that he come down from the cross if he possesses that royal dignity. In John (12:13), at Jesus's entry into Jerusalem, the crowd pay him homage with this title in addition to the Synoptic *Vorlage* (Mark 11:9–10 and par.). They thus make him their own. So, in our passage, Nathanael appears to be the precursor of this confession. At the same time, he formulates it with the confession of John's community of Jesus as "Christ, the Son of God" (John 20:31).

In John's Gospel, we have to distinguish among three messiahs: the Jewish, the Samaritan, and the Christian. Frequently, the subject is the messiah in the sense of Israel's expectation at the time of the Second Temple. The dominant picture here is that of a messiah from the house of Judah as the king and eschatological redeemer of Israel. With this messianic picture, we should compare John 1:19–21, 25 with John the Baptist's reference to "the one who is to come" (John 1:27), as well as John 7:26, 31, 41–42; 9:22; 10:24; 12:34 in the controversies over Jesus's identity.

This messiah is to be distinguished from that of the Samaritans. Thus, the woman of Samaria asks whether Jesus is the "one that is to come," with a possible allusion to the Taheb, the Samaritans' messiah (John 4:29).

---

85. Cf. Beutler, "'Ich habe gesagt.'"

In John, we find the description of Jesus as "Christ" or messiah in the Christian sense almost uniformly linked to that of "Son of God." Here there is a progressive development from "We have found the Messiah" (John 1:41) to Nathanael's confession "Rabbi, you are the Son of God, you are the King of Israel!" (John 1:49). Both titles are encountered together in Martha's confession (John 11:27), as well as in the original conclusion to John's Gospel in John 20:31. Moreover, as mentioned, Jesus's royal dignity is recognized by the Passover pilgrims in Jerusalem (John 12:13) and even, in fact, by Pilate (John 19:12, 15–19: the inscription on the cross). For Christians, "Jesus Christ" becomes the proper name of Jesus and the epitome of his mission (cf. John 1:17; 17:3).

**1:50–51** One could think that Nathanael's confession "Rabbi, you are the Son of God, you are the King of Israel!" forms the climax of the christological titles of dignity in John 1:35–51. This is not the case, however. Jesus promises Nathanael that he will see still greater, more sublime things than the revelation of his heart's secrets: "You will see heaven opened and the angels of God ascending and descending upon the Son of Man." Who is this Son of Man?

Clearly, Gen 28:12 is being thought of here: the ladder up to heaven on which Jacob sees the angels of God ascending and descending. Instead of "on it" referring to the ladder, John refers it to Jesus. According to Schnackenburg,[86] three categories can be distinguished among the texts in John's Gospel that speak of the Son of Man:

- the Son of Man, who comes from and goes back to heaven (John 3:13; 6:62)
- the lifted-up Son of Man (John 3:14; 8:28; 12:34c)
- the glorified Son of Man (12:23; 13:31–32).

Together with the texts in John 6 concerning the Son of Man as giver of the living bread from heaven, our text from John 1:51 belongs to the first group of texts that speak of a Son of Man who comes from God, remains united with God, and goes back to God.

The immediate source of the Johannine concepts of the Son of Man is to be found in the Synoptic Gospels and there, above all, in the texts that speak about Jesus's forthcoming passion and death and resurrection. Of course, John reveals the influence of the Old Testament texts that speak of

---

86. Schnackenburg, 1:412.

the "servant," and his future "lifting up" and "exaltation" (Isa 52:13 LXX). In John, he is identified with the Son of Man.[87]

In John 1:51, it remains open when the disciples (or the reader) will see the greater things and the angels of God ascending and descending over the Son of Man. The following account of the marriage at Cana suggests itself as a possibility: it is certainly to be understood as the beginning of the revelation of Jesus in his signs. In fact, in this sign, the disciples see the glory of Jesus so that they are able to come to belief (John 2:11). This display of his glory is repeated (cf. John 11:4) and intensified until the perception of his glory in his lifting up to the Father (cf. John 13:31–32; 17:24).

## III

In the account of the call of the disciples in John 1:35–51, John gives us two models of discipleship. Disciples come to Jesus on account of the testimony of other disciples who have previously come to him. However, there can also be an emphasis on the authority of Jesus who approaches someone on his own initiative and invites him to follow him.

Jesus's free initiative is shown in the calling of Philip in John 1:43. He "finds" Philip for himself and calls him to follow him. This demonstrates an essential element of the call to faith and following that is also presupposed in the other accounts. Even when there is human intervention, Jesus remains the one who calls.

In the other call scenes in our section, it is this human intervention that stands in the foreground. John the Baptist points out Jesus to the first two disciples; one of them, Andrew, does the same for his brother Cephas/Peter, as does Philip, after his calling, for Nathanael. Thus, human conditions contribute to the transmission of faith. Andrew, the "other disciple," Peter, and Philip all hail from the same place, Bethsaida. Furthermore, Andrew and Peter are brothers.

For his part, Jesus takes into consideration human limits and prejudices in his call of the first disciples. That is shown in the call of Nathanael. At first, he expresses reservations about a man who comes from Nazareth, and these too are credited to him. Jesus counters Nathanael's skepticism with his own positive judgement. Nathanael's further skepticism as to how Jesus knows him is also overcome, and so Nathanael can formulate his con-

---

87. Cf. Beutler, "Greeks"; Beutler, "Griechen."

fession of faith. Thus Nathanael is taken seriously with all his reservations, something that also encourages the Gospel's readers to allow themselves to persevere through their own possible reservations until they come to confess their faith in Jesus Christ.

Basic to the account of the call of the disciples in John 1:35–51 remains Jesus's question to the first two prospective disciples in John 1:38: "What do you want?" Clearly, Jesus does not come across as being intent primarily on advancing his own concerns. He desires to enter into the deepest wishes of the men whom he meets and whom he wishes to follow him. So when the disciples say: "Rabbi, where do you live?," he invites them to come with him and see his lodgings. They then "remain" with him for the rest of that day. In entering into the desire of his future disciples, he gives them a new home while letting them take an active interest in his own "abode." Here too, the readers of John's Gospel can feel themselves addressed over the years. A new existence is not being imposed on them, but they are being invited to experience the fulfillment of their innermost desires in communion with Jesus.

## 4. The First Sign of Jesus in Cana (2:1–12)

[1] On the third day, a marriage took place in Cana of Galilee, and the mother of Jesus was there. [2] Jesus and his disciples had also been invited to the wedding. [3] When the wine ran out, Jesus's mother said to him: They have no wine. [4] Jesus replied: Woman, what do you want from me? My hour has not yet come. [5] His mother said to the servants: Do whatever he tells you! [6] Standing there were six stone water jugs, complying with the Jewish rites of purification; each held about twenty or thirty gallons. [7] Jesus said to the servants: Fill the jugs with water! And they filled them to the brim. [8] He said to them: Draw now, and bring it to the president of the feast. They brought it to him. [9] He tasted the water that had become wine. He didn't know where the wine came from; but the servants who had drawn the water knew. Then he had the bridegroom called in [10] and said to him: Everyone serves the good wine first and only the less good when the guests have drunk too much. But you have kept the good wine until now. [11] Thus Jesus did his first sign, in Cana of Galilee, and manifested his glory, and his disciples believed in him. [12] After this he went down to Capernaum with his mother, his brothers and his disciples. There they remained for some time.

*The Divine Word Enters the World (1:1–4:54)*

*I*

The account of the changing of water into wine at the marriage of Cana closes the section of the call of Jesus's first disciples and at the same time opens a new section that extends at least to Jesus's second sign in Cana: the healing of the royal official's son in John 4:46–54.[88] At the end of John 1:35–51, it was said: "You will see something still greater. . . . You will see heaven opened, and angels of God ascending and descending upon the Son of Man" (John 1:50–51). A first realization of this announcement takes place precisely in Jesus's first sign as the manifestation of his glory before his disciples (John 2:11). On the other hand, however, this sign also opens a whole new section in John's Gospel that exegetes like to call "The Book of Signs" (John 2–12), with the raising of Lazarus (John 11:1–44) as its climax and conclusion. Apart from this hinge function, our text exhibits links with other sections of the Gospel in John 13–21. Michèle Morgen points to connections of the communal meal in John 2:1–11 with Jesus's Last Supper with his friends in John 13:1–30 and the significance of such meals in the Jewish and early Christian world.[89] Moreover, the presence of Jesus's mother at the wedding of Cana forms an inclusio with the scene at the cross at which his mother is present once again and he once more uses "woman" as a form of address—a remark that only seems cold, but in reality is not (John 19:25–27). Mary—who is not named as such—is perceived in her womanly role in salvation history that transcends her individuality. The theme of Jesus's glory points forward to its fulfillment in the one who will be glorified in his death on the cross and in his resurrection.

The account of the changing of water into wine at Cana has been the object of more investigations and hypotheses than other texts in John's Gospel. Until very recently, literary-critical questions were discussed, especially in connection with the difficult dialogue between Jesus and his mother in verses 3–4, its aporias being solved by distinguishing sources or strata. Furthermore, the cultural and religious-historical background to the story remains disputed. Is it to be sought in the Bible (with its symbolism of the marriage between God and his people and the sacred meal) or in

---

88. Brown, 1:xi sees in John 2–4 a separate subsection "From Cana to Cana." Moloney, 62f., sees in it a symmetrical construction framed by the two Cana pericopes. This shows Jesus only in an encounter with a Jew in Jerusalem, then with the Samaritans. Kierspel, "Religion," finds here instead a chiastic construction with its center in the dialogues and speeches of John 3.

89. Morgen, "Le festin."

the Greco-Hellenistic milieu with parallels of wonderful gifts of wine by the god Dionysus? Such questions will be dealt with in the concluding excursus.

Regardless of its pre-history, the text here meets with similarly differing exegeses. For some authors, the meaning of the story of the wine miracle in Cana is, above all, christological; for others, it is Marian, and for others still it is salvation-historical. Lastly, for some, it has significance from a feminist perspective, at least in addition to other meanings. Which is to be preferred? In answering this question, one starts out, logically, from semantic observations on the text. Overall, we can distinguish four semantic fields that give the text its character: 1) the motif of wedding and marriage, 2) that of the meal, 3) the motif complex of human relations in dialogue, and 4) a temporal sequence of "before" and "after" (water to wine, poorer wine to better wine, and lack to fullness). We shall come across these again in the detailed exegesis.

The construction of the section emerges, chiefly, from a series of dialogue scenes. In verses 1–3a, there is a narrative introduction to the story. There follows, in verses 3b to 4, the dialogue between Jesus and his mother, succeeded in v. 5 by the mother's word to the servant. Then, in v. 6, we have a narrative preparation for the miracle. This begins with a word of Jesus to the servant and its fulfillment in v. 7. There follow a second word of Jesus and its fulfillment in v. 8. Here, the president of the feast is introduced. He detects the unexpected abundance of the "best" wine and calls for the bridegroom in v. 9, acknowledging that the latter has kept back the best wine until then (v. 10). The story closes, not with a word of Jesus, but with a theological comment from the evangelist who makes clear the deeper meaning of the event in v. 11. The section ends with information about Jesus's setting out from Cana to Capernaum in v. 12.[90]

## II

**2:1–3a** The opening verses contain the unfolding of the narrative. Information regarding place and time comes first. The "third day" could refer back to the beginning of the call of the disciples in v. 35 or to the last reckoning of days in v. 43. The latter theory is the more probable. Cana in Galilee is also

---

90. A concentric construction for John 2:1–12 is seen by Girard, "Cana."

mentioned in John 4:46 and is shown to be one of the favorite early sites of Jesus's activity.[91] The mention of his mother before Jesus himself is astonishing and can be explained in either historical or theological terms. In the whole story, the bride is not mentioned, and it is Jesus's mother who, in a certain sense, replaces her, something that points to her role in salvation history. The running out of wine prepares for the governing theme of the narrative. The disciples are mentioned here as the event's witnesses who, in hindsight, were able to discern its deeper meaning. Within the narrative itself, they do not appear again.

**2:3b–4** The narrative proper begins with an exchange between Jesus and his mother. She is the one who begins to speak, something that suits her leading role within the narrative that we have already observed. She indicates to Jesus that the wine is beginning to run out. Jesus's answer appears harsh and dismissive, at least if one takes his words literally. In his defense, there are Old Testament parallels such as Judg 11:12; 2 Sam 16:10; 19:22; 1 Kgs 17:18.[92] "My hour is not yet come" should be taken as a statement and not as the question: "Has my hour not come yet?"[93] At first sight, Jesus's answer that his hour has not yet come appears not to correspond to his mother's request that he help the young pair. Thus, in the final analysis, the narrator binds the manifestation of Jesus's glory to his lifting up on the cross and to his Father. Cf. John 12:23; 13:31–32.

**2:5** Mary behaves as if she had not taken Jesus's answer on board. She asks the servants to fill the water jugs and so prepares for the miracle. In the given context, her behavior can also mean that the manifestation of Jesus's glory could begin at any point in time, perhaps as an anticipation of his coming glory at his "hour."

**2:6–8** The following verses render the dialogue between Jesus and the servants. Jesus now makes the preparations for performing the miracle of the changing of the water into wine. First, the empty jugs have to be filled with water. The reference to the purification customs of the Jews allows us to think of the sequence: old—new order of salvation. This sequence is characteristic of the entire narrative.[94] It indicates the fullness of

---

91. Bergler, *Von Kana nach Jerusalem*, 30, situates, once again, the location of this place in Hirbet-Kana, a site that is now abandoned, north of the Kafr Kenna shown to present-day pilgrims.

92. These texts are cited by Stramare, "La risposta," 185, who, however, gives Jesus's saying another, positive sense: "What is mine, is yours."

93. Stramare also goes with this meaning, but largely alone. See the previous note.

94. On the interpretation of these temporal categories in a salvation-historical sense

the water that has already been provided, and it prepares for the fullness of the gift of wine. Jesus now asks the servants to bring some of the water to the president of the feast. The text gives the impression that the water is first changed into wine when it is drawn and brought to the meal. The filling of the jugs did not in itself constitute the miracle.[95]

**2:9–10** That a miracle has taken place follows from the ensuing dialogue between the president of the feast and the bridegroom. Both appear not to know the origin of the wonderful wine that, contrary to custom, has been kept until then. The last word is not left to Jesus but to the president of the feast. Perhaps we have here a touch of "Johannine irony." In other "apothegms," it is the chief protagonist; in the Gospels, it is mainly Jesus who has the last word that brings the meaning of a narrative to expression. So, do we have a reference here to Jesus as "president of the feast"?

**2:11** The conclusion of the narrative has been formulated by the evangelist. As just mentioned, neither the president nor the bridegroom knew where the good wine had come from. Only the disciples seem to have understood what Jesus had done. In this first "sign" of his, Jesus unveils before their eyes his "glory" as Christ and Son of God. They have seen "something greater" just as had been announced to Nathanael (John 1:50)—and they will see things greater still when "the Son of Man ascends where he was before" (John 6:62). The readers are invited to share in this experience of the glory of the Son of Man. Thus, with the Gospel's entrance hymn, they can confess: "And the Word became flesh and lived among us, and we saw his glory, the glory of the only Son of the Father, full of grace and truth" (John 1:14).

**2:12** In a transitional verse, the narrator reverts once more to the beginning of his account (vv. 1–2). Jesus departs, and along with him his mother and his disciples. His brothers are also mentioned, having apparently been among the wedding guests. Otherwise, in John's Gospel, they play a wholly subordinate role (cf., though, John 7:3). Only in the disciples can the readers find their way to faith in Jesus. Apart from this passage, Capernaum is found in the Fourth Gospel only in John 6 (17, 24, 59) as the stage for Jesus's discourse on the bread of life. In John, Capernaum does not possess comparable significance to what it enjoys in the Synoptic Gospels. For the author of the Fourth Gospel, it is a lo-

---

in John 2:1–11, cf. Olsson, *Structure and Meaning*. The "Before" and "After" is also highlighted by Girard, "Cana," 102.

95. Cf. Ognibene, "L'ignoranza."

cation in Galilee from which Jesus departs on his journeys as a pilgrim to Jerusalem.

*Excursus:* The Origin of the Story
of the Miracle of the Wine at Cana

The story of the miracle of the wine stands alone as unique in the tradition. Moreover, upon careful reading, it leads to a host of difficulties that make it hard to understand. For a long time, it was literary-critical questions that were mainly being asked, and scholars attempted to eliminate the apparent tensions in the story by distinguishing sources and strata. Among other matters, discussion concerned the original place of the narrative in John's Gospel; the presence or not of Jesus's mother as well as of the disciples in the oldest account; the originality of the conversation between Jesus and his mother in verses 3–4 or also of the reference to the Jewish rites of purification; and, finally, the reckoning of signs at the close of the story. Walter Lütgehetmann has described these literary-critical discussions in detail, and so there is no reason to deal with them again here.[96]

More important seems the question as to how to explain the kernel of the narrative, the miracle of the wine in the context of a marriage feast from a historical point of view. Are there precedents, and where would we look for them? Here, the research divides into two basic directions. The first direction points especially to biblical precedents and parallels. It is found in Brown, among others.[97] Within the NT, the changing of water into wine points, above all, to the story of the miraculous multiplication of loaves. This tradition is found, not only in the three Synoptics (Mark 6:32–44 par.; 8:1–9 par.), but also in John's Gospel itself (John 6:1–15). Of course, the exegete recalls the differences as well as the agreements. In the multiplication miracle, Jesus has recourse to existing material and multiplies it. In the marriage of Cana, he bestows wine that previously did not exist. Moreover, that material is wine and not bread. Thus, there remain considerable differences.

Close to the text of John 2:1–11 are some stories from the cycle of the two great prophets, Elijah and Elisha, in the books of Kings. There is a precedent for the multiplication of bread in the cycle in 2 Kgs 4:42–44.

---

96. Cf. Lütgehetmann, *Die Hochzeit von Kana*, 41–122.
97. Cf. Brown, 1:101–10.

In this story, Elisha orders twenty barley loaves and fresh grain to be distributed to a hundred people, and there is enough for them, and more is left over. Similar texts are the miraculous gift of meal and oil for the widow of Zarephath by the prophet Elijah (1 Kgs 17:1–16), and of oil for another widow by the prophet Elisha (2 Kgs 4:1–7). All these miracles fall under the category of "gift miracles," and it is to this category that the majority of exegetes assign the changing of water into wine at Cana. Naturally, there also remain substantial differences between these Old Testament stories and John 2:1–11: none of these stories concerns a gift of wine, and in none of them is the gift bestowed without a small amount of existing material that is then simply multiplied.

Other biblical precedents come into play when one considers the motifs of the eschatological banquet and the wedding. The image of marriage for the relationship between God and his people is already found before the Exile. The oldest text is Hos 2:1–3:5 where a new, God-given fidelity succeeds Israel's unfaithfulness. In the exilic and post-exilic periods, the wedding comes to represent the loving covenant of God with his people in the messianic age (Isa 54:4–8; 62:4–5).[98] Jesus himself takes up the image of the banquet and the wedding in order to describe the coming salvation (Matt 8:11; 22:1–14; Luke 22:16–18).[99] The wedding also appears as an image of the messianic fulfillment in the Revelation of John (19:9). For wine as an element of an eschatological meal, cf. Isa 25:6.

All these elements are to be considered in the working out of the background of John 2:1–11. What struck us was the absence of the bride and the presence of Jesus's mother who was called "woman" (John 2:4). Thus, the story can be attributed a symbolic meaning: at the beginning of his public ministry, Jesus celebrates with his disciples the opening of a new era of salvation history, the inbreaking of eschatological joy at the climax of the covenant relationship, at the dawn of the new and everlasting covenant under the image of a marriage feast.

The alternative or rather the complement to a religious-historical derivation of the miracle of the wine at Cana from biblical parallels is offered by the reference to Hellenistic ones. In spite of the counter-arguments of Heinz Noetzel,[100] a growing number of scholars consider

---

98. On the relevance of this motif for John 2:1–11, cf. Varghese, *Imagery*, 39–97.

99. Garský, *Wirken Jesu*, 125–50, sees numerous connections between Mark 2:18–22 par. and John 2:1–11.

100. Noetzel, *Christus und Dionysos*.

## The Divine Word Enters the World (1:1–4:54)

likely an influence of the Dionysus cult on our narrative, just as had already been suggested by Bultmann in his commentary. More recently, among others, the contribution of the noted New Testament scholar from Tübingen, Hengel,[101] as well as the Frankfurt dissertation of Lütgehetmann[102] should be mentioned.

For the sake of convenience, it is permissible here to go over the influence of the cult of Dionysus on John 2:1–11 by following its treatment in *RAC*:[103]

> Already in the classical Greek tradition is Dionysus known as the giver of wine: sailors suddenly swim in it (Hymn. Hom. Bachh. 35–37 [77 Allen]), just as the Bacchae in a fit of ecstasy create milk and honey out of a river (Plato, *Ion* 534A). According to Euripides, the god would cause a spring of wine to stream out of the earth if a bacchant stuck her Thyrsis rod into the ground (*Bacch.* 706f); milk, wine and honey would stream from where the god trod the land (*ibid.* 142f. cf. 423f. 651. 773f); he is even himself present in wine (284f). According to Diodorus Siculus, he brings forth a spring of wine at regular intervals in Teos, something that the people of Teos reckon as a token of the birth of Dionysus in their city (Diod. Sic. 3.66.3). Two further texts belong, in fact, to the second century CE but contain traditions that may be older: according to Lucian, sailors at the Pillars of Hercules discovered an inscription: "Heracles and Dionysus came as far as this." Close by, there flowed a river of costly wine like that of Chios. It was regarded as a σημεῖον of a sojourn of Dionysus (*True History*, 1.7). According to Pausanias, on the feast of the Thyia in the temple of Dionysus in Elis, the priests set out three empty jugs and seal the temple in the presence of witnesses; the next morning, the jugs are filled with costly wine (6.26.1f). On Andros, annually, on the feast of Dionysus, wine flows out of his temple. Already in the first century AD, Pliny the Elder knows the same tradition for the Nones of January; the feast is called Θεοδοσία (*Natural History*, 2.231).

101. Hengel, "The Interpretation of the Wine Miracle."
102. Lütgehetmann, *Die Hochzeit von Kana*. Cf., since then, among others, Bergler, *Von Kana in Galiläa nach Jerusalem*, 80–140; Eisele, "Jesus und Dionysos." He extends the comparison with the Dionysius myth to the areas of wine, wedding, mother (foster-mother), disciples.
103. Beutler and Meredith, "Johannes-Evangelium (u. -Briefe)," 652f. Cf. Beutler, "Johannesevangelium, Johannesbriefe," 30f.

Now, one must keep in sight the fact that the Greek epics themselves know of the origin of Dionysus from the East. Dionysus is the son of Semele, the daughter of the Theban king's son Cadmos who came to Greece from Tyre (or Sidon). Greek coins from Syro-Palestine bear Dionysian motifs. This is true, among other places, of Skythopolis (Beth Shean), a city on the edge of Galilee that boasted itself to be the city of the birth and early childhood of Dionysus (cf. Pliny, *Natural History*, 5.74). A text of Achilles Tatius relocates to Tyre the Attic legend of Dionyus' gift of the grapevine to a hospitable shepherd (*Leucippe et Cliptophon*, 2.2.1–6). Therefore, there probably lurks behind Dionysus an old Oriental vegetation deity which is also attested in Phrygia by Ovid (*Met.* 8.679–83). So with M. Hengel, who has assembled this information, (...),[104] we can speculate on an Oriental origin behind the tradition of the Cana miracle.

If Jesus appears in our story in the role of Dionysus as the donor of joy and abundance, this picture meets with that gained from the Old Testament. Here too, Jesus gives a physical joy that can be experienced in the festive marriage meal that he has made possible.

### III

In John, at the beginning of Jesus's public ministry, there is no call to repentance and conversion nor even a verbal proclamation of the imminent kingdom of God. Jesus begins his activity by performing a sign that makes it clear just what he has come to bring: eschatological, nuptial joy through the gift of abundant wine to a couple at a wedding. In this way, contemporary readers can be more easily addressed than through repetition of Jesus's first words of proclamation. Precisely in a visually-oriented culture, the message of Jesus goes more easily into people's hearts in this way than in the simple repetition of his words. The picture of the wine miracle at Cana shows us a Jesus who gives joy in abundance and this at the celebration of a feast, a feast that more than all others rejoices the heart: the feast at a wedding.

---

104. See n. 101 above.

# *The Divine Word Enters the World (1:1–4:54)*

## 5. The First Passover: Cleansing of the Temple (2:13–25)

**13** The Passover feast of the Jews was near, and Jesus went up to Jerusalem. **14** In the temple, he found those who were selling oxen, sheep and doves, and the moneychangers who were sitting there. **15** He made a whip out of cords, and drove them all out of the temple together with the sheep and oxen; he scattered the changers' money, overturned their tables, **16** and said to the dove-sellers: Take these things away; do not make my Father's house into a market hall! **17** His disciples remembered that it was written: Zeal for your house has consumed me. **18** The Jews answered and said to him: What sign have you to show us for doing this? **19** Jesus replied: Demolish this temple, and in three days I will raise it up again. **20** Then the Jews said: This temple took forty-six years to build, and will you raise it up in three days? **21** But he meant the temple of his body. **22** When he was raised from the dead, his disciples remembered that he had said this, and they believed the Scripture and the word that Jesus had spoken.

**23** While he was in Jerusalem at the Passover feast, many came to believe in his name, for they saw the signs that he performed. **24** But Jesus himself had no faith in them, for he knew them all **25** and needed testimony about men from no one; for he knew what was in men.

### I

After the marriage at Cana, the account of the "cleansing of the temple" in John 2:13–22 comes rather unexpectedly. In the Synoptic Gospels, this event is recounted much closer to the passion of Jesus. In fact, it is made to appear as a possible ground for Jesus's arrest. In John, such a connection is not apparent, and so the question arises why he has placed this scene at the beginning of Jesus's ministry. An answer to this question seems possible only after a careful analysis of the text.

The question of the relation of our text to the Synoptic tradition raises itself also within our pericope. According to a study by Jarl Henning Ulrichsen,[105] we have to distinguish in this unit between a tradition about a "temple cleansing" and another about a controversy between Jesus and the Jewish authorities over his authority. The parallels to John 2:14–17 are to be found in Mark 11:15–17 par. Matt 21:12–13 and Luke 19:45–46. These Synoptic texts display stark differences not only over against the Johan-

---

105. Ulrichsen, "Jesus—der neue Tempel?"

nine versions but also among themselves. The difference consists, above all, in the situation that is presupposed. In Mark, the scene immediately precedes the passion narrative and seems to have provoked the arrest of Jesus, directly or indirectly. With Matthew, this connection already seems to have been loosened, and with Luke this is even more strongly the case. In any case, Jesus's behavior in the temple is not mentioned at his trial, but it lingers under the surface in the quotation of his alleged saying that he would destroy the temple and build another in three days (Mark 14:58). As Ernst Bammel remarks, this charge was without foundation just like the corresponding one against Stephen (Acts 6:13–14).[106] The fact that Jesus's action apparently played no part in his trial shows, according to Bammel, that the connection between this event and the passion of Jesus could be secondary. Of course, it also remains necessary to explain the place of the story of the cleansing of the temple in John. As will be shown, Jesus continues to visit the temple, and, in the following eight chapters, he makes it the preferred place for his teaching and preaching. A conflict in this place with the Jewish authorities is easier to understand at the end of Jesus's public life than at its beginning. Bammel speculates that the place of the story of the cleansing of the temple was found in the first half of John 11 in the pre-Johannine tradition. The danger to which Jesus exposes himself when he sets out to go to his friend in Bethany, and the readiness of the disciples to go and die with him (John 11:16), are more easily understood in connection with Jesus's action in the temple than in connection with the miracle of the raising of Lazarus. Bammel's proposal merits further study, but it invites us to look for the original setting of Jesus's cleansing of the temple (which is generally regarded as historical in its nucleus) at the end rather than at the beginning of Jesus's public life.

The actual account of the cleansing of the temple displays substantial differences not only among the three Synoptic compositions but also between them and the Johannine version. In none of the three Synoptic narratives is there any mention, as in John, of sheep and oxen, and the whip of cords is also missing. The saying with which Jesus justifies his behavior in the Synoptics is taken from the prophets Isaiah (56:7) and Jeremiah (7:11). In John, the disciples recall a verse from the Psalms (Ps 69:9). According to Mark (11:16), Jesus did not let anyone carry anything through the temple precinct. Luke remains very general and mentions neither the doves nor the fact that Jesus upset the tables of the money changers and the trad-

---

106. Bammel, "Die Tempelreinigung."

ers. The whole emphasis lies on Jesus's saying that the Scripture of Israel is being referred to. Despite these differences, a broad consensus today maintains that it is one and the same event that is being handled in these different accounts, and that it only appears to be especially elaborately portrayed and theologically reflected on in the Fourth Gospel.

For the following subsection on the demand for a sign, scholars refer to Mark 11:27–33 par. Matt 21:23–27 and Luke 20:1–8. In this account, Jesus answers the question of the chief priests, Pharisees, and scribes with a counter-question about John's baptism. Added to this is another text in which Jesus is asked about his authority: the pericope about the sign of Jonah (Matt 12:38–42; 16:1–2a, 4; Luke 11:16, 29–32). Here, Jesus speaks figuratively about his death and resurrection after three days. According to Bammel,[107] this text would stand behind John 2:18–22, together with Mark 14:57–59 par. Matt 26:60–61; cf. Acts 6:14, concerning the destruction and rebuilding of the temple.[108]

How far the evangelist has gone back to directly to the Synoptics in the present account of the cleansing of the temple still remains disputed. Tobias Nicklas[109] sees a connection to the Synoptics on the level of the reader and so opposes Labahn and Lang,[110] who would like to detect such a relationship on the level of the text. They seem to be correct.

How is the whole section, John 2:13–25, constructed? First, it is a good idea to separate the scene of the cleansing of the temple with its following question about authority, vv. 13–22, from the concluding verses, 23–25. The first group appears to be divided into two parts that both display a similar construction:[111]

(1) v. 13     Frame
(2) vv. 14–17     Cleansing of the temple
    vv. 14–15     Jesus's action
    v. 16     Jesus's saying
    v. 17     The disciples remember (a word of Scripture)

---

107. Bammel, "Die Tempelreinigung."
108. According to Stowasser, "Tempelaktion," what stands behind John 2:14–19 is an old tradition rather than the text of the Synoptic Gospels. Schleritt, *Passionsbericht*, 173, sees the pre-Johannine passion narrative that he advocates behind this pericope.
109. Nicklas, "Tempelreinigung."
110. Labahn and Lang, "Johannes und die Synoptiker."
111. Cf. the article by Ulrichsen, "Jesus—der neue Tempel?" and Frühwald-König, *Tempel und Kult*. We follow Ulrichsen here.

(3) vv. 18–22       Question about Authority
    v. 18           Reaction of the Jews
    v. 19           Enigmatic saying of Jesus
    v. 20           Misunderstanding of the Jews
    v. 21           Comment of the Evangelist
    v. 22           Memory of the Disciples

The concluding verses, 23–25, are connected with the previous context through the Passover feast (vv. 13 and 23) as well as the theme of "signs" (v. 11, v. 18, and v. 23) and of "faith" or "trust" (πιστεύειν, vv. 11 and 23–24).

## II

**2:13-17** The account of the cleansing of the temple begins with indications of time and place. Jesus is staying in Galilee, but starts off for the first time to go to one of the pilgrim feasts at Jerusalem. This will be followed by the unnamed feast of John 5:1 (probably the Feast of Weeks) and the Feast of Tabernacles, 7:2, before the last Passover feast in 11:55; 12:1, and 13:1. We presumed earlier that the Passover feast of 6:4 was added subsequently to this annual cycle of Jewish pilgrim feasts.[112] If it is removed from the series of feasts, Jesus's ministry according to John is set within four pilgrim journeys to Jerusalem in the annual cycle of Jewish feasts. Thus, Israel's holy seasons come to fulfillment in Jesus.

In what follows, we see how in Jesus the holy places of Israel also come to fulfillment. This seems to be the deeper meaning of the "cleansing of the temple" together with Jesus's concluding words about the "temple of his body." Of course, it is necessary here to warn against jumping to the conclusion of a theory of supersession. According to a series of authors, Jesus appears in John 2:13–22 as "the new temple." Ulrichsen subjects this interpretation to a critical appraisal that we shall associate ourselves with in the following.[113]

In Jesus's actions, which are described in verses 14 and 15, there is nothing about the abolition of the cult. Jesus is throwing out of the temple men who have introduced the secular into the sanctuary, the animal traders and the money changers. John adds the sheep and the oxen to the

---

112. See the introduction above.
113. Ulrichsen, "Jesus—der neue Tempel?"

*The Divine Word Enters the World (1:1–4:54)*

doves and thereby effectively combines those animals that were designated for the daily offerings in the temple together with the doves that served as the offerings of the poor (cf. Luke 2:24).[114] Jesus's words to the dove-sellers make it clear that he does not wish to abolish the offerings but only to remove all secular, business elements from the temple as a holy place. In this sense, it is correct to speak of a "cleansing" of the temple and not of its replacement. When Jesus calls the temple "my Father's house," he identifies himself in large measure with this place and this institution of Israel. The saying to which Jesus is referring is to be found in Zech 14:21 and thus in the last verse of the book of Zechariah.[115] This verse announces that no Canaanite or trader will be in the temple any more. The latter interpretation is clearly supposed in John 2:16.

The concluding verse 17 speaks of a "remembering" of the disciples, as does the corresponding verse 22. In v. 17, the disciples recall immediately a text from the Psalms: "Zeal for your house will consume me" (Ps 69:9), where the future tense is the work of the evangelist. The message for the readers is that Jesus—like the psalmist—will have to suffer in his service on behalf of the house of the Lord. This is far away from an abolition of the cult. Jesus takes a dedicated stand for the restoration of the holiness of the central cultic place of Israel, even at risk to his life.

**2:18–22** This second scene contains no further action but only a dialogue, and an incomplete one at that. To the "Jews'" question about his authority in v. 18, Jesus answers with an enigmatic saying (v. 19), which is misunderstood by the Jews as their new question (v. 20) shows. To this question, Jesus has no further reply; instead, the evangelist makes a comment that interprets the meaning of Jesus's saying (v. 21). The section ends with a further comment by the evangelist, who refers to the disciples and, in fact, to their understanding of Jesus's saying after his resurrection from the dead and to their belief at that point in time (v. 22).

The "Jews" were already mentioned in chap. 1 as the people who had sent a delegation to John the Baptist asking him who he was and why he was baptizing (John 1:19). In John's Gospel, these "Jews" are often presented as a central authority of the Jewish people and faith in Jerusalem whose job it was to keep watch over the orthodoxy of the Jewish faith. It is these

---

114. According to Hübenthal, "Wie kommen Schafe und Rinder," the oxen and sheep come from Ps 69, the psalm from which the quotation in John 2:17 is taken, and, there, from v. 31.

115. Cf. Hübenthal, *Transformation*, 322–67.

"Jews" who demand from Jesus a sign of his authority. Actually, such signs are mentioned for Jesus's activity in Jerusalem (cf. John 2:23; 7:31; 11:47; 12:37 after the opening sign of the marriage at Cana in John 2:1–11). There is a further demand for a sign in Jesus's dialogue with the crowd in John 6:30, which is surprising after the previously recounted miracle, cf. 6:26. In John 2:19, Jesus does not refuse to provide a sign, but offers one that the Jews do not understand. He challenges them to destroy this temple, and he will then rebuild it in three days. As already mentioned, Jesus uses here a saying that the "false witnesses" had quoted in his Jewish trial. For John, this saying has a deeper meaning, just like the other one ascribed to Jesus about the prophet Jonah who remained in the belly of the whale for three days and then came out of it again. The "Jews" are not able to understand Jesus's saying. The evangelist (as omniscient narrator) provides the meaning for the readers: Jesus was speaking about the temple of his body (v. 21). It has often been concluded from this meaning that, for the readers, Jesus's body had replaced the temple of Jerusalem. Against this notion, Ulrichsen argues that John wanted only to explain Jesus's enigmatic saying. For Jesus, the temple remains the point of reference for his future public ministry, beginning with his pilgrim journeys. The temple will also be the preferred place for his teaching (cf. John 18:20). Only after the destruction of the temple, which occurred before the Fourth Gospel was written down, was the risen body of Jesus, that is, Jesus himself, to become the sole place of God's presence among men.[116] This is the standpoint of verse 22, in which Jesus's saying is placed alongside that of Scripture (without becoming part of it). Only after Easter, under the guidance of the Holy Spirit, do Jesus's words and deeds become comprehensible (cf. John 16:12–15).

**2:23–25** The last three verses do not agree with the numeration of signs according to John 2:11 and 4:54 (cf. 21:4, according to J.-P. Heekerens a third sign that belongs to a sign collection of the Johannine redaction[117]). Those scholars who ascribe the numbering of the signs to the hypothetical "sign source" in John's Gospel see the hand of the evangelist at work in John 2:23. Of course, one can suggest the evangelist as the author of verses 23–25 without the theory of a sign source. Since John 2:11, there has been a presumed connection between the "seeing" of a sign and faith. Naturally, such faith still remains superficial. Jesus had no "faith" (οὐκ ἐπίστευσεν

---

116. This clarification should be taken into account in the Frankfurt dissertation of López Rosas, *La señal del Templo*, which is otherwise worth reading.

117. Heekerens, *Die Zeichen-Quelle der johanneischen Redaktion*.

ἑαυτόν, with a play on words) in men who arrived at a faith like this. He needed from no one a testimony about men, for he knew them and was aware of the depths of the human heart (cf. his knowledge of Nathanael before he met him, John 1:47–48, and the individual past of the Samaritan woman in John 4:16–18). If these three verses go back to the evangelist, they establish a certain skepticism on his part with regard to a too strong connection between Jesus's signs and belief in him that can already be observed in John 2:1–11. Just as in the story of the marriage at Cana the "hour" of Jesus serves as a hermeneutical key, so too in our present section the superhuman knowledge of Jesus, who is able to distinguish between a superficial form of faith based on his signs and a deeper one that also has a knowledge of the mystery of his person, serves as a hermeneutical key: the way predestined for him by the Father, which will lead him to a violent death and only thus to his resurrection.

## III

The relocation of the story of the cleansing of the temple to the beginning of John's Gospel lends high drama to this Gospel from its very opening. Conflict concerning Jesus and his mission does not arise gradually but right away from the beginning of the narrative. The starting point is the trading in the holy place. Jesus's violent intervention against it raises the question of his authority. As already in the story of the marriage at Cana, the true key to the mystery of Jesus is shown in his journey through life right to the end. He will be the new and abiding place of God's presence among men, his very body that will reach resurrection through the gate of death. The holy places of Israel will thereby not be abolished but "taken up" in the Hegelian sense of being preserved on a higher level.

## 6. The Dialogue with Nicodemus in Jerusalem (3:1–21)

¹ There was one of the Pharisees called Nicodemus, a leading figure among the Jews. ² He visited Jesus by night and said to him: Rabbi, we know that you are a teacher come from God; for no one can do the signs that you perform unless God is with him. ³ Jesus answered him: Amen, amen, I say to you: Unless one is born anew, one cannot see the kingdom of God. ⁴ Nicodemus replied: How can a man be born if he is already old? Can he return to his mother's womb and be

born a second time? ⁵ Jesus answered: Amen, amen, I say to you: Unless one is born of water and spirit, one cannot enter the kingdom of God. ⁶ What is born of the flesh is flesh; but what is born of the Spirit is spirit. ⁷ Do not marvel that I said to you: You must be born anew. ⁸ The wind blows where it wills; you hear its noise, but you do not know where it comes from or where it is going to. That is the case with everyone who is born from the Spirit. ⁹ Nicodemus replied: How can that happen? ¹⁰ Jesus answered: Are you the teacher of Israel and you do not understand? ¹¹ Amen, amen, I say to you: What we know, we speak, and what we have seen, that we witness, yet you do not receive our testimony. ¹² If I have spoken of earthly things to you and you do not believe, how will you believe when I speak of heavenly things to you? ¹³ And no one has ascended to heaven except the one who has come down from heaven: the Son of Man. ¹⁴ And just as Moses lifted up the serpent in the wilderness, so must the Son of Man be lifted up, ¹⁵ so that everyone who believes in him may have eternal life. ¹⁶ For God so loved the world that he gave over his only Son, so that everyone who believes in him might not perish but have eternal life. ¹⁷ For God sent his Son into the world, not to condemn the world but so that the world might be redeemed through him. ¹⁸ Whoever believes in him will not be condemned; whoever does not believe is already condemned because he has not believed in the name of the only Son of God. ¹⁹ For the condemnation lies in this: The light came into the world, but men preferred the darkness to the light because their deeds were evil. ²⁰ Everyone that does evil hates the light and does not come to the light so that his deeds may not be revealed. ²¹ But whoever does the truth comes to the light so that it may be manifest that his deeds are accomplished in God.

*I*

Jesus's dialogue with Nicodemus is distinctly marked off from the previous text. Occasionally it has been suggested to regard the section as opening already in John 2:23 since Nicodemus seems to belong to those Jews who began to believe in Jesus on account of his signs.[118] However, that is not stated explicitly in the text. Thus, the beginning of the pericope appears to be securely established in John 3:1. It is more difficult to identify the conclusion of the dialogue with Nicodemus. After his last word in v. 9, Nicodemus is not mentioned again and so appears to have left the stage as

---

118. So now Girard, "Le paradigme," also on the grounds of a chiastic construction in John 2:23–3:2.

Jesus's dialogue partner. Jesus's speech develops increasingly into a monologue that seems, in its turn, to become a speech by the evangelist. For this reason, numerous scholars fix the end of the dialogue in v. 12 where, for the last time, an address in the second person (here, plural) appears in Jesus's mouth. Schnackenburg goes beyond this theory and regards John 3:13–21 and 3:31–36 as "free-floating speeches"[119] that were connected only secondarily with the Nicodemus dialogue. On the basis of a literary and theological analysis of this passage, Schnackenburg comes to the conclusion that John 3:31–36 originally followed 3:1–12 and was followed, in turn, by 3:13–21. According to Bultmann,[120] John 3:31–36 originally followed 3:1–21. However, these suggestions have not been accepted in Johannine research, and so the traditional arrangement of the text remains in John 3. Thus, with Otfried Hofius as well one can regard John 3:13–21 as the continuation of Jesus's answer to Nicodemus's last question in v. 9.[121]

Occasionally too, the literary and theological unity of our passage has been disputed. Bultmann ascribed the new birth "from water" and not only from the Spirit in John 3:5 to his "ecclesiastical redaction."[122] His school went beyond this and held verses 19–21 to be partly secondary since, in them, human works appear as a condition of salvation. According to Becker,[123] these verses also display a dualism different from that of the evangelist: a horizontal difference between good and evil men instead of the evangelist's characteristic vertical difference between the world "above," of God and salvation, and the world "below" in which men live prior to salvation. In addition, there are problems like the presumed eschatology and the relationship between Christology and soteriology. Here, however, we also maintain the literary unity of the section and will argue for it in the following exegesis.

Up to v. 12, the construction of the section can be determined according to the criteria of narrative analysis. After the introduction in vv. 1–2b, with its naming of the people taking part in the dialogue and the temporal indication (it is night), the following verses divide into three spoken exchanges between Nicodemus and Jesus (vv. 2c–3, 4–8, and 9–12 or 9–21), in which Jesus's answer begins with the formula "Amen, amen, I say to you"

---

119. Schnackenburg, "Die 'situationsgelösten' Redestücke in Joh 3," taken up in Schnackenburg, 1:374–77.

120. Bultmann, 92f.

121. Hofius, "Das Wunder," 34f.

122. Bultmann, 98 with n. 2.

123. Becker, 1:173f. Here, Becker apparently confuses the sense of "horizontal" and "vertical" (which we have corrected).

(vv. 3c, 5b, and 11). The end of Jesus's third answer cannot be determined with certainty since, here, Jesus's words seem to blend into those of the evangelist who speaks of Jesus in the third person. From v. 12 to v. 17, a catchword connection can be observed just like the one that attracted our attention in the first five verses of the prologue (John 1:1–5):

| 12 | "heavenly things" | 13 | "heaven" |
| 13 | "heaven" | 13 | "Son of Man" |
| 14 | "Son of Man" | 15 | "eternal life" |
| 16 | "eternal life" | 16 | "Son" |
| 17 | "Son" | 17 | "condemn" |
| 18 | "condemn" | | |

In verses 18–21, no such connection is to be observed. The movement goes from "condemnation" (vv. 17–18) to "deeds" (vv. 19–21). Inasmuch as the theme of "condemnation" is introduced already in v. 17, it is not possible, without difficulty, to ascribe verses 18–21 or 19–21 to a different literary stratum from verses 12–17(18).

## II

**3:1–3** At the beginning of the chapter, the evangelist introduces the setting for the dialogue (vv. 1–2b) and records a first exchange of speech between Nicodemus and Jesus (vv. 2c–3). The way in which Nicodemus is introduced recalls the Septuagint (cf. 1 Sam 1:1). He belongs to the Pharisees and is called "a leading figure among the Jews." This description is not exact, but it allows one to think of a member of the Sanhedrin, something that is confirmed later in ch. 7 (vv. 48 and 50). John never describes the composition of the Sanhedrin accurately (by contrast with Mark 11:27), but speaks rather anachronistically of the "chief priests and Pharisees" (cf. 7:45). A member of this group comes to Jesus by night to question him. It is scarcely likely that he chose this late hour because the rabbis recommended study of the Torah at night. It is more probable that he had chosen this time because he did not wish to be observed.[124] This suits the picture that we have gained of him in connection with the aim of John's

---

124. This literal understanding of the coming of Nicodemus to Jesus "by night" is well established in Wiarda, "Scenes," 168–73.

Gospel.[125] Nicodemus comes first to Jesus by night, but then publicly, in the Sanhedrin, takes Jesus's side (7:50–51), and, at the end, shows the courage to ask for the corpse of Jesus, who had just been executed for high treason (19:39). From the beginning of this dialogue with Jesus, it is plain that Nicodemus represents the Jewish people and their religion. He addresses Jesus with the appellation "Rabbi." His expression "we know" suggests that he thinks he is able to classify Jesus. He holds Jesus to be a prophet, as is apparent from his words: "We know that you are a teacher come from God." According to Hofius,[126] Nicodemus thereby shows that he has not yet understood Jesus's mission: Jesus has not "come from God" but "proceeds from him" (ἐξῆλθον ... ἀπό ... ἐκ ... παρὰ τοῦ θεοῦ; John 8:42; 13:3; 16:27–28). God is not only "with him," but he is God (cf. 1:18; 10:30). His dignity is to be understood not only on the strength of the "signs" that he performs, but also and especially in receiving his word. At this point, we expect a direct question from Nicodemus, but this is not recounted. Hofius conjectures that there was one and that it concerned salvation since this is suggested by Jesus's answer.[127]

In his answer (vv. 2c–3), Jesus intuits this unspoken question of Nicodemus and, after a solemn introductory formula, explains that it is necessary to be born again in order to see the kingdom of God. The expression γεννηθῆναι ἄνωθεν is ambiguous: it can mean to be "born again" or "born from above." According to widespread opinion, the Johannine Jesus chooses this expression deliberately. However, new birth is probably what is meant here. In any case, it is this that is the subject of what immediately follows. The expression "see the kingdom of God" is not typically Johannine but has its parallels in the Synoptic Gospels (Mark 9:1 par. Luke 9:27). Here too we already have the basis for the notion that for entry into the kingdom of God it is necessary to become like children (cf. Matt 18:3; cf. Mark 10:15).[128] For its part, the phrase "kingdom of God" in this Gospel is

---

125. See the introduction above. Sevrin, "The Nicodemus Enigma," sees the figure of Nicodemus differently. He finds explicit faith lacking in Nicodemus and shows little interest in his courage in confessing Jesus publicly. Similarly, Hakola, "Burden."

126. Hofius, "Das Wunder," 38.

127. Hofius, "Das Wunder," 39f.

128. According to Morgen, "Jean 3," the whole section Mark 10:13–31 par, stands behind John 3:1–12. The first verses (Mark 10:13–16) are about "how to become/how to receive children"; in the account of the call of the rich young man, the topic is the entry conditions for the kingdom of God (Mark 10:17–27); in the concluding verses (Mark 10:28–31), there are promises for those who follow Jesus. All these elements are found in John 3:1–12.

confined to John 3 (vv. 3 and 5). Only in John 18:36–37. does the Johannine Jesus speak of "his" kingdom. The decisive concept of salvation in John is "life." When it says in our passage that, in order to see the kingdom of God, that is, to participate in eschatological salvation, one must be born again, become a new man, then this perspective contrasts with that of Judaism according to which participation in salvation is essentially a matter of human behavior.

**3:4–8** Nicodemus's question in v. 4 has found different explanations. According to one, Nicodemus is subject to a serious misunderstanding that lets him assume that a man who is to be born again has to go back into his mother's womb. According to the other, his question shows only that Jesus's saying about the necessary new birth remains incomprehensible to him.[129] This explanation is certainly preferable. Without faith, access to Jesus's message about the new birth remains barred to him.

Jesus's answer begins in v. 5, once more with the solemn formula: "Amen, amen, I say to you." The following verses are characterized by two oppositions: birth and rebirth as well as flesh and spirit. At the beginning, we have the theme of rebirth. According to Jesus's words, only the one who is born again from water and the spirit can enter the kingdom of God. The element of water is not taken up again in what follows and is considered by Bultmann as an addition of the ecclesiastical redaction.[130] Nevertheless, its presence can be defended in two ways. Firstly, water belongs to the elements linked to the new covenant according to Ezek 36:25–27; secondly, it is not only Catholic authors who see in it a reference to baptism. Certainly, when the theme of rebirth is taken up again in v. 8, water is not mentioned again. In its place, there is an image that is employed already by Qoheleth (11:5), namely, that no one knows from where the wind comes or to where it goes. If the Spirit is understood literally as breath, then one can say something similar about those who have been born again from the Spirit.[131] This Spirit is set over against the flesh, which is good for nothing (cf. John 6:63). Both concepts are more typical of Pauline rather than Johannine anthropology. In this contrast, the "flesh" signifies man as a creature that has not yet been redeemed.

---

129. This is the view of Hofius, "Das Wunder," 44–48.

130. Bultmann, 98 with n. 2. The same thesis is found, among others, in Schmidl, *Jesus und Nikodemus*.

131. According to Sandnes, "Whence and Whither," the mysterious origin of the one born from the Spirit and water corresponds to the mysterious origin of Jesus and his mysterious destination.

**3:9–12** Once more and for the third time, in v. 9, Nicodemus begins to speak. His question shows that he has not understood Jesus's words. He is stuck in a human way of thinking and thus is incapable of grasping Jesus's words about rebirth. It would be no use to explain the situation to him since it is only in faith that one can have access to Jesus's words of revelation.

In his answer in v. 10, Jesus marvels first that Nicodemus does not understand his words for he is "a teacher of Israel," to be more precise, "the teacher of Israel." Perhaps there is an allusion here to the description of Jesus as "teacher" at the beginning of the conversation in v. 2. In any case, for the readers, it is clear who the true "teacher" is. Along these lines, the plural in v. 11, "What we know we speak," could represent an echo of the "we know" in v. 2. This is preceded once more by the solemn formula "Amen, amen, I say to you." In fact, with the plural here, Jesus doubtless means himself.[132] This is the first time in John's Gospel that Jesus appears as a witness. He bears witness not to himself but to heavenly things. This perspective could be influenced by apocalyptic thought.[133] Just as, in the prologue, the light found no acceptance, so it is with Jesus's testimony that he is bearing witness to heavenly things that he has seen (with God). When he speaks of earthly things—probably with the teaching about the necessity for rebirth—and they do not believe him, how much less will they believe him when he speaks about heavenly things. These are, according to Hofius,[134] the truths that concern Jesus Christ and are contained in the following verses. Ultimately, it boils down to faith. Whoever comes to Jesus without faith will understand neither earthly nor heavenly things. Only in faith is there access to the mystery of salvation in Christ.

**3:13–17** In the following five verses, there is a movement away from the kerygmatic formulas of faith in Christ to soteriology. Indeed, the verb form "be redeemed" / σωθῆναι is to be found at the end, in v. 17. Something speaks for the fact, with Hofius,[135] that in these verses we should see the continuation of Jesus's dialogue with Nicodemus about salvation, even if this is no longer actually mentioned and Jesus's words increasingly become a monologue. By contrast with verses 1–12, it is scarcely possible to discover a Synoptic tradition underlying verses 13–17. There is only the

---

132. According to Hofius, "Das Wunder," 57, this was the style of heterosis.
133. Cf. Beutler, *Martyria*, ch. 7.
134. Hofius, "Das Wunder," 58f.
135. Cf. Hofius, "Das Wunder," 34f.

influence of some Old Testament and early Christian traditions that will be considered in their place.

In v. 13, Jesus speaks of himself in the third person for the first time. In so doing, he applies the expression "Son of Man" to himself. According to the apocalyptic tradition of the book of Daniel (7:14), this Son of Man is an other-worldly figure. Some authors see this Old Testament tradition as the basis for the Johannine Son of Man who ascends to heaven.[136] In between the Old Testament and John stands the Synoptic tradition of the Son of Man. The Synoptics know three kinds of sayings about the Son of Man: the Son of Man who will come to judge, the Son of Man present on earth, and the Son of Man who is to suffer and die and then rise again. The last usage seems to have influenced John most strongly. Evidently, John connects the title Son of Man with statements that, in Isa 42–53, refer to the Servant of the Lord, especially in Isa 52:13–53:12, in the so-called Fourth Servant Song.[137] Most relevant here is Isa 52:13 LXX, where it says that the servant will be "lifted up and glorified." This vision seems to be presupposed also in John 3:13, even if the following verse alludes to Num 21:8-9, the story of the serpent in the wilderness. In John 3:13, there is no mention yet of the "lifting up" of the Son of Man, only of his ascension, but it comes to expression in the following v. 14. For Jesus's ascension to the Father, cf. John 6:62; 20:17. In 3:13, the idea of the ascension is introduced with regard to revelation. Here the subject of "heavenly things" is introduced. Access to them is limited to the one who has come from God, from heaven, the Son of Man. Perhaps concealed here is a polemic against other great figures in the history of Israel who, in the time of the apocalyptic literature, had heavenly journeys to receive divine revelations ascribed to them, figures such as Enoch, Moses, Elijah, Isaiah, Baruch, or Ezra.

In v. 14, the subject passes from "ascension" to "lifting up." After the incarnation, soteriology comes into view. Of course, the meaning of "lifting up" is disputed. Some think that the Johannine Jesus is speaking here of his lifting up on the cross to be followed by his glorification;[138] others think of his lifting up in a broader sense that also includes his lifting up to the Father and his glorification.[139] This seems to correspond better with the Johannine viewpoint. In John 3:14, the subject is first of all the lifting up of

---

136. So, among others, Merklein, "Gott und Welt," 269f.

137. Cf. Beutler, "Greeks"; Obielosi, *Servant of God*, 197–214.

138. Thus, Hofius, "Das Wunder," 61–63, with Thüsing, *Die Erhöhung*, and Ruckstuhl, cited by Merklein, "Gott und Welt," 270 n. 37.

139. So Merklein, cf. the previous note, with Bultmann, Schnackenburg, and others.

the serpent in the wilderness to protect the Israelites from the poisonous snakes. For John, the comparison lies in the lifting up of something for the people's salvation. Here both Old Testament traditions come together: that of the wandering in the desert and that of the servant (Isa 52:13 LXX). The concept of salvation also comes to expression in the motif of the divine δεῖ / "must," the necessity of salvation according to God's plan.

Men find salvation not simply *ex opere operato*, without their own cooperation. This consists in faith in Jesus according to v. 15. The ἐν αὐτῷ "in him" is thus linked with the receiving of life and not with "believing in" Jesus.[140] The two verses 14–15 form a syntactical unit, which has been studied by Gundry,[141] and they have their climax in the final clause of v. 15. The lifting up of the serpent in the wilderness prefigures the lifting up of the Son of Man who is to bring eternal life to all who believe in him.

The construction of v.16 resembles that of vv. 14–15. Thus, v. 16cd corresponds to v. 15. Jesus's saying promises eternal life to all those who believe in the Son (here we find the expression πιστεύειν εἰς, which is lacking in v. 15). In place of the "lifting up" of the Son of Man comes the "gift" of the Son. This gift is the result of God's love for the world. This is a surprising thought since, normally in John, the "world" appears in opposition to God and the one whom he has sent (cf. John 1:10!). Our verse allows the conclusion that God's love for mankind applies without restriction and that his plan for salvation excludes no one.[142] What does this "gift" of the Son consist of? One could think of the giving up of the Son in his death on the cross, but then one would expect the term παρέδωκεν. Thus "gift" of the Son might mean his being sent to men.

How is v. 17 connected? According to Hofius,[143] verses 13–17 may contain a chiasmus: in v. 13, there is a glimpse of the notion of the incarnation, verses 14–16 concern the sending of the Son as far as his saving death, and, in v. 17, there is a return to the incarnation. This suggestion might come to grief owing to the fact that it understands ἔδωκεν in v. 16 in the sense of παρέδωκεν, which seems to be incorrect. In any case, there is a connection

---

140. With Nestle-Aland[28], we read ἐν αὐτῷ, just as it is found in the two ancient manuscripts P[75] and B. It is the *lectio difficilior* and on that account to be preferred. P[66] L read ἐπ' αὐτῷ, the majority of manuscripts have εἰς αὐτόν, probably in harmony with the Johannine usage with πιστεύειν.

141. Gundry, "The Sense and Syntax," 373–76.

142. Cf. Beutler, "So sehr hat Gott." According to Popkes, "Love of God," the verse is a Johannine creation.

143. Hofius, "Das Wunder," 59f.

between the "sending" of the Son as per v. 17 and the descent of the Son of Man to earth as per v. 13. The meaning of this sending is clear: it concerns the salvation of the world as the family of mankind.

**3:18–21** The following group of verses is not completely detached from the previous context as conjectured by Bultmann and his school. The introduction of the theme of "condemnation" in v. 17 already speaks against this, as does the emphasis on the necessity of faith, not only in v. 18, but also already in verses 15 and 16. If one regards John 3:13–21 as the continuation and elaboration of the dialogue with Nicodemus, then verses 13–17 could be entitled "New birth by virtue of faith in the Son sent from the Father" and verses 18–21 "New birth thanks to the deeds of truth."

Verse 18 resumes the previous verse and interprets it, just as previously v. 15 completed v. 14, and v. 16cd the lines v. 16ab. The only new feature is the notion of condemnation: whoever does not believe "in the name of the only Son of God" is already condemned. Here, for the first time, we come across Johannine eschatology, which has recently been investigated and described by Frey.[144] Characteristically Johannine is the conviction that the final judgement already follows in the hour of faith or of refusal of faith. Of course, this viewpoint is complemented by another, according to which judgement will follow only at the end (cf. John 5:25–27 with 5:28–29). It is better to view this tension as going back to differing traditions rather than to see it as the result of different literary strata, as is the case with Bultmann and his school.

Verse 19 takes the previous v. 18 for granted and develops the thought further that judgement or condemnation occurs in the present moment and not on the last day.[145] Now there is an account of the reason for the sins of the world and their condemnation: men preferred the darkness to the light because their deeds were evil. The two statements interpret each other reciprocally. The "evil deeds" do not signify actions that are morally reprehensible but the rejection of the light. For those who have read this Gospel from the prologue on, this light is given with the divine Logos.

The same thought returns in v. 20. Everyone who does evil hates the light and does not come to it. If they did, their evil deeds would be exposed. Here, exegetes discuss whether there have been evil men (in the evangelist's sense) on earth from the beginning and men of the light. On

---

144. Cf. Frey, *Die johanneische Eschatologie*, vols. 1–3.
145. "Judgement" here does not simply mean "deciding" but the sentence in the sense of vv. 17 and 18, as Gourges, "Hautē de estin," has correctly highlighted.

the one hand, there is an emphasis on the importance of predestination for salvation; on the other hand, on the fact that all men as such require forgiveness of sins and the salvation of grace. In the exegesis of John 3:18–21 caution should be allowed to prevail since this passage does not offer sufficient factors for solving the difficult relationship between divine predestination and human freedom.[146]

Just as those who perform evil deeds avoid the light so that their actions may not be exposed, so the children of light seek the light so that their good deeds may be manifest as such. "Doing the truth" is not a Greek but a Hebrew expression. It is found also in 1 John 1:6, where Brown in his commentary notes examples from the Hebrew Bible, the Septuagint, and the intertestamental literature.[147] Among other places, the expression is found in the Qumran texts (cf. 1 QS 8.1–2). In Hebrew, "truth" signifies, not the avenue to empirical or conceptual reality, but rather reality as it appears to be revealed by God. The one who "does the truth" is the one who is open to God's word. As a child of the light, he attains the light, and his deeds can manifest themselves as good.

## III

The notion of new birth has biblical roots but cannot be derived from them completely. In the section John 1:19–34, John announces a coming baptism with water and the Holy Spirit that Jesus will bestow (John 1:33). An eschatological cleansing in water and renewal in the Spirit rings out in Ezek 36:25–27. The rebirth of a man is rather familiar to syncretistic texts of Late Antiquity. Especially relevant here is Tractate XIII from the Corpus Hermeticum. Dodd has analyzed the similarities and differences with John's Gospel.[148] In both texts, man attains eternal life through a form of insight by virtue of a rebirth from the sphere of the body or of the flesh into that of the mind or the spirit. For this, both texts require a cleansing that is not, however, the final step. In both texts, man attains divine sonship with the help of the Logos. The role of Hermes as revealer thus corresponds to that of the Christ, the incarnate Son of God.[149] This Hermetic tractate shows

---

146. This freewill is disputed by Hofius, "Das Wunder," 79f., following Martin Luther.
147. Brown, *The Epistles*, 200.
148. Dodd, *The Interpretation*, 44–53.
149. Cf. Dodd, *The Interpretation*, 49.

how close philosophical reflection can come to the proclamatory stance of John's Gospel. Of course the differences here must be acknowledged. The Christian readers of John's Gospel attain salvation not simply through God-given gnosis but through faith. This is set out in all its distinctness in the section following from John 3:1–12. Moreover, they confess in faith not simply the Logos but the incarnate Logos who has to walk the path of suffering, something totally foreign to Hellenistic thought. It must be proclaimed and believed.

## 7. Jesus in Judaea: Further Testimony of the Baptist (3:22–36)

²² After this, Jesus came to Judaea with his disciples. There, he stayed with them and baptized. ²³ However, John was also baptizing then, and, in fact, at Aenon near Salim, because there was much water there; and people came and had themselves baptized. ²⁴ For John had not yet been thrown into prison. ²⁵ There a dispute arose over the question of cleansing between the disciples of John and a Jew. ²⁶ They came to John and said to him: Rabbi, the man who was with you on the other side to whom you bore witness is now baptizing and all are coming to him. ²⁷ John answered: No one can receive anything unless it is given to him from heaven. ²⁸ You yourselves are my witnesses that I said: I am not the Christ, only sent here before him. ²⁹ The one who has the bride is the bridegroom; but the friend of the bridegroom who stands beside him and listens to him is full of joy at the voice of the bridegroom. This joy has now been fulfilled in me. ³⁰ He must increase but I must decrease.

³¹ He who comes from above is above all; he who hails from the earth is earthly and speaks in an earthly way. He who comes from heaven is above all. ³² He bears testimony to what he has seen and heard, but no one accepts his testimony. ³³ Whoever accepts his testimony, has certified this, that God is true. ³⁴ For the one whom God has sent speaks the words of God; for he gives the Spirit without measure. ³⁵ The Father loves the Son and has given everything into his hand. ³⁶ Whoever believes in the Son has eternal life; but whoever does not obey the Son will not see the light, but the wrath of God rests upon him.

*The Divine Word Enters the World (1:1–4:54)*

*I*

The section John 3:22–36 presents the exegete with some problems. The beginning is clearly marked by information about place and time after the dialogue with Nicodemus. It is more difficult to determine the end of the passage. At the beginning, verses 3:22–30 separate themselves as a narrative unit in the form of a dialogue. They are followed, in v. 31 to v. 36, by statements of a general character that recall John 3:13–21. We saw that some authors bring them into connection with this section of speech. The continuation of the statements of the Baptist in vv. 27–30 would be seen as isolated in verses 31–36. Others hear the voice of Jesus here. Most commonly detected here, however, are statements of the evangelist to whom the text of the Gospel goes back anyway. In any case, they are connected with the previous rather than the following context and, as will be shown, exhibit links with its content so that it is reasonable to treat them both together.

In verses 22–30, it is surprising first of all that v. 22 reports that Jesus has arrived in Judaea after his stay in that area had been reported some time previously. How do we explain that it is first stated that Jesus baptized here (v. 22), while, a little later (John 4:3), this is disputed? Who is "the Jew" with whom John's disciples find themselves in dispute in John 3:25? Do we have here, perhaps, some damage to the text? And what is the connection between the theme of baptism and that of the bridegroom and his friend (v. 29)? How far are we dealing here with a unitary text and what is it trying to express on the literary and theological level?

Research has long tried to employ the difference between tradition and the evangelist's redaction to resolve the tensions that manifest themselves precisely in the first subsection (vv. 22–30). In this connection, the article of John W. Pryor is worth reading.[150] According to him, in verses 22–25, the majority of the text goes back to pre-Johannine tradition. John would only have converted the dialogue between the disciples of John and Jesus in v. 25 into one with a "Jew" in order to eliminate any competition between the Baptist and his disciples and Jesus. For the pre-Johannine tradition, a baptismal ministry of Jesus would have presented no problem. Verse 26 would then already constitute the transition to the text of the fourth evangelist.

For the image of the bridegroom, with reference to Jesus in v. 29,

---

150. Pryor, "John the Baptist."

scholars like to point to Mark 2:18-20 par. Matt 9:14-15. Thus, Trocmé[151] speculates that perhaps the Baptist had already employed the Old Testament image of the bride and bridegroom as a picture for the relationship of God and his people in his preaching of the end time. Mark had meant it then in a christological sense. It will not be easy to shed more light on this connection, but it is also not all that pressing for the interpretation of this Johannine text.

How is our passage constructed, and how can it be explained in a way that is manifestly observable in the text? Here the article by Nicklas is helpful.[152] According to this author, we have to distinguish first of all between the older literary criticism in the sense of analyzing sources and strata and the more recent type that interprets the text in question by observing its linguistic signals. In any case, such a procedure is advisable as a first step, and many tensions, which readily serve as the starting point for diachronic hypotheses, are shown to make sense through a more careful reading of the text. They can then be understood as "gaps" in the text that the author has created deliberately or allowed to stand to encourage his readers to think for themselves.

In his analysis of this passage, Nicklas also factors John 4:1-3 into this passage and sees a concentric construction there: verses 3:22-24 and 4:1-3 emerge, respectively, as the "frame" in which the "dialogue" between the Baptist's disciples and the Baptist in verses 3:25-30, 31-36 is embedded. On the other hand, however, it seems more reasonable to regard John 4:1-3 as an independent textual unit that introduces a new geographical context. This will be established when we reach that point.

Within the text unit John 3:22-36, verses 22-30 and 31-36 are separated from each other, as has already been shown. Verses 22-24 depict the baptismal activity of Jesus and the Baptist in Judaea and close with a parenthesis about John's not having been thrown into prison yet (v. 24). Then, in verses 25-30, there follows a dialogue between disciples of John and John himself concerning the baptismal activity of Jesus. It is not clear how far this extends. The exchange evidently ends in v. 30, and is followed by statements about Jesus as the one coming from above and faith in him in verses 31-36. These are connected only loosely to the previous context. This gives us, then, a rough arrangement for our passage.

---

151. Trocmé, "Jean."
152. Nicklas, "Literarkritik," 180f.

## The Divine Word Enters the World (1:1–4:54)

*II*

**3:22–24** With a characteristic "after this" (μετὰ ταῦτα, cf. 5:1; 6:1; 7:1), a new narrative unit begins. As in the Johannine miracle stories, a narrative section (here, vv. 22–24) is followed by a dialogue (here, vv. 25–30). In v. 22, after the temporal indication, the people taking part in the story are introduced: Jesus and his disciples. Since the "coming" and later also the "baptizing" are referred to Jesus in the singular, the disciples seem to have been added. Perhaps they are supposed to correspond to the group of John's disciples who appear in v. 25. The text recounts ingenuously that Jesus baptized, although this is contradicted by the correction in John 4:2. With Nicklas, one may see the readers' curiosity awakened here. Perhaps also strata have been superimposed. Theologically speaking, we have here another presentation of the opposition between baptism with water and that in the Holy Spirit.

Much guesswork has been triggered by the indication that Jesus and his disciples came to "Judaea." In John 2:13, his journey to Jerusalem, the capital of Judaea, had already been reported. Here, the text must be read with precision. Jerusalem is indeed the capital of Judaea but the region itself is not mentioned in John 2:13–3:21. Apparently, the evangelist sees Jesus in a movement from Jerusalem (2:13) across "Judaea" (3:22) and "Samaria" (4:4) as far as "Galilee" (4:43). His revelation as Word of God and Son of God embraces ever wider circles, ever wider from the center of Jewish faith to the periphery. The inhabitants of Sychar rightly see him as the "Redeemer of the world" (John 4:42). This movement would thus correspond to Jesus's commission to his disciples in Acts 1:8 to be his witnesses "in Jerusalem and throughout Judaea and Samaria and to the ends of the earth." "Galilee" would thus, for John, stand for these "ends of the earth."

In v. 22, the evangelist is thinking of an extended sojourn in the "land of Judaea" as his choice of the imperfect tense suggests. We must then think of the baptismal activity of Jesus as correspondingly extended. The baptism of John is spoken of in similar terms in v. 23. To this day, the location mentioned has not been able to be verified. However, more important than the concrete geographical place is the reference to the abundant water available in John's baptismal site, something that is supported linguistically by the name "Aenon" = "Spring." Thus, there is a double reference to John's baptism as water baptism, something that John himself had already indicated as characteristic of him (cf. John 1:26, 33). At the very least, the readers of the fourth evangelist will recall that, in John 1:33, it was already proclaimed who was the one who will baptize with the Holy Spirit. Thus, the "lacuna" is filled through the memory of the readers. It is narrated explicitly in v. 23 that "they," probably in droves, came to be baptized by John. That then leads to the ensuing enquiry by the Baptist's disciples.

However, before this is reported, in v. 24, the evangelist slips in a piece of information that anticipates the fate of the Baptist. Familiar with the Synoptic tradition (cf. Mark 1:14 par.), the readers are naturally aware of this fate. In John 5:35, the evangelist will assume John's arrest and execution are known. The anticipation here clearly serves the purpose of lending emphasis to the following testimony of the Baptist. It is the word of a man who will vouch for his testimony with his life.

**3:25–30** The ensuing dialogue between John's disciples and the Baptist himself is divided into small subsections. Verses 25–26 introduce the disciples' question, followed by the Baptist's answer in verses 27–30, with a loose connection to vv. 31–36. Clearly, John's disciples regard Jesus's baptism, which is very popular, as competition with their master's baptism. It is not clear, of course, with whom they are disputing. According to the text, it was a "Jew," though why, in this case, should he be responsible for replying on Jesus's behalf? The reading Ἰουδαίων ("Jews," plural) instead of Ἰουδαίου (" a Jew," in the singular) is widespread but lacks the support of the most important ancient texts. So one is left at best with the awkward expression "with a Jew" in v. 25. If we discern a geographical sense for Ἰουδαία γῆ, "land of Judaea," in v. 22, then the dispute would be between John's disciples and a Judaean, an inhabitant of Judaea who has journeyed from there; one can also imagine him to be a follower of Jesus.[153]

The subject of the dispute is similarly surprising, namely, "purification." "Purification complying with the custom of the Jews" was the subject in John 2:6. Is baptism being classified in such a connection here? Again, this is something for the reader to answer for himself.

When Jesus is described by the Baptist's disciples as "the one to whom you bore witness," this is a clear reference to John 1:19–34. This is also the purpose of the information "on the other side of the Jordan." Clearly, the Baptist's testimony to Jesus is now to be taken up and developed. In so doing, the main subject will be the relationship between the Baptist and Jesus. It is apparently regarded in a critical way by John's disciples. The success of Jesus's baptisms is being felt as damaging to the success of John's.

The Baptist's answer in 27–30 is able to draw on John's testimony in

---

153. The geographical sense of Ἰουδαῖος in John is stressed, among others, by Lowe, "Who Were."

John 1:19–34, in which Jesus is superior to him. If his own success is being surpassed, then this is only because God has willed it thus (v. 27; cf. 6:44; 19:11). John the Baptist is not himself the Messiah, but only the one sent by him to prepare his way (v. 28; cf. 1:20–23). He is only the friend of the bridegroom, who rejoices to hear the bridegroom's voice (v. 29). The latter must increase, but he himself must decrease (v. 30). The change of images invites the readers once again to creative cooperation. They will recall the biblical pictures of the nuptial relationship between God and his people, but also the scene of the wedding at Cana in John 2:1–12 with its symbolic world. The joy that the friend of the bridegroom experiences is now felt by the Baptist in his last testimony on behalf of Jesus. It is a perfect joy in which the readers are also to share.[154]

**3:31–36** As already stated in the introductory section (I), verses 31–36 are connected only loosely to the previous context. Instead of transposing them, it is better to explain them within their broader context. They then read as a *"relecture"* of John 3:1–30, to adopt the coinage of Zumstein. It is the statements of John 3:1–21 on new birth that are chiefly developed. Already in John 3:11–12, they led on to statements about Jesus as the one bringing a heavenly message. The theme of bestowal of the Spirit is also resumed in vv. 31–36 (v. 34), as well as the theme of testimony (vv. 32–33). The transition to the third person effects a demarcation from the Baptist's testimony in John 3:27–30. From v. 31, the speaker no longer speaks of himself in the first person.[155]

The verse groups show correspondences between verses 31–33, on the one hand, and 34–36 on the other. They can be presented as follows:

| | |
|---|---|
| [31] *He who comes from above is above all; he who hails from the earth is earthly and speaks in an earthly way. He who comes from heaven is above all.* [32] *He bears testimony to what he has seen and heard, but no one accepts his testimony.* [33] *Whoever accepts his testimony has certified this, that God is true.* | [34] *For the one whom God has sent speaks the words of God; for he gives the Spirit without measure.* [35] *The Father loves the Son and has given everything into his hand.* [36] *Whoever believes in the Son has eternal life; but whoever does not obey the Son will not see the light; rather, the wrath of God rests upon him.* |

---

154. The eschatological joy of the Baptist here is neatly laid out by Kempter, "Signification eschatologique."

155. Stare, "So nämlich liebte Gott die Welt," 74, sees in John 3:31–36 "the testimony of John the Baptist as an echo of the words of Jesus in the conclusion of his dialogue with Nicodemus," where John takes up again in John 3:31–36 the words of Jesus in John 3:9–21.

At the beginning, in both cases, there is a statement about the message that comes from above, from God, as testimony or word. This word or testimony is succeeded by a double kind of response: acceptance or rejection. In the first case, the believer who accepts the message "certifies" that God is true, and he receives the promise of eternal life (v. 36). The wrath of God is announced for the one who denies the faith. There was already a similar structure in the prologue of the Fourth Gospel. The statement that his own had not received the Word of God (John 1:5, 10) is corrected by the promise that all who believed became children of God (John 1:12–13).

At the beginning of the verse group vv. 31–33, there is a contrast between the one who comes from above/from heaven and the one who hails from the earth. We have already come across the expression ἄνωθεν in the dialogue between Jesus and Nicodemus in John 3:3, 7. There, it could mean to be born "from above" or "anew." The first meaning could be supported by our passage here. However, the correspondence should not be given undue weight. "Coming," with reference to Jesus Christ, has already been the subject of statements by John the Baptist (John 1:15, 27, 30). This Jesus Christ is the one who "comes from above." According to v. 34, he has been "sent from God." Opposed to this one who comes from above is the one who hails from the earth. Only a few authors see this as a reference to John the Baptist who, in comparison with Jesus, had an earthly and human message (Brown). The man who hails from the earth is better seen as every man who brings a purely human message. This is something that cannot be said of the prophetic message of John the Baptist, "the man sent by God" (John 1:6).

The one who comes from above is above all. Action follows identity. Since he is above all, he can also speak from above with the authority of the Most High.[156] This heavenly messenger not only "speaks" of heavenly things but also bears witness to them. This statement calls to mind John 3:11, in which Jesus says of himself that he "witnesses" to what he has "seen." His statement is thus worthy of belief. The concept of a witness of heavenly things is at home in apocalyptic texts. It is to be distinguished from John's wider concept of a manifold witness to Jesus and his being sent from the Father.[157] The text is not clear about the content of the heavenly

---

156. With Nestle-Aland, it is better to retain the repetition of ἐπάνω πάντων ἐστίν in v. 31, despite the square brackets. This is to be explained through the absence of the phrase in P75 ℵ* D etc.

157. Cf. Beutler, *Martyria*, 328ff. on John 3:11, 32; Beutler, "μαρτυρέω," *EWNT* 2:960-62; *EDNT* 2:391. The Qumran texts speak of a divine "witness." According to the War Scroll

message brought by Jesus. From the broad context of the Gospel, it can be concluded that the content of his testimony is given with his sending from the Father as Revealer. It is precisely this and only this which he has to proclaim and bear witness to.

The twofold response to the heavenly message in vv. 32–33 is found already in the prologue, as previously mentioned. The contradiction between the general statement that "no one accepts his testimony" and a group that nonetheless receives it is resolved with the indication that the acceptance of the divine message is dependent on divine predestination and grace (cf. John 6:44). Of himself alone, man is not able either to understand or to accept the divine revelation.

To those who accept the divine message, no promise is bestowed, but it is said of them that they have "certified that God is true." The alternative would be to make God a liar, 1 John 1:10 says of those who claim that they have not sinned. The term "certify" (σφραγίζειν) occurs again in John 6:27 where it says that God has "certified" the Son whom he sent into the world, that is, provided him with a seal or certificate of trustworthiness. Correspondingly, those who accept the testimony of the Son confirm his sending by the Father as Revealer and thereby the trustworthiness of the Father who sent him.

In verses 34–36, at the beginning, the "the one whom God has sent" corresponds to the "one who comes from above," the "one speaking the words of God" to the "testimony" (v. 34). Moreover, the statements of v. 34 correspond to those of verses 31–32, if also with some variations. The first consists in the fact that it is said of the Jesus sent from God: "He gives the Spirit without measure." In this way, the revealing word of the Son is linked to the gift of the Spirit and so the passage John 3:31–36 is associated with the conversation between Jesus and Nicodemus in John 3:1–12. In that the author is highlighting the "pneumatological" dimension of the revelation, he is emphasizing the Trinitarian dimension of salvation and so rounds off the whole of ch. 3.

The other difference in comparison with verses 31–33 consists in the statement that the Father loves the Son and has given everything into his hand (v. 35). The Father's love for the Son is something spoken of in the

---

(1 QM 11.7f.), the prophets are the "seers of testimonies" with reference to the revelation of the community's calendar. A similar use of "testimony" is found in the prologue to the *Second (Slavic) Book of Enoch*. In the NT, the Revelation of John is aware of this usage (cf. Rev 1:1–2).

Farewell Speeches (John 17:23, 26). That God has given everything into the hand of the Son is stressed in John 13:3 at the beginning of the Farewell Speech. This double agreement shows how close our text is to the Farewell Speeches in their final form (John 17 might belong to the final stratum of these speeches and of the Gospel together). In terms of content, one can conjecture for this motif the influence of the covenant theology of the Old Testament: Israel loves God and is loved by him to the extent that it remains true to his commandments (cf. Deut 7:8–9, 13).

The promise of eternal life for those who believe in the Son is a central motif of the Fourth Gospel (cf., most recently, John 3:16, 18 up to the concluding verse 20:31). The alternative to unbelief is described in v. 36 as "disobedience." It leads to the "wrath" of God—an expression that is found only here in John and for which "condemnation" is otherwise employed (cf. John 3:17–21). However, the concept of "wrath" occurs in the Synoptic tradition in John the Baptist's preaching of repentance (Luke 3:7). From this linguistic relationship, some authors conclude that John 3:31–36 belongs to the Baptist's speech that was begun in 3:27, but this remains only a possibility.

## III

What is the abiding message of John 3:22–36 that is valid for us today? The text invites the reader to embark on a movement. The starting point is "Judaea," the "land of the Jews." John the Baptist appears and gives his testimony to Jesus. Characteristic of that testimony are the "before" and "after" in verses 22–30. John was sent before the Messiah whom he proclaimed. The one coming after him is the bridegroom for the bride, the people of God. John himself is only the friend of the bridegroom who does not enter the bridal chamber. Jesus must increase, John must decrease. Here, the text remains strongly in the conceptual world of contemporary Judaism with its expectation of the eschatological, messianic salvation.

In verses 31–36, the perspective changes. What we have here is a *"relecture,"* a rereading of the previous section. A spatial dualism replaces the temporal one. Jesus is not coming after the man who preceded him, but, from his origin, stands in space over all things that speak of salvation. For that reason, he has a heavenly message. He has been sent from the Father. He therefore brings not just God's word and message, but also God's Spirit, without measure. That also connects with earlier texts. On the one

*The Divine Word Enters the World (1:1–4:54)*

hand, the evangelist is stamped here by apocalyptic concepts that knew of a "testimony" of a seer from the heavenly world. On the other hand, with the change from a temporal to a spatial perspective, he opens up the comprehension of his text to the Hellenistic reader who is familiar with the world of Plato. To the real world "above" is counterposed the unreal world "below." It is from this world "above" that the message and messenger of redemption come.

This change of perspective invites us to consider further updates for the message of salvation. Spatial concepts of the "heavenly world" as the real world and as the source of salvation often bump into incomprehension. Many things suggest that it comes across better today to take the temporal dimension of salvation into account more seriously. The Second Vatican Council took to itself as its own the "joy and hope" of the whole family of mankind. That opens the message of salvation once again to the future. It also leads back to the hope of salvation of Israel, of "Judaea."

## 8. Jesus in Samaria (4:1–42)

¹ Jesus learned that the Pharisees had heard that he was gaining and baptizing more disciples than John – ² mind you, it wasn't Jesus himself who baptized but his disciples; ³ he, therefore, left Judaea and went again to Galilee. ⁴ He had to take the route through Samaria. ⁵ So he came to a city of Samaria that is called Sychar and lay near the parcel of land that Jacob had given over to his son, Joseph. ⁶ Jacob's well was there. Jesus was weary from the journey and sat down beside the well; it was about the sixth hour.

⁷ There came a woman of Samaria to draw water. Jesus said to her: Give me something to drink! ⁸ For his disciples had gone into the city to buy something to eat. ⁹ The Samaritan woman said to him: How can you as a Jew ask water from me, a Samaritan woman? For the Jews have no dealings with the Samaritans. ¹⁰ Jesus answered her: If you knew wherein the gift of God consisted and who it is who is saying to you: Give me something to drink!, then you would have asked of him, and he would have given you living water. ¹¹ She said to him: Sir, you have no bucket and the well is deep; so from where do you have this living water? ¹² Are you greater than our father Jacob who gave us this well and drank out of it himself, as did his sons and his cattle? ¹³ Jesus answered her: Whoever drinks from this water will thirst again; ¹⁴ but whoever drinks from the water that I shall give him will never thirst again; rather, the water that I shall give him will be in him a spring whose water will well up to eternal life. ¹⁵ Then the woman

said to him: Sir, give me this water so that I may not thirst anymore and not have to come here to draw water.

[16] He said to her: Go, call your husband, and come back here! [17] The woman answered: I have no husband. Jesus said to her: You have rightly said: I have no husband. [18] For you have had five husbands, and the one that you have now is not your husband. In this you have spoken the truth. [19] The woman said to him: Sir, I see that you are a prophet. [20] Our fathers worshiped God on this mountain; but you say the place where one has to worship is in Jerusalem. [21] Jesus spoke to her: Woman, believe me, the hour is coming when the Father will be worshiped neither on this mountain nor in Jerusalem. [22] You worship what you do not know; we worship what we know, for salvation comes from the Jews. [23] But the hour is coming, and is already here, when the true worshipers will worship the Father in spirit and in truth; for thus the Father wishes to be worshiped. [24] God is spirit, and all who worship him must worship in spirit and in truth. [25] The woman said to him: I know that the Messiah is coming who is called Christ. When he comes, he will tell us everything. [26] Jesus said to her: I am he, the one who is speaking to you. [27] Meanwhile, his disciples had returned. They were surprised that he was speaking with a woman but no one said: What do you want, or: Why are you talking with her? [28] The woman now set down her water jar, returned to the city and said to the people: [29] Come, look, here is a man who told me all that I have done: Is he perhaps the Christ? [30] Then they went out of the city and came to Jesus.

[31] Meanwhile, his disciples urged him: Rabbi, eat! [32] But he said to them: I have food to eat that you do not know about. [33] Then the disciples said to one another: Has someone brought him something to eat? [34] Jesus said to them: My food is to do the will of the one who has sent me and to finish his work. [35] Do you not say: There are still four months until harvest? Look, I tell you: Lift up your eyes and see: the fields are white for the harvest. [36] The reaper is already receiving his wages and gathering fruit for eternal life so that the sower and the reaper may rejoice together. [37] For here the proverb is true: One sows, and another reaps. [38] I have sent you to reap that for which you have not labored; others have labored, and you have benefited from their labors.

[39] Many Samaritans from the city came to faith in Jesus on the word of the woman who had testified: He told me what I have done. [40] When the Samaritans came to him, they urged him to stay with them, and he stayed there for two days. [41] And still more people came to faith in him on account of his own words. [42] And they said to the woman: We no longer believe on account of your words, for we ourselves have heard and know: He really is the Savior of the world.

## The Divine Word Enters the World (1:1–4:54)

### I

Jesus's starting out from Judaea to Galilee and his stay in Samaria in John 4 is clearly the beginning of a new section. It is reasonable to take it as far as John 4:42 where Jesus's stay in Samaria comes to an end. Jesus's arrival in Galilee in John 4:43–45 would then represent a further section before the second sign in Cana of Galilee in John 4:46–54. After the beginning in Jerusalem (John 2:13) and in Judaea (John 3:22), we now see Jesus on his way to new areas of the Holy Land and to new groups of people.

The structure of the text emerges by applying narrative criteria. The first six verses can be understood as an introduction. Jesus reaches Samaria and, tired from the journey, sits down on the edge of Jacob's well. With the arrival of the Samaritan woman in v. 7, we have a new narrative section that recounts the dialogue of Jesus with her (John 4:7–26). It can be divided into two: the dialogue about the water that Jesus first requests and then promises (vv. 7–15), and the following one about the woman's husbands and the true place of worship, with the self-revelation of Jesus at the end (vv. 16–26). Verses 27–30 are characterized by a twofold movement: the woman's return to her city and the approach of the inhabitants of this city to Jesus. Verses 31–38 recount a dialogue between Jesus and his disciples who had gone off to get bread (v. 8). Its subject is Jesus's food and a transition to the theme of mission (vv. 31–38). Verses 39–42 bring the narrative to its conclusion: the testimony of the woman and then the declaration of Jesus himself lead to the belief of many in Jesus as the "Savior of the world."

This brief portrayal of the narrative lets us recognize a consistently constructed story. As such, at first sight, it offers few openings for hypotheses about sources and strata. All the same, there is no shortage of such suggestions even now. Older models of source and stratum analysis are tackled by Andrea Link[158] in her dissertation. The author herself endorses a model of four stages that distinguishes a signs source, a *Grundschrift*, the evangelist, and a post-Johannine redaction. Without accepting the *Grundschrift*, this proposal is found also in Becker[159] and Theobald.[160] The latter indeed sees a possibility of the redactor at work only in John 4:9c. However, these authors are increasingly being opposed by those who see a unitary text here and reject all hypotheses about origins. The latter in-

---

158. Cf. Link, *"Was redest du mir ihr?,"* 103–77.
159. Becker, 1:196–99.
160. Theobald, 1:304f.; cf. Theobald, "Abraham," 163–68.

clude Birger Olsson,[161] Teresa Okure,[162] and J. Eugene Botha.[163] More and more, scholars point to the importance of the biblical tradition for the understanding of Jesus's dialogue with the Samaritan woman.[164] In what follows, it is this aspect that is to be emphasized chiefly.

## II

### Jesus's Arrival at Jacob's Well (4:1–6)

The first six verses of John 4 lead to the ensuing dialogue that lasts until v. 42. Here, we have mainly a description of a change of place. Jesus leaves Judaea and arrives in Samaria where he sits down on the edge of Jacob's well. On closer examination, this small narrative unit may be divided into two parts. The first three verses describe Jesus's journey from Judaea to Galilee and explain the reasons for this journey. In verses 4–6, we see Jesus in Samaria and making his way to Jacob's well where he sits down because he is tired. Here, the first three verses could also be understood as the conclusion of a larger narrative unit that begins in John 3:22. The description of the baptismal ministry of Jesus and John in 3:22–24 and 4:1–3 forms a frame for the dialogue and speech section in 3:25–36.[165]

**4:1–3** Verses 1–3 form a single complex sentence with three subordinate clauses (ὡς... ὅτι... ὅτι) in v. 1 and the main clause in v. 3; v. 2 constitutes a parenthesis. The central statement of the first three verses occurs in v. 3: Jesus leaves Judaea and starts out for Galilee. The reason for his journey is given in v. 1: Jesus had learned that the Pharisees had received news that he was baptizing more people than John the Baptist.[166] He evidently saw that this was dangerous for his personal security and that of his disciples,

---

161. Olsson, *Structure*.
162. Okure, *Mission*.
163. Botha, *Jesus*.
164. There is a fine example of this in Ska, "Jésus." Cf. Theobald, "Abraham."
165. Cf. Nicklas, "Literarkritik," who sees in John 3:25–36 another, last, testimony by the Baptist.
166. We read ὁ 'Ιησοῦς here with Nestle-Aland[28] supported by P[66*] ℵ D Q 086 f[1] and other mss. against the reading ὁ κύριος in P[66c.75] A B C K L W[s] among others as well as the majority text. The replacement of the name of Jesus, which occurs three times, with "the Lord" is more probable than the reverse. In John's Gospel, the title of "Lord" is used only for the Risen One but is predominant in early Christianity.

## The Divine Word Enters the World (1:1–4:54)

and so he withdrew from Judaea. Clearly, it is still being assumed here that Jesus's baptism was on the same level as that of John and so a competitive situation could arise. This impression is obviously being corrected in v. 2: it was not Jesus that was baptizing but only his disciples. If one elects to utilize source or stratum analysis, then the evangelist has probably corrected an older *Vorlage* here. His view is that the baptism bestowed by Jesus is of a different kind from that of John. Jesus will bestow it, not with water but with the Holy Spirit (John 1:33). Thus, it surpasses John's baptism. In the light of narrative research, one can recognize in v. 2's correction of the statement in v. 1 another element of guidance for the reader. On the one hand, it is now important to distinguish the nature of Jesus's baptism that was spoken of in John 3:22–24;[167] on the other hand, the reader learns that the narrator is reliable since he is able to correct or explain statements. Thus, we have a "lacuna" that the readers can now fill out for themselves.[168]

The historical origin of the information about Jesus's return from Judaea to Galilee is unknown. Be that as it may, the return of Galileans back home from Jerusalem corresponds to the Jewish practice. On the way to Jerusalem, they preferred the route via the Jordan valley so as not to make themselves unclean in Samaria while on their way to the sanctuary. Hence also the scenes of Jesus's passage through Jericho (cf. Mark 10:46–52 par.). On the return journey, there was no need for such precautions.

**4:4-6** The verses that now follow can be understood in a narrower sense as an introduction to the conversation between Jesus and the Samaritan woman. In v. 4, the Samarian territory appears for the first time. It appears initially not as the object of Jesus's journey but only as a stopping place on the way. However, it will go on to appear as the stage for important encounters and dialogues. In this verse, the information about the location moves from the general to the particular. After the region of Samaria, the city of Sychar is named, then Jacob's well, and, finally, the edge of this well on which Jesus sits down exhausted by his journey. There then follows a temporal indication: it is about the sixth hour, the time of the greatest midday heat. According to Okure,[169] the conceptual world

---

167. Cf. Nicklas, "Literarkritik."

168. Cf. Botha, *Jesus*, 105. According to Müller, "Zeuge," in John 4:1–3, the evangelist employs the stylistic device of *synkrisis*, the comparison of two characters, as in the "*Vitae Parallelae*" of Plutarch, in which characters of ancient Greece and Rome are compared. Thus Jesus's superiority to the Baptist is displayed because he baptizes not with water but with the Holy Spirit.

169. Cf. Okure, *Mission*, 86, 91.

of the mission is being echoed here. Jesus is "weary" (κεκοπιακώς) from the journey. The expression chosen is employed otherwise in the NT for "being wearied" in the service of preaching and leading the community (cf. John 4:38; 1 Thess 5:12; 1 Cor 16:16). The entirety of the following scene serves to describe Jesus in this service of preaching and shows how others—the woman herself and the disciples—take part in this task.

Sychar was the capital city of Samaria after John Hyrcanus I destroyed Samaria in the year 129 BCE.[170] That Jacob gave his son Joseph a field in this area can be deduced from information in the books of Genesis and Joshua: According to Gen 33:18–19, Jacob acquired a field in the region of Shechem; according to Gen 48:4, he gave it over to his son Joseph; according to Josh 24:32, Joseph's bones were buried in the field that Jacob had given to his son. According to Theobald,[171] the word ἔδωκεν "he gave" in John 4:5 alludes to the same verb in Gen 24:32 LXX.

Jacob's well is not found elsewhere in the Bible. According to Jean-Louis Ska,[172] Theobald,[173] and others the motif of the "well" refers to the "well stories" that are found in three places in the Bible:

- Gen 24:10–21 Abraham's servant encounters Rebekah at a well close to the house of Nahor, her grandfather
- Gen 29:1–13 Jacob encounters Rachel at a well
- Exod 2:16–22 Moses meets Zipporah, her sisters, and the herdsmen of Jethro, his future father-in-law, at a well.

The elements in these betrothal scenes were subsequently described by Robert Alter[174] as follows[175]: The bridegroom journeys into a far-off land; there he meets a young woman (or several women) at a well. Someone draws water. The woman or women hurry back with the news of their encounter. A wedding is negotiated, usually in connection with a meal. M. W. Martin has introduced further elements such as the presentation of a gift to the bride and the self-introduction of the suitor.[176] Further elements are added. Thus, the influence of the biblical tradition on John 4

---

170. Cf., here and for the following, Theobald, "Abraham," 168–72.
171. Theobald, "Abraham," 168 n. 46.
172. Ska, "Jésus."
173. Theobald, "Abraham," 170.
174. Alter, *Art*, 47–62.
175. Cf. Martin, "Betrothal Journey Narratives," 597.
176. Cf. Martin, "Betrothal Journey Narratives," 508f.

*The Divine Word Enters the World (1:1–4:54)*

is assured.[177] From here too, it is possible to understand the motifs of the woman's five husbands and the true place of worship, provided that one recognizes the symbolic content of the marriage motif in Israel. For this, see below at vv. 16–26.

### *Jesus's Conversation with the Samaritan Woman about the Living Water (4:7–15)*

In v. 7, the woman of Samaria enters the scene and Jesus's dialogue with her begins, going on until v. 26. With good reason, this section is subdivided into verses 7–15, with the theme of the living water, and 16–26, with the theme of the woman's husbands, the true place of worship, and the identity of Jesus.

The construction of the group of vv. 7–15 emerges from an analysis of the flow of the narrative. We can isolate three exchanges between the woman of Samaria and Jesus, in verses 7–9 (v. 8 is a parenthesis), 10–12 and 13–15. At the end of v. 9, there is a comment by the evangelist. Under the semantic aspect, verses 7–15 show themselves to be dominated by the themes of "water" and "drinking." Between v. 7 and v. 15, there is also an inclusio with the expression "come to draw water." In this way, the group of verses appears to be a self-contained textual unit.

**4:7–9** Jesus's request "Give me something to drink!" corresponds to the literary genre of the well stories (see vv. 4–6 above). In John 4, this request can also be seen in connection with Jesus's labor and exhaustion, his hunger and thirst on his journey. Against the background of other texts of the Fourth Gospel, Jesus's request can be seen as the expression of his thirst for man's salvation. Relevant here are the words of Jesus immediately before his death on the cross: "I thirst" (John 19:28). They too are not an expression of Jesus's physical thirst only. This aspect of Jesus's request is confirmed by the interpolated verse, John 4:8: "For his disciples had gone into the city to buy something to eat." Jesus appears in our chapter as a man who experiences hunger and thirst, but these bodily needs also have their spiritual side. This will become clear in what follows when Jesus describes as his food doing the will of the one who has sent him, that is, to carry out the Father's plan of salvation (vv. 31–34).

---

177. The attempt by Arterbury, "Breaking the Betrothal Bonds," to reduce the so-called well stories to meal scenes is not convincing.

The woman of Samaria evades this deeper meaning of Jesus's words and also shows no interest in Jesus's request to give him something to drink. As happens continually in this episode, she sidesteps or shows her lack of understanding. Instead of addressing herself to Jesus's request, she begins a conversation about how it is that Jesus is asking her for a drink of water since he is a Jew and she is a Samaritan. The narrator adds here that the Jews and Samaritans have no dealings with one another.[178] From the narrative perspective, Jesus's request remains misunderstood and unfulfilled. At the same time, however, an important theme for the whole dialogue comes into play: the relationship between Jews and Samaritans. This theme is explicitly discussed in the following section (vv. 19–24).

The motif of water is common in almost all religions. Bultmann thinks here in John 4 of a source of Gnostic revelation discourses. It is more to the point to indicate the biblical background of the water theme in John 4. Relevant here is the beginning of Ps 42/43 where it says: "Just as the deer gasps for fresh water, so my soul gasps for you, O God. My soul is thirsting for God, for the living God. When may I come and see God's face?" This psalm seems to have been employed more than once in John's Gospel.[179] During the passage through the desert, God bestowed water on his people (Exod 17:1–7). This event is taken up again in Ps 105:41. In Ezek 47, the prophet describes the vision of a spring that wells up in the temple and grows into a river that causes the desert to bloom. In John's Gospel, two healing miracles are acted out close to pools: the healing of the paralytic in John 5 and that of the man born blind in John 9. The water motif plays a central role in John 7 at the Feast of Tabernacles. At the climax of this feast, Jesus cries out solemnly: "Whoever is thirsty, let him come to me, whoever believes in me, let him drink. As the Scripture says: Out of his inmost being will streams of living water flow" (John 7:37–38). We recall here again the words of the departing Jesus at the cross: "I thirst" (John 19:28). Jesus experiences his own thirst, but, at the same time, desires also to quench the thirst of men. He is thirsting for their salvation.

**4:10-12** In the second exchange between Jesus and the Samaritan woman, two new themes surface: the drink that Jesus is offering and his

---

178. John's chosen expression can also be translated: "the Jews and the Samaritans use no common vessels" (thus Daube, "Jesus and the Samaritan Woman: The Meaning of συγχράομαι"), but there are no convincing parallels for this usage (cf. Bauer, *Wörterbuch*).

179. Cf. Beutler, "Psalm 42/43 im Johannesevangelium."

## The Divine Word Enters the World (1:1–4:54)

person. Instead of persisting in his request for water, Jesus now offers the woman a drink that she does not yet know about and that is only understood when one knows who Jesus is. Instead of the water from the well, Jesus offers a "living water," a gift from God, the meaning of which is still hidden from the woman (v. 10).

Once again, the woman cannot understand what Jesus is saying. In her eyes, Jesus is just being silly. He has no bucket and the well is deep. This shows that the woman has understood Jesus's words in a purely physical and naturalistic sense without reckoning on their deeper and religious meaning. On the other hand, the woman introduces a new theme that will be important for the further course of the conversation: a comparison between Jesus and the patriarch Jacob who donated the well to his sons and their cattle. Is this unknown traveler who is sitting down on the edge of Jacob's well greater than the patriarch Jacob? Exegetes see in this question an example of "Johannine irony": for the readers, Jesus is indeed greater than the patriarch Jacob, even if this is not known to the woman who is asking the question.

**4:13–15** Jesus's answer mentions neither the bucket nor his relationship to the patriarch Jacob (of whom there will be talk somewhat later), but describes the singular quality of the water he is offering: it will be of such a kind that whoever drinks it will thirst no more. It will become a spring with waters that well up to eternal life. This promise by Jesus anticipates his declaration in the bread of life discourse in John 6:35: "I am the bread of life. Whoever comes to me will hunger no more, and whoever believes in me will thirst no more."[180] Of course, the woman is still far from such a perspective of faith and so answers with a request that is wholly oriented to this world and to its everyday needs: "Sir, give me this water so that I may not thirst anymore and not have to come here to draw water" (v. 15). Until now, the dialogue has made little progress. It will ultimately be Jesus who will break through the woman's lack of understanding as he passes over to a totally new theme that will define the following section (vv. 16–26).

---

180. Létourneau, "Durst," 520, points here to parallels in the Jewish wisdom literature that see in water an image for Wisdom and the Law. At the same time, there are differences alongside the similarities. Thus, in Sir 24:21, Wisdom says: "Whoever hears me, will hunger for more, whoever drinks me, will thirst for more."

## Jesus's Conversation with the Samaritan Woman about True Worship (4:16–26)

"Go, call your husband, and come back here!" Jesus's command is surprising at this point and demands an explanation. However, this is not the only inconsistency in our passage. What connection is there between the theme of the woman's husbands and that of the place of worship desired by God? And how do these themes hang together with the identity of Jesus as prophet and then possibly even messiah? Finally: how does the statement "For salvation comes from the Jews" (v. 22) fit into the perspective of the Gospel and, in particular, of the textual unit of John 4?

Historical-critical exegesis tried to solve these inconsistencies by distinguishing sources and strata. Central Europe was long under the influence of Rudolf Bultmann who distinguished between a pre-Johannine source (signs source) and the evangelist to whose work an "ecclesiastical redaction" had been added (to which, among others, v. 22 goes back, at least in part). Both the Evangelical[181] and Catholic[182] branches of the Bultmann school stuck to or stick to this line.

More recently, however, criticism of this "criticism" has grown. The text is to be explained as a rational whole so long as this is not excluded by irreconcilable tensions. In fact, our text can be understood as a thoroughly rational whole of this kind as has been shown in recent contributions by representatives of synchronic exegesis.[183] In what follows, this approach to the text is attempted. At the same time, we shall also point out biblical traditions that have influenced the text. They will help us to understand the inner coherence of the themes of the passage that at first sight seem very different.

The structure of the passage emerges out of the exchanges between Jesus and the Samaritan woman. From their thematic content, verses 16–18 show themselves to belong together, something that is generally accepted. These verses concern the husband or the husbands of the woman in the sequence: Jesus—Samaritan woman—Jesus. In what follows, the woman changes the subject and in verses 19–20 passes on to the question of the place of worship favored by God. Jesus answers this question in verses

---

181. Cf. the commentaries of Becker, Schulz, and Haenchen.
182. Cf. Richter, "Studien"; Link, "*Was redest du mir ihr?*"
183. Cf. O'Day, *Revelation*; Wessel, "Die fünf Männer"; van Belle, "Salvation"; Thyen, "Eine ältere Quelle."

## The Divine Word Enters the World (1:1–4:54)

21–24. There follows a final exchange between the woman and Jesus in verses 25–26. It is striking that, from v. 19 on, the order of speakers is changed. The woman seizes the initiative and places her questions that Jesus answers. In this narrative flow, it is possible to see the increasingly active role in the dialogue played by the woman being confirmed.

**4:16–18** Jesus's command "Go, call your husband, and come back here!" astonishes the readers. It also gives rise to various explanations. Gail R. O'Day[184] sees here a connection to the previous verse 15 with the catchword "here." The woman had asked Jesus to give her living water so that she did not have to come "here" any more. Jesus does not take up this request but, on the contrary, commands the woman to come "here" with her husband. The American scholar sees this double use of a word as an example of "Johannine irony." Jesus uses an expression that his conversation partner had used but in another context and with another aim. Botha is dissatisfied with this suggestion and counters it with another: Jesus deliberately changes the subject in v. 16 precisely so that the conversation with the woman can continue.[185] Until then, he had not managed to enter into a really personal conversation with the woman ("to get through to her," to use an expression of Hendrikus Boers[186]). He could obtain that through this sudden change of topic, thinks Botha, with a reference to "speech-act theory."

Without questioning such literary approaches to the text, it is appropriate here to examine the biblical background to the scene. We recall the article by Ska,[187] who, among others, points to the Old Testament well stories as parallels (Gen 24, Abraham's servant meets Rebekah; Gen 29:1–13, Jacob meets Rachel; Exod 2:16–22, Moses meets Zipporah and her sisters). These stories are love stories too. At the beginning, there is the request for water from the man or the woman; then, a conversation ensues; the woman takes the man with her back home; they have a meal; he asks for her hand; and they are married. The question arises why the conclusion is otherwise in our story here. According to Ska, the Samaritan woman in John 4 stands for the Samaritan people and their religion. This observation is supported by the woman's answer: she has no husband. Jesus picks up on this and clarifies it: actually, she has had five husbands and the one she has now

---

184. O'Day, *Revelation*.
185. Botha, *Jesus*, 139–41.
186. Boers, *Neither on This Mountain*.
187. Ska, "Jésus."

is not her husband. Ska takes this answer of Jesus in connection with the theme of Israel's unfaithfulness to her God. The Samaritan woman appears in the role of the wife of Hos 2, who was unfaithful to her husband and was rehabilitated by her "husband" through a new nuptial connection. In this way, it will not be the woman but the Samaritans who will be the "bride" of Jesus. This will be the fulfillment of the promise of new fertility in Hos 2.

There have been various explanations for the woman's five husbands. The following are the three most important: 1) The five men are really the woman's husbands. Since the rabbis permitted three consecutive marriages, she is a woman of dubious reputation. This is why her most recent partner is not her husband. 2) The five husbands stand for the gods of the Samaritans that, according to 2 Kgs 17:30–32, 41, the foreign immigrants brought with them into the land. The text itself speaks of seven deities, but Josephus (*Ant.* 9.288) speaks of only five. The Samaritans reverenced these gods and now worship the true God in a way that is displeasing to him. 3) The five husbands stand for the five books of the Pentateuch.[188] The woman stands for Samaria, which follows the tradition of the Pentateuch but has not remained faithful to this connection with God.

The first proposal is represented only seldom nowadays. It is the second and third ones that are discussed. They are not mutually exclusive. Within the Johannine dialogue scene, the theme of the woman's love life, understood as metaphor, could smooth the way to the next subject in the conversation, that of the place of worship desired by God.

**4:19–24** From now on, the order of speakers is altered. The woman takes the initiative and turns to Jesus with the question about the place of worship desired by God.[189] She addresses her question to Jesus respectfully, and calls him "Sir." She has recognized that he is "a prophet." According to the Samaritans' faith, only a prophet could reveal mysterious things. Thus, the conversation passes from the person of the woman to that of Jesus. It is not to be assumed that Jesus would have revealed the woman's sins to her in detail. His statement about her past life is to be understood also against the background of his knowledge of the human heart and his knowledge of the personal experiences of his conversation partner—one thinks only of his knowledge of the personal experiences of Nathanael (John 1:48) or his knowledge of men in general (John 2:24; cf. 13:21). The woman now asks

---

188. So Wessel, "Die fünf Männer."

189. The *Einheitsübersetzung* sticks here and in what follows to the translation "anbeten" or "worship." It is better, however, to speak of "reverencing" God.

about the place of worship desired by God. This was the chief battleground between Jews and Samaritans. This new subject can be explained by a metaphorical understanding of the woman's marital relationships. Perhaps the transition to the new theme is more simply explained by the fact that Mount Gerizim lay in the immediate neighborhood of Jacob's well.[190] Thus, the change of subject would be similarly understandable.

In Jesus's answer (vv. 21–24), we have to distinguish between his starting-off point and his end point. Jesus starts out from the worship that is supposed to take place in Jerusalem according to the will of God as laid down in Scripture. In this sense, "salvation comes from the Jews." The end point forms the pattern of worship in which the differences between the various places for prayer and sacrifices are transcended. The time in which this will happen is the end time. John uses two expressions to designate this time: "the hour is coming" (v. 21) and "the hour is coming, and is already here" (v. 23). It is reasonable to conclude from this that the two perspectives are complementary, and do not derive from two different levels of redaction.[191]

What is meant by "in spirit and in truth"? This has nothing to do with purely inner worship without liturgical assembly of the community, rites, and ministers, but with the worship of the end time. The Spirit will be God's "gift" to his people in the future, the time of the "new covenant" (cf. Ezek 36:26).[192] Similarly, "truth" in our passage is to be understood not as the "conformity between thought and reality" or the "revelation of things as such." In John, the concept of truth has a theological and not a philosophical stamp, as de la Potterie has demonstrated clearly against Bultmann in his dissertation.[193] In John, the concept of truth has Old Testament and early Jewish features with parallels also in the Qumran texts. It derives from the Hebrew root *'emet* and describes a relationship between persons (God and his people) rather than one between abstract quantities, namely, God's reliable self-revelation.

Jesus's saying "salvation comes from the Jews" does not mean that this salvation stems from the Jews until the appearance of Jesus Christ and since then comes only from him and from the Christians. Salvation comes from the

---

190. Cf. O'Day and Olsson, quoted approvingly by Botha, *Jesus*, 143f.

191. Cf. the three-volume monograph of Frey, *Die johanneische Eschatologie*.

192. In her Roman dissertation *Worshiping*, Jojko sets out the Trinitarian dimension of John 4:20–26.

193. de la Potterie, *Vérité*.

Jews for all ages, as Wengst,[194] among others, has shown along with Calvin. Paul speaks of the branches that are grafted on to the olive tree of Israel (cf. Rom 11:16–20). The branch does not bear the root but the root the branch.

As already mentioned, Bultmann and his school dispute the origin of John 4:22 from the evangelist John. The statement that salvation stems from the Jews would have been added by the "ecclesiastical" or "Johannine redaction." It is not quite clear, however, just what motive the increasingly Gentile Johannine community at the end of the first century would have had for adding this sentence. It is better, therefore, to reject this hypothesis.

**4:25-26** In a final exchange, the woman comes still closer to the mystery of Jesus: the Messiah will come and teach the people about the kind of worship favored by God. According to Gail R. O'Day,[195] it is possible to detect here a final example of Johannine irony: without knowing it, the woman is repeating the faith conviction of John's Christian community, except that the Messiah will not only come, for he is already there. Furthermore, he is no unknown figure but the Jesus who is standing before her and speaking with her. It is just this that Jesus declares: "I am he, the one who is speaking to you" (v. 26). Jesus is the "Taheb," the "coming" Messiah of the Samaritans but also the Messiah of the Jews, and he will be revealed, at the same time, as the "Savior of the world," as the Samaritans will proclaim after their encounter with him (v. 42).

The exegetes ask whether Jesus's words "I am he" mean more than his identification with the coming Messiah of whom the woman had spoken. This expression suggests itself as an example of the "I am" sayings with which God has introduced himself in the Old Testament (from Exodus to Ezekiel). If this observation is correct, then Jesus's words in v. 26 go beyond messianism and turn out to be Johannine Christology in the fullest sense: Jesus reveals himself as the presence of God among men.

### *The Departure of the Woman.*
### *The Arrival of the Disciples and the Samaritans (4:27–30)*

The short ensuing section is characterized by "coming" and "going." Here, we can distinguish a threefold movement: the coming of the disciples to Jesus (ἦλθαν, v. 27), the departure of the woman (ἀπῆλθεν, vv. 28–29) to

---

194. Wengst, 1:174f.; cf., also, van Belle, "Salvation."
195. O'Day, *Revelation*.

## The Divine Word Enters the World (1:1–4:54)

bear witness about Jesus, and the departure of the inhabitants of her city (ἐξῆλθον, v. 30) in order to meet Jesus. From this short survey, it is already clear that Jesus stands in the middle of this short passage. The movement goes out from him and then leads back to him after a first, reticent, testimony of the woman to him.

At the beginning, we have the arrival of the disciples who had gone off to the city to get some bread (v. 8). As Bultmann noticed, the return of the disciples at this moment allows them to witness the conversation between Jesus and the Samaritan woman. Here, the theme of food does not yet come into view but rather there is mention of a question put by the disciples, namely why Jesus is speaking with a woman. For Boers,[196] the fact that Jesus is speaking with a woman does not fit in with the complex of themes in this passage. With the help of a semantic analysis, therefore, he omits the verse. It is appropriate, however, not to limit the extent of the themes that come to expression here. In John 4:1–42, Jesus appears as one who breaks with the customs of his people under various aspects. The most important is the conflict between the Jews and Samaritans but to this is added the relationship of men and women in that society. Both these aspects, among which Jesus forges new ways, already come to expression in v. 9 where the woman expresses her amazement that Jesus, a Jew, should speak to her, a woman of Samaria. So the astonishment of the disciples in v. 27 is prepared for well in advance. The text in v. 27 does not say simply: "Why are you speaking with her?," but names as the content of the disciples' unexpressed question to Jesus: "What do you want?" or "What are you talking about with her?" Edouard Cothenet[197] sees in these words an expression of Jesus's "seeking" after the salvation of the woman in which God's seeking after man's salvation is being expressed.

According to v. 28, the woman leaves her jar behind and returns to her city to report on whom she has met. In this feature, exegetes mostly see an expression of the haste with which the woman goes on her way. One can, however, read it as an expression of the learning process through which the woman has passed since the beginning of her conversation with Jesus. At least for the readers, the woman no longer needs the physical water that she had come to seek after she has met Jesus, the source and the bestower of living water that quenches man's thirst in a deeper sense. The woman's message to the inhabitants of her city is in two parts: she has met

---

196. Boers, *Neither on This Mountain*.
197. Cothenet, "Nourriture."

a man who has told her everything she has done. From this experience it follows that he must be a prophet at least (v. 19). In the second half of her testimony, the woman goes beyond this and poses the question whether or not he could be the Messiah. Scholars are not united regarding the meaning of this question. Some are skeptical.[198] The μήτι "whether perhaps" leads rather to the expectation of a negative answer (cf. the same word in John 8:22; 18:35). According to others,[199] the expression remains open, even if it does not actually allow for a positive answer.[200] In the light of the narrative analysis, a hunch on the woman's part that Jesus is the Messiah (after the witness of v. 26) appears more probable than the opposite. It is precisely for this reason that the inhabitants of Sychar come out to Jesus (v. 30).

### *Jesus's Conversation with His Disciples about His Food and about the Harvest (4:31–38)*

The return of the disciples leads to a conversation between them and Jesus over his food. To the disciples' request to Jesus that he eat (v. 31), there follows Jesus's answer about his food that lasts until v. 34. It passes into Jesus's sayings about the coming harvest, which continue until v. 38. For the detailed exegesis, it is a good idea to interpret verses 31–34 and 35–38 on their own, respectively, and thereby to demonstrate their connection.

**4:31–34** The first four verses of this section focus on the themes of food and eating. As in the two previous sections of the dialogue of Jesus with the Samaritan woman (cf. Jesus's request in v. 7 "Give me something to drink" and his command in v. 16 "Call your husband, and come back here"), this section too begins with a request. In our case, it is the disciples who ask of Jesus: "Rabbi, eat!" Just as in the previous examples, the person receiving the request does not act on it. Jesus's reaction recalls the conversation about the water in verses 9–15. By contrast with this earlier conversation (and John 6:35), however, Jesus speaks here not of a food (or a drink) that he bestows, but of one that he receives. This food too is to be understood figuratively: for Jesus, his food consists in carrying out the will

---

198. Thus Danna, "A Note."

199. Cf. Bauer, *Wörterbuch*; Blass-Debrunner, *Grammatik*, 427.2; Schnackenburg, 1:478.

200. Boers, *Neither on This Mountain*.

of the one who has sent him: the Father (v. 34). The disciples are unable to understand his meaning and ask one another whether, in the meanwhile, someone has brought him something to eat (v. 33). They cannot understand what is the true food of Jesus (v. 32). The similarity of Jesus's conversation with the woman is obvious. On the other hand, the theme of Jesus's true food is related to that of his thirst in the metaphorical sense. We recall that, at the beginning of the narrative, a thirsty and exhausted Jesus had sat down on the edge of Jacob's well and asked the woman of Samaria for a drink of water (vv. 6–7). Looked at more deeply, this concerned his thirst for the salvation of men, which would be with him until his last words on the cross (cf. 19:28).

Jesus thirsts to do the will of his Father. The Father's will is the salvation of men, the "eternal life" in Jesus's name. That leads us to the Farewell Prayer of Jesus in John 17. In the first verses of this prayer, this purpose of the life and mission of Jesus is brought to expression. Here (in John 17:4), the subject is the "work" (ἔργον, in the sing.), which Jesus has "to finish" (τελειοῦν) or "has finished" in the same wording as in John 4:34. With that, we already find ourselves in the semantic field of "mission" terminology that will define the following four verses.

**4:35–38** The concept of the "harvest" that dominates the following verses is not found elsewhere in John but in an eschatological or missionary sense in other places in the NT. In the Synoptic Gospels, this concept is found in Jesus's parables to give a pictorial description of the eschatological gathering of the fruit of salvation or of damnation (Mark 4:29; Matt 13:30, 39), or else of the mission (Matt 9:37–38 / Luke 10:2 = Q). In this last sense, the expression of John in John 4:35–38. is used within a proverb, according to which it is possible to calculate the time between the blooming of the ears and their fruit in the harvest. In the real world, this distance in time has disappeared: with the flowers, the time of maturity has already arrived, harvest time is already there—in Jesus. In v. 36, the contrast between sower and reaper is introduced. Both will rejoice. Here another proverb is brought in, one that takes up the difference between sower and reaper (v. 37). Jesus applies this difference to the present situation: others have sown, and the disciples will reap a harvest that they themselves have not sown. They will only share in the "labor" of the sowers (v. 38). This usage points back to the "labor/weariness" at the beginning of the narrative of his dialogue with the Samaritan woman (4:6 κεκοπιακώς). We recall that, since 1 Thess 5:12, this expression has been used as a technical term for pastoral work.

Scholars differ over the question as to who is meant by "the others who have labored." Some see here the Father, others John the Baptist, still others the woman of Samaria. In answering the question, one has to keep in mind that the text presumes missionary activity in the land of the Samaritans at the time of the evangelist. In this sense, one could think here also of the first missionaries of this area—according to the Acts of the Apostles, Philip (Acts 8:4–8) before the arrival of the apostles Peter and John (Acts 8:14–17).[201]

Looking back, the question of the thematic unity of Jesus's conversation with the disciples in John 4:31–38 comes to the fore once again. Our view, in accordance with that of more recent authors, is that what we have in John 4:1–42 is a symbolic narrative.[202] Above all, Olsson and T. Okure have highlighted the central role of Jesus's "work" in this section. It can be shown that the missionary aspect plays a role in the narrative of John 4 from the beginning, from the moment when Jesus, weary and thirsty, sits on the edge of the well and says to the woman: "Give me something to drink" (4:7). In the final section (4:31–38), this theme is brought to a close.

### Many Samaritans Come to the Faith (4:39–42)

In this group of verses, the account of the stay and deeds of Jesus in Samaria comes to a close. Already, a rich harvest can be gathered. This small section divides into two. First, it is reported that on account of the testimony of the woman whom Jesus had met, many Samaritans from her city came to the faith. Jesus came and spent two days there (vv. 39–40). His preaching among them brought still more inhabitants of the city to the faith, and this faith gained in certainty after they had heard Jesus himself and received his word (vv. 41–42). However, it is worth taking a closer look at the Johannine narrative.

**4:39–40** In a first step, the Samaritans arrive at faith in Jesus (as we understand with the majority of the manuscripts) because of the testimony of the woman who had reported that Jesus had told her everything she had done. This faith is not considered satisfactory by the evangelist; it remains open to deeper understanding.[203] This is made possible by Jesus's two-day

---

201. This is also the understanding of Theobald, "Die Ernte ist da."
202. Cf. Olsson, *Structure*; Okure, *Mission*; Boers, *Neither on This Mountain*.
203. There is no sufficient reason to ascribe these two verses to a "signs source" on

stay in the Samaritans' city. This stay is also mentioned at the beginning of the next section in John 4:43. It allows Jesus to address his word to the Samaritans and bring them to a deeper knowledge of his person and his mission.

**4:41–42** At the beginning of the second part of the section, it is precisely this word of Jesus that is adopted as the reason why a still greater number[204] came to believe in him. Thus, Jesus's word has replaced that of the woman. Of course, the text does not state that the woman's word had become redundant. It says only that the Samaritans "no longer" (as before) believe on account of the word of the woman, but (now) on account of their personal encounter with Jesus and his word that leads to their faith that he really is the Savior of the world.

## III

The story of Jesus and the Samaritan woman is also characterized by a movement. The starting point is formed by Jesus's request for a drink of water. He will also need bread in order to be able to continue his human journey. In John, however, man does not live by bread alone, nor by daily drinking water. The woman and with her the readers will be led out of their everyday needs to the true drink, to Jesus as the source of living water, and to the true food, the accomplishment of God's plan of salvation.

This plan desires salvation also for the Samaritans, the "separated brethren" of the Jewish people. Separate sanctuaries and separate traditions are no longer to be a cause of separation from one another. Indeed the time is near, and is breaking out with Jesus when the true worshiper will reverence God everywhere. That will become possible in the Spirit and in Jesus, and thus he is indeed "the Savior of the world" (v. 42).

If Jesus reveals himself in Samaria first and especially to a woman, this is also not without significance. In the ancient world and in early Judaism, there are barriers between men and women to observe and to follow. Jesus overcomes such barriers to the amazement of his disciples. His example remains for all times as a challenge in the double sense of that word: first,

---

account of their belief based on a prophetic word, as is done by Bultmann and his school. They are only recognizable steps of the Samaritan coming to belief.

204. That they believed "more" in Jesus is allowed only by P[75] with several Old Latin manuscripts, and is not original.

perhaps, outrage, but then invitation to follow his example in overcoming prejudices towards women. If the woman from Sychar is the preacher of the message of salvation for her contemporaries, then she also remains an example for women in the service of that preaching to the present day.

## 9. Jesus in Galilee (4:43–45)

⁴³ After these two days, he went from there to Galilee. ⁴⁴ For Jesus himself had attested: A prophet is not honored in his own homeland. ⁴⁵ When he came to Galilee, the Galileans welcomed him, because they had seen everything that he had done in Jerusalem at the feast; for they too had gone to the feast.

### I

In John 4:43–45, the account of Jesus's journey towards Galilee is resumed from John 4:1–3 and taken further. This is commonly recognized by exegetes. If one reads verses 43 and 45 together, a coherent meaning emerges: Jesus sees himself threatened in Judaea, sets out for Galilee, and arrives there after the interlude in Samaria. In Galilee, Jesus is received with open arms on account of his reputation, which had preceded him because of the signs that he had performed in Jerusalem. These had been reported by the pilgrims who had returned from the feast.

The problem lies in v. 44. Jesus appeals to a proverb for his journey: no prophet is honored in his homeland. In this connection, the conjunction γάρ, "for," is especially difficult. Classical literary criticism tried to solve the problem by distinguishing sources and strata. A recent representative of this school of exegesis is Becker. According to him, what we have in John 4:44 is the late gloss of a scribe that has subsequently crept into the text. However, this proposal has seldom been taken up, and the majority of exegetes read the text as a unity. This raises the questions as to what is the πατρίς "homeland" of Jesus and what sense the γάρ "for" could have.

The oldest exegesis sees Jesus's homeland in John 4:44 as Judaea or Jerusalem. This interpretation is found already in Origen[205] and Theodore of Mopsuestia,[206] and lies at the basis of the present exegesis. In recent

---

205. Origen, *Comm. Jo.* 13.54–55.236–43.
206. 68 (edition of Vosté).

research there has been a preference for Judaea/Jerusalem especially in Anglo-Saxon circles, but also among some continental exegetes.[207]

The meaning of Jesus's "home town" as Nazareth or his "homeland" as Galilee is usually supported by the Synoptic parallels Mark 6:1-6 par. Matt 13:53-58; Luke 4:16-30. In that connection, one must bear in mind, of course, that the logion of the prophet without honor in his own country and that of the physician who can perform no healings among his own people are found, though without a narrative framework, in the Gospel of Thomas (31) and in POxy 1.6. However, this setting probably goes back to the Synoptics, especially Luke (in whom the motif of the physician is found). Those who show a preference for Nazareth/Galilee are chiefly in the German-speaking sphere, but not only there.[208] The difficulty for this meaning lies in the fact that the γάρ, "for" in v. 44 seems to refer to what goes before, namely Jesus's journey from Samaria to Galilee. If Jesus is journeying to Galilee and his reason is that a prophet is not honored in his homeland, then he is literally seeking rejection. Of course, according to v. 45, the Galileans welcome him with open arms, but their faith is imperfect since it is based on seeing signs. So, in the proverb of v. 44, we would be dealing with a case of "Johannine irony." The readers know that Jesus is not concerned with human respect but with fulfilling the will of God. According to this interpretation, the γάρ could even be rendered with "nonetheless."[209]

Occasionally, other interpretations of Jesus's "homeland" are found. Thus John Chrysostom[210] suggests Capernaum, others think of Palestine,[211]

---

207. Cf., among others, Hoskyns; Dodd, *Interpretation*, 352; somewhat different, *Tradition*, 238-41; Lindars; Marsh; Smith; Barrett; Moloney; Rebstock; Schwank; Keener; Thyen; Willemse, "La patrie"; Meeks, "Galilee"; Olsson, *Structure*, 27-29, 143-47; Fortna, "Locale"; Bassler, "Galileans"; von Wahlde, 2:205-9, for the first two steps of the redaction of John's Gospel. For extensive and complete documentation of this perspective and the opposing one, cf. van Belle, "Faith"; cf. Thyen, 284f.

208. Cf., among others, Weiss; Bauer; Bultmann; Brown; Schnackenburg; Blank; Kysar; Morris; Beasley-Murray; Wengst; Wilckens; Schenke; Schnelle; Theobald; McHugh; von Wahlde, 2:205-9, for the third step of redaction of John's Gospel; van Belle, "Faith"; Stimpfle, "Das 'sinnlose γάρ,'"; Heil, "Jesus"; Garský, *Das Wirken*, 151. According to Corley, "Dishonoured Prophet," the logion would have referred initially to John the Baptist and his home region in Peraea, but then later to Jesus and his homeland in Galilee.

209. Thus, Stimpfle with older authors.

210. According to Bergler, *Kana*, 160, the indication referred to Capernaum in a first draft of John's Gospel.

211. Loisy.

others still the Jewish people (Judaeans and Galileans) by contrast with the Samaritans who stand here for Christians,[212] according to yet others, heaven.[213]

## II

As Theodore of Mopsuestia saw a long time ago, verses 4:43–45 resume John 4:1–3. A threatening situation had emerged for Jesus in Judaea that suggested to him that he return to Galilee. The section about his encounter with the Samaritan woman and her compatriots in 4:4–42 is thus a parenthesis.[214] At its close (v. 40), a two-day stay of Jesus in the Samaritans' city was mentioned. Verse 43 returns to these two days. The "leaving" of v. 3 then becomes the "coming from" the city of the Samaritans. Galilee is named once again as the goal of the journey. This territory is more important for the evangelist than detailed place names, as the occurrence of the word in the following verses (45, 47, 54) also shows.

Jesus's journey to Galilee is explained with a causal clause (γάρ). According to what has already been stated, this explanation is best correlated with verses 1–3, which mention the increasing anxiety of the Pharisees about Jesus's success in baptizing. When and where Jesus is supposed to have "attested" the saying about the prophet who is not honored in his own homeland cannot be discerned from the text. Be that as it may, this is the reason given for his journey from Judaea to Galilee. From this it follows that it is preferable to see Judaea or Jerusalem as the "homeland" of Jesus. To be sure, Jesus did not hail from this city, but it is precisely the latter that was the center of his activity according to John's Gospel. This is the homeland of the prophets, and this is where their fate was always fulfilled. Origen cites here the fate of the prophets according to Heb 11:37 and Acts 7:52, but also the clamor of the Jews for the crucifixion of Jesus in John 19:15 and the adorning of the tombs of the prophets without repentance in Matt 23:29 and Luke 11:47.[215] According to Origen, the wise men and sages of Greece fared no better; they too were not honored in their homeland and were not seldom threatened, if not actually executed.[216]

212. So Augustine, *Tract. Ev. Jo.* 16.3. Similarly, Pryor, "John 4:44," with Hirsch.
213. Lightfoot, 34–36: 35; as a possibility also in Morris.
214. 68 (edition of Vosté).
215. Origen, *Comm. Jo.* 13.54–55.236–43.
216. Concrete examples are found in vol. 3 of the Origen edition by Blanc, 241 n. 3.

## The Divine Word Enters the World (1:1–4:54)

If the tenor of Jesus's saying in John 4:44 is in broad agreement with that of Mark 6:4; Matt 13:57; Luke 4:24, then it does not necessarily follow that the same "homeland" is meant. Already in POxy 1.6 and Gospel of Thomas 31 the logion is being transmitted in isolation. John could also have used it in a freer form in order to explain the rejection of Jesus in the center of the Jewish faith and people.

From this, it has often been suggested that, for the Fourth Gospel too, Jesus hails from Nazareth or Galilee. However, it is necessary to bear in mind to whom statements of this kind are ascribed. In John 1:45–46 it is Philip and Nathanael, where the latter is taking offense at Jesus's origin from Nazareth. In John 7:41, 52, it is the Jews at the Feast of Tabernacles or the members of the Sanhedrin who cannot imagine a Messiah from Galilee. In the view of the evangelist, without faith, Jesus's origin is unknown (cf. John 7:27–29; 8:14; 19:9–11); in fact, he comes from the Father.

Jesus's departure for Galilee is followed in v. 45 by his arrival there. The Galileans welcome (ἐδέξαντο) him readily, recalling the formulation in Luke 4:24 (δεκτός ἐστιν), but here expressed positively. This is explained by the memory of the things that the Galileans had seen as pilgrims to the feast in Jerusalem. There is often an attempt to play down this statement in view of Jesus's critical position over the sign-based belief of the Judaeans in John 2:23–25. Moreover, according to John 4:48, a faith based on signs and wonders alone is not sufficient. However, signs can definitely lead to faith. That is true for the disciples at the marriage of Cana in John 2:11 and is also formulated, in conclusion, as an aim of the Gospel in John 20:30–31. The official from Capernaum testifies to his faith in the power of Jesus already before the miraculous healing of his son (John 4:47, 49) and believes Jesus on his word alone (v. 50), before his faith and that of his whole household is stated conclusively (v. 53). Thereby, the faith of men is recorded for the second time in Cana of Galilee. Thus, the "Galileans" (cf. v. 45) feature positively in John throughout, by contrast with the "Judaeans" who increasingly close themselves off from Jesus and his claim.[217]

---

217. Cf. Bassler: "Galileans symbolize those who receive the Word, Judeans symbolize those who reject it" ("Galileans," 253). Note also John 4:45, 7:52 (when Nicodemus puts in a good word for Jesus, he is asked whether he is a Galilean). Those Galileans who will not accept the words of Jesus will later turn out to be "Ioudaioi" (John 6:41, 52).

## III

The section John 4:43–45 brings us close to the end of the first major section of John, which we have entitled "The divine Word enters the world" (John 1:1–4:54). After the prelude in the Jordan valley in Judaea with the first disciples, a cycle began that has sometimes been entitled "From Cana to Cana" (John 2–4). After the account of the marriage at Cana (John 2:1–12), we see Jesus on a journey that takes him first to Jerusalem (John 2:13–3:21) and then to the whole of Judaea (John 3:22–36). On the way to Galilee, Jesus turns first to the Samaritans (John 4:4–42). Only then does he finally depart for Galilee. Now, already, his reception in Jerusalem and Judaea contrasts with that in Samaria. The citizens of Jerusalem come only to an imperfect faith; for his part, Nicodemus remains a questioner. The further Jesus distances himself from the center of Jewish faith, the more readily he is received. That is illustrated by his arrival in Galilee.

The Johannine Jesus does not simply break with Judaism but rather questions it in its traditional form and so detaches himself from the Jerusalem authorities. Only those who recognize him have understood the meaning of the religious tradition of Israel and its cult. This is understood better by those "on the margin" than those who consider themselves to be at the center of the faith of Israel.

Our short passage thus constitutes an invitation to think about "center" and "periphery." Just as, according to the Synoptics, Jesus shows his preference for those on the social margins, tax collectors and prostitutes, so he does also, according to John's Gospel, for those who, religiously speaking, are outcasts: Samaritans and Galileans. Here there is a lasting demand on all those who carry the torch for the message of Jesus today.

## 10. Jesus's Second Sign in Cana of Galilee (4:46–54)

[46] Jesus came again to Cana in Galilee where he had changed the water into wine. In Capernaum, there lived a royal official whose son was ill. [47] When he heard that Jesus had come to Galilee from Judaea, he sought him out and begged him to come and heal his son, for he was on his death-bed. [48] Then Jesus said to him: Unless you see signs and wonders, you do not believe. [49] The official begged him: Sir, come down before my child dies. [50] Jesus replied to him: Go, your son will live! The man believed the word that Jesus had said to him, and went on his way. [51] While he was still going down, his servants came to meet him and said: Your son lives. [52] Then he

asked them for the precise hour in which the improvement began. They answered: Yesterday, at the seventh hour, the fever left him. [53] Then the father knew that it was exactly the hour when Jesus had said to him: Your son will live. And he became a believer with his whole household. [54] Jesus thus performed his second sign after he came from Judaea to Galilee.

## I

The account of the healing of the royal official's son in John 4:46–54 appears to be traditional but, at the same time, puzzling. From the point of view of content, the story fits in with other, similar accounts of Jesus's miraculous healings. In this respect, its relationship with the narrative of the healing of the centurion's servant from Capernaum in Matt 8:5–13 and Luke 7:1–10 is striking. Naturally, the problems already begin here. Exegetes enquire after the origin of the Johannine story and its connection with the similar account in the Synoptics. If one can demonstrate a literary dependence of the Johannine text on the reports of Matthew and Luke, the further questions arise whether John depends directly on the two Synoptics or rather on a previous source common to them both, the hypothetical, so-called "Q." In the latter, the story of the centurion from Capernaum would be the only example of a miraculous healing. A series of authors disputes John's dependence on the Synoptics and reckons instead with another source or tradition. This has led chiefly to the theory of a "signs source" gaining currency.

Alongside the questions of compositional history, the question arises, above all, regarding the meaning and function of the Johannine text in the context of John's Gospel. What does the evangelist want to impart to his reader with this story at the end of the first four chapters of his Gospel? What task does this passage perform before the transition to the great controversies of chs. 5–10? The answer to these questions will help us to look back once more at chs. 1–4 of the Gospel and enquire after the function of this chapter in the overall construction of John's Gospel.

The starting point for the various literary-critical hypotheses in the sense of classical literary criticism (distinguishing sources and strata) is formed, on the one hand, by the above-mentioned parallel texts and, on the other hand, by this text's having a certain lack of coherence and logical sequence. Here, not least, the dialogue between Jesus and the royal official (vv. 48–49) is significant. A more careful reading reveals that the official had certainly not asked Jesus for a sign as the basis for his faith, but only Jesus's help for his son who was gravely ill. To that extent, Jesus's answer does not fit the context well. In the following verses, the problems continue. What the official says in v. 49 has nothing to do with what Jesus has said but only repeats the request he had already expressed that Jesus be so good as to heal his son before it was too late. When, in v. 50, Jesus promises him his son will live, the faith of the royal official is bound up with the word of Jesus. In this way, he displays precisely the faith that Jesus had spoken of shortly before. In turn, that does not then match the concluding information that the royal official "became a believer with his whole household" after he had been convinced by the healing that had occurred (v. 53).

The classic answer to these problems consists in the theory of the employment of a "signs source" or a "*semeia* source" by the fourth evangelist. This source, the existence of which was first conjectured by Alexander Fauré,[218] gained currency chiefly through Rudolf Bultmann and his school. Characteristic of this source was its Christology of Jesus as a "divine man" (Θεῖος Ἀνήρ), who manifested his divine origin and power through miracles that led to faith in him as a man sent from God (cf. John 2:23–25; 4:45 or the saying of Nicodemus in John 3:2). In the face of such a path to belief and such an imperfect faith, the evangelist would have remained skeptical and expressed his reservations through redactional comments that would have corrected the inadequate theology of the *semeia* source. An example of such a correction, according to Bultmann, would be in the already mentioned dialogue that would have been added in John 4:48–50. The Bultmann school would see a further example in the conversation between Jesus and his mother in John 2:4–5, where the link between Jesus's miracle and his "hour" is registered.

Today, the acceptance of a "*semeia* source" is no longer widespread.[219] There remains the problem of reconstructing a hypothetical source for which there is no direct evidence, and this chiefly on the basis of theological criteria. An improvement would be signified by John's dependence on the source "Q" in the composition of John 4:46–54. It too remains hypothetical but can be deduced from Matthew's and Luke's common material

---

218. Fauré, "Die alttestamentlichen Zitate," 107–12, cited by Bultmann, 78 n. 4.
219. The most recent representative is Theobald.

in addition to Mark.[220] On the other hand, it remains a possibility that the core of John 4:46–54 goes back directly to the two accounts of the Capernaum centurion in Matthew and Luke themselves. This thesis is powerfully represented by Neirynck.[221] It too appears plausible. A strong argument in favor of the direct dependence of John 4:46–54 on the Synoptics lies in the fact that John directly takes up Matt 8:13, a verse that clearly belongs to Matthean redaction (and not to "Q"), with the motif of the healing "at that hour." A further theme that is often regarded as a Johannine insertion is Jesus's refusal to grant a request for "signs and wonders." Neirynck points his readers to Mark's Gospel for this motif, more precisely Mark 7:26–29; 8:11–12; 9:19; 13:22. These texts have recently been taken up by Beasley-Murray and Udo Schnelle in their commentaries.

How are the differences between John and the Synoptic tradition to be explained? For John, the "royal official" is not a (Roman) Gentile but evidently a Jew (*contra* Becker and Schnelle). For this reason, it was appropriate to make him, not an officer of the occupying power, but an official of the ruling king, Herod Antipas. Jesus's words about the future salvation of the Gentiles thus became superfluous. John replaced them with the dialogue about faith in Jesus's word. The substitution of Cana for Capernaum is understandable from the author's intention to increase the distance between the location of Jesus's word and that of its fulfillment. Furthermore, Cana could serve as a pointer to Jesus's first miracle in Galilee and thus draw a line between the two, and this at a particular moment of the Johannine account of the public work of Jesus. Thus, there emerges the arch "from Cana to Cana," which was already so dubbed by Henri van den Bussche and since then taken up by numerous authors, among whom is Brown in his commentary.


## II

When we now turn to our passage, the narrative may be divided into two parts that correspond with each other: after Jesus's arrival in Cana, that of the royal official, his conversation with Jesus, and his journey back to Capernaum (vv. 46–50).[222] A similar sequence of events ensues: the jour-

---

220. Thus, Lindars, "Capernaum."
221. Neirynck, "Jean 4,46–54," among others, against Landis, *Das Verhältnis*.
222. Cf. the powerful narrative analysis by van Aarde, "Narrative Criticism."

ney of the royal official to Capernaum, his conversation with his servants, and the conclusion of the narrative with the conversion of the whole of the official's household (vv. 51–54). This twofold division will be taken as a basis of the following.

**4:46–50** Verses 46–47 contain the explanation for the narrative. Twice Jesus's return to Galilee is mentioned. This part of the Holy Land has played a positive role in Jesus's experiences until now. In Judaea, he experienced opposition (cf. 4:1–3). In Samaria, he found faith, but he could not stay there, for he came from Galilee. In Galilee, he was welcomed with open arms (4:43–45), even if the form of faith that he found there was not yet perfect. This is the context of our story. It can be read as an introduction to the nature of true faith.[223] The opportunity for this is offered with the arrival of the royal official from Capernaum, the city to which Jesus had gone down once before (2:12). The royal official begs Jesus to accompany him and heal his son who is gravely ill. He does not ask Jesus for any "sign," and perhaps not even a miracle, but he sees in Jesus a man who performs extraordinary deeds, no more, no less. This is how to understand Jesus's saying: "Unless you see signs and wonders." The man does not yet understand the meaning of Jesus's words but sticks to his confidence. Jesus could heal his son, and so he repeats his entreaty. Jesus does not agree, but promises the anxious father that his son will live (using Elijah's words to the widow of Zarephath in 1 Kgs 17:23). The father believes the word of Jesus and returns to Capernaum.

**4:51–54** The journey of the royal official from Capernaum to Cana is matched in the second scene by his journey from Cana to Capernaum. Once again, a dialogue is reproduced, this time between the royal official and his servants. They inform him that his son "lives." In answer to the official's question, they report to him the hour when the boy began to improve: it was the seventh hour. The official recognizes that this was the hour when Jesus said to him that his son lived and he came to faith (in Jesus) with his whole household. It is mentioned, in addition, that this was the second sign that Jesus performed after his arrival in Galilee from Judaea. It is clear that the central theme here is authentic faith in Jesus. In verse 53 another aspect of this faith—the communal element—is revealed: "And he became a believer with his whole household." It is the only time the formula "one and one's household" appears in the Gospels, but in the Acts of the Apostles it is found repeatedly in connection with piety, sal-

---

223. van Aarde, "Narrative Criticism."

vation, or the faith of an entire family (Acts 10:2; 11:14; 16:15, 31, 34; 18:8: Becker). Certainly one cannot speak here yet of the establishment of a "Christian house community." However, already in the account of the faith of the woman of Samaria and her fellow citizens, there has been a sketch of a time in which "the fields are white for the harvest." Such a moment seems to be heralded also by the encounter with Jesus in Galilee.

## III

With the account of the healing of the son of the royal official in John 4:46–54, we see the closure of several concentric circles.

### From Cana to Cana

Jesus's second sign in John 4:46–54 recalls again the first from John 2:1–11 in several ways. It was because of this sign that Jesus's disciples came to faith in him (2:11). Of course, the nature of this faith still remains undefined, and so long as it relies on visible signs, an element of imperfection clings to it. Jesus's long journey in John 2:13 until 4:45 is also a description of a path in the formation of faith. Many from Jerusalem come to faith in his name, but in so doing they rely on the signs he has performed. So he has no faith in them (John 2:23–25). They are not able to understand the all-surpassing sign of his death and resurrection, and even the disciples cannot do this (2:22). Nicodemus appears as representative of the imperfect faith of the Jerusalemites (3:1–3), and we do not learn to what kind of understanding of faith his (more open) dialogue with Jesus led. We also have an example of a faith journey with the Samaritans and their representative, the woman of Samaria. From acknowledging Jesus as a prophet, since he has revealed to her the secrets of her life, the woman comes to an incipient belief in him as Messiah, which leads also to the faith of her compatriots who recognize Jesus as the Savior of the world (4:42). We can observe a similar process at work among the Galileans. They come first to a primitive faith because of the signs that Jesus performed in Jerusalem (4:45), but then they are invited to deepen this faith. In the figure of the royal official, the Galileans turn aside from this path. From a faith based on Jesus's signs, he reaches a faith dependent on Jesus's word. It is in this way that Christian communities in Samaria and Galilee become possible.

### The Pattern of Faith for the Disciples

Read from the end of ch. 4, the account of the first disciples in John 1:19–51 acquires a deeper sense. In chs. 2–4, the disciples are not in the foreground, but they are present the whole time. Their role is highlighted above all on the occasion of Jesus's first sign in Cana of Galilee. Following this event, they are mentioned occasionally (3:22), more particularly in ch. 4 (4:8, 27, 31–38). In the deepening of the faith of the royal official, they are also able to discover a pattern of faith for themselves: a journey from faith based on Jesus's signs to a faith based on his word.

### The Offering of Life

The word with which the evangelist brings to expression the healing of the son of the royal official and his freeing from the threat of death: "Your son will live" (4:50, 51, 53) seems to have been chosen with some care. Looking back, we can discover another point of contact with this key word: a connection with the Johannine prologue (John 1:1–18). "What came into being through him was life, and the life was the light of men. And the light is shining in the darkness, and the darkness has not grasped it" (John 1:3–5). This life, bestowed by Jesus, the divine Logos and only-born Son of God (John 1:1, 18), allows all who believe in him to become children of God (John 1:12–13). Read from this perspective, Jesus's word in John 4:50, "Your son will live" acquires a deeper sense: it is in the only-born Son that the life that makes us children of God, the light of men, is bestowed. This message is valid for all time and also expressly contemporary when men are concerned with their necessities for life.

# Jesus Reveals Himself to His People (5:1–10:42)

The first four chapters of John's Gospel announce the entry of the divine Word into the world. He became flesh in Jesus of Nazareth and wishes to arouse faith. In John's account of this, after the call of the first disciples at the Jordan, there emerge concentric circles "from Cana to Cana" in John 2–4. Jesus begins his activity in his homeland of Galilee, but then leaves it for Jerusalem to go to a first Passover feast (2:13). Here he reveals himself in word and deed but finds little faith in his word. Journeys to Judaea (3:22–36) and Samaria (4:1–42) follow before Jesus arrives again in Galilee (4:43–45). The further Jesus removes himself from Jerusalem, the more easily he finds the faith that is due him. Finally, the outstanding example of this faith is that of the royal official in the second miracle at Cana (4:46–54). It is this that closes a first circle.[1]

The following section of John's Gospel appears structured by Jesus's pilgrim journeys to the chief feasts of the Jews before the final Passover in 11:55. In John 5, we see Jesus at an unnamed feast that could well be the Feast of Weeks. In John 7:1–10:21, Jesus takes himself to a pilgrim feast in Jerusalem, named in John 7:2 as the Feast of Tabernacles. At the Feast of the Dedication of the Temple in John 10:22, he is already present in Jerusalem. All these chapters are characterized by revelation discourses of Jesus and by conflict dialogues with the "Jews." So it is that we can entitle this section "Jesus reveals himself to his people." Jesus contends for the faith of the Israelites from Jerusalem and Judaea and thereby provokes increasing opposition. The sections concerning faith in Samaria and Galilee appear

---

1. For the construction of John 1–4 in light of the structure of the entire Gospel, see the previous section of exegesis.

to point to a rather later date when the message of Jesus will one day find faith there.

We are now in a position to classify chap. 6 in the picture as a whole. The feast named as that of the Passover in John 6:4 disrupts the space and time frame of the broader context. It comes between the feasts of Weeks and Tabernacles. Moreover, Jesus does not appear to go to Jerusalem on pilgrimage for it. Since the chapter is otherwise inserted with difficulty into the wider context of the text, it is proposed here that it be regarded as a *"relecture"* of its context that also breaks the previous Passover framework.[2] In terms of time, this chapter ushers us into the period of the early Church, when the Passover tradition was already being increasingly loosened from its Jewish roots and acquiring a specifically Christian character.

Chapters 11 and 12 belong, on the one hand, to the structural theme of "Jesus and the Chief Feast of the Jews" since they lead to the last Passover in 11:55. On the other hand, however, these chapters lead already to the theme of the suffering and death of Jesus as well as his resurrection. Thus, with more recent authors, we have decided to consider it as a transitional section that deserves its own title.

## 1. Jesus at the Feast of Weeks (5:1–47)

[1] After this, there was a feast of the Jews, and Jesus went up to Jerusalem. [2] Now, in Jerusalem, next to the Sheep Gate, there is a pool with five porticoes; this pool is called Bethesda in Hebrew. [3] In these spaces, there lay many sick people, including the blind, lame and paralyzed. [4] [5] A man was lying there who had been sick now for thirty-eight years. [6] When Jesus saw him lying there and knew that he had been sick for a long time now, he asked him: Do you want to be well? [7] The sick man answered him: Sir, I have no one to carry me into the pool as soon as the water surges up. While I am dragging myself there, another climbs in before me. [8] Then Jesus said to him: Stand up, take your mat and go! [9] Immediately, the man was healed, took his mat and went.

However, that day was a Sabbath. [10] Then the Jews said to the man who was healed: It is the Sabbath; you are not allowed to carry your mat. [11] He replied to them: The man who healed me said to me: Take your bed and go! [12] They asked him: Who is this man who told you: Take your bed and go? [13] The man who was healed did not know who it was, for Jesus had left the scene because there was

2. Cf. Beutler, "Joh 6."

## Jesus Reveals Himself to His People (5:1–10:42)

a great crowd there. ¹⁴ After that, Jesus met him in the temple and said to him: Look, you have been healed; sin no more lest something worse happens to you. ¹⁵ The man went off and informed the Jews that it was Jesus who had healed him. ¹⁶ Consequently, the Jews persecuted Jesus because he had done this on the Sabbath. ¹⁷ Jesus retorted: My Father works until now, and I also work. ¹⁸ For this reason, the Jews sought even more to kill him because not only did he break the Sabbath but also called God his Father and so made himself equal with God.

¹⁹ Jesus said to them, however: Amen, amen, I say to you: The Son can do nothing on his own, but only when he sees the Father doing something. For what the Father does, the Son does in the same way. ²⁰ For the Father loves the Son and shows him all that he does, and he will show him still greater works so that you will be astonished. ²¹ For just as the Father raises the dead and gives them life, so the Son also gives life to whom he will. ²² Moreover, the Father judges no one, but has given over all judgement to the Son, ²³ so that all may honor the Son just as they honor the Father. Whoever does not honor the Son does not honor the Father who sent him. ²⁴ Amen, amen, I say to you: Whoever hears my word and believes him who sent me has eternal life; he does not come to judgement but has passed out of death into life. ²⁵ Amen, amen, I tell you: The hour is coming and now is when the dead will hear the voice of the Son of God; and all who hear it will live. ²⁶ For just as the Father has life in himself, so has he also given the Son to have life in himself. ²⁷ And he has given him the authority to deliver judgement because he is the Son of Man. ²⁸ Do not marvel at this! The hour is coming when all who are in their graves will hear his voice ²⁹ and come out: Those who have done good will rise to life; those who have done evil will rise to the judgement. ³⁰ Of myself, I can do nothing; I judge as I hear from the Father, and my judgement is right because I am not seeking my own will but the will of him who sent me.

³¹ If I bear witness to myself, my testimony is not true; ³² there is another who bears witness to me, and I know: the testimony that he bears witness to me is true. ³³ You sent to John, and he bore witness to the truth. ³⁴ However, I accept no human testimony, but I am saying this so that you may be saved. ³⁵ He was the lamp that burns and shines, but you wanted to rejoice in his light for only a short while. ³⁶ However, I have a more important testimony than that of John: The works that my Father has committed to me to fulfill, these works I am performing bear witness that it is the Father who sent me. ³⁷ Moreover, the Father himself who sent me has borne witness to me. You have never heard his voice or seen his form ³⁸ and furthermore, his word does not dwell in you because you do not believe in him whom he has sent. ³⁹ You search the Scriptures because you reckon that in them you have eternal life; it is precisely they that bear witness to me. ⁴⁰ And yet you do not want to come to me to have life.

⁴¹ I do not accept honor from men. ⁴² But I have come to know that you do not have the love of God in you. ⁴³ I have come in my Father's name, and you do not accept me. But if another comes in his own name, then you will accept him. ⁴⁴ How can you come to faith when you accept honor from one another but do not seek the honor that comes from the one who alone is God? ⁴⁵ Do not think that I shall accuse you before my Father; it is Moses, on whom you have set your hope, who accuses. ⁴⁶ If you believed Moses, you would have had to believe me also; for he wrote about me. ⁴⁷ But if you do not believe what he wrote, how then can you believe my words?

## I

To divide up John 5, it is reasonable to join narrative with linguistic criteria. Genre criticism can be usefully added too. After the introductory v. 1 about Jesus's pilgrimage to Jerusalem, verses 1–9c tell of the healing of the paralytic at the Pool of Bethesda. Jesus's dialogue with the sick man belongs to the miracle story. The passage belongs to the genre of miracle healing story.

The mention in v. 9d that the healing took place on a Sabbath leads to a series of dialogues between the "Jews" in Jerusalem, the man who was healed, and Jesus in verses 10–18.

In v. 19, there is a speech introducing the beginning of a long section that renders the words of Jesus although without mentioning to whom he is talking. This lasts to the end of the chapter in v. 47. Here, naturally, subsections can be detected according to linguistic criteria. Verses 19 to 30 are held together through the peg "the Son can do nothing on his own"/ "of myself I can do nothing." This section is matched by the following one, which is introduced with the words: "If I bear witness to myself, my testimony is not true" (v. 31). The theme of "testimony" lasts until v. 40. Based on this previous section, it then says in v. 41: "I do not accept honor from men." This theme of honor defines the group of verses in 41–45. Here, honor from men is set over against that of honor from God. If someone seeks honor from men, then he cannot understand the witness of God to Jesus in the writings of Moses. This is the subject of the concluding verses 46–47.

As before, the composition history of John 5 enjoys no agreement among exegetes. Among the proponents of a pre-Johannine tradition or source, three models can be recognized: the theory of a "signs source," the theory of an independent tradition, particularly in the healing story, and the theory of John's dependence on the Synoptic Gospels.

## Jesus Reveals Himself to His People (5:1–10:42)

Still widespread is the theory that, in the composition of John 5, John was going back to a *"semeia"* or "signs source." In the form represented by Bultmann, the hypothesis is that the source in question contained both the healing story of John 5:2–9c as well as parts of the ensuing dialogue up to v. 18. The evangelist would have added the element of the Sabbath dispute, and verses 19–47 also go back to him with the exception of the statements that reflect a future eschatology in John 5:28–29, which belong to the "ecclesiastical redaction." Later representatives of his school follow the line of Bultmann's suggestion.[3] Related to Bultmann's approach is that of Robert T. Fortna, who proposes a "signs gospel" from which the miraculous healing in John 5:2–9c would stem, without the succeeding dialogue. As the last of Jesus's "signs," the narrative would have brought the cycle to a close before the transition to the passion.[4]

According to other authors, the narrative of the healing of the paralytic goes back to an independent tradition or written source that does not have the extent of the *semeia* source. Schnackenburg favors this idea.[5] He sees certain points of contact in wording with the Synoptic tradition of the healing of the paralytic in Mark 2:1–12, such as the mention of the "mat" (κράβαττος) or the connection between sickness and sin. However, he does not think that these are enough for a theory of the direct literary dependence of John on the Mark tradition. It remains a question of the point of contact. Brown's judgement is similar. On account of some narrative details (such as the paralytic's failure to obtain timely assistance), he sees a possible later reworking of earlier primitive Christian narrative tradition that could still be recognized as a historical event.[6]

The serious and increasing alternative to these schemes is the theory that, in the story of the healing of the paralytic also, John has gone back to the Synoptic tradition, though naturally in a very free form as is otherwise the case in his account of the public life of Jesus before the passion. Chief

---

3. Becker, 1:276f. ascribes John 5:9d–16 to the *semeia* source that would have taken over the even older miracle story in vv. 2–9c. Vv. 17f. like v. 1 would have been added by the evangelist to whom the speech section would also be due. This is also the model retained by Theobald, 1:367f. There is a critical survey of the *semeia* hypothesis in van Belle, *The Signs Source*.

4. Fortna, *Fourth Gospel*, 113–17.

5. Schnackenburg, 2:117f. The miracle story of John 5 could go back to the same source as that of John 9. Schnelle also accepts a source or tradition that is independent of the Synoptics.

6. Brown, 1:208–10.

representative of this direction in exegesis is the Louvain scholar of the New Testament, Neirynck, followed by many of his pupils and colleagues. According to Neirynck,[7] there is a series of agreements in content and language between John 5:1–18 and Mark 2:1–3:6. To the correspondences in Jesus's order for the sick man to take up his "mat" (κράβαττος) and go, the connection between sickness and sins, and the motif of the Sabbath dispute can be added. To it there correspond in Mark the story of the disciples' gleaning ears of corn on the Sabbath with the ensuing controversy dialogue in Mark 2:23–28 and that of the healing of the man with the withered hand on the Sabbath in the synagogue in Mark 3:1–6. The "Jews" in John (5:10), therefore, correspond to Mark's Pharisees (2:24; 3:6). In both Gospels, the conflict leads to the death sentence against Jesus (cf. Mark 3:6 with John 5:18). The main difficulty of the theory of the fourth evangelist's dependence on the second in our narrative lies in the different setting: the location at the Pool of Bethesda with its five porticoes at the Sheep Gate of Jerusalem cannot in any way go back to the scene of the house in Galilee with its roof removed in order to let the paralytic down with ropes at Jesus's feet. Here, additional tradition must have been adopted such as does not allow John to be understood as a "fourth Synoptic," not even as seen from the Louvain perspective.

Recently, it has been claimed that we should once again take the contribution of the evangelist to the whole narrative more seriously.[8] This is something that can be recognized as early as the account of the healing of the paralytic in John 5:2–9c. Probably John has combined the Markan story with a Jerusalem tradition of a healing of Jesus at the Sheep Gate, but added some details of his own. This could be the case with the motif of the man's lack of readiness to be healed, possibly as an example of Johannine "misunderstanding." The invalid is seeking only the physical healing for which someone must carry him down to the surging water. Deviating from the genre of the miracle story, the sick man remains without companions and the dialogue is played out between him and Jesus alone. Similarly absent is the "Final Chorus" with which, at the end, the crowd praises God for the mighty act they have experienced. In John, this is replaced by the ensuing dispute about the Sabbath. Here too, then, the hand of the evangelist shows itself. It is striking, though, in this Johannine story that it is not Jesus but the healed man who is the first to transgress the Sabbath

---

7. Neirynck, "John 5,1–18."
8. Cf., esp., Witkamp, "The Use of Tradition."

## Jesus Reveals Himself to His People (5:1–10:42)

command. This could be a reflection of the situation of the Johannine communities who, with their freer interpretation of the Torah, were in conflict with their Jewish environment.

### II

#### The Healing of a Paralytic at the Pool of Bethesda (5:1–9c)

At the beginning of the chapter stands the account of the healing of a paralytic at the Pool of Bethesda in Jerusalem. The narrative shows typical features of a healing-miracle story, as Labahn,[9] among others, has stressed: introduction of the characters; description of the illness; an indication of the seriousness of the case; conversation between the invalid and the healer; the healing itself and its proof—the healed person takes his mat away by himself. All these elements point to a pre-Johannine tradition. Naturally, there are also cursory deviations from the literary form. The information about place and time seems to have been added, as well as the duration of the illness and more precise details about the location of the healing.

Another approach emerges from the comparison of this healing miracle with the other "sign" stories in John such as the wine miracle in Cana in John 2:1–11 and the healing of the son of the royal official in John 4:46–54.[10] Here, the following story line emerges:

- a person turns to Jesus with the request for his help
- Jesus rebuffs the request
- the person perseveres with the request
- Jesus gives instructions relating to the request
- the conversation partner obeys Jesus's instructions, and the miracle takes place
- the sign is confirmed by a third party
- a response of faith follows the miracle

Of course, in our passage there are variations from this sequence. Thus, no one requests the healing from Jesus, but he approaches the sick man on his

---

9. Labahn, "Spurensuche."
10. Culpepper, "Un exemple."

own initiative. Jesus also rebuffs no request, but the sick man at first turns aside Jesus's offer with his reference to his negative experiences. Thus, there is no question of the sick man persevering in anything; it is Jesus who stands by his offer. The healing takes place before any response of faith or obedience on the part of the invalid. Even after the healing, the latter expresses no direct act of faith but simply names ("announces") Jesus's name to the Jewish authorities, something that leads to conflict between Jesus and the "Jews" in Jerusalem.

We can divide the passage into an introduction with the time and place of the event as well as the given situation (vv. 1–3; for v. 4, see below); the dialogue between Jesus and the sick man (vv. 5–7); and the healing (vv. 8–9c).

**5:1-3** The opening verses of the narrative are defined with information about time and place. An unnamed feast of the Jews is imminent. It appears to be a pilgrim feast, for Jesus "goes up" to Jerusalem in order to be able to celebrate the feast. In the context of the Gospel, the "after this" refers to the second sign in Cana of Galilee, which has just been recorded (John 4:46–54). On the possible transposition of chs. 5 and 6, it is better to refrain from speculation.[11] The wording of the text gives nothing away as to which feast is in question. Some manuscripts attempt to fill the gap, but these details cannot be regarded as original.[12] Recent exegetes waver between Passover,[13] Weeks,[14] and Tabernacles.[15] Against Passover and Tabernacles is the fact that then the same feast would follow twice consecutively, which would then exclude the public ministry of Jesus from taking place within a single year of the Jewish cycle of feasts. The theory that what we have here is the Feast of Weeks can be supported by additional information.[16] On the one hand, in the previous context (John 4:35–38), the subject is the "harvest," and this would suit the Feast of Weeks well, as it was a harvest feast at the time of the firstfruits. On the other hand,

---

11. Thus, in Bultmann, Schnackenburg, Becker, and Wilckens. However, see in this connection the introduction above (section 4) on the secondary character of John 6.

12. Codex 131 reads here ἡ σκηνοπηγία "Tabernacles"; numerous manuscripts, beginning with the Codex Sinaiticus, read ἡ ἑορτή "the feast," which likewise could mean Tabernacles. However, the *Greek New Testament* gives the version without additions the badge of certainty "A" since we are clearly dealing with a later attempt at clarification.

13. Thus, Bultmann, 179; Wilckens, 113.

14. So, Mollat, 90; Schnackenburg, 2:118.

15. Thus, Manns, "La fête."

16. Cf. Rigato, "Era festa."

## Jesus Reveals Himself to His People (5:1–10:42)

in early Jewish tradition, the Feast of Weeks is connected with the commemoration of the giving of the Torah and with the Feast of the Covenant Renewal at Qumran. This would fit well with the Torah or the writings of Moses that gain in importance as the speech of Jesus continues (vv. 39–47). We shall, therefore, start from the position that John 5:1 concerns the Feast of Weeks.[17]

The information as to the location in v. 2 is also not quite so simple to define and explain. The text edition of Nestle-Aland holds the reading "Betzata," with the most ancient Greek manuscripts, as the oldest and best attested.[18] The more common "Bethesda" is found in the translations since the Codex Alexandrinus. Similarly, the expression ἐπὶ τῇ προβατικῇ is disputed on text-critical grounds. Most probable is the theory of an ellipsis, that is, through the omission of "gate": "In Jerusalem there is by the Sheep Gate a pool." This pool had five porticoes. For a long time the puzzle of this pool had been solved because in 1865 two pools were found near St. Anne's Church that were connected by porticoes. According to more recent archaeological results, however, this construction dates from after the destruction of Jerusalem. It remains still a double pool that was clearly too deep for someone to be able to go down into it easily. According to Antoine Duprez, there would have been further, smaller pools here, hewn out of the rocks, and these would have been used for the cult of a god of healing (Asclepius or the Oriental Serapis).[19] It is difficult to imagine a movement of water in this complex, and so Devillers suggests adopting an early version of the story that recounted a miracle at the Pool of Siloam, which is fed from the spring of Gihon.[20] Here, such a surge of the water would have been possible. The evangelist would then have relocated the miracle to the Pool of Bethesda in order to be able to recount two miracles of Jesus at pools in Jerusalem and demonstrate Jesus's superiority over the gods of healing. Such questions will no doubt continue to be discussed. Verse 4, which explains the surge of the water as being caused by an angel, is regarded by text critics as a later clarification.

After the information about place and time, the account turns, in v. 3, to those taking part. At the Pool of Bethesda lie a crowd of invalids,

---

17. Felsch, *Feste*, 96–170, adds further arguments to the interpretation of John 5:1 as the Feast of Weeks; besides, she also sees elements of the New Year festival in this feast.

18. This reading is now also supported by the fact that the evidence added for "Bethesda" from 3Q15.11–12 is to be read otherwise; cf. Ceulemans, "Name."

19. Duprez, *Jésus*.

20. Devillers, "Une piscine."

waiting for a healing. They are blind, lame, and crippled. This list is probably not fortuitous. Matthew and Luke tell of a deputation sent by John the Baptist from prison to ask Jesus whether he is the coming one. Jesus answers: "Go and tell John what you hear and see: the blind see again, the lame walk; lepers are made clean, and the deaf hear; the dead are raised, and the poor have the Gospel preached to them" (Matt 11:4–5; cf. Luke 7:22). Jesus is seen here as the one who fulfills the promises of the prophets. Healing is promised to the blind and lame in Isa 35:5–6, to the blind also in Isa 29:18. The raising of the dead is promised in Isa 26:19. This is the key to the miracles in John 5, John 9, and John 11 with the healing of the paralytic and the man born blind, and the raising of Lazarus. Jesus is the one in whom the promises of the prophets are fulfilled.

**5:5–7** In v. 5, one of the invalids is singled out from the crowd. The narrator knows that he has already suffered for thirty-eight years. The readers will perhaps think of the thirty-eight years that the people of Israel wandered through the wilderness before they were able to reach the Promised Land (cf. Deut 2:14). The initiative for the healing does not come, as usual, from the invalid or his companions but, according to v. 6, from Jesus. He sees the lame man lying there, is aware of the length of his infirmity, and speaks to him. Clearly what is being stressed here is not only the defining role of Jesus but also his knowledge of men (cf. John 1:48; 2:25; 4:18). The question to the sick man, whether he wants to be well, is a surprising one. The lame man's answer in v. 7 shows that it was justified. The answer sounds like an evasion. Despite his answer, the lame man's desire for healing is, of course, presupposed by Jesus, for only then can he speak the word that saves the sick man.

**5:8–9c** According to v. 8, Jesus's healing word consists of a command to the sick man. He should and can now become active: "Stand up, take your mat and go!" The same sentence is also to be found almost word for word in the healing of the paralytic in Mark 2:11; cf. Matt 9:6; Luke 5:24, only there, the healed man is commanded to go home. The "walking around" (περιπατεῖν) in John corresponds to that of the paralytic in Matt 11:5; Luke 7:22; cf. Acts 3:6; 14:10 and probably corresponds to the firmer narrative tradition with its resort to the Isaianic promise. The motif of healed paralytics taking up their beds or whatever is also attested outside the Bible.[21] It serves as a proof of the successful healing. In John, however, it also leads into the accusation of Sabbath transgression, the subject of

---

21. Cf. Labahn, "Spurensuche," 163.

*Jesus Reveals Himself to His People (5:1–10:42)*

the following section. In v. 9a–c, Jesus's command is matched by its exact execution by the paralytic: he gets up, takes his mat, and walks around. The motif of "getting up/rising" (ἐγείρειν) may have a deeper meaning in John. It anticipates the authority of the Son, like that of the Father, to raise the dead (cf. v. 21). In the story of the raising of Lazarus in John 11, this authority will be demonstrated visibly.

### *The Dialogue over Sabbath Observance (5:9d–18)*

The account of the healing of the paralytic at the Pool of Bethesda is followed by a controversy between the man who was healed, Jesus, and the Jewish authorities over the legitimacy of the healing since it occurred on a Sabbath day. The fact that it does not say until v. 9d "However, that day was a Sabbath" is considered by many exegetes as indicating that this motif was added only subsequently by the evangelist or a source that is not identical with the one that reports the miraculous healing.[22] Other authors, such as those associated with the Louvain school (cf. Neirynck), point, of course, to the fact that the connection between Jesus's miracle and the Sabbath motif is already present in the Synoptic tradition (cf. Mark 2:1–3:6; Luke 13:10–17).[23] According to Peder Borgen, there already occurs a connection between an event carried out on the Sabbath and an ensuing controversy in Philo of Alexandria.[24] Philo also discusses the difference between God who, according to the interpretation of Gen 2:2–3, can work on the Sabbath, and man, who has to observe the Sabbath (cf. *Migr.* 89–93). Thus, the Sabbath-healing connection probably belongs already to the pre-Johannine tradition, something that is also transparent in John 7:21–24.

Less probable is Tom Thatcher's theory that the Sabbath motif, added only later in John 5:9d, is an example of an "unstable irony," that is, a deliberate deception not only of those present at the time of the action ("stable irony"), but also the later readers and so is a case of "a Sabbath trick."[25] The suggestion founders on the fact that the Johannine irony invariably refers to the tension between the revelatory words of Jesus or

22. See above.
23. Discussion above.
24. Cf. Borgen, "The Sabbath Controversy."
25. Thatcher, "The Sabbath Trick."

statements about Jesus and their being misunderstood by the hearers. This is not the case here. Nowhere else does the fourth evangelist deliberately lead his readers into error.

For the genre of our section (and similarly in the course of John's Gospel), the suggestion has been made to see here the pattern of the lawsuit attested in the OT, a lawsuit between God and his people.[26] A lawsuit of this kind is distinguished by the fact that there is no judicial authority to decide the dispute. It is the better arguments alone that count. Despite all the closeness of John's Gospel to the Old Testament, and, not least, to its prophetic tradition, the employment of this literary model for the controversies between Jesus and his opponents in Jerusalem is not really convincing. On the one hand, Jesus does not simply stand in the place of God; on the other hand, in John, judicial authority is not absent. On the political level, there are the judicial organs of the people of Israel that are in the position to exclude from the community or even to impose the death penalty. From the theological perspective, Jesus reveals himself as the true judge or, at least, as the one who performs the divine judgement on all who oppose him and, in the final analysis, as God himself.

With R. Alan Culpepper,[27] after the first conversation between Jesus and the man at the Pool of Bethesda in John 5:5–9a, we can make out further conversation units in the following verses: the "Jews" and the man who was healed (5:10–13), Jesus and that man (5:14), the man and the "Jews" (5:15) as well as Jesus and the "Jews" (5:16–18). The latter also make up the addressees of the following speech of Jesus in 5:19–47.

**5:9d–13** The scene is introduced with the information: "However, that day was a Sabbath" (v. 9d). The statement recalls the same detail in John 9:14 (cf., also, 19:14). Stylistically, it points to the evangelist. For the disputes of the following verses, incidentally, it is rather beside the point whether the day of healing was a Sabbath since, according to Jewish Law, the feast days were treated on the same basis as Sabbath days.

In v. 10, the "Jews" come on the scene for the first time. By contrast with John 4:22, where the expression describes the Jewish religious community, here it appears to stand for a group within Judaism. It was first mentioned in John 1:19 in connection with the members of the mission sent to question John the Baptist about his person and his activity. Clearly, it concerned the Jewish authorities in Jerusalem, without these being spec-

---

26. Cf. Asiedu-Peprah, *Johannine Sabbath Conflicts*.
27. Culpepper, "Un exemple," 143.

## Jesus Reveals Himself to His People (5:1–10:42)

ified in greater detail.[28] These "Jews" rebuke the man who had been healed for carrying his mat on the Sabbath. The bearing of burdens was one of the thirty-nine "works" that were considered to be forbidden by the Law of Moses.[29] From the point of view of narrative flow, it is significant that the first accusation is addressed to the man and not to Jesus. Of course, the latter is being criticized indirectly as will become immediately apparent.

The man gets himself out of the picture by transferring the accusation to Jesus who had commanded him to take his mat and go. Here, the expression "healthy" (ὑγιής) is striking. This adjective, which was already used in v. 6, appears also again in v. 14. It probably originates from the pre-Johannine tradition and serves to connect the healing miracle with the ensuing controversies. The word is encountered in Hellenistic accounts of healing miracles, as already noted.[30] Thus, Jesus appears as "dieu guérisseur" (healing divinity).

On the basis of the man's answer, the "Jews'" question turns into an investigation into the person who healed him. The man explains that he does not know who the man was who healed him. The narrator adds that, at the scene of this exchange, there was a crowd and that Jesus had disappeared into it.

**5:14** After a meeting between the man who was healed and the "Jews," there occurs a meeting between him and Jesus. Here, it is not he who finds Jesus, but Jesus who finds him (as he "found" Philip, John 1:43) "after that" (μετὰ ταῦτα, a Johannine expression) and exhorts him to sin no more. This command has been much discussed. A connection between sickness and sins seems to have been presupposed in Jewish circles, as perhaps the disciples' question in John 9:2 indicates. Similarly, the Synoptic tradition in Mark 2:1–12 knows this connection, even if not in a causal sense. Jesus first forgives the sick man his sins before he heals him. A connection is not stated directly. According to a widespread opinion, Jesus's command could be explained by a glance at the man's biography. He had not taken all the opportunities to be healed, and could or would not give any information about his healer.[31] This explanation is, of course, excluded by the following verse.

---

28. The identity of this group and the problems of the expression are widely discussed in Beutler, "The Identity."

29. Cf. the reference to Mishnah Šabb 7.2 in Barrett: according to Šabb 10.5, a man can carry another on a bed or mat on the Sabbath also since, in the final analysis, he is carrying someone who is sick. However, this was not the case in John 5.

30. See the discussion above on v. 6. See also n. 19 above.

31. Metzner, "Der Geheilte."

**5:15** After the man's meeting with Jesus, he takes himself to the "Jews" in order to inform them that it was Jesus who healed him. This detail has been very differently interpreted by the exegetes, as Rainer Metzner shows in his article.[32] It appears that the man probably went to the "Jews" in order to denounce Jesus. So far, he had shown no positive relationship to Jesus, and so it remains open whether he had come to faith in him. Against this, of course, another view is increasingly represented today that perceives the man who was healed in a more positive light.[33] If he goes to the Jews in order to "proclaim" that it was Jesus who had healed him, then it is necessary to take seriously the meaning of the word ἀναγγέλλω, which does not mean "denounce" but "proclaim." The healed paralytic of John 5 is thus a precursor of the healed man born blind of John 9 who, after his healing, comes to a fearless acknowledgment of Jesus and a full confession of faith. This fits in with the fact that the paralytic plays a role in the baptismal cycles of early Christian frescoes, as is shown by the examples in the Cappella Greca in the Catacombs of Priscilla or the Chapel of the Sacraments in the Catacombs of Callistus, both in Rome.[34]

**5:16–18** Verse 16 could have been an original ending for the narrative in the pre-Johannine tradition. The "Jews" persecuted Jesus as a transgressor of the Sabbath.[35] The imperfect signifies a lasting rather than a one-off conflict. The word chosen recalls the future persecution of the disciples (John 15:20). Just as the "Jews" persecuted Jesus, so will they also persecute his disciples.

Verse 17 already anticipates the revelation discourse of Jesus (and on this account is already also ascribed to the evangelist in every respect). Jesus describes his activity as "work" and thus justifies it at the same time, for he has performed this work in union with the Father. According to Jewish thought, attested by Philo, God also works on the Sabbath, and thus Jesus's "work" is justified.[36]

According to v. 18, the "Jews" sense this claim of Jesus to make himself equal with God and want to kill him on account of his blasphemy.

---

32. Metzner, "Der Geheilte."
33. Cf. Scholstissek, "Mündiger Glaube"; Straub, "Alles ist durch ihn geworden," 164f.
34. Cf. Metzner, "Der Geheilte," 182 n. 19, following an interpretation of the baptismal scenes by Cullmann.
35. A series of older manuscripts add here "and sought to kill him" (A K N Γ Δ Θ Ψ [$f^{13}$] 700 1424 M e q sy$^{p.h}$ bo$^{pt}$ [f r$^1$]). However, the oldest Egyptian text witnesses are against this. The statement is obviously taken over from v. 18.
36. Note reference above by Borgen to Philo's interpretation of Gen 2:2–3.

## Jesus Reveals Himself to His People (5:1–10:42)

This purpose exceeds the "persecuting" of Jesus in v. 16, but it finds its basis already in the Synoptic tradition of Mark 2:1–3:6 (cf. Mark 3:6!). The Hellenistic parallels to divinity have been studied by Wayne A. Meeks.[37] Relevant here is the case of Apollonius of Tyana, whose life was described by Philostratus. Before the Emperor Domitian, he justifies the title "god," which a disciple had bestowed on him. First, Apollonius demonstrates his superhuman qualities by suddenly disappearing before the eyes of his audience. Then he also justifies himself in words. Men honor good people as gods since they embody the image of God. How much more, then, can a person who is endowed with the powers of Apollonius be described as God.[38] The argumentation is similar to that of John 5, but also to that of John 10, where Jesus (in v. 34) quotes in his own favor Ps 82:6 where all Israelites are called "gods and sons of the Most High."[39] According to Jewish tradition, all the Israelites who heard the voice of God at Sinai and experienced his instructions became divine. It was only through their sin in worshiping the golden calf that they lost this privilege. Only in perfect faithfulness to the Law will they be able to claim this privilege again (relevant here is the making of the second covenant in Exod 34). Jesus could have been referring to such a tradition. It will be taken up again in John 10:34–36 (see there).

### Jesus Does Nothing on His Own (5:19–30)

John 5:19 opens the last part of the chapter. From here on, it is only Jesus who speaks. The miracle story (vv. 1–9c) and the dialogues (vv. 9d–18) are now followed by a revelatory speech of Jesus. The style of verses 19–47 is Johannine, as is the theology. The author is going back to traditions rather than written sources. For the possibility of a later layer in verses 28–29, see the commentary there.

As already mentioned, verses 19–30 form an independent subsection. This is framed by the statement that the Son can do nothing by himself but works continually in union with his Father (vv. 19 and 30). The two outstanding works of God, the Father, are the bestowal of life in the resurrection of the dead and the judgement. With this twofold statement,

---

37. Cf. Meeks, "Equal to God."
38. Cf. Meeks, "Equal to God," 96.
39. Cf. Beutler, "Ich habe gesagt."

Jesus is referring again to Jewish tradition. The two works mentioned are those that God can also perform on the Sabbath. From this viewpoint, our section develops the previous one further and brings it to its conclusion.

The composition of the section is simple. Verses 19–20 introduce the principle that the Son can do nothing other than what he sees the Father doing. This image could stem from the world of craft-work in which the son takes over his father's trade. In verses 21–28, the work that the Son has taken over from his Father is clarified: they are the two works of bestowing life in the resurrection and judgement. They are the two works reserved to God that are entrusted to the Son. In verse 21, the subject is the bestowal of life, in verses 22–23, judgement.

In verses 24–28, the work of the Son is clarified. The promise of life and the exercise of judgement apply in the present moment: "The hour is coming and now is" (v. 25). In verses 28–29, the same theme returns again. However, the promise is valid now only for the future: "The hour is coming" (v. 28). The exegetes discuss the significance of this doublet. It will come up in our exegesis of verses 28–29.

**5:19–20** Jesus's actual speech begins with the typical Johannine affirmation: "Amen, amen, I say to you." They lend a special weight to the following words. The first two verses are characterized by the image taken from craft-work, that the son learns his father's trade in that he watches him at his work and then imitates him. This metaphor is noted and described by Dodd.[40] This approach explains the concepts of "watching," "showing," and "doing." The father-son relationship is not only a professional one, but also of a familial kind: the father loves his son. This two-fold aspect allows the image to be taken over easily into the relationship between the heavenly Father and Jesus. The latter too can do nothing by himself but only what the Father shows him and entrusts him with. To the works entrusted to the Son by the Father belong the work of creation (cf. John 1:3), but also the work of redemption. Both have their climax in the eschatological works. These are the "greater works" that the Son will perform to the astonishment of Jesus's contemporaries.

**5:21–23** The previous verses have set out the dependence of the Son on the Father. The Son does nothing except what he sees the Father doing. By contrast, verses 21–23 highlight the dignity of the Son. Thus, they end with the statement that everyone who honors the Father also honors the Son. The dignity of the Son is demonstrated by his participation in the

---

40. Cf. Dodd, "Une parabole."

## Jesus Reveals Himself to His People (5:1–10:42)

works reserved to God alone: to raise the dead and to execute the judgement. Indeed, the judgement is actually reserved exclusively to the Son so that God himself does not take part in it. In these verses, Johannine theology comes to expression as an early reflection of the church on the dignity of Christ. John's view comes close to that of Paul and his tradition (cf. the hymn used by Paul in Phil 2:6–11 or the beginning of the Letter to the Romans, Rom 1:3–4; similarly, the Trinitarian formula 2 Cor 13:13). A related view is also found, of course, in other layers and writings of the New Testament (cf. Matt 11:25–27; Mark 1:11 par.; 9:7 par.; Heb 1:1–4). For the judgement committed to the Son of Man, cf. Mark 13:26–27 par.; Matt 25:31–46.

From the beginning, Jesus's divine sonship has provoked opposition. From early on, Jews and perhaps also Jewish Christians were opposed to this point of view. The great controversies of John 5–10 have their basis here. Later on, Arius challenged Jesus's divine sonship. According to him, Jesus is a creature and not equal to God. Nowadays, there is opposition to the family metaphor that comes to expression in talk about God the Father and God the Son. M. Eugene Boring brings this concern to expression for the Western world.[41] According to him, talk of "Father" and "Son" expresses a certain patriarchalism that is placed in question not only from a feminist perspective but also from people nowadays who mount a critical challenge to the authority of fathers as such. Such questions are to be taken seriously, though naturally one has to consider that they originate especially in the Western world.

**5:24–27** In the verses that follow, the twofold work of Jesus, of the Son, is described from two different perspectives: that of men and that of the Son. In verses 24–25, the subject is life and judgement from the human point of view. The usage here is influenced by wisdom literature, which promises men salvation if they meet specific demands. Verses 26–27 take on a more firmly dogmatic tone and describe the dignity of the Son.

First, vv. 24–25. In these verses, eternal life is promised to those who hear the word of Jesus and believe the God who sent him. More precisely, eternal life is not promised here; rather, it is explained that all who hear the word of Jesus and believe the Father have already passed from death to eternal life (Greek perfect!). These men do not come to judgement. This is an expression of the "realized eschatology" that is typical of the fourth evangelist. According to the traditional Jewish conception, every

---

41. Cf. Boring, "John 5:19–24."

man goes first to his death at the end of his earthly life. Then, some day, according to the Pharisaic idea of the resurrection of the dead (or of the righteous), there will be judgement and eternal life for the righteous. For John, true death is the separation from God, the source of life. From this death, one can now already pass over to the true, eternal life if one believes in Jesus and in the one who sent him. Whoever does this does not come into judgement. This notion is found also in other places in John's Gospel (cf. 3:15-18, 36; 6:40, 47; 12:46-47). The promise of "eternal life" is found already in Dan 12:2. Here it is promised to the righteous on the day of final judgement when they arise out of their graves. In John, the role of the archangel Michael is taken over by the "Son of God" as "Son of Man" (cf. v. 27; Dan 7:13-14). The expression "the hour is coming" is completed in v. 25 with "and now is." From here, then, the concepts of "death" and "life" are interpreted anew. "Death" consists in separation from God as the source of life; "life" is "eternal life" insofar as it comes from God. The future, which is spoken of here in terms of the eschatological hearing of the voice of the Son, the resurrection and life, loses its sense as an indication of time and is more of a logical nature: what is to happen, happens now, in the "hour" of faith.

In v. 26, the evangelist abandons for a moment the traditional world of eschatological notions and speaks of Christ as the source of life in more theological language. The Father has life in himself, and he has also handed over this power to the Son. Here the prologue of the Gospel comes to mind (John 1:4), where the divine word appears as bearer and source of life. In v. 27, the author returns to the conceptual world of apocalyptic. Exegetes see in this verse an echo of Dan 7:13-14, although there it is not judgement that is mentioned but rather dominion until the end of time. Confirmation of the dependence of John on Daniel here could lie in the absence of the article in v. 27: "because he is a Son of Man."

**5:28-29** The command at the beginning of v. 28: "Do not marvel at this!" can refer, as happens not infrequently, to the previous context. In that case, the following ὅτι probably has a causal sense, such as could be expressed with a colon. However, the command can also refer to the following context with the possibility that ὅτι would then be understood as declarative. This is the understanding, more or less, of Hans-Christian Kammler.[42] The difference in sense is negligible.

Verses 28-29 refer back to v. 25, something that is generally noticed.

---

42. Cf. Kammler, *Christologie*.

In fact, the verses correspond on the level of form as the following table demonstrates:

| | |
|---|---|
| ἔρχεται ὥρα καὶ νῦν ἐστιν | ἔρχεται ὥρα |
| ὅτε οἱ νεκροὶ | ἐν ᾗ πάντες οἱ ἐν τοῖς μνημείοις |
| ἀκούσουσιν τῆς φωνῆς | ἀκούσουσιν τῆς φωνῆς αὐτοῦ |
| τοῦ υἱοῦ τοῦ θεοῦ | καὶ ἐκπορεύσονται οἱ τὰ ἀγαθὰ |
| καὶ οἱ ἀκούσαντες ζήσουσιν. | ποιήσαντες |
| | εἰς ἀνάστασιν ζωῆς, |
| | οἱ δὲ τὰ φαῦλα πράξαντες |
| | εἰς ἀνάστασιν κρίσεως. |

The main differences between the two passages are the following: verses 28–29 say: "the hour is coming" without adding "and now is"; they have: "all who are in their graves" instead of "the dead"; and the judgement appears to be bound up with works that have been achieved. How are we to explain these differences? Three interpretive models should be considered.

The first model is that of "realized eschatology." Its chief representative is Bultmann in his commentary that came out in 1941; numerous authors have followed.[43] According to these authors, the text of John 5:28–29 speaks of a future resurrection of the dead on the day of judgement. John's "realized eschatology" appeared too adventurous to the emerging church at the end of the first century, and so it was completed by the "classical" Jewish model of eschatology that is also found in the other NT writings (Synoptics, Paul at least partly). In this way, the Fourth Gospel was "rescued" for the post-apostolic church.

The second model is that of two complementary layers in John's Gospel. It is the model favored by the great commentaries from Great Britain,[44] the United States of America,[45] and numerous authors from the continent of Europe.[46] According to these authors, the evangelist John himself reformulated his characteristic realized eschatology once again

---

43. Cf. Becker, 1:291 with reference also to Schnackenburg (but cf., below, n. 46) and Richter. Most recently, this suggestion is followed by Theobald, 398–400; Theobald, "Futurische versus präsentische Eschatologie?"

44. Cf. Dodd, *Interpretation*; Lindars; Barrett; Beasley-Murray.

45. Cf. Brown; Moloney.

46. However, here Schnackenburg is probably to be mentioned as well as his pupil, Blank, in his commentary and in his monograph, *Krisis*, 172–83. Among the newer commentaries, cf. Schnelle and Schenke.

as a future eschatology. Here, one does not necessarily have to start out from the Jewish apocalyptic or early Christian model of the end-time resurrection of the dead. John speaks, indeed, not of the "dead" who rise but of "those who are in their graves." The "dead," as before, are those who already in this life through their decision against God have separated themselves from him. This observation is found already in Josef Blank. Recently, in his three-volume work on Johannine eschatology, Jörg Frey has been a powerful advocate for the thesis that both eschatologies in John are to be regarded as complementary.[47] Without the future eschatology, the Johannine kerygma would be incomplete. Bultmann is right that the "works" of which the Johannine text speaks are not the "good" or "evil works" of Judaism or early Christianity but faith in Christ or the lack thereof (cf. John 3:16–18; 6:29).

A third model interprets John 5:25–29 as strictly unitary, and, in fact, from the point of view of realized eschatology.[48] Even verses 28–29 can be interpreted in a realized sense if one reads and understands them correctly despite their traditional formulation. The future would be similar to that in v. 25; cf., also, John 10:16. According to this suggestion, Jesus is speaking of the time after Easter when the end-time promises will be fulfilled.[49] This proposal merits deeper study that also incorporates other "eschatological" texts of John such as John 6:39, 40, 44, 54. In favor of this suggestion it can be pointed out that, in John 4:21, 23, there appears to be no semantic difference between "the hour is coming" (ἔρχεται ὥρα) and "the hour is coming and now is" (ἔρχεται ὥρα καὶ νῦν ἐστιν).

**5:30** Just as Jesus bestows life in complete dependence on his Father, so too does he execute justice. That is the message of verse 30. Jesus does not seek his own will but that of the one who has sent him (cf. John 8:28). It is precisely for this reason that his judgement is right. From a literary point of view, this verse brings the text unit John 5:19–30 to an efficient close through the resumption of v. 19. At the same time, it prepares the transition to the next section.

---

47. Frey, *Johanneische Eschatologie*, vols. 2 and 3; cf., now, O'Donnell, "Complementary Eschatologies."

48. Cf., again, Kammler, *Christologie*; similarly, Stimpfle, *Blinde sehen*.

49. Cf. Kammler, "Jesus Christus."

## Jesus Reveals Himself to His People (5:1–10:42)

### Jesus Does Not Bear Testimony to Himself (5:31–40)

In its composition, this section is similar to the previous one (Jesus does nothing on his own, vv. 19–30) and the following one (Jesus does not seek his own honor, vv. 41–47). Each time, the basic principle is placed at the beginning of the whole section and so the theme of the passage is announced. Jesus is continually denying that it is for himself that he is claiming honor and authority. All his power, his recognition, and his honor come from God. It is precisely on this basis that he stands above all human authority. God himself works in him, authorizes him, and honors him.

The paragraph John 5:31–40 is characterized by the semantic field of "testimony."[50] In v. 31, Jesus denies bearing witness to himself (in John 8:12–20, another point of view will prevail!). It is another who bears witness to him: it is the Father, who is not yet named here (v. 32). Furthermore, there occurs here the testimony of John the Baptist on Jesus's behalf. John is now a figure of the past (vv. 33–35). In v. 36, the testimony of the "other" about Jesus is taken up again; now it is quite clearly the Father. He endows Jesus with the astonishing works that bear witness to him (v. 36), and he also bears direct testimony to Jesus (vv. 37–38), as he has done already through the Scriptures of Israel (v. 39). Of course, in order to grasp this manifold witness, it is necessary to let oneself be led to Jesus and so to have life (v. 40).

**5:31–32** The two introductory verses are formed to match v. 19 and v. 41 and express the total dependence of Jesus, the Son, on the Father, but also his authority, which is bestowed on him by the Father. For the "truth" of this witness, we can also compare John 19:35; 21:24; and 3 John 9.

**5:33–35** According to the evangelist, next to God himself, who has empowered Jesus for his mission in word and deed, it is John the Baptist who is the most important witness to Jesus. He appears as witness in favor of Jesus from the prologue on (John 1:6–8, 15). The narrative part of the Gospel begins with a long section concerning the witness of John the Baptist to Jesus in John 1:19–34. This witness is presupposed and developed in the conversation between John's disciples and Jesus in John 3:22–30: he is none other than the friend of the bridegroom, who rejoices when he hears the bridegroom's voice coming out of the bridal chamber (John 3:29), since he is only the herald of the Messiah and not the Messiah himself (John 3:28). The role of John to be Jesus's witness is so dominant for

---

50. Cf., for this section, Beutler, *Martyria*, 254–64.

the fourth evangelist that he never speaks of him as "Baptist" but always only as witness. In his capacity as "companion" of Jesus, he is superseded by Lazarus in chs. 11–12 and by the beloved disciple in chs. 13–21.

At the time of the controversy of Jesus with the "Jews" in Jerusalem following the healing of the paralytic, John has already completed his career. Jesus now speaks of him in the past. The "Jews" had sent a delegation to him to find out who Jesus was, but they had not been willing to accept his testimony. Indeed, they put up with him for a short time only then to snuff him out. The evangelist expresses this experience with the image of the candlestick. The "Jews" had been prepared to rejoice in his light for only a short time. In language and content, the difference from Jesus is striking here: John is the "candle"; Jesus is the light of the world (cf. John 1:4–5, 9; 8:12; 9:5; 12:46).

**5:36** In what follows, Jesus passes on to the witness borne by the works that the Father has bestowed on him. These works have led to astonishment and faith, as was shown in Jesus's first two signs that were reported in the Gospel (John 2:1–12 and 4:46–54; cf. 2:23; 3:2). One could add the works of which Jesus speaks in John 5:17–30, especially giving life to the dead and executing judgement in God's name. Naturally, these works are visible only to those with faith.

If one asks for literary precedents to the Johannine concept of the witness of works to Jesus, one comes across texts related to Hellenistic Judaism that speak of God's witness for Moses. Both Josephus and Philo speak of one such witness in reference to the "signs" that Moses performed during the Exodus of Israel from Egypt, at the crossing of the Red Sea, and during the passage through the desert (cf. Philo, *Mos.* 3.263–81; *Leg.* 2.55; Josephus, *Ag. Ap.* 2.53).[51] In the NT, this theme is employed in a christological sense in Acts 14:3 and Heb 2:4.

**5:37–39** Just as the Father has borne witness to Jesus in the works he has bestowed on him, so also he has borne witness to him in his word. This word was issued in the old covenant. It remains true, of course, that the Israelites could not hear it, just as they did not see the face of God. However, they possessed the divine witness to Jesus in their holy Scriptures. They only had to search through these, and then they would have discovered their witness on Jesus's behalf.

The "testimony" of Scripture to Jesus is, once more, a characteristic theme of John's Gospel, but not without precedents and parallels in

---

51. Cf. Beutler, *Martyria*, 152f.; Beutler, "μαρτυρέω," *EWNT* 2:960; *EDNT* 2:391.

## Jesus Reveals Himself to His People (5:1–10:42)

the other writings of the NT. The Synoptic tradition knows mainly of the fulfillment of particular passages of Israel's Scripture in Jesus, in his life, and, above all, in his passion. John demonstrates this procedure—in correspondence with the Synoptics—above all in his passion narrative. John 12:38 marks the first occasion of the formula: "This was to fulfill the word." More characteristic of John is the use of Scripture as testimony for Jesus without reference to a specific biblical text.[52] It is not this or that passage but Scripture as such that bears witness for Jesus. John 5:39 is the classical text for this perspective, but cf. also John 1:45; 5:45–47; 10:34: a psalm citation as testimony from "the Law."

**5:40** If the Israelites have not succeeded in hearing the testimony for Jesus that is in their own Scripture, then that is not the fault of Scripture. Rather, the readers are not ready to open themselves to the message of Scripture. Thereby, however, they are withdrawing from the source of life.

### Jesus Does Not Seek His Own Honor (5:41–47)

The last section of Jesus's speech can be divided into two: Jesus does not seek his own honor (vv. 41–44), and it is not Jesus who accuses the "Jews" but Moses (vv. 45–47).

**5:41–44** This group of verses is framed by the theme of "honor"[53]: Jesus does not seek his own honor (v. 41). This is what his opponents do: they receive honor from one another and not from the one God (v. 44), so that they are incapable of coming to Jesus and believing in him. Verses 42–43 put forward a deeper reason that defines the misguided behavior of Jesus's opponents: they do not have the love of God in them. Thus, they receive the one who comes in his own name, but not the one who comes in the name of God, to wit, Jesus.

If we are not misguided in our interpretation, then our group of verses has made use of the faith confession of Israel, "Hear, O Israel," from Deut 6:4–5.[54] In this central text of Judaism, God commands his people to acknowledge him as the only God and to love him with their whole heart. The influence of this text on John 5:41–44, as also on John 8:41–42, has scarcely been recognized until now. In both cases, the unity of God is

---

52. Cf. Beutler, "Der Gebrauch."
53. Cf. Beutler, "Die Ehre Gottes."
54. Cf. Beutler, "Das Hauptgebot."

bound up with love for him or for Jesus as the one whom the Father has sent. An echo of this Deuteronomic command is found in John 21:15–17 (Peter's love for Jesus, as the expression of his fundamental relationship with him, makes possible the commission to shepherd the Lord's flock).

If this interpretation is correct, then it follows for John 5:42 and similar texts in this Gospel that the expression ἡ ἀγάπη τοῦ θεοῦ is to be understood as an objective genitive. In John's Gospel, it is a matter of the right relationship to God, even as a member of the people of Israel. Whoever does not love God, will not love Christ, his Son, and will seek his own glory. In the First Letter of John, the situation is different. The author finds himself in controversy with a group that, to a high degree, claims the possession of the Spirit for themselves, imagine themselves to be above the Law, and think that they can maintain that they know God and love him. In the First Letter of John, such men are told that they are first loved by God before they are able to say that they love God (cf. 1 John 4:7–21; further, 2:15; 3:16–17).

**5:45–47** Various reasons can be given for the transition from the theme of honor to that of Moses. Already in John 5:39, Jesus claimed that the Scriptures speak of him. These Scriptures are the Torah, mediated by Moses, the prophets, and the other writings, especially the Psalms. In this sense, the theme of Moses who accuses the Israelites has already been prepared for in the immediate context. The text also recalls John 7:19–23 where Jesus, in connection with his healing performed on the Sabbath, argues from the Law of Moses that permits circumcision on the Sabbath. Thus, we can also see, in John 5:45–47, a reference to the controversy over the healing performed by Jesus as a discussion over the use of the Law of Moses.

The conviction that Moses wrote about Jesus (v. 46) is to be considered from the consistent viewpoint of John according to which the whole of Scripture, read correctly, speaks of Jesus. A first example of this viewpoint occurs in John 1:45 in the words of Philip: "We have found the one whom Moses in the Law and also the prophets have written about: Jesus, the son of Joseph, from Nazareth."

The Israelites believed in God and also in Moses, as it says in Exod 14:31, after the account of the Exodus of Israel from Egypt and of the passage through the Red Sea. The Israelites of Jesus's time stand in this tradition. At them is aimed the saying of Jesus that it is not enough to believe in Moses, but that one has also to read his Scriptures correctly: as a testimony to Jesus. Whoever believes in Moses must also believe in Jesus, for Moses

*Jesus Reveals Himself to His People (5:1–10:42)*

wrote about Jesus. Whoever does not believe in Jesus cannot claim that he has believed the words of Moses. In this way, ch. 5 closes with a stirring accusation against Jesus's audience. The conflict will continue in chs. 6 and 7–8.

### III

In chs. 2–4 of John's Gospel, Jesus takes his message ever more strongly from the center to the peripheries of the land of Israel. Then, in ch. 5, he returns to the center once again where there is an altercation concerning his mission to the inhabitants of Jerusalem and the leaders of the Jewish people. A miracle that arouses astonishment, the healing of a man who had been lame for thirty-eight years, leads to a controversy over his conduct on the Sabbath, but then increasingly to the question of his person. For the first time now, the "Jews" appear in a longer section as the opponents of Jesus. Jesus's claim to act in union with his heavenly Father admits only the conclusion that he is making himself equal to the Father in power and dignity. This claim has engendered opposition, and not only at the time of the evangelist. If it is to be rightly understood, it is worth going back once more over Jesus's discourse in John 5:19–47.

On a more careful reading, it is striking that Jesus always points away from himself and avoids putting himself in the middle of the picture. Jesus does nothing by himself (vv. 19–30), he does not bear testimony to himself (vv. 31–40), and he also does not seek his own honor (vv. 41–45 or 47). It is God who allows him to share in his work, who keeps him within the limits for him, and who honors him. Looked at in this way, the discourse section in John 5:19–47 is not only, or even primarily, oriented towards Christology. It is and remains theological. In the best tradition of Israel, the fourth evangelist and, within his work, the Christ of his Gospel refer back all action to God, the Father. He works in the Son, he supports him, and he honors him. It is not by chance, therefore, that in the closing verses, 42–44, we come across the chief commandment, the confession of Israel in one God, and the summons to love him. It is from this point that we should reconsider the claim of Jesus in John 5 as well as in the great controversies of John 5–10 taken as a whole.

## 2. The Passover in Galilee (6:1–71)

¹ After this, Jesus went to the other shore of the Sea of Galilee, which is also called the Sea of Tiberias. ² A great crowd followed him because they saw the signs that he was performing on the sick. ³ Jesus went up the mountain and sat down there with his disciples. ⁴ The Passover, the feast of the Jews, was near. ⁵ When Jesus looked up and saw that so many were coming to him, he asked Philip: Where are we to buy bread so that these people may eat? ⁶ He said this only to put him to the test; for he himself knew what he intended to do. ⁷ Philip answered him: Two hundred denarii's worth of bread is not enough if each of them is to have even a little piece. ⁸ One of his disciples, Andrew, the brother of Simon Peter, said to him: ⁹ Here is a small lad who has five barley loaves and two fish; but what is that for so many? ¹⁰ Jesus said: Make the crowd sit down! Now there was much grass there. So they sat down; there were about five thousand men. ¹¹ Then Jesus took the loaves, spoke the thanksgiving and distributed it to the people, as much as they wanted; he did the same with the fish. ¹² When the crowd had been satisfied, he said to his disciples: Gather the fragments that are left over so that nothing is spoiled. ¹³ They gathered and filled twelve baskets with the fragments that were left over from the five barley loaves after the meal. ¹⁴ When the crowd saw the sign that he had done, they said: This is truly the prophet who is to come into the world. ¹⁵ Then Jesus realized that they would come to seize him and make him king. Therefore, he went back up the mountain again, by himself only.

¹⁶ When evening came, his disciples went down to the sea, ¹⁷ got into a boat and went over the water to Capernaum. It was already dark, and Jesus had not yet come to them. ¹⁸ Then the sea became rough with a heavy storm. ¹⁹ When they had gone about twenty-five or thirty stadia, they saw Jesus coming over the sea and approaching the boat; and they were terrified. ²⁰ But he called to them: It is I; do not be afraid! ²¹ They wanted to take him into the boat, but the boat was already at the shore that they had been intending to reach.

²² The next day, the crowd that had remained on the other shore saw that only one boat had been there and that Jesus had not got into the boat with his disciples, but that his disciples had left by themselves. ²³ Other boats came from Tiberias close to the place where they had eaten the bread after the Lord's prayer of thanksgiving. ²⁴ When the people saw that neither Jesus nor his disciples were there, they got into the boats, made for Capernaum, and looked for Jesus. ²⁵ When they found him on the other side of the sea, they asked him: Rabbi, when did you come here? ²⁶ Jesus answered them: Amen, amen, I say to you: You do not seek me because you have seen the signs but because you have eaten the bread and been filled. ²⁷ Do not labor for the food that perishes, but for the food

that lasts to eternal life and that the Son of Man will give you. For God the Father has certified him with his seal.

²⁸ Then they asked him: What have we to do if we are to perform God's work? ²⁹ Jesus answered them: This is the work of God, that you believe in him whom he has sent.

³⁰ They said to him: What sign do you do, then, so that we may see and believe you? What kind of work do you perform? ³¹ Our fathers ate manna in the desert, as it says in Scripture: He gave them bread from heaven to eat. ³² Jesus said to them: Amen, amen, I tell you: It was not Moses that gave you bread from heaven, but my Father gives you the true bread from heaven. ³³ For the bread that God gives comes down from heaven and gives life to the world.

³⁴ Then they asked him: Sir, give us this bread always! ³⁵ Jesus answered them: I am the bread of life; whoever comes to me will never be hungry, and whoever believes in me will never thirst.³⁶ However, I have told you: You saw, and yet you did not believe. ³⁷ All that the Father gives to me will come to me, and whoever comes to me, I will not cast out; ³⁸ for I have come down from heaven, not to do my own will but the will of the one who has sent me, ³⁹ and this is the will of him who sent me, that I let none of those that he has given me perish but that I raise them up at the last day. ⁴⁰ For this is the will of the Father, that whoever sees the Son and believes in him has eternal life and I will raise him up at the last day.

⁴¹ Then the Jews murmured against him because he had said: I am the bread that has come down from heaven. ⁴² And they said: Isn't this Jesus, the son of Joseph, whose father and mother we know? How can he now say: I have come down from heaven? ⁴³ Jesus said to them: Do not murmur! ⁴⁴ No one can come to me unless the Father who has sent me draw him; and I will raise him up at the last day. ⁴⁵ It is written in the prophets: and they shall all be taught by God. Everyone who hears the Father and learned from him will come to me. ⁴⁶ No one has seen the Father except the one who is from God; he alone has seen the Father. ⁴⁷ Amen, amen, I say to you: Whoever believes has eternal life. ⁴⁸ I am the bread of life. ⁴⁹ Your fathers ate manna in the desert and died. ⁵⁰ But this is the bread that comes down from heaven: If someone eats of it, he will never die. ⁵¹ I am the living bread that has come down from heaven. Whoever eats this bread will live for ever. The bread that I shall give is my flesh for the life of the world.

⁵² Then the Jews disputed among themselves: How can he give us his flesh to eat? ⁵³ Jesus said to them: Amen, amen, I say to you: unless you eat the flesh of the Son of Man and drink his blood, you have no life in you. ⁵⁴ Whoever eats my flesh and drinks my blood has eternal life, and I will raise him up at the last day. ⁵⁵ For my flesh is truly food, and my blood is truly drink. ⁵⁶ Whoever eats my

flesh and drinks my blood, dwells in me and I in him. ⁵⁷ As the living Father has sent me and I live because of the Father, so will everyone who eats me and drinks me. ⁵⁸ This is the bread that has come down from heaven. It is not like the bread that your fathers ate and died. Whoever eats this bread will live for ever. ⁵⁹ Jesus spoke these words as he taught in the synagogue at Capernaum.

⁶⁰ Many of his disciples who heard him said: This is a hard saying. Who can listen to it? ⁶¹ Jesus knew that his disciples were murmuring about it and asked them: Are you taking offense at this? ⁶² What will you say when you see the Son of Man ascending where he was before? ⁶³ It is the spirit that gives life; the flesh is useless. The words that I have spoken to you are spirit and life. ⁶⁴ But there are some among you who do not believe. In fact, Jesus knew from the beginning who were the ones who did not believe and who it was who would betray him. ⁶⁵ And he said: That is why I said to you: No one can come to me unless it is given by the Father.

⁶⁶ After that, many of his disciples drew back and no longer went about with him. ⁶⁷ Then Jesus asked the Twelve: Do you want to go away also? ⁶⁸ Simon Peter answered him: Lord, to whom should we go? You have words of eternal life. ⁶⁹ We have come to believe and have recognized: You are the Holy One of God. ⁷⁰ Jesus replied: Have I not chosen you, the Twelve? And yet one of you is a devil. ⁷¹ He spoke of Judas, the son of Simon Iscariot; for he was to betray him: one of the Twelve.

## I

At first sight, John 6 is included in the context of John's Gospel only with difficulty. It is assumed at the beginning of the chapter that Jesus is in Galilee, close to the Sea of Tiberias, while the last thing recounted in ch. 5 was his discourse before the "Jews" subsequent to his healing of the paralytic at the Pool of Bethesda in Jerusalem. There is reference back to this healing on a Sabbath in John 7:14–24. As early as John 7:1, as a reason for a stay of Jesus in Galilee, it is indicated that the "Jews" were seeking to kill him in an allusion to John 5:18. In the course of the twentieth century, these difficulties in fitting the whole thing together led eminent commentators to suggest reversing the sequence of John 5 and 6.⁵⁵ In this way, a more comprehensible text would emerge. Just as at the end of John 4, Jesus finds himself in Galilee at the beginning of John 6. If ch. 5 followed ch. 6,

---

55. Cf. the commentaries of Bernard, Bultmann, Schnackenburg, and Becker.

## Jesus Reveals Himself to His People (5:1–10:42)

then the double reference back to ch. 5 in John 7 would be comprehensible. However, in more recent times, this proposal has not been accepted. Respect for the text before us does not easily permit such or similar conjectures of transposition, and the manuscripts give no kind of evidence for this. At the same time, it is also possible to get some sense out of the present order of the text if one proceeds from the fact that, at least for the final author, geographical and chronological standpoints did not have to constitute the decisive criteria for the sequence of the text.

As already suggested, there are good reasons for considering John 6 an interpolation in John's Gospel. This would likewise solve the problem we have observed in the sequence of the text.[56] The starting point for this is the chapter's literary unity. Only in this chapter of John is the subject the Eucharist, and it is missing in the passion narrative in John 13. Here, in John 6, Jesus apparently does not go to the Passover feast mentioned in v. 4. A Christian Passover seems to replace the Jewish pilgrim feast. Jesus celebrates it in Galilee, homeland of the first Christian communities. His opponents the "Jews" come on the scene from v. 41; they otherwise confront him only in Judaea. In the whole of ch. 6, John appears to be strongly influenced by the Synoptic tradition, especially by Mark 6:32–56 and 8:11–33, as the following table makes clear:

| | | |
|---|---|---|
| Multiplication of bread | Mark 6:32–44 | John 6:1–15 |
| Walking on the water | Mark 6:45–52 | John 6:16–21 |
| Meeting of Jesus with the crowd | Mark 6:53–56 | John 6:22–25(29) |
| Demand for a sign | Mark 8:11–13 | John 6:30–31 |
| Bread discourse | Mark 8:14–21 | John 6:32–58 |
| Identity of Jesus | Mark 8:27–30 | John 6:60–66 |
| Peter's confession | Mark 8:29 | John 6:67–69 |
| One of the disciples is a Satan | Mark 8:31–33 | John 6:70–71 |

The section Mark 7:1–8:10 has no counterpart in John, and thus he also has no second multiplication miracle, though this is also the case with Luke. Within John 6, John follows the Markan or Synoptic text, at times to the very letter. Such details include the two hundred denarii for buying the bread, the number of loaves and fish, the description of Jesus's gestures, the twelve baskets with the remaining bread, and the number of those who had been miraculously fed. Nowhere else in his Gospel does John display

---

56. See the introduction above; cf. Beutler, "Joh 6."

such closeness to the Synoptic tradition. The closest comparison is with the account of the passion, death, and resurrection of Jesus, but here there remain significant differences, beginning with the different chronology of the Last Supper and the death of Jesus. Since John 21, regarded by many as the supplement to the reputed final chapter, reveals strong connections with the Synoptics (cf. for the miraculous catch of fish, Luke 5:1–11 and for the sons of Zebedee, Mark 1:19 par.), it immediately suggests itself that, similarly with John 6, we adopt a somewhat later date of composition by contrast with its context in John's Gospel.

Not least on account of the section concerning the eucharistic gifts of Jesus, the past century often saw doubt cast on the literary unity of the chapter. Thus, Bultmann[57] distinguishes four different layers in John 6: a "signs source" to which we owe the stories of the multiplication of the bread and the stilling of the sea (6:1–15, 16–21); extracts from a Gnostic-inspired source of revelatory discourses occurring, above all, in the bread discourse of John 6:27–51c; the revising hand of the evangelist, similarly, chiefly in the christological part of the bread discourse; and the ecclesiastical redaction containing the "eucharistic" section 6:51d–58, but also the reference to the future resurrection of the dead in 6:39, 40, 44. A similar adjudication of sources continues in the exegesis inspired by Bultmann even if the hypothesis of a Gnostic-influenced "discourse source" appears to have been abandoned.[58]

A simpler model of composition history for John 6 is put forward by Fortna.[59] He ascribes the narrative material of John 6:1–25 to his speculative "signs source" or "predecessor" of John's Gospel, the rest to the evangelist.

A fresh multilayered model is advocated by Paul N. Anderson that starts out from the deposits of the different conflicts that follow one another in John 6.[60] There would have been a first conflict with the crowd about the true food (vv. 25–40); a second with the "Jews" about the Torah and the bread from heaven (vv. 41–51); followed by a schism with the predominantly Gentile disciples of Jesus concerning his true bodiliness (vv. 51–66); and, finally, a controversy about the right place of the Johannine group between the Johannine community and the great Church as

---

57. Bultmann, 154–79.
58. Cf. Becker; Richter, *Studien*; Theobald. Also Schnackenburg, without the theory of an ecclesiastical redaction.
59. Fortna, *Fourth Gospel*; Fortna, *Gospel of Signs*.
60. Anderson, "Sitz im Leben."

represented by Peter (vv. 67-70). Less complicated is the model of Painter,[61] according to whom a "quest story" is taken up first in John 6:1-40 in which the crowd seeks Jesus and finds him. According to him, there then follows, in vv. 41-66, a series of "rejection stories" that were added secondarily. Verses 67-70 would serve the purpose of reconciling the members of the Johannine community with the members of a Christian group for whom the figure of Peter had a decisive significance.

Whether and how far the Fourth Gospel depends directly on the Synoptic Gospels is a matter of continuing controversy. At a conference on the relationship of John's Gospel and the Synoptics in Louvain, François Vouga argued for a direct dependence of John 6 on the Synoptics.[62] Other authors remain more cautious here and reckon rather on the influence of the Synoptic tradition on the composition of John 6.[63]

Alongside the working out of sources for John 6 and the stages of the chapter's composition, there are also studies of its cultural and religious background. In recent decades, such studies have gained in importance. In his work *The Prophet-King,* Meeks starts out from the observation that the Jews want to make Jesus their king after they have seen the sign of the miraculous multiplication of bread—a sign that is rather characteristic for a prophet of Israel (cf. John 6:14-15). Meeks follows the connection between these two titles in the contemporary Jewish literature and finds it chiefly in the figure of Moses as he appears in Hellenistic Judaism. For his part, Borgen investigates the technique of Midrash in Hellenistic Judaism in order to show that John employs these methods in ch. 6 of his Gospel in order to declare Jesus as the bread of life.[64] In the homilies of this period, a Bible text was treated in two sections and then connected with another text. In John 6, John would have treated Ps 78:24 in two parts: "He gave them bread from heaven" (vv. 31-47) and "to eat" (vv. 48-58). Isaiah 54:13, quoted in v. 45 in its Septuagintal form, would have then been the second preaching text. This suggestion provides an alternative to Bultmann's proposed division of the bread discourse according to theological criteria.

Alongside, if not in the place of, investigations of the composition history of John 6, some recent scholars treat the final form of the text

61. Painter, "Jesus and the Quest."
62. Vouga, *Le quatrième évangile.*
63. Cf. Ruckstuhl, "Die Speisung"; Dunderberg, *Johannes und die Synoptiker*; Labahn, *Jesus,* 265-304; Labahn, *Offenbarung.*
64. Borgen, *Bread.*

either from the point of view of narrative research or in an examination of its structure. Culpepper has pursued such contributions and they can be found, among other places, in the volume edited by him that documents a seminar of the Studiorum Novi Testamenti Societas (SNTS).[65] Robert Kysar sees in John 6 a teaching about faith that is based not on human effort but on the grace of God that precedes all human effort.[66] Gail R. O'Day emphasizes the significance of the account of Jesus's stilling of the sea (John 6:16–21), which is often neglected and represented as an interruption of the account of the bread of life.[67] The Johannine account of Jesus's sea miracle differs from that of the Synoptic narratives in that it puts the stress on the theophany and not on the power of Jesus over the wind and waves. This christological reading fits in well with the orientation of the whole chapter.

Francis J. Moloney observes the use of "prolepsis," that is, the anticipation of themes in the narrative strategy of John 6.[68] Thus, the "fragments" of the five loaves, which have to be gathered up after the multiplication of the bread, are already announcing the eucharistic bread provided by Jesus according to verses 51–58. The same goes for Jesus's declaration in v. 27 that he will "give" bread to the disciples and not just be bread for them. With this technique, the author creates the literary unity of the chapter and ensures its coherence.

In his survey,[69] Culpepper is able to note that all the participants in the seminar collection edited by him were in agreement that verses 51c–58, which speak of the eucharistic bread provided for the disciples, belong to the original context. Thus, the theory of Bultmann and his pupils that we have here a later insertion differing from the theology of the evangelist has been abandoned. Numerous exegetes highlight the christological significance of verses 51c–58 such as, for example, M. J. J. Menken in a further article in this collection.[70] Jesus continually forms the center point, in these verses too, which prepare for the mystery of his salvific death.

Fundamental for the synchronic exegesis of John 6 is the determination of the structure of the chapter. On the basis of a suggestion of

65. Cf. Culpepper, *Critical Readings*.
66. Cf. Kysar, "Dismantling."
67. O'Day, "John 6:15–21."
68. Moloney, "Function."
69. Culpepper, "Current Research."
70. Menken, "John 6:51c–58."

## Jesus Reveals Himself to His People (5:1–10:42)

G. A. Philipps,[71] further development is possible here.[72] In the development of the construction of John 6, it is reasonable to start out from the scenic construction of the chapter and not from catchwords or concepts. In the individual scenes, there are indications of place and time, people involved, and plot. Moreover, the discourse of Jesus in verses 22–59 can be divided according to the exchanges between Jesus and his conversation partners.

At the beginning and at the end there are two scenes, both of a narrative nature: at the beginning, we have the accounts of the multiplication of bread (vv. 1–15) and the walking of Jesus on the water (vv. 16–21); at the end, the exchange between Jesus and the disciples subsequent to the discourse on bread (vv. 60–66) and the discourse with Peter over Jesus's identity (vv. 67–71). The first scene (vv. 1–15) and the last (vv. 67–71) match each other in the fact that in them we encounter named disciples. Insofar as these two scenes frame the entire narrative, they highlight the meaning of the chapter for its Christian readers. In the second and penultimate scene, we encounter Jesus and the group of disciples.

Jesus's discourse at the synagogue in Capernaum can be divided into six parts on the basis of the change of speakers: vv. 22–27; 28–29; 30–33; 34–40; 41–51; and 52–58. Furthermore, these sections appear to correspond in a mirror-like fashion. The strongest agreements are found between verses 22–27, on the one hand, and verses 52–59, on the other, with the motifs of the "Son of Man" (vv. 27 and 53), the "gift" of food by Jesus (vv. 27 and 51–52), the "food" itself (vv. 27 and 55), and the theme of "lasting/dwelling" (vv. 27 and 56). Similarly, if not so strong, are the cross-references between the sections 28–29 and 41–51 as well as 30–33 and 34–40. Then, in the center of these discourse sections, stands the saying of Jesus "I am the bread of life" in its first occurrence in v. 35. That does not mean, of course, that the focal point of the chapter would lie simply in this statement. From the pragmatic point of view, the chapter has a linear construction leading to the decision and confession of the disciples as brought to expression by Peter in an exemplary manner: "We have come to believe and have recognized: You are the Holy One of God" (John 6:69).

---

71. Phillips, "Hard Saying."
72. Beutler, "Struktur."

## II

### *The Miraculous Multiplication of Bread (6:1–15)*

The section John 6:1–15 marks the beginning of the cycle of Jesus's activity in Galilee according to John 6:1–71. As already noted, this sequence of scenes does not fit readily into the context of John's Gospel because of the journey by Jesus from Jerusalem to Galilee that is presumed in the text but not recorded. On the other hand, the exegetes also point to connections between chs. 5 and 6 in the Gospel as we have it: in his extensive discourse in John 5:19–47, Jesus refers repeatedly to Moses as a witness in his favor, especially at the conclusion of this discourse (5:45–47). Through this reference, the role of Moses as giver of manna in the desert (John 6:32) is prepared. Israel's wandering through the desert constitutes the background for the entire controversy in John 6:31–58. In this way, John develops the previous chapter further. The authority of Moses will be of key significance in John 7, beginning with v. 19. In this chapter, then, continuity between all three chapters is established.

Also with the account of the miraculous multiplication in John 6:1–15, scholars' opinions of the relationship of the Johannine account to the Synoptics are divided. Among the more recent authors, three models can be distinguished:

- John is independent of the Synoptics; both versions would then have gone back to a common source[73]
- John depends on a proto-Mark[74]
- John uses the Synoptics, mainly Mark, but in greater freedom within the frames of his narrative strategy and his theological aims[75]

We decide in favor of the third model for which important reasons are mentioned by the authors cited. The detailed exegesis will confirm this view.

For the structure of John 6:1–15, there is an attractive proposal by

---

73. Cf Riniker, "Jean 6,1–21"; Barnett, "Feeding."
74. Cf. Fuchs, "Verhältnis."
75. Cf. Konings, "Dialogue"; Mackay, *Relationship*. The model in Labahn, *Offenbarung*, according to whom John would possibly have gone back to Mark after a process of re-oralization, can be reconciled with this point of view. Cf. Labahn, "Jesus," 294 ("secondary orality").

## Jesus Reveals Himself to His People (5:1–10:42)

Johan Konings.[76] The author first notes the affinity of the text with its Synoptic parallels but also those in Exodus and in the Elijah-Elisha cycles. The text itself is arranged concentrically in John: in the beginning, in 6:1–4, there is the *exposition* of the story with the introduction to the scene, the people taking part, etc. The ensuing dialogue of Jesus with Philip and Andrew in 6:5–9 sketches the *problem*, namely the hunger of the crowd. The central part, 6:10–11, sees the *solution* of the problem by Jesus himself. He arranges for the crowd to sit down, blesses the food that they have, and orders it to be distributed. Corresponding to the second part, the fourth, 6:12–13, recounts the *confirmation* of the miracle through the collecting of the pieces left over. The fifth part reverts to the motif of the first and describes the *reactions* to the miracle: the messianic fever of the crowd on account of the sign (cf., already, v. 2) and the withdrawal of Jesus up the mountain mentioned at the outset (v. 3): 6:14–15. It leads over to the following section.

**6:1–4** The first four verses of the narrative introduce the spatial and temporal framework and mention the people taking part. The information about Jesus's change of place takes over traditional motifs (only the "Sea of Tiberias" is Johannine: cf. 21:1), but it stands in tension with the wider context in John as already observed. Jesus is found unexpectedly in Galilee, and, in fact, as it appears, on the west bank of the Sea of Tiberias, and crosses over the sea. The presence of the crowds is not the reason for his withdrawal but rather its consequence. The temporal indications are of a strongly Johannine stamp: the characteristic "after this" (μετὰ ταῦτα) and the mention of the closeness of the Passover feast. John's "mountain" replaces the "lonely place" of the Synoptics. It forms a hook with the mountain to which Jesus returns at the end of the story (v. 15). Also Johannine is the motif of the crowd who follow Jesus because they have seen his signs in the healing of the sick. The only concrete case of this was the healing of the son of the royal official in John 4:46–54. Thus, this reference to the crowd who followed Jesus because they had seen his signs sounds rather traditional (cf. John 2:23; 3:2). The apologists for the hypothesis of a signs source see in this reference a proof for the use of this source in John 6:1–21.

The reference to the imminent Passover feast of the Jews in v. 4 is surprising here. It disrupts the series of Jewish pilgrim feasts since the first Passover of John 2:13 and what we have taken as the Feast of Weeks in John 5:1, and, indeed, Jesus seems not to have set out for Jerusalem for this feast.

---

76. Cf. Konings, "Dialogue," 257.

We have speculated that what we have here in this feast is a Christian *"relecture"* of the Jewish Passover feast under the influence of the "eucharistic" verses, John 6:51c–58, but also of other eucharistic elements in John 6.[77]

**6:5–9** In the following verses, we can observe some features where the fourth evangelist has dramatized an existing story.[78] On the one hand, he singles out individual characters from a group of people; on the other, he creates groups opposed to each other. In the present case, these groups are the disciples and the crowd, and this opposition defines the whole narrative flow of John 6. Thus, the evangelist first picks out from the group of disciples mentioned in v. 3 Philip and Andrew—probably not by chance the same persons mentioned in John 1:43–45 and 12:20–36. It could be added that these disciples with their Greek names were especially suitable as a "bridge" between Jesus and his future disciples. The reference to Peter in v. 8 points back to 1:40–42. Peter will be the disciples' spokesman at the close of the chapter in 6:67–71.

Already, in v. 5, there appears the initiative of Jesus that leads to the miracle. Jesus looks up, sees the huge crowd, and asks Philip how it would be possible to feed so many people or, more precisely, where one could buy provisions for so many. The buying belongs, naturally, to the tradition. John uses the motif so that Jesus can test the faith of the disciples, since he knows already how he is going to satisfy the hunger of the crowd (v. 6). The conversation of Jesus and the Samaritan woman in John 4:6–15 comes to mind here where Jesus is thinking of a drink of which the woman is not yet aware. The question "Where are we to obtain?" recalls Num 11:13 LXX where Moses asks the Lord where he is to obtain the meat to satisfy the crowd.[79]

In Philip's answer, there appears to be a difference between the Synoptic account and that of John: according to the Synoptics, two hundred denarii worth of bread would be enough to satisfy the crowd; for Philip—according to John—it would not be enough. Thus, the motif is intensified. Andrew's contribution in verses 8–9 displays agreements and

---

77. Bergler, *Von Kana in Galiläa nach Jerusalem*, 237f., detects in the Passover feast of John 6:4 "the feast," that is, the Feast of Tabernacles. Daise, *Feasts*, 3f., suspects behind John 6:4 in the original version of John's Gospel (which was more strongly committed to Judaism) a reference to Num 9:9–14. This text mentions a transferred feast of the Passover that was no longer connected with the Feast of Unleavened Bread. This harmonizes badly with the fact that John 6:9 mentions the barley loaves brought by a young lad.

78. Konings, "Dialogue," 572f.

79. Konings, "Dialogue."

## Jesus Reveals Himself to His People (5:1–10:42)

disagreements vis à vis the Synoptic tradition. In both versions, the talk is of five loaves and two fish. In the linguistic expression there are, of course, differences. John speaks of "barley loaves" (ἄρτους κριθίνους) with a specificity not encountered in the Synoptics but certainly found in an account of a multiplication of bread by Elisha in 2 Kgs 4:42 (twenty barley loaves for one hundred people). The description of the fish (ἰχθύες) in John with ὀψάρια shows these as prepared for eating, that is, boiled or roasted (cf. the same expression in John 21:9).

The chief difference between the Synoptic and Johannine accounts lies in the fact that, in John, all the initiatives proceed from Jesus and not from the disciples.

**6:10-11** The instruction for the crowd to sit down belongs to the traditional stock of the narrative. John lacks the detail that the people had to sit down in groups of ten and fifty men. It possibly stems from the dividing up of the people of God during their march through the desert. For its part, the desert does not appear in John; rather the mention is of a place with much grass. In the performance of the miracle itself, John displays several differences with the Synoptic tradition:

- the role of the disciples as helpers is missing
- in John Jesus takes only the bread in his hands, not the fish, which is only mentioned later; the reason is the emphasis on bread in the chapter as a whole
- it is not mentioned that Jesus raised his eyes to heaven, but this motif was already mentioned previously in v. 5
- it is not said that Jesus "broke" the bread before distributing it

Otherwise, regarding the distribution, John uses the same expressions as the Synoptics: Jesus "took the loaves," "spoke the thanksgiving" and "gave" them to the disciples for the distribution. Exegetes point here to the eucharistic tone of what Jesus does (cf. Mark 14:22 par.; 1 Cor 11:23–26). It is even clearer in the Synoptics and Paul, but yet still recognizable in John.

**6:12-13** The miracle itself is not narrated, by contrast with the Synoptics that record that they all ate and were filled (Mark 6:42 par.). John says only: "When the crowd had been satisfied," as though it were the most natural thing in the world for five thousand men to be satisfied with five loaves and two fish. The circumstance is explained certainly by the fact that the miracle was well known from the common Christian tradition. Another deviation from the Synoptic tradition is that Jesus instructs the disciples to gather together the pieces that were left over after the meal. The exegetes see in this element an emphasis on the role of the disciples and, perhaps, at the same time, a eucharistic element as well.

**6:14–15** The end of the Johannine account has no counterpart in the Synoptic texts. The miracle performed by Jesus is "seen" by the men and discerned as a "sign" with an expression that has already been encountered at the beginning of the chapter (v. 2). Instead of seeing in this expression proof for the use of a "signs source," it may be sufficient to recognize this understanding of Jesus's action as the messianic and eschatological belief of the crowd who had not yet reached a mature faith in Jesus—in the sense of the Fourth Gospel—as the consubstantial Son of the Father sent for the salvation of men. Jesus is not a new Moses, prophet, and king, but the only-born Son of God; but, at the same time, he is the Son of Man who will have to be lifted up from the earth in order to draw all to himself (cf. 12:32). For this reason Jesus returns up the mountain, all alone.

From the dramatic point of view, this last scene is surprising. Jesus remains all alone on the mountain. He was alone also at the beginning but followed by the crowd. This crowd surrounded him and led to dialogue with the disciples. In the middle of the narrative, Jesus is surrounded by this group of disciples. Then the crowd follows again and receives Jesus's miraculous food. At the end, after the collection of the remaining pieces, Jesus remains alone once more, having returned up the mountain. This is an indication of the christological orientation that defines the whole chapter. The readers ask themselves: who is this Jesus who does not wish to be the prophet-king of his people, and where does his future path lead? The following sections of the chapter will answer such questions. This goes especially for the closing section, 6:67–71, which, as we have seen, forms a bracket with 6:1–15. Peter will confess Jesus as the Holy One of God. However, the reference to Judas will also introduce the subject of Jesus's forthcoming death.

*Jesus's Walking on the Sea (6:16–21)*

At first sight, the narrative of Jesus's miraculous crossing of the Sea of Tiberias seems a foreign body within John 6. There are only sparse references to the previous context with its miraculous multiplication of bread and to the following one with its discourse on the bread of life. The element that links the section most strongly with the basic theme of the bread of life is

## Jesus Reveals Himself to His People (5:1–10:42)

the formula by which Jesus identifies himself to the disciples in the boat: "It is I" (v. 20). As will be shown, this formula is of great significance for the connection of the account of the walking on the sea with the following discourse of Jesus in which Jesus describes himself with the words: "I am the bread of life" (John 6:35, 48, 51), a formula that draws on the linguistic treasury of the Old Testament.

All exegetes are agreed that in the sequence of scenes in John 6, John is following the outline of Mark. Thus, in his Gospel too, the story of the multiplication is followed by that of the walking on the water (cf. Mark 6:45–52 par. Matt 14:22–33). It still remains open here whether John is following this sequence simply because of tradition or whether he is also linking it up with his own theological insights.

For the prehistory of the present passage there exist in scholarship the same models that have already been indicated in the introduction to chapter 6.[80] Right up to the present, source-critical explanations are being proposed. For Bultmann and the authors following him, but also for Schnackenburg, the story of the walking on the water goes back to the hypothetical "signs source" in which it would have followed the account of the multiplication of bread. Other authors think that John would have used the Synoptics, albeit in freer form. Today, this theory meets with increasing agreement. John writes for a community or a group of communities in which the Markan tradition can be presupposed. Of course, times have changed. The role of the disciples must be delineated afresh— from the hearers of Jesus with little understanding and belief in Mark to a paradigmatic role of faith in John. The Christology too has to conform to the characteristic form of confession of the Johannine community. In the Johannine account, therefore, one may expect not just variants of those of Mark or Matthew but should see in it a *"relecture"* of their texts in the light of the faith experiences of the Johannine community. According to this model, John will not simply be a "fourth Synoptic," despite quite a few verbal agreements, but reveals himself to be an interpreter of the Synoptic tradition in the light of his time.[81]

Various suggestions as to tradition- and form-history have been made as to the background of the Johannine story of the walking on the water.

---

80. Cf. the first chapter of Madden, *Jesus' Walking*.

81. Madden, *Jesus' Walking*, sees the origin of the Johannine sea story in John 21:1–14, thus in a post-Easter appearance story. The appearance and walking "on the shore of the Sea of Tiberias" (ἐπὶ τῆς θαλάσσης τῆς Τιβεριάδος) would have become an appearance and walking "on the Sea of Tiberias."

Bultmann points to parallels in Buddhism where the motif of the crossing of the waters by men with superhuman powers is found.[82] Closer to the New Testament environment are the examples of this motif in Hellenistic texts.[83] These texts belong to the genre of epiphanies that can be experienced by a group of seafarers in peril on the sea. An example may be adduced here: Diodorus Siculus narrates in his book (4.43) the experience of seafarers who were in danger one night. They implored the gods of Samothrace for help. At this moment, the stars became visible again in the sky. This experience was explicitly credited to the Dioscuri.[84] In other texts, the Dioscuri were carried over the sea by their horses.[85] Correspondingly, the heroes also had this ability.[86] In some cases, the credibility of such powers was debated, perhaps as in a well-known passage of Lucian.[87] A positive example was also ascribed to Xerxes by Dio Chrysostom.[88] This example is significant since it seems to link the capacity to cross water with Xerxes' kingly dignity. Thus the question arises whether Jesus's ability to cross the water is perhaps connected with the attempt to make him king (v. 15), an attempt that Jesus rejects but will later reinterpret (cf. John 18:36–37).

Passages from the Old Testament-Jewish tradition have at least the same weight as these Hellenistic texts. For the walking on the water and the rescue of the disciples in the boat from their peril on the sea, scholars point to biblical passages as well as to the intertestamental Jewish literature. The book of Job is sometimes indicated where it says: "It is he who alone stretched out the heavens and walks about the sea as on dry land" (Job 9:8 LXX). The crossing through the Red Sea (Exod 14) and the passage over the Jordan by Elijah and Elisha in 2 Kgs 2:8, 14 also come to mind. A further, often quoted text is Ps 107:23–30. Here, there is praise of God who gives his presence and help to a group of sailors so that they can safely reach their harbor.

This last element is important for John Paul Heil.[89] According to him, the basis of the account of the sea miracle is a literary genre of "Rescue-Epiphany-Stories." More particularly, with the last cited text, as with sim-

---

82. Cf. Bultmann, *Geschichte*, 252.
83. Cf. Bultmann, *Geschichte*, 251f.; Labahn, *Offenbarung*, with examples, 202–10.
84. Cf. Labahn, *Offenbarung*, 205.
85. Cf. Alkaios.
86. Cf. Euphemos.
87. Cf. Lucian, *Philopseudes*, 13, cited in Labahn, *Offenbarung*, 207.
88. *Or.* 3.31.
89. Heil, *Jesus Walking*.

ilar ones such as Testament of Naphtali 6.1–10, the subject is rather the rescue of a group of sailors from a storm though divine intervention. This motif is found in Mark 4:35–41 par., less clearly in Mark 6:45–52, and almost not at all in John 6:16–21.

Moreover, because the history of religions derivations proposed for the sea miracle in John 6:16–21 are not entirely satisfactory, more recent attempts at exegesis start out from the present Johannine text. Already, in his commentary, Schnackenburg saw the connection between the reported epiphany of Jesus in our text with the repeated "Ego eimi" ("It is I") and the following bread discourse. Giblin opposes the explanation of the scene through a "rescue-epiphany-story" genre whose very existence he questions.[90] In John 6:16–21, the emphasis lies chiefly on the disciples. Jesus "appears" to them and causes them to reach the shore, also a symbol of their vocation as apostles. Other similar contributions start out similarly from the present text.[91]

In what follows, our exegesis will be aligned above all with those authors who allow the text to speak for itself in its present form. With Giblin,[92] we can divide the passage into two subsections: vv. 16–18 the situation of the disciples before Jesus's arrival and vv. 19–21 his actions on behalf of the group of disciples. This division is supported by the observation that John 6:16–21 is written mainly from the point of view of the disciples.

**6:16–18** The small textual unit is framed by information as to place and time. After the multiplication of bread, it is late (v. 16), indeed, already dark (v. 17). In John's symbolic world, such information also has an emblematical character. Nicodemus comes to Jesus by night (John 3:2), not yet enlightened by the teaching of Jesus. Similarly, when Judas leaves the group of disciples in order to betray Jesus, it is at night (John 13:30). In John 6, the night signifies the time of fear and danger. This symbol is well matched with that of the sea, since the oldest times a world of menace and of powers revolting against God. This threat is supplemented by the strong wind spoken of in v. 18. This wind forms part of the scenery, without becoming a dominating motif, as will be shown in what follows (at the moment of Jesus's arrival, it does not say that the wind is stilled, by contrast with Mark 4:35–41 par.).

---

90. Giblin, "Miraculous Crossing," in a critical dispute with Heil, *Jesus Walking*.
91. Cf. O'Day, "John 6:15–21"; Mackay, *John's Relationship*; also, Labahn, *Offenbarung*, at the end of its section in 202–10; Marguerat, "Le point de vue," 95.
92. Giblin, "Miraculous Crossing."

As noticed by Giblin,[93] the information from the scene and regarding the situation of the disciples frames the statement in v. 17 that Jesus had not yet come to the disciples. With respect to style, one can identify a prolepsis here, an anticipation of the arrival of Jesus that is recounted in v. 19. Looked at rhetorically, a contrast emerges between the situation of the disciples before and after the coming of their Lord. As for the semantic field, the disciples' situation before the coming of Jesus is characterized by the night (disorientation and danger) and by the high sea (a hostile element to men who dwell on the land). The wind is added to this hostile and threatening element. This wind whips up high waves that assail the disciples' boat and threaten to capsize it. Distance is also important in this account in that still, as from the beginning of v. 19, the disciples find themselves far from shore.

**6:19–21** Verses 19–21 describe the disciples' situation after the arrival of Jesus. At this moment, they are still well out at sea, about 25 to 30 stadia, that is, 4.5 to 5.6 km from the shore. Then they see Jesus walking on the sea and approaching their boat (v. 19). The sight of him fills them with terror. Then Jesus calls out to them: "It is I. Do not be afraid" (v. 20).

Exegetes propose two models for understanding this scene. Its first meaning is clearly christological. A representative of this meaning is O'Day.[94] According to her, the meaning of this scene lies in the words with which Jesus lets himself be recognized by the disciples and not in his walking on the water. These words are not a formula of identification as in the parallel Synoptic accounts in which the terrified disciples believe that they have seen a ghost. John has changed this formula of identification into one of revelation: "It is I." This recalls similar expressions in Deutero-Isaiah with which God reveals himself to his people as their redeemer (Isa 43:25; 51:12; 52:6). In a related formula, God commands his people not to be afraid (Isa 43:1; 44:2, 8). The appearing of the divinity and the command not to be afraid belong to the genre of epiphanies (cf. Gen 15:1; Luke 1:30). The epiphany of Jesus in John 6:16–21 fits well in the context, between the discourse of Jesus about his dignity and his participation in the works reserved to God in John 5:19–30 and the self-revelation discourse of John 6:22–58.

Other authors, such as Giblin,[95] see the main emphasis in John 6:16–21 on the disciples. Before the arrival of Jesus, they are well out in the lake.

---

93. Cf. the previous note.
94. O'Day, "John 6:15–21."
95. Giblin, "Miraculous Crossing."

*Jesus Reveals Himself to His People (5:1–10:42)*

On seeing Jesus, they are overcome with terror (v. 19). Jesus's word gives them courage after his appearance has frightened them. They have not yet understood what it means for them to have Jesus with them. Thus, they want to take him into the boat. They have not understood that with Jesus they have reached the other shore. Instead of seeing in his sudden arrival simply a "mini-miracle within the miracle," it is better to recognize John's symbolic world in this detail: united with Jesus, the disciples have reached their goal. Giblin recalls two similar texts here: the fruit that Jesus promises to those vines that remain joined to him (John 15:5), and the joy of the harvest that he promises to the laborers (John 4:35–38).

### *Jesus's Bread of Life Discourse (6:22–59)*

The account of the miraculous multiplication of bread (John 6:1–15) and Jesus walking on the Sea of Tiberias (John 6:16–21) is followed by a longer section of John 6 that is characterized by dialogues and by speeches of Jesus. In John 6:22–59, scholars often speak of the "bread of life discourse." This can be justified, though the section consists rather of a series of dialogues. Earlier on (see above, I), dividing John 6:22–59 into six exchanges of speech between Jesus's conversation partners and himself was suggested: vv. 22–27; 28–29; 30–33; 34–40; 41–51; 52–59. Only a few authors choose this means of division, but it is recommended by a look at the narrative structure of the section.

There are still some authors who reckon on a development of the text even in the bread of life discourse of John 6. Bultmann's suggestion to regard the eucharistic section, John 6:51c–58, as an interpolation of the "ecclesiastical redactor" is still influential.[96] As already mentioned, of course, all the participants of a seminar of the SNTS were agreed that these verses are an integral part of the chapter.[97] Painter's suggestion,[98] to distinguish in John 6 a "quest story" in verses 1–40 and a "rejection story" in verses 41–58 in which the words of Jesus are rejected by the Jews, was an isolated contribution within the seminar. At the same time, Painter also thinks that John 6:51c–58 belongs to its literary context (from v. 41).

---

96. He is followed, among others, by Roulet and Ruegg, "Étude de Jean 6"; cf., also, the commentary of Theobald.
97. Cf. Culpepper, *John 6*.
98. Painter, "Jesus."

In what follows, John 6:22–59 will be read as a coherent text. Here, two possibilities are considered. The first reads the text with a focus on its content. Christology forms the midpoint of the section. This method is preferred by the majority of exegetes. Naturally, one can also treat the text from the point of view of the readers. This kind of treatment (the so-called reader's response) is chosen by Kysar.[99] He investigates John 6:25–71 from the point of view of the faith journey of the readers. Two kinds of faith can be distinguished: faith as one's own effort, and faith as the gift of God. The evangelist certainly prefers the second and negates the first. It is a good idea to keep this kind of treatment in view in the interest of the working out of the textual pragmatics.

There is no agreement about the beginning of the so-called bread of life discourse. Some think that it begins in v. 30 with the question of the crowd and Jesus's answer that mentions for the first time bread from heaven given by the Father. Others reckon that the discourse begins in v. 25 with the first question of the crowd. In the following, we shall choose a third possibility: joining together the introduction to the scene in verses 22–25 with the following exchange of speech. In fact, verses 22–25a prepare the question of the crowd in v. 25b. In verses 22–25, we already find important concepts that will be significant for the discourse or the following dialogues. In particular, we have here a preparation for the eucharistic theme of verses 52–59. In this connection, we should recall the concentric construction of John 6 from which this correspondence results.

Alongside these concentric structures a linear structure can be detected.[100] In the first four verbal exchanges between John 6:22 and 6:40, Jesus finds himself in conversation with the crowd. From v. 42 on, he is in dialogue with the "Jews," from 6:60 with the disciples, and from v. 67 with the "Twelve." Thus it is possible to observe an increasing relevance with regard to the personal concerns of the readership.

**6:22–27** In the verses that lead to the bread of life discourse, there is, first of all, an account of the arrival of Jesus and that of the crowd that will form his audience. The meaning of these introductory verses is much discussed, and there are one or two text-critical problems to deal with. The scene is not so implausible as occasionally observed. The crowd remaining after the departure of the disciples and Jesus's withdrawal up the mountain deduces the departure of the disciples on account of the absence

---

99. Kysar, "Dismantling."
100. Cf. Kysar, "Dismantling."

## Jesus Reveals Himself to His People (5:1–10:42)

of their boats (with the exception of one boat). The arrival of other boats from Tiberias allow them—as a "deus ex machina"—to cross the sea. The question as to how a crowd of five thousand men (and their families) could cross the sea with a few boats does not trouble the narrator. For him, other details are more important: The crowd is looking for Jesus. The boats arrive at the place where the crowd had eaten "the bread" (in the singular, perhaps as an announcement of what is to follow) that Jesus had given them after "the Lord's prayer of thanksgiving" (v. 23). This element too has a eucharistic tone.

When the crowd has found Jesus, they ask him: "Rabbi, when did you come here?" It is worth comparing the question of the crowd with Jesus's answer. The crowd are interested in the time of Jesus's arrival. Jesus does not answer this question but alters the line of questioning. For him, what is significant is the reason for their arrival. They have come because they have received from Jesus enough physical bread to satisfy them. From this kind of receiving, they must progress to the desire for the true food, that of eternal life, which the Son of Man will hand over to the crowd.

In the structure for John 6 and the bread of life discourse that we have previously suggested, we have seen that verses 22–27 correspond to the last section of the discourse, verses 52–58, the so-called eucharistic section. Among others, the lexical correspondences between the two sections are ἄρτος ("bread"), βρῶσις ("food"), ὁ υἱὸς τοῦ ἀνθρώπου ("the Son of Man"), ζωὴ αἰώνιος ("eternal life"), and διδόναι ("give"). Both sections deal with the bread that the Son of Man gives or will give, not with that with which he identifies himself (as in 6:35–51b). It is also recalled where the crowd had eaten the bread "after his prayer of thanksgiving," a further eucharistic feature.

**6:28–29** The following short section shows the continuation of the misunderstandings. The crowd has grasped that one must do the will of God in order to attain eternal life. At the same time, the people in the crowd understand the will of God in the sense of the Mosaic commandments: doing the works of God. The only question that then remains is, which works are these? Jesus's answer does not follow this paradigm. To attain eternal life, the works of Jewish piety are not necessary; only one work is required: to believe in Jesus as the one sent by God. "The works" are thus replaced by "the work." For this idea, cf. John 4:34, where Jesus says: "My food is to do the will of the one who has sent me and to finish his work," and 17:4 in Jesus's last prayer: "I have glorified you on the earth and finished the work that you gave me to do." The will of God consists not in a number of good or prescribed works but in the total commitment to God in obedience (for Jesus) and in faith (for the others), a faith that finds its only reference and focal point in Jesus as the one sent from God.

**6:30–33** The next exchange leads to the theme of the bread from heaven. The theme of "believing/faith" provides the cue. The crowd remain with the paradigm of the "prophet-king" corresponding to Moses. So they demand a sign from Jesus to justify his claim about the kind of faith required. In their choice of example, as pointed out by Zumstein,[101] the crowd refers to the literary background of the whole of ch. 6: the account of the Exodus and the gift of manna. Thus, they take as their example the gift of manna from heaven as recorded in Ps 78(77):24, a text that relies on Exod 16:4, 15. It was through a sign like this that Moses received his legitimacy. What similar signs will Jesus work? (vv. 30–31).

Jesus does not reject this demand for a sign, but he corrects the Exodus tradition as reported by the crowd and interprets it anew.[102] With a solemn introductory formula, he explains that it was not Moses who gave the bread from heaven, but his (i.e., Jesus's) Father, and not just once sometime in the past, but now. As Borgen has noticed,[103] John employs here the rabbinic technique of "read not this but that." Do not read "gave," but "gives." Moreover, Jesus corrects the crowd's conception that it was Moses who gave the bread from heaven; it was not Moses but God who gave it. The third difference underlined by Jesus lies in the fact that the Father gives the bread from heaven, "for the life of the world," not just for Israel on its march through the desert. This bread is identified with the bread that has come down from heaven to give life to the world. There remains a further difference to be added: John's Jesus is speaking not of the bread that was "given" from heaven but of a bread that "comes down" from heaven (ὁ καταβαίνων ἐκ τοῦ οὐρανοῦ). Thereby, the Johannine vocabulary of Jesus coming or coming down is adopted (cf. John 3:13; 6:38, 41–42, 50–51, 58), the one that corresponds to his "ascent" to the Father (cf. John 3:13; 6:62; 20:17).

According to Borgen, this is the beginning of a passage that was conceived to correspond to the Jewish homily.[104] The preacher begins with a quotation from Scripture or the tradition. According to Borgen,

---

101. Zumstein, "Schriftrezeption."
102. Zumstein, "Schriftrezeption," 131–34.
103. Borgen, *Bread*, 62.
104. Borgen, *Bread*, 33–43.

## Jesus Reveals Himself to His People (5:1–10:42)

it would have been a *haggadah*; according to Menken,[105] it would have been Ps 78(77):24-25. In verses 32-47, Jesus exegetes the first half of the quotation: "He gave them bread from heaven"; in verses 48-58, the second half: "to eat." As the homily progresses, the first text is expounded by at least a second one. In our case, this would be Isa 54:13, which is quoted in John 6:45. Zumstein is not convinced by this suggestion since the style of the dialogue between Jesus and the crowd or the "Jews" is not that of the homily.[106] His reasons have to be taken seriously. It is reasonable, therefore, to see in John 6 first and foremost a *"relecture"* of the Exodus cycle in general and of the gift of manna in particular (with Exod 16 as "Hypotext" and John 6 as "Hypertext").[107]

**6:34-40** The following exchange leads to the theme of the true bread. It begins once again with a misunderstanding. The crowd have thought that Jesus has promised them a bread from heaven that gives life. So they ask Jesus to give them this bread forever (v. 34). The request recalls that of the woman of Samaria in John 4:15: "Sir, give me this water so that I may not thirst anymore and not have to come here to draw water." The woman had not understood that the water Jesus had offered to her was of another nature. Similarly too, the crowd in John 6 remains preoccupied by everyday needs and has not understood that what Jesus is giving is himself. Jesus repeats anew his promise to the woman of Samaria: "Whoever drinks from the water that I shall give him will never thirst again" (John 4:14). This promise corresponds to that of John 6:35: "I am the bread of life; whoever comes to me, will never be hungry, and whoever believes in me, will never thirst." Texts like these are inspired by wisdom literature,[108] but go beyond it as the comparison with Sir 24:21 shows ("those who eat me will hunger for more, and those who drink me will thirst for more"). The deeper reason for this difference lies in the fact that Jesus not only gives, but also is, the bread of life.

The following section speaks of access to this bread of life (vv. 36–40). These verses are framed by the "seeing" of Jesus, the Son of Man (vv. 36 and 40). The crowd have seen Jesus but not believed in him (v. 36). The reason for this lies less in the crowd themselves than in the fact that they have not been called by the Father (v. 37). All that Jesus has been

---

105. Menken, *Quotations*, 47–65.
106. Zumstein, "Schriftrezeption," 130f.
107. Cf. Zumstein, "Schriftrezeption."
108. Cf. Strotmann, "Die göttliche Weisheit."

given by the Father he accepts and he rejects no one. But whoever is not chosen by God and has not been sent to Jesus by the Father does not come to Jesus, the source of life. We are here confronted with the Johannine version of predestination, which is not easy to unravel. In this place, it may be sufficient to indicate that nowhere is there predestination to the loss of eternal life. The texts confine themselves to the statement that no one comes to Jesus who is not drawn by Jesus and taught by the Father (cf. 6:45). Jesus's mission is something positive: he has come to fulfill his Father's will, and this will consists in the gift of eternal life for all who have been given to Jesus to be saved (vv. 38–40). This gift of eternal life is consummated in the resurrection of the dead. According to Bultmann and his school, the words "I will raise him up at the last day" in verses 39, 40, and 44 would be an addition of the "ecclesiastical redaction" of the Fourth Gospel. Today, especially after the studies of Frey,[109] this notion has but a few champions. One can ask whether, in these verses, the preposition ἐν belongs to the original text given that it is missing in credible ancient witnesses (like Papyri 66 and 75 as well as in Codex Vaticanus) and correspondingly is put into brackets by Nestle-Aland[28]. If the text is read without the preposition, the dative could be understood in the sense of "raise up *for* the last day." Such an understanding of Jesus's word would be easier to reconcile with John's realized eschatology. The suggestion is put forward here only as a hypothesis.[110]

**6:41–51** The ensuing exchange is divided between the "murmuring" of the Jews and their offense at Jesus's claims in verses 41–42, and Jesus's answer to the unspoken question in verses 43–51. There is no reason to assign the passage, which begins now and goes on to the end of the bread of life discourse, to a more recent literary layer, perhaps on the ground that the "Jews" appear here for the first time as Jesus's increasingly critical audience.[111] If from here on the "crowd" becomes "the Jews," then we probably have Johannine usage to thank for this. The "Jews" have been Jesus's classical opponents in John since the first chapter (1:19). They are otherwise at home in Jerusalem, which is one of the reasons for regarding John 6 as a "*relecture.*" If and insofar as Jesus's conversation partners refuse to come to faith, they become "Jews." This is apparent in the scenes that

---

109. Frey, *Eschatologie*; see the comments above on John 5:28–29.

110. Less plausible appears the proposal of Seitz, "Wann werden die Toten auferstehen?," to refer the "last day" to the last day of the dead person's life.

111. Thus the suggestion of Painter, "Jesus."

## Jesus Reveals Himself to His People (5:1–10:42)

follow the healing of the man born blind in John 9. Here, the talk is first of the "Pharisees" (vv. 13 and 15) and then of the "Jews" who show themselves to be without faith (v. 18; cf. 22).

The "murmuring" is part of the Exodus theme.[112] According to Exod 16:2, the Israelites "murmured" against Moses and Aaron in the desert because they had no bread and lusted after the fleshpots of Egypt (διεγόγγυζεν πᾶσα συναγωγὴ υἱῶν Ἰσραήλ). The agreement of vocabulary and content supports the thesis of Zumstein that the whole chapter of John is a hypertext on the hypotext Exod 16.[113] The reason for the Israelites' protest against Jesus is naturally different from that of the children of Israel. Jesus is not being reproached for the lack of bread but for his claim to be the bread that comes from heaven. This claim appears to be incredible because his father and his mother are known.

Jesus's answer to the reproach (which is not uttered in express terms) consists of two parts. In the first part (vv. 43–47), Jesus stresses the necessity for the grace of faith in order to be able to understand his claims. In the second part, Jesus claims anew that he is the bread come down from heaven, and strengthens the impact of this claim with the statement that the bread that he will give is his flesh for the life of the world (vv. 48–51).

The disbelief of the "Jews" meets with no direct answer from Jesus. At the beginning of his words, Jesus shows that he knows about the murmuring of the Jews. Thus, once again, he shows his knowledge of hearts as he has already done in his conversation with Nathanael (1:47–48) or with the woman of Samaria (4:18–19; cf., also, 2:24–25; 6:15). Already on this ground, Jesus has no need to demonstrate his credibility in order to claim that he is the bread from heaven. The problem lies not in the fact that his claim is unverified but in the incapacity of his audience to understand and accept his message. The deeper ground for this incapacity lies in the fact that all who are not able to believe in him have not been drawn to him by the Father in order to have the eternal life that will be perfected at the day of resurrection. For the one who comes to him, the prophecy of Isaiah must be fulfilled: "They will all be taught by God" (Isa 54:13), a promise from the time of the Exile that is related to that of the New Covenant according to Jer 31:33.[114] In this element of the "all" there also lies some

---

112. Cf. Labahn, "Die Wüste lebt."
113. Cf. Zumstein, "Schriftrezeption."
114. According to Witmer, "Overlooked Evidence," John has allowed the quotation from Isa 54:13 to begin with "and" as in the original text. He replaces only "your sons" with

encouragement. Of itself, the divine plan of salvation excludes no one. It is enough to hear the voice of the Father and allow oneself to be instructed by Jesus in order to come to him. Jesus remains the sole means of access to the Father whom no one else has ever seen (cf.1:18!).

According to Borgen, v. 48 marks the second half of the homily that would be supporting the *haggadah* of John 6:31: "He gave them bread from heaven to eat."[115] While verses 32–47 would be treating the first half of the Jewish (according to others biblical) tradition, verses 48–58 concern the second half of the text: "to eat." The suggestion retains its weight even if our text does not correspond fully to the Jewish preaching of this period. The small text unit of vv. 48–51 is framed by the twofold statement of Jesus: "I am the bread of life" (v. 48) or "I am the living bread that has come down from heaven" (v. 51). The arguments that were brought against the claims of Jesus are not refuted with reasons but simply rejected with the repeated statement of who Jesus is. The fact that the fathers died in the desert shows the inadequacy of the bread imparted to them. The bread that Jesus promises and that he himself is leads to eternal life and protects against death.[116] That this bread leads to eternal life is not something one can understand with reason, but is accepted in faith.

The section ends with an unexpected twist: "The bread that I shall give is my flesh for the life of the world" (v. 51c). It is better not to be too quick in ascribing a eucharistic sense to this statement. Anderson underlines the aspect of giving for his own that comes to expression in the Johannine formula.[117] Jesus surrenders his flesh on the cross and becomes an example for all who believe in him and are invited to surrender their lives in trust to the will of God.[118] On the other hand, the eucharistic tone of the verses is indisputable. Especially striking is the influence of the words of institution of the Eucharist according to Luke (22:19) and Paul (1 Cor 11:24). The formula "for you" (ὑπὲρ ὑμῶν) in Luke and Paul is replaced in John with "for the life of the world" (ὑπὲρ τῆς τοῦ κόσμου ζωῆς), just as the evangelist also replaces "body" (σῶμα) with "flesh" (σάρξ)—an expression

---

"all" and clarifies the eschatological meaning with ἔσονται. The new interpretation of the new covenant here is highlighted by Theobald, "Gottes-Gelehrtheit."

115. Borgen, *Bread*, 35.
116. The dimensions of this life are unfolded by Stare, *Durch ihn leben*.
117. Anderson, "Sitz im Leben."
118. Sapiential interpretations of the eucharistic section in John 6 are also presented by Menken, "John 6:51c–58." He himself disputes a eucharistic meaning for these verses and interprets them metaphorically.

that is not found in this connection in the Synoptic tradition or in Paul, but in Ignatius of Antioch and Justin.[119]

**6:52–59** The last exchange of the discourse on the bread of life concerns the question of how Jesus can give his flesh to eat. Verse 52 leads into this line of questioning in which it soon becomes apparent that no genuine dialogue is taking place here. The Jews' murmuring in verses 41 and 43 has a double aspect: discussion among themselves and protest. The verb γογγύζω and the substantive γογγυσμός are used consistently by John in this sense (cf. 6:61; 7:12: difference of opinion; 7:32). The word μάχεσθαι in v. 52 has a similar sense: "Then the Jews disputed among themselves: How can he give us his flesh to eat?" A careful reading of the text reveals that the "Jews" are protesting against a claim that Jesus has not actually made. He had spoken of his self-surrender as bread of life and identified this bread with his flesh without expressing the need for eating this flesh in a physical sense.

If this interpretation is correct, then one can say that, in his answer from v. 53 on, Jesus is responding to a misunderstanding. We could paraphrase his answer thus: "I have not said that you must eat my flesh, but, if you want, we can stick with that: yes, you have to eat my flesh and drink my blood in order to have eternal life." This statement is introduced with a solemn formula ("Amen, amen, I say to you") and linked with a title that simultaneously expresses the humanity and the divine majesty of Jesus: the "Son of Man." Many exegetes understand this title in the sense of John 3:13: the Son of Man who has descended from heaven is returning to heaven. Moloney criticizes this view and would prefer to understand the Johannine Son of Man from Dan 7:13–14, 15–27.[120] The sovereignty of "one like a Son of Man" is identified with the sovereignty of the sons of the Most High after the victory over the empire of the beast. The "Son of Man" would thus be a title that is connected with suffering and only then with salvation and majesty. Closer, perhaps, is a view of the Johannine Son of Man drawn from the servant. According to Isa 52:13 LXX, the latter must be "lifted up and glorified," two key concepts of Johannine Christology.[121]

In verses 55–57, the evangelist deepens the instruction of Jesus in verses 53–54. In a causal statement, the Johannine Jesus repeats his statement that

---

119. Cf. Ignatius, *Rom.* 7.3; *Phld.* 4; *Sm.* 7.1; Justin, *1 Apol.* 66.2, cited by Menken, "John 6:51c–58," 188. There too for the eucharistic sense of αἷμα.

120. Cf. Moloney, *Johannine Son of Man*.

121. Cf. Beutler, "Griechen."

his flesh is truly food and his blood is truly drink (v. 55). The adverb "truly" can have different meanings. In John, it is often employed for what is real and of lasting value as against mere appearance. In John 6:55, the sense is rather: my flesh is really food to eat, not just a symbol. Whoever eats the flesh of Jesus and drinks his blood dwells in him and vice versa (v. 56). The formula of "dwelling in" anticipates a theme that will be developed further in the farewell discourses of Jesus in chs. 13–17, especially in 15–17.[122] The most graphic text is the *Bildrede* of the vine and the branches in 15:4–8. However, the theme is also deepened in Jesus's prayer in John 17.

The verb τρώγω "chew" is even more radical than "eat" (ἐσθίειν and φαγεῖν) and is found in John only here and in the quotation of a psalm in John 13:18. In the face of the concrete nature of this expression, it is difficult to agree with the metaphorical understanding of Menken.

Just as in the farewell discourses the basis of the unity of the disciples with Jesus is Jesus's own union with the Father (cf. the texts cited above), the same goes for John 6:57. The closeness of John 6:52–58 to Jesus's farewell discourses, especially to John 15–17, supports the theory that John 6 was added in a secondary revision of the Gospel.

In v. 57, we should note the identification of Jesus with the gift that he is handing over, that is, his flesh. One could say: "Whoever eats me." The giver is present in the gift. This identification is significant for understanding the closing verses of the discourse.

The identification of Jesus with the bread he gives for salvation is continued in the last verse of the discourse: v. 58. The formula: "This is the bread that has come down from heaven" takes v. 50 literally, and the contrast with the fathers in the desert who ate and died goes back to v. 49. It is possible to recognize in this (chiastic) restatement the technique of inclusio that holds together the section of verses 48–59. This would confirm the proposal of Borgen,[123] according to whom these verses form the second part of Jesus's "homily" about the bread of life after the first part in verses 32–47. This would also be made clear by the catchword "bread," which does not appear again after v. 51. At the same time, we are prepared for the objection of the "disciples" that Jesus is claiming to have come down from heaven (vv. 60–65).

The concluding note in v. 59 is similar to other conclusions in John 1:28; 8:20. From the literary point of view, the mention of Capernaum con-

---

122. Cf. Scholtissek, *In ihm sein*.
123. Cf. Borgen, *Bread*, 35.

firms the inclusio of John 6:52–59 with 6:22–25 and the nature of 6:22–25 as an introduction to the discourse on bread instead of these verses forming an independent section.[124]

Jesus's teaching "in the synagogue" is presupposed in his answer to the high priest (John 18:20), but otherwise never mentioned. This feature is developed more strongly in the Synoptics, but retains some significance for John too.[125]

### Jesus and the Disciples (6:60–66)

The last twelve verses of John 6 throw up a series of questions. The first is why, in v. 60, we have another change in the description of Jesus's audience: after the "crowd" (vv. 20–40) and the "Jews" (vv. 41–59), it is the turn of the "disciples," and then, again in v. 67, 70–71, the "Twelve." The exegetes ask whether these "disciples" are those known from the previous chapters (cf. John 2:2, 11–12, 17, 22; 3:22; 4:1–2, 8, 27, 31, 33). More probable is the assumption that we are dealing here with Jesus's audience in verses 25–58 as men with an incipient faith in Jesus.

Connected with this identification of the "disciples" is the further problem of identifying what crisis of faith could have been the difficulty for them. According to some, the crisis would be put down to Jesus's words about his coming down from heaven as the "bread of life"; others think that the crisis mirrors a disagreement within the Johannine community concerning right belief in Jesus. Both views coalesce in the suggestion of Schenke, in which it is recognized that the scandal provoked by Jesus's discourse leads to the refusal of Jesus's Jewish audience to see in him more than a messianic figure: a divine being who has come down from heaven.[126] At first glance, this proposal is convincing, but it loses its force when Schenke identifies the crisis of faith with the split in the community presupposed in the First Letter of John (1 John 2:18–19; cf. 4:1–3). There, the theme is probably rather the true humanity of Jesus in the face of docetic challenges, something that does not seem to be the case in John 6.[127]

124. Thus, in Stare, *Durch ihn leben*.
125. Cf. Olsson, "All My Teaching."
126. Schenke, "The Johannine Schism."
127. Cf. Beutler, *Johannesbriefe*. The fundamental problem of the opponents in 1 John seems to have been their self-understanding. They believed themselves to be so filled and anointed with the spirit that they had no need of a Christ who became flesh and died on the

Finally, John 6:60–71 raises the problem of the relation of these verses to the Synoptic Gospels in general and to Mark in particular. Here, the investigation of Ian D. Mackay throws light on the composition of the Johannine text.[128] He shows convincingly how John used Mark 6–8 in a free and creative manner. Any additional source for the Johannine text remains highly hypothetical. It is justifiable, therefore, to carry out the diachronic analysis with the use of Mackay's results.

The section John 6:60–66 can be divided up according to narrative criteria. At the beginning, there are a narrative piece of information and an indirectly reproduced saying of many disciples of Jesus in v. 60. These are followed by Jesus's answer with its narrative introduction into verses 61–65 and the narrative conclusion in v. 66.

**6:60** Jesus's words are perceived as having been "hard." But which of Jesus's words have activated the protest? According to some, it is Jesus's words about the Eucharist, that is, about the need to eat his flesh and drink his blood—shocking words indeed. Jesus's answer shows, however, that the reason for the protest did not lie here. He recalls the necessity to believe in him as the one who has come from heaven and who will again ascend to heaven to the Father (v. 62). Thus, the faith crisis appears to have been triggered by the whole of Jesus's discourse about himself as the bread come from heaven, which is also promised to the disciples in sacramental form. This view is gaining ground today.[129] So the "disciples" were those who had questioned precisely these words of Jesus. Thereby the "Jews" come into the meaning of "disciples" since, according to earlier passages in the Gospel, they had come to an (incipient) faith in Jesus (cf. John 2:23; 7:31; 8:30–31; 10:42; 11:45; 12:42).

**6:61–65** In v. 61, Jesus reveals himself once more as the one who knows the hearts of men and what is hidden (cf., above, at verses 43 and 53). He also knows their "murmuring" (v. 41) and their disputing (v. 52). The theme of "murmuring" links this passage with the previous one (vv. 41–58) and compares the protesting of the disciples with the people of Israel in the rebellion against Moses and Aaron, against God himself in the final analysis. They were challenged to make up their minds without arguments to support their decision of faith. In fact, the challenge is aug-

---

cross. They were thus on the way to docetism, which denied the incarnation completely, and to gnosis. The opponents of John 6:60–66 are at best on the way to this.

128. Mackay, *John's Relationship*.
129. Cf. Culpepper, *Critical Readings*.

mented: if they are scandalized at a Christ who has come as bread from heaven, how much greater offense will they take if they see him ascend to the Father from whom he has come? At first glance, the point of this argument is not evident. It is reasonable, however, to detect in this saying a play on the double meanings of the "ascending" and "lifting up" of Jesus: on the cross and to the Father. No matter what, the cross will be the stumbling block for Jews who expect a victorious Messiah. However, the ascent to the Father also appears shocking to the Jews since Jesus is known to them as the son of Joseph and Mary (cf. 6:42). So the scandal is not lessened but heightened.

If faith is made impossible on account of a shocking message, it has to be made possible by a power given from above. This is the subject of v. 63. The word of Jesus is itself spirit and life. While the flesh cannot of itself bestow divine and eternal life, the Spirit is indeed able to give this life since he is the Spirit of life. We recall the exchanges between Jesus and the Jews in verses 41–58, in which Jesus explains that one has to be drawn by the Father in order to come to him (v. 44). The same content is being expressed in our verse with reference to the Spirit who is identified with the word of Jesus.

In the following verses 64 and 65, Jesus refers expressly to this his previous statement that no one could come to him unless he is drawn by God, that is, on account of a gift of God. In other words, one has to be chosen by God for grace and life (v. 65). Jesus knows right from the beginning who will have this grace and who not, indeed, who will be the betrayer (v. 64).

**6:66** The verse brings the small section to a close. Already it is also preparing for the following and last section. While in v. 60 many disciples merely "say" that this word is hard and difficult to accept, at the end of the following words of Jesus, they push their judgement to its conclusion. He has not facilitated their decision of faith but only demonstrated that it is a decision made possible through faith. Instead of turning to God and asking for this grace, the audience abandons Jesus and gives up their project of faith in him. The readers should not follow their example but accept the invitation of Jesus to believe in him with the power of the grace given to them by God.

With regard to composition history, John appears to be indebted to Mark's Gospel, as Ian D. Mackay has shown.[130] According to him, John

---

130. Cf. Mackay, *John's Relationship*.

has reversed the order of themes and passages in Mark 8:27–9:1. Peter's confession appears at the end (John 6:67–69); the theme of the lifting up of the Son of Man at the beginning (John 6:62). It looks as if the stumbling block of the descent and ascent of the Son of Man in John stems from the first announcement of the passion, death, and resurrection of Jesus in Mark 8:31–33. The description of Peter as "Satan" in Mark 8:33 becomes the characterization of Judas in John 6:70. In John, Peter becomes an example of faith, and so his characterization as "Satan" in Mark is not compatible here.

*Jesus and the Twelve (6:67–71)*

Again, from the perspective of composition history, verses John 6:67–71 appear to have been influenced by Mark 8:27–30, together with the following verses in Mark 8:31–9:1. Jesus's two questions in Mark 8:27, 29 are matched by that of John 6:67: "Do you want to go away also?" Here, a decision of faith is required. In both texts, Peter is named as the spokesman for the disciples' confession of faith. The title with which Peter confesses his faith in Mark 8:29: "You are the Messiah" is unsatisfactory as far as John is concerned. This title would be too similar to the idea of the crowd who, in John 6:15, wanted to make Jesus a king, a messianic king who satisfies the material needs of the people of God. So John chooses another title, that of "the Holy One of God." The choice is somewhat astonishing since, in Mark (1:24), this description is employed by a demon on the occasion of Jesus's first act of exorcism.[131] Mackay lists the reasons for this *"relecture"* in John.[132] If this is an isolated instance of this title in John, it is highly suitable nonetheless to express the dignity and the eminence of Jesus. John thus avoids an anticlimax and leads the readers to a deeper confession that agrees more firmly with the theology of his Gospel. The understanding of this title transcends human knowledge and belongs to the supernatural world. In that respect, both titles correspond.

**6:67** The group of the "Twelve" makes an appearance in John only here (vv. 67 and 71: Inclusio) and in John 20:24. We should consider this expression in connection with the course of the focalization in John 6:22–71: from the "crowd" to the "Jews," from the "Jews" to the "disciples," from

---

131. In the Old Testament, the expression occurs only twice in the Septuagint: Judg 13:7; 16:17 B of the Nazirite Samson as such. Thus, it has no primarily messianic stamp.

132. Mackay, *John's Relationship*.

## Jesus Reveals Himself to His People (5:1–10:42)

the "disciples" to the "Twelve," and from the Twelve to individual named apostles (Peter, Judas). Earlier, we noticed the concentric structure of John 6. In John 6:1–21, the groups mentioned are in reverse order (vv. 16–21: disciples, 1–15 individual, named disciples). In Mark, it is easier to identify the group of "disciples" with the Twelve (cf. Mark 8:27); John does not make this identification, and the group of disciples extends further than the Twelve (cf., above, 6:60). The question of Jesus whether the Twelve too will go away is not far from the words with which, in Mark 8:34–9:1, he requires his disciples to follow after him to the most extreme consequences.

**6:68** Peter answers with a confession of faith expressed with a messianic title as in Mark (8:29). Peter expresses his faith in Jesus in Johannine language: there is nowhere else for him to go. Only Jesus has the words of eternal life (cf. v. 63).

**6:69** The words: "We have come to believe and have recognized: you are the Holy One of God" have found different explanations. In the present context, they admit no doubt that they are expressing a certainty and knowledge of faith that has been acquired on one occasion and been maintained from then on (note the perfect tense). In the "we," Peter is speaking not just for himself but as spokesman for the group of the Twelve and for the community that is arising. One can ask why Peter appears in this place in John as spokesman for the faith of the Twelve. Two reasons can be mentioned. A first lies in John's dependence on Mark at this point. This dependence is closer here than in other parts of the Gospel and this is probably because of the later composition of John 6. This leads to the other reason for the role of Peter in John 6:67–71: the closeness of John 6 to John 21. This closeness has been investigated by Benedikt Schwank, among others.[133] In both chapters, we are on the shore of the Sea of Tiberias. Jesus appears to his disciples and prepares a miraculous meal for them on the beach. An important role falls to Peter, whether in the confession of his faith and trust or as spokesman and guarantor of the faith of the community. This text probably takes us to a moment at the end of the apostolic period in which the faith of the Johannine community could no longer rely exclusively on the testimony of the beloved disciple but increasingly also on the confession and the proclamation of the faith through Peter in harmony with the rising post-apostolic church.[134]

---

133. Cf. Schwank, 2:37.

134. Wucherpfennig, "Petrusamt," 98, conjectures that there is an ancient tradition independent of Matthew in the role of Peter in John 6:67–69 and 21:15–17.

**6:70–71** Membership of the group of the "Twelve" does not guarantee faith in Jesus or faithfulness to him. All have been chosen by Jesus (cf. John 13:18; 15:16; Mark 3:13–14 par.), but not all will persevere in this faith. Indeed, one of them will become the betrayer and will receive the name of "Satan," "eschatological opponent." We recall that this description has been transferred from Peter to Judas (cf. Mark 8:33). The fact that he belongs to the group of the Twelve is mentioned expressly. As highlighted by Mackay, for John the image of a Peter who opposed Jesus to such an extent that he earned the title "Satan" was no longer acceptable. Peter had to serve as an example for the believers of the reading community. His threefold denial had to be reported because of the tradition. However, John's Peter shows remorse and returns to faith in Jesus and back to his original love before he is commissioned as shepherd of the sheep (John 21:15–17).

The negative picture of Judas in the New Testament reaches its high point in John's Gospel. He is a *diabolos* (v. 70), the "betrayer" (v. 71; 13:2). At the anointing of Jesus, he is portrayed as the administrator of the disciples' common purse, not for altruistic motives, but because he was a thief and misappropriated the money entrusted to him (John 12:6).[135] This tendency to present Judas in dark colors continues during the course of the church's history right up to the "Legenda Aurea" of the Baroque period. According to the study of Hans-Josef Klauck,[136] it is time to see that more justice is done to Judas and to reconstruct the picture of this member of the Twelve as a disappointed disciple of Jesus, who was certainly not lacking in goodwill in every respect.

## III

We started with the observation that John 6 is a later *"relecture"* of the Passover framework of the Fourth Gospel. Jesus no longer goes to the pilgrim feast of his people and his fellow believers at the temple in Jerusalem but celebrates a new Passover in Galilee, home of the early Christian communities. Passover would continue to remain important but it receives a new meaning. It becomes the feast recalling Jesus's Last Supper with his own disciples, his return home, and his resurrection. It is not by chance that, in

---

135. This opposition is pointed out by Gruber, "Zumutung," 656–58.
136. Klauck, *Judas*.

## Jesus Reveals Himself to His People (5:1–10:42)

this chapter (and only here in John), we meet with statements about the body and blood of Jesus that will be applied to the Eucharist. Future Christians who celebrate the Last Supper will remain conscious of the Jewish roots of their celebration, and will think back on the words of institution with which Jesus interpreted his gifts of bread and wine as father of his own household. They will need to go on pilgrimage to Jerusalem no longer. In assembling for the sacred meal, they will enter into the sanctuary, meet God in Christ, and receive eternal life.

There is no antithesis between the figurative discourse of Jesus about the bread of life, which he himself is and which is received in faith, and the bread in which he hands himself over as food. To receive Jesus in faith means to open oneself totally to him and experience the one who has given himself over for his own. It is only a step from here to the faithful receiving of the Lord's Supper. The Lord offered in death is received in faith in his word but also in the sacrament. Word and sacrament complete each other and must not be played against each other. That is good ecumenical theology.

Similarly, there is no antithesis between the salvation that Jesus now gives through faith, and the eternal life that is to be revealed once for all at the end of time. If the Evangelist juxtaposes statements about present salvation and the resurrection at the last day, one should understand these statements as complementary. It is the same salvation and the same eternal life that Jesus now gives to his own and is to be revealed at the end of history.

At the same time, John 6 leads to the personal decision of faith on the part of the readers. It has been shown that underlying the chapter are both a concentric and a linear structure. At the beginning of the chapter, individual disciples were mentioned by name; then the subject was, successively, the disciples as a group, the crowd of people, and the "Jews." Then, from v. 60, the disciples came into play again, next the Twelve, and, at the close, once again, individual named disciples: Peter and Judas. This movement towards ever smaller groups and towards individuals is significant for the readers also. They have to decide for themselves—for Peter's confession of faith and against the betrayal of Judas: "Lord to whom should we go? You have words of eternal life. We have come to believe and have recognized: You are the Holy One of God."

## 3. Jesus at the Feast of Tabernacles (7:1–10:21)

### *Jesus at the Feast of Tabernacles in Jerusalem (7:1–52)*

¹ After this, Jesus traveled around Galilee; he did not wish to stay in Judaea because the Jews were seeking to kill him. ² The Jews' Feast of Tabernacles was at hand. ³ Then his brothers said to him: Leave here, and go to Judaea so that your disciples may also see the works that you are doing. ⁴ For no one works in secret if he wants to be known publicly. If you do these things, show yourself to the world! ⁵ for even his brothers did not believe in him. ⁶ Jesus said to them: My time has not yet come, but for you the time is always right. ⁷ The world cannot hate you, but it hates me because I witness that its deeds are evil. ⁸ Go up to the feast by yourselves; I am not going up to this feast because my time has not yet been fulfilled. ⁹ He said that to them and remained in Galilee. ¹⁰ However, when his brothers had gone up to the feast, he too went up, though not openly but in secret. ¹¹ At the feast, the Jews were looking for him and saying: Where is he? ¹² And among the crowd there was much discussion back and forth about him. Some said: He is a good man. Other said: No, he is leading the people astray. ¹³ But no one spoke openly about him for fear of the Jews.

¹⁴ The first half of the week of the feast was already over when Jesus went up to the temple and taught. ¹⁵ The Jews were amazed and said: How can he understand the Scripture without being instructed in it? ¹⁶ So Jesus answered them: My teaching does not stem from me but from the one who sent me. ¹⁷ Whoever is ready to do the will of God will know whether this teaching stems from God or whether I am speaking on my own account. ¹⁸ Whoever speaks on his own account seeks his own honor; but whoever seeks the honor of him who sent him is true and in him there is no falsehood. ¹⁹ Did not Moses give you the Law? Yet none of you keeps the Law. Why are you seeking to kill me? ²⁰ The crowd answered: You really are possessed by a demon – who is seeking to kill you? ²¹ Jesus answered them: I performed only a single work, and you all marveled at it. ²² Moses gave you circumcision – not that it stems from Moses, of course, but from the fathers, and you circumcise a man even on the Sabbath. ²³ If a man may receive circumcision on the Sabbath so that the Law of Moses is not broken, why are you angry with me because I have made a man completely whole on the Sabbath? ²⁴ Do not judge by appearances, but judge rightly!

²⁵ Then some people from Jerusalem said: Is not that the man they are seeking to kill? ²⁶ And yet he is speaking in complete openness and they are letting him do as he pleases. Has the Supreme Council really recognized that he is the Christ? ²⁷ But we know where this man comes from; yet when the Christ comes, no one will know where he comes from. ²⁸ While Jesus was teaching in

*Jesus Reveals Himself to His People (5:1–10:42)*

the temple, he cried out: You know me and know where I come from; but I have not come on my own account but he who sent me is true. Him you do not know. ²⁹ I know him because I come from him and he has sent me. ³⁰ Then they sought to arrest him; but no one laid a hand on him because his hour was not yet come.

³¹ Many people in the crowd believed in him; they said: When he comes, will the Christ do more signs than this man has? ³² The Pharisees heard what the people were saying about him furtively. Then the chief priests and the Pharisees sent officers to have him arrested. ³³ However, Jesus said: I am still with you for a short time; then I am going away to the one who sent me. ³⁴ You will seek me and you will not find me; for where I am you cannot come. ³⁵ Then the Jews said to one another: Where will he go then, that we shall not find him? Will he go, perhaps, to the Diaspora of the Greeks and teach the Greeks? ³⁶ What does it mean when he says: You will seek me but not find me; for where I am you cannot come?

³⁷ On the last day of the feast, the great day, Jesus stood up and cried: Whoever is thirsty, let him come to me, and let him drink, ³⁸ whoever believes on me. As the Scripture says: from deep within him will flow streams of living water. ³⁹ With this he meant the Spirit that all who believe in him were to receive, for the Spirit had not yet been given because Jesus had not yet been glorified. ⁴⁰ When they heard these words, some of the people said: This is truly the Prophet. ⁴¹ Others said: This is the Christ. Still others said: Does the Christ come from Galilee? ⁴² Surely the Scripture says: The Christ comes from David's line and from the village of Bethlehem where David lived. ⁴³ Thus there arose a division in the crowd on his account. ⁴⁴ Some of them wanted to arrest him; but no one laid a hand on him.

⁴⁵ When the officers returned to the chief priests and the Pharisees, the latter asked: Why haven't you brought him here? ⁴⁶ The officers answered: No man ever spoke like this. ⁴⁷ Then the Pharisees replied to them: Have you also let yourselves be led astray? ⁴⁸ Has even one of the Supreme Council or of the Pharisees come to believe in him? ⁴⁹ But these people, who know nothing about the Law, are cursed. ⁵⁰ Nicodemus, however, one of their own councilors who had previously sought out Jesus said to them: ⁵¹ Surely our Law does not judge a man without hearing him and determining what he is doing. ⁵² They retorted: Are you from Galilee also? Check up and see: No prophet comes from Galilee.

### *Jesus and the Adulteress (7:53–8:11)*

⁵³ Then they all went home. 8 ¹ Jesus, however, went to the Mount of Olives. ² Early in the morning, he betook himself again to the temple. All the people came to him. He sat down and taught them. ³ Then the scribes and Pharisees brought a woman who had been caught out in the act of adultery. They placed her in the

midst ⁴ and said to him: Master, this woman was taken in the very act of adultery. ⁵ In the Law, Moses prescribed that such women be stoned. What do you say? ⁶ With these words, they wanted to put him to the test so that they might have a reason to accuse him. Jesus, however, bent down and wrote on the ground with his finger. ⁷ As they continued to question him doggedly and repeatedly, he straightened up and said to them: Whoever of you is without sin, let him be first to cast a stone. ⁸ And he bent down again and wrote on the ground. ⁹ When they heard that, they went away one after the other, beginning with the eldest. Jesus remained behind alone with the woman who was still standing in the middle. ¹⁰ He straightened up and said to her: Woman, where are they? Has no one condemned you? ¹¹ She answered: No one, sir. Then Jesus said to her: Neither do I condemn you. Go and sin no more!

*Jesus's Disputes in Jerusalem. Jesus and Abraham (8:12–59)*

¹² As Jesus was speaking to them on another occasion, he said: I am the light of the world. Whoever follows me will not walk in darkness but will have the light of life. ¹³ Then the Pharisees said to him: You are bearing witness about yourself; your witness is not true. ¹⁴ Jesus replied: Even if I am bearing witness about myself, my witness is true. For I know where I have come from and where I am going to. But you do not know where I have come from and where I am going to. ¹⁵ You judge as men judge; I judge no one. ¹⁶ But if I judge, my testimony is true; for I am not judging alone, but I and the Father who sent me. ¹⁷ And in your Law it stands written: The witness of two men is true. ¹⁸ I am one who bear witness to myself, and also the Father who sent me, he bears witness to me. ¹⁹ Then they asked him: Who is your Father? Jesus answered: You know neither me nor my Father; if you knew me, then you would also know my Father. ²⁰ He said these words while he was teaching in the temple beside the treasury. But no one arrested him; for his hour had not yet come.

²¹ Another time, Jesus said to them: I am going away, and you will seek me, and you will die in your sins. Where I am going, you cannot come. ²² Then the Jews said: Is he going to kill himself perhaps? Why would he say otherwise: Where I am going you cannot come? ²³ He said to them: You are from below; I am from above. You are from this world; I am not from this world. ²⁴ I said to you: You will die in your sins; for if you do not believe that I am he, you will die in your sins. ²⁵ So they asked him: Who are you then? Jesus answered: Why am I still talking to you at all? ²⁶ I would still have much to say about you and much to judge, but the one who sent me is true, and what I have heard from him I am saying to the world. ²⁷ They did not understand that he was talking here of the Father. ²⁸ Then Jesus said to them: When you have lifted up the Son of Man, then

## Jesus Reveals Himself to His People (5:1–10:42)

you will know that I am he. You will know that I do nothing of myself but say only what the Father has taught me. ²⁹ And the one who has sent me is with me; he has not left me alone because I do always what pleases him. ³⁰ When Jesus said that, many came to faith in him.

³¹ Then he said to the Jews who had come to believe in him: If you remain in my word, you will be truly my disciples. ³² Then you will know the truth, and the truth will set you free. ³³ They retorted: We are the descendants of Abraham and were never slaves. How can you say: You will be free? ³⁴ Jesus answered them: Amen, amen, I say to you: Whoever commits sin is the slave of sin. ³⁵ But the slave does not remain in the house for ever; only the Son remains for ever. ³⁶ So, if the Son sets you free, then you are really free. ³⁷ I know that you are the descendants of Abraham. But you are seeking to kill me because my word finds no place in you. ³⁸ I say what I have seen with my Father, and you do what you have heard from your father. ³⁹ They answered him: Our father is Abraham. Jesus said to them: If you were Abraham's children, you would do the works of Abraham. ⁴⁰ But now you seek to kill me, a man who has announced to you the truth that I have heard from God. Abraham did not behave like this. ⁴¹ You perform the work of your father. They retorted: We were not born from adultery, but have only the one Father: God. ⁴² Jesus said to them: If God were your Father, you would have loved me; for I proceeded and came from God. I have not come on my own account, but he sent me. ⁴³ Why do you not understand what I am saying? Because you are not able to hear my word. ⁴⁴ You have the devil as your father, and you want to do what your father desires. He was a murderer from the beginning. And he does not stand in the truth; for there is no truth in him. When he lies, he says what comes from him himself; for he is a liar and the father of lies. ⁴⁵ But you do not believe me because I tell the truth. ⁴⁶ Which of you can convict me of a sin? If I tell the truth, why do you not believe me? ⁴⁷ Whoever is of God hears the words of God; therefore, you do not hear them because you are not of God.

⁴⁸ Then the Jews answered him: Are we not right in saying: You are a Samaritan and possessed by a demon? ⁴⁹ Jesus retorted: I am not possessed by any demon, but I honor my Father; and you dishonor me. ⁵⁰ I am not seeking my own honor; but there is one who seeks and who judges. ⁵¹ Amen, amen, I say to you: If anyone keeps my word, he will never see death. ⁵² Then the Jews said to him: Now we know that you are possessed by a demon. Abraham and the prophets are dead, but you are saying: If anyone keeps my word, he will never suffer death. ⁵³ Are you greater than our father Abraham? He is dead, and the prophets are dead. Who are you claiming to be? ⁵⁴ Jesus answered: If I glorify myself, my glory is nothing. It is my Father who glorifies me, the one of whom you say: He is our God. ⁵⁵ But you have not known him. I know him, however, and if I said: I do not

know him, I would be a liar like you. But I know him and I keep his word. **56** Your father Abraham rejoiced because he was to see my day. He saw it and was glad. **57** The Jews retorted: You are not yet fifty years old and are you supposed to have seen Abraham? **58** Jesus answered them: Amen, amen, I say to you: Before Abraham was, I am. **59** Then they took up stones to throw at him, but Jesus hid himself and left the temple.

## *The Healing of the Man Born Blind. Controversies about Jesus (9:1–41)*

9 **1** As he was on his way, Jesus saw a man who had been blind since birth. **2** Then his disciples asked him: Rabbi, who sinned? He himself or his parents so that he was born blind? **3** Jesus answered: Neither he nor his parents sinned, but the works of God have to be revealed in him. **4** As long as it is day, we must perform the works of the one who has sent me; the night is coming when no one can work any more. **5** As long as I am in the world, I am the light of the world. **6** When he had said this, he spat on the ground; then with the spittle he made some clay, spread it over the eyes of the blind man **7** and said to him: Go and wash in the Pool of Siloam! The translation is: The one sent. The man went away and washed. And when he came back, he was able to see.

**8** The neighbors and those who had seen him previously as a beggar said: Isn't this the man who sat here and begged? **9** Some said: It is he. Others said: No, he only seems to be like him. But he himself said: It is I. **10** Then they asked him: How have your eyes been opened? **11** He answered: The man who is called Jesus made some clay, spread it over my eyes and said to me: Go to the Pool of Siloam and wash! I went, washed and can see. **12** They asked him: Where is he? He said: I don't know.

**13** Then they brought the man who had been blind to the Pharisees. **14** However, it was on the Sabbath day that Jesus had made the clay and opened his eyes. **15** The Pharisees too asked him how he had become able to see. He answered: He laid some clay on my eyes; then I washed and now I see. **16** Some of the Pharisees said: This man is not from God because he does not keep the Sabbath. But others said: How can a sinful man do such signs? Thus there arose a division among them. **17** Then they questioned the blind man once again: What do you say about him? After all, it is your eyes he opened. The man said: He is a prophet.

**18** However, the Jews did not want to believe that he was blind and had become able to see. So they called the parents of the man who had been healed from blindness, **19** and asked them: Is this your son, who you say was born blind? How does it come about that he now sees? **20** His parents answered: We know that this is our son and that he was born blind. **21** How it comes about that he now sees we do not know. And who has opened his eyes, that too we do not know. Ask him himself. He is old enough and can speak for himself. ²² The parents said that because they feared the Jews; for the Jews had already decided to expel from the synagogue everyone who confessed him as the Christ. ²³ That is why the parents said: He is old enough, ask him himself.

²⁴ Then, for the second time, the Pharisees called the man who had been blind and said to him: Give God the glory! We know that this man is a sinner. ²⁵ He answered: Whether he is a sinner I do not know. I know only one thing, that I was blind and now I see. ²⁶ They asked him: What did he do with you? How did he open your eyes? ²⁷ He answered them: I have already told you, but you did not listen. Why do you want to hear it again? Perhaps you also want to become his disciples, is that it? ²⁸ Then they berated him: You are a disciple of this man; but we are disciples of Moses. ²⁹ We know that God spoke to Moses; but we do not know where this man comes from. ³⁰ The man answered them: This is really astonishing: you don't know where he comes from; yet he opened my eyes. ³¹ We know that God does not hear sinners; but whoever fears God and does his will, him he listens to. ³² It has never yet been heard of that someone has opened the eyes of someone born blind. ³³ If this man were not from God, then he would certainly not have been able to achieve anything. ³⁴ They retorted: You were born totally in your sins, and do you mean to teach us? And they threw him out.

³⁵ Jesus heard that they had thrown him out, and, when he came across him, he said to him: Do you believe in the Son of Man? ³⁶ Then he answered and said: Who is he, sir, that I may believe in him? ³⁷ Jesus said to him: You have already seen him; it is he who is speaking with you. ³⁸ He said: I believe, Lord! And he threw himself down before him. ³⁹ Then Jesus spoke: I came into this world in order to judge: so that the blind might see and those who see become blind. ⁴⁰ Some Pharisees who were near him heard this. And they asked him: Are we also blind then? ⁴¹ Jesus said to them: If you were blind, you would be without sin. But now you say: We can see. That is why your sin remains.

### The Good Shepherd and His Antitheses (10:1–21)

10 ¹ Amen, amen, I say to you: Whoever does not enter the sheepfold through the gate but climbs in some other way is a thief and a robber. ² But whoever goes through the gate is the shepherd of the sheep. ³ The gatekeeper opens the gate for him and the sheep hear his voice; he calls each of the sheep who belong to him by name and leads them out. ⁴ When he has brought out all his sheep, he goes before them, and the sheep follow him because they recognize his voice. ⁵ However, they will not follow a stranger but will flee from him because they do not know the voice of strangers. ⁶ Jesus told them this parable; but they did not understand the meaning of what he had said to them.

⁷ Again Jesus said to them: Amen, amen, I say to you: I am the gate to the sheep. ⁸ All who came before me are thieves and robbers; but the sheep did not listen to them. ⁹ I am the door; whoever enters through me will be saved, and will come in and go out and find pasture. ¹⁰ The thief comes only to steal, to slaughter and to destroy; I have come that they may have life, and have it to the full.

¹¹ I am the good shepherd. The good shepherd gives his life for the sheep. ¹² But the hired man who is not the shepherd and to whom the sheep do not belong sees the wolf coming, deserts the sheep and flees; and the wolf seizes the sheep and scatters them. He flees, ¹³ because he is a hired man and has no concern for the sheep. ¹⁴ I am the good shepherd; I know mine and my own know me, ¹⁵ just as the Father knows me and I know the Father; and I lay down my life for the sheep. ¹⁶ I have other sheep that are not from this fold; I must lead them too, and they will listen to my voice; then there will be only one flock and one shepherd. ¹⁷ For this reason the Father loves me, because I lay down my life in order to take it up again. ¹⁸ No one snatches it from me, but I give it up out of my own free will. I have power to give it up, and I have power to take it up again. This is the command that I have received from my Father.

¹⁹ On account of these words, there was a division once more among the Jews. ²⁰ Some of them said: He is possessed by a devil and is talking rubbish. Why are you listening to him? ²¹ Others said: No one possessed speaks like this. Can a demon open the eyes of the blind?

## I

The narrative basis of John's Gospel lies in the cycle of Jewish pilgrim feasts for which Jesus goes up to Jerusalem. Once we exclude the Passover feast in Galilee in John 6:4, which simultaneously ruptures this cycle and takes it forward, then the first Passover feast of John 2:13 and what we have taken to be the Feast of Weeks in John 5:1 are now followed in John 7:2 by the Feast of Tabernacles to which Jesus goes up after initial hesitations. Research is increasingly establishing that the whole section John 7:1–10:42 is stamped and determined by this feast. Moloney sees the influence of the Feast of Tabernacles chiefly in John 7–8.[137] Our knowledge of this feast rests mainly on the Mishnah tractate Sukkah, but also on other rabbinic and biblical witnesses. For the exegesis of John's Gospel, three basic elements of this feast prove to be significant:

---

137. Moloney, "Narrative."

## Jesus Reveals Himself to His People (5:1–10:42)

- the daily rite of the drawing of water at the Pool of Siloam (Sukkah 4:9–10)
- the rite of light (Sukkah 5:1–4) and
- the rite of the orientation towards the temple (Sukkah 5:4)

The first rite consisted of a daily procession to the Pool of Siloam in order to draw water and bring it to the temple. This procession was accompanied with chants and the recitation of the Great Hallel (Pss 113–118) and ended in the temple precinct. There, the priest entrusted with the temple service poured this water together with some wine into two perforated vessels, out of which the liquid flowed on to the altar. At the time of the prophet Zechariah, this rite had also a messianic tone (Zech 14).

The second rite consisted of the nightly illumination of the Court of Women in the temple by four huge lamps that were fed with oil. The light was brought to the temple by the Israelites with music that was made up chiefly of pilgrim songs. According to Suk 5,3, there was no court in the city of Jerusalem that was not illuminated by the light that came from the temple. The whole feast was full of joy, and the people danced. In Zech 14:6–8, the light is interpreted eschatologically. This rite of light recalled the tradition of the pillar of fire that accompanied the Israelites on their nocturnal departure from Egypt (cf. Exod 13:21).

The third rite, which is described in Sukkah 5.4, consisted of a prayer that was performed at the east gate of the temple with faces to the west and thus with backs to the sun. At this moment, the participants in the procession said: "Our fathers, when they had come to this place, turned their backs to the temple, set their faces to the east and worshiped the sun, turned to the east. But our eyes are turned towards the Lord."

For Moloney (and other authors too with regard to the first two rites), these rites are of the greatest significance for the understanding of John 7–8. In this way, both the words of Jesus about the streams of living water in John 7:37–38, as well as the saying of John 8:12, "I am the light of the world," are easier to understand. In addition, with a glance at these rites, it is easier to understand Jesus's exhortation not to worship other gods but only the one God who is revealed in him.[138]

The extensive dissertation of Devillers has much in common with

---

138. The coherence of John 7–8 is also examined by Cory, "Wisdom's Rescue." Behind both chapters the author sees the myth of Wisdom that is treated with hostility but justified in the end.

the article of Moloney but ranges wider.[139] Among other things, the two studies differ in that Devillers also includes John 9:1–10:39. On the one hand, the chapter about the healing of the man born blind (John 9) with the directly ensuing good shepherd discourse (John 10:1–21) follows immediately on the account of Jesus's presence at the Feast of Tabernacles. On the other hand, Jesus's saying "I am the light of the world" in John 9:5 and the image of "light" and "blindness/night" within ch. 9 fit well with the theme of light in John 7–8. According to Devillers, the mention of a further feast, that of the dedication of the temple in John 10:22, does not absolutely signify the end of the section defined by the Feast of Tabernacles. Jesus is still in Jerusalem. His audience is still the same. The theme of the good shepherd is taken up again (John 10:26–29). In this connection, we have also to remember that, from the beginning, the Feast of the Dedication of the temple was regarded by the Jews as a second Feast of Tabernacles.[140] The Johannine cycle begun with the Feast of Tabernacles ends, according to Devillers, in John 10:39, that is, the moment when Jesus finally leaves the temple to go back again to the area on the other side of the Jordan where he is received with faith (John 10:40–42).

A similar demarcation of the text is reached by Schenke[141] with the help of his working out of the dramatic structure of the section. In opposition to Bultmann, who conjectures a disturbed textual series in John 7–10, he is of the opinion that the present form of the text is easy to understand and logical. According to Schenke, the text can be divided as follows:

(1) Prologue: 7:1–9
    Scene: Galilee. Time: shortly before the Feast of Tabernacles.
    Content: Conflict with Jesus's brothers.
(2) First Act: 7:10–8:59
    Four scenes can be distinguished (7:10–31, 32–44; 7:45–8:20; 8:21–59). At the end of the first scene, there is the attempt to seize Jesus; at the end, the attempt to stone him.
(3) Intermezzo (9:1–10:21)
    In John 9:1–39, we find ourselves in the "narrated" world; in 9:40–10:21, in the "reflective" one. There is a division.
(4) Second Act: 10:22–39

---

139. Devillers, *Fête*.
140. Cf. Devillers, *Fête*, 41.
141. Schenke, "Joh 7–10"; cf. Schenke, *Kommentar*, 144–206.

## Jesus Reveals Himself to His People (5:1–10:42)

The controversies of John 7:10–8:59 are taken up again. The same happens with the shepherd discourse of John 10:1–18. At the end, there is the attempt to stone Jesus.

The unity of the text is also displayed in a series of back and forward cross-references within our section. Thus the readers remember and also prepare themselves for further guidance. An impressive example is formed by the "lifting up" of the Son of Man in John 8:28. The talk about this event is understandable only with a view to the death and resurrection of Jesus.

With the last-named authors, we recognize the textual unity of John 7:1–10:39 (with 10:40–42 as a narrative conclusion). Dissenting from them, however, we prefer to let a new subsection begin again with the Feast of the Dedication of the Temple in John 10:22. The reason lies in the structural significance of the Jewish festal cycle for the construction of John's Gospel. Of course, the Feast of the Dedication of the temple is not one of the three prescribed pilgrim feasts, and Jesus does not go up to it but finds himself in the city of Jerusalem already. Nevertheless, it makes sense to mark out as such the passage that begins with the mention of the Feast of the Dedication of the Temple in John 10:22. Before the last Passover feast in John 11:55, then, Jesus will have gone through the whole festal cycle of his faith community once.

## II

### Before the Feast of Tabernacles (7:1–9)

According to our previous interpretation, John 6 goes back to a later "*relecture*" of the Jewish festal cycle in John's Gospel. Originally, therefore, ch. 7 followed ch. 5. A careful reading confirms this view. Thus, the details of place and time at the beginning of John 7 make good sense. After the conflict in John 5 and the threat of the "Jews" in John 5:18 to kill him, Jesus prefers to remain in Galilee and not appear in Judaea, at least not in public. The Feast of Tabernacles fits organically after the feast of John 5:1 that we interpret as the Feast of Weeks. We considered the Passover in John 6:4 as a later insertion.

The larger section, John 7:1–13, which describes Jesus's hesitant departure for the Feast of Tabernacles, can be divided into two subsections as it appears in various commentaries and also in the divisions of the editions of the Greek text. In verses 1–9, Jesus does not go to the Feast of Tabernacles, at least not openly. He is in conversation with his brothers. In verses 10–13, Jesus goes to the feast, but secretly. There is an account of the discussion about him among the crowd. This division of the passage results in a difference as to the actors in the two subsections: first, Jesus and his brothers; then, the "Jews" and the crowd. In the first scene, Jesus speaks; in the second, he acts.

In John 7:1–9, an inclusio can be recognized with the statement that Jesus remained in Galilee although the Feast of Tabernacles was at hand (vv. 1 and 9). Together with v. 2, v. 1 forms the narrative introduction to the section, which corresponds to the conclusion in v. 9. In verses 3–4, there follows the challenge of Jesus's brothers for him to go up to the feast, beginning with a narrative introduction. Verse 5 contains a commentary by the evangelist on this challenge by Jesus's brothers. In verses 6–8, there follows Jesus's answer with its narrative introduction.

The section is characterized by various oppositions. The most important concern place and time; added to these are those of "in secret" and "openly." These oppositions stand in relationship to each other: Jesus has to go from Galilee to the Feast of Tabernacles in order to appear openly before his disciples. However, Jesus rejects this challenge, since his "moment" (καιρός), one could also say his "hour," had not yet come.

**7:1–2** The "after this" (μετὰ ταῦτα) is a typical Johannine phrase and recalls the same expression in John 5:1 and 6:1. In the present version of the Gospel, the formula relates to the events recorded in the previous chapter; in the conjectural foundational text, it refers to the controversies reported in ch. 5 with the threat of the "Jews" to kill Jesus. This connection makes more sense, for the hostility of the Jewish authorities in Jerusalem recorded in John 5 explains the fact that Jesus prefers to remain in Galilee where he had been better received (cf. John 2:1–12 and 4:43–54).

The statement in v. 1 that Jesus did not "wish" to go to Judaea is subject to text-critical considerations. A well-attested variant (W it sy[c] Chrysostom) reads εἶχεν ἐξουσίαν ("could") instead of ἤθελεν ("wished"). However, the external attestation for "could not" is weaker than that for "did not wish." Internally, an emendation from "did not wish" to "could not" is easier to explain since the reason why Jesus did not wish to go to the feast was that he reckoned that his hour had not yet come.[142]

The Feast of Tabernacles mentioned in v. 2 has recently been com-

---

142. Cf. Riesner, "Joh 7,1."

*Jesus Reveals Himself to His People (5:1–10:42)*

mented on comprehensively in an essay by Siegfried Bergler.[143] The starting point are three letters from Bar Kochba that were discovered in Nahal Hever in the Judaean desert. These letters go back to the last year of the revolt against Hadrian and so to the time 134–135 CE. In this correspondence, which is preserved in Aramaic and Greek, Simon Bar Kochba urgently requests that he be sent the indispensable branches (*Lulab* and *Etrog*) for the feast of Tabernacles. One can ask why, in an especially tense military situation in conflict with the Roman occupying power, these branches should have had such an importance. Bergler's answer to this question consists in pointing to the fact that Bar Kochba wanted to celebrate the feast in Jerusalem as the eschatological fulfillment of the feast described in Lev 23:33–43. Indeed, the feast had already received an eschatological significance in Zech 14.

**7:3–5** For the second time in this Gospel, we come across the "brothers" of Jesus. They were already present at the wedding at Cana, and it was recounted that they, with Jesus, his mother, and his disciples, went down to Capernaum (John 2:12).

Jesus's brothers urge him to go up to Jerusalem in order to manifest his power there openly, to perform great "works" in the name of God. Their request is supported by human experience and wisdom: no one wants to remain hidden, everyone seeks to be known. However, it is precisely this wisdom that, in the light of the Fourth Gospel, is revealed as contrary to the wisdom and will of God. Moreover, the human wisdom of Jesus's brothers is a sign of the inadequacy of their belief in the divine mission of Jesus.

Who, then, were these "brothers of Jesus"?[144] The answer to this question is made harder because of the lack of agreement among the Gospels and the other writings of the New Testament concerning Jesus's origin. The infancy narratives in Matt 1–2 and Luke 1–2 report the birth of Jesus from the Virgin Mary, and this conviction found its way into the creed. Bound up with this at an already early date was the conviction in the Greek Church that Mary was a virgin before, during, and after the birth of Jesus. As a result, full brothers and sisters of Jesus are ruled out. Here, of course, the early development of doctrine goes beyond the New Testament. In the Western church, with the Protoevangelium of James

---

143. Bergler, "Jesus."
144. Cf. Beutler, "Brüder Jesu"; Beutler, "ἀδελφός," *EWNT* 1:69; *EDNT* 1:29, each with bibliography.

(9:2; 17:1–2; 18:1), it was suggested that the brothers and sisters of Jesus were children of Joseph from a previous marriage; since Jerome, the Latin church saw them rather as the cousins or relatives of Jesus. Naturally, this can scarcely be justified linguistically. In any case, John seems unembarrassed by the mention of Jesus's full brothers. Four of them are mentioned by name in the Synoptic tradition (Mark 6:3 par. Matt 13:55).

More recently, defining the role of the family of Jesus and his brothers in John more closely from a sociological perspective has been attempted.[145] A first glance reveals that, from the beginning, Jesus's family exercised an influence on him that was not insignificant. Jesus's mother (whose name is never mentioned) accompanies him from the beginning (John 2:1–12) right to the end (John 19:25–27). In both texts, Jesus addresses her with the appellation "woman," which shows that Jesus views her as an equal partner in conversation and in action. In John 2, Jesus's brothers are mentioned before his disciples, who were probably inserted later. These brothers think that Jesus should reveal himself in his power and dignity before his disciples and the people (John 7:1–9). After this section of the text, they show that they have not arrived at true faith in Jesus. One should not conclude from that, however, that they were hostile to Jesus's claim of having been sent by God.

Here there comes to mind the scene that Mark records towards the beginning of his Gospel (Mark 3:31–35; cf. Matt 12:46–50; Luke 8:19–21). The mother and brothers of Jesus come to bring him back home since he is out of his mind. Such an assessment is absent in John. Right up to the crucifixion, Jesus is close to his family, and his family to him. Here, we should also recall those texts that speak of the role of the brothers of Jesus and his mother after Easter: Acts 1:14; Gal 1:19; 1 Cor 9:5. According to John 7:1–9, Jesus's brothers already belong to the Jesus movement even if their understanding of his mission still remains limited and human.[146]

**7:6–9** In verses 6–8, Jesus gives his answer to the suggestion of his brothers; in v. 9, we have the narrative conclusion of this group of verses. Jesus's answer is framed by his statement about the "time" that has not yet come or been fulfilled. Three times, Jesus contrasts himself linguistically with his brothers ("you," "your"). If he does not wish to go up yet to the feast at the present moment, the reason is that he sees that his "present moment," his "time," has not yet come. The word employed here, καιρός,

---

145. Cf. Destro and Pesce, "Kinship."
146. Cf. Destro and Pesce, "Kinship."

is found in John only in John 7:6, 8. It is used by Matthew (26:18), perhaps in a similar sense, with reference to the imminent passion. In John, there is repeated mention of the "hour" of Jesus, which at first is still to come (cf. John 2:4; 7:30), but then has come (13:1; cf. 12:23, 27; 17:1).

What is only hinted at by the opposition between the "time" of Jesus and that of his brothers (their time is always right) is next developed fully in a theological manner. With their esteem of prestige and recognition, the brothers are thinking the thoughts of the world and arouse no challenge. Jesus wages his conflict with the world in that he confronts it with its evil deeds and thereby provokes it to hatred. The thought is probably about the provocation that Jesus's championing of God's will and God's glory above human honor brings with it (cf. John 5:41–44; 12:43). Evil deeds in connection with hatred of the light were the subject in John 3:19–20; John 15:18–19, 23 speak of the hatred of the world for Jesus and his disciples. The background is formed by Mark 13:13 par. Matt 10:22; 26:21; Luke 21:17.

In v. 8, Jesus draws the conclusion from the difference between him and his brothers: they want to go up to the feast only because their time has always come; he will not do it because his right moment has not yet been "fulfilled," as it says with a typically Johannine expression (otherwise repeated with "fulfilled joy": John 3:29; 15:11; 16:24; 1 John 1:4; 2 John 12). Thus, as is next narrated in v. 9, Jesus remains in Galilee. The naming of the area underlines once again its significance in the overall construction of John's Gospel. It is also the more secure location for Jesus.

### Jesus at the Feast of Tabernacles. Opinions about him (7:10–13)

**7:10** The information that, after the departure of his brothers, Jesus likewise left for the feast appears to contradict his words that he was not going there. The contradiction is resolved through the fact that Jesus went up to the feast not openly but secretly. It remains true, therefore, that his hour had not yet come. A little later, Jesus appears openly at the feast (John 7:14). It seems that now the hour is getting close. In the course of chs. 7–8, the conflicts with the Jewish authorities are repeated, and, at the close, it is noted that Jesus hid from the "Jews" who took up stones in order to stone him (John 8:59). Jesus proclaims the arrival of his "hour" only in John 12:23 after his entry into the city for his last Passover (cf. John 13:1; 17:1).

**7:11** Once again (after John 7:1), the "Jews" are introduced. They ask where Jesus is. After the information in v. 1, it is evident that no good intention lies behind this question. The "Jews'" question is characteristic: they ask where Jesus is. The question recalls John 6:25 where the crowd ask when Jesus arrived at the other side of the Sea of Tiberias. In both cases, the questions remain on the physical levels of place and time. John's Jesus appears to be uninterested in such questions, as shown by Jesus's answer to the crowd in John 6:26–27. The real question is who he is and how one can come to faith in him in order to be saved.

**12–13** Once again, the evangelist distinguishes between the "Jews" and the "crowd." The "Jews" have already shown themselves to be a group hostile to Jesus and his claim. The "crowd" remains more open, as has already been shown in ch. 6 (cf. the dialogue between Jesus and the "crowd" in verses 22–40 and that with the "Jews" in verses 41–58). Once again, there is mention of "murmuring" (γογγυσμός) about him, this time among the people and not (as in John 6:41, 43) among the "Jews." In John 7:12, the word does not seem to have a hostile nuance as in Exodus, as rebellion against Moses, Aaron, and, ultimately, God himself. Here, the word expresses discussion about Jesus without his taking part in the conversation. Two opinions come to the surface: "He is a good man" according to some; "No, he is leading the people astray" according to others. The positive judgement is vague, but at least open. Jesus's pre-eminence as the one coming from God has not yet been revealed, but the judgement of the crowd does not actually exclude it. The negative judgement rests on the verdict concerning the false prophets in Deut 18:20–22. Already in this text it is laid down that the false prophet must die.

The climate of the controversy is fraught. Out of "fear of the Jews," it cannot be conducted freely. This fear is mentioned several times in John's Gospel. A classic text is John 9:22, where it is mentioned that the parents of the man born blind whom Jesus had healed did not have the courage to acknowledge Jesus as the one performing the miracle for fear of the "Jews," who had already decided to exclude from the synagogue anyone confessing faith in Jesus. In John 12:42, the subject is of some leading men among the Jews who believed but did not confess this faith for fear of being thrown out of the synagogue. Again, on Easter Day, the disciples are assembled behind closed doors "for fear of the Jews" (John 20:19). Thus, in John 7:12–13, the people are in fact speaking about Jesus but not openly for fear of the consequences in the social network of the synagogue.

For the readers of John's Gospel, the controversy about Jesus at the Feast of Tabernacles is of the greatest significance. Again and again, the evangelist brings before his readers' eyes the "splits" in the Jewish people

## Jesus Reveals Himself to His People (5:1–10:42)

with regard to their judgement of Jesus. Alongside the already cited texts in John 6, we should think here of the controversies among the people in John 7:30-31 and 7:40-44, in the Supreme Council in 7:45-52, among the "Jews" in John 9 and in John 10:19-21, as well as in the Supreme Council again in John 11:45-53. In these texts, the author is inviting the readers to come to their own decision. The readers are confronted with the question of who Jesus is for them and what consequences they are prepared to suffer for their faith in Jesus and the confession of that faith.

### Jesus Begins His Teaching in the Temple (7:14–24)

Exegetes usually regard the section John 7:14-24 as a text unit complete in itself. Jesus has arrived at the Feast of Tabernacles. After the first assessments of him (John 7:10-13), he himself begins to speak. The conversation partners in this section are the "Jews" who are named for the first time in v. 11. Once again, they appear to be hostile to Jesus and his mission. In the following subsection (John 7:25-36), various actors appear: "some people from Jerusalem" (v. 25), "people in the crowd (v. 31), "the Pharisees" (v. 32), "the chief priests and the Pharisees" (v. 32) and "the Jews" (v. 35).

The subsection John 7:14-24 is divided into a narrative introduction (vv. 14-15a) and two exchanges between the "Jews" and Jesus in verses 15-19 and 20-24. Verses 14-18 concern the authority of Jesus to teach although he has not studied. In v. 19, Jesus himself changes the subject and passes on to the authority of Moses and his Law. Jesus thus goes on the attack. The "Jews" had turned against him over the compliance with the Law of Moses of a healing performed by Jesus on the Sabbath. They do not appear credible, however, since none of them keep this Law. Instead, they are trying to kill Jesus. The sequence of thought seems somewhat convoluted. Nevertheless, a new theme comes to the surface: the observance of the Sabbath according to the Law of Moses. This theme too is involved. The "Jews" dispute with Jesus the possibility of healing a man on the Sabbath; at the same time, they allow, with Moses, a man to be circumcised on the Sabbath. Only a detailed analysis of this passage can render it comprehensible.

Verses 14-19 deal with Jesus's power to teach with authority. These verses display a certain coherence not just from the narrative point of view but also in their vocabulary. The determining concept introduced in v. 14 is that of "teaching." The "Jews" marvel that Jesus teaches with authority without having studied. In v. 21, there appears the idea that will determine the dialogue of verses 20–24: Jesus's behavior. Such an alternation between the words and works of Jesus is found repeatedly in the Fourth Gospel and appears to belong to the thought world of the fourth evangelist. We should think, perhaps, of John 14:10–11: the disciples should believe in Jesus on account of his words and on account of his works; but also in John 15:22–24: the Jews should have believed in Jesus on account of his words but also on account of his astonishing works, which no one before him had performed. However, they were not ready to receive this twofold witness.

**7:14** Verse 14 introduces the scenery of the next dialogue. In John 7, the evangelist follows the course of the Feast of Tabernacles. At the beginning, Jesus does not appear at the feast. He goes there only subsequently and appears there openly for the first time when the middle of the eight-day feast has been reached. He declares his final great word of revelation on the last day of the feast when this celebration reaches its climax (John 7:37). The place of encounter between Jesus and the "Jews" is the temple. It is there that the sequence of scenes between John 7:37 and 8:59 will take place, up to the moment when Jesus withdraws to avoid being stoned. John speaks of an ascent of Jesus to the temple once more in John 10:22 in connection with the Feast of the Dedication of the temple. The encounters with the "Jews" in this place end with the final retreat of Jesus (John 10:39). In this way, then, the great section of controversies between Jesus and the Jewish authorities in John 5–10 is ended.

A "teaching" of Jesus is also mentioned in John 18:20, where Jesus explains before the high priest that he has been teaching openly in the temple and in the synagogues. This practice of Jesus is also emphasized by the use of the imperfect in John 7:14. Luke 19:47 reads similarly (with reference to the temple). The "synagogues" allow one to think of John 6:59.

**7:15** The "Jews" marvel at Jesus's teaching since he has not studied. The reason for their amazement lies in the fact that they are judging the teaching of Jesus by the standards of their earthly teachers. Jesus will not sanction the validity of this view, as immediately becomes clear.[147] There is a similar scene in the account of the teaching of the twelve-year-old Jesus in the temple (Luke 2:47). Here, the same principles apply.

**7:16** Jesus rejects the critical question with a twofold argument: his teaching does not stem from human authority but from God, and so is

---

147. Cf., for this tension between Jesus and his lack of education, Keith, "Claim." According to Keith, historical memories of Jesus could still be active here.

## Jesus Reveals Himself to His People (5:1–10:42)

fully justifiable; and its justifiability will be seen when the test of praxis is applied. Moreover, Jesus is not seeking his own honor, but the honor of the one who sent him. Thus, his teaching must be accepted. To go back to the first argument: for the content of his teaching Jesus invokes the authority of the one who sent him. This statement is not alone in the Bible, as R. W. L. Moberly has shown.[148] Already in Jeremiah it says: "The words of Jeremiah . . . the word of the Lord came to him" (Jer 1:1–2). Paul speaks with the same authority when he writes to the Thessalonians: "Therefore, we also thank God constantly for this, that when you received the word of God that you heard from us, you accepted it not as the word of men but as what it really is, the word of God" (1 Thess 2:13). Naturally, the mission of Jesus transcends those of the prophets and apostles, for he himself is the incarnate "Word" of God (John 1:14).

**7:17-18** In support of Jesus's teaching there is also the argument of the proof from practice. As Moberly remarks, this argument can also lead to circular reasoning: the "work" that counts in John's Gospel is faith in Jesus as the one sent from God (cf. John 6:29, a text quoted by many authors).[149] So the justification of faith is demonstrated by faith. This circular structure of the argument has been noticed from Augustine to Bultmann and Ernst Haenchen. However, not every circle is a vicious one. One can also enter into a circle as an ascending spiral. The proof through praxis throws new light on the reliability of the teaching received. From the theological point of view, one must remember that faith is a gift, and no one comes to the truth unless he is already, in a certain sense, a child of the truth (cf. John 18:36–37[150]). A further argument is added: Jesus is not seeking his own honor (cf. John 5:41–44; 8:50, 54) and is, therefore, credible on this account. In this way, Jesus distinguishes himself from all those who seek their own honor (cf. John 5:44; 12:43).

**7:19** The connection of these verses with the previous context is not apparent at first sight. That is why it is occasionally linked to the following verses. What binds this verse to the previous ones is the thought of teaching with authority. Jesus speaks in his own name since he declares his word in the name of God. For the "Jews," it is Moses who is the mediator of God's word. At first, Jesus allows the argument to have some force but then makes it irrelevant through the observation that the "Jews" themselves do

---

148. Moberly, "How Can We Know the Truth?"
149. Moberly, "How Can We Know the Truth?"
150. Moberly, "How Can We Know the Truth?," 252.

not take the word of Moses seriously. Thus, they are not justified in killing Jesus on the basis of the Law of Moses.

**7:20** The second part of the section John 7:14–24 in verses 20–24 is divided into a statement of the "Jews" (v. 20) and Jesus's answer (vv. 21–24). The dominating theme is that of Jesus's behavior in contrast to his teaching, which is the subject of verses 14–19. Again, the figure of Moses takes center stage. From an earlier narrative of John's Gospel (John 5), it will be remembered that Jesus healed a lame man on the Sabbath.

The charge thrown against Jesus in v. 20 that he is possessed returns again in John's Gospel at 10:20. Synoptic parallels are found in Mark 3:30: Jesus has a demon; he drives out demons with the aid of Beelzebul: Mark 3:22 par. Matt 12:24; Luke 11:15. The question of the "Jews": "Who is seeking to kill you?" is clearly hypocritical in view of their decision reported in John 5:18.

**7:21** In his answer, Jesus refers to the authority with which he acts. This authority corresponds to that with which he speaks. His word, like his work, arouses astonishment as it says in v. 21 in exact agreement with v. 15 (ἐθαύμαζον, θαυμάζετε).

**7:22–24** The following verses are full of exegetical problems. A first question concerns the connection of the introductory "therefore" (διὰ τοῦτο) with the preceding or following context. In newer editions and translations of the text, the phrase is linked to the following verses even if it is not easy to make out the sense of this. One could see here a resumption of v. 19: "Did not Moses give you the Law?" Just as Moses gave the Israelites the Law, so he also gave them the commandment of circumcision (Lev 12:3). However, this commandment goes back as far as the patriarch Abraham (Gen 17:10–12). As the foundational commandment of the people of God, the prescription for the circumcision of a male Israelite eight days after birth takes precedence over the Sabbath commandment. In the application of the example of the legitimate practice of circumcision on a Sabbath to the healing of a paralytic on the Sabbath, more recent exegetes like Brown see an argument "from light to heavy": if an operation on a human member is allowed on the Sabbath, how much more justifiable is the healing of an entire man on the Sabbath?[151]

However, this argument is not without its problems.[152] On the one hand, the employment of the exegetical rule "from light to heavy" assumes the use of two Scripture texts and not just one, as in the present case. On

---

151. Cf. Brown, 1:313.
152. Cf. Derrett, "Circumcision."

## Jesus Reveals Himself to His People (5:1–10:42)

the other hand, it is not exactly obvious how the removal of the foreskin of a male Israelite can be compared with the healing of a paralytic. As a solution to this problem, it is suggested that for the Jewish tradition Abraham's circumcision was bound up with the thought of perfection. In Gen 17:1, the account of the covenant of God with Abraham begins with the words: "I am God, the Almighty. Live in my presence and be perfect." In the Targum tradition, this expression is rendered with "undamaged" or "whole." Against this background, Jesus's thought process is more comprehensible: If one receives perfection on the Sabbath through circumcision, then why not also through a healing?

### Different Opinions about Jesus (7:25–36)

The following section has garnered less attention among interpreters. Thus it can be interpreted for the most part on its own terms. In the construction of John 7, the section stands between the first appearance of Jesus in the middle of the Feast of Tabernacles together with his words about his word and his work in John 7:14–24, and the revelatory saying of Jesus on the last day of the feast in John 7:37–39 with the ensuing controversies in John 7:40–52.

The construction of John 7:25–36 emerges with the aid of narrative and semantic criteria. From this double perspective, the section appears to be divided into two parts: vv. 25–30 and 31–36.

From the narrative flow, the subsection John 7:25–30 emerges as a self-contained text unit. The remarks of the inhabitants of Jerusalem in verses 25–27 are followed by the saying of Jesus in verses 28–29 and the evangelist's comment on the attempt to seize Jesus in v. 30.

The following group of verses displays a divergent construction. The beginning contains a double reaction to the person of Jesus: a positive and a negative. The latter leads to the attempt to seize Jesus (vv. 31–32). There follows a saying of Jesus concerning his impending departure (vv. 33–34), followed by the question for the audience as to what Jesus's words could mean (vv. 35–36).

Both groups of verses have in common the controversy as to who Jesus is. In verses 25–30, the focus is on where Jesus comes from. If he is the Christ, then one cannot know where he comes from. By contrast, people know where Jesus comes from and so he cannot be the Messiah. It will be shown how the evangelist employs the stylistic devices of misunderstanding and irony to convey his point of view.

In verses 31–36, the debate is whither Jesus is going. The attempt to seize him (vv. 30, 32) leads to the question as to where he is going. Once again, the author makes use of expressions with a double meaning in order to convey his message: Jesus's "departure" is understood as a departure for a journey to the land of the Greeks. This also contains an element of truth, but the meaning of Jesus's words is of a totally different nature. He will be going home to the Father.

We turn first to verses 25–30. The reference to the words and works of Jesus in the previous verses leads to the question who Jesus is. According to John, the answer to this question does not correspond to the criteria of human society. Thus, it cannot be known who he is when all that is known about him is his earthly father or mother or native city. According to John, Jesus comes from his heavenly Father and is going back to him. This fact leads to a series of misunderstandings in this and the following subsection.

**7:25–27** Jesus's argument against the accusation of the "Jews" that he has broken the Sabbath has apparently impressed his audience in Jerusalem. Thus, they begin to ask whether perhaps he is the Christ. The expression "some people from Jerusalem" is not found elsewhere in John but it fits the situation. John distinguishes in his description of Jesus's audience and their relation to Jesus and his message:

- the "crowd" (vv. 12, 20, 31–32, 40, 43, 49) remains basically open to Jesus's claim and asks about his identity; related to this are
- "some people from Jerusalem" (v. 25);
- the "Jews" appear hostile to Jesus and ready to get him out of the way (vv. 1, 11, 13, 15, 35); a different use of Ἰουδαῖοι is found only in v. 2;
- the "Pharisees" seem similarly hostile to Jesus (vv. 32, 45, 47–48); they form the Sanhedrin together with
- "the chief priests" (vv. 32, 45); together they can be called
- "the leaders" (ἄρχοντες, vv. 26, 48) who are in command of
- "the officials" (ὑπηρέται, vv. 32, 45–46); sometimes, there also appear
- "some," who are not explained more precisely, mostly in connection with the Jewish authorities who are seeking to arrest Jesus (vv. 25, 30).

These different groups help the readers to find their own position and to set up their own decision of faith (cf., above, v. 3, on the mention of Jesus's "disciples" after his "brothers").

## Jesus Reveals Himself to His People (5:1–10:42)

The "people from Jerusalem" mentioned in v. 25 appear as undecided and independent from the opinion of the leaders. Their question is concerned less with the identity of Jesus than with the opinion of the leaders' group about him. The basis for their question lies in the fact that Jesus is preaching openly without having to undergo any examination (cf. John 18:20). The hostile position of the Jewish authorities against Jesus is known to the readers. For the decision to kill Jesus, cf. John 5:18.

The description of Jesus as "Christ" is not found often in John's Gospel but it occurs in prominent places (cf. the first conclusion in John 20:31, the confession of Martha in 11:27 and of the man born blind in 9:22, as well as that of the Samaritan woman in 4:25, 29; cf., also, 1:41; 3:28). In John, this title appears to be still ambiguous and needing of explanation so that it is not misunderstood as being purely political or social (cf. the confession of Martha and the first conclusion of the Gospel in 20:31: "the Christ, the Son of God" ).

Against the confession of Jesus as "Christ," it can be objected that his origin appears to be known while, according to Jewish tradition, the origin of the Messiah is to be unknown. Scholars debate how far back this tradition of the "unknown Messiah" goes. R. E. Brown deals with this question in his commentary.[153] On the one hand, the Messiah has to come from Bethlehem, the city of David (cf. John 7:42; Matt 2:5). On the other hand, his identity can remain hidden and be revealed only by God (cf. Matt 16:17). In his *Dialogue with Trypho* (8.4; 90.1), Justin assumes the argument of the unknown Messiah and tries to answer it as an argument against Jesus as Messiah. According to Trypho, Elijah must come for the anointing of the Messiah. Close to this idea, there is also the apocalyptic tradition of the book of Enoch concerning the unknown Son of Man who is unknown at first and only revealed in the end time. John could have known both traditions.

**7:28–29** Jesus's answer is introduced with a solemn formula. Jesus does not "speak" but cries out with a loud voice. The verb κράζειν is employed by John for such solemn declarations, whether from the mouth of John the Baptist (John 1:15), or from the mouth of Jesus (John 7:28, 37; 12:44). The assertion that the audience knows him and knows where he comes from must be understood in light of "Johannine irony." In reality, Jesus's hearers do not know him just as they do not know the one who sent him (v. 29). His origin, from which one could deduce his identity, is not

---

153. Brown, 1:53.

earthly but heavenly: He comes from the Father who has sent him. The latter is "true," a predicate that is reserved for God and his revelation in John's Gospel (cf. John 17:3; a secondary use is found in John 19:35). The audience does not know God, but Jesus knows him because it is God who sent him.

**7:30** Here, for the first time, we come across the verb πιάζω, "seize," "arrest" (cf. John 7:32, 44; 8:20; 10:39; 11:57). With the claim to come directly from God, Jesus has exposed himself to the accusation of blasphemy. For this reason, the Jewish authorities attempt to arrest him. These authorities are not named explicitly, something that lends a Kafkaesque feature to this arrest. At this moment, however, no one is yet able to lay a hand on Jesus "because his hour was not yet come." The hour of Jesus will be that of his lifting up and glorification on the cross, and this hour is decided by the Father alone (cf. John 2:4; 8:20; 12:23, 27; 13:1; 17:1).

**7:31-32** Whereas verses 25–30 deal with the question of where Jesus comes from, so now in verses 31–36 the question is where he is going. Before the next saying of Jesus, it is reported that "many" of the audience believed in him. The reason for this faith lies less in the words of Jesus than in his spectacular deeds that could recall the Messiah (according to the rabbinical principle that the second Moses will perform the same works as the first; cf., also, Matt 11:3–5 par.). Such a faith based on Jesus's works is found elsewhere in John's Gospel (cf. John 2:23; 3:2); in other texts, there is faith in the word of Jesus, often set in contrast to a rejection of Jesus (cf. John 6:60; 7:40–44; 8:31; 10:19–21; 11:45–46; 12:9–11, 17–19, 42–43). These texts serve the function of preparing the readers for a responsible decision about Jesus. In John 7:32, the text speaks only of a "murmuring" about Jesus (cf. John 6:41, 43, 61; 7:12). That is already enough, however, to alarm the chief priests and Pharisees as members of the Sanhedrin and to cause them to have Jesus arrested by their officials. In v. 30, they were still anonymous.

**7:33-34** Jesus's saying that he will be only a short time longer with his conversation partners is to be considered in connection with his hour, which has not yet come but is drawing near (cf., above, v. 30). The formula "still only for a short time" that Jesus will be with his hearers returns again in John 12:35 and 13:33—addressed, in the first case, to the Jews, in the second, to the disciples. In the latter text, we find an express cross-reference back to our text in John 7:33: Jesus is going to a place where his hearers cannot come because he is going to the Father. Thus, just as his origin remains hidden from his hearers, so it will also be with his end. It is from this double perspective that his divine origin is revealed.

**35-36** Once again, Jesus's hearers are unable to understand his

*Jesus Reveals Himself to His People (5:1–10:42)*

words.¹⁵⁴ So they react with a further misunderstanding. They have understood that Jesus is going to a place they cannot reach. However, they understand these words in a physical sense and ask whether he intends perhaps to go to the Greek diaspora. This idea is another example of "Johannine irony." Of course, Jesus is not speaking of his departure for the Greek diaspora, but the idea of the hearers makes sense on a deeper level: Jesus will indeed get to the Greeks through proclamation, his death and his resurrection for the salvation of men. The section John 12:20–24, with the arrival of the Greeks who wish to see Jesus, will confirm this. The fields are white for the harvest (cf. John 4:35).

### *Jesus's Word of Revelation on the Chief Feast Day. Different Opinions about Him (7:37–52)*

The following section fits well into the previous context. Jesus has gone up to the Feast of Tabernacles only after its opening. He makes his first speech when the feast has reached its midpoint (John 7:14). He begins to speak again on the last day of the feast (John 7:37–38, with a comment of the narrator in v. 39). This is concluded with various reactions to Jesus and his claim in verses 40–44 and 45–52. In what follows, the story of Jesus and the woman taken in adultery is inserted (John 7:53–8:11). The setting of Jesus's next speech is not quite clear. It begins in John 8:12 and extends with different dialogue scenes as far as John 8:59. If one assumes that the story of the woman taken in adultery is an insertion into the Fourth Gospel, then Jesus's discourse that is begun in John 7:37–38 would continue until John 8:12. It would thus still belong to Jesus's discourse on the last day of the Feast of Tabernacles. This impression is confirmed by the fact that, in John 8:12, Jesus employs the symbol of light that we have already seen to belong to the Feast of Tabernacles. Thus, the scene of Jesus's speech would extend to John 8:59. The gift of sight to the man born blind in John 9 would fit well into this symbolic world. Since the good shepherd discourse in John

---

154. In v. 36, there are some uncertainties in the text. The ὅτι before ζητήσετε is too weakly attested to be taken into consideration. The με is absent in Nestle-Aland²⁶ but favored in the following editions on account of the ancient Egyptian tradition that attests it. ὑμεῖς is absent, as is the με, in P⁶⁶, but is adequately attested in the rest of the tradition and can so be considered original. Interesting is the insertion of John 7:53–8:11 at this spot in the Greek minuscule manuscript 225. In any case, this attestation confirms the uncertain home of this piece of text in the original Gospel of John.

10:1–18, with the reaction in 10:19–21, follows ch. 9 organically, the cycle of the Feast of Tabernacles would extend right up to John 10:21 before the Feast of the Dedication of the Temple in John 10:22.

From the narrative perspective, the passage John 7:37–52 divides into three subsections: verses 37–39 contain Jesus's short speech on the last day of the Feast of Tabernacles; in verses 40–44, there follow the reactions of the people with an attempt to arrest Jesus; and verses 45–52 enclose the controversy concerning the legitimacy of arresting Jesus.

**7:37–39** Before any exegesis, it is necessary to establish a reliable text form, especially for verses 37 and 38. Most editions of the text place a full stop after v. 37.[155] The expression "whoever believes on me" in v. 38 is then drawn to what follows. However, with the Jerusalem Bible and the *Einheitsübersetzung*, it is better to link the expression "whoever believes on me" with the previous context: "Whoever is thirsty, let him come to me, and let him drink, whoever believes on me." The parallelism is better preserved, and verse 38 contains a comprehensible christological interpretation.[156]

The group of vv. 37–39 divides into the narrative introduction in v. 37a–b, Jesus's discourse in vv. 37c and 38, and the comment of the evangelist in v. 39.

First, the narrative introduction (v. 37a–b): The setting in the temple and the time of the last, great day of the Feast of Tabernacles lend the scene considerable weight. The "great day" of the feast was the eighth day that had been added to close the feast week with special rites, including those of the drawing of water in the Pool of Siloam and the procession to the temple with the water that had been drawn. Jesus's saying is lent especial weight by the verb "cried" (κράζειν), which had already been used in v. 28.

Jesus's invitation in vv. 37c–38 is constructed chiastically. The twofold invitation is situated at the end of the first line and the beginning of the second; the characterization of the person invited in the first half of the first line and in the last half of the second. The form of Jesus's saying is synonymous parallelism. "Is thirsty" corresponds to "believes," "comes to Jesus" corresponds to "drink." Some scholars ask how one can be thirsty if one believes in Jesus. Perhaps the answer lies in the dynamic that comes

---

155. Cf. Nestle-Aland[28] and the Greek New Testament.

156. An alternative suggestion is found in Menken, "Rivers." According to him, one should put a full stop after "and drink." In the following sentence, the clause "whoever believes in me" would be a *nominativus pendens* and have to be translated: "of whom it is true: streams of living water will flow from him." However, this would refer to Christ.

## Jesus Reveals Himself to His People (5:1–10:42)

to expression in our verses: Whoever is thirsty is invited to come to Jesus and drink. If and insofar as he does, he presents himself already as one who believes.

In assuming the division of the text proposed above, the scriptural quotation refers to Jesus as the source of living water in a way that makes sense. Readers will recall the promise to the Samaritan woman of a source that will quench all thirst. One is also led to think, however, of the water and blood that flowed from the side of Jesus according to John 19:34.

This small section ends with the evangelist's comment in v. 39. He sees a relation between the promise of Jesus in John 7:37–38 and his death and resurrection as the moment of his "glorification."[157] A connection between the promise of living water and the gift of the Spirit appears in John 4 (cf. 4:23–24 about the true worshiper in spirit and truth); in John 4, the gift of the Spirit is also bound up with the "hour" of Jesus (cf. 4:21, 23).

The original of the scriptural quotation in John 7:38 is unknown (cf. the question "*unde*" in the margin of the text edition of Nestle-Aland). If one favors the reference of the quotation as being to Jesus and not to the believer, then exegetes today think especially of the rock from which, in the time of Moses, water sprang for the relief of Israel on its march through the desert. The relevant passages in the Pentateuch are Exod 17:1–7 and Num 20:8–13, taken up again in Ps 78:16–20. According to Menken,[158] who has studied this text the most extensively, the Johannine text is closest to Ps 78:16–20. Here, the "streams" of water and the verb "flow" are in evidence. The expression "deep within" could come from a revocalization of the Hebrew since this expression can signify "source/spring" as well as "body." Cf. Ps 114:8 cited by Menken as the "bridge" between Ps 78:16, 20 and John 7:38. A similar process of thought is found in the work of Joel Marcus.[159] Behind John 7:38, he sees the verse Isa 12:3, with a play on words with "source/spring" and "body," "Jesus" and "help."

With Menken, we can recall that the source of living water at the Feast of Tabernacles exhibits a reference to the passage of the temple source/spring in Ezek 47, which is then taken up in Zech 14:8. Jewish tradition knows of an eschatological and messianic interpretation of this source/spring.[160]

---

157. This connection is also emphasized by Weidemann, "Der Gekreuzigte."
158. Cf. Menken, "Rivers." For Moses and the gift of water in ancient Jewish tradition, cf. Bienaimé, *Moïse*.
159. Marcus, "Rivers."
160. Cf. the reference in Menken, 197.

We should point out that, in the New Testament, Paul in 1 Cor 10:4 compares Christ with the water from the rock that was given to the people of Israel in the desert. This water is called a "spiritual drink." We are very close here to the Johannine passage. The closeness of both texts is underlined by the fact that Paul speaks of "spiritual drink" in parallel with "spiritual food" (1 Cor 10:3). In John, it is precisely this theme of the manna that is encountered in a christological sense in the previous ch. 6 in a discourse characterized by Jesus as filled with "spirit and life" (John 6:63).

**7:40-44** As ever, Jesus's words arouse controversy among his hearers as to who he is. In verses 40-41, a positive reaction is reported, and in verses 42-43 a negative one that, in v. 44, leads not only to a reaction against Jesus's teaching but also to the attempt to arrest him.

First, the positive opinion in verses 40-41b. In the words of Jesus, the audience has heard the claim that he is the bringer of eschatological salvation, the true source of living water, the temple, and a messianic figure. Thus, some of them at least ask whether Jesus is not "the prophet," an eschatological figure who was expected according to Deut 18:18, or even the Messiah. Such expectations are attested not only in the Synoptic tradition (cf. Mark 8:27-30 par.), but also in John, as is shown by the text of the interrogation of John the Baptist in John 1:19-21.

The two positive reactions of the "crowd" are followed by a skeptical one in verses 41c-44: when the Christ comes, is he not to come from Bethlehem, the city of David? For David's descendants, one should think of 2 Sam 7:12; for the origin of the Messiah from Bethlehem, texts such as Mic 5:2 (quoted in Matt 2:6) or Ps 89:3-4. This argument was already employed by Nathanael in John 1:46. If one can assume a knowledge of the Synoptic Gospels in John, then the question of the "skeptics" could be another example of "Johannine irony." According to the infancy narratives of Matthew and Luke, Jesus does indeed come from Bethlehem. However, elsewhere, the fourth evangelist displays no awareness of this tradition. Humanly speaking, Jesus hails from Nazareth (cf. John 1:45-46; 18:5; 19:19).[161] However, his true place of origin is the Father and not this or that city (cf. above, John 7:25-29). The "division" that arises on his account is characteristic for chs. 5-12 of John's Gospel and reflects the different opinions about Jesus during his lifetime. At the same time, however, it serves to guide the readers. They must get on with their decision of faith. Among those listening to Jesus, one has to imagine the representatives of

---

161. Cf. Heil, "Jesus."

## Jesus Reveals Himself to His People (5:1–10:42)

the highest Jewish authorities in Jerusalem (cf. v. 45). They try to arrest Jesus (as already previously in v. 30, cf. 32). At this moment, they cannot achieve this since the time (the "hour") for Jesus has not yet come (cf., above, to John 7:30).

**7:45-52** The debate among the people is followed by a further one in the Sanhedrin. The account of this can be divided into two: the exchange between the officials of the Sanhedrin and the Sanhedrin itself (vv. 45–49), and that between the majority of the Sanhedrin and Nicodemus (vv. 50–52).

In v. 45, the "officials" appear as sent from the "chief priests and Pharisees," with a typical Johannine expression in which the "chief priests" refer to the time of Jesus and the "Pharisees" rather to the time of the evangelist.[162] In Mark, the composition of the Sanhedrin is described as "chief priests, scribes and elders" (Mark 11:27). For the members of the Sanhedrin, their own opinion, as "leaders" of the people, is more important than that of the crowd (cf., above, John 7:26). The basis of their judgement lies in their knowledge of the "Law" that, however, is brought into question by Nicodemus (v. 51). The reaction of the officials matches that of those who are mentioned in John 18:3 who were sent out to arrest Jesus but fell to the ground as Jesus identified himself with the solemn "I am he" (John 18:6). In both cases, the words of Jesus unleash fear and awe.

At this point, a division within the Sanhedrin itself is reported (vv. 50–52). Nicodemus, a member of the Sanhedrin, begins to speak. The readers know him already: it is recalled that it was he who came to Jesus by night (John 3:1-2). If it is assumed that Nicodemus came to Jesus by night out of fear of being seen, then his initiative here exhibits both courage and candor. He appears to have matured. Nicodemus reminds the other members of the Sanhedrin that, according to the Law, an accused person must be given a hearing (cf. Deut 1:16–17). The other members of the Sanhedrin do not take up his argument but only repeat the idea already known to the readers that no prophet comes from Galilee (cf., above, vv. 41–42).

The figure of Nicodemus appears to have a significant role in John's narrative strategy. Coming to Jesus first at night out of fear of the "Jews," he now appears as a man who courageously takes the part of Jesus before the highest Jewish authorities. Later, he will once again play a role at the scene when Jesus is taken down from the cross. With Joseph of Arimathaea, he takes himself to Pilate to beg the body of Jesus for an honorable burial.

---

162. Cf. Martyn, *History*, 71–73.

One can suspect that, for John, Nicodemus was one of those "crypto-Christians" who believed in Jesus without confessing this belief openly (cf. John 19:38–39). For John's readers, both these men serve as examples for fearless confession of faith in a hostile environment.[163]

The question "Who is Jesus?" also dominates ch. 7 of John's Gospel. If one listens attentively, however, it should be framed more correctly as: "Who is Jesus for the believer?" Thus, it is not a question of Jesus in himself but Jesus for the believer. This comes to expression in the central saying of Jesus in John 7:37–38: "Whoever is thirsty, let him come to me, and let him drink, whoever believes in me." The setting of the Feast of Tabernacles recalls the sacred symbols of water and light. They are taken up here and in John 8:12 as well as John 9. In this way, Christology is at the service of soteriology, the teaching about man's salvation.

One cannot speak of the salvation that Jesus brings, however, so long as it is an open question who he is. Thus, the dialogues and controversies of ch. 7 lead ever more urgently to the question as to who Jesus is. The answer is attached to the question of where he comes from and where is he going. It is thus rooted in Jesus's origin from the Father and his return to the Father. The Christology is grounded, therefore, in the theology.

It is precisely theology, teaching about God, that also links our chapter with Judaism. Jesus is the eschatological fulfillment of the Feast of Tabernacles. From him, as from the new temple, the salvific water of life is given and the light of the world shines out.

In this way, faith in Jesus is not simply a purely personal and rational agreement with his claim. It is taken up and lived in communion/community and has to be openly confessed. That is why Nicodemus appears at the end of the scenes. Like him, the readers have to be ready to confess their faith in Jesus without fear. Then, under the cross, they will experience his salvation. It is precisely for them that streams of living water flow from the opened heart of Jesus.

### Jesus and the Woman Taken in Adultery (7:53–8:11)

The pericope about Jesus and the woman taken in adultery appears like a meteorite in the narrative flow of John's Gospel. The passage interrupts the dialogues between Jesus and the "Jews" in the temple area of Jeru-

---

163. Cf. Beutler, "Faith and Confession."

*Jesus Reveals Himself to His People (5:1–10:42)*

salem. The theme appears unusual for John's Gospel. Jesus's behavior is different from that which he displays in the chapters before and after this incident. Jesus restrains himself and begins to speak only at the end of the episode. The literary form of the section is that of the so-called paradigm or apothegm, a genre rarely attested in John. Within the narrative, characters appear who are otherwise not encountered in John's Gospel, such as the "scribes" (John 8:3). The style is not really Johannine. The gentleness of Jesus causes one to think of that same quality that he shows in Luke (one thinks of the story of Jesus and the woman who was a sinner in Luke 7:36–50). In the early centuries, the attestation of the text is poor and its place in the order of the text inconsistent. Thus, we are confronted with the problem of the text's authenticity. On the other hand, the Council of Trent declared that the disputed sections of the New Testament are fully part of it and confirmed their canonicity and inspiration (DS 1504). What, then, is the meaning of this section?

First, we have the textual problem. More recent text editions place the passage in square brackets or put it in small print. It thus belongs to the text, but as an element that is disputed or uncertain. The Greek New Testament awards the exclusion of the text a grade "A," the highest degree of certainty. The reason for this judgement lies chiefly in the weak external attestation of the text, which is not witnessed by any Greek manuscript before the fifth century. Texts that do not include the pericope are both the Greek papyri ($P^{66}$ and $P^{75}$), Codex Sinaiticus, and, apparently, Codex Alexandrinus, Codex Vaticanus, and other ancient uncials according to the information of the apparatus in Nestle-Aland$^{28}$ and in the Greek New Testament, a greater part of the lectionaries, the ancient translations, and the Church fathers of the first millennium. Some newer works[164] have once again checked the attestation of the pericope from scratch but come to no result that is substantially different. The only new insight is that this story is considerably more ancient than modern editions of the text let one suppose. Thus, according to Eusebius, Papias knew the passage and ascribed it to the Gospel of the Hebrews. Codex D (Bezae), the oldest witness to the Greek text of the pericope, does not appear to be the basis for the later tradition since its text was not adopted by later manuscripts. Everything speaks for the fact that this pericope goes back to the first centuries. What is difficult to explain is its uncertain position in the Gospels. The majority of manuscripts transmit the text after John 7:52, the minuscule 225 after

---

164. Cf. Robinson, "Preliminary Observations"; Keith, "Initial Location."

John 7:36 (see there); other manuscripts put it after John 21 or after Luke 21:38 or 24:53. The lectionaries partly include only John 8:3–11, and this is marked with an obelisk by other manuscripts that, according to Maurice A. Robinson, does not mean that the text would have been regarded as secondary. Thus, we must account for the ancient nature of the passage despite its changing location in the Gospels.

How can we explain that a passage that goes back to the first centuries has such weak attestation? The reason seems to lie in the content. In a treatise on marriage, Augustine expresses his concern that the story could mislead Christian wives into not taking adultery seriously. Next to murder and apostasy, adultery was one of the three worst sins for the early Church, and there was no certainty that the Church could forgive them. This could explain why it was only with difficulty that the text could find acceptance in the canon of sacred books and a place in the canonical Gospels.

As to the content of the pericope, there are different approaches. First, there is the question of the historical probability of the scene. Thus, Alan Watson attempts to imagine the real life situation in which the passage could have originated.[165] The text throws up a series of questions that cannot easily be answered on the assumption of an actual incident in which the judgement of a woman caught in adultery takes place. From the beginning, it is not clear whether a formal trial preceded the question to Jesus. In the scene itself, there is an absence of a series of elements that were necessary for the trial of an adulteress. Why is there no mention of the man in question who, according to the Pentateuch, had equally to be brought before the court (cf. Lev 20:10)? Why is there no mention of witnesses? When Jesus asks "Has no one condemned you?," why can the woman answer, "No one, sir"? All of this does not fit with the idea that we are dealing here with the real case of a woman who has been caught committing adultery.

For Watson, the solution to this puzzle lies in the theory that the woman brought to Jesus was a wife who had been divorced according to the Mosaic Law and who had married again. According to the Synoptic Gospels (Mark 10:12 par.), such a woman would be committing adultery. If the scribes and Pharisees were bringing a woman like this to Jesus, then they were confronting him with the consequences of his rigorous teaching. The point, then, was not to see that justice was done for the woman, but to put Jesus to the test. If he forgave the woman, then he would be con-

---

165. Watson, "Jesus."

tradicting himself; if he condemned her, then he was acting against the gentleness that he otherwise advocated.

Watson's suggestion is ingenious but not fully convincing. He himself sees the problem: nowhere does the text of John 7:53–8:11 speak of a divorced woman. So it is better to proceed from a real case of adultery and not from a divorce that Jesus explained to be impermissible.

Increasingly worth consideration are attempts to approach the passage of Jesus and the woman taken in adultery with the means of narrative criticism. At the same time, feminist viewpoints can play a role here. This perspective is dominant in a volume edited by Larry J. Kreitzer and Deborah W. Rooke.[166] Not all the findings can be reported here. Some may be mentioned briefly. To these belong the already mentioned early attestation and the presumed reason for the exclusion from the canonical text, namely the problem for the morality of marriage resulting from the text. The pericope could find acceptance only after the church's position on the morality of marriage was adequately established. The scene itself shows male domination: men are judging a transgression that, by its very nature, concerns both a man and a woman. At the same time, the woman's guilt is presumed rather than demonstrated, just like Susanna who was unjustly accused by the elders.

For the exegesis of the passage in its present form, we need, first, to place it in its context. On the one hand, the insertion of the pericope in its present place is arbitrary; on the other hand, it also makes sense. In John, there are various passages that concern women. In the other cases, the women appear as disciples (like the woman of Samaria in John 4 or Mary Magdalene in John 19–20) or linked to Jesus through family friendship (like the sisters of Lazarus). Our case here is different but fits the positive image of women in the Fourth Gospel.

The context in John 7–8 is suitable for the insertion of this pericope. Jesus is speaking repeatedly here of judgement; one thinks of the controversies over the Sabbath in John 7:19–24, the debate in the Sanhedrin over the trial of Jesus in John 7:45–52 and the resumption of the theme of judgement in John 8:12–20 (with the motif of the two witnesses). The mention of the Mount of Olives in John 8:1 is understood not only from the Synoptic tradition but also from Zechariah 14, a passage to which the account of the Feast of Tabernacles alludes (cf. John 7:37–38). This Mount will be the scene of the Last Judgement.

---

166. Kreitzer and Rooke, *Ciphers in the Sand*.

The construction of the passage emerges from the application of narrative criteria. John 7:53–8:2 contains the narrative introduction of the pericope. In verses 3–6b, the question of the scribes and Pharisees is recounted, in verses 6c–8, the reaction of Jesus. Verses 9–11 describe the conclusion of the narrative.

**7:53–8:2** This small section introduces the scene and presents the characters. In verses 7:53–8:1, the preceding incident comes to a conclusion. The information about Jesus's conversation partners, who go back home, seems rather banal; the details about Jesus are inspired by the Synoptic tradition, according to which Jesus resorted to the Mount of Olives at night (Luke 21:37). In John, Jesus receives hospitality from his friends in Bethany (cf. John 11) and betakes himself to the "Garden of Gethsemane" at the foot of the Mount of Olives only on the last night (John 18:1). The place of the teaching of Jesus on the following day corresponds to the setting of the previous chapter and lends his words a greater authority. He "sits down" as the teacher of the Law and teaches (Greek imperfect for a lasting or repeated event).

**8:3–6b** The actors here are the scribes and Pharisees, the woman (brought in by them), Jesus, and probably a crowd listening to his teaching. This is the presupposition when it says that the woman was placed "in the midst." The scribes are encountered only here in John's Gospel and are one of the strongest indications of the non-Johannine origin of the story. The Fourth Gospel speaks rather of "chief priests and Pharisees" (cf. 7:45).

The passage assumes that the woman brought in by the scribes and Pharisees was indeed an adulteress. This can be questioned. In any case, the woman appears to be an adulteress in the eyes of her accusers. Thus, they are determined that the Law of Moses is to be executed, following Lev 20:10 (cf. Deut 22:22–24, which envisage the stoning not only of the woman but also of her partner). Watson has guided our attention to the fact that in this case all the elements that were necessary for the woman's trial are lacking: evidence and witness statements.[167] Of her partner, there is no word. In the end, Jesus will ask: "Has no one condemned you?" and the woman will say: "No one, sir." So the elements of a trial are absent.

The accusers ask Jesus for his opinion, but they do this, not out of concern for the woman, but only to put Jesus to the test. Thus, the scene has the traits of a school dialogue or a conflict dialogue over questions of Law. However, the further development of the scene excludes assign-

---

167. Cf. Watson, "Jesus."

ing the narrative to such a genre. As already noted, the narrative displays rather the traits of a paradigm or apothegm that reaches its climax in Jesus's saying.

**8:6c–8** In school and conflict dialogues, Jesus answers the question with a counter-question. The dialogue partners answer this counter-question and so allow Jesus to deliver his concluding answer. Our dialogue does not follow this pattern. Instead we see a small scene of concentric construction: Jesus bends down and writes with his finger on the ground; the woman's accusers insist that he give an answer. Thereupon, Jesus bends down again and writes on the ground. What is the meaning of Jesus's writing on the ground? Still today, exegetes ask about the text that Jesus, perhaps, was writing on the ground. Jeremiah 17:13 is often suggested as the text: "Those who turn away from you shall be written in the earth, for they have forsaken the Lord, the fountain of living water." The saying is addressed to Israel. Thus Jesus would be referring to the judgement that the prophet is proclaiming for all who turn away from the Lord. However, this proposal remains purely speculative. We have to acknowledge that we do not know what Jesus was writing on the ground. If the text says nothing about it, one has the impression that the content is scarcely of importance. So it boils down to the gesture that Jesus wrote on the ground. Thomas O'Loughlin has drawn our attention to the significance that Augustine suggests for this gesture.[168] The Bishop of Hippo sees a semantic opposition between Jesus's writing on the earth and the Decalogue's being written on stone as the basis for the accusation against the woman. This proposal seems very convincing. The Law of Moses may not be used as a rigid instrument of execution. One must write in the sand, handle it flexibly, and have regard for the situation and the people to whom it is being applied. In this case, what is relevant is that the accusers are themselves involved in sin. Whoever is without sin (ἀναμάρτητος, hapax in the NT), let him be the first to cast a stone at her.

**8:9–11** There now follows the conclusion of the narrative. The reaction of the accusers was predictable: they withdraw, one after the other. The expression "beginning with the eldest" reminds us of the elders who accused Susanna. Precisely on the basis of this correspondence, one asks whether one should not assume the innocence of the alleged adulteress in John. In fact, Jesus does not condemn the woman who had been condemned by no one else. His warning: "Go and sin no more" certainly does

---

168. O'Loughlin, "A Woman's Plight."

not assume the woman's guilt just as such guilt is not presupposed in the same saying he addresses to the paralytic who has been healed in John 5:14.

Augustine underlines the contrast between the just Jesus and the sinful woman. This view is rightly criticized. Jesus condemns the sin, not the sinner. The true antithesis lies in the hypocritical condemnation of the scribes and Pharisees and the demeanor of Jesus, full of understanding. Thus Jesus appears as the representative of a God who desires the life of a sinner and not his death. It could even be that the woman's sin is not unequivocally certain, and so more justice must be done to her in Christian exegesis.

Here we can take a further step by emphasizing the woman as the subject in our text. The traditional exegesis is almost exclusively interested in the role of Jesus by contrast with that of the religious representatives of his people. The woman herself remains the object, whether of the accusation of the scribes and Pharisees or of the defense by Jesus. Perhaps this is the moment to discover in this story an autonomous personality who deserves to be taken seriously and rehabilitated.

Where the historicity of the passage is concerned, the picture of Jesus it imparts is a good match with that of the Synoptic Gospels. Despite some circumstances that are difficult to explain, the situation is conceivable. Thus, a historical kernel of the narrative deserves to be considered as a possibility.

### *Jesus's Testimony about Himself (8:12–20)*

The following section does not seem to be inserted into its context intelligibly without further explanation. Jesus's last words were addressed to the woman with the command not to sin again. In John 8:12, Jesus turns again to an unnamed group—"they," probably his audience in 7:37–39, who, in 7:40–44, were described as "crowd" or "some" of the crowd. The adverbial "on another occasion" (πάλιν) recalls a similar previous discourse of Jesus without having to have a strong temporal sense (cf. the same adverb in v. 21). An indication of the location of the scene follows at the end of the section in v. 20. Jesus spoke his words in the temple when he was teaching "beside the treasury." This location lends a solemn character to Jesus's discourse.

The construction of the section John 8:12–59 is not easy to determine. At the beginning, the stage directions are helpful. Thus, verses 12–20

*Jesus Reveals Himself to His People (5:1–10:42)*

start off clearly. A further section follows with words of Jesus and, with the observation that many of the hearers believed in Jesus because of his words, lasts until v. 30. In the following section, vv. 31–59 lack any stage directions. Only at the close, in v. 59, is there an account of the listeners' reaction: they take up stones to throw at him.

From the semantic point of view, we can make out, with Jacques Cazeaux,[169] in verses 12–30 a first part of the section that focuses on the person of Jesus and his identity, followed by a second part in verses 31–59 concerned with his activity.

Examined in more detail, John 8:12–59 contains the following themes:

- the testimony of Jesus about himself (vv. 12–20)
- the origin and the goal of Jesus (vv. 21–30)
- the message of Jesus: the truth that makes free (vv. 31–36)
- the sons of Abraham (vv. 37–47)
- Jesus and Abraham (vv. 48–58)
- the attempt to stone Jesus (v. 59)

We must admit that these themes do not follow one another in a strictly logical order. As in a conversation, things go from one theme to the next by contrast with a treatise from which one would expect a logical sequence.

A certain development can be observed in Jesus's audience. At the beginning, his listeners are mentioned only in the third person without being named more specifically (v. 12). In v. 13, the "Pharisees" appear on the scene. Later, the text speaks of the "Jews who had come to believe in Jesus" (v. 31). However, the tone becomes ever more tough towards these groups, and, from v. 31 on, mention is made only of the "Jews" who are increasingly presented as hostile to Jesus (vv. 48, 52, 57).

The verses John 8:12–20 display the characteristic peculiarity of the revelatory discourses of Jesus in John's Gospel. In these speeches, Jesus is often interrupted by his conversation partners. In the light of the juridical character of the present section, one can also speak of a hearing, with accusations against Jesus and his defense. The theme of testimony confirms this legal aspect of the present section.

**8:12** Jesus's saying "I am the light of the world" could have been triggered by the Feast of Tabernacles during which the Court of Women in the

---

169. Cf. Cazeaux, "Concept ou mémoire?"

temple was illuminated by huge lampstands that bathed the whole city in light. According to its form, Jesus's saying is one of the so-called revelation sayings that have been studied by Schulz.[170] At the beginning stands the self-revelation of the revealer. There follow an invitation to the hearers and a promise. For Jesus as the light of the world, we should compare John 9:5; 12:46 in accordance with the prologue 1:4-5, 9, and John 3:19. The form of the saying in John 8:12 is the same as that in John 6:35 concerning Jesus as the bread of life. The Old Testament–Jewish background for the light metaphor in John 8:12 and the other places appears to be decisive. The psalmist's question "The Lord is my light and my salvation, whom should I fear?" (Ps 27:1) brings Israel's conviction to expression. Of God's servant, the text says: "I shall make you a light to the nations so that my salvation may reach the remotest parts of the earth" (Isa 49:6). From here it is but a step to Jesus's saying in John 8:12. Comparative Gnostic texts express the thought of the promises more clearly, but none of them is older than John's Gospel. The later they are reckoned to be, the more probable it is that they depend on John.[171] "Light" and "darkness" dualism is already in evidence in the Qumran texts (cf. the War Scroll [1 QM 1.1-17; 13.5-16] and the Rule of the Community [1 QS 3.13-4.26]) and is characteristic of John's Gospel (cf. John 1:4-5; 12:46). Here, to "follow" Jesus means to believe in him.

**8:13-14** The Pharisees answer Jesus's self-revelation with the objection that Jesus is bearing witness about himself and so his witness is not true (v. 13). The audience could here be invoking the speech of Jesus in John 5:31, where Jesus had admitted that a witness he would bear to himself would not be true. However, in ch. 8, the situation is different. Jesus is not just any witness but one who has been sent by God (v. 14).

According to this passage, Jesus can call on the testimony of two witnesses: his own and that of his Father who bears witness to him. It is not difficult to imagine Jesus's bearing witness to himself. He knows where he comes from and where he is going. But how can Jesus declare that the Father bears witness to him? Exegetes usually point here to the passage John 5:31-40, which has already been discussed. Here, Jesus speaks of the witness the Father bears to him. Above all, it is the Scriptures that speak of him if one reads them correctly. Alongside the Scripture of Israel (Moses) are the works with which Jesus is endowed by the Father that show his

---

170. Cf. Schulz, *Komposition*, 85-90.
171. Cf., extensively on this, Koester, "Gnostic Sayings," with texts especially from Nag Hammadi, who also reckons with parallel traditions.

sending to be legitimate (corresponding to the ten "signs" of Moses before Pharaoh and his wonders during the passage of Israel through the Red Sea and through the desert). In the exegesis of John 5:31-40, we pointed to some corresponding texts of Hellenistic-Jewish literature, especially to some treatises of Philo of Alexandria and Josephus that speak of the "testimony" of such signs on behalf of a person, in this case of Moses.

**8:15-18** The passage now turns to the theme of "judgement." Jesus appears to be facing judgement, but, on further examination, it is he who is the judge. He does not wish to judge on his own account (v. 15), by contrast with his conversation partners who judge "after the flesh," that is, as men judge. If Jesus judges, then he does so with justice since he is acting in union with the Father (v. 16). Thus, he is also meeting the prescription of the Torah according to which every matter is to be determined on the basis of the statements of two witnesses (Deut 17:6; 19:15; Num 35:30). He and the Father are the two witnesses (vv. 17-18).[172] In that way, the testimony of the Father in v. 18 is thought of as ongoing, by contrast with John 5:36-37.

**8:19-20** The audience remain skeptical and ask who this Father of Jesus is (v. 19a-b). They have not understood the allusion in v. 14 according to which Jesus knows where he comes from and where he is going. Thus Jesus is obliged to state that his hearers know neither him nor his Father (v. 19c-f). The hearers have no answer to this. They would rather have arrested him on account of blasphemy, but his hour was not yet come (v. 20; cf., above, 7:30).

The section John 8:12-20 is without parallels in the Synoptic Gospels. For the "great trial" between Jesus and the Jewish authorities concerning his mission there are no real analogies among the Synoptics. With his portrayal of things, the fourth evangelist is requiring his readers too to take a clear position on behalf of Jesus on the basis of the Scripture of Israel but also on the self-testimony of Jesus. This summons is timeless.

### The Origin and the Goal of Jesus (8:21-30)

The next section progresses the dialogue of Jesus with his Jewish audience concerning his claim and his mission. Thus, just as the section 8:12-20 takes up from ch. 5 with the theme of testimony, so the present section draws on ch. 7, especially 7:25-36 with the questions about the origin and goal of Jesus.

---

172. Cf. for this and the whole section, Beutler, *Martyria*, 265-71 (esp. 270).

**8:21–24** The first four verses of the section are determined by a conversation of Jesus with his dialogue partners (according to v. 13, the "Pharisees"). A saying of Jesus (v. 21) is followed by a reaction of his Jewish listeners, who speculate among themselves (v. 22), and a new saying of Jesus (vv. 23–24). We are not dealing here with a real dialogue since the partners are addressing one another and not Jesus. The theme of the section is similar to John 7:25–36 with the themes of the departure and origin of Jesus. Verse 21 partly takes up John 7:34 with the themes of the departure of Jesus and the inability of the Jews to go where he is going. However, a new motif is added: Jesus's hearers will die in their sins. However, the latter do not take this as an invitation to repentance and faith but ask one another whether Jesus perhaps intends to kill himself (v. 22). They thus display their lack of understanding just as Jesus's audience in John 7:3 has already asked if he is intending to go to the Greek diaspora.

In answering his audience's doubt (vv. 23–24), Jesus shows the reason for their lack of understanding. Just as he hails from above, from God, so are they from below, from this world and thus prove themselves to be incapable of understanding the meaning of Jesus's words of revelation. The content of faith demanded are the simple words: "I am he." In this formula, exegetes see an allusion to the formula with which God revealed himself to his people in the old covenant, especially in connection with the proclamation of eschatological salvation (cf. Isa 41:4; 43:10, 25; 45:18, 22; 46:4, 9; 48:12; 51:12; 52:6; Jer 24:7; Ezek 6:7, 13, etc.).[173]

**8:25–30** If verses 21–24 deal mainly with the question of the origin and goal of Jesus, the following verses are concerned with the question of who Jesus is. In response to the last saying of Jesus, the listeners pose a question that is understandable in the overall context of John's Gospel, but is not really appropriate here: "Who are you?" What they should have asked is who they were and why they were proving themselves unable to understand the words of Jesus. Thus, Jesus's answer shows that their question does not seem relevant to him: "Why am I still talking to you at all?" (v. 25)."

The question reproduced here is mostly reproduced in this form by exegetes today. However, other possible interpretations have been and are considered, and this led already early to textual variants. With Nestle-Aland[28], we are reading τὴν ἀρχὴν ὅ τι καὶ λαλῶ ὑμῖν. The editions of the text that support this question—from Westcott-Hort to the margin of the

---

173. Cf. Schnackenburg, vol. 2; Zimmermann, "Das absolute Ἐγώ εἰμι."

## Jesus Reveals Himself to His People (5:1–10:42)

Jerusalem Bible—are listed in the first apparatus of the Greek New Testament, and the German *Einheitsübersetzung* and Schnackenburg can be added to this. However, this apparatus also contains the supporters of a statement rather than a question (from the Textus Receptus to the Revised Standard Version; cf. Brown). The expression τὴν ἀρχὴν has various meanings. What cannot be justified is the meaning of the Vulgate, which understands the expression as a nominative and the words of Jesus taken as an answer to the question posed to him in v. 25a "Who are you then?" with the result:"The beginning who is speaking to you" / "Principium, qui et loquor vobis."[174] With Max Zerwick, it is advisable to take τὴν ἀρχὴν as an adverb: "Ante omnia, prorsus, omnino" ("especially, altogether, at all"). If one understands the following words as a question, they produce a good sense: "Why (ὅ τι = ὅτι) am I still talking to you at all?" This is the reading of the *Einheitsübersetzung* with Schnackenburg. The proposal of Edouard Delebecque is strongly under the influence of the Western doctrinal tradition: "Depuis le Principe, tout cela même que je vous livre."[175] In this, the author is taking Jesus's words as a direct answer to the question of the Jews in v. 25b. "Depuis" is, thus, interpretation. Chrys C. Caragounis understands the sentence similarly: "[I am] from the beginning!—precisely what I have been saying (speaking) to you." Here, the "I am" is supplied.[176]

"Why am I still talking to you at all?"—as the one sent by the Father, Jesus would have much to say to his conversation partners, but he sees almost no point in prolonging the dialogue with them (v. 26). They have not at all grasped that he was speaking to them of his heavenly Father (v. 27). Thus, they understand neither themselves nor Jesus nor the Father. They will be able to understand the mission of Jesus only when it is too late—when they have lifted him up on the cross. Only then will they recognize that Jesus was sent by the Father and that he carried out the Father's commission in word and deed to the end (vv. 28–29).

These words finally seem to have made an impression on the audience. It says that many of his hearers came to faith in him (v. 30). Perhaps it was the radical way in which Jesus had expressed his readiness to pursue his way to the end that had finally convinced his listeners. The readiness of Jesus had its basis and its strength in the fact that the Father was with him and had not left him alone.

---

174. Cf. Zerwick, *Analysis philologica*.
175. Delebecque, "Autour du verbe."
176. Caragounis, "What Did Jesus Mean by τὴν ἀρχὴν?," 129.

## The Message of Jesus: The Truth That Makes Free (8:31–36)

The next section begins with a weighty problem of interpretation. What does it mean in v. 31: "Then he said to the Jews who had come to believe in him"? Some think that the perfect πεπιστευκότας refers to Jews who had once believed in him.[177] This suggestion founders on the fact that the Greek perfect represents an action in the past that continues to have an effect in the present. So it is advisable to think of a group of people who had come to believe in Jesus and still believed (cf. John 7:31). How then can we explain that the tone with regard to this group becomes increasingly severe in what follows and right to the end of the chapter? Scholars have given different answers to this question. A first answer would be that, in verses 30–31, we are faced with a redactional sentence.[178] This suggestion, however, is followed by only a few authors. Others see a difference between the πιστεύειν εἰς in v. 30 and the πιστεύειν with the dative in v. 31: the latter expression would be weaker and would signify no real belief in Jesus. Still others see a shift between v. 32 and v. 33. The people to whom Jesus turns in v. 33 are the "Jews" hostile to him. However, such a break does not arise from the text. Consequently, we are dealing rather with men who have found an elementary faith in Jesus but who later prove themselves to be unable to penetrate fully into his mystery. People like this were already presupposed in John 2:23–25 and 7:31; from the pragmatic point of view, they have the function of bringing the readers of John to a mature faith in Jesus.

As for the construction of the group of verses: from the semantic point of view, verses 31–36 form a unit of text defined by the theme of "freedom" introduced in v. 32. From the narrative perspective, these verses do not stand alone since they continue the discourse of Jesus in v. 38. In what follows, the semantic division is taken as a basis.

**8:31-32** As suggested above, Jesus's hearers are Jews who have attained an initial faith in Jesus. They now have the duty to keep this faith—by remaining in the word of Jesus—and deepening it. This deeper penetration into Jesus's word will make them truly his disciples, and, as such, they will recognize the truth and obtain freedom. In John, the truth is the reality about God revealed by God in Jesus Christ. It is no philosophical concept. This is shown in the conversation between Jesus and Pilate in

---

177. So, among others, Swetnam, "The Meaning."
178. Thus Brown.

John 18:37–38. Jesus is "the way, the truth and the life" (John 14:6)—in other words, the way to life through the truth contained in the revelation received in faith. The meaning of the "freedom" promised by Jesus is not yet clear but will soon be made accessible.

**8:33** The promise of "freedom" has irritated Jesus's listeners. As Jews, they are the sons and daughters of Abraham and have never been the slaves of anyone. This observation derives from their religious self-image, for it was well known that Israel had lived for four hundred years in the "house of slavery" in Egypt. The scriptural basis for the awareness of the Israelites as free and the children of free parents is found in chs. 16 and 21 of the book of Genesis. The Israelites are children of Sarah, the freewoman, and not of Hagar, the slave (a theme taken up by Paul that he applies to the Christians, see below). The same claim—"We are children of Abraham"—is found Luke 3:8 in the mouth of John the Baptist as part of his preaching of repentance. Here too it is a question of the pride of Israel in being the chosen and favored people.

**8:34–36** Jesus's answer is introduced with the solemn formula: "Amen, amen, I say to you," which lends his word great weight. According to Jesus, freedom must be proved by works. Whoever sins is shown to be the slave of sin (cf. the same thought in 2 Pet 2:19). The consequence of slavery is seen in the exclusion of the slave from the house of his master when the time comes (cf. the case of Abraham who cast out the slave woman with her son according to Gen 21:8–21). The son, on the other hand, always remains in his father's house. The Son spoken of in v. 35 seems to be Jesus. According to v. 36, in him his audience too can live as free men, freed by the Son.[179]

In exegetical discussion, the question arises as to the tradition-historical background of the Johannine theme of freedom. As already indicated, biblical traditions have influenced our text, especially that of Sarah and Hagar in Gen 16–21. Influence from Gal 4 or, at least, a tradition common to both texts cannot be ruled out. The exegetes of John 8 point also to the Exodus-experience as the foundational experience for liberation and freedom in Israel.

Alongside these biblical traditions, some authors have also pointed to other cultural areas that could have influenced the theme of "freedom" in John 8. A first cultural area is found in Buddhist texts. According to

---

179. This connection between the sonship of Jesus, the divine adoption of believers, and the freedom of the Son/children is well analyzed by Tuñí Vancells, *La verdad*.

J. Duncan M. Derrett, John shows a kinship with Buddhist texts, and an influence of these writings on the Fourth Gospel cannot be excluded.[180] His collection of these parallel texts is impressive, but the question remains how on earth this Indian culture could have influenced the biblical one.

More probable is the influence of the Hellenistic world on the Johannine (and Pauline) concept of freedom. The closeness of the Johannine notion of freedom to Hellenism was already seen by Bultmann in his commentary (at John 8:31–36).[181] In the Stoa, one attained the freedom in which reason was allowed to explore and discover its own roots. This thought was taken up again in German idealism. By contrast with this conception, John sees the attainment of freedom not in the discovery of one's own rationality but in openness towards the divine word of revelation.[182]

*The Sons of Abraham (8:37–47)*

The section John 8:37–47 is probably the most debated section of the Gospel, if not of the whole of the New Testament. The reason for that lies in the description of the "Jews" as "sons of the devil" in v. 44 and in the demonizing of the "Jews" throughout the section. Ever since the Holocaust, there has been discussion of the possible anti-Judaism, if not anti-Semitism of John that could have contributed to the "Final Solution of the Jewish Question" under the domination of the National Socialists in Germany. It is not possible to cite here and discuss all of the literature on this theme. A first view can be gained from a volume that goes back to a colloquium at the University of Louvain in January 2000.[183] The date at the turn of the millennium was probably chosen deliberately.

With regard to the construction of the passage, the words of Jesus and those of his conversation partners can be distinguished from the nar-

---

180. Derrett, "Oriental Sources."

181. Cf. Bultmann, 334.

182. On the fundamental role of "freedom" in the ancient world of Greece and Rome, cf. Dautzenberg, "Freiheit." The author investigates the relationship between "freedom" in the Pauline Letters and in Hellenism, and demonstrates agreements and disagreements. A similar comparison can be made between John and the Hellenistic concept of freedom. See above, for Bultmann.

183. Bieringer, Pollefeyt, and Vandecasteele-Vanneuville, eds., *Anti-Judaism and the Fourth Gospel*. See there, among others, Beutler, "The Identity."

rative point of view. The section begins with the continuing discourse of Jesus in v. 37 that lasts until v. 38. In v. 39a–c, the "Jews" reply, and then Jesus answers them in vv. 39d–41a. After a new reaction of the "Jews" in v. 41b–d, there follows a final bit of speech by Jesus in verses 42–47. From this perspective, verses 37–38 can be distinguished as the continuation of the present section, followed by two exchanges between Jesus and his conversation partners in verses 39–41a and 41b–47. This division has the advantage of allowing two main themes to be recognized: kinship with Abraham in verses 39–41a (prepared in vv. 37–38) and the kinship with God and the devil in verses 41b–47.[184]

**8:37–38** In the next part of his discourse, Jesus takes up a saying of his conversation partners reported in v. 33: "We are the descendants of Abraham." Jesus does not in the least dispute their physical descent from Abraham but puts its foundation in question. The true children of Abraham have to recognize in Jesus the one sent by the Father who declares the words of the heavenly Father. His interlocutors follow the words of their father—a first allusion to their kinship with the devil. Instead of accepting the message of Jesus, they are trying to kill him.

**8:39–41a** The conversation partners have understood the allusion to a descent from the Evil One and repeat their earlier declaration (vv. 32 and 37) that they are the children of Abraham. In his answer, Jesus puts this declaration to the proof. If they were children of Abraham, then they would have to behave like Abraham. In concrete terms, that means that they show themselves obedient to the word of God that Abraham honored. Instead, they do not accept the word addressed to them in Jesus, but seek to kill him, the messenger. With the concluding statement: "You perform the work of your father" in v. 41a, Jesus is already preparing the transition to the twofold fatherhood, that of God or the devil, which will be the theme of the following subsection in vv. 41b–47.

**8:41b–d** From the theme of Abraham's descendants, the dialogue changes now to that of the descendants of God or the devil. Those taking part in the conversation have perceived this change of subject. They, therefore, explain that they are children of one Father, God, and not—on account of an act of adultery—of any other god. The image of adultery for Israel's relations outside faith in the only God was introduced from the time of the prophets (cf. Hos 1–2 or Ezek 16). The mention of the "one"

---

184. This change of subject has been recognized by different authors, thus, among others, by Schnackenburg; note also von Wahlde, "You Are of Your Father."

God reminds us of the chief commandment in Deut 6:4: to love the LORD as the one God of his people.[185]

**8:42-43** Jesus's answer presupposes the chief commandment. The conclusion is simple. If, as they declare, the "Jews" worship the true God, they must also "love" Jesus, that is, worship him, since he has proceeded from the Father. And since he comes from the Father, he also speaks the words that the Father has entrusted to him. If the "Jews" do not accept his words, it is not simply their fault but also indicates their inability to understand him. In v. 43, we are close to "double predestination," to salvation or damnation, but it can be inferred from the context that the hearers still have the possibility to come to the repentance God holds out to them (cf. John 6:44; 12:32), because of his love for the world (John 3:16) in his Son, the light of the world (John 8:12; 9:5; 12:46).

**8:44-45** The alternative to descent from God is descent from the devil. According to the author, the power of the devil has two characteristic features: violence and lies. Satan has exercised his influence since the beginning of human history with Cain's murder of his brother, Abel. The same theme is found in 1 John 3:12-15. It could go back to a common tradition. The theme of lies is found early in connection with Satan, probably because of the account in Genesis of the deceiving of our first parents by the serpent (Gen 3), which precedes that of Cain and Abel (Gen 4). According to v. 44, the devil is a liar from the beginning and the father of lies. Insofar as Jesus comes from the Father with his true and trustworthy message, he deserves faith. However, that is what his hearers are denying him (v. 45).

Verse 44 stands in the middle of the present debate over anti-Judaism in John. How on earth can an evangelist call the Jews (with or without quotation marks) "children of the devil"? The reception history of this text has shown that it has been commonly understood as a judgement by Jesus regarding the Jewish people and the Jewish religion. In the face of such a conclusion, however, it is worth recalling one or two things.

A first aspect has already been mentioned. In the previous verses, the theme of faith had already been introduced with a reference to Israel's confession of faith, the *Shema Israel* of Deut 6:4-5. Thus, one cannot claim that, in our text, the Jewish religion has been replaced by the Christian one. The question is only who the true Israelite is in whom there is no guile (cf. John 1:47).

---

185. Cf. Beutler, "Das Hauptgebot."

## Jesus Reveals Himself to His People (5:1–10:42)

The tone and the language of our passage are explained, at least partly, by the accepted form of polemic in the circle of the Fourth Gospel. This appears plausible from the above-mentioned article of Urban von Wahlde.[186] According to this author, the polemic between Jesus and his conversation partners in John 8 forms an example of the controversies such as we find in contemporary Judaism and early Christianity. The texts studied by von Wahlde are those from Qumran, especially 1 QS 3.13–4.26, Testaments of the Twelve Patriarchs, and the First Letter of John (1 John 2:29–3:10; 4:1–6). The texts first mentioned are both of Jewish origin and go back to the second century BCE; the third text is Christian but makes use of the tradition. According to von Wahlde, these texts have five common elements:

- Different protagonists (in Qumran, the Spirits of Truth and Lies; in the Testaments of the Twelve Patriarchs the spirit of God or Belial)
- The work of God or of the devil is being carried out
- The general traits of each group are listed (on the one hand, the sins and the lies; on the other hand, the works of virtue)
- The particular traits of each group are listed (cf. T. Levi, T. Jud., T. Naph., and T. Ash.), such as, for example, sacrilege, lack of obedience to God's commandments, etc.
- There is an ethical rather than an absolute dualism. There is always the possibility of repentance so that one can speak rather of a "decisional dualism" rather than a metaphysical one.

What is to be registered from this list of elements that are common to the Qumran texts, Testaments of the Twelve Patriarchs, and the First Letter of John is that the first two are clearly from literary circles that are Jewish. Thus, one cannot say that, in using such polemic, John is betraying an anti-Jewish attitude. The controversy is more concerned with the question as to who is a true Israelite. Moreover, it is to be kept in mind that the controversy of John 8:31–58 is taking place between Jesus and a group of Jews who had come to believe in him. The tone of the controversy is explained by the danger of apostasy that threatened the first Christian communities.

Furthermore, in the early Church, there was also a "demonizing" of opponents in conflicts concerning the true doctrine.[187]

---

186. von Wahlde, "You Are of Your Father."
187. Cf. Pedersen, "Anti-Judaism."

**8:46-47** The fact that the message of Jesus found no acceptance is not founded in the limitations of Jesus or in his message itself. Jesus can take pride in not having committed a sin, and his message is pure truth. The guilt, therefore, lies with his hearers. They deny him their faith. This failure has a deeper reason in the origin of the listeners that is not from God, but from elsewhere. If they came from God, then they could accept the message of Jesus. The readers will recall the prologue where it says: "But to all who did receive him, he gave the power to become the children of God, all who believe in his name, who were born not from blood, nor from the will of the flesh, nor from the will of man but from God" (John 1:12-13).

### Who Are the "Jews" in John?

We may recall here the contribution in the proceedings of the Louvain conference.[188] The authors distinguish four different ways in which the word Ἰουδαῖοι is used in John:

- the Jews as a people
- the Jews in antithesis to the Gentiles
- the Jews as the contemporaries of Jesus with their customs and feasts
- the Jews as the opponents of Jesus

The problem lies in the fourth use of the word. In general, these opponents seem to be identical to the Jewish authorities in Jerusalem. The two single exceptions, in John 6:41, 52, can be explained through the probably later date of composition. The coincidence of the "Jews" in the typically Johannine sense with the authorities in Jerusalem can be demonstrated especially clearly in John 9 where, in v. 22, it says that the "Jews" had already decided to exclude from the synagogue those who believed in Jesus. This statement makes sense only if the subject is a group of Jewish people with legal power, since the man born blind himself, his parents, and his neighbors are all Jews. A connection of that group with the province of Judaea is not thereby excluded.[189]

Once again, one should mention here that the first readers of John's Gospel could fully understand the special meaning of the Johannine ex-

---

188. Cf. Beutler, "The Identity."
189. Cf. Beutler, "The Identity"; Lowe, "Who Were the Ἰουδαῖοι?"

pression "the Jews" in the sense of a group among the Jewish people in Jerusalem who were hostile to Jesus. The situation was altered with the inclusion of the Gospel into the corpus of the New Testament. In all the other books, as can be shown, the expression οἱ Ἰουδαῖοι describes the members of the Jewish people or the Jewish religious community. This led to the fact that the readers of John's Gospel as part of the New Testament almost inevitably identified Jesus's opponents in John with the "Jews" in the general sense of the word. The consequences were incalculable, from the pogroms of the Middle Ages and the present day through the ghettos in the "Christian" cities (including Rome), to the ostracism and eventual extermination of the Jews in the concentration camps of the Nazi era. One cannot claim that the New Testament was the main reason for anti-Judaism in so-called Christian countries, but, equally, one can hardly dispute that this Christian anti-Judaism also had an influence on the hatred of the Jews in the twentieth century.

### Jesus and Abraham (8:48–59)

Already in the previous section (John 8:37–47), the talk had passed from the question concerning the true descendants of Abraham to that of the true children of God. In the present section, the theme changes again. Jesus will now speak of his relationship to Abraham, and, as a result, the dialogue reaches a theological depth hitherto unplumbed. However, Jesus's testimony about himself encounters a hostile reception and he narrowly escapes the hands of those who wish to stone him for blasphemy.

It is easy to make out the composition of the section: a first exchange between Jesus's conversation partners and himself in verses 48–51 is followed by a second in verses 52–56 and a concluding one in verses 57–58. A comment of the narrator in v. 59 marks the conclusion of the section.

At the beginning of the first two exchanges, the accusation against Jesus is surprising: he is possessed (vv. 48 and 52). This kind of language is still in the memory of the readers. Shortly before, Jesus had declared that his conversation partners came from the devil (v. 44). Now they direct the same accusation against him. Whoever reads this passage with one eye on the religious controversies of that time will not be astonished at the accusation raised against Jesus (cf. above at v. 44).

**8:48–51** Once again, Jesus's origin is at the center of this exchange between Jesus and his conversation partners. The starting point for the

"Jews'" accusation against Jesus does not lie in the pre-eminence he is claiming for himself but in his statement that they do not come from God (v. 47). In their answer, the "Jews" turn the argument around and dispute that Jesus comes from God. He appears to be a Samaritan or one possessed (v. 48). An explanation of the accusation of being possessed has been given shortly before (see above, the introduction to this section). The accusation that Jesus is a Samaritan is found in John and in the whole of the NT only here. In his commentary, Beasley-Murray[190] gives a survey of the suggested meanings: a) The Samaritans were regarded by the Jews as heretics since they rejected the worship of God and claimed to be performing a cult established by God; b) the Jews seem to have considered the Samaritans to be magicians; c) Samaria was the home of prophets who claimed divine dignity for themselves, such as Dositheus, who saw himself as the son of God, and Simon Magus, who reckoned himself to be "the great power"; d) the Jews could consider Jesus as a Samaritan because his teaching seemed similar to that of the Samaritans.[191] It cannot be excluded that reasons different from these come into play.

In his reply, Jesus does not deal with the first accusation (he is a Samaritan) and answers the second one (he is possessed) with the assurance that he came not from the devil but from God. He seeks the honor of God—that God to whom they do not wish to render any honor while they do not wish to believe in the one whom he has sent. In John's Gospel, the verb τιμάω is found relatively seldom (apart from here, it is found only four times in John 5:23 and once in John 12:26). More frequently attested is the verb δοξάζειν "glorify" that refers to the suffering servant. In John 13:31–32 and 17:1–5, the thought of the mutual glorification of the Father and the Son is found. This idea is also presupposed in John 8:49–50. The Father who honors his Son will also be the judge of those who have denied Jesus, the Son of God, the honor due to him. The word of judgement is followed by a promise: whoever keeps the word of Jesus will never see death. Occasionally, a reference to the first logion of the Gospel of Thomas is seen here.[192] This does not mean, of course, that there is any literary dependence here whether of John's Gospel on Thomas or vice versa. A common tradition

---

190. Beasley-Murray, 136.
191. Here, however, caution is required, cf. Thyen, "Die Ἰουδαῖοι."
192. Cf. Koester, "Gnostic Sayings"; Beasley-Murray, 173, who points to the fact that the expressions "taste death" and "see death" are found both in the Gospel of Thomas as well as in John (for the former logion 1, cf. John 8:52; for the second logion 18, 19 and 85, cf. John 8:51).

would be enough. For "keeping the word" of Jesus, cf. John 14:23; 15:20; 17:6. This expression originates in the language of covenant theology.¹⁹³

**8:52-56** In their reply, the "Jews" turn back to the theme of Abraham who was last mentioned in v. 40. This marks the start of a twofold line of thought that is connected with Abraham: to have been heard by Abraham or to have seen Abraham or been seen by him. The dialogue begins with the hearing or keeping of the word of Jesus. According to v. 51, one who has accepted the word of Jesus will never die. Applied to Abraham, this would mean that he would never have died. The same goes for the prophets. The argument of Jesus's conversation partners is incomprehensible unless we presuppose an allusion to Jesus's claim in v. 58 that he was before Abraham. In v. 53, the conversation partners confine themselves to questioning Jesus's claim to be immortal and in this sense to stand above time. If this were the case, then Jesus would indeed be superior to Abraham and the prophets who had to die. For the question: "Are you greater than our father Abraham?" cf. the similar question of the Samaritan woman: "Are you greater than our father Jacob?" (John 4:12). The drift of the Johannine texts is the same in both cases: Jesus indeed stands over the patriarchs.¹⁹⁴ For Isaac, see below at v. 56 (ἠγαλλιάσατο, he rejoiced).

In his answer, Jesus takes up the theme of the honor that the Father and Son render to each other (cf., above, vv. 49-50), now with the stronger Johannine vocabulary of mutual "glorification." The Father "glorifies" the Son since the latter remains true to his mission to make the Father known. If the "Jews" claim to know him, they are not simply mistaken but they are lying since they are deliberately speaking the opposite of the truth. This marks a return to the theme of lying that had already been addressed in connection with the devil's kindred (cf. above, v. 44).

Abraham rejoiced since he was to see the day of Jesus. At first sight, this statement is not comprehensible. Clearly, the Jewish and rabbinic notion is being presupposed here, according to which Abraham foresaw the days of the Messiah. Johanan ben Zakkai was of the opinion that God revealed only this world to Abraham; Rabbi Akiva, by contrast, reckoned that he also revealed the future world to him. Other rabbis too express themselves along these lines. Abraham's "rejoicing" is explained by his laughter at hearing the news that, despite his advanced age, he would still beget a son (Gen 17:7), or by the name given to this son, "Isaac," "he

---

193. Cf. Beutler, *Habt keine Angst*, 55-62.
194. Cf. Theobald, "Abraham."

laughed." In this expression of "rejoicing" one can also find an eschatological dimension.¹⁹⁵ There is a parallel text in John 5:35, where it says that the Israelites wished to enjoy this delight only for a short time.

**8:57-59** Already in v. 56, there has been a transition from "hearing" to "seeing." This idea is taken up by Jesus's conversation partners in their reply. They had picked out that when Jesus spoke of Abraham having seen his days, he must have seen Abraham (if we do not follow the variant that reads Jesus was seen by Abraham¹⁹⁶). This seems impossible, however, since Jesus was not yet fifty years old.¹⁹⁷ Scholars ask why John inserted this particular age. It is difficult to reconcile with the statement of the Synoptic tradition that when Jesus began his ministry he was about thirty years old (Luke 3:23). Two grounds are offered for this Johannine number. On the one hand, those who had achieved the age of fifty, after the end of a professional and social career, had reached old age. On the other hand, fifty years lead up to the so-called Jubilee or Jubilee Year according to Lev 25:8-12 as the year of grace and remission (cf. Luke 4:19). In particular, the book of Jubilees sees the whole of history parceled out in a series of jubilees. The argument of Jesus's conversation partners could have been that Abraham did not experience four jubilees and, therefore, Jesus, who had not yet experienced a jubilee once, could scarcely have seen Abraham. For the role of jubilees for Abraham, cf. Jub 23:10, 11, 15; a descendant of Abraham is announced in 16:1ff. Cf., also, 11Q Melch for the announcement of the Messiah.

In his reply (v. 58), Jesus explains with a solemn formula that he *is* before Abraham *was*. With this statement, Jesus's revelation to his hearers reaches its climax. In John 10:30, there is a similar climactic statement towards the end of Jesus's final revelatory discourse in the temple: "I and the Father are one." How is the "I am" in v. 58 to be explained? The same expression has already been met with in John 8:24, 28. Here, we already re-

---

195. Cf. Mörchen, "Johanneisches 'Jubeln.'"

196. In v. 57, the vast majority of the manuscripts read ἑώρακας and a small group, which, however, goes back to an early time (P⁷⁵ 070 *א sy⁸ sa ly pbo), reads ἑώρακέν σε. To the manuscripts listed by Nestle-Aland²⁸ should be added the *Diatessaron* of Tatian in its original form, as Baarda, "John 8:57b," has highlighted whereby this reading can be traced back to the middle of the second century in Rome. Baarda, therefore, maintains this reading as original. However, it might be advisable, with Beasley-Murray, to remain cautious about this hypothesis. It could be that an early copyist changed "saw" to "was seen" because of the logical difficulty offered by "saw."

197. On the problematic nature of the verse, cf. Delebecque, "Jésus contemporain."

ferred to the absolute use of "Ego eimi" as a Johannine revelatory formula going back to the prophets of the Exile, especially Deutero-Isaiah. Scholars refer also to the self-revelation of God in the burning bush according to Exod 3:14. In both cases, it is indicated that God is revealing himself not simply as absolute Being but as the one who is there for his people. Thus, in the last analysis, the formula is soteriological. Jesus exists forever, and is forever present for his own and for the world he came to save.

The "Jews" cannot, of course, accept this claim of Jesus but attempt to stone him on account of his blasphemy (cf. 10:39). So Jesus has to spirit himself out of the temple, just as also later at the end of ch. 10. Just as he had "secretly" gone up to the Feast of Tabernacles (cf. 7:10), so he hides himself once more, in order to await the "hour" of his coming home to the Father.

### The Healing of the Man Born Blind (9:1-7)

Further scenes in Jerusalem ensue. The action takes place first on the streets, squares, and public areas of the city before being transferred back to the temple precincts in ch. 10. The story of the healing of the man born blind with the dialogues that follow is clearly in contrast to the previous context. New people and groups appear on the stage. The passage is defined by a new plot. Thus, scholars are agreed that a new episode begins in John 9:1, despite the fact that one has to bear in mind the larger context since the beginning of the Feast of Tabernacles in John 7:1.

It is not quite so easy to determine the end of this story. Until not so long ago, the story was read, for the most part, as ending in John 9:41, with a new episode concerning the good shepherd beginning in John 10. Occasionally, in fact, the shepherd discourse or a part of it was seen, at first glance, to be a text unit foreign to John's Gospel that had been inserted here, or else the discourse was treated as an insertion by the redactor (see below). Added to this were attempts to relocate the shepherd discourse within the Fourth Gospel, and to abandon its connection with ch. 9 altogether.

For the original connection between John 9 and 10, it is significant that the division of the New Testament into chapters goes back only to the early thirteenth century (by Stephen Langton, Archbishop of Canterbury, 1206). A glance at the great uncials of the New Testament (such as Codex Vaticanus, Alexandrinus, or Codex Bezae Cantabrigiensis) shows that, in their reproduction of the text, John 10:1 follows directly on 9:41. Thus, the drastic caesura between the two chapters that is often accepted must first be established by exegetical means. The decisive reason for a closer connection between chs. 9 and 10 lies in the fact that Jesus's conversation partners at the beginning of John 10 remain the same as those in 9:39–41: cf. the "I say to you" in 10:1 and the first conclusion of Jesus's discourse in 10:6: "Jesus told them this parable." This view is confirmed by the cross-reference back to the healing of the blind man in 10:19–21.

One of the first authors in more recent times to emphasize the connection between John 9 and John 10 was Dodd.[198] He sees in John 9:1–10:21 a sequence of "narrative" (9:1–7) and "dialogue" (9:8–41) that passes more firmly into Jesus's discourse in John 10:1–18, 22–30. A similar sequence can already be observed in John 5.

Moreover, with a view to the more recent contributions on John 10, of which we have still to speak, it is advisable to see a close connection between John 9 and John 10. Above all, the closing section in John 9:39–41 is clearly forming a bridge between the two chapters and occupies a key position for understanding them.

In German-speaking research especially, questions of composition history are also in the foreground in John 9. Thus, first of all, a distinction is made between the story of the healing miracle in verses 1–7 and the following dialogue. In the former, traditional material is generally accepted in verses 1 and 6–7, thus establishing the kernel of the healing story as the most ancient traditional material.[199] Not infrequently, the ensuing dialogue is also ascribed, though in a different way, to the pre-Johannine tradition, something like the "signs source."[200] The linguistic and conceptual material of the evangelist come to expression especially in verses 2–5 or 3b–5 and 39–41.[201] Here, then, there extends the arc of Jesus as the bestower of light

---

198. Dodd, *Interpretation*, 354–62.

199. So, approximately, Becker, 1:370; according to Schnackenburg, 2:304f and Schnelle, 186, vv. 2–3a could also belong to the tradition.

200. According to Brown, in John 9, it underlies the text as far as v. 17; according to Becker, until v. 34; and according to Reim, "Joh 9," until v. 39.

201. Among others, this is emphasized by Haenchen, 383. He ascribes the rest of the narrative to a "Grundschrift." According to Painter, "John 9," the evangelist would have expanded an original healing story in verses 1–3, 6–7, 8–11 in two phases: first, in verses 4–5 and 12–39 (with traditional material) with the aim of encouraging secret Christians to renounce their anonymity and confess their faith in Christ openly, and then, after the separation of church and synagogue, in verses 40–41, which could only further pronounce judgement on the "Jews'" lack of faith. The Christian community could thus go on its way undeterred. The separation of the text into phases remains too speculative to prevent the increasing ascription of the text to the evangelist.

to the man born blind and to the believers in that those who believe they can see are increasingly shown to be blind.

However, in saying that, we have already arrived at the treatment of the text in its final form. This is increasingly the interest of scholars in more recent exegesis. The object of a study by Venance Bacinoni,[202] probably under the influence of French structuralism, is precisely the thought of the progressive path to light of the man who was formerly blind with the simultaneous darkening of the sight of Jesus's opponents. Not only does the blind man obtain his sight, but he also comes by steps to the confession of Jesus as Messiah and Son of God, while the Pharisees get ever deeper into darkness on account of their lack of faith. Thus, the readers are confronted with the question of their own faith decision. Similarly from Rome, there has emerged the work of Santos Sabugal on the dramatic structure of John 9.[203] This allows the recognition of the leading interest in the messianic-eschatological dimension of the passage. In John 9 different levels of Christology can be made out, and these can lead the readers to the confession of Jesus as the Christ: from "man" (v. 9) by way of "prophet" (v. 17) and one who "comes from God" (v. 33), to the "Son of Man" (vv. 35–38). Jesus is thus revealed gradually as the "light of the world" (v. 5). This view of things makes sense and makes difficult any dividing up of the passage according to different Christologies in successive redactional stages.

A very helpful francophone contribution is the structural analysis by Michel Gourges.[204] The six scenes of the narrative (vv. 1–7, 8–12, 13–17, 18–23, 24–34, 35–41) can be grouped in pairs. The first two scenes deal with the "deed," the third and fourth with the "trial," and the two last with the "judgement." The trial contains three questions: the miracle, how it happened, and who performed it. Scenes 2–5 focus on these questions. This creates a movement from "miracle" to "sign." Four types of reaction can be distinguished:

(1) of those who ask no questions (the neighbors of the man born blind)
(2) of those who ask but do not believe (the Pharisees)
(3) of those who believe but do not witness to this faith (the parents)
(4) of those who ask, who believe, and who witness to this faith (the man born blind himself; cf. the different stages of his christological confession)

202. Bacinoni, "L'aveuglement."
203. Sabugal, "La curación."
204. Gourges, "L'aveugle-né."

Gourges too sees the inclusio between verses 4–5 and 39–41 through the motif of light and the notion of judgement.[205]

In more recent times, there have been an increasing number of suggestions that see a path to faith and to light depicted in John 9, while the Pharisees, despite their evident ability to see, become ever more blind in that they close themselves off to faith.[206]

After these introductory remarks to John 9, we turn to the first seven verses. These contain the account of the healing. On closer examination, it appears that the narrative begins not in John 9:1, but in 8:59. There it says: "But Jesus hid himself and left the temple." From the Greek, we should read a coordinate clause here: ". . .and, as he was on his way, he saw a man who had been blind since birth." Thus, John 8:59 contains two elements that are absent in 9:1: the grammatical subject and an indication of the place where the encounter with the blind man occurred. The narrative flow of the section can thus be determined more easily.

The scene of action appears to be an area outside the temple in Jerusalem. The time of the larger context is given as the Feast of Tabernacles. More exactly, probably, it is the "great day" mentioned in 7:37 and so the day on which Jesus described himself as the "light of the world" (John 8:12; the section 7:53–8:11 probably does not belong to the original form of the text, see there). As for the persons mentioned in the text, we have to distinguish between the narrative and the narrative world. Within the narrative, only a few active characters appear. Jesus is clearly center stage here. At the beginning, in v. 1, he sees the blind man. The disciples ask him who was responsible for this blindness (v. 2), and he gives the answer (vv. 3–5). Then Jesus addresses himself to the healing of the blind man. He forms some clay, smears it over the eyes of the blind man (v. 6), and sends him to the Pool of Siloam to wash there and be healed (v. 7). In the "narrative world"

---

205. We should also mention contributions from the United States that study the chapter with the methods of rhetorical criticism. Bishop, "Encounters," studies the chapter from the perspective of "encounter" between the man born blind and Jesus, Resseguie, "John 9," takes the thought further and examines an inner growth on the part of the man born blind to a more mature identity in the course of his emancipation from his parents' home and his former faith community and his acceptance by Jesus. From the Indian perspective, Soares-Prabhu, "Der Blindgeborene," sees Jesus as the giver of light for men who are seeking God but also for the suffering and those who are physically thirsty.

206. Cf. Zumstein, "Wissenskrise"; Labahn, "Der Weg eines Namenlosen"; Labahn, "Blinded by the Light"; Scholtissek, "Mündiger Glaube"; Theobald, "Missionarische Gestalten," 480f.; Wright IV, *Rhetoric*.

*Jesus Reveals Himself to His People (5:1–10:42)*

other subjects also appear: alongside the blind man and his parents, Jesus and his disciples, the works of God, day and night are mentioned (vv. 3–5). In v. 7, the Pool of Siloam is interpreted by the narrator.

The core element of the narrative in verses 1 and 6–7 enables the recognition of a healing miracle story typical of such accounts in Judaism and Hellenism: at the beginning is the exposition with the description of the sickness (v. 1). Then come the action of the healer, including the employment of saliva (v. 6), the word to the blind man, its explanation, and, finally, the declaration of the successful healing (v. 7). Pools or other bodies of water could play a role in healings, not only in John (cf., also, John 5), but also in the Old Testament, as is shown by the story of the Syrian leper, Naaman, and his healing by the prophet Elisha in 2 Kgs 5:10.[207] What is striking is the absence of a "choral conclusion" at the end of the miracle story as is otherwise often the case ("Who is this?," "a great prophet is risen up among us"). Instead, John recounts various reactions of the witnesses of the miracle and so offers the readers different models with which to identify.

The dialogue between Jesus and his disciples over the cause of the blindness in verses 2–5 does not match the pattern of the healing miracle story. It appears to reflect a later hand, although that does not have to be the actual hand of the evangelist. In any case, the latter is responsible for verses 3c–5. This is confirmed by the syntax. The story itself consists of a series of main clauses linked by "and" (9:1, 2, 6 twice, 7 twice). At the beginning of v. 3, the lack of connection (asyndeton) is striking. Subordinate clauses are found only in verses 2–5. Otherwise, there is only an explanatory relative clause in v. 7. The tense employed for the narrative is generally the aorist. The present is encountered in vv. 4–5. The dominant person is the third, but in v. 4 we also meet the first person plural and, in v. 5, the first person singular plus the second person in the word to the blind man in v. 7. Thus, yet again, the difference in verses 4–5 is manifest.

**9:1** As mentioned, the narrative really begins in John 8:59c–d. Jesus hides from his enemies and leaves the temple. On the way, he sees a man who was born blind. By contrast with the other New Testament stories of healings of the blind (cf. Mark 8:22–26 par.; 10:46–52 par.), the blind man of John 9 was blind from birth. This heightens the marvel and allows for more theological depth: men who by their nature cannot see, recover on their encounter with Jesus.

207. Cf. Brodie, "Jesus."

**9:2–3** The disciples' question as to who was responsible for the blind man's condition breaks the bounds of a miracle story. It is occasionally suggested that this question and the first part of Jesus's answer in v. 3a–b should be ascribed to a pre-Johannine source or tradition. However, the impression remains that verses 2–5 build on one another linguistically and logically and cannot easily be separated out into two compositional strata. Indeed, the theme of "guilt" is emphatically resumed in v. 41 at the conclusion of the narrative, and so frames the whole section. In opposition to widespread notions (one thinks of Job's friends), Jesus sees no causative connection between sin and sickness (despite a sentence in John 5:14), but sets the expected healing in the context of his "works" as the works of God (cf. John 5:36; 7:3, 21; 10:25; 14:11). The "revelation" of these works belongs equally to Johannine language (cf. John 1:31; 2:11; 17:6; 21:1, 14).

**9:4–5** At that point, the "works" are taken completely literally as actions one can perform in the light of day. John 5:19 comes into mind where the Son observes his father in the workshop and learns his trade. When night comes, activity stops (cf., similarly, John 11:9–10). Jesus uses this idea as an image of the time remaining to him.[208] Since his first sign at the marriage of Cana (John 2:1–11, cf. v. 4), there has been a connection between the works of Jesus and his "hour." This connection will be renewed and strengthened by the last "sign" or "work" of Jesus, the raising of Lazarus (John 11:1–44), which signified in advance Jesus's imminent end and his own resurrection.

**9:6–7** Reflection on the sickness, its cause, and its healing at the appropriate time is followed by completion of the story of the healing miracle. The pattern is firmly traditional. Thus the element of the saliva that Jesus smears over the eyes of the blind man is found in Mark 8:23 (cf. the same element with the healing of the deaf mute in Mark 7:33). The requirement to wash in some waters has its precedent in the word of Elisha to the Syrian Naaman that he go and wash seven times in the Jordan in 2 Kgs 5:10. The element of saliva was probably understood early rather as an expression of folk medicine that reduced the impact of Jesus's miraculous power just as happened with the gradual healing of the blind man in Mark 8. Thus, the story of the healing of the blind man from Bethsaida in

---

208. With Papyri 66 and 75, Sinaiticus in its oldest version, Vaticanus, and other old manuscripts, we should allow the "we" at the beginning of v. 4 to stand (so too Nestle-Aland[28]). Jesus would then be associating himself here with his disciples (and the readers). With the clause "who has sent me," the text returns again to Jesus.

## Jesus Reveals Himself to His People (5:1–10:42)

Mark 8:22–26 is without parallels in the other Synoptics. John makes free use of the elements of folk medicine but sets them in the larger context of his theology of revelation.

While the washing in some healing water could belong to the topic of healing miracle stories (see above, with reference to 2 Kgs 5:10), we need to explain Jesus's command to the blind man to wash in the Pool of Siloam. An article by K. Müller could shed some light on this.[209] It could probably be made out that behind the name "Siloam" lies a Jewish interpretation of Jacob's blessing in Gen 49:10. In this text, there is mention of a mysterious word that can be translated with "to whom it belongs" or with a proper name. The Septuagint in its usual rendering and modern translations following it decide for "to whom it belongs."[210] However, in addition, the ancient Jewish tradition—and this probably in the period before Christ—knows the interpretation as a proper name, as is shown, among others, by a text from Cave 4 from Qumran. This would then be identified with the "cool Siloam's shady rill" of Isa 8:6, in which case, a substitution of the Hebrew letter $h$ with $ḥ$ would be assumed. The messianic interpretation of Shiloh seems thus to go back to Gen 49:10, the (etymologically contestable) interpretation as "sent" to Isa 8:6. However, the latter cannot invoke Jewish tradition.[211]

As already shown, the pre-Johannine story of the healing of the blind man already exhibits a messianic orientation. At the same time, it remains an open question whether a messianic understanding of "Siloam" was already present at this level. In any case, the accounts of the healings of the blind men in Mark 8:22–26 and 10:47–52 par. had already had the aim of leading to a deeper faith among the disciples as the context shows in its details. The messianic orientation of the pre-Johannine story can be inferred, among other things, from a saying of the Logia source in Matt 11:2–6 par. Luke 7:18–23 in which Jesus, on being asked by the Baptist whether he is the awaited Messiah, points to his deeds: "The blind see, the lame walk, lepers are cleansed." Here, there are echoes especially of passages from Isaiah (26:19; 29:18; 35:5–6; 61:1), and their fulfillment is announced.

The evangelist broadens this perspective: Jesus is not only the Mes-

---

209. Müller, "Joh 9,7."

210. Somewhat dissenting now is the new German translation of the Septuagint: "until what is preserved for him comes." In any case, here too, no proper name is introduced.

211. Reim, "Joh 9," sees a confirmation of the reference in John 9:7 to Gen 49:10 in the element of the "prostration" that is found both in John 9:38 and in the Hebrew text of Gen 49:10.

siah of Israel but the "light of the world" (v. 5)—a light, however, that is threatened by the powers of darkness. In this sense, the story is already a prelude to the passion. The vocabulary here of "day," "light," and "night" is related to that in the parallel text John 11:9 at the beginning of the story of the raising of Lazarus.

The idea of "light" appears in John 9 already in the metaphorical sense of "light of faith." In this connection, it is probably of significance that, according to v. 1, the blind man was "blind from birth." This blindness describes the situation of people from their birth on before they have caught sight of Jesus, the "light of the world." This is a theme that will be developed further in the course of the chapter.

On the side of "darkness" and "not seeing" belongs "sin" as well (vv. 2–3). This topic was already the subject repeatedly in the previous chapter (cf. 8:21, 24, 34, 46).

On the other side stands the "work" of God that Jesus performs. Jesus involves his disciples in this work through the "we" in v. 4. This theme too has already been introduced from ch. 7 on (cf. 7:3, 7, 21; 8:39, 41).

### Controversies about Jesus (9:8–41)

With the declaration of the successful healing, the story of the man born blind could come to an end. But this is not the case. There now ensue long scenes of dialogue that last until the end of the chapter. They have not only been ascribed to another hand than that of the kernel of the healing story but more often also parceled out to two stages of the redaction.[212] A messianic interpretation would thus have been followed further along the lines of Johannine Christology, and the break with the synagogue seems to be presupposed.

Here, we are of the view that the dialogue scenes in John 9:8–41 can be understood as a unitary composition of the evangelist, as may have been the case all along with his source material. The unity of the text is already indicated by the connection of the separate sentences. These are linked throughout with καί ("and"), οὖν ("now"), or δέ ("but") right to the end of the chapter. One of John's characteristic ways of joining sentences is "asyndeton," that is, a sentence that begins without a conjunction. This takes place no less than twelve times in John 9 between v. 9 and v. 41.

---

212. See above at John 9:1–7.

*Jesus Reveals Himself to His People (5:1–10:42)*

Moreover, pronominal forms pervade the whole chapter and contribute to its unity. They are absent only in v. 32 where a general principle is being enunciated (cf., also, v. 39).

The healing of the man born blind in John 9 is constructed in seven scenes. For the sequence of the scenes, indications of time and place are not important. In the center of the narrative are the people or groups taking part. The action is defined by Jesus's miracle of the healing of the man born blind and the consequent question as to his identity. This controversy includes the question about remaining in the synagogue after a public profession of faith in Jesus.

According to exegetes, this chapter is usually divided into seven scenes:

1) Jesus, the disciples, and the blind man who was healed (1–7)[213]
2) The neighbors and the man (8–12)
3) The Pharisees and the man (13–17)
4) The "Jews" and the man's parents (18–23)
5) The "Jews" and the man (24–34)
6) Jesus and the man (35–38)
7) Jesus and some Pharisees (39–41)

There are good grounds for seeing in John 9 a concentric structure in which the scenes correspond as follows:

| | |
|---|---|
| 1) 1–7 | 7) 39–41 |
| 2) 8–12 | 6) 35–38 |
| 3) 13–17 | 5) 24–34 |
| | 4) 18–23 |

The points of contact between verses 1 and 7 are often noticed and, in German-speaking literary criticism, readily explained with the hypothesis of a Johannine interpolation in verses 4–5 and the Johannine origin of verses 39–41. However, these links could proceed from the final form of the text, particularly in view of the structural unity of the chapter as a whole. In the first and seventh scenes, there are linguistic correspondences among the concepts of "light" and "world" as well as "blind" and "see." In

---

213. Moloney, 290f., divides vv. 1–7 into two: 1–5 Jesus and the disciples, 6–7 Jesus and the man born blind, but the latter appears already in v. 1.

both scenes, the concepts of "blind" and "see" are images for the reality of faith. In both scenes, Jesus is in the center of the narrative.

The links between the second and sixth scenes are less close although, in both scenes, the man who was healed takes part. Both scenes concern the person of Jesus: in v. 11 as "the man who is called Jesus"; in verses 35–38, as the "Son of Man" whom the man that had been blind confesses.

The strongest correspondence occurs between the third and fifth scenes. Already, from the formal point of view, the fifth scene refers explicitly to the third, beginning, as it does, with the words: "Then, for the second time (ἐκ δευτέρου), the Pharisees called him." Added to this, we can observe further correspondences of language and content. Both scenes see the healed man in conflict with the Jewish authorities (the Pharisees who are called the "Jews" in v. 18), and the subject is the "how" of the healing. Moreover, the dialogue develops into the question of Jesus's origin. For the blind man, Jesus comes from God and is a prophet; for the Pharisees/"Jews," he does not come from God but is a sinner. For both sides, the criterion lies in whether he is doing God's will: in the first scene, Jesus has to demonstrate this by his observance of the Sabbath; in the second, the question is more generally as to whether he fears God and does his will. According to the opinion of the formerly blind man, this can be predicated of Jesus. Thus, the same criterion leads to an opposing judgement about Jesus.

According to the structure proposed here, the fourth scene stands at the center of the chapter.[214] Here, we can also observe a peripety or turning point in the narrative. The people taking part are the blind man's parents and the "Jews." The dialogue concerns the identity of their son, the means of his healing, and the identity of the one who healed him. The parents answer only the first question and refuse to answer the second and third with the indication: "He is old enough." In v. 22, the attitude of the parents is explained by the "omniscient" narrator in a parenthesis. This interruption is significant for the narrative flow, for the narrator is here placing himself in direct contact with his readers. Clearly, we have here content that is important for the readers. What at first glance appears to be a digression turns out to be decisive for the readers: it is a question of reaching a mature, grown-up confession of Jesus as the Christ. This focus

---

214. The suggestion of Brown, 1:380, to see it as added from a later point of view does not convince since the danger of exclusion from the synagogue pervades the whole chapter (cf. vv. 22–23, 34–35) and indeed the Gospel (cf. 12:42; 16:2; here probably post-Johannine).

could correspond very precisely to the needs of the reading community of John's Gospel.[215]

**9:8-12** In the first dialogue scene, we find the neighbors of the blind man and the man himself in conversation. The neighbors stand for those people who do not ask serious questions. If one looks at them in the light of the overall plot,[216] then their opinions already differ as to whether they recognize the man who was healed as the blind man they had known before or not. When they recognize him again, they enquire after the circumstances of his healing or also, in addition to that, about his healer. However, they do not ask who this healer is. The question of his identity does not seem to interest them. However, it is precisely to this that the narrator turns. At this stage, the man who has been healed himself describes Jesus as "the man who is called Jesus." With that, he puts himself at the beginning of his journey of faith, as perhaps also the first readers.

**9:13-17** The second scene is prompted by the information added in v. 14 that it was the Sabbath day on which Jesus healed the blind man (cf. similarly John 5:9). Involved here are the blind man and the Pharisees as one of the groups who, in the mind of the evangelist, were responsible for Torah observance in Jerusalem. In the context of John 9, at least a part of them stand for those who ask, but who do not come to faith. The Pharisees too ask first about the circumstances of the healing, and the formerly blind man tells them. Part of the healing consisted of the fact that Jesus prepared some clay and smeared it on the blind man's eyes. In the mind of strict Jewish piety, that could count as work, and so a part of the Pharisees come to the conclusion that this man does not come from God since he does not keep the Sabbath. However, others see in Jesus's deed a "sign" that presupposes that he cannot be a sinner. Thus a "division" arises among them in their controversy about Jesus, something John records elsewhere (cf. John 7:43; 10:19). Once again, the readers are confronted with the question of Jesus's identity. The blind man himself has taken a step forward. According to him, Jesus is "a prophet" (v. 17).

**9:18-23** The Pharisees who have not come to faith are now, in v. 18,

---

215. The reference here to the "reading community" and not the "Johannine community" is deliberate. Wright IV, *Rhetoric*, correctly questions the approach of Martyn, *History and Theology*, according to which John 9 is to be read on two levels: that of the time of Jesus and that of the time of the evangelist and his community that was threatened with exclusion from the synagogue. Skepticism with regard to a "Johannine community" is expressed also by Thyen, "Joh 9,22."

216. Cf. the mention of Brémond, *Logique du récit*, 131, in Egger, *Methodenlehre*, 123.

described as "Jews" (cf. the similar linguistic twist in John 6:41 that does not justify assuming a new group of people). At the beginning of the new scene, they fall back on their first question in the opening scene as to whether the man who had been healed was really the one who was previously known to be blind. So they summon the man's parents. The latter stand for people who recognize the man as such and also come to the recognition of the identity of Jesus but do not want to stand up for it openly. Their reason is fear of the "Jews" (v. 22). Thus, the parents represent those Jews who, on the one hand, believed in Jesus but who did not want to profess this faith since they feared that this would lead to their exclusion from the synagogue (cf., also, John 12:42-43 and the designation of Joseph of Arimathaea in John 19:38; further, 16:2). It is the widespread opinion that the evangelist is writing here under the influence of the situation of his time in which Jews who confessed their faith in Jesus as Messiah had to fear that they would be excluded from the synagogue.[217]

A pointer as to how the readers had to behave themselves is found in the words of the parents: "He is old enough. Ask him himself," which the text repeats twice within a short time (vv. 21 and 23). The blind man has reached the age of majority and so can speak for himself. For this reason, he can also confess his faith in Jesus with free responsibility, and he does this gradually as the narrative progresses. He thus becomes the prototype of all those who, as mature men, stand up for their faith in Jesus. The early Church read the story of the healing of the man born blind at the beginning of Lent as part of the preparation of the catechumens for their baptism at the Paschal vigil. One could also look at it, however, in connection with confirmation when young people, on the threshold of adulthood, confess their faith in Christ and to that end ask for and receive the power of God.

**9:24-34** The fourth dialogue scene now follows and harkens back strongly to verses 17-22. Once again, we find the Pharisees and the healed man in conversation. This time, the interrogation of the man begins with the person of Jesus. He is alleged to be a sinner. However, according to the man, that is impossible since Jesus has healed him. So, yet again, the

---

217. According to Martyn, *History*, 34-38, the "Cursing of the Heathen" (Birkat ha-minim) in Ber 28b could be evidence for an exclusion of heretics, in this case Christians, from the synagogue on account of a decision of the so-called Synod of Jamnia. Since then, the reference to Christians has been doubted and scholars reckon more on a local exclusion of Christians at different times. Cf. Kimelman, "Birkat ha-Minim." Cf. on this, once again Wright IV, *Rhetoric*, 1-56, who suggests a new way of reading John 9 on two levels: the literal and the figurative.

healing is investigated. But the man has already described this to the Pharisees once. Why, then, are they asking him about it again? In the manner of Johannine irony, he asks the Pharisees if, perhaps, they want to become his disciples. The Pharisees deny this vehemently with the information that they are disciples of Moses, and no one knows where "this man" comes from. In response to the reference that God spoke through Moses, the man counters with the fact that clearly God has worked in Jesus. It is impossible, therefore, to say that no one knows where Jesus comes from. Jesus is, at least, "one who fears God and does his will" (v. 31) and is certainly no sinner. Indeed, he comes from God (v. 33). This confession is enough for him to be thrown out of the synagogue (v. 34). The multiple repetitions within this section, as also with regard to the previous scenes, strengthen the readers' impression that it is not enough to stand still for all time with the event of the healing of the blind man and its circumstances, but it is necessary to understand it as a deed of God in Jesus. However, the Pharisees contradict this view insistently. Thereby, sin emerges again as a theme. It was already introduced in vv. 2-3. Neither the man who was formerly blind nor his parents sinned and so caused his blindness, although this is disputed by the Pharisees (v. 34). Jesus too is no sinner since he acts with the power of God (v. 31). The true sinners are exposed much more as those who refuse faith in Jesus (v. 41). They then show themselves also to be the truly blind.

**9:35-38** In the penultimate dialogue scene, Jesus and the man he has healed meet again. Already, after the healing of the paralytic, the text said in John 5:14 that Jesus "met" him in the temple. It was an open question whether he found faith in Jesus. He heard only the exhortation not to sin any more lest something worse befall him. The blind man who was healed has by now a path of faith behind him and has just been thrown out of the synagogue on this account. Thus, Jesus can lead him along the path of the faith that he has begun and witnessed to its end. When Jesus "meets" him, he asks him: "Do you believe in the Son of Man?" Even now, the man does not know who this is, but Jesus reveals himself to him with the words: "You have already seen him; it is he who is speaking with you" (v. 37). Thereupon the man gives his answer of faith, falls down before him, and expresses his words of worship.

Instead of seeing a new literary stratum here, it is advisable to see in these verses the conscious and deliberate conclusion of the faith journey of the man born blind. It begins with "the man who is called Jesus" (v. 11) and leads to the "prophet" (v. 17) and "a man from God" (v. 33). With the title of "Son of Man," with which Jesus now introduces himself, the man has reached the full confession of faith of the Johannine reading community. For the deliberate leading of the blind man and, ultimately, the reading community to this point there is a significant parallel in John 1:35–51. At the beginning here, we have the puzzling "Lamb of God" (John 1:29, 36). After their first meeting, Andrew and the other disciple with him confess Jesus already as the "Messiah" (v. 41). Philip describes Jesus as "the one whom Moses in the Law and also the prophets have written about" (v. 45). Nathanael's confession goes further: "Rabbi, you are the Son of God, you are the King of Israel" (v. 49). Here too, the title of Son of Man forms the conclusion, and, here too, it is Jesus who reveals himself with this title full of majesty: "Amen, amen, I say to you: you will see heaven opened, and the angels of God ascending and descending over the Son of Man" (v. 51).

Jesus's self-revelation in John 9:37 recalls the scene at the conclusion of the conversation with the Samaritan woman. When she utters her conviction that the Messiah will come, Jesus says to her: "I am he, the one who is speaking to you" (John 4:26). The formula is the same here, word for word.

Occasionally, the original status of John 9:38–39a has been questioned because of its rather insecure textual attestation.[218] The passage could be understood as a later insertion under the influence of liturgy.[219] The man prostrates himself before Jesus like the candidate for baptism coming to faith. However, the scant attestation cannot take us so far. Rather, vice versa, this feature serves as the model for the account of Christian candidates for baptism.

**9:39–41** As already in the second and fourth dialogue scenes, the Pharisees now appear on the stage again in the sixth and last scene. They have heard a saying of Jesus in which he announces that he has come into the world for judgement so that the blind may see and those who see become blind. From that they have drawn the conclusion that it is they who could have been meant. According to Jesus's final reply, their guilt lies, not in their blindness, from which they could have been healed, but in their claim to be able to see. This small section brings the whole narrative to an effective end. The theme of judgement is new, but it is related to the theme of sin that is being taken up again. John 9:2–3 was concerned with the sin either of the blind man or his parents, with an echo in v. 34, and vv. 24–25 with Jesus as a possible sinner. Now the subject turns to the involvement in sin of those Pharisees who do not believe in Jesus. Thus, the theme per-

---

218. Verses 38–39a are missing in P$^{75}$ ℵ$^2$ W b (l) sa$^{ms}$ ly cw.
219. Cf. Porter, "John IX,38.39a."

vades the whole chapter—a further reason for refraining from parceling it out into different literary strata. The result is a transfer of attention from the possible sin of the blind man to the sin of the Pharisees who do not believe in Christ.

The motif of seeing is related to the motif of sin, and this too pervades the whole chapter, but with a linear development from the beginning of John 9 to the end. On the one hand, the whole account deals with seeing in the literal sense. At the beginning (v. 1), it has to do with someone who is physically blind from birth. His healing by Jesus occupies all the scenes. It is not until v. 39 that the blind man's ability to see serves as a contrast with the established blindness of the Pharisees who do not believe in Jesus. It is here that we first come across a clearly figurative use. However, this can then be recognized retrospectively as exegetes have increasingly noticed. As a result, there is a continual movement of the man born blind to the recovery of his sight, but also to the light of faith in Jesus. There is a corresponding movement from a group who think they can see but at the end are shown to be the truly blind. This antithesis defines not just the opening and closing verses of chapter 9 (which are then often ascribed to the evangelist in a special way), but the whole course of the narrative. Without the controversies that precede it, the closing judgement of Jesus is left up in the air. It arises precisely as a result of the increasingly clear refusal of the group of Pharisees to draw the only correct conclusion from the healing of the man born blind.

Insofar as the Pharisees (or "Jews") appear here as representatives of the Jewish authorities, the opening verses of John 10 follow seamlessly. This will be recalled later at the appropriate place.

What purpose links the narrator of John 9 with his story here? The question cannot be answered by pointing to one or the other texts. Rather, the answer must be comprehensive. On the one hand, on several occasions, the narrator emerges from his anonymity to insert explanations such as the interpretation of the Pool of Siloam as "the one sent" (= Christ, v. 7) or the information that the healing took place on a Sabbath (v. 14). The guiding of the readers is especially obvious where the narrator adds that the "Jews" had already decided to exclude from the synagogue anyone who confessed Jesus as Messiah (v. 22). At this point, the text contains particles and causal constructions that betray the author's concern with the understanding of the readers.

The question as to the persons or groups within the text with which the narrator identifies himself points in the same direction. The answer permits no doubt: it is the blind man himself. He shows that he has decided to believe in Jesus and to confess this faith without fear. In this sense, he is an exemplary disciple. This view is matched by the observation that Jesus's disciples are already introduced into the story in v. 2, even if there they have less understanding about his identity and his works. In the conversation between the "Jews" and the man who was healed, the question of discipleship is raised again: the man asks ironically whether the Pharisees also wish to become disciples of Jesus. The answer is that *he* can do that; *they* are the disciples of Moses (vv. 27–28). The readers are in a position to understand the deeper irony of this exchange: in fact, it concerns the right sort of discipleship—not vis à vis Moses, but vis à vis Jesus.

The narrative, therefore, opens a window into a situation in which one should arrive at the confession of faith in Jesus even at the cost of being excluded from the synagogue for this reason. Such a situation is reflected in a double saying of the logia source (Luke 12:8–9, 11–12 par. Matt 10:32–33, 19–20: the saying about the one who confesses and the one who denies, and the encouragement for the moment in which the disciples are brought before the court). This belongs more to the period of the Fourth Gospel than to the lifetime of Jesus. In its formulation, Luke 6:22–23 comes even closer to the synagogue exclusion in John 9 since it expressly speaks of the "exclusion" of the disciples for Jesus's sake.[220]

### The Good Shepherd and His Opposites (10:1–21)

The section John 10:1–21 closes the section of the Fourth Gospel that is defined by the Feast of Tabernacles. With the mention of the Feast of the Dedication of the temple in 10:22, a new section begins that lasts until the end of the chapter. The themes of John 10:1–21 are also taken up again in part in this later section, and so it is appropriate and practical to treat and expound ch. 10 as a whole.

We have already mentioned the connection of John 10 with the previous story of the healing of the blind man in John 9. It is accepted more generally today than a short time ago. The transition is constituted by the verses John 9:39–41 with Jesus's settlement of accounts with those Pharisees who have not reached faith in him. It is precisely they who are addressed at the beginning of John 10 and are meant as conversation partners in 10:6.

---

220. Cf. Thyen, "Joh 9,22," 577.

## Jesus Reveals Himself to His People (5:1–10:42)

At least in German-speaking research, however, the context of John 10:1–18 has not always been seen and acknowledged. Additionally, more often, a stratification has been identified within the shepherd discourse. Here, theological criteria were mainly in operation. Sometimes the orientation of the discourse towards a collective group, the flock or the people of God, was felt to be problematic in a Gospel that was considered to be only about Jesus and faith in him. Rudolf Bultmann ascribes the discourse in its final form to the evangelist but sees in it the discourse source of Gnostic inspiration that he used. According to Bultmann, the text has not been transmitted in its original sequence, which would have been: John 10:22–26, 11–13, 1–10, 14–18, 27–39.[221] However, no manuscripts can be listed for this reconstruction, which thus remains purely hypothetical.

In more recent times, the Johannine origin of the shepherd discourse or some of its sections has been questioned, chiefly on account of their ecclesiological orientation. Here, Becker goes furthest and sees the whole passage John 10:1–18 as an insertion by Bultmann's "ecclesiastical redaction."[222] Becker sees here an "ecclesiastical determinism," according to which God or Jesus know in advance that sheep belong to him. Such a view is also adopted for John 15–17. Verses 10:26–29 (with their resumption of the shepherd motif) and 10:34–36 (with the argument from Scripture that looks to have been inspired by Judaism rather than by gnosis) are also regarded by Becker as secondary. He reckons that verses 10:40–42 could stem from the "signs source" since they refer to John 1:28—a verse that, according to this view, would come from the same source.

Some authors maintain that the metaphorical saying about the "gate" in John 10:7–10 is an interruption of the text between the *Bildrede* of vv. 1–6 and the shepherd discourse in the narrower sense in verses 11–16. This is roughly how Ferdinand Hahn sees it.[223] For him, the saying about the good shepherd who knows his own sheep and gives his life for them (vv. 14–15) stands in the center of the shepherd discourse from the theological and literary points of view. Hahn, therefore, ascribes verses 7–10 to the Johannine redaction, which has allegorized a motif from the main *Bildrede*. The view of Haenchen is similar.[224] According to him, v. 9 or the whole section John 10:7–10 goes back to the post-Johannine redaction.

---

221. Cf. Bultmann, 274.
222. Cf. Becker, 1:366, with Langbrandtner, *Weltferner Gott*.
223. Cf. Hahn, "Die Hirtenrede."
224. Cf. Haenchen, 389–94.

The mention of "other sheep" in v. 16 is also regarded by the aforementioned authors as a foreign element within the context. According to this view, here and only here does the problematic relationship between Christians who come from Judaism and those who had come from paganism occur. Thus, Becker[225] ascribes the verse to a further redaction subsequent to the first; Hahn[226] and Haenchen[227] hold the verse to be an insertion of the ecclesiastical or post-Johannine redaction.

In evaluating such literary-critical hypotheses, two criteria are important. On the one hand, there is the question whether, alongside the reasons of content (theology), linguistic grounds can also be identified for such a division of the text into strata. In this case, we must then take into account the composition of the whole passage and its individual subsections. On the other hand, we have to check whether the ecclesiological orientation is to be ascribed exclusively to the "ecclesiastical" or "post-Johannine" redaction. It could actually be the case that the notion of the people of God was important for the evangelist too. This will be taken as foundational in what follows.[228]

A successful study of the composition of the passage has been made by Odo Kiefer under the supervision of Schnackenburg in Würzburg.[229] According to this study, the strongest structural signal of the passage consists in the repeated "I am" of Jesus. Twice, Jesus describes himself as "the door" (vv. 7 and 9), and twice as "the good shepherd" (vv. 11 and 14). From this there emerges a well-structured whole. That the door sayings come first is explained by the fact that, in John 10:7-18, the evangelist is taking up two important catchwords from the preceding *Bildrede* in vv. 1-6 and, in fact, in the sequence in which they occur: first, the door (v. 1) and then the shepherd (v. 2).

Here it has already been assumed that, in John 10:1-18, two different genres or figures of speech are encountered. The first five verses are described by the evangelist in v. 6 as "paroimia." This expression is encountered twice more in ch. 16 (vv. 25 and 29). There, it describes a figurative discourse that needs explanation. For this type of speech, the similitudes and parables of Jesus in the Synoptics are usually indicated as the closest paral-

---

225. Cf. Becker, 1:389.
226. Cf. Hahn, "Die Hirtenrede," 198.
227. Cf. Haenchen, 394.
228. A rigorous critique of excessive "literary criticism" in John 10 is found in Thyen, "Zu den zahllosen Versuchen." Here, Thyen starts out from the literary-critical suggestions of Ashton, *Understanding John; Studying the Fourth Gospel*.
229. Cf. Kiefer, *Die Hirtenrede*.

*Jesus Reveals Himself to His People (5:1–10:42)*

lels. Where John is concerned, we think here also of Jesus's discourse about the "true vine" (John 15:1–8). By contrast with the Synoptics, however, the Johannine *Bildreden* of John 10 and John 15 have to do with more than one point of comparison, without their having to be reckoned as allegories on that account. In John, the levels of image and reality interpenetrate so that here the expression "*Bildrede*" or "extended metaphor" is chosen.[230]

The contrast between Jesus and the false shepherd has polemical traits in John 10, and, in fact, from the first five verses on. From the beginning, we meet negative images that set the false door and the false shepherd against the true door and the true shepherd. The question, therefore, arises as to what this polemic is referring to.

According to A. J. Simonis,[231] the polemic of the shepherd discourse is explained by the time and circumstances of the life of Jesus. The images of the discourse should be understood and interpreted with reference to these contextual aspects. According to Simonis, the "thieves and robbers" stand for the Zealots who wished to bring the temple area under their control by violence without worrying about the effects on the population. The weakness of this exegesis lies primarily in the fact that it contradicts John's normal speech usage. For John, Jesus's opponents are the "Jews" in the sense of the Pharisees (cf. John 9:41). Moreover, the suggested conflict is probably too quickly located to the time of Jesus, a position that is contradicted by the current view of the circumstances in which the Fourth Gospel arose. Interesting here is a comparative glance at 1 Enoch 89 where the powerful in Israel are portrayed as the leaders of the blind sheep of the people. This passage (1 Enoch 83–90) probably stems from the time of the Maccabees. It would scarcely have had a direct influence on John's Gospel; more likely is the possibility that both it and John 10 go back to the same Old Testament roots.

It is most probable that this passage arose in the situation of the Fourth Gospel. In this case, the opponents would be the Pharisees as the most important representatives of contemporary rabbinic Judaism. The majority of contemporary exegetes have good grounds for this interpretation.

A third possibility is advocated by Pius-Ramon Tragan.[232] According

---

230. Thus Kiefer in the work mentioned; cf. for John 15:1–8, Borig, *Der wahre Weinstock*. However, it is advisable here not to speak of a genre in the proper sense since extra-Johannine examples are lacking; cf. Zimmermann, *Christologie*, 288.

231. Cf. Simonis, *Die Hirtenrede*.

232. Cf. Tragan, *La parabole*. Beside other authors, this view is assumed also in Heckel, *Hirtenamt*, 108–23.

to him, the shepherd discourse of John 10 is about the proper service of shepherds in the community. To this end, he quotes some comparable texts from the NT about "shepherds." The study of the text will reveal to what degree a view like this can be commended for John 10.

**10:1-6** The "shepherd discourse" begins with the introduction of the motif of the shepherd and sheep in verses 1–5. Joined to it is the motif of the thief or the robber who climbs over the wall. From the beginning, the good shepherd and his opposite number are set against each other, and thus it is not advisable to place the whole section straight away under the theme of "the good shepherd." Above all, what we have here is not a pastoral idyll. Already, from the beginning, the emphasis of the words of Jesus is striking linguistically: "Amen, amen, I say to you" (v. 1). To this is added the polemical tone that already characterizes the first section. Repeatedly, the negative statements come before the positive ones and so determine the color of the section. The critical debate will then determine the rest of the shepherd discourse until v. 18.

The language of this first section is stamped with a simple style. As a rule, main clauses follow one another. Subordinate clauses occur only in verses 4–5 in the form of causal and temporal clauses, something that already shows the emphasis of the narrator and his concern for the understanding of the readers. Here, however, the antithesis is between "shepherds" and "strangers."

The vocabulary of the first five verses is clearly stamped with the world of pastoral imagery. The motif of "calling" with the "voice" is already preparing the transition to the level of lived experience. Verse 6 records the reaction of the hearer to the "paroimia" described in the previous verses and exhibits Johannine style.

The understanding of the section depends decisively on its construction. Verses 1–5 display a mirror-image ("chiastic") construction. First, we can make out two parts. At the beginning, we have verses 1–3a with the theme of "the coming of the shepherd." This is followed by verses 3b–5 about the "conduct of the shepherd." Parallel to this sequence is another that shows the contrast between the shepherd and the thief and the robber, and then the stranger. In v. 1, the subject is the thief and the robber who does not get to the sheep through the door. Verse 2 follows with the opposite figure of the shepherd who enters the sheepfold through the door. The description of the activity of the shepherd and the stranger displays the reverse sequence. First comes the description of what the shepherd does in verses 3a–4, followed by the description of the conduct of the stranger, whom the sheep do not follow, in v. 5. This results in the following construction:

1 The entry of the stranger
  2–3a The entry of the shepherd
  3b–4 The activity of the shepherd, the reaction of the sheep
5 The conduct of the stranger, seen from the perspective of the sheep

The section is characterized by sharp antitheses, as is shown by the portrayal of the shepherd and his opposite number, but also by explanatory clauses. Thus one can speak of an "argumentative text."[233] The literary genre of the section is mostly taken to be a *Bildrede* or "paroimia" (cf. at v. 6) by which is meant a genre or figure of speech that stands midway between the similitude or parable (with only one point of comparison) and the allegory (with more points of comparison). Characteristic of this genre or figure of speech is the interpenetration of image and reality.

The dominating vocabulary is that of shepherd, sheep, and sheepfold. In v. 6, in his own words, the narrator comments on the success of the speech that has just been delivered.

For the pragmatic of the text, that is, the guidance of the reader, it is significant that the text presupposes a reading community that (by contrast with the Pharisees) is in a position to understand the figurative speech of Jesus. The text is thus oriented ultimately to the Christian readers of the evangelist's community. It is being explained to them wherein the difference lies between the "shepherd," Jesus, and the "stranger."

It is not easy to answer the question as to the origin of the extended metaphor of the shepherd in John 10:1–5. There are no satisfactory indications for the employment of a written source, although the vocabulary does not point to the evangelist. Most likely what we have here is a tradition that has influenced the passage.

Later on in John's Gospel (21:15–19), we again encounter the *motifs* of the "shepherd" and the "sheep." However, we can observe a semantic shift to the shepherd of the community. The antithesis to the "shepherd" of Israel has disappeared. Similar texts about "shepherds" of the community are found in Acts 20:18–35 and 1 Pet 5:1–4.

Shepherd and sheep are also the subject of the Synoptic parable of the Lost Sheep in Luke 15:3–7 par. Matt 18:12–14. We cannot exclude some

---

233. Cf., for this description, Berger, *Exegese*, 77.

influence of this parable on the Johannine text whereby a stronger emphasis on Christology can be observed in the new context. This comes to the surface especially in the antithesis of the good shepherd and the bad.

The contrast with the bad shepherd can be explained by the influence of the Old Testament on our text. One thinks especially here of Jer 23 and Ezek 34. Both passages go back to the Exilic or post-Exilic periods and the judgement oracles on the wicked shepherds of Israel. God will depose these wicked shepherds because of their transgressions and will himself become the just shepherd of his people. According to another view, he will send his people a new David who will safeguard the good of his flock in his name. The detailed study of John 10:11–18 will show a partial agreement of the Johannine text with these texts of the prophetic tradition.

The redactional work of the evangelist appears especially in the detailed working out of the relationship between the shepherd and the sheep. This relationship is based on the mission entrusted to Jesus by the Father. Hence it is important to discern where the good shepherd comes from (v. 2). Kiefer points here to texts like John 7:27–28; 8:14; 9:29–30; 19:9.[234] Whoever is open to the voice of the revealer "hears his voice," as it says in verses 3–5 with regard to the sheep vis à vis the shepherd. According to John 3:29, the friend "hears the voice" of the bridegroom; according to John 5:25, 28, men "hear the voice" of the Son of Man; according to John 18:37, everyone who is of the truth "hears the voice" of Jesus. The personal element of the relationship between the sheep and the shepherd is also shown in the fact that he "calls" each of them "by their names" (v. 3) and "leads them out." Later, he will "bring them out" and "go before them" (v. 4). From the side of the sheep, the "following" of the sheep corresponds to this (vv. 3–4).

As already at the beginning (v. 1), so too at the end (v. 5), the action of the "stranger" is contrasted with that of the shepherd. The difference is shown indirectly in the reaction of the sheep: they will not "follow the stranger," but "flee," since they do not know his voice. The future here could be looking forward to the time of the church, if it is not simply a logical future. With this, the passage returns to its beginning with the statements about the "thieves and robbers."

With the reference to the audience in v. 6, the passage returns to its starting point. That the audience "did not understand" the words of Jesus is repeatedly stated in John's Gospel; the observation in John 10:6 is especially sharp. We recall here Jesus's conversation with Nicodemus (John

---

234. Kiefer, *Hirtenrede*, 42.

## Jesus Reveals Himself to His People (5:1–10:42)

3:1-12) and with the Samaritan woman (John 4:10, 22, 25). Jesus has a food of which the disciples are not aware (John 4:32). It appears that the "Jews" know who Jesus's parents are (6:42) and where he comes from (7:27), but they do not know the Father (7:28-29); so Jesus remains hidden to them. There are similar statements also in John 8:14, 19, 55; 9:21-30; 14:17 (about the Spirit).

**10:7-10** A double metaphorical saying about Jesus as the gate comes next. It appears to interrupt the discourse about the shepherd and the sheep in verses 1-5 and 11-18, and is occasionally rejected as secondary.[235] There are not sufficient textual grounds for this, however, and the gate motif can be understood as the resumption of v. 1 before the motif of the shepherd is taken up again from v. 2 in verses 11-18.

The key to the construction of this small unit lies in the double saying of Jesus "I am the gate of the sheep" in verses 7 and 9. This metaphor forms the semantic axis of the unit. At the beginning, in v. 7, we have the narrative introduction of the section before the Johannine formula with which Jesus begins his discourse: "Amen, amen, I say to you." As in verses 1-5, v. 8 also has a negative statement at the beginning of the section about unlawful access to the people of God. Verse 9 follows with a positive statement about Jesus. The behavior of the sheep with regard to the intruder in v. 8b is matched by their behavior with regard to Jesus in v. 9b. A final antithesis between the "thief" and Jesus in v. 10 closes the section. At the same time, the promise of Jesus in v. 10 extends way beyond the previous controversy and summarizes the mission of Jesus in an unsurpassable way.

With the division of the passage into two parallel sections, it is assumed that, both in v. 7 and also in v. 9, the correct reading is: "I am the gate." An ancient reading of v. 7 reads not "I am the gate" but "I am the shepherd."[236] Even today, this occasionally has its appeal,[237] since it would be a way of sustaining the shepherd theme. However, its poor attestation and the nature of "gate" as *lectio difficilior* militate against this reading.

In v. 7, the text does not allow us to make out clearly whether the genitive "of the sheep" is to be understood as "for the sheep" or "to the sheep." With the *Einheitsübersetzung* the second possibility is preferable. The reason lies in the context. Already in verses 1-6, the subject of the

---

235. Cf. Hahn, "Die Hirtenrede."
236. It is found in P[75] as well as in the Coptic texts sa ac and cw.
237. Thus, in Haenchen, who also strikes out v. 9 as secondary; similarly, in Busse, "Open Questions," 10.

sentence was the proper access to the sheep. In v. 10, the "coming" of the thief to the sheep is the subject. However, the possibility also remains of understanding Jesus in v. 7 as gate "for the sheep." Then, according to v. 9, it would be through Jesus that they would go in and out to find pasture.

In v. 8, we have another textual problem. In some manuscripts, it says "all who came" instead of "all who came before me." Probably, there is an attempt here to confront the difficulties in understanding this passage, since it is not clear to whom Jesus is referring. On this ground alone, it is advisable to read the longer text with Nestle-Aland[28].

After clearing up these preliminary questions, the lines of meaning and oppositions of the section can be studied better. On the one hand, there are the "thieves and robbers" who have no legal access to the sheep (v. 8), whom the sheep do not listen to, and who come only "to steal, to slaughter and to destroy" (v. 10). On the other side, there is Jesus. He does have legal access to the sheep (vv. 7, 9), and he is the gate through which the sheep go and can find good pasture (vv. 9–10). In this context, we also find some of the evangelist's characteristic expressions such as "be saved" (v. 9) and "have life" (v. 10).

The literary genre or property of this group of verses is like that of the paroimia of vv. 1–5. Once again, image and reality interpenetrate, as in the case of the "saving" of the sheep through Jesus, the "gate" (v. 9), or of their "slaughter" and "destruction" by the thief (v. 10). Insofar as verses 7–10 take up elements of verses 1–5 and develop them, we can also speak of the literary genre of midrash.

Where does the ultimate intended message of this short passage lie? The question can best be answered in connection with the understanding of those who "came before (Jesus)" and who are none other than "thieves and robbers" in v. 8. Precisely since it is a question here of people who came "before" Jesus, one can exclude any reference to unworthy shepherds of the Christian community.[238] Jesus's saying can refer only to false Jewish saviors. A reference to the leading figures of Israel's history, to the patriarchs, kings, and prophets, can also be excluded here in view of the positive role of Abraham, Moses, David, and Isaiah in the Fourth Gospel. It is advisable, therefore, with the "thieves and robbers" to think of the contemporaries of Jesus

---

238. According to Öhler, "Der 'Mietling' Petrus," the motif of the "hireling" who runs away when danger threatens is taken up again in John 21:15–17 and applied to Peter. Witetschek, "Ein Räuber," sees a correspondence between Barabbas, the robber in the shepherd discourse John 10:1, 8, 10, and the figure of Judas who is portrayed in John 12:6 as a thief.

or the evangelist. The suggestion of Simonis[239] to see in them the Zealots of Jesus's time has little to recommend it. John's Gospel is in continual dispute with the Pharisees who in the evangelist's day had become the normative authorities. It is advisable, therefore, to understand the polemic of our passage as part of the debate with this Jewish school of thought. This is corroborated by the mention of the Pharisees in John 9:40 as the addressees of the words of Jesus without any subsequent mention of a change of audience.

What is the origin of the gate motif in John 10:7–10? Occasionally, the finger is pointed at Ps 118:20: "This is the gate of the Lord; only the righteous enter here." Moreover, this psalm appears to have been understood in a messianic sense in New Testament times.[240] However, there is no connection here with the shepherd metaphor characteristic for this section of John. In the New Testament, Luke 13:24 is indicated: "Strive to enter through the narrow gate." But the same applies here: there is no christological reference. However, one could think of a similar development to that in John 12:24, where John, by contrast with the Synoptics in the parable of the sower, interprets the grain of wheat christologically. A Synoptic similitude thus takes on a christological interpretation. The Church fathers too know the image of the gate for Jesus, and the Gnostics use this image for the revealer. The Bahai religion call their nineteenth-century founder "el Bab"—"the gate/door." His grave is venerated in Haifa in Israel.

In our passage, the literary and theological work of the evangelist is most in evidence where he abandons the image in favor of the reality. This is especially the case in the opposition between "death" and "life." On the one hand, the activity of the thieves and robbers leads to "destruction" (v. 10); on the other hand, the work of the shepherd leads to "saving/salvation" (v. 9) and "life"—"to the full" (v. 10). This is the point where we reach the particular vocabulary that the evangelist uses to describe Jesus's gift of salvation.

**10:11–18** Verses 11–18 mark the climax of the shepherd discourse of John 10. In place of the "thieves" and "robbers" there now enters the "hired man." However, the positive statements predominate here. The governing theme of the section, repeated five times, is Jesus's statement that the good shepherd "gives up his life" for his sheep.

The clause structure within the section exhibits some differences. In general, main clauses are construed paratactically. In some verses, how-

---

239. Cf. Simonis, *Die Hirtenrede*.
240. Cf. Schnackenburg, 2.365, with reference to John 12:13 par.; Mark 12:10; Matt 23:39 par.

ever, we can discern more clearly through a sentence's syntactical complexity the author's emphases. This can be observed in vv. 12, 13a as well as in v. 17. In the first case, the hired man is described. Here, we find a participle, a relative clause, three main clauses, a parenthesis, and a causal clause. Apparently, the identity and characteristic conduct of the hired man are of great importance for the author. Here, it is striking that the attributes of the hired man are almost all negative, by contrast with those that describe the person and conduct of the shepherd. In v. 17, the relationship between Jesus and the Father is described explicitly. For this, there are a causal clause (introduced with "therefore" διὰ τοῦτο) and a final clause. Here too, we can recognize the emphasis of the author. The case is similar in the comparison of v. 15a.

The vocabulary of the section is strongly determined by the imagery of the shepherd. The behavior of the hired man is contrasted with that of the "good" shepherd (a single adjective with the exception of "own" in v. 14 and "other" in v. 16). Going beyond this vocabulary are those statements describing the mutual relationship of shepherd and sheep with the expression of "knowing" and that of Jesus and the Father with the expressions of "knowing" and "loving" (cf. vv. 14–15, 17–18 about Jesus's obedience to the Father's command).

The semantic analysis of the section can begin with the previous observations. Characteristic statements describe the "good shepherd" on the one hand, and the "hired man" on the other:

| | |
|---|---|
| shepherd (ποιμήν) | hired man (μισθωτὸς, οὐκ ὢν ποιμήν) |
| good (καλός) | - |
| gives his life (τίθησιν τὴν ψυχήν) for the sheep (ὑπὲρ τῶν προβάτων) | sees the wolf coming (θεωρεῖ τὸν λύκον ἐρχόμενον) deserts the sheep (ἀφίησιν τὰ πρόβατα) flees (φεύγει) |
| mine (τὰ ἐμά) | not his own (οὐκ ἴδια) |
| knows (γινώσκω) | has no concern for them (οὐ μέλει αὐτῷ) |

The statements about the "good shepherd" and the "wolf" can also be contrasted:

| | |
|---|---|
| lead (ἀγαγεῖν) | seizes (ἁρπάζει) |
| one flock, one shepherd (μία πόιμνη, εἷς ποιμήν) | scatters (σκορπίζει) |

On the other hand, there is a positive correspondence between the relationship of Jesus and the sheep on the one side and Jesus and the Father on the other:

| | |
|---|---|
| know mine (γινώσκω τὰ ἐμά) | know the Father (γινώσκω τὸν πατέρα) |
| my own know me (γινώσκουσί με τὰ ἐμά) | the Father knows me (γινώσκει με ὁ πατήρ) |

Added to that, we have only to notice that statements about the mutual knowing in verses 14–15 are arranged in a chiastic (mirror-image) order. Jesus's "knowing" stands at the beginning and end, the "being known" twice in the middle. Such correspondences, which are introduced with καθώς and describe the relationship between Jesus and his followers on the one hand and Jesus and the Father on the other, are characteristic of the fourth evangelist.[241] In the course of this, the particle "as" goes beyond being a comparison and also specifies the reason for the relationship: the relationship of Jesus to his followers is founded in his relationship to the Father (cf. John 6:57; 13:34; 15:9–11, 12; 17:11, 18, 21).[242]

The construction of the passage is similar to that of verses 7–10. Just as in that section, here also there are two "I am sayings," which take up and develop a catchword from the *Bildrede* of verses 1–5. At the beginning, as in verses 7–10, stands a first "I am saying," followed by a negative statement about Jesus's counter-image. The second "I am saying" is followed by a positive statement about Jesus. One should not conclude from this that

---

241. Cf. de Dinechin, "Καθώς."
242. For this correspondence, cf. Scholtissek, *In ihm sein*, 372, etc.

verses 12–13a are secondary vis à vis v. 14.²⁴³ What is revealed is much more a structure that resembles verses 7–10:

> the good shepherd and the sheep (11)
>     the hired man and the sheep (12–13)
> the good shepherd and the sheep
>     knowledge (14)
>     giving up of life (15, 17–18)
>     leading other sheep (16)

The "leading" of other sheep interrupts the thought process between v. 15 and v. 17, as it has been envisaged by different authors, but caution is due with literary-critical operations. In verses 17–18, it is the relationship of Jesus and his Father that is the subject, and thus the passage ends with a theological train of thought.

The figure of speech employed in this passage can again be described as a "*Bildrede*." As in verses 7–10, a key concept of the *Bildrede* in verses 1–5 is taken up again and developed: that of the "shepherd." In the present section too, image and reality interpenetrate, especially where the imaginative world of the shepherd is left and the subject is the mutual "knowing" of the shepherd and the sheep corresponding to the Father and Jesus; similarly where the theme of the laying down of the life of the shepherd for the sheep is raised. Here, the text is already speaking from the experience of Christian faith.

What is the purpose of this passage? There are essentially two answers to this question. One view sees here a controversy concerning false shepherds of the Christian community;²⁴⁴ the other reckons that this is a controversy about the "shepherds" and leaders of Israel.²⁴⁵ A diachronic study will show that the latter version is preferable.

At the same time, there is the question of the tradition-historical background of the passage. Depending on whether the imagery of the shepherd or the theme of mutual knowledge is taken as the central point, different answers result.

According to numerous authors, the evangelist was inspired by the imagery of the Old Testament, Judaism, and the Synoptic Jesus tradition.²⁴⁶

---

243. Thus Hahn, "Die Hirtenrede."
244. Cf., above, for Tragan, *La parabole*, among others.
245. Thus representing Schnackenburg, vol. 2.
246. In this sense, Jeremias, "ποιμήν"; Schnackenburg, vol. 2; Barrett; Brown, vol. 1, among others.

## Jesus Reveals Himself to His People (5:1–10:42)

Another interpretation sees the background of the shepherd imagery in Hellenism and gnosis.[247] For a judgement that turns especially on the Gnostic background of the discourse, it is worth following the advice of Joachim Jeremias who points out that the texts invoked by Bultmann are later and presuppose John's Gospel.[248] Overall, the comparative material from the Bible would facilitate a more coherent interpretation of the shepherd discourse than pointing to extrabiblical texts.

As already suggested, the background of the discourse about the good shepherd might be sought especially in ch. 23 (vv. 1–8) of Jeremiah as well as ch. 34 of Ezekiel, with possible contributions from Ezek 36 and 37, not to mention Zech 11 and 13.[249] The motif of the wicked shepherds, who abandon the sheep to the wild animals, is found in Ezek 34:5, 8. The future king (David) will not allow this to happen any more (34:28). Concern for the sheep condemned to slaughter (πρόβατα τῆς σφαγῆς) is also spoken of by Zechariah in Zech 11:4, 7.

The motif of the "scattering" of the sheep (John 10:12) is found in the judgement on the wicked shepherds in Jer 23:1–2 (διασκορπίζομαι). It is also encountered in Ezek 34:5 as well as with the betrayal of the wild animals in 36:19. In Ezek 37 (cf. verses 12 and 21), it becomes a starting point for a new "gathering" of Israel; cf., also, Zech 10:9 (σπείρω); 11:16 (διασκορπίζομαι); and 13:7. That the wicked shepherds do not care for the sheep (John 10:13) is already found in the judgement in Ezek 34:1–10 (cf. 17–22).

The "scattering" of the sheep because of their abandonment by the wicked shepherd to the ravages of wild animals is matched by their "gathering" and "being led" by God or a shepherd over the whole of Israel whom he has appointed. For that, cf. Jer 23:7–8 (ἀνήγαγεν, συνήγαγεν), Ezek 34:13 (ἐξάξω, συνάξω, εἰσάξω); 37:12, 21 (the same verbs); Zech 10:10 ("lead them," "into Lebanon"). It becomes clear, then, that the "leading" of other sheep in John 10 also has its precedents in the Old Testament even if these texts are not thinking yet of a union and gathering with the Gentiles but rather with that of the sons and daughters of Israel from the diaspora.

The gathering and homecoming of Israel lead to a new union of the people. "One flock, one shepherd" (John 10:16) comes from Ezek 37:12, 21–22, 24 (ἔθνος ἕν, ἄρχων εἷς, ποιμὴν εἷς) in a context the describes the "new

---

247. So Bultmann, Becker, *Die Reden*, Schulz; cf., further, Hahn, "Die Hirtenrede." An examination of the Gnostic material is found in Turner, "The History."

248. Cf. Jeremias, "ποιμήν," 495f.

249. Cf. for this and the following, Beutler, "Der alttestamentlich-jüdische Hintergrund."

covenant," the "covenant of peace" (37:26). The Gentiles come into play here insofar as God proves himself to them as present and almighty (v. 28).

What are we to gain from the formula repeated five times that the good shepherd "gives/lays down" his life for his sheep? Here, we are helped by a text out of the Synoptic passion narrative (Mark 14:27 par. Matt 26:31) that interprets the beginning of Jesus's passion and the subsequent scattering of the disciples: "I will strike the shepherd, then the sheep will be scattered." The quotation reproduces (somewhat freely) Zech 13:7. In Zechariah, a positive connection between the death of the shepherd and the saving of at least a part of the people is implied. That the Johannine school knew this text emerges from John 16:32 where reference is made to the prophetic text. In John 10:12, different from Zech 13:7 LXX, the verb "σκορπίζω" is used, recalling Mark 14:27 par. For this reason, the influence of the Markan tradition on John is probable here.

There is also a Synoptic parallel for the motif of the gathering of the sheep of Israel in Matt 15:24; 10:6 where the connection with Ezek 34 is especially prominent.

The notion that Jesus is fulfilling the "command" of the Father and, therefore, is "loved" by him (John 10:17–18) is formulated in the language of covenant theology, as is shown elsewhere.[250] The dedication of the life of Jesus "for" his sheep appears to stem from the Fourth Servant Song, Isa 52:13–53:12. This text has influenced both the Synoptic tradition (cf. Mark 10:45 par. and the account of the Last Supper, Mark 14:24 par.) and also John (cf. John 6:51c; 15:13 and the present passage). Thus, for John 10, it is important that, in Isa 53:6, the people for whom the servant dies are identified with the "straying sheep," and that the image of the sheep has also been applied to him (53:7): like a sheep he was led to the slaughter, and as a sheep that is dumb before its shearers, so he did not open his mouth.[251]

On account of the close connection with the imagery of the context, it is advisable not to assign this verse to another, later stratum of the Gospel,[252] but to maintain its origin from the evangelist.

**10:19–21** The good shepherd discourse concludes with the description of its effect on the listeners. In this way, the narrator points back to

---

250. Cf. Beutler, *Habt keine Angst*, ch. 3.

251. The giving of the life of the shepherd for the sheep emerges from the parallels in John as well as the "giving up" and renewed "taking up" of the life of Jesus in vv. 17–18. Cf. Zimmermann, *Christologie*, 390ff.

252. So, approximately, Becker, 1:389.

## Jesus Reveals Himself to His People (5:1–10:42)

the previous story of the healing of the man born blind, underlining once more the cohesiveness of the two texts.

The grammatical construction of this small unit merits notice. After a short account of the different reactions of the listeners to the words of Jesus in v. 19, there follows an antithesis of what "many" say (v. 20) and what "others" say (v. 21). The two reactions have the same construction: at the beginning, there is the expression of an opinion, and this is followed by a question. In the first case, the question appears rhetorical, in the second, genuine. From this comparison, it is clear already with which answer the narrator identifies himself.

The accusation that Jesus is "possessed by a devil" (δαιμονιζόμενος) is the key concept. This accusation is not new but has appeared already in John 7:20; 8:48. It too stems clearly from the Synoptic tradition. It appears for the first time in Mark 3:22, 30 together with the accusation of Jesus's relations that he is out of his mind (Mark 3:21)—both accusations are brought together in John 10:20. Cf., also, Matt 12:24–32; Luke 11:15–23. In Matt 9:34, the accusation surfaces again, in this case in connection with the exorcism of a demon by Jesus and before a saying about Jesus's compassion on the people whom he saw "like sheep without a shepherd" (Matt 9:35–36).

The function of the text is revealed in the "division" elicited by Jesus (v. 19; cf. 7:43, but also 9:16) and in the different reactions of the listeners to the discourse. Just as the words of Jesus presented a faith decision then, so now the readers find themselves placed before such a decision. It is necessary to decide between the rejection of every divine operation in Jesus by the "many," and an opening to the call issuing from his word and work.

## III

Within the cycle of Jewish feasts, the section of John's Gospel that is characterized by the Feast of Tabernacles takes up the most space (7:1–10:21). In chs. 7 and 8, Jesus reveals himself in his word. In the background, however, there are activities like the rite of water drawing at the spring of Gihon or the illumination of the city from the temple that point to Jesus as the "light of the world" (John 8:12, cf. 9:5) and the source of "living water" (John 7:38). In John 9, Jesus then emerges as actor. He heals the man born blind. In him is shown the path of one, who has not yet come to believe, to arrive at faith in Jesus. This is parallel to the path of the Pharisees who, from their supposed ability to see, sink ever further into the blindness of their denial of faith. With them too is the controversy over faith in Jesus carried out in John 10:1–21. They who ought to be the true shepherds of the people of Israel prove themselves unworthy of this task. There is only one good shepherd: Jesus himself to whom Israel's Scriptures pointed. With his death, he will seal the faithfulness of his mission. However, this will become a source of new life "to the full" (John 10:10).

The question as to who are meant by Jesus's opponents and the antithesis of the good shepherd in the real, historical world may not be the crucial one. John is writing his Gospel, not as a report of the protagonists and groups of the time of Jesus but as a manual of instruction for his readers. Moreover, this is not to be identified with a reconstructed "Johannine community" whose existence is increasingly doubted today. It is better to speak of John's reading community, which is open to the future and so also to the present. In this way, it is not simply a question of a model of responsible leadership of the Christian community but the assumption of social responsibility and the translation of faith into the area of society and politics.

## 4. Jesus at the Feast of the Dedication of the Temple. His Withdrawal over the Jordan (10:22–39, 40–42)

[22] About this time, the feast of the dedication of the temple took place in Jerusalem. It was winter, [23] and Jesus was walking up and down in the temple in the portico of Solomon. [24] The Jews gathered around him there and asked him: How long will you keep us in suspense? If you are the Christ, tell us openly! [25] Jesus answered them: I have told you, but you do not believe. The works that I perform in my Father's name bear witness to me; [26] but you do not believe, because you do not belong to my sheep. [27] My sheep hear my voice; I know them, and they follow me. [28] I give them eternal life. They will never perish, and no one will seize them out of my hand. [29] My Father who gave them to me is greater than all, and no one can seize them out of my Father's hand. [30] I and the Father are one.

[31] Then the Jews took up stones again to stone him. [32] Jesus replied to them: I have shown you many good works on behalf of my Father. For which of these works do you wish to stone me? [33] The Jews answered him: It is not for a good work that we are stoning you but because of blasphemy; for you are only a man but are making yourself into God. [34] Jesus replied to them: Is it not written in your Law: I said, "You are gods"? [35] If he called those men gods to whom the word of God came, and if Scripture cannot be abolished, [36] can you say of the one

whom the Father sanctified and sent into the world: You are blaspheming – because you said: I am the Son of God? ³⁷ If I do not perform my Father's works, then do not believe me. ³⁸ But if I do perform them, then at least believe the works, even if you do not believe in me. Then you will know and understand that the Father is in me and I am in the Father. ³⁹ Again they sought to arrest him; but he escaped their grasp.

⁴⁰ Then Jesus went away again to the other side of the Jordan to the place where John had first been baptizing; and there he stayed. ⁴¹ Many came to him. They said: John did no signs; but everything that John said about this man has turned out to be true. ⁴² And many came to faith in him there.

I

The shepherd discourse ends with an epilogue: a conversation in the temple on the occasion of the Feast of the Dedication of the temple during the winter. With that, Jesus has almost run the course of the Jewish festal cycle to the end. Now he enters the temple for the last time. For John, the cleansing of the temple has already been carried out (John 2:13–22). Thus, Jesus's visit to the temple, as it is recorded in John 10:22–39, is of especial significance. This impression is confirmed by the content of the controversy between Jesus and the "Jews": Jesus's statements about himself reach a new, final climax. At the same time, it is shown who the "Jews" are who refuse to believe in him. The final scene in the temple forms a bracket with the cleansing of the temple narrated in John 2:13–22; the report of the return of Jesus over the Jordan and the reference to John the Baptist provide a cross-reference back to John 1:19–28. This is the last mention of John the Baptist in the Gospel. This confirms the impression that the first part of John's Gospel closes with ch. 10.

The last section of John 10 is divided first into the controversy in the temple in John 10:22–39, and then the return of Jesus to the area on the other side of the Jordan in 10:40–42. We stay first with the section that deals with Jesus's final controversy with his hearers in the temple in John 10:22–39.

To many exegetes, it appears that the order of the text in John 10:22–39 has been disturbed. The reason lies especially in verses 26–29 in which the theme of the good shepherd is taken up again rather unexpectedly. A number of authors suspect, therefore, a disturbance in the text that they try to reassemble. Thus J. H. Bernard suggests inserting verses 10–18 after verses 26-29. Schnackenburg is sympathetic to this suggestion as is also Alfred Wikenhauser, who suggests inserting verses 1-18 after John 10:24. The far more advanced suggestion of Bultmann to reconstruct the discourse totally has already been mentioned. Similarly radical is the suggestion of Blank,[253] according to whom ch. 10 originally began with verses 19-21, 22-26. The double metaphorical saying of verses 7-10 would have come next, followed by the *Bildrede* of verses 1-6. The double word about the good shepherd in verses 11-18 would have followed before verses 27-30. Verses 31-42 would have stood at the end.

The authors who oppose such hypotheses of transposition point especially to the close connection between the shepherd discourse of John 10 and the controversies of John 9. This is the position, above all, of Dodd,[254] following E. C. Hoskyns.[255] The text sequence that has been transmitted was also endorsed by the participants in the seminar of the SNTS in 1985 and 1986.[256] It will be taken as a basis in what follows. It is also supported by the syntactical structure of the present section as well as its semantic unity.

The syntactic analysis of the passage shows this to be an argumentative text as far as v. 38. At the beginning, there are main clauses without a conjunction or joined together with a simple "and," "but," or "therefore" (καί, δέ, οὖν). With the exception of two relative clauses (vv. 25, 29), there are few subordinate constructions. They are found in v. 26 (causal clause) and especially in verses 35-38: in v. 35 conditional and relative clauses; in v. 36 relative and causal clauses; in v. 37 conditional clauses; in v. 38 two conditional clauses, a final clause, and some indirect speech. The nominal clauses within the section also contribute to its understanding: they concern the identity of Jesus (v. 24), that of the Jews (v. 26); of the Father (v. 29); and Jesus together with the Father (v. 30) in the first part of the passage. In the second half (if we leave out the participial construction of v. 34), we have Jesus as a man (v. 33), the Israelites as gods (v. 34), and Jesus as Son of God (v. 36). At the end, there is a statement about the mutual indwelling of Jesus and the Father (v. 38). These nominal clauses carry the weight of the argument to a large extent.

This look at the nominal clauses has already prepared us for the se-

---

253. Cf. the commentaries for the authors mentioned.

254. Dodd, *Interpretation*, 354-62.

255. Cf. Hoskyns. In the same sense, cf. Lightfoot, Brown, and Strathmann. Also, Mollat in the Jerusalem Bible as well as, now, Thyen in his commentary and in "Zu den zahllosen Versuchen."

256. Cf. Beutler and Fortna, eds., *The Shepherd Discourse*.

mantic analysis of the text, of the words and word fields employed. The (good) works of Jesus are the theme that pervades the whole section. It occurs for the first time in v. 25, defines the interaction of verses 31–32, and prepares for the following and final section of verses 33–38 (vv. 33, 37–38). The words of Jesus are placed beside his works (from vv. 24–25 until the end in v. 36). The theme of "faith" also dominates the whole section (from v. 25 until vv. 37–38). Cross-references back to the shepherd discourse are found exclusively in verses 26–29 (belong to the sheep, hear the voice, follow, not perish, not be seized from Jesus's hand; cf., also, the gift of life in v. 28). If we keep in mind that the shepherd in John 10 means the messianic king of Israel in the language of the OT, then there is no opposition between the question about Jesus's messianic character in v. 24 and his answer with shepherd imagery.

Verses 31–32 recount an attempt to stone Jesus with his answer about his (good) works. In verses 33–38, the vocabulary is almost exclusively theological. It concerns Jesus's claim to be the Son of God, and its basis in Scripture. The statement in v. 30 that Jesus and the Father are one corresponds to that of v. 38 that the Father is in him and he in the Father.

The structure of the text revealed by linguistic analysis is as follows:

| | |
|---|---|
| 22–23 | Information about time and place |
| 24–30 | First exchange |
| | 24 Question of the Jews |
| | 25–30 Jesus's answer |
| 31–32 | Second exchange |
| | 31 Attempt to stone Jesus |
| | 32 Jesus's question about the motive |
| 33–38 | Third exchange |
| | 33 Answer of the Jews |
| | 34–38 Jesus's answer |
| 39 | Conclusion. Attempt to arrest Jesus; Jesus's escape |
| 40–42 | Return of Jesus over the Jordan; many believe |

The guiding of the readers is revealed above all in the clauses with an argumentative character, i.e., in verses 26–29, and especially in the closing section vv. 35–38. It is, then, a question of faith in Jesus as the Son of God, one with the Father, as God, in fact, against Jewish contradictions. Thus, the "stage directions" have their weight: the scene of action is the temple; the time is the last Jewish feast before the next Passover, the Feast of the Dedication of the temple; the season is winter—perhaps symbolic for the climate of the debate. The decision for or against Jesus, therefore, has dramatic aspects, and this drama occurs also in the attempt to stone Jesus or arrest him.

To understand this section, it is necessary to enquire after its roots in the tradition. For a long time it has been suggested that the Jewish trial in the Synoptics seems to lie behind John 10:22–39.[257] The strongest contacts turn out to be with Luke 22:66–71. In detail, these are:

- if you are the Messiah, then tell us (εἰ σὺ εἶ ὁ χριστός, εἰπὸν ἡμῖν, Luke 22:67; John 10:24)
- if I tell you, you will not believe me (ἐὰν ὑμῖν εἴπω, οὐ μὴ πιστεύσητε, Luke 22:67; John 10:25)
- an argument from Scripture, more specifically from the Psalms (Luke 22:69: Ps 109:1 LXX; John 10:34–36: Ps 81:6 LXX)
- the Son of God (ὁ υἱὸς τοῦ θεοῦ, Luke 22:70; John 10:36)

In his account of Jesus's Jewish trial, John mentions Jesus's teaching in the temple only briefly (cf. Luke 22:53; 19:47; also, John 10:24 "tell us openly"). The content of this teaching is made clear in John 10:22–39.

With his quotation from the Psalms in John 10:34–36, the Johannine Jesus is arguing "from light to heavy," that is, with Jewish methods of argument.[258] Only the first half of the text, Ps 81:6 LXX, is quoted; the second half, which would have strengthened the argument further, is omitted: "You are all sons of the Most High." Originally, this saying represented a judgement on the gods as unjust judges.[259] In the Second Temple period and in early Judaism, four different exegeses replaced this interpretation.[260] It was referred to the angels; to Melchizedek (cf. 11QMelch); to the judges of Israel; or to the people of Israel at Mount Sinai. With good reasons from numerous midrashic texts, Neyrey has made a plausible argument that it was this fourth interpretation that was probably presupposed by John.[261] According to Jewish understanding, with the bestowal of the Law at Sinai, Israel received the dignity of the first human couple in Paradise, "after the image of God," which the first parents had lost, and possessed "eternal

---

257. Cf. Sabbe, "John 10"; further, Dauer, "Spuren."
258. Cf., for this section, Beutler, "Ich habe gesagt."
259. Cf. Jüngling, *Der Tod*.
260. Cf. Neyrey, "I Said." Since then, there is a thorough exposition in Maier, "Das jüdische Verständnis."
261. Cf. Neyrey, "I Said." This interpretation is also adopted by Felsch, *Feste*, 239–43.

life." Just as Adam and Eve lost their immortality because of their sin, so too did the Israelites on account of their worship of the golden calf. Jesus is the positive counter-image as "Son of God." He receives life because of his obedience and can pass it on to others.

Against the background of the tradition, the Johannine redaction can be worked out more clearly. We begin with the framework and the first exchange of speech in verses 22–30.

## II

**10:22–23** The action takes place during the last major feast of the Jews. Originally, this was a transferred Feast of Tabernacles after the restoration of the cult in 165 BCE (cf. 2 Macc 1:9).[262] For this reason too, the temple is the suitable stage for the controversy between Jesus and the "Jews." The "portico of Solomon" will later become the meeting point for the Christians in the process of their gradual separation from Judaism (cf. Acts 3:11; 5:12).

**10:24–26** The "Jews" "gather round" Jesus, apparently with a hostile attitude. Their demand for Jesus to explain "openly" who he is is perhaps alluding to Jesus's way of talking in images and similitudes (cf. John 16:25, 29 and what is said above at John 10:6).

When Jesus maintains in v. 25 that he has already said that he is the Messiah, this presupposes the messianic-eschatological interpretation of the good shepherd discourse in John 10:1–18. Cf., also, perhaps v. 16 with its statement about one flock and one shepherd. However, Jesus understands his identity as Messiah in the sense of divine sonship. This sonship is exhibited in his union with the Father in word and work. The "testimony" of the work has already occurred in John 5:36.[263] The argument could stem from Jewish-Hellenistic apologetic in which the divine sending of Moses was proved by the signs performed by him.

In v. 26, the thought shifts from the content of faith in Jesus to its enabling. The talk of "election" at that point is not to be thought of as post-Johannine, as is occasionally conjectured, but simply goes back to the *Bildrede* in verses 1–18, as is shown in the following.

---

262. There is a thorough description of the Feast of the Dedication of the temple as the background to John 10:22–39 in Felsch, *Feste*, 221–45. Poirier, "Hanukkah," would like to see the controversy dialogues and discourses of Jesus from John 8:12 as composed under the influence of Hanukkah. For this reason, in John 10:22, he reads ἐγένετο δέ, with difficulty.

263. Cf., for this theme, Beutler, *Martyria*, 260ff., 272ff.

**10:27–30** The image of the shepherd and sheep in v. 27 points back to John 10:1–18. For the motif of hearing a voice and following, one thinks of verses 3–5 and 16, and for the knowing of the sheep, verses 14–15.

Verse 28 starts out from verses 11–15 but is recalling verses as early as 9–10. In v. 10, it says that the thief steals, slaughters, and destroys; in v. 12, that the wolf seizes them and scatters them. By contrast, it is said in v. 10 that Jesus had come so that the sheep, i.e., those entrusted to him, might have life to the full.

According to the *Einheitsübersetzung*, v. 29 speaks of the superiority of the Father to every human power so that no one is able to seize the sheep entrusted to Jesus from the Father's hand. However, the text at the basis of the *Einheitsübersetzung* is not certain. The text tradition that is probably most ancient (represented by Papyri 66 and—so it appears—75, as well as Codex Vaticanus, Codex L, the Syrosinaiticus, not to mention the proto-Bohairic tradition) reads the text that Nestle-Aland[28] adduces as the main text and the *Einheitsübersetzung* offers as an alternative: "What my Father has given me, is greater than all, and no one can seize it from my Father's hand." In content, there is no great difference between the two readings. The marked assurance in the verse already presupposes that there is a full agreement between Jesus and the Father when it comes to action. The sheep entrusted to Jesus are ultimately led by the hand of the Father and are secure with him. This union in action is followed by the climactic saying in v. 30: "I and the Father are one."

Although the statement in v. 30 starts out from the union of the Father and the Son in action, it must nevertheless be understood as a statement about the unity of the Father and the Son in their being. Father and Son are not one person but nonetheless one in being. This statement is not all that surprising for the reader of John's Gospel since it is taking up the framing verses of the prologue, John 1:1, 18, which find their echo in the confession of Thomas in John 20:28, that is, in the confession of Jesus's divinity. Here, opinions are divided to the present day.

The second and third exchanges (John 10:31–39) are closely connected to each other and can be discussed together here.

**10:31–32** The reaction of the "Jews" to the words of Jesus follows, not in words but in deeds. They take up stones to stone him—the death penalty prescribed by the Mishnah for blasphemy. In reply, Jesus not only asserts his innocence but also points to his good work of healing the man born blind and other good works that preclude his being stoned.

**10:33–36** The "Jews" do not now repeat their accusation but try to make it more specific: Jesus is claiming divine dignity for himself. Jesus answers this accusation with an argument from Ps 81/82:6 (see above, I). Dorit Felsch suggests that the notion of "blasphemy" was linked with the celebration of the Feast of the Dedication of the temple from the beginning. The feast was established to celebrate the liberation of the temple from its desecration by Antiochus IV Epiphanes.[264] The accusation against Jesus that he is blaspheming God does not have the desired effect since he appears to be fully in union with God the Father. It was by God that he was "sanctified and sent into the world" (v. 36). Thus, he is without fault.

**10:37–38** The witness to Jesus from the word is followed again by that from his works (cf. v. 25). The point of this reference does not consist in the fact that faith in the word of Jesus can be replaced through an understanding of his person based on his works. Rather, God reveals himself in Jesus's works also, and here too the correct response is one of faith.[265] In this way, the correct understanding of the works of Jesus is inferred only on the basis of his revelation in his words. A similar connection between the word and work of Jesus is expressed also in John 14:10–11 and 15:23–25.

**10:39** This exchange too ends not with a concluding response from Jesus's listeners but with violence. They try to arrest Jesus. Attempts of this kind have already been mentioned in John 7:30, 32, 44; 8:20. These places represent a dramatic anticipation during his public life of the final apprehending of Jesus at the beginning of the passion narrative. Thereby, the judgement of the world is enacted (John 12:31), and the one judged appears as judge.

Chapter 10 closes with the information about Jesus's return to the area on the other side of the Jordan and the faith of many there (John 10:40–42).

**10:40** Jesus leaves the temple. He will not enter it again, and will return to Jerusalem only for the raising of Lazarus and his own passion. The area "on the other side of the Jordan" is the same as that where John the Baptist worked (John 1:28; 3:26) as is explicitly highlighted by the text. Thus a full circle is completed.

**10:41–42** In this way, for a last time, there is a reference to the testimony of John the Baptist to Jesus (cf. John 5:33–35). The significance

---

264. Cf. Felsch, *Feste*, 228–32. According to the author, the messianic expectations were especially strong at this feast. This also explains the demand that Jesus say clearly whether he is the Messiah.

265. For the immanence formulas in this place ("the Father in me" and "I in the Father") and elsewhere in John, cf. Scholtissek, *In ihm sein und bleiben*.

of John the Baptist consists not in miracles like those of Jesus but in his testimony on Jesus's behalf (cf. John 1:6–8, 15, 19–34; 3:26–30). Thus John's Gospel is wholly oriented towards Jesus, and the Baptist is consistently subordinate to him.

The short conclusion: "and many came to faith in him there" in v. 42 is to be understood against the background of the controversies that define the previous chapters. According to John 10:20, "many" had taken offense at him, and only a few had contested this judgement (John 10:21). Now, "many" come to faith in Jesus. However, the location is no longer Jerusalem, but "there," on the other side of the Jordan, not far from the region of the Gentiles. Thus, once again, there is an announcement of the opening of Jesus's work of salvation to the Gentiles, as has already been declared in John 10:16: "I have other sheep."

## III

The controversies on the Feast of the Dedication of the temple mark the climax and conclusion of the controversy dialogues and discourses of Jesus in chs. 7–10. The subject is continually the divine mission of Jesus and his claim to be the Son and Savior sent into the world by the Father. In the concluding section, John 10:22–39, a peak has been reached insofar as the theme is now, in an unparalleled way, Jesus himself and his union with the Father. The two climactic statements "I and the Father are one" (v. 30) and "the Father is in me and I am in the Father" (v. 38) sound like short formulations of Johannine Christology. Opinions on them differ dramatically.

These climactic statements of Johannine Christology have lost nothing of their provocative character. Over the centuries, the church has tried to fill them out thoughtfully and with precise terminology, a process in which Greek thought became as a godfather. Today, we are discovering anew the roots of Johannine Christology in the faith of Israel. The Johannine Jesus argues from the Psalms as part of the "Law," that is, the Scripture of Israel, and the tradition of the dignity of Israel before their falling into sin with the golden calf and their eschatological promise can help to recognize Jesus as Son and representative of his people and embrace him in his unique connection with the Father. The temple is the appropriate stage for this. If Jesus now leaves it for good, he has nonetheless promised that he will rise again in the body that he has given up (cf. John 2:19–22). It is the body the good shepherd will lay down for his (John 10:11, 17–18).

# Jesus on the Way to His Passion (11:1–12:50)

There are good grounds for seeing chs. 11–12 of John's Gospel as a separate main section that provides a transition from the preaching of Jesus before his people to the story of his passion.[1] With John 10:40–42, the Baptist has finally left the stage as a witness for Jesus. Lazarus will enter temporarily in his place. In John 11:55, Jesus is on the threshold of his final journey to Jerusalem for the feast of the Passover. Instead of the question as to who Jesus is, which reached its unsurpassable climax in ch. 10, this section deals with his destiny and its fulfillment. The raising of Lazarus, who had lain in the grave for three days, points towards the resurrection of Jesus on the third day (John 11:1–46). The decision to kill Jesus already belongs to the story of the passion (John 11:47–54), and Jesus's final Passover forms its framework (John 11:55–57). Jesus's anointing follows with a look towards his imminent death (John 12:1–11). His entry into Jerusalem reveals a contrast between the ovation of the crowd and the reaction of the Pharisees who now see that the moment has arrived to prepare the end-game (John 12:12–19). Jesus then sees the coming salvation of the Greeks, something that presupposes his death (John 12:20–36), and the evangelist can only observe and try to understand the rejection of Jesus by a large part of Israel before Jesus summons them to faith in him for the last time (John 12:37–50).

---

1. For this, cf. the introduction to the commentary, section 2.

## 1. The Raising of Lazarus (11:1–46)

¹ A man was sick, Lazarus from Bethany, the village of Mary and her sister, Martha. ² Mary was the one who anointed the Lord with oil and dried his feet with her hair; her brother, Lazarus, was sick. ³ So the sisters sent Jesus the news: Lord, the man you love is sick. ⁴ When Jesus heard that, he said: This sickness will not lead to death, but serves the glory of God: through it the Son is to be glorified. ⁵ Jesus loved Martha, her sister and Lazarus. ⁶ When he heard that Lazarus was sick, he remained for two more days in the place where he was staying.

⁷ After this, he said to the disciples: Let us go again to Judaea. ⁸ The disciples said to him: Rabbi, just now, the Jews sought to stone you, and are you going there again? ⁹ Jesus answered: Are there not twelve hours in the day? If anyone walks about during the day, he does not stumble because he sees the light of this world; ¹⁰ but when anyone walks about during the night, he stumbles because the light is not in him. ¹¹ He spoke thus. Then he said to them: Lazarus, our friend, is sleeping; but I am going to rouse him. ¹² Then the disciples said to him: Lord, if he is sleeping, then he will get better. ¹³ However, Jesus had been speaking about his death whereas they thought he was speaking of sleep as usual. ¹⁴ So Jesus said to them plainly: Lazarus is dead. ¹⁵ And I am glad for you that I was not there; for I want you to believe. However, we shall go to him. ¹⁶ Then Thomas, who was called Didymus, said to the other disciples: Let us go with him so that we may die with him.

¹⁷ When Jesus arrived he found that Lazarus had already lain in the tomb for four days. ¹⁸ Bethany was close to Jerusalem, about fifteen stadia away. ¹⁹ Many Jews had come to Martha and Mary to comfort them on account of their brother. ²⁰ When Martha heard that Jesus was coming, she went to meet him, but Mary remained sitting in the house. ²¹ Martha said to Jesus: Lord, if you had been here, my brother would not have died. ²² But I know even now: Whatever you ask of God, God will give you. ²³ Jesus said to her: Your brother will rise again. ²⁴ Martha said to him: I know that he will rise at the resurrection on the last day. ²⁵ Jesus said to her: I am the resurrection and the life. Whoever believes in me will live, even if he dies, ²⁶ and whoever lives and believes in me will never die. Do you believe that? ²⁷ Martha said to him: Yes, Lord, I believe that you are the Christ, the Son of God, who is to come into the world.

²⁸ After these words, she went away and called her sister Mary secretly and said to her: The master is here and is calling for you. ²⁹ When Mary heard that, she got up immediately and went to him. ³⁰ For Jesus had not yet reached the village; he was still in the place where Martha had met him. ³¹ The Jews who were with Mary in the house and were comforting her saw her suddenly getting up and

going out. Then they followed her, because they thought she was going to the grave to weep there. ³² When Mary came to the place where Jesus was and saw him, she fell at his feet and said to him: Lord, if you had been here, my brother would not have died. ³³ When Jesus saw how she wept and how the Jews who had come with her also wept, he was greatly moved and distressed. ³⁴ He said: Where have you laid him? They said to him: Lord, come and see! ³⁵ Jesus wept. ³⁶ The Jews said: See how he loved him! ³⁷ But some said: If he opened the blind man's eyes, could he not have prevented this man here from dying? ³⁸ Then Jesus was greatly moved again, and he went to the grave. It was a cave that was closed off with a stone. ³⁹ Jesus said: Take the stone away! Martha, the dead man's sister, said to him: But, Lord, he will already stink, for it is now the fourth day. ⁴⁰ Jesus said to her: Have I not told you: If you believe you will see the glory of God? ⁴¹ Then they took away the stone. Jesus, however, raised his eyes and spoke: Father, I thank you that you have heard me. ⁴² I knew that you always hear me; but I have said it on account of the crowd who are standing round me so that they may know that you have sent me. ⁴³ After he had said this, he cried with a loud voice: Lazarus, come forth! ⁴⁴ Then the dead man came out; his feet and his hands were tied with bandages, and his face was wrapped in a towel. Jesus said to them: Untie the bandages and let him go! ⁴⁵ Many of the Jews that had come to Mary and seen what Jesus had done came to faith in him. ⁴⁶ But some of them went to the Pharisees and told them what he had done.

*I*

Jesus's last great "sign" before his death and resurrection is the raising of his friend Lazarus from the dead. This event anticipates the destiny of Jesus and introduces the reader more deeply into the evangelist's view of the theology of "death" and "life."

At first glance, the narrative of the raising of Lazarus appears a unity, but, on closer examination, different levels of the account are revealed, showing a slow growth in the text that has been transmitted. Indications of such a growth could include the following:

- different information about the characters (Mary and Martha as sisters *tout court*, as sisters of Lazarus, or simply as women from the same village);
- contradictory information about the place (Jesus comes to the place where Lazarus lived, v. 17, and has not yet arrived, v. 30);

- the two sisters address the same words to Jesus on his arrival in Bethany (in v. 21 Martha and in v. 32 Mary); only once do these develop into a dialogue (vv. 22–27);
- the narrative is repeatedly interrupted by dialogues (vv. 7–16 with the disciples, vv. 21–27 and again vv. 39–40 with Martha);
- the narrative is also interrupted with comments from the narrator;
- the text exhibits theological tensions. Where does the narrator's interest lie: in the astonishing miracle of Jesus, in the introduction to his passion, in the deeper sense of the "life" bestowed by Jesus, or in something else?

More recent authors have propounded hypotheses of strata in the Johannine text in order to resolve these tensions. Thus, it is possible to offer four different options for how the sources are distinguished from one another:

- signs source – (Gnostic) revelation discourses – evangelist[2]
- signs source – evangelist[3]
- *Vorlage* – signs source – evangelist[4]
- tradition – *Grundschrift* – evangelist – ecclesiastical redaction[5]

Since the hypothesis of a source of Gnostic revelation discourses in John has been abandoned and the discussion over the existence of a "*Grundschrift*" or "signs source" has still not yielded accepted results, it is advisable in what follows to distinguish between pre-Johannine tradition and Johannine revision. This is especially noticeable in the dialogues between Jesus and the disciples (vv. 7–16) as well as Jesus and Martha (vv. 21–27 and 39–40). However, the whole text in John 11:1–46 in its final form is to be viewed and expounded as a Johannine text, since the parts of the text that have been taken over are component parts of the text of the final hand and to be understood as belonging to him.

For this reason, in more recent times, there have been an increasing number of suggestions to give a synchronic exegesis of the Lazarus story, that is, on the basis of the present text in its final form. Thyen still considers the Synoptic Gospels to function as sources that were then newly inter-

---

2. Thus Bultmann.
3. In this sense, Nicol, *Semeia*; Stenger, "Auferweckung."
4. So Becker; cf. Wilkens, "Die Erweckung des Lazarus."
5. In this sense, Wagner, *Auferstehung*, from the school of Hainz and Richter.

preted.⁶ Other authors abstain from such proposals and expound the text from the perspective of its theological train of thought⁷ or its guidance of the readers.⁸

The construction of the narrative emerges from narrative criteria, that is, with the aid of information as to time, place, characters, and action.⁹ This is what results:

| | |
|---|---|
| 11:1–6 | Introduction |
| 7–16 | Dialogue of Jesus with the disciples. Departure |
| 17–27 | Dialogue with Martha |
| 28–32 | Mary runs to meet Jesus, followed by the Jews |
| 33–37 | Mary and the Jews with Jesus |
| 38–44 | Jesus goes to the grave. The miracle of the raising |
| 45–46 | Results of the miracle |

In determining the genre of the narrative, we have to take into account that it probably has a long process of growth behind it. If one omits the dialogue scenes on this basis, then there emerges the core of a story about the raising of a dead person as found elsewhere in the Bible.¹⁰

The two New Testament parallels from the Gospels are the raising of Jairus's daughter and that of the son of the widow of Nain. The story of the raising of the daughter of the ruler of the synagogue, Jairus (Mark 5:21–43 par. Matt 9:18–26; Luke 8:40–56), is characterized by its link with the story of the healing of a woman suffering from an issue of blood (Mark 5:25–34). This connection may already have been pre-Markan and created room for the girl's death to occur in the meantime. Apart from that, the story of the raising follows the scheme of miracle healing stories with the exposition, the mention of the doubtful situation (the bystanders only laugh when Jesus says the child is sleeping, v. 40), the choice of witnesses, and the words of healing (v. 41), the success and proof of the healing (twofold here: the girl walks around and eats). Mark 5 lacks the "concluding chorus," the praise of God

---

6. Cf. Thyen, "Erzählung."
7. Thus, for instance, Kremer, *Lazarus*.
8. Along these lines, Wuellner, "Putting Life Back"; Moloney, "Can Everyone Be Wrong?"; Dennis, "Conflict and Resolution"; Manzi, "Resa credente"; Hofius, "Auferweckung"; Labahn, "Bedeutung"; Zimmermann, "The Narrative Hermeneutics"; Zimmermann, "Narrative Ethik."
9. Most authors offer a similar division. Cf., among others, Kremer, *Lazarus*.
10. Cf. Bultmann, *Geschichte*, 228–30.

or the exclamation of astonishment at the miracle that has been performed. It is omitted here and replaced by the typical Markan injunction to silence.

The other comparable text is that of the raising of the son of the widow of Nain (Luke 7:11–17). This narrative is peculiar to Luke. It lacks the motif of delay that marks the story of the raising of Jairus's daughter but also the raising of Lazarus. The typical elements include the death of the son of a widow (cf., for this, the raising of the son of the widow of Zarephath by Elijah in 1 Kgs 17:17–24) and the dead man's being borne out of the city on a bier.[11] Characteristic also are the crowd of bystanders, the word of healing, the realization and proof of the healing or raising (the young man begins to speak), as well as the explicit "choral conclusion."

When these observations are applied to the story of the raising of Lazarus in John 11:1–44, then it emerges that the older Johannine narrative is similar to that of the raising of the young man of Nain but the expanded narrative is closer to that of the raising of the daughter of Jairus on account of the motif of delay. According to Thyen,[12] there would have been direct influence on our evangelist from the story of the raising of the young man of Nain but also from the pericopes of Martha and Mary in Luke 10:38–42 and of the poor man, Lazarus, in Luke 16:19–31. For the final form of the narrative including the dialogues, the only possible parallels are from John's Gospel. Especially relevant here are the healing stories in John 5 and John 9.

On the basis of the proper names found in John's story of Lazarus, two accounts are mentioned that could have exercised influence on John 11:1–44. First, there is the story of the rich man and poor Lazarus in Luke 16:19–31. In fact, most authors deny any direct influence of this story on John 11, yet there are striking agreements: a man called Lazarus dies and wishes to return to the living (to warn his brothers and relations). In Luke, the return from the dead is only the object of a conversation; in John it occurs in reality—although only with the consequence of reinforcing the unbelief of the "Jews."

The other passage is the pericope that we have mentioned about the two sisters Martha and Mary in Luke 10:38–42. They are mentioned together here but there is no talk of a family relationship to Lazarus. In the center of this story—by contrast with John, but perhaps in agreement with the pre-Johannine tradition—stands the figure of Mary. This is also the case in the story of the anointing of Jesus in John 12:1–8 (cf. Mark 14:3–9 par.

---

11. Cf. Bultmann, *Geschichte*, 230 and 236, with Hellenistic parallels.
12. Cf. Thyen.

*Jesus on the Way to His Passion (11:1–12:50)*

Matt 26:6–13; Luke 7:36–50—in this tradition, the woman anointing Jesus is unnamed; it is only Christian tradition that has made the identification with Mary Magdalene).

The orientation that the evangelist wished to give to his story is especially noticeable in his additions to the tradition, although not everywhere with the same certainty.

The least certain Johannine motif is that of the "glorification" of God's Son in v. 4. The majority of exegetes ascribe it to the evangelist,[13] but they have occasionally prefaced this with the warning not to ascribe the glorification of Jesus through his signs too quickly to the evangelist since, according to the advocates of a "signs source," this is precisely what is supposed to be characteristic of this source.[14] The same goes for v. 40. However, as long as the "signs source" remains a hypothesis, the motif of Jesus's "glorification" in his final and greatest sign is not easily denied to the evangelist. In any case, it should be put down to the last hand responsible for the text.

We can be more certain that the motif of suffering in Jesus's dialogue with the disciples in verses 1–6 and especially 8–10 as well as 16 goes back to the evangelist. This observation is confirmed by the fact that the Lazarus story appears close to John's account of the passion.

The language and theology of the fourth evangelist occur most strongly in Jesus's words of revelation to Martha within the course of the dialogue in John 11:21–27: "I am the resurrection and the life." Here the Christology and eschatology of John's Gospel find their purest expression. Jesus is the bringer of light and life from the Father (for the motif of "light," cf. John 9). This life is not, as Martha first supposes, a new life after bodily death, but an opening up of the meaning of existence that is granted here and now. In view of this gift, sickness and death lose their meaning.

## II

*The Sickness of Lazarus—"Not to Death" (11:1–6)*

The first 16 verses of the Lazarus story serve as an introduction to the account of the raising of Lazarus. "Sickness" and "death" appear connected there. The first six verses concern the sickness of Lazarus that could lead to

---

13. To them belongs also Becker.
14. Along these lines, Richter, *Studien*, 284–86.

his death; verses 7–16 are about the departure of Jesus for Bethany, which could mean his own death.

The passage has a simple grammatical construction. Generally, there is a succession of main clauses. Apart from some relative clauses and the temporal clause of v. 6, especially striking among the subordinate clauses is the final clause of v. 4: "so that through it (the sickness) the Son of God will be glorified." This finds its structural correspondence in the final clause of v. 15: "so that you may believe." In this way, important objectives are already expressed, and it is these that determine the whole narrative complex. Within the first six verses the action starts, after some nominal clauses, in v. 3 with the transition to the narrative aorist. The comment in v. 5 is in the imperfect.

As for the use of language, in the first six verses, there are three chief word fields that are especially significant:

- "sick" (ἀσθεν-) in all verses except v. 5,
- "brother/sister" (ἀδελφός, ἀδελφή) in verses 1–3 and 5 as well as
- "love" (ἀγαπάω/φιλέω) in verses 3 and 5.

Added to this are the themes of "death" (vv. 2 and 4) and the "anointing" in view of death (v. 2).

How is our passage narrated? The narrator is encountered in all the verses. Twice, there is a comment or explanation in the imperfect. In the first case, we have the explanation about Mary (v. 2); in the second, that of Lazarus and his sisters (v. 5). In the center stand the communication of the sisters in v. 3 and Jesus's reply in v. 4. This gives the following narrative construction:

1 Narrator
2 Narrator (comment)
3 Narrator, sisters
4 Narrator, Jesus
5 Narrator (comment)
6 Narrator

The construction is thus concentric, with the words of the sisters and Jesus in the center.

**11:1–3** The narrative begins with the exposition of the story of the raising. The most important catchword occurs right at the beginning: Lazarus is "sick." In this way, the story starts out, like other Johannine signs, from everyday experience. The place Bethany recalls the Bethany on the other side of the Jordan where John the Baptist began his activity (John 1:28; cf. 10:40). Perhaps here too an arc is being registered deliberately. A new cycle opens. Lazarus now enters instead of the Baptist. He is someone whom Jesus loves (v. 3), and so prepares the transition to Jesus's beloved disciple who, from ch. 13, appears at Jesus's side and becomes his witness.

There is a development in the identification of the two sisters, Mary and Martha. According to v. 1, they only hail from the same village; according to v. 2, they are sisters of Lazarus. Here the growth of the tradition is still visible. The narrator's comment in v. 2 that Mary is the same person who anointed Jesus with oil anticipates John 12:1–8 and presupposes readers who have a view of the whole text. As regards content, this reference connects the raising of Lazarus with the imminent death of Jesus. Here, the hand of the evangelist may be detected.

**11:4** We certainly see the evangelist at work in v. 4. Linguistically speaking the text passes from "being sick" (verbal) to "sickness" (nominal). This will not lead to death but is to serve for the glorification of God. In this way, a central note of John's Gospel is struck. The "glorification of God" takes place in the "glorification" of God's Son.[15] Almost throughout the Gospel, this theme is linked to the death and "lifting up" of Jesus (cf. John 7:39; 12:16, 23, 28; 13:31–32; 17:1, 5). Isaiah's servant (52:13 LXX) seems to stand in the background. It is also not necessary to see, in John 11:4, the theology of the "signs source" or the "*Grundschrift*," which connects the glorification of Jesus with his earthly signs. What is the concern here is the last great sign of Jesus, which directly prefigures his own departure. In John 9:3–4 too, the sign of the healing of the blind man was seen in connection with the self-revelation of Jesus in the "work" but also with his imminent end.

**11:5** We hear the evangelist's language also in v. 5. Whereas it says in v. 3: "The man you love is sick" (with the verb φιλεῖν, with a root that expresses rather a relationship of friendship, cf. John 15:13–15), it is now said that Jesus "loved" his sisters and him (ἠγάπα), with the verb that, in John, has its biblical note and expresses more than a purely human relationship. Here again, there is probably an echo of the beloved disciple.[16]

---

15. Instead of "God's Son," P[45] with part of the Itala as well as the Coptic and Syriac text tradition reads "his son," probably under the influence of the context. P[66] omits the genitive construction since, apparently, the correct reading was already no longer certain. Our exegesis follows the text in Nestle-Aland[28].

16. Cf. Thyen, "Die Erzählung," who warns, however, against an identification of the two figures on the real level.

**11:6** After the double interruption in verses 4 and 6, the narrator takes up the thread again. From the "sickness," we pass back to the "being sick" of Lazarus. Jesus hears of it, but remains two days after receiving the news before he sets out for Bethany. Here, we encounter the motif of delay, which is not foreign to the genre. It creates room for Lazarus's death to take place in the meantime but also for his miraculous raising. When with the third day, we reach the departure of Jesus, there is probably an echo here too of his own resurrection on the third day. Human considerations, such as whether Jesus could not have hindered his friend's death by an earlier departure (cf. the saying of Martha in v. 21 and that of Mary in v. 32), are irrelevant to the Johannine narrator. Only Lazarus's death makes possible the experience of the power of God over death.

### The Departure of Jesus (11:7–16)

The following passage is often proposed to begin with v. 6. There are good reasons, however, for seeing it as beginning only at v. 7:

- the syntactic coherence of vv. 1–6 (see above)
- the double temporal indication in v. 7 (ἔπειτα, μετὰ τοῦτο) "after this"
- the author's eschewal of a δέ in v. 7 after the μέν of v. 6
- the new concentric structure of vv. 7–15 with v. 16 as its conclusion (see below)
- the semantic coherence of the passage and its orientation towards Jesus and the disciples

A glance at the grammatical construction of the passage shows that, again, this consists broadly of main clauses. Coordination outweighs subordination. The style is more markedly Johannine than in the previous verses with the "after this" (μετὰ τοῦτο) in verses 7 and 11, the "so" (τότε οὖν) in v. 14, and the asyndeton in verses 8–9. There are conditional clauses, followed by a causal clause in verses 9–10. and a further conditional clause in v. 12. It is, again, the final clauses that are significant: in v. 11, Jesus gives the purpose of his departure for Bethany; in v. 15, the reason for his joy despite the death of his friends: it is a matter of the disciples' faith.

The narrative construction of the passage is concentric like that of the previous one. Thus, the passage is framed by the catch-phrase "Let us go" (ἄγωμεν):

| v. 7 | Narrator, Jesus | ἄγωμεν |
| v. 8 | Narrator, disciples | |
| vv. 9–10 | Narrator, Jesus, Metaphor | |
| v. 11 | Narrator, Jesus, Metaphor | |
| v. 12 | Narrator, disciples | |
| vv. 13–15 | Narrator, Jesus ("plainly") | ἄγωμεν |
| v. 16 | Narrator, Thomas | ἄγωμεν |

In the middle stands the double metaphor, at the beginning a clear statement of Jesus and at the end an explanation of one of the metaphors. The frame is formed by Jesus's saying "Let us go" in v. 6, which he takes up again in v. 15, and by Thomas as spokesman for the disciples in v. 16. The meaning of the text emerges most easily from the individual analysis of the verses:

**11:7** With Jesus's summons to depart with him for Judaea, one of the central themes of the passage is already registered, and it is linked to the second. This departure is the commencement of a risk as will immediately be revealed. Jesus's departure is connected to the theme of death, and, in fact, not only the death of his friend, Lazarus.

**11:8** This is shown by the disciples' pointing to the attempt to stone Jesus in Judaea. There, where his friend has died, Jesus could also lose his life and also expose the disciples to danger.

**11:9–10** Jesus is aware of his own death, but it has its day and its hour. It is the hour prescribed by the Father. This is conveyed by the image of the onset of night, when the light yields to the darkness and feet stumble. The same image is encountered again in John 12:35, applied there to Jesus's hearers who have only a short time that has been allotted to them.

**11:11–13** A further saying of Jesus replaces the night with sleep, it too an image for the world of the dead as will be made explicit in v. 13. That Jesus will go and wake Lazarus from sleep is misunderstood by the disciples at first.

**11:14–15** What the narrator has already explained in v. 13, Jesus now says openly to his disciples: Lazarus has died. However, he is glad for the sake of the disciples that this has happened. The raising of Lazarus is to strengthen their faith. Therefore they have to set out with him for Judaea—in this way, the summons in v. 7 is taken up again and the passage rounded off.

**11:16** Thereupon, Thomas makes himself a spokesman for the disciples and urges the other disciples to go with Jesus and die with him. It has occasionally been doubted whether to take Thomas's words seriously since they sound similar to the boastful words of Peter in John 13:37 that are then followed not by deeds but by the triple denial.[17] However, everything speaks for the fact that Thomas's words should be taken seriously. In other places too, Jesus commands the disciples to be faithful to him until death (cf. John 12:25–26; 21:18–19), and predicts for them a coming persecution to the death (John 15:26–27; 16:1–3). Within the section, John 11:7–16, the words of Thomas stand at the close and, with recourse to the double saying of Jesus, encapsulate the whole passage. It is improbable, then, that what we have here are supposed to be empty words. For the readers, Thomas's words contain a clear message: to be ready to go with Jesus even to death in order to find life.[18]

### *Jesus's Arrival in Bethany and His Conversation with Martha (11:17–27)*

The long story of the raising of Lazarus is characterized by an exchange of narrative and dialogue. This is also the case in the present section. At the beginning stands the account of Jesus's arrival in Bethany (vv. 17–20). This is followed by the theologically dense and central dialogue of Jesus with Martha (vv. 21–27).

A first examination of the text confirms the division of the passage into two. The first four verses are of a narrative type, reporting Jesus's arrival in Bethany. This provides information about time and place. Alongside the indication of the time that had elapsed since the burial of Lazarus, we are given information about the place where he was buried and about the people taking part. Separate from this group of verses is the following one with the conversation between Jesus and Martha in verses 21–27. They are the only people involved here. Both subsections are held together by the "coming" of Jesus and thus are shown to belong together: Jesus, who comes to Bethany, is the one who is to come into the world (vv. 17 and 27).

The two subsections are also differentiated linguistically. The first

---

17. Cf. Beutler, "Lasst uns mit ihm gehen," nn. 1–2. The skeptics have now been joined also by Moloney, "Can Everyone Be Wrong?," 512.

18. Cf. Beutler, "Lasst uns mit ihm gehen."

four verses are marked especially by verbal clauses, interrupted only by the parenthesis in v. 18, which states the distance between Bethany and Jerusalem. In the second subsection (vv. 21–27), there are three nominal clauses (vv. 21, 25, 27) alongside the verbal clauses. It will be shown that these nominal clauses are of great significance. In this sequence, as we shall see, they describe a whole pathway of faith (from what Jesus could be to what he actually is).

An examination of the tenses employed leads in the same direction. In the verses that frame the first subsection (vv. 17 and 20), we find narrative tenses. The parentheses of verses 18 and 19 employ the imperfect or pluperfect. In the second half, there is a movement from what could have been, by way of what will be, to what is (prepared for by the "I am" of Jesus in v. 25).

The subsections are separate and build on each other semantically as well, as is shown in the detailed analysis.

**11:17-20** In the first four verses, the subject is "coming" in its everyday sense. Related to it is the "meeting" between Jesus and Martha in v. 20, which prepares for the dialogue. By contrast with this movement, we have the "remaining" of Mary in the house (v. 20) as a static element. The theme of the following verses (21–27) is prepared in the first four verses by the "lying" of Lazarus in the grave (v. 17). Here belong also the "four days" and "Jerusalem" (vv. 17–18) as pointers forward to the passion of Jesus, and the intention of many Jews to comfort the sisters in their sorrow (v. 19).[19]

**11:21-27** The following group of verses is marked especially by verbs of saying (vv. 21, 23, 24, 25, 27). Martha begins the dialogue and also ends it. Thus, the text starts with her situation and leads to her confession.

"Death" and "resurrection" are the antithesis in what follows, and they define the section. Here, there is a movement from "would not have died" (v. 21), by way of "even if he dies" (v. 25), to "will never die" (v. 26). Another line of meaning begins with the indirect request of Martha (v. 22), continues with Jesus's declaration that her brother will rise again (v. 23), is taken up again and interpreted in the sense of the Jewish hope in the resurrection of the dead (v. 24), and leads finally to the "I am" saying of Jesus (vv. 25–26). In this he describes himself as "the resurrection and the life" and promises immortality to those who believe in him.

---

19. How the "Jews" were seeking to comfort the sisters remains an open question according to Theobald, "Trauer um Lazarus." The narrator has created a lacuna here that is to be filled by the reader.

Here we can pick up again on the ascending sequence of nominal clauses that refer to Jesus in verses 21–27. In v. 21, Martha's speech about what would have happened if Jesus had been there (in Bethany) is construed as an unreal condition of the past. The "if you were here" is matched by the "I am" of Jesus in v. 25. It is not about what he would do (v. 22: ask), but about what or who he is now. However, this change of perspective must be adopted by Martha. In a wholly personal way, she makes the "I am" of Jesus her own (v. 27), in that she makes it "you are" and formulates it in the sense of the confession of faith of the Johannine community (cf. John 20:30–31).

At the same time, we can observe progress in Martha's path to faith. She starts out from a place of "knowing" (cf. οἶδα) that glimpses in Jesus a kind of "intercessory omnipotence" (v. 22), but yet remains in the traditional (Pharisaic-rabbinic) belief in the resurrection of the dead on the last day (v. 24). Jesus leads her to faith (πιστεύειν) in him as the embodiment and the sole bringer of "resurrection" and "life" (v. 26). When Martha makes this truth of faith her own (v. 27), her path of faith has reached its goal, and is thus also representative of the readers who will follow her. "Life" has here its full Johannine sense as the epitome of salvation, corresponding to the "kingdom of God" in the Synoptics or "justification" in Paul. It is John's favored concept for eschatological salvation.[20]

With her confession of Jesus as Messiah and Son of God "who is to come into the world" Martha resumes the theme of "coming" from verses 17–20. Now it is no longer a question of the "coming" of Jesus to the grave of his friend, but of his "coming" into the world and for the world (cf. John 1:9; 12:46; 16:28; 18:37).[21]

Looking back, we can recognize the narrator's aim in John 11:17–27 as guiding the readers to the acknowledgment and confession of Jesus as the embodiment and bringer of "life" in the fullest sense. That is why he has "come."

It is perhaps not by chance that this confession of faith in the sense of John's Gospel is attested here by a woman.[22] It forms a parallel with the confession of Peter in John 6:68–69, and this too may be no accident. Through its positioning in the center of John's Gospel, this confession of Mary gains extra weight.

---

20. Cf. Beutler, *Habt keine Angst*, 79–81.
21. The attempt of Moloney, "Can Everyone Be Wrong?," 513f., to locate Martha's faith as imperfect does not convince on the ground of what has been said.
22. Cf. Beutler, "Frauen und Männer."

*Jesus on the Way to His Passion (11:1–12:50)*

Apart from the christological significance of the passage, it can also be of help for those who are suffering or will suffer grief.[23] Perhaps they will experience the care of people who wish to "comfort" them. In this case, another help may be a reliance on prayer (personal or that of Jesus). What is to be overcome above all is the orientation towards the past and to what could have been if... This is Martha's attitude in v. 21. It is already being overcome tentatively through the "but I know even now" of v. 22. Here, Martha's hope is already oriented to the future.

The decisive point is reached when Jesus reveals himself to her in his significance in the present for those who believe, and when they make this "now" their own (v. 27). True help for life is only possible when people are able to disengage themselves from a fixation on the past and on what could have been. The word and work of Jesus free people for life in the present moment.

### Jesus and the Power of Death (11:28–37)

The climax and the end of the narrative of the raising of Lazarus are characterized by a change of scene and of the people taking part. Of especial significance are the two similar sections that report the reaction of the "Jews." In verses 36–37, there are different interpretations of Jesus's weeping; in verses 45–46, of his action with Lazarus. The response of faith of the many is contrasted with the reaction of "some of them" (τινὲς δὲ ἐξ αὐτῶν). These differences offer the readers a help in finding their own identity. According to this double comment, the remaining section of the Lazarus story can be divided into two subsections: "Jesus and the power of death" (vv. 28–37) and "Jesus's power over death" (vv. 38–46). It is to the first ten verses that we now turn.

From the point of view of clause construction, what is striking in these verses are the differences from the previous dialogue between Jesus and Martha in verses 21–27. Again, the narration is in the aorist or historic present. But, in v. 28, the repeated present with reference to Jesus and, in vv. 36–37, the double imperfect are striking: the "Jews" puzzle over Jesus's weeping. Verbal clauses are dominant over nominal clauses. Nominal clauses referring to Jesus concern his physical presence (imperfect in v. 30, unreal condition of the past in v. 32). Subordinate clauses are rather rare.

---

23. Cf. Beutler, "Unterwegs von der Trauer zur Hoffnung."

The only exceptions are the intricate verse 31 and the similarly more richly structured verse 32. All these observations point to a strong influence of the pre-Johannine tradition on the present group of verses, probably with the exception of the reference to the reaction of the "Jews" in verses 36–37.

The word fields show a difference between verses 28–32 and verses 33–37. In verses 28–32, verbs of movement predominate ("go away," "get up," "come," "follow," "fall at the feet") with their corresponding substantives ("place," "house"). In verses 33–37, it is verbs of emotion that predominate ("greatly moved," "distressed," "weep"). Added to this are the comments of verses 36–37 ("say"). The verbs of movement are confined to v. 34. In both groups of verses, the subject at the end is the "death" of Lazarus (vv. 32 and 37).

**11:28–32** Initially, verses 28–32 betray no awareness of the previous encounter between Jesus and Martha and their dialogue in verses 17–27. In their substance, therefore, they are mostly considered older from the point of view of tradition history. Verses 28–29 thus serve as a transition and join up the two encounter scenes. Verses 17–18 recorded that Jesus had already come to Bethany, and this is taken up again in v. 30. The Jews mentioned in v. 31 appear as a homogeneous group and simply as mourners, not as examples of different positions with regard to Jesus as in verses 36–37 or 45–46. Mary's encounter with Jesus is dramatized even more strongly than that of her sister according to v. 20: she falls at Jesus's feet. Her words, however, are the same as those reported of Martha in v. 21:[24] if Jesus had arrived early enough, then her brother would not have died. The theory that Mary's saying would have served the evangelist as the template for Jesus's dialogue with Martha is highly probable. It does not have to be reflected on in a theological way here. Instead there is a strong account of the emotional reaction of Jesus.

**11:33–37** Jesus appears to be deeply moved by the grief of Mary and her friends and their weeping. According to v. 33, he is greatly moved and distressed. Then he asks to be shown the place of Lazarus's burial. At that point, he bursts into tears. However, this is interpreted in different ways by the Jews who are present. They could show how much he loved his friend, but they could also allow the question to be raised as to why he let him die when he was so close to him (vv. 36–37).

The verbs with which Jesus's emotions are described already in v. 33 are not so easy to interpret and, in the course of time, have been vari-

---

24. Only the placing of the pronominal adjective μου ("my") is altered.

ously understood.[25] The first verb ("was greatly moved"; ἐνεβριμήσατο) actually means something more like "becoming angry." The second verb ("distressed"; ἐτάρασσεν ἑαυτὸν) seems originally to mean a consciously directed movement of the mind. In the first verb, the Church fathers saw a spontaneous emotion on Jesus's part and in the second one a consciously willed emotion, thus finding here evidence for the two natures of Jesus: as man, Jesus is subject to spontaneous emotions; as Son of God, he stands above such things A similar partition is found in the medieval theologians like Thomas Aquinas who, however, reversed the allocation, probably because of the Latin rendering of the two verbs. More recently, the problem has been approached mainly with philological methods. If the wrath of Jesus had an object, what was it: human suffering and death or the unbelief of the Jewish spectators? Or was it only a question of the excitement of the miracle worker before his intervention, or even no concrete object? This is the direction suggested by the use of ἐμβριμάομαι and similar verbs in New Testament miracle stories (cf. Mark 1:43 and Matt 9:30 — the highly emotional exhortation after the healing of a leper or two blind men with the same verb; Mark 7:34 — the "sighing" of Jesus on the occasion of the healing of a deaf mute; Mark 3:5 — the "anger" of Jesus before the healing of the man with the withered hand). Jesus's "anger" in John 11:33, 38 could stem from an older *Vorlage* and have led to interpretive problems for the evangelist.

It could be that the evangelist, at his own discretion, has weakened and interpreted the difficult expression through the second verb. In doing this, however, perhaps he went back to an earlier tradition.[26] This is the possibility favored here. The evangelist would thus have been referring (as in John 12:27; 13:21; 14:1, 27) to the Synoptic Gethsemane tradition that, in its turn, went back to Ps 42/43. In Mark 14:34, there is a quotation from Ps 42:5, 11; 43:5, the refrain of the double psalm. John seems to employ this verse in John 12:27; 13:21 and perhaps in John 14:1, 27, possibly in connection with Ps 41:7 LXX (or 42:6 MT). If John is going back to Ps 41 LXX in John 11 (there are no other reflexive cases of ταράσσειν in the New Testament), he is able to give the emotion of Jesus a theological significance that is supported by the tradition and that interprets the "excitement" of Jesus as an experience of the suffering righteous who is entering into his own suffering. Perhaps Jesus's "weeping" in v. 35 (δακρύειν instead of the oth-

---

25. For this and what follows see Beutler, "Psalm 42/43."
26. Cf. Beutler, "Psalm 42/43"; Beutler, *Habt keine Angst*, 25f.

erwise employed κλαίειν) comes from Ps 41:4 LXX δάκρυα (cf. the "tears" of Jesus in Heb 5:7, where there is an echo of the Gethsemane tradition).[27]

In verses 36–37, there is an account of the double reaction of the Jews who were witnesses of Jesus's distress. Some are simply affected at how close Jesus was to Lazarus. Others ask critically whether he could not have actually prevented his death, since he opened the blind man's eyes. It is precisely this reference that shows that the question is being placed on the level of the evangelist. For him it is a matter of demonstrating two different ways of reacting to Jesus's distress: recognition of Jesus's compassion or critical challenge. In this way, the readers too are faced with the question whether they give credit to and are generally open to him or not.

### Jesus's Power over Death (11:38–46)

In the following verses, the climax and the conclusion of the Lazarus narrative are reached. Now Jesus appears to be distressed no longer at the power of death but is presented as Lord over death. The narrative is in the aorist or—when leading to direct speech—in the historical present. The account is worded chiefly in main clauses into which fit the short dialogue of Jesus with Martha in vv. 39–40 and Jesus's prayer in vv. 41–42. Here there are also subordinate clauses and richer grammatical constructions. The same goes for the concluding verses (45–46). We have good reason to recognize the hand of the evangelist here, marking the traditional account with his personal stamp.

The word fields also show a change from the previous group of verses. In verses 38–46, only once is there any mention of Jesus's emotion (Jesus is "greatly moved again," v. 38a); in what follows, Jesus appears as a man

---

27. The discussion over the puzzling verb ἐμβριμάομαι in John 11:33, 38 continues. Story, "Mental Attitude," understands the τῷ πνεύματι in v. 33 as dative object: Jesus is agitated at his own spirit that has misled him into letting his friend Lazarus die. Against this with good reasons, Lindars, "Rebuking," maintains that the ἐμβριμάομαι in v. 33 still has the original meaning of "to be or to become internally excited." The source would have referred this emotion to a demon, who was still part of the original narrative; the evangelist, by contrast, would have understood the verb as reflexive and interpreted it in the sense of the equally reflexive expression ἐτάραξεν ἑαυτὸν. Thus it came to express an inner emotion of Jesus. Moloney, "Can Everyone Be Wrong?," 518, abandons tradition-critical considerations and interprets the double expression as Jesus's anger and his emotion about the general lack of faith. There is reference to Moloney in Zimmermann, "Narrative Ethik," 164; cf. Zimmermann, "Narrative Hermeneutics," 94.

*Jesus on the Way to His Passion (11:1–12:50)*

who speaks and arranges things after he has "come" to the grave (v. 38). He "raises his eyes" in prayer, "thanks" the Father, and "knows" that the Father always hears him (vv. 41–42). Now, after the verses that attest his lowliness and humanity (vv. 28–37), his majesty and divinity emerge (vv. 38–44).

Similar to the previous section, this passage is divided into the report about Jesus (vv. 38–44) and the Jews' reaction to his behavior (vv. 45–46).

**11:38–44** Jesus now appears again as complete master of himself. Unflinchingly and confidently, he goes to the grave of Lazarus and has the stone sealing the tomb removed (vv. 38–39b). Martha's information that her brother has already lain in the tomb for four days is not simply ignored but serves as the impetus for a revelatory saying of Jesus that betrays the hand of the evangelist (v. 40). In the dialogue of verses 21–27, Jesus did not promise Martha she would, if she believed, see the glory of God, but, much more, that her brother would rise again (v. 23). Thus, here, in v. 40, Jesus's words on receiving the news of the sickness of his friend are probably being recalled—that Lazarus's death would not lead to death but would serve the glory of God. The Son of God is to be glorified through it (v. 4). As the sister of Lazarus, Martha must also have heard this saying of Jesus. If behind the Son of God of v. 4, one also sees the servant of Isaiah (52:13 LXX), then the connection between the raising of Lazarus and the lifting up and glorification of Jesus becomes clearer. At the same time, it is no longer possible to distinguish a glorification of Jesus through his "signs" in the sense of a "signs source," and a glorification through his cross and resurrection in the sense of the evangelist.

The prerequisite for Martha seeing the glory of God in the work of Jesus is her faith. This brings us to the mention of a decisive catchword for this section of the Gospel. It will occur straightaway in Jesus's prayer (v. 41–42) and so prepares for the decision of the witnesses of the miracle whether they are ready to believe in Jesus or not (vv. 45–46). For guiding the readers too, this will be a decisive catchword.

In our passage, faith is associated with "seeing." In v. 45, many Jews come to faith after they have seen Jesus's work on Lazarus. Conversely, in v. 40, Jesus promises Martha that if she believes, she will see the glory of God. Clearly, seeing leads to believing, but faith also leads to a new way of seeing.[28]

The actual raising of Lazarus is briefly related (vv. 43–44). It goes further than the Synoptic raisings insofar as here (other than with Jairus's

---

28. Cf. Traets, *Voir Jésus*; Manzi, "Resa credente," 115–18.

daughter in Mark 5:39) we have to do with a really dead person who has already lain in the grave for four days, and the pure word of power from Jesus summoning the dead man from his grave is sufficient without any gesture (as reported in Mark 5:41; Luke 7:14). From this point of view, therefore, this "sign" of Jesus stands unsurpassable at the close of his public ministry.

**11:45-46** The double reaction of the Jews to the mighty act of Jesus corresponds to their different reactions when they see Jesus weeping (vv. 36-37). Only now it is clearer what this is all about: faith in Jesus. Jesus's sign leads many Jews who witnessed it to faith in him. The counterpart of this is not lack of faith but sheer hostility. So one group of witnesses goes off to the Pharisees, the opponents of Jesus in the Sanhedrin, in order to accuse him. They consider Jesus to be a sorcerer and a seducer of the people, as has already been expressed (cf. John 7:12; 8:48, 52). Thus, a neutral attitude to Jesus is impossible. "Whoever is not with me is against me" (Matt 12:30; Luke 11:23).

The historicity of the Lazarus story is pursued by Jacob Kremer, among others.[29] It seems scarcely possible to understand it simply as a dramatization of the story of the rich man and poor Lazarus in Luke 16:19-31 since, for its part, this seems rather to presuppose a historical figure. Thus, behind it, could stand a healing miracle that was thus interpreted as the raising of a dead man, or a similar powerful act of Jesus that was considered as such. There is no direct access to the historical event either here or anywhere else in the New Testament. It is transmitted to us through the word of witnesses who are always constrained by the limits of human language.

## III

The message of the Lazarus story in general and of its closing section in verses 38-46 in particular can be tied down, above all, to the dialogue of Jesus with Martha in verses 39c-40, the prayer of Jesus in verses 41-42, and the conclusion of the narrative in verses 45-46. The short exchange between Jesus and Martha before the raising of her brother guides the readers' attention to the initial theme of the narrative according to v. 4: Jesus's deed is to serve the glory of God, and he himself is to be glorified by it. The prayer of Jesus before his command to Lazarus to come forth

---

29. Cf. Kremer, *Lazarus*, 109.

*Jesus on the Way to His Passion (11:1–12:50)*

from the grave shows him working in union with the Father. Faith in him is to be made possible and strengthened by the sign. Without this faith, even the most astonishing mighty acts of Jesus remain incomprehensible, offensive even. The reading community is summoned to grow in this faith in Jesus and also, when the opportunity arises, to confess it. The alternative would signify a switch into the camp of Jesus's enemies.

## 2. The Decision to Kill Jesus (11:47–54)

**47** Then the chief priests and Pharisees summoned a meeting of the Sanhedrin. They said: What should we do? This man is performing many signs. **48** If we let him go on, everyone will believe in him. Then the Romans will come and take away our holy place and our nation. **49** One of them, Caiaphas, the high priest that year, said to them: You understand nothing at all. **50** You do not consider that it is better for you if one man dies for the people than for the whole nation to perish. **51** He said this, not on his own account; but, because he was the high priest that year, he spoke from prophetic inspiration that Jesus would die for the people. **52** But he was to die not only for the people, but also to gather together again all the scattered children of God. **53** From this day on, they decided to kill him. **54** From now on, Jesus no longer moved openly among the Jews but went back from there to the area close to the desert, to a town called Ephraim. There he remained with his disciples.

*I*

There is a double reaction to the raising of Lazarus. Many Jews come to faith in Jesus; some, however, go to the Pharisees so that they may intervene against Jesus (John 11:45–46). The following passage sketches the consequences of this complaint and Jesus's subsequent reaction (vv. 47–54). There follows a pointer to the imminent feast of the Passover, the Passover of Jesus's return to the Father, which can be regarded as a small subsection by itself.

In the exegesis of this passage, greater weight is commonly placed on its relation to the Synoptic parallels. The subject here is the tradition of the decision of the Jewish authorities to kill Jesus before the feast of the Passover, in Matt 26:3–5; Mark 14:1–2; Luke 22:1–2, cf. 19:47. It is true that only Matthew and John know of a formal convening of the Sanhedrin for this purpose. One can guess that there is a connection between the Synoptic tradition and the Johannine text. The later Gospels make a special attempt to render the death of Jesus historically comprehensible. Even in the mention of the "chief priests and Pharisees," John is close to Matthew's formulation (Matt 27:62; 21:45). In fact, the Sanhedrin was made up of the chief priests or the chief priests and elders (cf. Matt 26:3), and the latter were composed of Pharisees and Sadducees together. The scribes were also members (cf. Mark 14:1; Luke 22:2). Towards the end of the first century, however, this composition of the Sanhedrin was no longer in effect, and the only surviving group that still had any influence was the Pharisees. From the historical point of view, it is probable that the Sadducees were involved in the decision to get Jesus out of the way more than all the other groups.[30]

Between the Synoptic texts cited and John's account there is a series of linguistic correspondences. Mark: "Passover," two "days," "chief priests," "arrest" (κρατέω for πιάζω in John); Matthew: "Caiaphas," "assemble" (συνάγεσθαι), "people/nation" (λαός), "arrest" (cf. Mark ), "kill" (ἀποκτείνω); Luke: "people/nation" (λαός in both texts), they did not know "what they should do" (τί ποιήσωσιν, 19:48).

What are the limits of the Johannine passage about the decision to kill Jesus? Some editions of the Bible allow a new section to begin with v. 54, extend it until v. 57, and place it, for instance, like the *Einheitsübersetzung*, under the theme of "Jesus's Flight Renewed." The French Jerusalem Bible connects v. 54 with the previous context and then begins a new long section: "The Final Passover (11:55–19:42). Before the Passion (11:55–12:20)." This suggestion merits consideration and approval in view of the role of the Jewish pilgrim feasts for the overall construction of John's Gospel. On account of the caesura at the end of John 10, it was advisable to see the Lazarus story as already an opening of the passion narrative with chs. 11–12 of the Gospel as a transitional section.

The linguistic structure of John 11:47–54 reveals a stylistically revised, argumentative text. In this way, it is already distinguishable from the Synoptic *Vorlagen*. The initial question of the chief priests and Pharisees (vv. 47–48) finds an answer in the saying of Caiaphas. Here (vv. 49–50) and in the closing reflection of the narrator (vv. 51–52), there are repeated final conjunctions and twice we encounter the preposition

---

30. Cf. Beutler, "Die 'Juden'"; Beutler, "The Identity"; von Wahlde, "The Johannine 'Jews.'"

## Jesus on the Way to His Passion (11:1–12:50)

"for" (ὑπέρ), which has its own final sense. In this way, the issues are made comprehensible.

The words and word fields employed are best shown as we review the text.

## II

**11:47–48** The decisive catchword of the whole passage may be given right at the beginning: "Then the chief priests and Pharisees summoned (συνήγαγον) the Sanhedrin." This is matched by the same verb at the close of the section in the comment of the narrator that Jesus would die not only for the people but "to gather together (συναγάγῃ εἰς ἕν) again all the scattered children of God" (v. 52). Through this framing catchword, the whole passage is defined by a pervasive opposition. On the one hand, the apparatus of power assembles to consider how it can protect itself. On the other hand, one person is ready to give up everything, even his life for the salvation of others.[31]

The proposal to see this passage John 11:47–54 as defined by this "inclusio" may be surprising, but it appears to be justified in view of the employment of similar frames in other parts of John's Gospel. Already in the prologue (John 1:1–18), the description of Jesus as "God" in the first and last verses is striking. It thus frames the prologue and gives it its decisive catchword. The following section is framed by the catchword of "testimony," which is found at the beginning (John 1:19) and at the end (1:32, 34), and represents the theme of the whole section. A little later, there is a longer section that commentators like to label "From Cana to Cana" after the scenes at the beginning (John 2:1–11) and at the end (4:46–54). The long discourses of Jesus, which strongly betray the hand of the evangelist, show the same procedure in what follows. John 5:19–30 is framed by the saying of Jesus that he does nothing "on his own," John 5:31–40 by the statement that "he is not bearing witness to himself," and John 5:41–44 by the thought that Jesus "is not seeking his own honor." Such frames can be pursued further in John's Gospel, not only in sections of discourse but also in narrative passages.[32] An example is the catchword "garden" at the beginning (John 18:1) and at the end (John 18:26) of the first major part

---

31. Cf., for this and what follows, Beutler, "Two Ways"; Beutler, "Zwei Weisen."
32. Cf. Beutler, "Zur Struktur."

of the passion narrative. It is encountered again at the transition to the Easter narrative (John 19:41; cf. 20:15). The Johannine letters too employ this stylistic feature.[33]

The reason for the summoning of the Sanhedrin by the chief priests and Pharisees (as the only influential group at the time of the evangelist) lies in the retention of power. "Faith" in Jesus, the goal of John's Gospel for its readers, is seen as a threat. A twofold fear comes to expression: the Romans could come and take away the "place" and people from the leading group. As for the "place," this is mostly understood to be the temple.[34] However, the word (τόπος) could also signify social status.[35] This too would make good sense. The word chosen for "people" (ἔθνος) is somewhat astonishing. It returns in vv. 50–52, and, in v. 50, it is parallel to the more common expression for the people of God (λαός). Clearly, in v. 48, the people (as ἔθνος) has more of a political dimension. If the evangelist seizes upon this expression, one should not conclude from this that, for him, Israel had lost its dignity as the people of God. Rather, this is another catchword frame within the passage.

**11:49-50** In the following verses, a new catchword occurs: "one." Caiaphas is "one" of them, that is, of the chief priests and Pharisees. According to his judgement, it is better that "one" man die for the people than that the whole nation perish.[36] In the first case, the "one" is set against the group of the powerful; in the second case, the "one" is set against the whole people, even, in fact, the whole multitude of the scattered children of God. The meaning of this connection will be explained by the evangelist in the following verses. The *realpolitik* consideration of Caiaphas will thus become transparent to the salvific dimension of Jesus's death for the many.

**11:51-52** When Caiaphas is mentioned as "high priest that year" (cf. John 18:13), this does not mean that John was supposing an annual changeover of the high priesthood. The meaning could also be that

---

33. Cf. Beutler, *Johannesbriefe*.

34. In the background stands the thought of Jesus as the new temple; cf. Dennis, "Restoration," 54ff.; Theobald, "Heilige Orte," 395–99.

35. Cf. Umoh, *The Plot*, 89–92, among others, with the rationale that τόπος in the sense of "holy place" is generally specified. This is not the case in John 11:48. Cf. Umoh, "The Temple," 329–32. Here, he also indicates the fact that "take away (αἴρω)" would not have the temple as a suitable object.

36. On Jewish texts for the argument of Caiaphas (one for many), cf. Aus, "The Death of One." He also sees the linguistic correspondence of "gathering" in v. 47 and v. 52 but does not develop this idea.

*Jesus on the Way to His Passion (11:1–12:50)*

Caiaphas was also and precisely high priest in this year. As such, in the mind of the evangelist, he is speaking prophetically. He thus not only declares the future but interprets it in the sense of the divine plan of salvation.

The death of Jesus for the many is also one that is encountered elsewhere in John's Gospel. It marks especially the conclusion of the shepherd discourse (John 10:11, 17-18). The good shepherd, Jesus himself, gives his life for his sheep. As already noticed for this passage, behind this "for" stands Isaiah's servant who dies representing the many and for the salvation of the many (Isa 53:11-12). Among others, the thought is taken up again in the tradition of the Last Supper (cf. Mark 14:24 par.), in John, Jesus's giving his flesh "for the life of the world" (John 6:51). It returns in the farewell discourses (John 15:13): The greatest love is shown when a man lays down his life "for his friends."

It is especially the good shepherd that is recalled by the saying of the evangelist that Jesus will "gather together again the scattered children of God," or, more exactly, "bring them together into oneness." Thus, just as the flock is scattered in its flight from the wolf (John 10:12), so the good shepherd brings it back together (John 10:16), and so does the one who dies for the salvation of the many. As in John 10:16 and even more clearly than there, the view here goes beyond that of God's people of Israel: through his death, Jesus will gather the scattered people of God. Here there is an echo of a universalism that seems to be presupposed elsewhere in John (cf. John 1:9-10; 3:16; 4:42; 6:51).[37]

In the Synoptic tradition, there is mention of the "gathering" of the people of God, among other places, in a saying of Q: "Jerusalem, Jerusalem, you kill the prophets and stone the messengers who are sent to you. How often would I have gathered your children to me, as a hen takes her chickens under her wings; but you would not" (Matt 23:37 par. Luke 13:34). Here Jesus refers to himself what was supposed to be the eschatological work of God according to the Exilic and post-Exilic prophets: gathering the sons and daughters from the diaspora and bringing them to Zion.[38]

---

37. Cf. Beutler, "So sehr." Van de Sandt, "Purpose," points to the motif of gathering in a eucharistic context in *Did.* 9.4 (cf. 10.9; Ign., *Eph.* 20.2).

38. Cf. Isa 27:12; 35:10; 40:11; 43:5; 49:5, 18; 52:12 LXX; 60:4, 7 [22 LXX]; Jer 23:8 LXX; Bar 4:37; 5:5; Ezek 11:17; 28:25; 34:12-13; 37:21; 38:8, 12; 39:27; Hos 1:11; Mic 2:12; 4:6, 12; Zeph 3:19 (gathering of the scattered); Tob 13:15 etc. According to Isa 11:12, the gathering of the scattered will be the work of the Anointed One. Cf., also, for the theme of the gathering, Dennis, "Restoration"; Dennis, *Jesus' Death*.

Of especial significance for John 11:51–52 are the texts that speak of the gathering of the non-Israelites on Mount Zion. This notion is found both in Trito-Isaiah (Isa 56:8; 66:18) as well as in Jeremiah (3:17) and, in a slightly different form, also in Ezekiel (29:13: God will gather the Egyptians in order to bring them to Egypt). In passages like these, one can see a preparation for the statement about the gathering of "the scattered children of God" in John 11:52.

The proposal to see Gnostic texts behind the gathering of the children of God in v. 52 has not been generally accepted, not least on account of the late dates of the relevant texts.[39]

**11:53–54** After these comments, the narrator turns again to his account. Caiaphas's proposal had clearly won agreement. The Sanhedrin has now decided to kill Jesus and, indeed, this decision was in effect "from this day on." The intervals of time are compressed. Caiaphas was "priest that year." At the same time, the year was coming to an end in which Jesus had performed his works according to the Jewish festal cycle from Passover to Passover. Now, it is only a matter of days (cf. 9:4). Soon, it will become hours (cf. 11:9; 19:14). Then "Jesus's hour" will have arrived.

In the concluding verse 54, information about place replaces that about time. From becoming aware of the decision of the Sanhedrin to kill him, Jesus no longer risks appearing among the Jews or Judaeans but returns to the area of the town of Ephraim at the edge of the desert.[40] At the center of the Sanhedrin scene stood the "place" (Jerusalem or the temple) where many gather and to which, according to v. 55, many pilgrims streamed. Jesus's path leads from the holy city and the holy place into isolation, at the edge of the desert. From now on, he is increasingly alone (cf. 16:32).

### III

In v. 54, Jesus is still accompanied by his disciples. They are also significant for the readers of the Gospel. They are to be with him, not only to attest their solidarity with him but also to stay in his school until the end—a

---

39. Cf. Ménard, "Le 'rassemblement.'"
40. For the Ephraim mentioned here, the Old Testament Ephraim (2 Sam 13:23; 2 Chr 13:19) or Ophrah (Josh 18:23; 1 Sam 13:17) east of Bethel are indicated; cf. *Neues Bibel-Lexikon*, 404.

*Jesus on the Way to His Passion (11:1–12:50)*

school in which it is a question of grasping the life and death of Jesus for many in its deepest sense. At the same time, the disciples are forming the core of a renewed, eschatological people of God. If, in his dying for many, Jesus will bring together God's people, Israel, but also, above and beyond Israel, all the scattered children of God, then this movement of gathering will begin with his disciples and be carried forward by them.

### 3. The Last Passover (11:55–57)

⁵⁵ The Passover feast of the Jews was near, and, already before the Passover feast, many came from the whole land to Jerusalem to purify themselves. ⁵⁶ They looked for Jesus, and while they stood together in the temple, they said to one another: What do you think? He will surely not be coming to the feast. ⁵⁷ For the chief priests and Pharisees had instructed that if anyone knew where he was staying, he must give notice of it so that they could arrest him.

*I*

Apparently, the cycle of Jewish pilgrim feasts determines the construction of John's Gospel. In this way, the span of Jesus's public life stretches from a first Passover (John 2:13) to a last one that is mentioned in John 11:55. This works, at least if, as is suggested in this commentary, the Passover of John 6, with the whole of ch. 6, has been added. In fact, it is not mentioned there as a pilgrim feast to which Jesus went up. Through the early story of the cleansing of the temple in John 2:13–22 with its potential for conflict and its pointing to the death and resurrection of Jesus, the evangelist has created a frame into which the whole public life of Jesus is dramatically inserted.

*II*

**11:55–56** Once again, there is an opposition between a crowd that is initially open to Jesus and the group of leaders in Jerusalem. The pilgrims to the feast flow in great numbers to Jerusalem and ask themselves whether Jesus will come to the feast (cf. John 7:11–12, where the pilgrims seek Jesus at the feast). They look for him in the temple where Jesus last showed himself in public without appreciating that, with the conclusion of the discourse in John 10, Jesus had taken his leave of the temple. Thus, the readers know more here than the pilgrims.

"Seeking" (ζητεῖν) is a Johannine catchword. Jesus asks the first disciples: "What are you looking for" (John 1:38). Men can seek Jesus because he has given them bread (6:26). When and insofar as they do not understand him, his origin and destination remain hidden: "You will seek me but not find me," says Jesus to people like this (7:34; cf. 7:36; 8:21; 13:33). The opponents of Jesus seek him in order to arrest him (18:4, 7–8). However, the right kind of seeking can lead to a true encounter with Jesus, as the story of Jesus and Mary Magdalene shows in John 20:1–2, 11–18. In John 11:56, what is meant is probably no more than a curious search for the wonderworker and sensational orator.

**11:57** The attitude of the chief priests and Pharisees towards Jesus is not neutral. They have clearly aligned themselves with the proposal of Caiaphas in John 11:49–50 to sacrifice Jesus in order to protect their holy place and also their position, and this decision has already begun to be implemented in the issue of an arrest warrant against Jesus. His "arrest" (πιάζω) has already been attempted on several occasions (cf. John 7:30, 32, 44; 8:20; 10:39). Now it is imminent (18:12). The fate of Jesus takes its course.

### III

At this point, the readers are invited to "seek" Jesus in the right way. This is not a matter of curiosity but the desire for a more truly salvific encounter. Here, there can be no neutral attitude. For the enemies of Jesus are already preparing to make an attempt on his life. Jesus's final Passover should and will bring a decision.

### 4. The Anointing of Jesus in Bethany (12:1–11)

[1] Six days before the Passover, Jesus came to Bethany, where Lazarus was whom he had raised from the dead. [2] There they prepared a meal for him; Martha served, and Lazarus was among those who were with Jesus at table. [3] Then Mary took a pound of pure, precious oil of nard, anointed Jesus's feet and dried them with her hair. The house was filled with the scent of the oil. [4] However, one of his disciples, Judas Iscariot, who later betrayed him, said: [5] Why was this oil not sold for three hundred denarii and the proceeds given to the poor? [6] But he said

this, not because he was concerned for the poor, but because he was a thief; in fact, he had the purse and embezzled the funds. ⁷ Jesus said, however: Leave her alone; she has treasured it for the day of my burial. ⁸ The poor you have always with you, but me you do not have always.

⁹ A great crowd of the Jews had learned that Jesus was there, and they came, not for the sake of Jesus alone, however, but also to see Lazarus whom he had raised from the dead. ¹⁰ But the chief priests had decided to kill Lazarus also, ¹¹ for many Jews were going away and believing in Jesus.

*I*

As has emerged from the previous exegesis, different opinions about Jesus increasingly mark the Johannine text. That can be seen from the following table:

- 9: The faith of the man born blind, 35–38; the unbelief of the Pharisees, 39–41
- 10:1–18: First part of the shepherd discourse: 19–21 division among the Jews
- 10:22–38: Second part of the shepherd discourse: 39 attempt to arrest Jesus; 40–42 faith
- 11:1–44: Lazarus; 45: faith of many Jews, 46: complaints about Jesus by others; 47–53: decision to kill Jesus

After the information about the withdrawal of Jesus in John 11:54 and the transition to the last Passover feast in 11:55–57, this rhythm continues:

- 12:1–8: anointing in Bethany; 9–11: a crowd comes to Jesus and Lazarus; the death of both is decided
- 12:12–16: Jesus's entry into Jerusalem; 17–19: witness of the crowd to Jesus; resentment of the Pharisees
- 12:20–36: The Greeks (open to Jesus) come to Jesus; final summons of Jesus to the Jews to believe in him
- 12:37–41: Unbelief of the Jews vis à vis Jesus; 42–43: faith of many; critical word for those who believe in Jesus without confessing this faith
- 12:44–50: Promise of light and life for all who believe; announcement of judgement for those who do not believe

Thus the double structure is preserved right to the end of the evangelist's narrative before the passion.

The delineation of the section is already clear from the previous table. According to John, the anointing of Jesus in Bethany is no detached event but belongs together with the verses about the "arrival" of Jesus in Bethany in John 12:1 and with those about the "arrival" of many Jews in the same place as well as the decision to kill not only Jesus but also Lazarus whom Jesus had raised from the dead (12:9–11).

A first linguistic approach to the text detects a difference between the narrative verses in the aorist and comments that are kept in the imperfect. Here, background information is given that is important for the readers' understanding. These comments are found in verses 2, 6, and 11. Thus, in v. 2, it says that Martha was serving at table while Lazarus reclined there. In v. 6, the readers learn that Judas was a thief and regularly misappropriated money from the common purse. According to v. 11, many Jews believed in Jesus on account of his raising of Lazarus. In the first case, a connection is established with the story of the raising of Lazarus. In the second case, a reason is offered for Judas's saying about the alleged waste while, in the third, it is explained why the chief priests decide to kill Lazarus too.

Further information for the readers is contained in appositions and subordinate clauses. To the characterization of Judas in v. 6 belongs also the double apposition in v. 4 that describes him as a disciple of Jesus but also as the future betrayer. As for Lazarus, it is important that he is "the one whom Jesus raised from the dead" (relative clauses in verses 1 and 9). The final clauses express what was to be permitted to Mary: to perform a gesture that anticipated Jesus's death (v. 7), and why the Jews came out to Bethany: not to see Jesus only, but also Lazarus (v. 9).

For their part, connections on the word level show the inner cohesiveness of the opening verses with the closing ones 9–11 and thereby of the whole section John 12:1–11:

> double mention of Jesus in v. 1, closing mention of Jesus at the end of v. 11
> "come" (to Bethany) in vv. 1a and 9
> mention of Lazarus in vv. 1 and 9b
> description of Lazarus as the one "whom Jesus had raised from the dead" in vv. 1 and 9

Thus, the anointing of Jesus is seen and interpreted in the light of the raising of Lazarus—a miracle that had led many Jews to faith in Jesus. It is to be kept in mind that the fourth evangelist never speaks of the "resurrection" of Jesus, with the exception of the account of the cleansing of the temple in John 2:19–22 (and the supplementary chapter in John 21:14). He speaks rather of the "lifting up" or "glorification" of Jesus (cf. John 11:4, 40; 12:28, 32, 34, 41). This "lifting up" or "glorification" of Jesus encapsulates the "work" of Jesus for his own (cf. 12:24, 32). The raising of Lazarus, therefore, has a christological significance: it announces the resurrection of Jesus without explicitly mentioning it. In the present narrative, this connection is made explicit through the decision to kill not only Jesus but also Lazarus (vv. 10–11).

The similar narrative in the Markan tradition (Mark 14:3–9 par. Matt 26:6–13) probably served as the *Vorlage* for the anointing story. Both texts have in common the time (Passover) and the place (Bethany), the sitting at table, the threefold description of the anointing oil, the words of protest (three hundred denarii, sale for the benefit of the poor), the words of Jesus: "leave her" (plural) or "leave her" (singular) with a reference to his burial as well as a double saying about Jesus and the poor. There are also differences, however: these concern the participants in the scene, the anointing of Jesus not on the head (Mark/Matt), but on the feet, the protest coming not from one (John), but from some, the "*more than* three hundred denarii" (Mark), among others. With the anointing of Jesus by a woman who was a sinner in Luke 7:36–50, the Johannine scene has but little in common. This includes the anointing of Jesus's feet and the drying of them with the woman's hair. Otherwise, it is variants that predominate, especially in the setting: in Luke, the meal is hosted by a Pharisee, the woman is a sinner, and the interpretation of the scene by Jesus/Luke is also different.

The construction of this group of verses in John can be divided according to the principal actors. After the narrative introduction, the action of Mary is recounted in vv. 1–3. This leads to the reaction of Judas in verses 4–6. This is followed, in vv. 7–8, by Jesus's assessment of the situation with which the passage ends initially. Insofar as the whole section leads up to the explanatory and conclusive word of Jesus, it could be ascribed to the literary genre of the "apophthegma." Verses 9–11 close the anointing story to the extent that they refer to Lazarus and illustrate the different ways in which people can react to the raising of the dead.

## II

**12:1–3** "Bethany" as the place of Jesus's "friends" is already known to the readers (cf. 11:1, 18). The "house" of his friends replaces the "house of his Father" (2:16), after Jesus has abandoned the temple in 10:39, following the fierce controversy in ch. 10. The naming of the siblings (though not as such) expressly recalls the miracle that has been experienced in their midst. The temporal indication "six days before the Passover" inserts the anointing once again into the Jewish festal cycle. Now, Jesus's last week is beginning, the week of his "glorification" as the Jerusalem Bible puts it.

The picture of Martha serving at table has its precedent in the scene of Martha and Mary in Luke 10:38–42. In John, however, Mary does not sit at Jesus's feet, but sets about anointing them. Here, the wastefulness of her gesture is underlined: a liter of fine oil signified a fortune, and, moreover, it is "pure",[41] "precious oil of nard." Its scent fills the whole house. At first the evangelist refrains from commenting on this extravagant gesture of Mary, but Jesus excuses it in his concluding saying (vv. 7–8).

**12:4–6** In John, there follows a protest, not by "some" (Mark 14:4), but by an individual, namely Judas. Here, it is highlighted that he was a disciple of Jesus but also the one who was to betray him. His saying that the oil could have been sold and the proceeds given to the poor stems from tradition, but in what follows it is characterized as hypocritical since, according to John, Judas was a thief and used to misappropriate donations from the common purse. This ascription of the words of protest to Judas can be put down to the Johannine redaction. It is the expression of a growing tendency in the Gospels to place Judas in a bad light. The later Christian tradition makes him the villain par excellence. From time to time, it also sees in him the paradigm of the rapacious Jew. Only in recent time has there been an attempt to counteract this bias and to see in Judas once again what he originally was, and also what he is in our text: "a disciple of the Lord,"[42] though a misguided one.

At this point, it is worth paying attention to the difference between the presentation of Mary and of Judas in John's text. Mary acts; Judas only speaks. She takes the precious oil and anoints Jesus's feet with it. Judas speaks only of what could have been done. She shows extravagant devo-

---

41. The adjective πιστικός there can mean "pure," but also derived from a pistachio or something similar. Cf. Bauer, *Wörterbuch*.

42. Cf. Klauck, *Judas*.

tion to Jesus. Judas appears as the egoist who diverts contributions to the common purse to his own use. Through these antitheses, the narrator is also offering role models even if they are painted in black and white tones that are hardly realistic.

**12:7–8** In his closing saying, Jesus takes up a position with regard to Mary's action. The twofold rationale is specified in the tradition. Mary has anointed Jesus in view of his imminent burial (after his death, in fact, this anointing was not carried out), and so it was a matter of urgency. While there will always be poor people among the people of God, Jesus has only a short time left among his own.[43] Here again the difference between Mary and Judas is revealed, here now in Jesus's pronouncement: she has treasured the oil and not given it away. She prepared tenderly for the death of Jesus that Judas is scheming to bring about. Moreover, she has understood that haste is required while Judas sees no urgency.

**12:9–11** The next verses connect the anointing story with the wider context of the raising of Lazarus. He is, then, mentioned twice. It is in his house that the anointing of Jesus has been performed. This house has become the object of the influx of crowds who want to assure themselves of the miracle. In John, crowds like this are generally neutral with regard to Jesus. In the mind of the evangelist, their motivation here is not sufficient because they seek something else in addition to Jesus, probably because of their thirst for wonders. However, the chief priests are deeply suspicious of this influx, and so they decide to get Lazarus out of the way as well as Jesus out of concern that the crowd could come to faith in Jesus on account of the Lazarus miracle. Thus, this passage too, like all the preceding one, closes with a double opinion about Jesus, and thus opens again to the readers the choice set before them.

### III

A look back at the anointing story invites a threefold reflection. First, we have in this story a further example for women, who, in John's Gospel, show a special relationship to Jesus.[44] That is already clear with the Samar-

---

43. The verse is missing in Codex D and in Syrosinaiticus, the most important witnesses of the Western text, its second half in some further manuscripts. However, it is extensively attested (cf. Nestle-Aland[28]).

44. Cf. Brown, "Die Rolle der Frau im vierten Evangelium"; Schneiders, "Women

itan woman in John 4:1–42, who came to faith in Jesus and brought her fellow citizens to this faith. Martha acknowledged and confessed in Jesus the Messiah and Son of God who was to come into the world (John 11:27). Later, Mary Magdalene will be the first witness and proclaimer of Jesus's resurrection (John 20:1–2, 11–18). Mary, the mother of Jesus (although not specifically named), stands at the beginning and end of Jesus's public life (John 2:1–11; 19:25–27). Such female figures lead today to the question of the position and office of women in the church.

Also, the manner of the devotion of Lazarus's sister, Mary, to Jesus invites consideration. Perhaps we have a mixture here of the idea of the anointing of Jesus for burial with the motif of a messianic anointing.[45] At the same time, however, the manner of Mary's devotion is by no means self-evident if it has also been affected by the Lukan tradition. Above all, the drying of Jesus's feet with the hair signifies a sensuous form of devotion that already causes furrowed brows in the Pharisees' house in Luke 7. In John, there are also elements of nuptial imagery as has been shown already in the encounter between Jesus and the Samaritan woman. In the biblical tradition, such "well stories" are courtship stories. Motifs in the Johannine anointing story seem to stem from the Song of Songs, especially the scent of perfume filling the whole house.[46] Later (John 20:15; cf. 19:41), the encounter between Jesus and Mary Magdalene will take place in a garden, another motif from the Song of Songs.[47] In the biblical tradition, motifs like these are by no means rare or surprising.[48] Only today are they perceived more clearly for what they are.

Finally, Jesus's saying that the disciples would always have the poor with them prompts consideration. Clearly, it refers back to Deut 15:11. From this it is not to be asserted that care for the poor has its own time and is not a priority. The verse in Deuteronomy itself does not say that. It

---

in the Fourth Gospel"; Karlsen Seim, "Roles of Women"; Morgen, "Les femmes"; Beutler, "Frauen und Männer."

45. Rigato, "La sepoltura regale."

46. The scent from ointment, balm, or oil of nard is part of the love imagery of the Song 1:3, 12 (nard); 2:13; 4:10–11; 7:8, 13; cf. 8:14. Cf. Calduch-Benages, "La fragancia"; Luzárraga, "El nardo."

47. The garden here is a symbol for the bride or for the abode of the bride or bridegroom: Song 4:12, 15, 16; 5:1; 6:2; 8:13.

48. Cf., also, above for the marriage of Cana, John 2:1–11, and for the word of John the Baptist about the friend of the bridegroom, John 3:29. From the more recent literature, cf. Varghese, *The Imagery of Love*, 59–204.

is a matter, therefore, of a wholly concrete priority that is established by the imminent death of Jesus. Moreover, Christian communities will not simply resign themselves to the fact that there will always be poor people. Through the community of goods, attested by the Acts of the Apostles, a powerful tool was and is given to overcome poverty in the community. The purse belonging to Jesus's disciples was clearly a prototype of this. The one who belongs to Jesus shares.

## 5. Jesus's Entry into Jerusalem (12:12–19)

¹² The next day, the great crowd of people who had come to the feast heard that Jesus was coming to Jerusalem. ¹³ Then they took palm branches, went out to welcome him, and cried: Hosanna! Blessed is he who comes in the name of the Lord, the king of Israel! ¹⁴ Jesus found a young donkey and sat down on it – as it says in the Scripture: ¹⁵ Fear not, daughter of Zion! Look, your king is coming; he is sitting on the foal of a donkey. ¹⁶ At first, his disciples did not understand all this; but when Jesus was glorified, then it became known to them that it thus stood written of him and that this had been what had been done to him. ¹⁷ The crowd who had been with Jesus when he called Lazarus out of the grave bore witness to him. ¹⁸ That is precisely the reason why the crowd went out to meet him: because they had heard that he had done this sign. ¹⁹ The Pharisees said to one another: You see! You are not achieving anything; the whole world is running after him.

I

The story of the anointing is followed by the account of Jesus's solemn entry into Jerusalem. The basic structure of the sections before Jesus's return home to the Father is maintained here too. Once again, at the beginning stands an account of an event that leads the way for the suffering of Jesus: Jesus's triumphal entry into Jerusalem (John 12:12–16). Once again, it is concluded with the contrast between the crowd (ὄχλος) and the Pharisees with the latter remaining in their rejection of Jesus.

The scriptural quotations are important for this passage: the double quotation in verses 13 and 15, and the information about the disciples' lack of understanding in v. 16.

Verbs of movement are especially characteristic of this section: Jesus "comes" as king to this city (in v. 12 and in both the scriptural quotations of verses 13 and 15), the crowd "goes out" (13) and "goes out to meet" (13 and 18) or "runs after him" from the perspective of the Pharisees (19).

For its part, the sentence structure allows us to make out more of the character of the passage. Subordinate clauses are found chiefly in the explanatory verses 16–19. The preferred tense is the aorist with the narrative changing to the imperfect only occasionally (with the cry of the crowd in v. 13). In the comment in v. 17, the imperfect is found once again right at the beginning. In v. 18, an aorist with the meaning of a pluperfect and a perfect infinitive similarly for the pluperfect appear. Here we are more on the reflexive levels. We only return to the present with the concluding refection of the Pharisees in v. 19.

The question of the literary genre of the passage cannot be answered without a comparative glance at the same narrative in the Synoptic Gospels. Taken by itself, the story of Jesus's entry into Jerusalem in John cannot easily be fitted into a known literary genre. At best, the "biographical apothegm" could be relevant here, though the concluding saying of Jesus is lacking. In fact, in this passage, Jesus does not utter a word. A comparative look at the Synoptic parallel texts, Mark 11:1–10/Matt 21:1–9/Luke 19:28–40, shows, however, that the account of the entry of Jesus into Jerusalem was originally joined to the story of the cleansing of the temple. This is especially the case in Matthew where both stories occur as a continuous text.[49] This would suit the narrative of the cleansing of the temple in John 2:13–22. This account in verses 13–16 finds its climax in a saying of Jesus and a consequent question of the Jews to which is added information about the "remembering" of the disciples (v. 17). Moreover, the subsequent demand for a sign leads to a saying of Jesus, a further question of the Jews, and another note about the "remembering" of the disciples (after Easter: v. 22). The relationship with John 12:12–16 is obvious.

If the evangelist does not report the cleansing of the temple in ch. 12, then that is because Jesus has already been recorded as having a last, highly dramatic, encounter with the "Jews" in John 10:22–38 at the Feast of the Dedication of the temple. Since this moment, Jesus has not entered the temple any more. From now on, he is the sanctuary of Israel and the place of God's presence (cf. 2:18–22 and 1:51 with the allusion to Gen 28:12).

John has in common with the Synoptics the following:

---

49. Cf. Lohfink, "Der Messiaskönig."

*Jesus on the Way to His Passion (11:1–12:50)*

- Matt: the mention of the crowd (ὄχλος) that came out to meet Jesus, and the quotation from Zechariah
- Mark : the mention of "many"
- Luke: the reference to the disciples; the crowd of people who "came" to Jesus; the mention of the Pharisees and their reaction

The chief difference from the Synoptics consists in the fact that John does not know of or report the disciples' search for the donkey. In this way, on the one hand, the initiative of Jesus is emphasized; on the other hand, the initiative of the "crowd of people" is emphasized.[50]

An alternative definition for the literary genre of the entry story consists of seeing it as a "quest story." Painter, who otherwise acknowledges quest stories to have a huge significance in John, does not cite our text among his examples.[51] However, it contains numerous elements of this genre: someone or a group of people seek Jesus (or help from Jesus); what is more, the motif of searching is central in the cry of the crowd in v. 13 (see II below); the description is detailed; the greeting of Jesus has a theological meaning; other elements are lacking in our text.

According to the people who act or speak, the unit can be divided as follows:

- 12–13 The crowd come to meet Jesus, scriptural quotation
- 14–15 Jesus enters his city as a king, scriptural quotation
- 16 The disciples' post-Easter understanding of the Scripture
- 17–18 The reason for the crowd's arrival
- 19 The hostile reaction of the Pharisees

## II

**12:12–13** The time of the following story is linked to the imminent feast of the Passover and so also to the passion of Jesus. In John, unlike the Synoptics, Jesus's entry into Jerusalem is not carefully planned through the instruction to find him a mount but takes on its solemn messianic character spontaneously. At the same time, elements of a "quest story" are

---

50. More extensively on the relation of the Johannine entry story to the three Synoptic accounts, cf. Morgen, "Le roi d'Israël."
51. Cf. Painter, "Quest and Rejection Stories"; cf. Painter, "The Quest."

revealed. The crowd coming to Jerusalem for the feast hears that Jesus is on his way to the city and goes out in a great multitude to meet him and pay homage to him. The Johannine text knows nothing of a spreading of clothes, but it knows of the homage of palms,[52] which the pilgrims cut down from the trees and bear before him in his honor. Palm branches are mentioned in connection with the Feast of Tabernacles (Lev 23:40; 2 Macc 10:7), something which occasionally leads to speculation that the scene had originally taken place on that feast. However, this conclusion is not persuasive since what we have here is more probably a messianic motif from the orbit of the Passover feast.[53] This is shown by the people's cry, which comes from the last psalm of the Great Hallel (Ps 118:25–26). "Hosanna" actually means: "save, please," but is probably intended here as a cry of homage. It is applied to the one "who comes in the name of the Lord, the king of Israel." The "king of Israel" here might stem from Zeph 3:15, a post-Exilic messianic text that is expressly quoted by the evangelist in v. 15.[54] Luke also (19:38) inserts the royal title; Mark (11:10) speaks only of the "coming kingdom of our father David."

**12:14–15** According to John, Jesus simply "found" the donkey and sat on it. The evangelist interprets this event with a scriptural text, the kernel of which stems from Zech 9:9, although he shortens this text (similar to what happens in Matt 21:5) and alters the introduction.[55] "Rejoice greatly, daughter of Zion" becomes "Fear not, daughter of Zion." In this way, the dignity of Jesus is further emphasized. In John, this address could originate with Zeph 3:16 in the immediate context of the reference to Zeph 3:15 in v. 13. Not only may the crowd rejoice; they may also draw courage in the face of the conflicts unleashed by the raising of Lazarus.

**12:16** Here, it is assumed that Jesus's disciples were present and that they had played a part with him. According to our verse, they did not understand at first what they had done. They would recall it only after the

---

52. The Greek expression means, literally, "palm branches of palms."

53. For the messianic meaning of palm branches in the context of the Maccabean revolt according to 1 Macc 13:51; 2 Macc 10:7, cf. Menken, *Old Testament Quotations*, 87. See also, Menken, *Old Testament Quotations*, 88f. and 94f., for the "foal of a donkey" as a messianic mount in connection with Gen 49:10–11 LXX.

54. In detail on the scriptural quotation, see Menken, *Old Testament Quotations*, 79–97. According to him, the "Fear not" could come from Isa 40:9 in the context of the proclamation that God, like a shepherd, will gather his flock (40:9–11).

55. For the reception of Zech 9:9 in the New Testament and in John, cf. Hübenthal, *Transformation*, 111–64; further, Kubis, *Book of Zechariah*.

## Jesus on the Way to His Passion (11:1–12:50)

"glorification" and then come to understanding. Here again, an event that anticipates the coming "lifting up" and "glorification" of Jesus evades the understanding of the disciples during his lifetime. This had already happened in connection with the cleansing of the temple and Jesus's saying in John 2:19 about the destruction of the temple, and, in fact, of the temple of his body and of its raising anew after three days according to John 2:22. The disciples can come to the full understanding of the "lifting up" of Jesus in its double sense (as lifting up on the cross and to the Father) and his "glorification" only through the gift of the Spirit (cf. John 7:39) after Easter. In this way, the disciples also stand for the future readers who will find their access to faith in Jesus only after Easter and from then on.

Again, it is here assumed that behind the "lifting up" and "glorification" of Jesus in John stands the servant of Isaiah to whom this is just what is promised at the beginning of the Fourth Servant Song (Isa 52:13 LXX). In John, the "lifting up" and "glorification" of Jesus is consistently connected with the title of "Son of Man." Behind that, there certainly stands the Synoptic tradition of the suffering and resurrection of the Son of Man.

**12:17–18** As is constantly in the foreground of the Johannine passion narrative, this account too has a double reaction at its conclusion that seems, for its part, to be included with a view to the readership. A first crowd consists of witnesses to the raising of Lazarus. They bore "witness," and so a key Johannine concept is taken up (v. 17). Here, this is probably a matter of witness to the actual event of this powerful deed of Jesus, but also, naturally, signifies an opinion in favor of Jesus. This crowd is to be distinguished from another who had only heard about the raising of Lazarus. By itself, this had not been enough to prompt them to go to pay homage to Jesus. With that, the narrative circle from v. 12 also comes to a close.

**12:19** The Pharisees who now come on to the stage remain outside the scene and act only in the background. The decision to kill Jesus had been approved by the chief priests and Pharisees in John 11:47–53. The decision to kill Lazarus too went back to the chief priests according to John 12:10. Now, in 12:19, it is the Pharisees who appear as protagonists. To them, the goings-on around Jesus appear indisputably suspicious and provide the reason to proceed against him without delay. In the process, their judgement is formulated along the lines of Johannine irony: "the whole world is running after him" or, more exactly: "the world has run after him." This is true not only on the pejorative level but also has its deeper sense according to the evangelist. The Messiah, who is here entering into his city, will also manifest himself as Savior of the nations. This is shown by the Greeks among the pilgrims at the feast who, according to the following verse, desire to see him. Their salvation is now at hand.

### III

Looking back at the Johannine story of the triumphal entry, we can discern three main points that are significant for the readers.

First and foremost, this account deals with a personal encounter with Jesus. None of the Synoptics says that the crowd went "to welcome" Jesus. Even the exodus of the crowd from the city is a feature peculiar to John's Gospel. From that, it comes across as decisive to be with Jesus (cf., also, v. 17). This is more important than staying in the sanctuary of the temple.

A further message of the Johannine text is that one can understand the messianic dignity of Jesus correctly (in the sense of the traditional entrance stories of the Synoptics) only in connection with his imminent "glorification" in his death and his "lifting up" to the Father.[56]

Finally, the Johannine text shows that the leaders of Israel and the representatives of the "daughter of Zion" do not need to fear this king. Jesus's rule is gentle. In his entry into the city, he does not ride on a warhorse and is not surrounded by a troop of soldiers. The extract from Zechariah highlights this aspect explicitly. The only ones who fear Jesus fear to lose the people whom they regard as their possession to be guarded.

## 6. The Coming of the Greeks (12:20–36)

[20] Among the pilgrims who wished to worship God at the feast, there were also some Greeks. [21] These came to Philip, who hailed from Bethsaida in Galilee, and asked him: Sir, we would like to see Jesus. [22] Philip went and told Andrew; Andrew and Philip went and told Jesus. [23] Jesus answered them: The hour has come for the Son of Man to be glorified. [24] Amen, amen, I say to you: Unless the grain of wheat falls into the earth and dies, it remains alone; but when it dies, it brings forth much fruit. [25] Whoever loves his life, loses it; but whoever has little concern for his life in this world, will keep it to eternal life. [26] If anyone will serve me, let

---

56. Here, John takes his Synoptic *Vorlagen* further; cf. März, "Siehe, dein König kommt zu dir . . . ," 11.

him follow me; and where I am, there will also my servant be. If anyone serves me, the Father will honor him. ²⁷ Now my soul is distressed. What am I to say: Father, save me from this hour? But it is for this that I have come to this hour. ²⁸ Father, glorify your name! Then a voice came from heaven: I have already glorified it and will glorify it again.

²⁹ The crowd that stood by and heard said: It has thundered. Others said: An angel has spoken to him. ³⁰ Jesus answered and said: This voice was not for my sake but for you. ³¹ Now judgement is being delivered on this world; now the ruler of this world is being cast out. ³² And I, if I am lifted up from the earth, will draw all to me. ³³ He said this in order to indicate what way he would die.

³⁴ However, the crowd responded: We have heard from the Law that the Christ will remain forever. How can you say that this Son of Man must be lifted up? Who is this Son of Man? ³⁵ Then Jesus said to them: The light is with you for only a short time more. While you have the light, walk in the light so that the darkness will not take you unawares. Whoever walks in the darkness does not know where he is going. ³⁶ While you have the light with you, believe in the light so that you may be the children of the light. Jesus said this. And he went out and hid from them.

## I

The narrative of the solemn entry of Jesus into Jerusalem in John 12:12–19 already had the character of a "quest story." Precisely characteristic for the Johannine understanding of this episode was the circumstance that a crowd came out from Jerusalem to meet Jesus. The following section is also such a story.[57] "Greeks" come and want to see Jesus. According to their literary genre, the quest stories belong to the so-called apophthegma or "pronouncement stories." They consist of a narrative introduction and a concluding word of the protagonist or a comment on the success or lack of it of the search. In the entrance story, this conclusion is more a note about the different outcomes of the searching of the crowds. In the report of the coming of the Greeks, the concluding saying is still quite recognizable (in John 12:23b–28a), although it is followed by further narrative elements and dialogue scenes (12:28b–36). Here too until the end, an assessment is being made of the seeking movement of the Greeks and the public behavior of Jesus.

---

57. Cf. the previous section at n. 51 for the genre of the quest story.

From the narrative point of view, the section John 12:20–36 can be divided into three that all are closed by a saying of Jesus:

a) *The Greeks Come to Jesus 12:20–28a*
    Account of the narrator 12:20–22
    Saying of Jesus 12:23–28a
b) *The Voice from Heaven 12:28b–33*
    Account of the narrator 12:28bc
    Interpretation of the voice by the crowd and by "others" 12:29
    Interpretation of the voice by Jesus 12:30–32
    Interpretation of Jesus's interpretation by the narrator 12:33
c) *Question and Answer 12:34–36*
    Question of the crowd 12:34
    Answer of Jesus 12:35, 36a–c
    Account of the narrator 12:36d–e.

The middle subsection merits special attention. In it, we meet again the "crowd" of Jewish pilgrims to the feast. By contrast with the "coming" of the Greeks to Jesus, this group remains sitting on the fence where Jesus is concerned. The last subsection of the passage is also marked by this uncertainty. At the close stands a final, powerful appeal by Jesus.

The syntax of the passage shows again the occurrence of subordinate clauses in Jesus's speeches (vv. 23–28a, 32, 35–36). Here then we have an argumentative text. For their part, nominal clauses indicate the high points (vv. 26, 31, 35). They concern the existence of the disciples with Jesus, but also his presence with men until the hour of decision. It will be emphasized once more by both the closing final clauses (vv. 35–36).

The composition of the text emerges also from the employment of the catchwords and word fields. "Say/tell" (11x), "answer" (3x), and "be" (6x) are frequently found here. Other important words include "coming" (ἔρχομαι, 5x, together with "coming to" or "going away," once each). "Glorify" (δοξάζω, 4x) seems to be of structural significance along with "honor" (τιμάω, 1x). Related in meaning here is "lift up" (ὑψόω, 2x). Both verbs (δοξάζω and ὑψόω) pervade the whole section, something that is to be explained later. They seem to form the "semantic axis" of the section. The most important substantives in the passage are "light" (φῶς, 4x), "world" (κόσμος, 3x), "voice" (φωνή, 2x), but also "hour" (ὥρα). This catchword is found three times in all, and frames the first subsection.

*Jesus on the Way to His Passion (11:1–12:50)*

Allowing for the semantic observations, the present passage can be divided as follows:

a) vv. 20–28a
    21 (προς)έρχομαι
    22     ἔρχομαι
    23     ἔρχομαι ὥρα    δοξάζω
    24
    25
    26                        τιμάω
    27     ἔρχομαι ὥρα
    28                        δοξάζω
b) vv. 28b–33
    28 (ἔρχομαι, φωνή)    δοξάζω
    32                        ὑψόομαι
c) vv. 34–36
    34                        ὑψόομαι
    35
    36 (ἀπ)έρχομαι

In the first scene, the "coming" of the Greeks to Jesus leads to the "coming" of their intermediaries to him. Jesus himself sees that his hour has "come." It is the hour in which the Son of Man is to be "glorified." The subsection also closes in verses 27 and 28a with the catchwords "coming," "hour," and "glorification." Whoever serves Jesus will be incorporated in the "honor" of Jesus (v. 26).

The second scene takes up the theme of "glorification" from v. 28a and interprets it in what follows as "lifting up" (v. 32).

With this catchword, the third and final scene begins. The word is found again in the mouth of the crowd in v. 34. However, the latter are asking about the Son of Man not about his glorification, which leads to the concluding saying of Jesus (vv. 35–36). Following this, "Jesus goes out" (v. 36).

After this introductory analysis, it is now possible to follow the text as it goes along.

## II

### *The Greeks Come to Jesus (12:20–28a)*

**12:20–22** The first three verses of the narrative set the scene. The stage is Jerusalem, the place to which the pilgrims have come for the feast; the time, the imminent feast of the Passover with its messianic expectations. In all probability, these "Greeks" are not simply Greek-speaking Jews from the diaspora, whom one would probably call Ἑλληνισταί as in Acts 6:1, but God-fearers from the diaspora (cf. the Ἕλληνες in John 7:35). Here, it is striking that it is they who want to "see," but this can probably be explained satisfactorily with a look at the tradition-historical background of the passage.

The "Greeks" do not turn to Jesus directly but to intermediaries close to him. These are the apostles Philip and Andrew. In John, they also play a prominent role in other places (cf. 6:7–8), probably on account of the fact that they bear Greek names, belong to the first of those called to follow Jesus, and hail from Bethsaida on the Sea of Gennesareth (cf. John 1:43–44), a city from the dominion of the tetrarch Herod Philip in the area of East Jordan with Greek cultural influence. John locates it, erroneously, in Galilee, the area in which Jesus had often revealed himself publicly. The two apostles were clearly important key persons for new converts from the Greek diaspora.

**12:23–24** According to all the Gospels, Jesus's mission to the Gentiles is opened definitively only with his death and resurrection. This is certainly true of John. With the approach of the Greeks, according to v. 23, Jesus sees that his "hour" has also come, not simply, however, as the hour of his death but as the "hour" of the "glorification of the Son of Man." From the beginning of the Gospel, this "hour" had been a topic. Already at the marriage of Cana, it was connected with Jesus's coming "glory" (cf. John 2:4, 11). It comes up again in John 7:39; 8:20. It then marks off the passion event according to John 13:1; 17:1. The future "lifting up" of the Son of Man had already been a topic in John 3:14 and 8:28. It is taken up again in 12:32, 34. It occurs together with the "glorification" of Jesus or the Son of Man, of which the Gospel speaks in John 7:39; 12:16 and will speak in 12:28; 13:31–32; 17:1. For the "coming" of the "hour" of the "Son of Man," a saying of Jesus from the end of the Gethsemane pericope (Mark 14:41 par.) plays a role. His "glorification" is comprehensible only against the background of the underlying Old Testament tradition, of which we shall say more later.

The saying about the grain of wheat that has to die and only thus brings forth much fruit, could be going back to the Synoptic parable of the sower in Mark 4:1–30. Here, attention is drawn especially to the interpretation of that parable in Mark 4:13–20 and the parable of the seed growing by itself in Mark 4:26–29. What was true of the word of God is true now of Jesus. He has to fall into the earth and so bring forth much fruit (for the formulation, cf. John 15:2, 8, 16, there, of the disciples).

**12:25–26** The sayings about following in vv. 25 and 26 take up Mark 8:35 par. and 8:34 par. in freer form. In John, readiness to serve includes that of following. "Denying oneself" and "taking up the cross" is replaced by being with Jesus (v. 26). To this is added that the Father will "honor" the faithful servant. "Saving one's life" in the Synoptics[58] becomes in John more clearly to "keep one's life" and, in fact, unto "eternal life" (v. 25), by the "hatred" of one's life, that is, the putting last of the physical life in favor of the life of faith "in this world."

On theological grounds, these two verses are occasionally denied to the evangelist and ascribed to the Johannine redaction. While it is the evangelist's view that salvation comes from faith in Jesus, it appears to depend here on the disciples' readiness to give up their life for the faith.[59] However, this opinion, which does not take seriously the continuity between John and the Synoptics, is possibly reading Paul into John and overlooks the fact that readiness for the most dire consequences for the faith belongs entirely with the core of the Fourth Gospel. One example of many here is the man born blind who puts up with expulsion from the synagogue for the sake of confessing Jesus (John 9:34). Another is the saying of Thomas: "Let us go with him, so that we may die with him" in John 11:16, which is certainly to be taken seriously.[60]

**12:27–28a** From the disciples, the thought returns to Jesus once more. His "soul" is "distressed." Such "distress" on Jesus's part was also registered in connection with his arrival at the grave of his friend Lazarus (John 11:33). It will also be mentioned once again in the Cenacle (John 13:21). Later, Jesus will urge his disciples not to let their heart be distressed (14:1, 27). As already noted for John 11:33, behind this formula there prob-

---

58. Cf. Schmidt, "Zum Paradox." He shows how the double saying of "losing" and "finding" one's life that appears to go back to Jesus need not necessarily have had an original reference to martyrdom. The saying receives this sense only from its context in the Gospel, also in John.

59. Cf. Becker, 2:466–68.

60. This saying is not denied to the evangelist by Becker, 2:419f.

ably lies Ps 42/43 in which, in the refrain (Ps 42:6, 12; 43:5), the worshiper bolsters up his courage, not to let his soul be "distressed," before he confesses "his soul is distressed" (Ps 41:7 LXX). Mark 14:34 probably goes back to the same verse when Jesus says "my soul is troubled even to death." That points to a connection between John 12:27–28 and the Gethsemane tradition which has long been recognized.[61] The scene of Jesus's prayer on the Mount of Olives is absent in John but could have been replaced by the saying of Jesus in John 12:27–28. In John too, Jesus is distressed in the face of his imminent death. As in the Synoptic tradition, he could pray for deliverance from this looming danger. He says this himself with a phrase that seems to stem from Ps 6:4.[62] However, his prayer has a different tone.

Jesus has not arrived at the hour of testing in order to be rescued from it again but in order to go through with it and thus remain faithful to his mission. It is precisely in this way that the hour is to come in which the Father will be glorified through him and in which Jesus himself will receive this glorification. That will be the leitmotiv at the beginning of the farewell discourses (cf. John 13:31–32; cf. 17:1, "I have glorified your name").

### The Voice from Heaven (12:28b–33)

**12:28b–29** Jesus's prayer is heard straightaway through a voice from heaven in which the Father is the speaker. Such heavenly voices belong to the mindscape of the Bible and of early Judaism (which speaks of the "Bat Qol"). In them, God himself is the speaker. In the Synoptics, this voice rings out, to be heard by all, in Jesus's baptism at the beginning of his earthly ministry with the proclamation of Jesus as the "beloved Son," probably already an allusion to the servant (cf. Mark 1:11 par.), and also in Jesus's Transfiguration, here already in the wider context of the passion between the first and second passion predictions (Mark 9:7 par.). Within the Gethsemane tradition, Luke has the detail that an angel gave Jesus strength and assurance in his agony (Luke 22:43). Here, in John, God lets a voice ring out that gains attention for Jesus's prayer. That the Father glorifies Jesus was already stated in John 8:54. Jesus will restate this in his farewell discourse in John 13:31 and, at the same time, in his farewell prayer

---

61. Cf. Brown, "Incidents"; Schnackenburg, 2:484f.
62. Already in this psalm, v. 3 says: "My soul is deeply distressed" (καὶ ἡ ψυχή μου ἐταράχθη σφόδρα).

in John 17:1, 5, make it the object of his prayer. The glorification of Jesus by the Father is bound up with the "hour" of Jesus (cf. John 12:23; 17:1), and this "hour" has now come for Jesus. If, at the same time, the glorification of Jesus is yet to come, the thought is probably of the complete fulfillment of this hour in the passion, death, and resurrection of Jesus. In Johannine terms, it is his "lifting up" on the cross to the Father.

**12:29** The voice from heaven is probably not to be understood without a religious significance. In any case, in its double interpretation, the "crowd standing by" (cf. John 11:42) fails to appreciate the true reality of it. As thunder, the voice perhaps is recalling the Sinai event (cf. Exod 19:16, 19); as the voice of an angel, it comes distinctly closer to the reality of the event. Exegetes point here to the comforting of Jesus in Gethsemane by an angel in Luke 22:43.[63] However, in that case, the significance of the heavenly voice still remains open.

**12:30-32** Only Jesus can understand and communicate this significance. He explains the voice from heaven in its relation to the surrounding crowd, in its significance for this world and its ruler, and its salvific significance for all. In this way, there is a movement from the theme of "glorification" in the voice from heaven to that of the "lifting up" of Jesus in v. 34. This will then define the last verses of the section.

In Jesus's explanation, the voice from heaven signifies not simply a message of salvation but an announcement of a certain time: now is the judgement of this world being enacted. Its ruler is now being cast out. Insofar as the subject here is not the judgement before which the individual is placed but that of "this world" and its ruler (cf. John 14:30; 16:11), this announcement of time shows itself to be a message of salvation.[64] The "now" of Jesus's distress in v. 27 is transformed into the "now" of his imminent glorification (cf. John 13:31) and of the salvation of men.

Once again, the announcement of salvation is connected with something in the future. The "hour" of Jesus, the "now" of salvation, is made concrete in the moment of his "lifting up from the earth" (for the "lifting up of the Son of Man," cf., already, John 3:14; 8:28). The expression is deliberately open. For knowledgeable readers, the reference to Jesus's lifting

---

63. This connection is pointed out by Kühschelm, "Gericht," 135, and Clivaz, "D'autres disaient," 174–77. The author follows clues back to Zech 1–2 and forward to notions of a possession of Jesus by an angel according to "Ebionite" texts on the way from early Judaism and Christianity to gnosis.

64. Dennis, "The Lifting Up," 690, sees a common apocalyptic tradition in the disempowerment of Satan by the Son of Man in John and in the Parables of Enoch.

up on the cross cannot be missed. There, lifted up on the cross, Jesus will draw all to himself. The formula lets us think of the bread of life discourse (John 6:44); the coming universal salvation expressed here pervades the whole Gospel (cf. John 1:9; 3:16; 4:42; 12:19).[65] It finds here its unsurpassable expression.

**12:33** For all those who had not yet understood the allusion, the narrator explains the enigmatic words of Jesus once more. The reference is to the "lifting up" of Jesus on the cross. It remains open how far the listeners in the "crowd" could reach this insight. Normally, the words and actions of Jesus that anticipate his death and resurrection are understood only after Easter and then by his disciples (cf. John 2:22; 12:16). Their circle is being opened to John's community of readers.

### Question and Answer (12:34–36)

**12:34** The thought has passed on from Jesus's "glorification" to his "lifting up." The crowd, however, remain with the question as to who it is that is to be "lifted up." If it is the Messiah, then he cannot be taken away; yet, according to Jesus, the Son of Man will be lifted up. Here again, knowledgeable readers are being presupposed. At the same time, a knowledge of the belief in the remaining of the Messiah can most likely be assumed. The language and the thought world of the Fourth Gospel already presuppose the identification of the Messiah with the Johannine Son of Man, and it is precisely this Son of Man to be lifted up who is presumed from John 3:14; 8:28.

**12:35–36** In his answer, Jesus does not elaborate on speculations about the Messiah, the Son of Man, and his being lifted up. They seem to him to distract from the need to render the decision of faith now. Thus, as already in v. 31, Jesus recalls this hour of decision once again with exceptional emphasis. Here, the decisive catchword is that of the "light," which occurs no less than five times. Jesus, this light, will be with his listeners for only a short time longer. That has already been said in John 7:33. When Jesus takes up the saying once more in the farewell discourse in John 13:33, it will only be the disciples who hear it. Time has run out.

Here, the metaphor of light has different aspects to it. It could mean the light of day and so a narrowly defined period of time, just like the "day"

---

65. Cf. Beutler, "So sehr."

in John 9:4–5. However, it could also stand for the illumination of existence through the word of Jesus as has usually been the case in John since the prologue (John 1:4–5, 9). The darkness is opposed to it. If, in John 1:5, the meaning is probably that the darkness has not seized/grasped the light, then the sense now is the exhortation not to let the darkness overpower the light. This happens through the faith decision of Jesus's hearers. This signifies not simply an intellectual assent to a message of faith that has been heard but an orientation of one's whole existence, in biblical terms a new conversion or "way of walking" (περιπατεῖν).

Jesus's command is linked to a promise. Whoever becomes aligned with him, the light, will become thereby a child of the light. Of course, this recalls the circular movement that is already visible in the prologue: becoming children of God in faith is promised to all those who, for their part, have already been born of God (John 1:12–13).

After this concluding saying, Jesus goes out and hides from his hearers. The note is reminiscent of John 8:59 where Jesus escapes from the threatened stoning and leaves the temple, and 10:39 where he does this definitively after a renewed threat. Here, in 12:36, it is only the crowd that Jesus is evading, leaving them alone with the question of how they will decide about him.

The "lifting" and "glorification" of Jesus emerged as a theme of our passage. As already observed earlier, these two themes seem to go back to the beginning of the Fourth Servant Song in Isa 52:13 LXX.[66] There it says "See, my servant shall understand and be lifted up and glorified exceedingly" (ὑψωθήσεται καὶ δοξασθήσεται σφόδρα). We came across these themes as consistent structural features throughout the section. Seemingly, John has placed the two basic statements at the center of his Christology and also the center of the present passage. In this way, he explains Jesus as Isaiah's suffering servant. That this has been noticed only recently probably lies in the fact that the fourth evangelist does not employ the servant title but replaces it with that of the Son of Man. He found the latter in the Synoptic tradition in the three passion predictions in Mark 8:31–32 par.; 9:31 par.; 10:33–34 par. In the probably later phase of Christology reached in John's Gospel, it was apparently possible to exchange the different christological titles with one another or link them together. Thus, in John 12:20–43 the pervasive, heavy influence of the book of Isaiah is demonstrable.

In the following section, John 12:37–43, Isaiah plays a key role as we

---

66. Cf. Beutler, "Greeks"; Beutler, "Griechen"; Obielosi, *Servant of God*, 242–55.

shall soon see. Both the fact of and the reason for the unbelief of Jesus's hearers are enshrined and presupposed in this book.

Once the influence of Isaiah and especially Isa 52:13–53:12 on John 12:20–43 has been established, it seems reasonable against this background to ask the question why, in John 12:20, the subject is of the Greeks wanting to "see" Jesus.[67] The expression is not self-evident, and one might rather expect verbs such as "meet" or "hear." With a new, more careful reading of Isa 52, the verse Isa 52:15 leaps to sight. There the subject is the peoples and kings who will shut their mouths out of astonishment or fear. According to the original text, this will be because they will see something they have never seen before and hear something they have never heard before. The relative pronoun will thus refer to the object of the seeing and hearing. The Septuagint has referred it to people who have never seen or heard something like the fate of the servant. It translates thus (and is grammatically correct): "for those to whom nothing has been disclosed about him will see, and those who have not heard will come to understanding" (ὅτι οἷς οὐκ ἀνηγγέλη περὶ αὐτοῦ, ὄψονται, καὶ οἳ οὐκ ἀκηκόασιν, συνήσουσιν). If we proceed from the fact that John has the Greek rather than the Hebrew text of the OT in his memory, it can be supposed that, in John 12:20, he was going back to Isa 52:15 LXX. However, in the overall context he had in view the book of Isaiah in general and the Fourth Servant Song in particular. The Isaiah verse would then be understood as the proclamation of salvation for those who had not yet heard of and not yet seen Jesus, the servant. It is precisely the Greeks who wished to "see" Jesus in John 12:20. Their wish was fulfilled.

Confirmation of this interpretation lies in the fact that Paul quotes the cited verse in its Septuagint form at the end of the Letter to the Romans in Rom 15:21. Paul solicits the Romans' understanding for the fact that his plans to visit them have not yet worked out. He surveys his missionary task in the whole of the Greek world as far as Illyria, in all places where the word has not yet been preached. This task was entrusted to him "that those who have not yet had him [for Paul: Christ] preached to them might see, and those who have not yet heard might hear." This text is also of significance for the understanding of John 12:20. It shows that Isa 52:15 LXX could be used in the early communities in a missionary sense. The coming of the Greeks to "see" Jesus could receive confirmation from this.

---

67. Cf. Beutler, "Greeks"; Beutler, "Griechen"; Lee, *Signore, vogliamo vedere Gesù*, 169–72.

*Jesus on the Way to His Passion (11:1–12:50)*

*III*

The present passage brings to a close Jesus's preaching to his people. The immediate sequel is a critical taking stock. The majority of Israel have not accepted his message. However, at the same time, this has opened a door for the salvation of the Gentiles. The Greeks come to see Jesus. The price of their salvation will be the servant's death. On the cross, he will draw all to himself.

Readers from the Gentile world will also see their salvation being proclaimed here. At the same time, they will thereby hear the invitation to hate their own life, with Jesus, before they can gain it properly. The grain of wheat that falls into the earth does not remain alone. It will bring forth fruit. Just as the servant experiences disgrace but in it and from it is lifted up and glorified, so the one who follows Jesus to shame and death will be honored by the Father and attain eternal life.

## 7. Look Back on the Activity of Jesus and Final Summons to Faith (12:37–50)

37 Although Jesus had performed so many signs before their eyes, they did not believe in him. 38 Thus was to be fulfilled the word that the prophet Isaiah had spoken: Lord, who has believed our message? And the arm of the Lord — to whom has its power been revealed? 39 For they could not believe, because Isaiah had said in another place: 40 He has blinded their eyes and hardened their heart, so that they may not see with their eyes and may not come to understanding with their heart, lest they return and I heal them. 41 Isaiah said this because he had seen the glory of Jesus; for he had spoken about him. 42 Nevertheless, in fact, many of the leaders came to faith in him but, on account of the Pharisees, did not confess him openly lest they be thrown out of the synagogue. 43 For they loved the honor of men more than the honor of God.

44 But, for all that, Jesus cried out: Whoever believes in me, believes not in me but in the one who sent me, 45 and whoever sees me, sees the one who sent me. 46 I have come as light into the world, so that everyone who believes in me may not remain in the darkness. 47 Whoever only hears my word and does not follow it, I do not judge him; for I have not come to judge the world but to save the world. 48 Whoever despises my words and does not accept them already has his judge: the word I have spoken will judge him on the last day. 49 For I have not spoken on my own account, but the Father who sent me has commanded me

what I should say and speak. ⁵⁰ And I know that his commandment is eternal life. Thus what I say, I say as the Father has said to me.

## I

John's Gospel knows a series of "quest stories." A first example is the account of the calling of the first disciples (John 1:35–51). Further examples of this kind are the narratives of Jesus's conversations with Nicodemus (3:1–21) and with the Samaritan woman (4:1–26). In the closer context of John 12, the Johannine form of the entrance story (12:12–19) has traits of a quest story. Distinctly belonging to this genre is the passage about the Greeks who come to see Jesus (12:20–36). This story appears to have considerable significance for the evangelist despite its open outcome. The opening of the Greeks to Jesus is matched on the negative side by a section that records the refusal of the "Jews" to believe in Jesus or to confess such a faith openly (12:37–43). It includes, however, a final summons to faith by Jesus (12:44–50), so that it does not remain on a negative note.

There are hypotheses of literary stratification regarding the section John 12:37–43. Often, the reference in John 12:37–38 to the "signs" performed by Jesus which should have inspired faith is taken, together with John 20:30–31, as the close of the hypothetical "signs source."[68] This source intended to lead to faith in Jesus on account of his signs. Another opinion ascribes the whole section 12:37–50 to the Johannine redaction,[69] yet another, verses 44–50.[70] According to a further view, verses 12:37–43 stem from the hypothetical *Grundschrift* used by the signs source in verses 37–38. Verses 39–40 go back to the evangelist.[71] However, before the text is parceled out into sources and layers of this kind, it is advisable, at least at first, to embrace it and explain it in its present form. The more it seems to have been constructed in a focused and meaningful way, the more theories about strata seem to be rather redundant.

In tracking down the structure of the present section, a glance at the syntax employed is useful. In verses 37, 39 and 42, the imperfect occurs, by contrast with the narrative aorist employed elsewhere. In v. 37, it is

---

68. Thus Bultmann, followed by numerous authors.
69. So Haenchen.
70. Thus in Boismard, Schnackenburg, Becker, and Kühschelm, *Verstockung*.
71. Along these lines, Richter, *Studien*, 397, 400.

*Jesus on the Way to His Passion (11:1–12:50)*

observed that Jesus's hearers do not believe in him although he had performed so many and such great signs. In v. 39, the reason for this is given: they did not believe in Jesus because they could not believe. In v. 42, it is observed that of those who came to believe in Jesus, many did not muster the courage to confess this faith openly since they loved the honor of men more than the love of God. This indicates the framework of the passage up to v. 43. From v. 44, there is a continuous discourse of Jesus that is similarly introduced with the aorist. In it, the present is predominant with occasional resort to the narrative aorist or the future.

The references to the prophet Isaiah contribute to the structure of the section up to v. 43. They confirm the division given above corresponding to the three imperfects in verses 37, 39 and 42. A reference to Isa 53:1 LXX in v. 38 gives the reason for the fact that many did not come to faith in Jesus. That they were not even in a position to do this is explained in v. 40 with a reference to Isa 6:10. Isaiah's name is repeated in v. 41, and there a theological reason for his prophetic word is given. Verses 37–38, 39–41, and 42–44 are thus revealed as belonging together in focusing on: the fact of unbelief, its basis, and the failing of many to confess this faith openly. The theme of "honor" is also found already in v. 41 and returns again, doubled, in v. 43, thus conferring on verse 41 a hinge role between the second and third and last subsection. The theme of "faith" occurs as a central feature in all three subsections and gives the whole passage its semantic framework. It then leads into the closing section, 12:44–50, where it retains its dominant role even when it is semantically modified.

## II

### A Look Back on the Activity of Jesus (12:37–43)

**12:37–38** Since John 5, there have been increasing reports of the different reactions of the Jewish hearers or opponents of Jesus to his word. The previous case began with the desire of the "Greeks" to see Jesus (John 12:20–36). It already led to Jesus's solemn warning not to neglect the moment of faith in him. There, it is the Jewish conversation partners of Jesus that are again being presupposed. They are asking about the relation between the Messiah and the Son of Man (v. 34). Thus, the closing exhortations up to v. 36 were probably meant for them.

If it is not stated in v. 37 who it is who have finally not believed in

Jesus despite his signs, then it is the recently named Jewish hearers of Jesus who are meant. That "they" did not believe in Jesus is a sweeping statement in which, however, we must keep in view that some of them did indeed come to faith. This is also stated in v. 42 in connection with the confession of faith. Thus, it concerns the majority of Jesus's Jewish hearers and certainly also their leaders (at least a majority of them) who opposed the claims of Jesus and had already decided on his death (cf. 11:47–53).

The signs of Jesus that should have led to faith in him had reached their unsurpassable climax in the raising of Lazarus (John 11:1–44). They are not the only way to faith in Jesus, but they are recognized and presented by the evangelist as a legitimate path to faith (cf. John 2:11, 23; 3:2; 6:2, 14, 26; 12:18; 20:30).

If the lack of faith in Jesus's hearers is conveyed in the imperfect, that serves to emphasize that it is not isolated incidents that we are dealing with but a fundamental decision that is meant to last.

The evangelist sees this lack of faith as being foretold by Isaiah. In this connection, he quotes Isa 53:1 in the Septuagint version. If our hypothesis is correct that in John 12:20 he has already developed from Isa 52:15 LXX the wish of the Greeks to "see" Jesus, this would now be the second time the evangelist has gone back to the Fourth Servant Song as it was read and understood in the Greek-speaking communities. In the Septuagint, Isa 53:1 begins with the address "Lord," which is absent in the Hebrew original. The recourse of the Fourth Gospel to the Septuagint is thus revealed clearly here.

Similarly, in Rom 9–11, Paul quotes the Septuagint version of Isa 53:1 in connection with the unbelief of Israel and its hoped-for salvation. Here too, in Rom 10:16, the saying from the Fourth Servant Song is employed in a christological fashion.

The form that introduces the Isaiah quotation in John 12:38 is met here in John's Gospel for the first time. It emerges clearly from this that a saying of the Old Testament is being quoted here in the immediate context of the passion.[72] Such "fulfillment quotations" are encountered first in the Synoptic tradition in connection with the passion narrative and have probably found their way from there into the Johannine passion narrative too. If in the previous narrative section the "Scripture" has served to legitimate Jesus's claim to having been sent by God, the narrator thus sees

---

72. Cf. Evans, "The Function"; Evans, "Quotation Formulas."

*Jesus on the Way to His Passion (11:1–12:50)*

the passion of Jesus and some of its details as enshrined in Scripture. In this way, as in the Synoptics, the impression is countered that the passion of Jesus had been outside the realm of the knowledge and will of God. Here, however, we are not concerned with a detail of the passion but with Jesus's rejection *tout court* by his people or their representatives. To that extent, our text stands between the Synoptic tradition and the Johannine perspective.

**12:39–41** That Jesus's Jewish hearers were not even able to believe is something the evangelist sees fixed in a further saying from Isa 6:10. This saying (or Isa 6:9–10) is found also in the Synoptics in Mark 4:11–12; Matt 13:14–15; Luke 8:10; and Acts 28:26–27. The Septuagint form is found in Matthew and in Acts. Mark offers an abbreviated text which, however, shares with the Septuagint the use of a *passivum divinum* from which God can be inferred as the one who "hardened" the hearts. This tendency is strengthened in John (where God appears directly as the subject of blinding and hardening). In the original text of Isaiah, it was the prophet who was commanded to "harden" the people. The Isaiah saying (in its Septuagint form) probably belonged to a collection of early Christian testimonies with which the early communities tried to explain the unbelief of Israel. The allusion to the text in Rom 11:8 belongs already in this connection. It is noticeable that John does not mention the ears and the hearing. Perhaps that is because he has already spoken of the message (ἀκοή) in the scriptural quotation from Isa 53:1 in v. 38.

In v. 41, the evangelist introduces a new key concept: "glory." According to him, Isaiah had seen the "glory" of Christ. Here, the Johannine insight that whoever sees Jesus also sees the Father (John 14:9) is enlisted in the interpretation of the call vision of Isaiah according to which the prophet, at his call, saw the "glory" of the Lord. Thus, the prophet already saw the glory of Christ (Abraham comes to mind here for according to John 8:56, he saw the days of Jesus).

**12:42–43** The small group of verses that follows also leads to the theme of "glory" or "honor." First, it is clear that not all the Jewish people closed themselves to faith in Jesus. "In fact, some of the leaders" came to faith in Jesus, which implies that other members of the people of God were open to faith in Jesus. Such members of the ruling class have already been mentioned previously and recur in John 7 (v. 48). Nicodemus belonged to them and showed, later on in the Gospel, that he could also stand up for this faith (John 3:1; 7:50; 19:39). Within the groups of the Sanhedrin, it is the Pharisees who appear as the most decided foes of Jesus. From fear of them and the danger of being thrown out of the synagogue at their instigation, clearly many members of the Sanhedrin did not dare to confess their faith in Jesus. This exclusion from the synagogue had already been mentioned in connection with the story of the healing of the man born blind (cf. John 9:22, 34; the theme returns in 16:2). From the evangelist's point of view, a fundamental decision is being made here: to seek the "honor" of God or that of men.[73] This too has already been mentioned (cf. John 5:41–44; 7:18). For John's reading community, this theme is of crucial significance. Probably already in a situation of persecution, they are summoned to confess their faith in Jesus fearlessly, whatever the consequences.[74]

### Final Summons to Faith (12:44–50)

**12:44–45** The section of John that leads into the passion narrative does not end with the statement of the unbelief of a great part of Jesus's hearers or their lack of readiness to confess their faith but with a final summons by Jesus to faith. On the one hand, it appears to be inserted without information as to place and time, but, on the other hand, it fits reasonably into the narrative flow and is of great significance for the readers at this point.[75]

The introduction to the small section states that Jesus "cried out" the following words. The term employed for this (ἔκραξεν) signifies a cry uttered with the most exceptional emphasis. It has already been used twice in connection with the account of the appearance of Jesus at the Feast of Tabernacles (John 7:28, 37) and appears first of all in the prologue with a confession of the Baptist (John 1:15). It is always attached to sayings of great weight.

Within the discourse of Jesus, there is a movement from statements about believers in Jesus (vv. 44–45) to statements about Jesus himself, and the consequences for those who do not believe in him (vv. 46–48), culminating in closing words about the mission of Jesus from the Father, which gives the decision about him the ultimate weight (vv. 49–50).

At the beginning stands the double saying about those who believe in Jesus and those who see him. For this evangelist, faith in Jesus and faith in God belong together, as is also shown by a saying from the farewell dis-

---

73. Cf. Beutler, "Die Ehre Gottes."
74. Cf. Beutler, "Faith and Confession."
75. This meaning is highlighted also by Becker, 2:481.

courses (John 14:1). Similarly, seeing Jesus and seeing the Father belong together as will likewise be explained in John 14 (v. 9). On the one hand, in John, the seeing, even of signs, can and should lead to faith (cf., most recently, vv. 37–38); on the other hand, there is a seeing that grows out of faith and lets the Father be recognized in Jesus, as is the case here. Whether there is still a thought of the "Greeks'" desire to "see" Jesus (John 12:20) has to remain open.

**12:46–48** Similar to the "I am" sayings a promise is associated with a threat. In fact, the opening of the next group of words recalls the saying of Jesus in John 8:12: "I am the light of the world" and is probably also referring to it (cf., also, John 9:5). Since the prologue (John 1:4–5, 7, 9), the light metaphor for Jesus has been familiar to the readers of John's Gospel. It signifies the illumination of existence as the door to life, as is immediately explained (v. 50). Already in the prologue, the light was opposed to the darkness (John 1:5). When the theme is taken up again later, the theme of judgement also emerges (John 3:19–21). Thus, John 12:44–50 also reads as a summary of the preaching of Jesus to this moment.[76] Jesus has come, not for judgement but for salvation and redemption (cf. John 3:17). Nevertheless, whoever rejects him and his message will be judged by the words of Jesus "on the last day." Here, once again, eschatological statements which refer to the present stand beside those which refer to the future. Here, as in John 5:24–29, it is not easy to infer the additions of an "ecclesiastical redaction," but the statements can be understood as complementary. Salvation and judgement now find their fulfillment and ratification in salvation and judgement in the future.

**49–50** Jesus's word is decisive for salvation and damnation since it has been given and commanded to him by the Father. Thus, he does not speak on his own account (cf. John 8:28). The word handed down by Jesus is precisely a "commandment" that has been commanded to him by the Father. The theme will be modified later in the farewell discourses: when Jesus speaks of entering upon his passion, he is acting just as the Father has commanded him (John 14:31). The word which the Father has commanded Jesus stands for eternal life. With this promise of salvation the final summons of Jesus to faith comes to a close before the account of his passion, death, and resurrection.

---

76. Thus, among others, Kühschelm, *Verstockung*, who works out the literary and theological unity of the passage.

*III*

The two parts of the passage John 12:37–50 complement each other. There is no lingering on the observation that a large part of Jesus's listeners refuse to come to faith in him or, at least, have not mustered the courage to confess their faith in him. The last word is reserved for Jesus himself who, disconnected, so to speak, from space and time, issues one more time an urgent call to faith in him. Precisely here, John's Gospel is revealed as a text intended not simply as a record but as a tool of communication between the author and his readers.

Both subsections pose the problem of divine predestination and human freedom. It is difficult to convey to contemporary readers that God himself would harden human hearts so that they could not come to faith. The problem returns in the second subsection as the dualism of light and darkness in which men are involved. Where the concept of hardening is concerned, we have to take into account that the Bible does not generally distinguish clearly between divine permission and divine predestination. Everything that happens is ultimately rooted in the will of God so that the relationship between divine determination and human freedom is not solved in a speculative manner. More often, statements on the predetermination of God and on human freedom of decision are set side by side so that they complement each other. This goes also, then, for the dualism of light and darkness in the second part of the passage. John is sometimes spoken of as having a "decision dualism." If someone finds salvation, then this is wholly the work of God but never without the cooperation of the one called to faith. The ultimate aim of the divine work of salvation is the "salvation of the world" (v. 47).

# Jesus Bids Farewell (13:1–17:26)

John 13:1 marks the beginning of a section of John's Gospel characterized by the farewell discourses. They belong to the distinctive character of the Fourth Gospel even if a shorter parallel, perhaps even a precedent, is found in Luke 21:20–38. In a broader sense, one could entitle the whole section John 13:1–17:26 as "Jesus's farewell discourses," in a narrower sense, the section from John 13:31 or 14:1 to 16:33. At the beginning stands the narrative of the washing of feet in John 13:1–20, followed by the account of the announcement of the betrayer in John 13:21–30. Jesus's prayer in John 17 closes the farewell discourses both thematically and linguistically but can be counted as part of them in a broader sense.

To this day, it remains controversial just how far we are faced with a unitary text here. Synoptic influence can be traced at least in ch. 13, but not only there. At this point in the commentary we shall prescind from more extensive source hypotheses and also from transpositional hypotheses that are supposed to lead to a more logical textual sequence.[1] In the view of this commentary, it is possible to trace a layer in which some parts of the text are being "re-read" and developed for a new set of readers. On this model of the so-called *"relecture,"* it is not a question of postulating different authors,[2] but of different texts that are connected with one an-

---

1. They often aim to locate the "departure signal" in John 14:31 at the end of the discourse. Bernard, 1:xx–xxvi, conjectures the original order as: John 13:31a; 15–16; 13:31b–14:31; 17. Bultmann, 348–51, suggests John 13:1–30; 17; 13:31–35; 15–16; 13:36–14:31.

2. In Bultmann's school, the evangelist versus "ecclesiastical redaction" distinction was applied to the farewell discourses by Becker and Richter with Hainz as the editor. Chapters 15–17 are no longer concerned primarily with Christology but with the community, likewise probably the earlier sections John 13:12–20 and 13:34–35. In their

other in such a way that an earlier text leads on to a further one in which the early text is "re-read."[3] In what follows, it will be assumed that chs. 15 to 17 develop chs. 13 to 14, more particularly that John 14 is taken further by John 16:4e–33, with John 15:1–16:4d as a transitional passage with, perhaps, its own prehistory. John 17 then presupposes the whole set of farewell discourses and brings it to a literary and theological conclusion. Important for the theory of this process of growth is the significance of the "departure signal" in John 14:31: "Rise, and let us be going." In its place, it will be shown that it is to be taken completely literally and finds its natural continuation in Jesus's departure to the brook Kidron in John 18:1, contrary to spiritualizing attempts intended to preserve the literary unity of the whole farewell discourse.

If chs. 15–17 are seen as a *"relecture"* of John 14 or 13:31–14:31, then the question emerges whether John 13 was constructed to include John 13:31–38 or not. A series of authors sees the first farewell discourse or the farewell discourses in general beginning in John 13:31.[4] They are opposed by others who regard ch. 13 as an independent literary unit. This is the position of the commentaries of Ulrich Wilckens[5] and Moloney,[6] as well as contributions from Mary L. Coloe[7] and Jean-Noël Aletti.[8] The last two authors especially see the chapter as an elaborately formed text of a concentric construction.

According to Coloe, after an introductory section (vv. 1–5), at the beginning and end of the main section (vv. 6–38), there is a dialogue of Jesus with Peter (vv. 6–11 and 36–38). There follows, at the beginning and preceding the end, a section about the instruction and gift of Jesus (vv. 11–15 and 34–35). In the middle are corresponding sections that deal with Judas (vv. 16–20 and 21–30). In his structural analysis, Aletti starts immediately with v. 1 and sees a correspondence between the opening verse 1 and the closing verses 31–38 with regard to Jesus's departure to the Father. Further

---

commentaries, Brown und Schnackenburg proceed from a Johannine redaction, similarly Wilckens and Frey.

3. Cf., for this model, the introduction, section 4.

4. See the discussion at John 13:31.

5. Wilckens, 204–19, who treats John 13:1–20, 13:21–30, 13:31–38 before the farewell discourse in John 14:1–31.

6. Moloney, 370–91, who summarizes John 13:1–38 under the catchwords "Making God Known, the Footwashing and the Morsel."

7. Coloe, "Welcome"; Coloe, "Sources."

8. Aletti, "Jn 13."

in, there follow sections that deal with the possession of Judas by the devil (vv. 2 and 21–30). In the center would stand the verses that tell of the preparation for the washing of the feet (vv. 4–5) and its accomplishment by Jesus with the relevant explanation (vv. 6–11, 12–20). The corresponding sections display, partly, the same vocabulary (cf. for the first and last segments, ἀγαπάω "love," θεός "God" and ὑπάγω "go away").

However one divides John 13, the chapter in any case displays a certain coherence that is revealed not only in the vocabulary employed but also, from the narrative point of view, in the people taking part (Jesus, disciples, Judas, Peter). The central text is the washing of feet within the framework of the Last Supper with its interpretations and the ensuing dialogues.

## 1. The Footwashing (13:1–20)

¹ It was before the feast of the Passover. Jesus knew that his hour had come for him to go from this world to the Father. Since he loved his own who were in the world, he loved them to the highest degree. ² A supper was taking place, and the devil had already put it into the heart of Judas, the son of Simon Iscariot, to betray him. ³ Jesus, who knew that the Father had given everything into his hand, and that he had come from God and was going back to God, ⁴ got up from the supper, laid aside his garment and girded himself with a linen cloth. ⁵ Then he poured water into a basin and began to wash the feet of the disciples and to dry them with the linen cloth with which he was girded. ⁶ When he came to Simon Peter, the latter said to him: Lord, do you want to wash my feet? ⁷ Jesus said to him: What I am doing, you do not understand now; but you will grasp it later. ⁸ Peter replied: You are never going to wash my feet! Jesus answered him: If I do not wash you, you have no share with me. ⁹ Then Simon Peter said to him: Then not only my feet, Lord, but also my hands and my head. ¹⁰ Jesus said to him: Whoever has bathed is completely clean and only needs his feet to be washed. You too are clean, but not all. ¹¹ For he knew who would betray him; that is why he said: You are not all clean.

¹² After he had washed their feet, got dressed again and taken his place, he said to them: Do you understand what I have done to you? ¹³ You call me Master and Lord, and you call me this with reason; for that is what I am. ¹⁴ If, then, I, your Lord and Master, have washed your feet, then you must also wash one another's feet. ¹⁵ I have given you an example so that you may do what I have done to you. ¹⁶ Amen, amen, I say to you: The slave is not greater than his master, and the

one who has been sent is not greater than the one who sent him. ¹⁷ If you know that — blessed are you if you act accordingly. ¹⁸ I am not saying this about all of you. I know whom I have chosen, but the saying of Scripture must be fulfilled: The one who ate my bread has betrayed me. ¹⁹ I am telling this to you now before it happens so that when it happens you may believe that I am he. ²⁰ Amen, amen, I say to you: Whoever receives the one whom I send receives me; and whoever receives me, receives the one who has sent me.

## I

At the beginning of the Johannine account of Jesus's return home stands the amply developed story of the footwashing. It has in common with the Synoptic accounts of the passion, death, and resurrection of Jesus that it describes a farewell supper of Jesus with his disciples directly before the feast of the Passover. However, John gives no clue that this could have been a Passover meal. The themes of such a meal appear in the Passover feast that Jesus celebrates with his disciples in John 6:51c–58. There, the Passover feast has already been Christianized.

The starting point for the Johannine scene could have been a saying from the forerunner of the farewell discourse in Luke 22:27.[9] Here, there is a report of a struggle for precedence among the disciples. Jesus points towards his own disposition: "Which of the two is greater: the one who sits at table or the one who serves? The one who sits at table, of course. I have come among you as one who serves." This saying seems to be presupposed in John.

How is the text constructed? Verse 1 appears to serve as the "title" for the Johannine passion narrative. This is commonly accepted. In a narrower sense, the verse also introduces the following narrative of the washing of the feet. This begins with the account of Jesus's actions (vv. 2–5). Next comes the dialogue between Jesus and Peter (vv. 6–11) before the instruction of the disciples (vv. 12–20). The introduction to this instruction takes up in reverse order the verbs with which Jesus's actions were described in verses 4–5. The ensuing scene with the description of the traitor and his leaving the supper in verses 21–30 is marked again by dialogues.

One of the striking features of the narrative is the repeated mention of Judas. After the introductory verse 1, Judas is mentioned directly or

---

9. The relation between the two texts was already seen by Origen.

*Jesus Bids Farewell (13:1–17:26)*

indirectly in all three of the following subsections: in v. 2, in verses 10–11, as well as in verses 18–19. The emphasis on the figure of Judas is part of the Johannine dualism but also reinforces the dramatic element of the Johannine account.

The instruction of the disciples in verses 12–17 or 12–20 is not seldom regarded as a continuation of the dialogue between Jesus and Peter in verses 6–10. It is no longer a question of the meaning of Jesus's action on behalf of the disciples, probably as a kind of anticipation of the passion the fruit of which is to be acquired in faith, but a matter of the actions of the disciples following the example of the Jesus who serves. The detailed exegesis will have to show how far to distinguish continuity and change here, and also how both elements can be explained in their relation to each other from the point of view of composition history.

## II

### *The Action of Jesus (13:1–5)*

The sentence construction allows us to divide this small narrative into verse 1, then 2–4, and, finally, verse 5. Historic present and aorist alternate, a feature that probably goes back to the narrator's intention to communicate a lively presentation.

**13:1** The opening verse serves as the title not only for the following narrative but for the entire Johannine account of Jesus's homecoming to the Father. It is formed with very distinctive language. At the beginning stands a temporal indication which is to be understood not only in a chronological but also in a liturgical sense. What Jesus is now doing and experiencing is unfolding within the frame of the chief Jewish feast of salvation. Two participles state the knowledge and disposition with which Jesus goes to the consummation of his life and work. Jesus knows that as of now his "hour has come to go from this world to the Father." This is the Johannine way of saying that the "hour" of his farewell has come.[10] The disposition with which Jesus approaches this hour is that of love to the utmost or to the end. By virtue of the fact that the participial verb is taken up again as the main verb, it assumes emphatic weight. In the first farewell

---

10. The aorist ἦλθεν is better attested than the perfect ἐλήλυθεν, and also corresponds to Johannine language.

discourse, Jesus will resume the theme of his love for his own and promise it to those who love him (John 14:21). Here, at the beginning of the farewell discourses, Jesus's love for his own is expressed unconditionally.

**13:2–4** The symbolic action that follows is meant to bring this to expression. The long sentence of verses 2–4 begins in the same way with an indication of time which also provides the frame for the action described in what follows: a supper. Two participles set Judas[11] and Jesus in opposition to each other. The former, inspired by the Evil One, has just decided to betray Jesus; the latter, Jesus, is aware of his farewell from the world and his return to the Father in order to complete his work of salvation (vv. 2–3).

That said, the main action can be described. This happens briefly but vividly. Jesus first equips himself for his service by rising from the meal, removing his over-garment and girding himself (v. 4). He thus takes up already the servant's role. Previously, Luke 22:27 had distinguished between the one who remains at table and the one who serves at table.

**13:5** However, the action being described goes beyond service at table. Jesus proceeds to wash his disciples' feet and then to dry them. In the ancient world, such service was restricted to the servants or slaves. This understanding of things is encountered in the instruction for the disciples in John 13:13–16. Perhaps the formulation also echoes the anointing of Jesus's feet by Mary in John 12:3. Mary too "serves" at supper. If she anointed Jesus's feet and dried them with her hair, this was honoring and a service of love. In view of the introduction to our passage in John 13:1, such an element could also be resonating in the footwashing scene.[12]

### The First Interpretation (13:6–11)

At the moment when Jesus wishes to carry out his service for Peter too, his action is followed by a threefold dialogue between the two men, which also divides this subsection. Here, we have a first expression of an interpretation as to what Jesus is about in his symbolic action. At the conclusion, the traitor comes into focus.

**13:6–8** The beginning contains a double refusal of Peter to allow

---

11. Judas's full name is not securely attested here. The text of Nestle-Aland[28] gives the description of "Iscariot" to Judas's father, something that we have accepted along with the *Einheitsübersetzung*.

12. Against this background, Gruber, "Zumutung," 56, stresses the reciprocal nature of the loving service of Jesus and of Mary as a member of the circle of disciples.

## Jesus Bids Farewell (13:1–17:26)

Jesus's act of service to happen to him. For the evangelist, Peter is the most important representative of the group of disciples. On the one hand, he confesses the disciples' faith in Christ in an exemplary manner (cf. John 6:68–69); on the other hand, he also reveals the typical weakness of the disciples as is shown in his triple denial of Jesus (which will already be announced in John 13:35–38).[13] The positive view of Peter in John 6 is, possibly, to be ascribed to a later *"relecture,"* as is noted in the exegesis of that chapter.

In our passage too, Peter shows that he has not understood Jesus's action and his mission. He understands Jesus's gesture on a purely human level. So, in his first reaction to this deed, he refuses Jesus. He cannot comprehend the declaration that he will understand at a later point what Jesus has done. He replaces Jesus's "later," with a "never" since he does not realize that the understanding of the life of Jesus is revealed only from the time of his "hour." Peter comes to some understanding of what Jesus is doing only after Jesus has threatened that he will have no share with Jesus if he does not allow Jesus to wash his feet.

**13:9–11** However, Peter still labors under a misapprehension. He understands Jesus's action on the physical level: the more of him that is washed, the closer will be his connection with Jesus. Peter does not understand that Jesus's action is meant to interpret the disposition with which he enters upon his passion. Therefore, the symbolic washing of the disciples' feet is sufficient.[14] If and insofar as they agree to the symbolic action of Jesus, they are clean. They have understood his message. In this sense, it can also be said later that Jesus's disciples are clean because of his word (cf. John 15:3).[15]

At the end, there is a reference to the disciple who is to betray Jesus. He remains the dark background to this Last Supper of Jesus with his own. The repeated references to him serve not least the aim of showing that Jesus went to his death in awareness of his fate. The powers of the Evil One are not at work without the knowledge and will of God. Thus, Jesus goes to his passion in full knowledge of what is awaiting him. The scene in John 13:21–30 will show this clearly once more.

---

13. Cf., recently, Schultheiß, *Petrusbild*.

14. The Greek wording of "needs his feet to be washed" in v. 10 is not totally secure in the Greek: some Mss. insert an "only," but it is absent in the preferred text of Nestle-Aland[28]. There too, we do not find the omission of εἰ μὴ τοὺς πόδας νίψασθαι that is encountered in part of the text tradition.

15. This is emphasized strongly by Bultmann.

### The Second Interpretation (13:12–20)

After Jesus has already interpreted for Peter the symbolic action of the footwashing, it is surprising that a second interpretation follows. If it is still the case that Peter cannot now understand Jesus's action but only later (John 13:7), how can Jesus now be asking his disciples whether they understand what he has done to them, a question which assumes that they could do just that (v. 12)? Various suggestions have been made to solve this apparent contradiction, and the different proposals have been thoroughly collected by Schnelle.[16] The first model hypothesizes that the first interpretation given by the evangelist has been corrected in the second by the "ecclesiastical redaction." Christology and personal faith is no longer the main concern but correct behavior in the community. This would already be an adumbration of the perspective of chs. 15–17.[17] A second model recognizes in the two interpretations different ways in which the evangelist has interpreted Jesus's symbolic action. A third model is related to the second, is endorsed by Schnelle himself, and has indeed good grounds for it. Its position is that, in the second interpretation, the evangelist employs traditional material that allows him to recognize in Jesus's action an additional dimension that is important for the community and which complements the first (christological-soteriological) meaning. Insofar as the second interpretation presupposes and develops the first, one can recognize in it a further example of "*relecture*," the rereading of the first interpretation in the light of the situation of the community.[18]

The division of the passage can no longer be achieved by means of narrative criteria since after the narrative introduction, it is Jesus alone who speaks. However, without any difficulty, a division emerges based on semantic criteria. Verses 13–17 are about ruling and serving; verses 18–20 are once again about the one who would betray Jesus, causing it to appear, at first glance, as if verse 20 does not belong to the context.

**13:12** The introduction to the following discourse of Jesus shows clearly that it is formulated in the light of the previous narrative of the footwashing. Verse 12 records in reverse sequence what Jesus did as ser-

---

16. Cf. Schnelle, 239.
17. In Beutler, "Die Heilsbedeutung," I have put forward a similar view, however without accepting an "ecclesiastical redaction" correcting the perspective of the evangelist.
18. For this model, see, above the introduction to the section "Jesus Bids Farewell (13:1–17:26)."

## Jesus Bids Farewell (13:1–17:26)

vice for the disciples according to vv. 4–5. Thus, after he has washed the disciples' feet, he puts his clothes back on and sits down for the instruction that follows.

At the beginning, Jesus asks if the disciples have understood what he has done to them. This is a surprising question since Peter has already had to hear that he could not now understand Jesus's symbolic action but would understand it later. It is permissible to conclude that the instruction for the disciples which now follows concerns commands of Jesus which ultimately presuppose the light of Easter. Correspondingly, they are now addressed also to all disciples. They have to do with the way the community lives.

**13:13–17** In case the disciples have not understood the service of Jesus, he now gives them the meaning of it. Here, the most important catchword is "do." It was already introduced at the end of v. 12 and closes the section in v. 17 within the framework of a macarism. In between, it is encountered twice in v. 15. The most important substantives are "Lord" and "Master" as well as "servant." Additionally, a tension is revealed between "being" and "doing."

Jesus's instruction has the form of an argument *a fortiori*. If the one whom the disciples rightly call "Lord" and "Master" washes their feet, how much more must they be ready to wash one another's feet. It is precisely for this reason that he has given the example.

For his argument, Jesus can rely on a generally recognized principle: the slave is not greater than his master, and the one sent is not greater than the one who sent him (v. 16). This proverb appears in the Gospels in different forms. Similarly to its form in John, it is found in Luke 6:40 towards the end of the Sermon on the Plain. There, the Jewish origin of the saying is still recognizable. It applies to the teacher-pupil relationship. The pupil can never rise above his teacher. If he learned everything, he would be like his teacher. So, then, perhaps John's saying is to be understood more generally in the sense that the pupil can never rise above the level of the teacher. In Matthew (10:24–25), the saying is modified to the principle that the pupil should not fare better than his teacher. He will thus have to put up with the same injury. The saying appears also in the same sense in John's farewell discourses (15:20) where Jesus points back to his previous statement in John 13:16. Within John's Gospel, the saying is thus employed and explained on several occasions.

That the one who has been sent is not superior to the one who sent him but can become equal to him is equally a recognized Jewish-rabbinic principle (the so-called "Shaliach" principle).[19] Jesus employs it here in the sense of status: the one sent can never set himself above the one who has sent him. Through the linking of the idea of "sending" with the motifs of "Lord" and "Master," the evangelist is establishing a connection to a fundamental theme of his Gospel: that of the "sending" of Jesus by the Father.

The disciples are not blessed when they have understood this teaching of Jesus but only when they also carry it out. Here too, we are not far from the Synoptic tradition (cf. Luke 10:28, 37).[20]

**13:18–20** However, Jesus's macarism does not apply to all the disciples in that he has explained that they are "not all" clean (v. 10). Once more, there is an indication of the traitor within the circle of the disciples. Jesus again appears to be aware as to who belongs to him ultimately since he knows those whom he has chosen (cf. John 6:70; 15:16, 19). However, it is not only he who is aware of his coming fate. It was also foretold in the Scriptures as is expressed in the reference to Ps 41:9. The quotation is a free form of Ps 40:10 LXX ("loaf"/"bread" instead of "loaves" and "has lifted his heel against me" instead of "magnified," the meaning is probably "go behind"). Here, we have an anticipation of the following story of the announcement of the betrayer (John 13:21–30: vv. 26–27) that does not have its own biblical quotation. Thus, the rooting of Jesus's betrayal in the Scripture is expressly stated here in v. 18 and so anchored, ultimately, in the will of God. It is remarkable that the prophetic saying of Jesus here (and not only here) is treated with equal weight to that of Scripture. Here, we come across an already advanced doctrine of "Scripture" which sets the word of Jesus alongside the word of God in the Old Testament.[21]

Jesus's foretelling of his betrayal by one of those at table is to lead the disciples after their fulfillment, and probably after Easter ultimately, to the belief that "I am he" (v. 19). This "absolute ἐγώ εἰμι" is familiar to

---

19. The more recent exegetes and translations speak here not of "apostle" but of "one sent" following Bultmann, 364, who here refers to Rengstorf, "ἀπόστολος." Dissenting from that, Luise Abramowski prefers the meaning "apostle" and interprets it as a reference to the apostle Paul whose understanding of the Eucharist is supposed to be being criticized here. For her, the footwashing is a sacrament alongside baptism and the Eucharist. Cf. Abramowski, "Apostel."

20. Vignolo, "Il Quarto Vangelo," 132, emphasizes the structural significance of the two macarisms in John, here and in John 20:29, at the beginning and end of the account of the passion. On the first occasion, we have a blessing of behavior, in the second a blessing of an insight of faith.

21. Cf. Beutler, "Der Gebrauch von 'Schrift'"; Labahn, "Jesus und die Autorität."

*Jesus Bids Farewell (13:1–17:26)*

the readers; it has already been encountered in the great controversies at the Feast of Tabernacles (cf. John 8:24, which is probably in allusion to the prophetic self-description of God in Isa 43:10.[22] It would then be being applied here by Jesus to himself).

The closing verse 20 remains a puzzle. Is Jesus thinking already of Judas, and is he speaking from a sense that he will betray him?[23] Or do we have here a recollection of the true mission of Jesus and the Presbyter against self-styled church leaders like Diotrephes?[24] Before any venture into the world outside the text, it is advisable to search in the text itself for information about the difficult saying of Jesus here. Sending was already mentioned in v. 16. There, the subject was the limits which cannot be crossed by the one sent by Jesus. Verse 20 expresses the same thing in a positive way: whoever receives someone whom Jesus has sent, receives him, and whoever receives him, receives the one who sent him. The two verses complement each other, with the positive statement at the end. Matt 10:40 par. could have been an influence here. Alongside v. 16, v. 20 also goes back to v. 18. There is a connection between the thought of choosing in v. 18 and that of sending in v. 20. The disciples chosen and sent by Jesus form the light background to the darker picture painted by the traitor Judas.

*III*

Images speak for themselves. That goes for prophetic symbolic actions too. Jesus's gesture on behalf of his disciples immediately before his passion is a vivid expression of the disposition with which he enters into his passion. Words will always fall short of the image.

Thus, the two interpretations that follow can only serve as examples as to how Jesus's act on behalf of his own at the farewell meal can be understood. They reveal dimensions of his homecoming. The explanation to Peter shows that the important thing is to appropriate Jesus's passion as his innermost act of salvation. That happens in faith. In the course of the history of exegesis, this has led to the notion of the sacra-

---

22. Cf. Hübner, "ΕΝ ΑΡΧΗΙ ΕΓΩ ΕΙΜΙ."

23. Lagrange, 358, interprets the verse along these lines as the beginning of a new section.

24. Thus Thyen, "Johannes 13"; Schnelle.

ment of baptism in which Christ effects salvation in the bath of baptism and in faith.

The second interpretation sees Jesus's action as an example for the disciples. Just as Jesus looks for the lowest place and performs the lowliest service, so also service and love for one another should mark the community of disciples. Already in Luke it is perceived that the struggle for status can threaten even the circle of disciples. Jesus's gesture here establishes an abiding benchmark.

John records the washing of feet in the place in which the other Gospels give an account of the institution of the Eucharist. On that note, John is describing—consciously or not—the inner aspect of the Eucharist. Where Christians congregate for Jesus's supper, this can only happen in the manner and in the disposition with which Jesus entered into his passion: in love and readiness for service. The footwashing is a clear expression of this. Paul will explain the Eucharist in exactly this sense for the community of Corinth (cf. 1 Cor 11:17–34).[25]

## 2. The Identification of Judas and His Exit (13:21–30)

[21] After these words, Jesus became distressed and testified: Amen, amen, I say to you: One of you will betray me. [22] The disciples looked at one another in bafflement, because they did not know what he meant. [23] One of the disciples was reclining at Jesus's side; it was the one whom Jesus loved. [24] Simon Peter nodded to him that he should ask about whom Jesus was speaking. [25] Then this one leaned back again on Jesus's breast and asked him: Lord, who is it? [26] Jesus answered: It is the one to whom I shall give the morsel of bread which I dip. Then he dipped the bread, took it and gave it to Judas, the son of Simon Iscariot. [27] When Judas had taken the morsel of bread, Satan entered into him. Jesus said to him: What you are planning to do, do soon! [28] But none of those who were present understood why he said that to him. [29] Because Judas had the purse, some thought that Jesus intended to say to him: Buy what we need for the feast!, or that Jesus was commanding him to give something to the poor. [30] When Jesus had taken the morsel of bread, he went out at once. And it was night.

---

25. For Coloe, "Welcome," the footwashing represents the reception into the household of God (411). In Jewish tradition, the prototype for the loving service in the footwashing is Abraham. Cf. Coloe, "Sources," and Coloe, *God Dwells with Us*.

*Jesus Bids Farewell (13:1–17:26)*

# I

The following section stands between the narrative of the footwashing and the beginning of the farewell discourses in a broader sense in John 13:31. The identification of the betrayer belonged already to the traditional passion narrative as it is attested in Mark 14:18–21. John develops this scene considerably in that, among other things, he introduces Peter and the beloved disciple.

From the narrative point of view, the passage is divided into three scenes, each beginning with a word or action of Jesus: Jesus's saying about the one who will betray him and the reaction of the disciples (vv. 21–25), his word again and his gesture towards Judas (vv. 26–27a), and a last saying of Jesus, addressed now to Judas directly, with some remarks about the disciples and about Judas's departure (vv. 27b–30).

The present passage is a classic example for source criticism. It was investigated in detail by Becker in his commentary.[26] Similarly to Georg Richter,[27] Becker distinguishes between pre-Johannine tradition, the evangelist, and the "ecclesiastical redaction" (a description introduced by Bultmann, although not employed by him for the present passage). According to Becker, the pre-Johannine tradition comprises verses 21b–22, 26–27, 30. It lacks the dialogues with the disciples and the reference to Peter and the beloved disciple. The evangelist would have inserted the introduction in v. 21a and the reference to the disciples' lack of understanding in verses 28–29. Verses 23–25 about the beloved disciple go back to the ecclesiastical redactor who was interested in the Johannine tradition as the basis for the faith of the Johannine community.

In more recent studies, the hypothesis of a pre-Johannine passion account has been almost entirely abandoned, mainly under the influence of Neirynck and his Louvain school. In fact, it appears more convincing to postulate a direct influence of the Synoptic Gospels on the Fourth Gospel. The starting point for the Johannine text would be Mark 14:18–21. The evangelist would have inserted Jesus's spiritual distress and his "testimony" at the beginning, then the scene with Peter and the beloved disciple, the action of Jesus offering the morsel to Judas, Satan's entering into the latter, Jesus's command addressed to Judas, and the deliberations of the disciples over the meaning of the words addressed to Judas; finally, the indication that it was night when Judas left the room. It is still true that the Johannine

---

26. Cf. Becker, 2:513–16.
27. Cf. Richter, "Die Fußwaschung."

account does not remain without tensions (thus, for example, the entry of Satan into Judas in v. 2 and v. 27, as well as the understanding of the disciples with regard to the action of Jesus, or the absence thereof, in v. 26 and v. 28); however, the reconstruction of a whole system of literary layers is also not without tensions and difficulties.

## II

**13:21–25** In the first scene, we have to proceed from the fact that Jesus's announcement that one from the circle of his disciples will betray him and the bafflement of the disciples as to who this is derive from the tradition. All the further elements of the scene would then go back to the evangelist. An ascription of all the texts about the beloved disciple in the Fourth Gospel to a post-Johannine redaction does not appear to be persuasive since they can be detached from the compositional context of John's Gospel only with difficulty and match the texts of the evangelist.

The hand of the evangelist can already be made out in the introduction to the scene in v. 21. He clearly wants to lend great weight to it. He achieves this, first by recounting powerful emotion on Jesus's part, renders his words as "testifying," and letting Jesus's words begin with the double "Amen" formula, thus bestowing additional weight to Jesus's words. We have already encountered Jesus's "distress" at the sight of the grave of his friend Lazarus in John 11:33. The word is encountered again in John 14:1, 27 and could come from Ps 42/43. It was probably mediated by the Synoptic Gethsemane tradition. Ps 42:6, 12; 43:5 is echoed in Mark 14:34. John seems to have Ps 42:6 (42:7 LXX) more in mind where the passive ταράσσεσθαι is employed and also the "soul" of the worshiper is mentioned ("spirit" in John). In the language of this psalm, Jesus appears as the suffering righteous man who brings his complaint before God. In John 14, however, he will also appear as the pilgrim who finds himself on the way to the heavenly sanctuary.

The reason for Jesus's distress is the fact that one of his disciples will betray him. The disciples do not understand what he says and look at one another in bafflement. In this way, the drama of the scene is further emphasized. None of the disciples has the courage to ask Jesus what his words mean. Only Peter summons up the courage and gets the "disciple whom Jesus loved" to ask Jesus. The readers still do not know this figure. To want to find him earlier in the "other disciple" who remains nameless in John 1:40 has no convincing basis in the text. It is more probable that this disciple is introduced first in the passion narrative. He is always beside Peter, but is superior to him in his very personal relationship with Jesus. While Peter denies knowing his Lord three times, the beloved disciple is the first to realize that Jesus is risen (John 20:3-10: v. 8), and, at Jesus's third appearance, he recognizes Jesus again before Peter (John 21:1-14: v. 7). In a certain way, he comes into the second part of John's Gospel in the place of Lazarus whom Jesus "loved" (John 11:5; 11:36). His closeness to Jesus is also expressed in the expression that he "leaned on Jesus's breast" (John 13:23-25), just as Jesus "rests on the Father's breast/in his heart" (John 1:18). In any case, whoever this disciple was, he was of huge significance for the Johannine tradition as the close of the Gospel shows (John 21:24).

**13:26-27a** The second scene is characterized by a word and an action of Jesus. He identifies the traitor by a word and an action. For the readers, it is clear that Jesus is fully aware of his situation and retains the initiative. After Jesus's action, Satan enters into Judas.

Jesus's word and deed clearly go back to the evangelist. From the Markan tradition (Mark 14:20), he takes only the "dipping." Jesus's common dipping with his enemy becomes an action of Jesus in which he dips a morsel into the dish and hands it to Judas in order to identify him. The whole thing bears only a distant resemblance to Ps 40:10 LXX. In his action, Jesus shows once again that he is sovereign Lord of the situation.

**13:27b-30** The third scene also begins with a saying of Jesus. It is followed by a reaction among the disciples before the exit of Judas. Jesus's words to Judas have no precedent in the other Gospels. It is to be understood from the theological perspective of the evangelist to paint Jesus as an active participant in the progress of his passion. It cannot proceed quickly enough.

The disciples are again portrayed as those who, before Easter, cannot understand Jesus's words about his coming fate (cf. John 2:22; 12:16). Thus, they interpret them along the lines of everyday experience.

Paradoxically, it seems to be only Judas who has understood what Jesus has said. So he goes out to his work. That it is night is certainly not merely an indication of time. It is the time of darkness with which the readers have been familiar since the prologue (cf. John 1:5; 8:12; 12:35, 46). It was under the protection of night that Nicodemus came to Jesus (John 3:2; 19:39). Night limits men's room for action and also that of Jesus (John 9:4). It is opposed to the day and the light in which a man finds the right path (John 3:19; 11:10). In harmony with Johannine dualism, Judas goes out to the place he belongs.

### III

In the scene described, Jesus appears wholly human and wholly divine. He is deeply distressed at his coming fate, and, in fact, not about the physical torments that await him but about the treachery of one of his loyal followers. However, he also appears to be sovereign as Lord of the situation. He knows his fate and he promotes it rather than delaying it. His disciples will understand his mystery only after his lifting up.

Access to the mystery of Jesus is offered by the "disciple whom Jesus loved." He forms the bridge between Jesus and the future community. He will also be the authority behind the Fourth Gospel, as the conclusion of the Gospel makes clear (cf. 21:24). Just as he rests on the heart of Jesus, so he provides access to the mystery of Jesus through the ages.

## 3. Transition to the Farewell Discourses (13:31–38)

³¹ When Judas had gone away, Jesus said: Now is the Son of Man glorified, and God is glorified in him. ³² If God is glorified in him, God will also glorify him in himself, and he will glorify him soon. ³³ Children, I will be with you for only a short time. You will look for me and, as I said to the Jews, I am saying now to you: Where I am going, you cannot come. ³⁴ I am giving you a new commandment: Love one another! As I have loved you, so should you also love one another. ³⁵ By this will everyone know that you are my disciples: if you love one another.

³⁶ Simon Peter asked him: Lord, where are you going? Jesus answered him: Where I am going you cannot follow me now. But you will follow me later. ³⁷ Peter said to him: Lord, why cannot I follow you now? I will lay down my life for you. ³⁸ Jesus retorted: Do you want to lay down your life for me? Amen, amen, I say to you: Before the cock crows, you will deny me three times.

### I

According to multiple authors, the actual farewell discourses of Jesus begin in John 13:31.[28] After the exit of Judas, Jesus explains that the hour of which he has spoken time and again is "now" come. One could also say that it is now dawning, and so Jesus also speaks in what follows of the "little while"

---

28. So, for instance, in Weidemann, *Der Tod*; Zumstein, vol. 2.

(μικρόν). Nevertheless, three reasons seem to indicate that the farewell discourses of Jesus in the narrower sense can be allowed to begin only in John 14:1. The first reason is the relative literary coherence of John 13. Thus, between the introductory speech and the discourse of John 14 there stands the dialogue between Jesus and Peter with the announcement of the latter's denial of Jesus. On the other hand, the discourse of John 14 displays strong contacts with the so-called "third discourse" in John 16:4e–33. For these reasons, John 13:31–35 can be understood as an "overture to the farewell discourses," with the announcement of Peter's denial as the last narrative unit before the farewell discourses proper. The introduction to the farewell discourses clearly shows the handwriting of the evangelist, not only in the announcement of the imminent glorification of Jesus and the Father but also in the saying about the "short time" that Jesus will still have among his own, and in the issuing of the commandment of brotherly love.

In the scene announcing Peter's denial, only the introduction might go back wholly to the evangelist (v. 36). The two following verses (vv. 37–38) show the influence of the Synoptic tradition (cf. Mark 14:29–31 par.). Here too, however, the redactional hand of the evangelist is also to be discerned.

## II

### The "Overture" to the Farewell Discourses (13:31–35)

The opening verses of our discourse are akin to the "overture" of an opera. In it, the audience is introduced to and put in the mood for the whole opera. This happens especially through the choice of the characteristic themes and motifs which mark the opera. Thus, the whole opera echoes already in the overture. A similar procedure can be observed in John 13:31–35. In verses 31–32, Jesus speaks of his coming "glorification." This theme has come up already in the section John 12:20–36 in verses 23 and 28. In 12:23, it was linked to the title of "Son of Man." This connection is encountered in our passage no less than five times (vv. 31 and 32) with minor variations. Clearly, the evangelist has set this theme as the title for the farewell discourses. It will re-emerge in John 17 (vv. 1–5), so that one can see a kind of "inclusio" between John 13:31–32 and the prayer of Jesus in John 17. The second theme of verses 31–35 is the imminent departure of Jesus and the inability of the disciples to follow their master, at least for the moment. This theme is taken up again extensively in the speeches in John 14 and 16:4e–33. The third theme, that of the mutual love of the disciples, prepares for John 15:12–17, and so for the second discourse in John 15:1–16:4d. It is possible to see a connection between the theme of love in John 13:34–35 and in the prayer of Jesus in John 17 and to add to the theme of love that of glorification.[29]

From the simple fact of the correspondence of John 13:31, 35 and the various parts of the farewell discourses, one cannot presume the literary unity of these discourses without further consideration. If, on account of the significance of John 14:31 and other observations it seems advisable to accept a process of growth in various stages for the discourses as well as the secondary character of chs. 15–17, it cannot be excluded that John 13:34–35 too, with the commandment of mutual love, has been added to the text later. However, the reverse theory, that the text in John 13 is preparing for the later echoes is not to be dismissed out of hand.

**13:31-32** With its fivefold repetition of the same verb, the small text unity is unique, not only in the Fourth Gospel but also in the New Testament (and probably beyond). We are thus presupposing the longer text including v. 32a, although these lines are enclosed in square brackets by Nestle-Aland[28]. It obviously makes sense after the two aorists that precede it and the two futures that follow. It is precisely this transition from the aorist to the future that is striking from the linguistic point of view. On the semantic level, the connection of the "Son of Man" title with the verb of "glorifying" needs clarification. It has already been suggested previously that the evangelist was apparently linking the tradition of the "Son of Man" who, according to the Synoptics following Dan 7:13–14 had to suffer, die, and rise again, with that of the servant of Isa 52:13–53:12, especially 52:13 LXX (the servant will be lifted up and glorified).

How can we now best explain the small text unit in which the theme of the "glorification" of the Son of Man returns five times?[30] It can be conjectured that the text unit is headed by a small hymnic fragment which reads simply: "Now is the Son of Man glorified, and God is glorified in him." One could imagine the origin of this couplet in the liturgy, perhaps in a community within the ambit of John's Gospel. Similar texts are found in the Revelation of John in which the introductory νῦν ("now") can be replaced by ἄρτι (cf. Rev 12:10). In Revelation, there are various texts which,

---

29. For this connection, cf. Simoens, *La gloire d'aimer*.
30. Cf. Beutler, "Die Überleitung."

in a cosmic liturgy, sing of the glory of God and the Lamb (cf. Rev 5:12–13; 7:12). If a verse like John 13:31 was sung in John's community, then the insertion of the couplet here leads to difficulties. In fact, Jesus is standing at the beginning of his passion and has to glorify the Father right to the end of his path of suffering. For this reason, the evangelist could have added the three lines that follow: As soon as the Son has glorified the Father to the end, the Father will also glorify him "in himself," and will do it soon.[31]

**13:33** Jesus had previously announced that he was departing for a place where he could not be reached. Verse 33 refers to John 7:33–34 where Jesus said to the Jews that he was going away, and where he was going they would not be able to follow him. In its place in John 7, Jesus's saying had more the sense of an urgent warning to listen to his words and accept them in faith. In John 13, it has more the task of preparing the disciples for their new situation in which Jesus would no longer be among them. In the thinking of Zumstein,[32] the saying in v. 33 has a double dimension: christological and soteriological. Jesus must depart in order to fulfill his role, and the disciples will be linked to him in a new way—no more in a physical and visible discipleship but through the new presence of Jesus among them in the Spirit. This reality will be taken up again in verses 36–38.

**13:34–35** Jesus's new commandment to love one another appears between the announcements of his departure in verses 33 and 36–38, and for this reason it has frequently been concluded that it has been inserted into this place subsequently. The question remains: at what point in time and from which hand was this interpolation carried out?

The content of the commandment comes from the Synoptic tradition (Mark 12:28–34 par.). The origin of the commandment of brotherly love is found in Lev 19:18, only, in John, the "neighbor" is replaced with the "others" belonging to the circle of disciples. The "as" (καθώς) thus signifies more than a comparison. Jesus's love for his own is not only the example for the love that the disciples ought to give to one another but at the same time is also its source. Correspondingly, the unity of the circle of disciples should become the mark of the fact that Jesus was sent from the Father

---

31. According to Chibici-Revneanu, "Variations," the author of the verse has deliberately left open to whom the "in himself" or "in him" respectively refers, in order to level the distinction between the Father and the Son. The change in the temporal perspective is rather played down by Ensor, "Glorification." That also links up with the fact that he understands the "glorification" of Father and Son strongly from the δόξα of the earthly Jesus.

32. Cf. Zumstein, vol. 2; Zumstein, "Die Logien"; Zumstein, "Jesus' Resurrection."

(John 17:21). These verses show that the Johannine community is not fully detached from its surroundings like a sect.

Why is Jesus's commandment a "new commandment"? Certainly, it does not mean new moral teaching.[33] Rather it is to be seen in connection with the new covenant. Just as Jeremiah in Jer 31:31–34 speaks of a new Law that will be written on the hearts of the Israelites, so the command of Jesus is also of a new kind that will be made possible through Jesus's "hour." For the First Letter of John (2:7), Jesus's commandment is simultaneously new and old; for Second John (5), it is no longer new but a commandment that the faithful have heard from the beginning.

### The Announcement of Peter's Denial (13:36–38)

After John 13:35, the farewell discourses could follow on immediately. However, the evangelist adds a section that stems from the tradition but also gives the opportunity for further reflection about Jesus's departure. From the narrative point of view, we can distinguish two sayings of Peter and two replies by Jesus. Peter's first saying is a question; the second consists of a question and an assertion that will then be called into question by Jesus. He foresees totally different behavior on Peter's part from that envisaged by the latter.

**13:36** The first dialogue shifts on to Peter, the disciples' spokesman, what Jesus had said previously to the Jews (John 7:33–34) and to all the disciples (13:33): where Jesus is going, they cannot follow. Peter will do so later—with an allusion to his violent death (cf. John 21:18–19). With Zumstein, we can see in this dialogue a reflection of the evangelist on the two ways of recognizing the presence of Christ—before and after his death and resurrection. At the moment of his "hour," no one can follow Jesus in the same way as before. The only way to follow Jesus in his "hour" consists of following him in his death and resurrection.

**13:37–38** The second dialogue takes up Synoptic material to a greater extent. The interest of the narrator is now strongly biographical. Peter will not only *not* lay down his life for his Lord but he will deny him three times as early as the next morning, before the cock crows.

---

33. According to Weder, "Das neue Gebot," 195, the new departure in the new command lies in the fact that it is Jesus's command.

## Jesus Bids Farewell (13:1–17:26)

The introduction to the narrative seems to have been altered from the Markan version (Mark 14:26–28; cf. Matt 26:30–32). According to these Synoptic accounts, Jesus speaks of Peter's denial after the Last Supper on the way to the Mount of Olives. By contrast, the frame of the Last Supper is attested by Luke (22:31–34) who here seems to lie at the basis of John. In the Synoptics, Jesus speaks first of the scattering of the sheep after the shepherd has been slain (with Zech 13:7). This part of Jesus's saying is not taken up here in John and appears only later at the end of the final farewell discourse in John 16:32. Thus the scene in John 13:36–38 is more strongly focused on Peter, as happened similarly in John 6:68 and 13:6–11. Peter's readiness to die for Jesus is expressed in a Johannine formulation: instead of "die with him" (συναποθανεῖν) cf. John 11:16), it says "lay down my life" (τιθέναι ψυχήν). This expression has already been used by Jesus who is "laying down his life" for his sheep (John 10:11, 15, 17–18). In John 15, Jesus will command the disciples to be ready to "lay down their life" for their friends (John 15:13) after his example as one who has loved his own to the utmost (John 15:12–13). If the evangelist is playing on this formula in John 13:37–38, he is recalling the connection between human readiness to surrender one's life and Jesus's laying down of his life that makes this readiness possible.

### III

This passage shows Jesus in full knowledge of what is before him from the part of men but also in full consciousness of what is now happening between him and the Father. Jesus sees himself not as someone who has been frustrated but as the "Son of Man" whose glorification is dawning as soon as he glorifies the Father in his return home.

By themselves, the disciples are incapable of understanding the deeper sense of his return home. Peter is still imagining himself at the side of Jesus when the latter is on the edge of leaving the world. He has to be told that he is falling miserably short.

The disciples are left with the task of remaining together in the love of Jesus. They will have to learn to understand the departure and return of Jesus ever more deeply. The following farewell discourses will serve this purpose. They will form a textual bridge to the future generations of believers. Thus, the fellowship of the believers with one another will always belong to their fellowship with Jesus.

## 4. The First Farewell Discourse (14:1–31)

¹ Do not let your heart be distressed. Believe in God, and believe in me! ² In my Father's house, there are many mansions. If it were not so, then would I have told you: I am going to prepare a place for you? ³ If I go and prepare a place for you, I will come again and take you to myself so that where I am you may be also. ⁴ And where I am going – you know the way. ⁵ Thomas said to him: Lord, we do not know where you are going. How then can we know the way? ⁶ Jesus said to him: I am the way and the truth and the life; no one comes to the Father except through me. ⁷ If you had known me, you would know my Father also. You already know him and have seen him. ⁸ Philip said to him: Lord, shows us the Father; that is enough for us. ⁹ Jesus said to him: Have I been so long with you, Philip, and you have not known me? Whoever has seen me has seen the Father. How can you say: Show us the Father? ¹⁰ Do you not believe that I am in the Father and that the Father is in me? I do not have from myself the words which I say to you. The Father who dwells in me performs his works. ¹¹ Believe me that I am in the Father and that the Father is in me; if not, then believe for the sake of the works themselves! ¹² Amen, amen, I say to you: Whoever believes in me will also perform the works that I perform, and he will perform greater ones than these because I go to the Father. ¹³ Everything that you ask in my name I will do, so that the Father may be glorified in the Son. ¹⁴ When you ask for something in my name, I will do it.

¹⁵ If you love me, you will keep my commandments. ¹⁶ And I will pray to the Father, and he will give you another adviser, who is to remain with you for ever, ¹⁷ the Spirit of truth whom the world cannot receive because it does not see him and does not know him. But you know him because he dwells with you and will be in you. ¹⁸ I will not leave you as orphans, I am coming to you. ¹⁹ Only a little while, and the world will see me no more; but you will see me, because I live and you will live also. ²⁰ On that day, you will know: I am in my Father, you are in me and I am in you. ²¹ Whoever has my commandments and keeps them, he it is who loves me; whoever loves me, will be loved by my Father and I too will love him and reveal myself to him. ²² Judas – not Iscariot – asked him: Lord, how is it that you will reveal yourself only to us and not to the world? ²³ Jesus answered him: If anyone loves me, he will keep my word; and my Father will love him, and we shall come to him and take up our dwelling with him. ²⁴ Whoever does not love me, does not keep my words. And the word that you hear does not come from me but from the Father who sent me.

²⁵ I have said this to you while I am still with you. ²⁶ But the advocate, the Holy Spirit, whom the Father will send in my name, will teach you everything and recall everything that I have said to you. ²⁷ Peace I bequeath to you, my peace I

give you; not as the world gives am I giving it to you. Do not trouble your heart and do not despair. ²⁸ You have heard that I said: I am going away and coming back to you. If you loved me, you would rejoice that I am going to the Father; for the Father is greater than I. ²⁹ I have said this to you now before it happens so that when it happens you may believe. ³⁰ I will not say much more to you; for the ruler of the world is coming. He has no power over me, ³¹ but the world should know that I love the Father and do what the Father has commanded me. Rise. Let us be going.

*I*

The arrangement of the Johannine farewell discourse into different, successive speeches of Jesus is not self-evident. This does not require that we must be dealing here with successive compositions, but results from the observation that the farewell discourses contain pieces of speech that are more or less self-contained linguistically and conceptually that build on one another or at least follow one another. Such a piece of discourse is John 14.

The separation of John 14 from the following context turns out to be rather easy. With the "departure signal": "Rise. Let us be going" in John 14:31, Jesus concludes his words to the disciples about his imminent departure, his return, and the abiding presence of the adviser or Paraclete. In fact, no further instruction is expected. So ch. 15 follows only loosely. The question of its origin and that of the following chapters will have to be dealt with later. Formally, we can observe an inclusio, an arch from Jesus's command "Do not let your hearts be distressed" in v. 1 to "Do not trouble your heart and do not despair" in v. 27. This holds together the whole chapter.

The demarcation of the discourse from the previous context is more difficult. Not a few scholars see in John 13:31 the beginning of the body of farewell discourses and so also of the first one in John.[34] Right at the beginning the dominant theological theme that will govern Jesus's return home reverberates: his glorification of the Father and his imminent glorification by the Father (John 13:31–32). Important themes of the following farewell discourses are announced: Jesus's imminent departure (v. 33) and his command of brotherly love (vv. 34–35). On the other hand, the foretelling of Peter's denial in verses 36–38 belongs more to the narrative context of

---

34. See above for John 13:31.

John 13, and, recently, the compositional unity of this chapter has also been pointed out, with Peter as the leading figure beside Jesus throughout.[35]

So it is probably a good idea to take John 13:31–38 as a transitional section, a kind of "overture" to the farewell discourses. We have already encountered such transitional passages in John 2:1–11 and John 11–12. They seem to belong to the evangelist's literary style.

Until now, the question as to how far we have a literary unity in John 14 has not always been answered along the same lines. Thus, within the chapter, we meet different conceptions of the end time and of Jesus's return. In verses 2–3, Jesus's return is painted in apocalyptic colors; in verses 18–19 and 23 as a new coming of Jesus to the disciples within their daily life and experience. Alongside the new coming of Jesus, his new presence through the Paraclete is announced (vv. 16–17), something that is then repeated (v. 26).

In verses 2–3, Jesus speaks of his eschatological coming in apocalyptic language. Instead of ascribing this to a Jewish-Christian *Grundschrift*, it is sufficient to postulate an early Christian tradition taken up here which is then newly interpreted in the sense of the evangelist in the following verses 4–24. Today, the attempt is hardly made any longer to trace back individual words of Jesus in this section to a Gnostic-inspired source of revelation discourses. Rather, the language and thought world of the evangelist lends itself as being inspired by the Old Testament and early Judaism. This makes it possible to demonstrate different spheres of origin for the main parts of the chapter.

The first four verses of the chapter introduce its theme: the departure of Jesus and his coming again to his own. Here, the evangelist seems to go back to early Christian notions of an eschatological coming of Jesus at the end of history that have been influenced by apocalyptic. He interprets these anew in the following verses up to v. 24.

Verses 5–14 talk, first, of the departure of Jesus and how an abiding link with him will be possible. It will be given in faith. It appears that, in the whole of the first part of the chapter, the evangelist has gone back to Ps 42/43, which we have already encountered from time to time.[36] Already, the command that the disciples should not be distressed seems to stem from this psalm, and its influence will be shown in the verses up to v. 14 as well.

---

35. Cf. Aletti, "Jn 13"; Coloe, "Sources."

36. See above for John 11:33; 13:21 as well as Beutler, *Psalm 42/43*; Beutler, "Habt keine Angst," 21–50: Beutler, *Do Not Be Afraid*, 23–47, 107f.

*Jesus Bids Farewell (13:1–17:26)*

In verses 15–24, Jesus announces his coming again. It appears that the evangelist mentions three different models as to how this can be conceived: a coming again of Jesus in the Paraclete (vv. 16–17), a personal coming (vv. 18–19), and a coming along with the Father (v. 23). We shall be able to show that, here, the evangelist is going back to the language and concepts of the covenant theology of the Old Testament, as it is found in the book of Deuteronomy and in the writings of the Old Testament and early Judaism dependent on it. It is also pointed to by the theme of "love" as the abiding link between Jesus and his own.

In verses 25–31, we can make out a concluding summary for the chapter. Jesus's departure and his coming again to his own are taken up again along with the command to be without fear and the theme of love.

The section John 14:25–29 is marked by Jesus's promises for the future with the promise of the Spirit-Paraclete, again at the beginning. The theme of joy is sounded and likewise that of peace. It will be shown that, here, the evangelist is probably going back to the traditions of the Exilic and post-Exilic prophets. These exhibit an affinity with other early Christian texts that deal with the kingdom of God.

With verses 30–31, the evangelist brings his composition of the discourse to an end. Jesus cannot speak to his disciples any longer now since his last encounter with his adversary is drawing near. Faithful to the command given him by the Father, he will not shy away from it. The evangelist's formulation here shows itself to be influenced by the Synoptic tradition, although he makes it serve his own literary and theological aims.

The question of the literary genre of John 14 cannot be answered easily. The chapter is related to the revelatory discourses of Jesus in the first part of the Gospel. However, it displays special features that point to the genre of the farewell discourse. The fourth evangelist shows little common material with such farewell discourses in Graeco-Roman and Gnostic texts.[37] More evident is the influence of texts from the biblical and early Jewish tradition that belong to this genre. They have been studied by Enric Cortès, among others.[38]

According to Cortès,[39] the following main elements of the genre can be established: "1. The one who is dying (or before his assumption)

---

37. Rather, what is indicated is the relationship of the Johannine farewell discourses with the Graeco-Roman consolation literature in general or in Seneca. Cf. Parsenios, *Departure*; Holloway, "Left Behind"; Lang, "Abschiedsreden."

38. Cortès, *Los discursos*; Cf., also, Nordheim, *Die Lehre der Alten*, I.

39. Cortès, *Los discursos*, 54.

calls his family to speak with him. 2. He gives his exhortations. Among these stand out, on account of their frequency, allusions to the works of mercy, to love and to brotherly love and concord. 3. The discourse ends with some sentences about the future of the community or the End time." These elements of content also correspond to some formal ones, thus: "1. The "calling" (καλεῖν) of the children and grandchildren; 2. The "command" (ἐντέλλεσθαι) to observe the laws; 3. The address "my children" (τέκνα [μου]), especially with the foretelling of the future."[40]

Likewise, according to Cortès, the biblical and post-biblical farewell discourses betray an influence from apocalyptic with the statements about the future under the influence of the present; the element of midrash with the reinterpretation or actualization of the biblical text; and a sapiential element with the search for the meaning of one's personal existence in respect of the creation and the creator.[41] It is probably this wisdom element that leads to the address "(my) children."[42] Within John 14, it is chiefly the second and the third formal elements that are attested. The characteristic ἐντέλλεσθαι, "command," is found, in fact, only at the close of the chapter in the command of the Father to Jesus, but the "laws" or "commandments" (ἐντολαί) play an important role in the middle section of the chapter (vv. 15–24), which deals with love for Jesus and the keeping of his commandments. The commandment of mutual love among the disciples was already called a "new commandment" of Jesus in John 13:34–35. There, in the "overture" to the farewell discourses, the address "children" (τεκνία) also occurred in 13:33.

The announcement of the future marks the whole of ch. 14. Jesus foretells his imminent departure but also his coming again to his own. The disciples should draw assurance from this and not despair.

The element of advocacy can similarly belong to the genre of the farewell discourse.[43] Within John 14, we encounter it both in Jesus's promise that he will campaign on behalf of his own with the Father (vv. 13–14), as well as in the announcement of the "Paraclete," the "advocate" in verses 16–17 and 26.

Important for the exegesis of John 14 are the contacts of the farewell discourse genre with midrash. Most Jewish texts that belong to this genre

---

40. Cortès, *Los discursos*, 56–61.
41. Cortès, *Los discursos*, 62–70.
42. Cortès, *Los discursos*, 69.
43. Cortès, *Los discursos*, 372–76.

## Jesus Bids Farewell (13:1–17:26)

stem from post-biblical times. So these post-biblical texts are happy to use accounts of the departure or assumption of the great men of the Old Testament in order to embellish the farewell discourses with them.[44] These could continue to have an effect in John's Gospel too. At the same time, there is not only the haggadic midrash, which employs narrative features, but also the halakhic midrash dealing with the correct exegesis of the Torah. They may play a role in the arrangement of the central section of the chapter around the love of Jesus and the keeping of his commandments. At the beginning, Ps 42/43 seems to have been taken up and reinterpreted; at the end elements of prophetic promise from the post-Exilic prophets are encountered.

## II

### Jesus's Departure and His Coming Again (14:1–4)

The first four verses of John 14 lead into the first farewell discourse and state its most important themes: the departure of Jesus and his coming back. At the beginning, in v. 1, there is an appeal to the disciples to have courage and trust. In verses 2–3, the evangelist mentions the basis for the disciples' assurance: yes, Jesus is going away, but only to prepare a place for his own. Then he will come back, to take his own to himself. In v. 4, the theme changes: the place which Jesus is preparing for himself and his own is replaced by the way there.

**14:1** The chapter and also the small section is headed by Jesus's appeal to the disciples not to fear but to believe in God and in him. This verse offers some linguistic peculiarities. The expression "your heart" is already striking since the pronominal adjective is in the plural and its noun in the singular. It is also unusual that Jesus departs from his customary usage in John's Gospel by asking for faith not only in him but also in God. Similarly, there is a question about the meaning of "believing" in v. 1. Here, it is probably being opposed to the bewilderment and fear of the disciples unleashed by Jesus's announcement of his imminent departure. However, that would mean that πιστεύειν is deviating from normal Johannine usage.

These observations can probably be best understood with a look at the traditions employed by the evangelist. It can be conjectured that

---

44. Cortès, *Los discursos*, 298–365.

here, above all, he was going back to Ps 41:6, 12; 42:5 LXX.[45] This psalm, to which attention has already been drawn in the exegesis of John 13:21, seems to have been used several times by John in his passion narrative. The "refrain" quoted is encountered three times in the double psalm (Ps 41:6, 12; 42:5 LXX) and, each time, closes a strophe. In this refrain, the psalmist appears to be full of trust in God. While in John 13:21 the evangelist is clearly going back to Ps 41:7 LXX, on the next occasion, in John 14:1 (as Mark in Mark 14:34), he goes back to the refrain. In doing this, he only replaces ψυχή "soul" with καρδία "heart," and ἐλπίζω "hope" with πιστεύειν "believe, trust" which is the more commonly used verb in John. This would thus explain why the evangelist straightaway and only here speaks of "belief" in God. Naturally, for him, faith in Jesus is, ultimately, the concrete form of faith in God.

**14:2–3** The two verses that follow belong closely together. This is shown already in the repetition of the expression "go to prepare a place for you" (πορεύεσθαι, ἑτοιμάσαι τόπον ὑμῖν). These lexical links stand in the middle of the sentence construction. At the beginning stands the promise of the many mansions for the disciples in the house of the Father; at the end, the announcement of Jesus that he will come again and bring his own to himself in these mansions. In v. 2, the connection and the meaning of the words "if it were not so" (εἰ δὲ μή) are debated. Some, like the scholars responsible for the *Einheitsübersetzung*, see in the words "I would have told you" a statement;[46] however, with good reason, the majority of exegetes see here a question. However, in this case it remains open when Jesus is supposed to have said he was going to prepare a place for his own. In any case, it is a matter here of encouragement. The disciples have to be sure that they will not be separated from their master for good but will be where he is too.

The exegesis of both verses remains disputed. Those who deny any future-oriented eschatology to the evangelist will try to give Jesus's words a spiritual or existential meaning.[47] On the other hand, however, it is advisable to take Jesus's announcement literally and understand it in the sense of a future-oriented eschatology, more precisely, the apocalyptic adopted by the earliest strains of Christianity.[48]

---

45. Cf. Beutler, "Psalm 42/43," 96f.; Beutler, *Habt keine Angst*, 28f.; Beutler, *Do Not Be Afraid*, 25f.

46. So, more or less, Bultmann, 464, who, however, remains undecided.

47. Cf. the relevant authors in Frey, *Johanneische Eschatologie*, 3.131–53.

48. Thus Frey himself, as well as Fischer, *Die himmlischen Wohnungen*.

*Jesus Bids Farewell (13:1–17:26)*

The key text for understanding the eschatology that comes to expression in John 14:2–3 is 1 Thess 4:13–18. Here, Paul refers explicitly to the Christian tradition, speaking of a "saying of the Lord." He is concerned to console the members of the community who have lost a relative or a friend. Those who have died in the Lord and the living will share the same destiny at the return of Christ. Just as the dead will be called out of their graves one day by the Lord, so will the Lord also come and look for those who are still alive in order to take them up with him into heaven, something that is obviously being thought of in very concrete terms. Certainly, Paul has taken this notion from the Judaism of his time and from earliest Christianity, as a comparative glance at the Synoptic Gospels shows (Mark 13 par.). These apocalyptic concepts were rooted in the book of Daniel and in the Jewish apocalyptic literature. The nearest thing to 1 Thess 4:13–18 is 1 Cor 15 (esp. 51–52).

Understandably, the concept of an "apocalyptic John" is a disconcerting one. There has been no lack of suggestions, therefore, to interpret John 14:2–3 in a spiritual or existential way. Thus, our verses can be read in the light of John 14:23 where Jesus promises that he and the Father will dwell with anyone who loves and believes. However, the movement there proceeds in the opposite direction, and the subject is not the dwellings Jesus will prepare for his own in the house of his Father. The attempt of Bultmann to interpret John 14:2–3 existentially is faced with similar difficulties. According to Bultmann, the evangelist is speaking here in a mythological language that has to be interpreted.[49] The aim of the group of verses is to lead the readers to a form of communion based on faith, and to help them to live this faith in the concrete moment.

With good reason, Frey[50] contradicts such attempts to make the text more flexible and comprehensible to the modern reader. According to him, one must leave the text in its original, apocalyptic sense. Things are no better if one goes back to the post-Johannine redaction here which would then have added the statements of future eschatology to the original Gospel (as John 5:28–29). Frey is of the opinion that the evangelist deliberately placed words of Jesus with an orientation towards future-oriented eschatology alongside others characterized by a present-oriented eschatology: Jesus comes now in the "hour of faith." The parade example of such a sequence is found in the following section, John 14:5–24, after verses 2–3. As a working

49. Cf. Bultmann, 463–65.
50. See n. 48 above.

hypothesis, it can be assumed that John is the result of a long process of growth that leads from the traditional eschatology of the first Christian communities to an eschatology that sees the events expected to occur in the future taking place already in the present. From this, Frey takes as his starting point that the different eschatological models in John do not replace each other in such a way that the model referring to the present is substituted for that oriented to the future. However, one gains the impression that the two models in John do not stand alongside each other on equal terms, but that the present eschatological model can be recognized as the evangelist's preference. This will be confirmed in the further course of John 14. Here too, one can speak of a *"relecture,"* as has proved to be a helpful hypothesis in our treatment of John 14–17 in other ways.

**14:4** From the narrative point of view, this verse still belongs to the opening of the first farewell discourse. Jesus continues to speak. In this verse, the content gives notice of a transition to a new view of the future connection between Jesus and his own, and the apocalyptic language, certainly incomprehensible to educated Greek and Roman readers, is laid aside. Once again, the starting point is Jesus's "departure" or "going away," which was already mentioned in verses 13:33 and 13:36–37. Now this going away is clarified with the help of a new concept, that of the "way." This new image may be surprising here. We should make the attempt in what follows to explain it too from the tradition that has been employed. Here Ps 42/43, already referred to in v. 1, is worthy of further consideration. As the exegetes stress, this psalm is, at one and the same time, the prayer of a suffering righteous person but also the pilgrimage song of an Israelite far from the sanctuary in Jerusalem, who "longs" for this sanctuary "as pants the hart for cooling streams." In Ps 42:3 LXX, the worshiper prays the Lord that he "lead" (ὁδηγεῖν) him to his holy mountain through his light and his truth. It will be shown that these ideas are encountered in what follows.

*Jesus's Departure and the Link with Him in Faith (14:5–14)*

From the narrative angle, a new section of the text begins in v. 5. For the division of the text, however, it is not sufficient to look at the succession of speakers. Philip's contribution in v. 8 appears to possess less weight than that of Thomas in v. 5. With a glance at the arrangement of the whole chapter, we can make out in verses 1–4 the introduction of the double theme of the going away of Jesus and his coming back again. Verses 5–14 develop the theme of the going away and verses 15-24 the theme of his coming back in which different models are offered with which to understand this coming back. In the closing verses, 25-31, both themes are taken up again from a new perspective (v. 28).

The theme of Jesus's going away is introduced in v. 5 and developed in what follows from the perspective of the abiding link of the disciples with Jesus through faith. Among the verbs that describe the behavior of the disciples, "believing" (πιστεύειν) seems to possess a special significance. It appears for the first time in v. 10 and is taken up again in vv. 11 (twice) and 12. In the following section (vv. 15-24) this verb is replaced by "loving" (ἀγαπᾶν) as the expression of the abiding link of the disciples with Jesus. Thus, it can be maintained that the central part of the chapter can be arranged into vv. 5-14, "the departure of Jesus and the link with him in faith," and vv. 15-24, "the coming again of Jesus and the link with him in love."[51]

The passage is divided principally by the exchanges of speech between Jesus and the disciples. A first group of verses begins with Thomas's question, followed by Jesus's answer (vv. 5-7). Some words of Philip follow with another answer by Jesus (vv. 8-11). As scholars have noticed, verses 12-14 follow, joined on loosely by a catchword connection on the theme of faith.

**14:5-7** The new subject begins already in v. 5 with the employment of the words Jesus has already used in v. 4. The shift in focus is from where Jesus is going to the way one gets there. For Thomas, this way is a means to get where Jesus is. Jesus sees himself as this way. In v. 6, there is a nominal clause referring to Jesus that will be followed by others later (vv. 9, 10 and 11). Thus, the perspective is modified: from Jesus's works and destiny to his presence and its significance. The relationship of the three terms "way, truth, and life" has been debated since the days of Augustine. From the Johannine point of view, Jesus is the way, insofar as he proclaims the "truth," the revelation coming from God, which leads to life. The structure of v. 6 corresponds to that of other "revelatory sayings" in John (cf. the other "I am sayings" in John 6:35; 8:12; 10:7, 9, 11, 14; 11:25; 15:1). They divide up into "self-presentation," "invitation," "promise," and "threat." One of the two last elements can be missing.[52]

In what follows, the going along the "way" is described as a process of perception. Whoever knows Jesus also knows the Father and has seen

---

51. Similarly, already Bultmann, 473.
52. Cf. Schulz, *Komposition*, 86f.

him. The row of three *motifs* or images with which Jesus is identified is best understood from the third and last *motif*, which is an expression of Jesus's promise: to be the giver of life, indeed to be life itself. Thus, the "way" focuses attention on the receiver of the promise, the "truth" on Jesus who both utters and fulfills it. That Jesus not only brings the truth—here, as revelation from the Father about himself and about men—but is himself the truth places serious difficulties not only before the ancient reader but also the contemporary one. Jesus's word sounds harsh, unacceptable, in fact, in view of the necessity of interreligious dialogue, then and now. In John's Gospel, Jesus reveals himself as the bringer, indeed as the incarnation of the "truth" (despite John 18:37), especially over and against God's people Israel. It is precisely here that new attention is required for the correct understanding of the "absolute claim" of Johannine Christianity, indeed of the Johannine Jesus himself.[53] Here, it will be crucial to see the Christianity proclaimed by John's Gospel, not in opposition to Israel but as its eschatological-messianic fulfillment.

In v. 7, an eschatological theme is struck with the "vision of God." Here, a transition is occurring from the future eschatology, which expects the return of Christ at the end of time, to the present eschatology, which considers the *visio beatifica* as already taking place now in faith. In these verses, scholars are correct in finding the expression of the characteristic Johannine view of eschatology. The only question that remains open is whether the evangelist intends to replace the model of future-oriented eschatology, as it appears in verses 2–3, by that of present-oriented eschatology, or whether he is deliberately causing the two models to be juxtaposed in a complementary manner. This latter theory might be more probable and fits better with the opening verses 2–3.

The vocabulary of verses 5–14 is strongly Johannine. The most important catchword is that of the "way." Apart from here, the word occurs in John only in John 1:23 in a scriptural saying from the prophet Isaiah so it does not belong to the characteristic Johannine vocabulary. Thus, the question arises as to its possible origin in the tradition. Our attention turns once again to Ps 42/43. It has already been shown that this double psalm belongs to two different genres: the lamentation of the righteous sufferer and the pilgrim

---

53. For this, see, out of the plethora of recent literature, the Zurich dissertation by Kirchschläger, *Nur ich bin die Wahrheit*, along with his article "Ich bin der Weg"; further, the commentary by Wengst, 2:120f. This warns correctly against the consequence that Israel has no access to the Father without Jesus.

## Jesus Bids Farewell (13:1–17:26)

song as the expression of desire for the sanctuary of Jerusalem on the part of the worshiper who is staying on Hermon, far from the sanctuary. For this reason, the worshiper speaks in Ps 43:3 in the original text in this way: "Send out your light and your truth that they may lead me; let them lead me to your holy mountain and to your dwelling." To that, there corresponds, at least in part, Ps 42:3 LXX: "Send out your light and your truth; they have conducted me and led me to your holy mountain and to your tabernacles." Here, the verb for "conduct" is ὁδηγεῖν, "lead a way." The "tabernacles" here might be the "mansions" mentioned in 14:2. The double psalm 42/43 is the only one in which the "house of God" (for John: "house of my Father") and "tabernacles" are found together. The "way" theme could stem from this psalm, particularly as it is linked with the theme of "truth."

The recourse to Ps 42/43 as expression of Jesus's desire for the heavenly dwellings is facilitated by the fact that, during the Second Temple period, an eschatological understanding of the pilgrim psalms had gained currency. This is shown by the exegesis of Pss 65:5 and 46:5 in the Targum. In the (later) midrash on the Psalms, Ps 43:3 is given an eschatological exegesis with a focus on the pilgrims who will come to God's mountain in the future. Consequently, the Johannine Jesus was able to rely on such traditions when he interpreted Ps 42/43 eschatologically. The psalm, then, would have been "fulfilled" in Jesus Christ himself as the bringer of "truth and life" and as the leader of the way to the holy dwelling of God.

The observation of the element of the "vision of God," which was prepared in Ps 42/3, points in the same direction. In John 14:7–9, this vision is taken up again and newly interpreted as the vision of Christ. Thus, in Ps 42/43, one can think of Ps 42:2 where it says: "When can I come and see the countenance of God?" This question corresponds to that of the worshiper's enemies in Ps 42:3: "Where is your God now?" Jesus answers these questions.

**14:8–11** In the following verses, the theme of the "vision of God" in the "vision" of Jesus is developed further. Philip's question serves the purpose of letting Jesus's revelatory speech progress. The deeper ground for the possibility of seeing God when one sees Jesus lies in the unity of being of the Father and the Son in their mutual "indwelling." This concept of a mutual immanence has no biblical roots but is found in Hellenistic Judaism.[54] As from v. 10c ("the words"), the mutual indwelling of Father and Son is specified by speaking and acting. In v. 10c–d, the unity of Father and

---

54. Cf., for this, more explicitly, Scholtissek, *In ihm sein und bleiben*.

Son is shown in their speech; in v. 10e, there occurs a transition to the unity of Father and Son in "work." The works that Jesus performs in the power of his Father can serve as a reason for believing in him (v. 11). This unity of the "words" and "works" of Jesus is also revealed in John 15:22, 24, where a close connection of these two elements is expressed as a basis of faith.

**14:12–14** Through a catchword connection, the author develops the link between faith and works. Whoever believes in Jesus performs his works; indeed, he will perform greater works. By this is certainly not intended more spectacular works than the healing of the man born blind (John 9) or the raising of Lazarus (John 11:1–44) but the characteristic works of the emerging church. The difference lies not in the quality of the works as such but in the time in which these works are carried out: the end time will be characterized by works that will wholly transcend the past on account of the power of the Spirit, which will be bestowed on the community and will open up for them horizons unimaginable until now (cf. John 16:13).

Jesus's promise in verses 13 and 14, that he will grant them everything that they ask of him, is to be understood against the eschatological background of this promise. Here too, we can discern biblical precedents.

Certainly, in the Old Testament, there are no parallels to the infallibility of prayer in the name of Jesus. For Abraham's intercession that is able to change God's mind, one can point to Gen 18:22–33. In the New Testament, we can recall the promise of Jesus in connection with the cursing of the fig tree in Mark 11:22–24. In John, it is Jesus himself who grants the request, and it is to be made in his name. Moreover, the idea that in this way God will be glorified matches Johannine language and thought (cf. John 17:1–5).

### Jesus's Coming Again and the Link with Him in Love (14:15–24)

With v. 15, the perspective in John 14 changes. It is now no more about the imminent departure of Jesus, but his coming again. Thus, the catchword "coming" is also of structural significance. It appears that the evangelist thinks of this new coming of Jesus as a coming in the Spirit-Paraclete; as a personal coming of Jesus; and as a coming together with the Father in order to dwell with the disciples.[55]

---

55. Thus, already, Boismard, "Évolution."

From the linguistic point of view, John 14:15–24 contains two kinds of clauses. The first are conditional or participial clauses which express a link between the "love" for Jesus, the keeping of his commandments, and specific promises connected to the fulfillment of the conditions. These clauses are found in verses 15, 21, 23 and 24. These verses can be described as "frame verses."

Beside these "frame verses," there are others with a divergent construction. This is especially true of verses 16–17. In this long sentence construction we find, after a double main clause, a final clause, an apposition, a relative clause, and a causal clause. An additional causal clause occurs after the next main clause in v. 17 (ὑμεῖς γινώσκετε αὐτό). In these clauses, Jesus speaks repeatedly of his future activity (vv. 16, 18 and 19) in connection with the fulfillment of the condition in the "frame verses" (v. 21 as preparation for v. 22, cf. ff.).

The "frame verses" and the promises of Jesus have, respectively, a different tradition-historical background as will be shown in what follows.

**14:15** In the introductory "frame verse," Jesus calls on the disciples to love him and keep his commandments. It is similar to the other "frame verses" in the course of the section. In verses 15 and 21, the keeping of the commandments is the fruit and badge of love for Jesus. In verses 23 and 24, the thought is the same except that the subject is now the "word" or "words" of Jesus instead of his "commandment": whoever loves Jesus will keep his word (v. 23); whoever does not love Jesus will not keep his words. Thus, the logical sequence can also be modified.

In v. 15, as with the "frame verses" taken as a whole, the vocabulary and the thought have their roots in biblical language.[56] The word-field "love" (God) and "keep his commandments" goes back to the oldest times of Israel. The earliest example is found in the Decalogue in connection with the first commandment. God promises his loyalty and fidelity to those who love him and keep his commandments (Exod 20:6; Deut 5:10). The word-field employed here is of fundamental significance for the theology of the book of Deuteronomy, especially Deut 5:11, which Norbert Lohfink has labeled "the chief commandment."[57] Moreover, this word-field can be followed back still further. Apparently, it belongs to the language and thought of the vassal treaties of the Ancient Near East in which a king was obliged to "love" a greater king and "keep his commands" as a basis for the "cove-

---

56. Cf. Beutler, *Habt keine Angst*, 55–62; Beutler, *Do Not Be Afraid*, 52–58.
57. Lohfink, *Das Hauptgebot*.

nant" of this great king with his vassal.[58] The significance of this world of language and thought for the Johannine literature has been demonstrated by Edward Malatesta in his dissertation for the Pontifical Biblical Institute.[59] The most important texts for "loving" (God) and "keeping his commandments" in Deuteronomy are Deut 5:10 (Decalogue); 7:9; 10:12–13; 11:1, 13, 22; 19:9 and 30:6, 16, 20. The foundational text is undoubtedly Deut 6:4–6 with the commandment to love God, with the keeping of his commandments in the introduction Deut 6:1–3 as also in the text itself (6:4–6) as fidelity to the "words" of the Lord. The link with the theme of the "covenant" is shown in Deut 7:9: "Know therefore that the LORD your God is God, the faithful God who keeps covenant and steadfast love with those who love him and keep his commandments, to a thousand generations."

The word-field appearing here is taken from the Deuteronomistic school and other later texts, cf. Josh 22:5; 1 Kgs 3:3; Neh 1:5; Dan 9:4. A sapiential application appears in Sir 2:15–16. Added to this are early Jewish texts like *Jub.* 20.7; 36.5ff.; *T.Benj.* 3.1, among others. In the Qumran community, Deut 7:9 is referred directly to the community (CD 19.1f., cf. 20.21f.; 1QH 16.7, 13, 17).

In the New Testament, it can be shown that love for God is almost always expressed in Old Testament language. We see this in Mark 12:28–34 par.; Rom 8:28; 1 Cor 2:9 (participial form). For the Gospel of John, this traditional linkage appears in John 5:42, 44 and 8:41–42, two places apparently influenced by the chief commandment of Deut 6:4–6.[60]

**14:16–17** These two verses emerge directly from v. 15 and contain a promise for the disciples if they love Jesus and keep his commandments. He will ask the Father on their behalf for the Spirit-Paraclete. As already shown in a preliminary way, the two verses exhibit a complex grammatical structure. It has the appearance of an early core that has been the object of Johannine development. Such additions could be: the fact that the Paraclete is requested from the Father by Jesus (cf. v. 26); his characterization as the "Spirit of truth" (cf. John 15:26; 16:13; 1 John 5:6), and the inability of the world, by contrast with the disciples, to see and recognize this Spirit. To the traditional material might belong the description of the Spirit as "Paraclete," "advocate," as well as the mention of him as a divine "gift" that is to be given to the disciples for ever.

---

58. Cf. McCarthy, *Treaty and Covenant.*
59. Cf. Malatesta, *Interiority and Covenant.*
60. Cf. Beutler, "Das Hauptgebot."

## Jesus Bids Farewell (13:1–17:26)

This last promise has its biblical basis in Ezek 36:26–27, a text that seems to have been influenced by the tradition of the "new covenant" in Jer 31:31–34.[61] According to the text of Ezekiel, God will, in the future, "give" his Spirit to his people and enable them to live according to his commandments by virtue of the Spirit given to them.

In the New Testament, the description of the Spirit as "Paraclete" is attested only in John (John 14:16, 26; 15:26; 16:7; 1 John 2:1).[62] In ancient extra-biblical usage, the word clearly has two dimensions: the "etymological" one, in the sense of a spokesman, and the "paratactical" in the sense of an advocate with a mandate.[63] The New Testament knows Jesus as "intercessor" for his own (Rom 8:34; Heb 7:25), and the Spirit performs this function on one occasion outside John (Rom 8:27). In John 14:16, Jesus is presupposed as a "Paraclete" for his own, something 1 John 2:1 seems to be taking up again. Now, in his place, "another Paraclete" appears, even the Spirit who will now support the disciples in Jesus's place.

**14:18–21** In the following verses, Jesus announces his coming again in different ways. He is coming not only as Spirit-Paraclete but also in a personal way to his own. That he will not abandon them as orphans is something he expresses as pertaining to the future, but his coming again is in the present. The word "coming" arouses attention. In New Testament texts, it is generally used in connection with the eschatological coming of Jesus at the end of days, as the "coming" of the Son of Man (cf. Mark 13:26 par., probably with reference to Dan 7:13, where already there is mention of "seeing"). In our text, there is clearly no thought of a distant future but of the coming of Jesus to his own in historical time. This is confirmed in John 20:19, 26 where, on the evening of Easter Day and then eight days later, Jesus "comes" to the disciples (an unusual expression for Easter texts which shows that, for John, the eschatological coming of Jesus takes place at or beginning with Easter). How one is to think of this "coming" again of Jesus remains here still open at first.

First, in v. 19, there follows a further saying about the "little while" (μικρόν). This was last mentioned in John 13:33. The word points back to John 7:33 where Jesus foretold to the Jews that they would soon see him no longer. In John 13:33, Jesus had then announced the same thing to the

---

61. Cf., for what follows, Beutler, *Habt keine Angst*, 62–69; Beutler, *Do Not Be Afraid*, 58–64, 109.
62. Cf. Porsch, "παράκλητος." Now, in more detail for this word, Pastorelli, *Le Paraclet*.
63. Cf. Pastorelli, *Le Paraclet*, 102–4.

disciples and foretold that they could not come where he was going. Now, in John 14:19, a difference is introduced between the "world" that will see Jesus no more and the disciples who will see him. Thus, it must be a matter of a perception in faith. This is further indicated by the linking of the promise with "life." In the future, and that means after Easter, the disciples will "live" and share in the "life" of Jesus.

In v. 20, "on that day" does not mean, as in the apocalyptic usage, the end of time, but the moment of the new, post-Easter presence of Jesus. Then the disciples will know that he is in the Father, they in him, and he in them. The thought of the immanence of Father, Son, and disciples has no immediate biblical precedents, but there are parallels to the idea in Hellenistic Judaism.[64] It will be taken up again repeatedly in the course of the farewell discourses (John 15:1–8; 17:21, 23) and also returns in the First Letter of John (1 John 2:5; 4:12).

Verse 21 takes up v. 15 once again and links it to a new promise. Now, the formulation sounds more strongly sapiential through the employment of the generalizing participles instead of the direct address to the disciples in v. 15. The promise that whoever keeps the commandments of Jesus will be "loved" by God and Jesus is prepared for in the book of Deuteronomy where it says that God will love those who remain faithful to his covenant (Deut 7:13). This promise fits well with the formulation of its condition as it appears already in John 14:15 and is now repeated. Jesus's "revealing himself" carries the promise further and is related to the "seeing" that was already the subject (v. 19). The verb used, ἐμφανίζω, is confined to our passage in John and is also rare in the New Testament. Matthew 27:53 uses it for the "appearing" of the risen dead from their graves at the death of Jesus, and so in an apocalyptic context that here in John appears to be modified again.

**14:22–24** From the question of Judas (not Iscariot) it emerges that Jesus's "revealing himself" is his being seen, a thing that in v. 19 was denied to the world. Only now it appears as the initiative of Jesus who shows himself. Why does he show himself only to the disciples and not to the world?

Jesus's answer in v. 23 begins with the assertion formula that invariably lends Jesus's words a special weight in John. Jesus links his coming back to his own and thus also his becoming visible again with love for him and the keeping of his word. His word appears to be identified with his "commandments." So once again it is a question of faithfulness to the

---

64. Cf. Scholtissek, *In ihm sein und bleiben*.

covenant. As already in v. 21, the love of the Father is promised to the one who loves Jesus and keeps his word. The text goes further, however. Jesus and the Father will come and take up their abode with the disciple. The thought is both new and yet goes back to an earlier announcement. In John 14:2–3, in fact, Jesus had promised that he would go away and prepare a dwelling for his own with God. What was formulated there in apocalyptic language now becomes a promise translated into the language and thought world of the evangelist and into the present of the believers. Now, they no longer obtain a dwelling with God in the heavenly tabernacles; it is God who pitches his tent with them (John 1:14 echoes here).

Here we have the presentation of the third model in which the evangelist envisages Jesus's coming again. The three models of coming again are: in the Spirit (John 14:16–17); as a personal coming again of Jesus (vv. 18–21); and as a coming of Jesus together with the Father (vv. 22–24).

In v. 24, Jesus's statement is reformulated in a negative way: whoever does not love Jesus does not keep his words. At the same time, a reason is offered why the one experiences the indwelling of Jesus and the Father, and the other does not: it is a matter of the accepting of the word of God that Jesus has imparted. It is decisive for the fate of men.

For this third way of describing the return of Jesus, reference can also be made to a preparation in the Old Testament.[65] The text edition of Nestle-Aland[28] gives here a reference to Ezek 37:27. In this passage, God announces through the prophet that he will one day take up residence among his people. The context is about the new covenant, as emerges from the mention of the "covenant of peace" in v. 26 as well as the use of the "covenant formula" in v. 27: "I will be their God, and they will be my people." Pertinent related texts are Ezek 43:7, 9; Lev 26:11; 1 Kgs 6:11–13.

The theme of "dwelling" points back once more to the first part of the chapter. God's "dwellings" in the temple have already been encountered in Ps 42/43 (43:3!). The evangelist has only replaced the Septuagint expression σχηνώματα "tabernacles" with the term more common to him, μοναί "mansions," since it fits the theology of the "dwelling" of Christ and in Christ better. The new interpretation of the apocalyptic theme of the divine "dwellings" would certainly have found a good reception with the Graeco-Roman educated readers of John's Gospel and also appears more comprehensible to contemporary readers.

Looking back, the influence of the covenant theology of the Old

---

65. Cf. Beutler, *Habt keine Angst*, 72–77; Beutler, *Do Not Be Afraid*, 67–70, 109.

Testament is revealed throughout John 14, which describes the coming back of Jesus. Both the conditions for Jesus's promises (love for him and keeping his commandments) as well as the promises themselves show the influence of covenant thought. Faithfulness to the covenant makes possible the experience of the love of God. This is revealed especially in the fulfillment of the promises of the "new covenant," a theme adopted since Jer 31:31 and spoken of also by Ezekiel. It is precisely according to the latter that God will "give" his people his Spirit (Ezek 36:26) and will dwell among them (Ezek 37:27). Against this background, the chain of thought in John 14:15–24 turns out to be quite coherent.

### The Close of the First Farewell Discourse (14:25–31)

With John 14:25–31, the first farewell discourse comes to a close. Some authors would like to push the second saying about the Paraclete in vv. 25–26 back into the previous context.[66] Others see it as a small text unit on its own.[67] It is advisable, however, to consider the two verses as the beginning of the last section in John 14.[68] This is signified formally by the introductory phrase "I have said this to you" in v. 25. As far as content is concerned, it will turn out that the promises of the Spirit and of peace and joy belong together both thematically and from the point of view of tradition history. In this way we can link vv. 25–26 to the following context.

Within this section, verses 25–29 and 30–31 belong together. The "I have said this to you" in v. 25 is matched by the "I have said this to you now" in v. 29. In both cases, the evangelist uses the perfect, and, in fact, only in these two places in Jesus's speech in John 14 (ταῦτα λελάληκα, νῦν εἴρηκα). Thus, the shaping of this group of verses is also shown linguistically. Here, Jesus is bringing his discourse to the disciples to its preliminary conclusion. In the last two verses (30–31), Jesus foretells what awaits him and that from now on he will not have (much) more to say to the disciples (οὐκέτι πολλὰ λαλήσω μεθ' ὑμῶν) since the ruler of the world is coming. However, the world should know that he enters into his passion in obedi-

---

66. Cf. Schnackenburg; Becker, vol. 2; Migliasso, *La presenza*; Scholtissek, "Relecture," 13f.

67. Cf. Schulz; Blank.

68. Cf., for this and the following, Beutler, *Habt keine Angst*, 87–104; Beutler, *Do Not Be Afraid*, 79–93, 109.

## Jesus Bids Farewell (13:1–17:26)

ence to the Father. Thus, he commands the disciples to get up and follow him to the scene of his arrest.

The first five verses of the passage (vv. 25–29) have a summary character. Here, themes from the previous verses are taken up again: the promise of the Spirit from v. 16–17 in v. 26; the theme of fear from v. 1 in v. 27; the themes of the departure and the coming back of Jesus from verses 2–3, 5–14, and 15–24 in v. 28; the themes of love (from verses 15, 21, 23–24, in v. 28) and of faith (from verses 1 and 10–12 in v. 29). There are also new themes, however, like that of joy (v. 28) or peace (v. 27). A glance at tradition history will show that the themes of peace, joy, and the Holy Spirit are already linked in the biblical tradition. In verses 30–31, traditional elements from the Synoptics show through.

**14:25–26** In their content, the first two verses of the section hang together. Once again, Jesus makes known his imminent separation from them, but he will not leave his own alone, even if he is not going to speak to them any more. The Father will send the Holy Spirit, the advocate, who will teach the disciples everything and recall for them everything that Jesus has said. By contrast with v. 16, the Spirit is no longer called here "another advocate." Thus, it is now taking the place of Jesus fully and adopting his role. The content of the Spirit's task, which remains open in the first saying, is now described. It will be the disciples' teacher, not independently or as the bringer of new revelations, but through the fact that it will recall the words of Jesus for the disciples.

**14:27–29** The promise of the Holy Spirit in verses 25–26 is addressed more firmly to the rational sensibilities of the disciples. In verses 27–29, Jesus appears to be more concerned with the inner composure of the disciples, with their joy and their peace. The peace of v. 27 is contrasted with the "trouble" in the same verse. It is seen in a dualistic way here, as peace that is not of this world. As in verses 1–3, the reason why the disciples must not be troubled lies in the fact that after his departure he will come back to them. He himself is setting off now for the goal of his life: the Father who is greater than him and whom he loves (cf. v. 31). If, for their part, the disciples love him, they will be filled with joy for him.

Thus, Old Testament–Jewish precedents can be demonstrated for Jesus's departure and the disciples' abiding link with him in faith. Similarly, these precedents exist for his return and the disciples' abiding link with him in love. The same is true for the section John 14:25–29. Here, we can recognize eschatological promises by Jesus that have their roots in the faith of Israel. The starting point for these observations is the fact that the concepts of "peace" and "joy" occur rather seldom in John's Gospel. The theme of "peace" is encountered again only in John 16:33 and then in John 20:19, 21, 26. In John 16, as in John 20:19–23, we encounter the expression within a word-field that is already found in John 14:25–29. The same observations can be made for the theme of "joy." We find it again in ch. 16, in verses 20–22, and in John 20:20. These observations already permit us to construct a traditional-historical hypothesis. This thesis assumes that in these texts John is dependent on a biblical tradition about the kingdom of God. The key text for this hypothesis is Rom 14:17. Paul rarely speaks of the reign or kingdom of God, and, when he does, then it is with reference to the biblical and Jewish or early Christian tradition. In Rom 14, Paul is debating with Christians for whom the rules about eating and drinking are of crucial importance. Paul's counter-argument is this: "The kingdom of God is not eating and drinking; it is righteousness, peace and joy in the Holy Spirit."

This verse, which has received scant attention in exegetical research, is of considerable interest, for it offers the only definition of the "kingdom of God" in the entire Bible. It can be shown that all four elements named by Paul occur in the passage John 16:4e–33. Only in this chapter, John too speaks of righteousness (16:8–10), something that is scarcely to be explained by internal exegesis of the text. In John 14:25–29 and 20:19–23, we find all the elements mentioned by Paul except for righteousness. We can speak here of the eschatological gifts of Jesus—promised in John 14:25–29 (as well as 16:4e–33) and bestowed in John 20:19–23 on Easter Day.

The biblical background to the gift of the Holy Spirit has already been demonstrated above in the discussion of vv. 16–17. The key text is Ezek 36:26–27, which contains an expression of the theology of the new covenant. The themes of righteousness, peace, and joy go back, above all, to the prophetic traditions of Israel for the eschatological future. A key text is quoted by Jesus in his so-called inaugural sermon in the synagogue at Nazareth: Isa 61:1–2, taken up in Luke 4:18–19. Filled with the Holy Spirit, Jesus announces to the remnant of Israel a future messianic kingdom with the liberation of the oppressed and the proclamation of a year of jubilee. The full text of Isaiah in Isa 61:1–11 speaks expressly of righteousness (vv. 3, 8, 10–11) but also of the joy the Messiah will bring (vv. 1, 3, 7, 10) and of the relationship with the neighboring peoples that will be regulated peacefully (vv. 5–7). An additional messianic text is Isa 11:1–10. These messianic texts have their roots in the royal ideology of the Ancient Near East that sees in the king the bringer of peace and justice for the joy of his people. This belief

## Jesus Bids Farewell (13:1–17:26)

comes into the open, above all, at the enthronement feast of the Ancient Near East ruler (as texts from Egypt and Mesopotamia show), with an echo in the Enthronement Psalms (93–100) of the Old Testament.[69]

**14:30–31** The previous subsection was shaped by the "I have said this to you" in v. 25 and the "I have said this to you" of v. 29. This is followed now in v. 30 by: "I will not say much more to you." The expression can scarcely be stretched so that these few remaining words of Jesus would include the following three chapters of farewell discourses and the prayer of Jesus.[70] Jesus's time is limited, for the adversary is near—for John, this is not Judas but the enemy par excellence, the "ruler of the world." Jesus knows that he is near, but he also knows that he is superior to him, not just in knowledge but in his inner strength. In the love for God to which he has urged his disciples, he himself enters into his passion and summons the disciples to follow him.

It is generally accepted that the last two verses of the chapter show the influence of the Synoptic tradition. In Mark, Jesus announces the arrival of the betrayer at the end of the Gethsemane scene (Mark 14:41–42 par. Matt 26:45–46); here, Jesus speaks of the closeness of the Evil One himself and commands the disciples: "Rise. Let us be going" (ἐγείρεσθε, ἄγωμεν ἐντεῦθεν). For John, the real adversary is not human but the Evil One in person who can be defeated in the strength of the love of God. This is precisely what Jesus will do for the world.

Scholars are divided about the significance of Jesus's saying in v. 31: "Rise. Let us be going."[71] This command of Jesus finds its natural continuation in John 18:1: "After these words, Jesus went out with his disciples, over the brook Kidron." Since ancient times, then, the majority of authors understand Jesus's command in John 14:31 literally as an invitation to the disciples to go with him on his way to the passion. This is already the view of Augustine,[72] followed later by Thomas Aquinas.[73] More recent exegetes follow this interpretation, especially in Anglo-Saxon scholarship.[74] In

---

69. Cf Beutler, *Habt keine Angst*, 103f.; Beutler, *Do Not Be Afraid*, 92f.

70. This suggestion is found in Schnelle, 263, with reference to Mark 14:43 "while he was still speaking" (καὶ ἔτι αὐτοῦ λαλοῦντος) at the scene of the arrest, something that presupposes a continuation from the speech of Jesus and that could have influenced John.

71. Cf., for what follows, Beutler, "Steht auf."

72. Augustine, *Tractatus*, 222; *Vorträge über das Evangelium des Heiligen Johannes*, III, 904/116.

73. Thomas Aquinas, *S. Th.* III, q. 47, a. 2, ad 1.

74. Cf. the commentaries of Brown and Barrett.

German-speaking research too, a literal understanding of Jesus's command is favored. This then leads, on the one hand, to transpositional hypotheses that relocate Jesus's saying to the end of a long discourse, or to the theory of a secondary layer of farewell discourses to which chs. 15–17 are to be assigned.[75] A modification of this suggestion is to see chs. 15–17 as a "*relecture*" of the first farewell discourse in John 14, a "*relecture*" which, for its part, perhaps grew up in stages. This model is plausible and will be taken as a foundation in the present commentary.

Since the commentary of E. C. Hoskyns in 1941, it has been popular to give a spiritual interpretation to Jesus's command: "Rise. Let us be going." According to this, Jesus's command would be about raising oneself to higher things such as those that will be expressed as the farewell discourses progress. Here, scholars generally call for support on Cyril of Alexandria in his commentary on John. However, this view does not stand up to examination. Cyril mentions two interpretations of Jesus's words,[76] one literal, the other figurative. For him, the literal stands in first place and implies quite simply that the disciples should now get up and follow Jesus to his passion. Cyril continues: "Moreover, I would interpret this place in yet another way with reference to ourselves. From the love of things, we should will to fulfill what pleases God, and, beyond that, reorient ourselves from slavery to the dignity of the adoption as children, from the earth to the heavenly city, from sins to righteousness through faith in Christ, from human shamelessness to holiness through the Spirit." Quite clearly, Cyril here is representing the literary exegesis of Jesus's words in first place, and the spiritual, which is strongly stamped with a homiletic character, only in second place. A similar spiritual interpretation is represented in a text ascribed to Epiphanius of Salamis[77] that gives a Platonic exegesis of Jesus's words: "Rise up, then, let us depart from here, from death to life, from perishability to imperishability, from the darkness to light etc." The liturgical occasion is Holy Saturday. The believers are to rise with their Lord to a new life. John 14:31 is being quoted here simply as the opportunity to introduce believers into the mystery of Easter.

If recent authors call on Cyril for the spiritual exegesis of John 14:31, then they would do well to take his full text into account with its clear starting point in the literal understanding of the text. A deeper meaning for Je-

---

75. See the introduction to John 13:1–17:26.
76. *In Joannis Evangelium*, 531ff. (edition of Pusey).
77. "In divini corporis sepulturam . . .": PG 43.439–64 (esp. 464).

sus's words within the frame of the present text of John 13–17 is not thereby excluded. If one takes the model of "*relecture*" as a basis, then chs. 15–17 could indeed open up a new perspective on John 14. More strongly than in John 14, they allow the post-Easter Jesus to speak. One can see in these discourses a movement from the question of the departure and return of Jesus to the question of the existence of the circle of disciples after Easter and its being threatened by persecution from without and through possible schism from within. If Jesus's command is read from this perspective, then one may also see in it an invitation to re-examining his message in each new situation.

## III

It is Christ who stands at the center of the first farewell discourse. He will leave his own, but he will come back to them. Precisely because the following farewell discourses will have a strong focus on the life and fate of the disciples, the anchoring of the ecclesiology in Christology is of fundamental significance.

John is not diffident about exploring new paths for the future expectation of the Christian community. He starts out from the very traditional concepts of a future return of Christ to take his believers home. He does not withdraw this but develops it into the thought that the disciples, by abiding in faith and love, remain linked to Jesus. In this way, they will already experience the awaited, eschatological vision of God. In looking at him in faith, they have already seen God.

Again and again, the evangelist takes up Israel's expectations of salvation. For the departure of Jesus and the abiding link with him in faith, he can go back already to the book of Psalms (Ps 42/43). What follows is strongly influenced by covenant theology. If the disciples love Jesus and keep his commandments, they will experience the promises of the new covenant. God will love them; he and Jesus will take up their abode with them; the eschatological Spirit will be bestowed on them and join them together permanently as his people.

In the concluding passage, the promises to God's people take on very concrete features. The promises for the coming kingdom of God ring out: peace and joy in the Holy Spirit. It is precisely here that the evangelist establishes a link to very ancient concepts about the king who brings righteousness and peace to his people and unleashes joy. It remains remarkable that the Gospel is probably the latest to be written and is readily placed close to gnosis and mystery, is also the Gospel that exhibits the most ancient roots, and points to the kingdom of God, righteousness, and peace in the power of the Spirit for the joy of the people of God who are in the midst of this world.

## 5. The Second Farewell Discourse (15:1–16:4d)

15 ¹ I am the true vine, and my Father is the vine grower. ² Every branch in me that produces no fruit he cuts away, and every branch that produces fruit he prunes so that it produces more fruit. ³ You are already clean because of the word I have spoken to you. ⁴ Abide in me, as I abide in you. Just as the branch cannot produce fruit on its own but only if it remains on the vine, so you too, unless you abide in me. ⁵ I am the vine, you are the branches. Whoever abides in me and I abide in him, he produces much fruit; for apart from me you can do nothing. ⁶ Whoever does not abide in me is thrown away like the branches and withers. The branches are gathered, thrown into the fire and burned. ⁷ If you abide in me and my words abide in you, then ask for anything that you want: you will receive it. ⁸ My Father will be glorified if you produce much fruit and become my disciples.

⁹ As my Father has loved me, even so have I loved you. Abide in my love! ¹⁰ If you keep my commandments, you will abide in my love, just as I have kept my Father's commandments and abide in his love. ¹¹ These things have I said to you so that my joy may be in you and so that your joy may be complete. ¹² This is my commandment: that you love one another as I have loved you. ¹³ There is no greater love than when a man lays down his life for his friends. ¹⁴ You are my friends if you do what I command you. ¹⁵ I am no longer calling you servants; for the servant does not know what his master is doing. Rather, I have called you friends because I have made known to you everything that I have heard from my Father. ¹⁶ You have not chosen me, but I have chosen you and appointed that you go out and produce fruit, and that your fruit remain. Then your Father will give you everything that you ask in my name. ¹⁷ This is what I command you, that you love one another.

¹⁸ If the world hates you, then know that it hated me before you. ¹⁹ If you belonged to the world, the world would love you as its own. However, because you do not belong to the world, the world hates you. ²⁰ Remember the word that I said to you: the servant is not greater than his master. If they persecuted me, they will also persecute you; if they kept my word, they will also keep your word. ²¹ But they will do all this to you for my name's sake; for they do not know the one

who sent me. ²² If I had not come and spoken to them, they would be without sin; but now they have no excuse for their sin. ²³ Whoever hates me, hates my Father also. ²⁴ If I had not performed among them the works which no other has performed, they would be without sin. Now they have seen the works, and yet they have hated me and my Father. ²⁵ But the word has to be fulfilled which is written in their Law: They hated me without a cause. ²⁶ But when the advocate comes whom I shall send from the Father, the Spirit of truth who proceeds from the Father, then he will bear witness to me. ²⁷ And you also will bear witness because you have been with me from the beginning. 16 ¹ I have told you this so that you do not take offense. ² They will throw you out of the synagogues, indeed the hour is coming in which everyone who kills you will think that he is performing a holy duty. ³ They will do this because they have known neither my Father nor me. ⁴ But I have told you this so that when the hour comes you will remember that I told you of it.

I

According to the view promoted in this commentary, the first farewell discourse in John 14 would find its natural continuation in John 18. Chapters 15–17 would thus appear as the completion of a text that was originally shorter, something that probably results from a long process of growth.

In the 1980s, the predominant proposals dealt with the different living conditions of the Johannine community(ies) that would have led to different passages in the farewell discourses. In his commentary, Becker sees five farewell discourses: John 13:31–14:31; 15:1–17; 15:18–16:15; 16:16–33; 17.[78] In the original and first discourse, the imminent farewell of Jesus is still standing in the foreground. In John 15:1–17, the community that has now been left on its own must learn to carry on, living in connection with Christ and in mutual love for one another. John 15:18–16:15 mirrors a situation of persecution for which the community hears words of comfort and encouragement; it is for them that the advocate will be sent and the world will be judged. The discourse in John 16:16–33 takes up the themes of the first and speaks of Jesus's return to the Father and of his coming back again to the disciples. Other authors divide the text similarly. Mostly, the section John 15:1–16:33 is divided into John 15:1–16:4d and 16:4e–33, with a sub-

78. Becker, vol. 2.

division into John 15:1–17 and 15:18–16:4d. This is how, in his dissertation,[79] Segovia divides John 15–16, deviating from Becker for John 16:4e–33. With Becker, Segovia accepts that the texts about the mutual love of the disciples (John 13:34–35; 15:12–17) presuppose the same living conditions as the First Letter of John: a community whose unity is threatened on account of ethical and christological disputes. By contrast with Becker, Segovia does not see this situation reflected in John 15:18–16:4d. According to him, this section rather preceded the conflict within the Johannine community.

Painter reckons with three discourses following on from John 14. At the time of the first discourse (John 15:1–16:4d), the community sees itself already thrown out of the synagogue, and, in fact, on account of the *birkat-ha-minim*, a measure taken by the Synod of Jamnia (c. 85 CE) to exclude heretics, regards itself as threatened.[80] Thus, the themes of the remaining in Christ and the loving connection with one another, on the one hand, match the experience of the hatred of the "world," concretely of the "Jews," on the other. At the time when John 16:4e–33 was written, this experience already belonged to the past, and the community shows itself to be heavily burdened by the absence of Christ, in grief and fear. Thus, the third discourse is an attempt to encourage and console this community through the renewed promises of the Spirit-Paraclete.

Today, decades after this phase of research, such attempts at reconstructing living conditions of the community on the basis of sections of the farewell discourse that follow one another have retreated into the background. It has become clearer that the exegete's task is to interpret the texts rather than to reconstruct historical circumstances. Thus, the historical paradigm has been replaced by the literary one.

In doing this, however, we should not lose sight of the purpose of the individual section. Indeed, one of the dimensions of the literary analysis of texts consists precisely in working out the narrative strategy of the text (in the United States through "reader response criticism," in continental Europe as "*Textpragmatik*"). From this perspective, different sections of the text can be distinguished in John 15–17, more or less along the lines of the proposals of Painter and Segovia. When the latter in his more recent monograph[81] arrives at a purely synchronic reading of the farewell discourses, he refrains from the possibilities afforded by his previous approach.

---

79. Segovia, *Love Relationships*.
80. Painter, "Farewell Discourses."
81. Segovia, *Farewell*.

More recently, the model of "*relecture*" has also been suggested for the relationship of the later sections of the farewell discourses to the earlier ones.[82] Jesus's earlier statements would then have been gradually actualized for the community's new situations. Here, however, the interest of the exegete would lie in the understanding of the text and not in the reconstruction of the living conditions of the community as has been the case in the socio-historical schemes since the 1980s.

A first subdividing of John 15:1–16:4d emerges already from the semantics of the text. A first subsection about the unity of the disciples (as branches on the true vine) and their "love" for one another in John 15:1–17 is matched in John 15:18–16:4d by "hatred of the world." Here, two basic concepts are being set over against each other. In the first part of the text, therefore, it is possible to distinguish, once again, the *Bildrede* or extended metaphor of the true vine in verses 1–8 from the words about the brotherhood of the disciples in love following the example of Jesus in verses 9–17. In the latter section, we can, again, separate from each other verses 9–11 (with a concluding formula) and 12–17 (bound together through an inclusio).

The section John 15:18–16:4d stands apart from the previous context on account of the catchword "hate," which is encountered for the first time in v. 18. The theme "hatred of the world" defines the section up to v. 24. In the occurrence of this catchword at the beginning in v. 18 (twice) and at the end in verses 23 and 24, it is possible to make out a linguistic and theological "inclusio" (framing) of this group of verses. The theme of "witness" in verses 26–27 is bound up with that of "hate," insofar as the disciples will experience the hatred of the world, above all in forensic situations and, here, the Spirit-Paraclete will support them. In verses 16:1–4d, there is a concrete example of the coming persecution. In this section again, we come across an inclusio with the formulam ταῦτα λελάληκα ὑμῖν ἵνα, which is employed in verses 1 and 4a. Thus, it appears to be justified to see in verses 1–4d a small subunit that is linked to the previous group of verses through the theme of hate and persecution.

With the connection of John 16:4d to 16:4e, a transition to a new subject is not apparent at first glance. The "I did not tell you this at the beginning" (ταῦτα δὲ ὑμῖν ἐξ ἀρχῆς οὐκ εἶπον) in 16:4e takes up the "I have told you this" (ταῦτα λελάληκα ὑμῖν) in 16:4a. However, from v. 5 on, the text leaves the themes of John 15:1–16:4d and returns to the themes of

---

82. Cf. Dettwiler, *Gegenwart*; Zumstein, *L'évangile*, vol 2.

John 14. Once again, the imminent departure of Jesus (ὑπάγω) becomes the main theme. With it, further themes from John 14 are taken up again, especially a new meeting between Jesus and the disciples (16:16), then the infallibility of prayer (16:23-24, 26) and, finally, faith (16:30). Above all, John 16:4e-33 contains again the "eschatological" themes that we encountered in John 14:25-28: the gift of the Holy Ghost (16:7-15) and the gift of joy (16:20-22) and peace (16:33). Added to this theme—as already in Rom 14:17—is that of righteousness (16:8-10). Because of this change of theme and perspective as well as the literary relationship, the section John 16:4e-33 will be considered here as a third farewell discourse which appears as a "*relecture*" of the first farewell discourse in John 14.

## II

### Jesus the True Vine (15:1-8)

This passage is characterized by the image of the "vine" and the verb of "abiding" or "remaining." The verb forms are found in the third person or in the second person plural; corresponding to them is the first person singular on the part of Jesus as speaker. Looked at as a whole, the text reveals a movement: from the description of a state of affairs (Jesus as vine, the Father as vine grower, the branches) to a dynamic process with the producing of fruit and pruning with the object of producing more fruit or even with the cutting off of branches that do not produce or promise any fruit.

To what genre can this passage be assigned?[83] In John 15:1-8, Jesus speaks figuratively. He compares himself with a vine, the Father with a vine grower, and the disciples with branches. Thus, scholars ask what kind of metaphorical speech it is that we are dealing with here. On the one hand, we do not have a parable or similitude typical of those ascribed to Jesus in the Synoptic Gospels. These texts make comparisons of the reality proclaimed by Jesus with an everyday experience or an individual case. Generally, they have only one point of comparison (like the Jewish *mashal*). On the other hand, one cannot assign John 15:1-8 to the allegory, for, in this genre, the figurative world is set over against the real world, detail by detail. Characteristic of John 15:1-8 is the interpenetration of the levels

---

83. From here to the exegesis of v. 8, extensive use is being made of Beutler, "5. Sonntag in der Osterzeit (B): Joh 15,1-8."

*Jesus Bids Farewell (13:1–17:26)*

of image and reality. Again and again, the speaker changes from one to the other. Such a procedure was found already in Jesus's discourse about the Good Shepherd in John 10:1–18. Since Kiefer[84] and Schnackenburg,[85] the best we can do here is to talk of a *"Bildrede"* or extended metaphor, something that is precisely characterized by the interpenetration of the levels of image and reality and can be assigned neither to a similitude or parable nor yet to an allegory. According to Scholtissek,[86] John 15:1–8 is a *"relecture"* of the *Bildrede* of John 10:1–18 in light of the focus on the disciples' link with Jesus.

How are we to explain the world of imagery in John 15:1–8? The suggestion of Bultmann[87] and Schweizer[88] to account for the metaphor of the vine with Gnostic and Mandaean parallels is today regarded as unsuccessful.[89] Instead of this, there has been general acceptance for the thesis of Rainer Borig that behind the vine metaphor stand Old Testament and Jewish precedents.[90] The prophets of Israel know the *motif* of the vineyard or vine for an Israel that is not producing fruit. The well-known parable of the vineyard in Isa 5:1–7 may be one of the oldest texts of this genre. Here already, alongside the vineyard (in v. 2), there is mention of the vine. This also belongs to the imagery of Isa 27:2–4; Jer 2:21; 6:9; Ezek 15:1–8; 17:1–10; 19:10–14; Hos 10:1 and Ps 80:8–19. Only Isa 27:2–4 speaks of the Lord's vine in a positive manner, within the frame of the later Isaiah apocalypse. The motif of the vine as a symbol for Israel is taken up by texts of the intertestamental period such as LAB 12:8; 18:10f. and *4 Ezra* 5:23. In the New Testament, cf. Mark 12:1–9 par. Matt 21:33–41; Luke 20:9–16. Since Ezekiel, one can also observe a tendency to link the vine with individual people. This is especially the case in Ezek 17:1–10 where the vine is identified with King Zedekiah. Then, in Sir 24:17, Wisdom is compared to a vine that puts out beautiful shoots and produces much fruit. We are close here to John 15:1–8.

It is interesting to look at the texts relating to John 15:1–8(17) in the rest of John's Gospel. Already in his commentary on John,[91] Bultmann

---

84. Kiefer, *Hirtenrede*.
85. Schnackenburg, 3.109.
86. Scholtissek, *In ihm sein*, 278.
87. Bultmann, 407.
88. Schweizer, *Ego eimi*, 39–41.
89. Cf. Dettwiler, *Gegenwart*, 87f.
90. Borig, *Der wahre Weinstock*.
91. Bultmann, 406.

was struck with the similarity of John 13:1-17 and 13:34-35, on the one hand, and John 15:1-17, on the other. The idea has been taken up again recently by Dettwiler who sees the text of John 15 as a *"relecture"* of that of John 13.[92] John 13 is headed by a symbolic action of Jesus to which the image of the true vine in John 15 corresponds. In John 13:6-10, it is followed by a first interpretation of the image which emphasizes its significance for the relationship between Jesus and the disciples. It is matched by the unfolding of the image of John 15:1-2 in 15:3-8. John 13 then concludes (in vv. 12-17 and 13:34-35) with the interpretation of the symbolic action for the relationship of the disciples among themselves, something to which the command of love in John 15:9-17 corresponds. This suggestion is appealing and to be retained. K. Haldimann sees as a text relating to John 15:1-17 both John 13:1-17 as well as the first farewell discourse, John 13:31-14:31.[93] More broadly conceived is the study of Christina Hoegen-Rohls.[94]

It is not easy to figure out the construction of the small text unit and so the proposals for the structure of our text differ. What leaps to the eye is the inclusio through the mention of "Father" in v. 1 and v. 8. At the same time, it is advisable to treat vv. 1-2 as belonging together. In vv. 3-4 and in v. 7, the metaphorical level is sometimes abandoned and reference made to the word of Jesus by virtue of which the disciples are linked with Jesus like the branches with the vine. In both parts of the text, reference is made to "abiding" in Jesus and his word. In the middle stand vv. 5-6. At the beginning, they take up the "I am saying" from v. 1 and develop it in a way corresponding to the genre of such "I am sayings" (which has been investigated, following Schweizer,[95] by Schulz[96]) in a twofold sense: through promise (v. 5b-c) and threat (v. 6). The only thing missing is the "invitation" that is otherwise typical of the genre. Thus, one could speak of a concentric structure which is built around the "I am saying" in vv. 5-6.

**15:1-2** The passage begins with a metaphor. By contrast with the parable, the similitude, or the allegory, our text does not have an initial metaphor that is then interpreted. Rather, the image and the interpretation are intertwined from the beginning (see, above, for the "genre"). The text begins with a characteristic feature of the Fourth Gospel; an "I am saying" with which Jesus describes himself in his salvific significance for believers

---

92. Dettwiler, *Gegenwart*, 60-110.
93. Haldimann, *Rekonstruktion*, 405.
94. Hoegen-Rohls, *Der nachösterliche Johannes*.
95. Schweizer, *Ego eimi*, 33, for the Johannine form of the "I am" sayings.
96. Schulz, *Komposition und Herkunft*, 86f.

## Jesus Bids Farewell (13:1–17:26)

(cf. John 6:35, 48, 51; 8:12; 9:5; 10:7, 9, 11, 14; 11:25; 14:6; further, 12:46). However, there is a difference that has been highlighted by Borig,[97] among others. While the "I am sayings" in John 6–14 employ images that describe a single reality (bread, light, gate, shepherd, the resurrection and the life, the way, the truth, and the life), John 15:1–8 makes use of an image that is primarily collective. This might fit in with the more strongly ecclesiological orientation of John 15–16 against the more heavily christological emphasis in the previous chapter. Thus, in John 15:1–8, Jesus applies to himself an image that first stood in the prophetic tradition of Israel. In a certain way, he incorporates the people of God in his own person and invites all people to incorporate themselves in him.

If Jesus describes himself as the "true" vine, then he is defining himself against other possibilities that could raise the claim to bring forth good fruit. In the same way, Jesus had already announced to his hearers in John 6:32 the true bread from heaven, just as the prologue had earlier spoken of the "true" light (John 1:9) that came into the world with Jesus. Some scholars see in this description a reference to the "truth" as paraphrase for the revelation brought by Jesus. The development of the vine image goes beyond the Old Testament examples. God the "Father" is described as the vine grower and his work on the vine is described in detail: he "prunes" the good branches and "throws away" those branches that do not produce fruit. The verbs employed are not typical of viticulture and are probably in keeping with the nonmetaphorical level of discourse (cf. v. 3). What is being thought of is the pruning of the vine in the spring with the cutting back of branches and the cutting away of sprouts that do not produce fruit at the grape harvest in autumn. For what follows, it is important that Jesus remains the true vine from the beginning and it is he who produces fruit. The branches do so only in so far as they remain joined to him.

**15:3–4** In verses 3–4, the metaphor from vv. 1–2 is partly explained, partly developed. Verse 3 takes up the theme of "pruning" from v. 2 and thereby leaves the metaphorical level. The disciples must not fear to be pruned again, since they are already pruned or clean because of the word Jesus has spoken to them. The parallel to John 13 is striking here. Peter and the other disciples were also declared to be clean by Jesus on account of his symbolic action for them (cf. John 13:10). In John 14:15–24, there appears a closer connection between the dwelling of Jesus and the Father in the

---

97. Borig, *Der wahre Weinstock*; along these lines, now also, Zumstein, "Bildersprache," 152.

disciples and the accepting of his word. This thought will be developed further (see also below, v. 7).

In v. 4, the indicative is now followed by the imperative, although linked with a promise. The verb "abiding" appears in our text for the first time. It will be of primary significance (cf., also, v. 9 at the beginning of the next section). In the emphasis on the necessity of "abiding" in Jesus and his word, scholars see a downturn in the fortunes of the Johannine community in the face of awakening division and a threat from outside. Jesus's command is clarified by a reference to the image chosen at the outset. Just as the branches bear fruit only if they abide in the vine, so the disciples can produce fruit only if they remain linked to Jesus. At this point, Scholtissek emphasizes that here, for the first time, there emerge in perfect clarity the "mutual indwelling expressions" that will be so characteristic of the Johannine theology in the following chapters until John 17: just as the disciples abide in Jesus, so he is in them, and just as the Father is in Jesus, so Jesus is in the Father.[98] Such expressions have no direct biblical precedents but find their parallels at best in the theology of the Hellenistic Judaism of Philo of Alexandria. In John 14, the idea of the "indwelling" of the Spirit, Jesus, and the Father in the disciples is prepared in the section vv. 15–24 (in an ascending Trinitarian sequence: the Spirit, v. 17; Jesus, vv. 18 and 20; Jesus and the Father, v. 23[99]). In John 14:20, there also occurs, for the first time, the thought of the mutual indwelling of Jesus and the disciples.

**15:5-6** With the repetition of the metaphor from vv. 1–2 in v. 5, the middle of the text has been reached. Compared with the previous occasion, minor shifts are evident. Jesus no longer describes himself as the "true" vine since this no longer needs to be clarified to the disciples who are already made clean through his word (v. 3). It is made clear only to the reader that the disciples are, in fact, the branches on the vine that is Jesus. From there, it then directly follows that they can produce fruit only if they remain connected to him. Newly added to the explanation of the image is that not only must the disciples abide in Jesus but that he too must abide in them. This goes beyond the image of the vine and is determined by the real level. Where production of fruit is concerned, the text knows only a radical antithesis: either the disciples abide in Jesus and he in them, and they then produce much fruit; or they separate themselves from him and

---

98. Scholtissek, *In ihm sein*, 290.
99. Cf. Beutler, *Habt keine Angst*, 62–77.

## Jesus Bids Farewell (13:1–17:26)

lose him, in which case they can do nothing, thus producing no kind of fruit. Between these two extremes, there are no degrees.

This negative possibility is further clarified in v. 6. An individual case is envisaged and so the text passes at first into the singular: if someone does not abide in Jesus, then he is "thrown away" (where? probably out of the vineyard as a symbol of the people of God), and withers. The branches are collected (the probably better reading now attests the plural again) and thrown into the fire where they are burned. Scholars take note of the well-known Synoptic language of judgement (cf. Matt 3:10–12; 5:22; 7:19; 13:40, 42, 50; 18:8–9; Mark 9:43, 48). However, the thought of fire is already found in some Old Testament texts, which deal with the vineyard or the vine (cf. Ezek 19:12, 14; Ps 80:16).

**15:7** Once again, as in v. 3, the text abandons the level of the image and speaks in nonmetaphorical terms. The mutual "abiding" of the disciples in Jesus and Jesus in the disciples is the basis of the promise that their prayer will be heard. At the same time, however, it is striking that the presence of Jesus in his disciples is now described as an abiding of his word in them. This notion was also prepared in v. 3. Previously in John's Gospel, Jesus had spoken of the abiding of God's word in his hearers and of their remaining in his word. Thus, he said to them in 5:38: "his word does not dwell in you because you do not believe in him whom he has sent." In 8:31, Jesus said to the Jews who had reached an initial faith in him: "If you remain in my word, you will be truly my disciples."

Whoever abides in Jesus and in whom his word finds room, to him is promised the hearing of all his prayers. Jesus had already promised this to the disciples in John 14:13–14. Probably what we have here is also a "*relecture*" of John 14. By contrast with that text, the subject in John 15:7 is no longer that the disciples' prayer has to be made "in the name of Jesus." In fact, what is presupposed is disciples who are closely connected with Jesus like the branches with the vine. The promise runs no more along the lines that Jesus will fulfill every one of the disciples' wishes in prayer but that their wish will be granted. One can detect here a reference to the Father who is the subject of the next verse (cf. also v. 16!).

**15:8** The closing verse takes the text back to the beginning. In v. 1, the Father was depicted as an agent. He is the vine grower who cuts down and prunes the branches so that they produce fruit. If and insofar as the disciples produce fruit, they glorify the Father, and he is glorified by them. At the beginning of the farewell discourses, Jesus had solemnly announced that now, at the moment of his entry into his passion, God was being glorified, and Jesus was being glorified in him (John 13:31). It is then explained that the glorification of the Son of Man will take place "soon," that is, in his passing over from this world to the Father (13:32; cf. 13:1). The high priestly prayer will take up this idea again (John 17:1, 5). According to John 14:13, God will be glorified by the fact that the disciples' prayers in the name of Jesus will be heard: the glory of Jesus redounds to the glory of God. In John 15:7–8, the idea of the glorification of God is not linked to the hearing of prayers but with the disciples' producing fruit. If one considers that the prayer of the disciples in Jesus's name has as its object chiefly their abiding in Jesus, then the difference is not substantial. Only, in John 15:8, it appears clearer that the connection of the disciples with Jesus is the actual reason for the glorification of the Father, not just the fulfilling of their wishes in prayer—in other words: that they will become and have become his disciples (cf., again, 8:31).

### The Commandment of Love (15:9–17)

John 15:1–17 is a very elaborate construction that boasts a series of networks.[100] Thus, the theme of the "fruit production," which belongs to the *Bildrede* of the true vine, lasts to the end of v. 16 and so to the end of the whole section, which is thereby shaped into a textual unit. In v. 9, the theme of "love" appears for the first time. It marks the whole of the following group of verses until v. 17 and holds it together from the thematic point of view. Within this section, vv. 9–11 and 12–17 again can be separated off as subunits. Vv. 9–11 speak of the love of Jesus for his own, and the need to abide in this love. As a way of abiding in the love of Jesus, the keeping of his commandments is indicated. At the close (in v. 11) stands the promise of perfect joy, introduced by a usage often encountered in these texts: "These things have I said to you," to which the statement "this is what I command you" in v. 17 corresponds. Vv. 12–17 are held together through the words "This is my commandment that you love one another" in v. 12 and "This is what I command you, that you love one another" in v. 17. In vv. 13–16, a further thematic development can be observed. The theme of "love" leads in vv. 13–14 to that of the "friend." In v. 15, the "friend" is contrasted with the "servant" and both are compared with each other. There follow, in v. 16,

---

100. From here to the exegesis of v. 17, the account follows extensively Beutler, "6. Sonntag der Osterzeit (B): Joh 15,9–17."

the themes of "choosing," "producing fruit," and "hearing prayer." From the syntactic point of view, v. 13 is distinguished from the remaining verses in that it speaks aphoristically in the third person, while the remaining verses of the section are characterized by the contrast between Jesus and his disciples, which is expressed in the second person plural. Also characteristic in v. 13 is the linking of "love" (ἀγάπη) and "friends" (φίλοι), which will be explained in what follows. Verse 13 is thus shown to be the key verse. It is key also from the fact that in it Christology and ethics, the conduct of Jesus and that of his disciples are linked especially clearly.

Generally, v. 17 is seen as the end of the section before the new text unit, John 15:18–16:4d, which is marked by the theme of the "hatred" of the world and persecution. Thus, Giorgio Giurisato[101] is able to show how the sections John 15:9–17 and 15:18–25 correspond in mirror-like fashion, with conceptual agreements between verses 9–11 and 23–25, then 12–14 and 21–22, next 15 and 20, and, finally, 16–17 and 18–19. This can easily be checked and speaks for the literary unity of the text unit being studied, even beyond v. 17.

**15:9-11** With v. 9, the Jesus of the farewell discourses leaves the image of the vine, the branches, and fruit production. What was previously expressed metaphorically is now uttered directly. This direct speech was already prepared for within the *Bildrede* in that the vine grower was identified with the Father (v. 1). The interpretation of the image thus goes beyond the demands of the metaphor. Between Jesus and the Father there is not only the relationship of vine grower and vine but also the personal bond of love. This is the archetype and source of the love between Jesus and his own and, at the same time, as the following passage will show, that of the disciples of Jesus among one another. For the Father's love for the Son, cf., already, John 3:35 and 5:20. Luther's text speaks here of the love of the Father and Jesus in the present: "As my Father loves me, so I love you." It makes sense, however, to allow the past tense of the Greek text to stand here since, in this way, the text's setting of imminent departure is taken into account better. The command: "Abide in my love!" is best understood from the previous clause. The point is that the disciples abide in the love demonstrated to them by Jesus—like the branches in the vine.

The correspondence in the relationship between Father and Son, on the one hand, and the Son/Jesus and the disciples, on the other, is continued in v. 16. Similar to John 14:15–24, the abiding of the Spirit, of

---

101. Cf. Giurisato, "Il comandamento."

Jesus, and of the Father in the disciples is linked with their abiding in their love for Jesus and keeping his commandments. The only difference is that now abiding in the love of Jesus is more strongly emphasized as the love demonstrated by Jesus. This shift may be connected with the changed situation of the community in which the assurance of the love of God and of Jesus was becoming more important in the face of dangers that threatened. The linkage of "keeping the commandments" and "love" stems from the language of the book of Deuteronomy, as a glance at that book shows, especially chs. 6–11.[102] It is there that the theology of the covenant of God with his people is expressed (cf. Deut 7:9, 12).

Not seldom, the formula "these things I have said to you" in v. 11 is employed to close sections of the farewell discourses (cf. 14:25; 16:33).[103] Jesus has spoken these words to his disciples so that his joy may be in them and come to perfection. This theme of joy has already appeared from time to time (cf. John 3:29; 14:28). It will be taken up once again in the farewell discourses as the eschatological joy of the disciples in the face of the "hour" of their master, using the image of the woman who sees that her hour has arrived (16:20–22). On Easter Day, the joy of the disciples at their meeting with the Risen One can be reported (20:20). Here too, the eschatological character of this joy is confirmed. For the "perfection" of joy, cf. also 1 John 1:4.

**15:12** Jesus's command to love one another is as simple as it is provocative. Whoever reads the Fourth Gospel after the first three will here expect the double command of love for God and one's neighbor as it is recalled by Jesus (cf. Mark 12:29–31 par.). However, we must bear in mind that this linking of love for God and neighbor probably goes back to the Hellenistic diaspora in which love of God in the sense of Deuteronomy was not something standing by itself. The proclaiming of faith by Jews and Christians had first of all to require the love of God and the renunciation of idols (cf. 1 Thess 1:9) before any mention of further obligations.[104]

Traces of an older understanding in which the center of the Torah was still simply brotherly love are found in Paul in Rom 13:8 and Gal 5:14. While the latter text speaks of love for the "neighbor," the former has an

---

102. Cf. Beutler, *Habt keine Angst*, 55–62. The connection between "law/commandment" and "love" does not emerge correctly in Fernando, *Relationship*.

103. The formula emphasizes, above all, the speaking subject, in this case Jesus, and less the object of his communication, something for which Pastorelli, "La formule," makes a plausible case.

104. Cf. Weiss, *Eine neue Lehre mit Vollmacht*.

## Jesus Bids Farewell (13:1–17:26)

understanding that comes very near to the text of John 15: "Owe no one anything, except to love one another. Whoever loves the other has fulfilled the Law." Why does Paul speak on one occasion of the "neighbor" and on the next of "the other"? In the composition of the Letter to the Galatians, as in Rom 13:9–10, Paul refers expressly to the Greek translation of the commandment of Lev 19:18, in which the "fellow" Israelite is rendered with "neighbor" (πλησίον) just as in the text from the Synoptic Gospels. It may be indeed that Paul, in Rom 13:8 like John in our text, is nearer to the original sense of Lev 19:18 since the Hebrew text of Lev 19:18 is thinking more of a fellow Israelite. For the biblical-Old Testament background of the love command in John, cf., among others the study of Jörg Augenstein.[105] The criticism is often made that, in the Johannine farewell discourses, Jesus limits the love command to the members of the community but also, and above all, knows of no command to love one's enemies, as expressed in Matt 5:44; Luke 6:27. However, one should bear in mind that the farewell discourse in John 15 explicitly forgoes the right of the disciples to answer the hate they experience with a return of hatred.[106]

**15:13** With a new image, Jesus explains his love for his own as the basis and example of the love of the disciples for one another: the image is that of a friend who lays down everything for his friend. The idea links up with the beginning of the farewell discourses. In John 13:1, the evangelist introduces the passion narrative with the information that Jesus, who had always loved his own who were in the world, loved them to the end. This is precisely the attitude with which Jesus carries out for his own the gesture of the footwashing as the expression of his loving service right to the end. What is new in John 15:13 is that this verse now expresses the love of Jesus for his own and his giving up of his life for them (cf. John 10:15, 17, 18) in terms of friendship. Here, a new language is being announced. A friend sacrificing his life for his friend is a frequent phenomenon in Greek literature. The New Wettstein offers here a rich choice of texts that range from Plato via Aristotle to the Pythagoreans, Epicureans, and Stoics.[107] In this connection, Augenstein[108] quotes a saying from the *Nicomachean Ethics* of Aristotle (1169a): "For an outstanding man, the simple truth applies: he

---

105. Cf. Augenstein, *Das Liebesgebot*. For the different images of love in John (nuptial, friendly, specified by the covenant) cf. Varghese, *The Imagery of Love*; more strictly theological remains Popkes, *Die Theologie der Liebe Gottes*.
106. Cf. Augenstein, *Das Liebesgebot*, 88.
107. Cf. Neuer Wettstein.
108. Augenstein, *Das Liebesgebot*, 72.

will again and again act on behalf of friend and fatherland and, if necessary, lay down his life."[109] Augenstein[110] points to the same ideas in Jewish texts, admittedly from the Hellenistic age, especially in the books of Maccabees. Judas goes to his death at the appointed time for the sake of his brothers (1 Macc 9:10). An elder from Jerusalem sacrificed himself to the utmost in life and limb for the sake of the Jewish religion (2 Macc 14:37). In fact, the martyrs laid down their lives for God, for the temple, and for the people (2 Macc 6:28; 7:9, 37; 8:21). Scholtissek points to the familial metaphors as a mirror for the relationships in the Johannine communities.[111]

**15:14** The disciples are friends of Jesus by virtue of his command. In this verse too, biblical and classical material is brought together. The implementation of what Jesus has "commanded" the disciples remains in the language of Deuteronomy. In Deuteronomy, the word ἐντέλλομαι is regularly used of Moses vis à vis the Israelites. The thought of friendship with God is found chiefly in Hellenistic-Jewish writings, beginning with the book of Wisdom (7:13–14, 27) up to Philo of Alexandria. A precedent is constituted by the description of Abraham as "friend of God" in 2 Chr 20:7; Isa 41:8; cf. Jas 2:23.[112]

**15:15** The disciples are friends of Jesus because they have fulfilled his word. Upon closer examination, however, Jesus can call them his friends because he has made known to them his message from the Father in full and thus has shared it with them. "Friends share everything"—so runs an ancient proverb that is fulfilled here. Here is revealed the difference from the servant or slave who does not know and understand what his master is doing. With the contrast between the figures of servant and friend, the fourth evangelist is taking up Jesus's word again from John 13:16. There, Jesus had based the action of the disciples in loving service in the fact that it is only right if the servant behaves as his master. In John 15:15, this perspective is abandoned and the disciples are deemed servants no longer. This comparison maintains the *"Neulesung"* or *"relecture"* of John 13:1–17 through John 15:1–17 suggested by Dettwiler following Bultmann.[113]

**15:16** The link of the disciples with Jesus is now developed a step further. They are joined to Jesus if and insofar as they carry out his com-

---

109. The same text is found in Neuer Wettstein.
110. Augenstein, *Das Liebesgebot*, 73.
111. Cf. Scholtissek, "Eine größere Liebe," 430f. For Hellenistic friendship ethics, see Repschinski, "Freundschaft."
112. Cf. Scholtissek, "Eine größere Liebe," 422.
113. See above.

mand (v. 14). Looked at more closely, they are joined to Jesus by virtue of the word addressed to them (v. 15). This connection has its basis and its root in Jesus's choice, behind which lies the choice of God himself (v. 16). The thought of the choice of the disciples has surfaced from time to time. It was uttered with respect to the circle of the twelve in John 6:70. Here already, Judas provided the occasion for this. He had indeed been chosen by Jesus but was to become his betrayer. Jesus's choice is the subject in the same context in 13:18. Here, the reference is to the eleven in contrast with Judas. In John 15:16—after the departure of Judas—Jesus's choice is now the subject in a positive sense only. The call of the first disciples may be echoing here (John 1:35–51). We are no longer concerned with warning but with assurance. Since the disciples have been called by Jesus, they should and will produce fruit (cf. 15:1–8), and their prayer is assured of a hearing (cf. 14:13).

**15:17** From the literary point of view, the renewed command of Jesus rounds off the section John 15:12–17. Looked at more closely, it is no mere repetition of the first mention of the commandment in v. 12. In the meantime, the disciples—and, with them, the reader—have been led a step further. Jesus has assured them of his closeness. They are his friends, connected with him by virtue of his word and enabled to produce fruit. Their prayers will be heard. Thus, they can receive Jesus's renewed command with confidence. In their fulfilling of his commandment, Jesus will not leave them on their own.

In the light of the present text, it is often thought that what we have here is a "sectarian ethic" in which the love command of Jesus is confined to the community to the exclusion of the neighbor and, *a fortiori*, the enemy. More recent scholarship is skeptical of this criticism. We could observe that Jesus's commandment to love one another derives from Lev 19:18, and that Paul knows a similar version of this commandment to that in John. An opening of the Johannine love command beyond the boundaries of the community is also visible in the parallel place to our text in John 13:34–35. There it says, in v. 35: "By this will everyone know that you are my disciples: if you love one another." Thus, the love lived out in the community is to be the mark of the disciples and also act as an advertisement to those outside (cf. John 17:21). In this way, the narrow circle of the community is broken open and the vista opened to all who are called to salvation in Christ.[114]

---

114. Cf. Beutler, "Kirche als Sekte."

### The Hatred of the World (15:18–16:4d)

**15:18–25** Despite the influence of the Synoptic tradition, which is still to be addressed, this section appears to be stamped with a typically Johannine style. The repeated conditional clauses ("*realis*" or "*irrealis*") lend the section a unitary syntactical structure. The governing theme is that of the "hatred" of the "world."

As we have seen above, this theme frames the section John 15:18–25. Thus, the hatred which the disciples experience is that of the "world." John locates the experience of hatred and persecution in a comprehensive dualistic context on the one side as a conflict between God, the one he has sent, and the disciples of the latter, and on the other the "world" opposed to God. From this it also emerges that the hate against the disciples is ultimately hate of Jesus and means against the one who sent him, the Father. Verse 19 develops this dualistic perspective: the world loves what belongs to it and hates what is opposed to it. On account of their calling by Jesus, the disciples no longer belong to the world but are hated by it. This experience of the disciples had been foretold by Jesus, as v. 20 maintains. The disciples are reminded of this by Jesus himself.[115] The author is probably thinking here of John 13:16. However, while the saying of Jesus in 13:16 serves to explain to the disciple that he, like his Master, should be ready for service, according to 15:20, he must be ready to suffer the same fate as his Master. This summons of Jesus is found at its clearest already in Matt 10:24–25. The behavior of the "world" with regard to the disciples repeats and mirrors its behavior with regard to Jesus—in the bad sense, but also in the good (cf. the end of v. 20). Finally, the behavior of the "world" with regard to the disciples is based on its lack of knowledge of Jesus and the Father (v. 21).

Verses 22–24 cohere. In word and deed, Jesus has shown that he was sent by the Father, but the world has not known him either. Thus the world has also hated Jesus and in him the Father (v. 23). This hatred was foretold in the Scriptures: it is a hatred without cause and without result (cf. Pss 35:19; 69:4).

The Johannine text about the hatred and persecution of the disciples has originated under the influence of the Synoptic tradition, as is evident in many ways.[116] The main text for comparison is Mark 13:9–13 where it says:

---

115. Theobald, "Erinnert euch," 267.
116. Cf. Beutler, "Synoptic Jesus Tradition," 171f.

## Jesus Bids Farewell (13:1–17:26)

"And you will be hated by all for my name's sake" (καὶ ἔσεσθε μισούμενοι ὑπὸ πάντων διὰ τὸ ὄνομά μου). By contrast with Mark, John speaks not only of the hatred of "all" but of the "world," as the summative designation of Jesus's opponents.[117] With Mark, the reason is also given for the hatred experienced: "for my name's sake" (διὰ τὸ ὄνομά μου, John 15:21). In John, this thought is deepened: the hatred against the disciples signifies hatred against Jesus and, ultimately, against the Father who sent him.

**15:26–27** We find a third saying inserted here about the Paraclete, one which is not too closely connected with the previous and following contexts. This has in common with the saying of Jesus in John 14:16, 26, that the Spirit-Paraclete appears to be sent by the Father. By contrast with this saying of Jesus, the advocate (again as the Spirit of truth as in 14:17) now has a task with regard to the world. He will support the disciples in a legal dispute by bearing witness for Jesus (with John's favored formula, cf. John 1:7–8, 15; 5:31–39; 8:13–14; 10:25[118]) and enable them, for their part, to bear witness also.

The witness theme belongs to the fundamental themes of John's Gospel. In the texts mentioned above, the evangelist or the Jesus of the Fourth Gospel refers to people and events that support Jesus's claim to be the Son of God sent by the Father. These witnesses are: the Scriptures of the Old Testament (5:39), John the Baptist (1:7–8, 15; 1:19–34; 5:33), the works of Jesus (5:36; 10:25), the Father (5:32, 37; 8:16–18), and Jesus himself (8:13–14, 18). In the time of the church, it will be the Spirit (cf. here) who will bear witness for Jesus together with the disciples. This juridical vocabulary fits in with the context of the "great trial" between Jesus and the world according to the Fourth Gospel. In it, Jesus appears as the accused and the condemned, but, ultimately, the world delivers judgement on itself.[119]

The promise of the Holy Spirit in John 15:26–27 is found already in Mark 13:11. There, it is announced that the Holy Spirit will provide the disciples with the right words before the courts of governors and kings so that they need have no anxiety about that. The concept of "testimony/witness" is also found in Mark: the appearance of the disciples in court will be a "testimony" "for" or "against" their accusers (Mark 13:9).

---

117. Thus, the dualistic Johannine perspective differs from that of the Synoptics who announce the coming persecution in an eschatological-apocalyptic perspective (cf. Mark 13:9 par. Matt 10:17–18; Luke 21:12–13); Zumstein, "Ils n'ont pas d'excuse," 168f.

118. Cf. Beutler, *Martyria*, 237–76.

119. Cf. Beutler, *Martyria*, and Beutler, "μαρτυρέω"; Beutler, "Zeuge, Zeugnis, Zeugenschaft."

**16:1–4d** As we have already seen, Jesus's announcement of a coming persecution of the disciples by the synagogues is framed by a saying of Jesus in which he declares his intention in imparting this information. The disciples must not take offense at the persecution and ought to remember the words of Jesus in their experience. The expression "remember" is important for the understanding of John's post-Easter perspective (cf. John 2:22; 12:16). The future exclusion of the disciples has been heralded already in the exclusion from the synagogue of the man born blind (John 9:22, 34–35; cf. 12:42); also, there has already been word of the possible death of the disciple for Jesus's sake (John 12:22–24). As spokesman for the disciples, Thomas had already declared himself ready to go with Jesus to Jerusalem and die with him (John 11:16). The same goes for Peter, although his readiness did not go beyond words (John 13:37). Now, this death for Christ has become a cruel reality. The persecutors will think that by killing the disciples they will be doing God a service, but all they show by this is that they know neither Jesus nor the Father. Again, the fate of the disciples is inserted into a theological dimension that leads down into the deep and indicates the deeper reason of the experience.

The persecution of the disciples by the synagogues is found already in Mark 13:9. However, Mark speaks of persecution by the synagogues and by secular courts, by governors and kings. In John, there occurs a concentration of the powers opposed to the disciples, above all in the Jewish institutions. The future death of some disciples is found in Mark (13:12) as in John (16:2).

*III*

With the poles of "love" and "hate," the fundamental dimensions of Christian existence are specified. After Jesus's departure, it falls to the disciples to remain linked to him and to one another. This means that remaining or "abiding" will, in fact, be a catchword. Thus, they also will be in a position to experience hatred and enmity.

The starting point is formed by Jesus's discourse about the true vine in John 15:1–8. Jesus describes himself here not simply as the "vine" but as the "true vine." With the emphasis on the authenticity of the vine in comparison with others, the text is also inviting the reader to vigilance and responsible judgement. Jesus is "the true light which gives light to every man" (1:9), "the true bread from heaven" (6:32), his flesh

## Jesus Bids Farewell (13:1–17:26)

is "truly food" and his blood is "truly drink" (6:55). In the same way, Jesus is the "true vine." In these characteristic Johannine expressions lies an element of choice, of decision. The believers must decide whether they accept Jesus as the source of their salvation and wish to remain linked to him in order to have life and to produce fruit, or else to reject this invitation.

If and insofar as the believers remain linked to Jesus, they will also be linked to one another in love. This is the theme of John 15:9–17. Apparently, this unity of the believers was soon under threat. From the Johannine letters, which might be contemporaneous with the later farewell discourses, we know of a division that threatened the community and also arose at a certain moment in time (1 John 2:19). The disputed matters were clearly the correct understanding of the faith in Christ and the ethical necessity to live according to Jesus's commandments. It is possible to seek an inner connection between these two elements in the understanding of the "secessionists" and discern it in their anthropology, their teaching about man: they were so convinced of being filled with the Holy Spirit that they no longer needed an "anointed one" or Messiah in the narrower sense to whom they owed salvation, and, at the same time, felt themselves to be raised above the commandments of Christ or God.

This notion has a certain contemporary feel. In fact, certain Pentecostal movements—outside and within the church—run the risk of overestimating their own charismatic gifts and so losing sight of others, their fellow Christians, and the social dimension of Christianity. Against such a danger, the command of mutual love proves its power—in openness to others, even those outside the community, and in the testimony of the Spirit of Christ who laid down his life for his own.

The experience of being hated by non-Christians has been a constant down the ages. From the Jewish side, the question has arisen recently whether the Fourth Gospel itself is not marked by a "grammar of hate."[120] The author observes that the Jews in John's Gospel are portrayed from the beginning as in opposition to Jesus, to the truth, and, ultimately, to God. They are the actual representatives of the "world" who oppose God and the one he has sent, and so are "children of the devil" (John 8:44). According to Adele Reinhartz, this is the language of hate. However, it is her opinion that, in the section John 15:18–16:4d, this form of hate does not occur directly, but that it becomes clear, in effect, that it is the Jews

---

120. Cf. Reinhartz, "Grammar of Hate."

who are the subject.¹²¹ This "grammar of hate," she thinks, is explained by the situation of the young community at the time of its separation from the synagogue. Be that as it may, the modern reader has to take into account Jewish sensibilities when he comes across the theme of "hate" in the farewell discourses.

Whether and how far the early Church experienced persecution on the part of the synagogue is still controversial. Beside the cases of Stephen (Acts 6:7–8:3) and James (Acts 12:1–2), there are few examples of martyrs for Christ at the behest of the Jewish authorities. If Paul is to be believed, he experienced various punishments from the synagogues in which he was preaching Christ. With John, one must reckon with the possibility that he took the experience of Roman persecution, of which we are aware from contemporary documents,¹²² and perhaps projected it on to the previously experienced opposition against Jesus and those believing in him on the part of the Jews.¹²³

## 6. The Third Farewell Discourse (16:4e–33)

16 ⁴ᵉ I did not say these things to you from the beginning, because I was with you. ⁵ Now, I am going to the one who sent me, and none of you is asking me: Where are you going? ⁶ Rather, sorrow has filled your heart, because I have said this to you. ⁷ But I am telling you the truth: It is good for you that I am going away. For if I do not go away, the advocate will not come to you; but I am going, and so I will send him to you. ⁸ and when he comes, he will convict the world and reveal what is sin, justice and judgement; ⁹ sin, because they do not believe in me; ¹⁰ justice, because I am going to the Father and you will see me no more; ¹¹ judgement, because the ruler of this world is being judged. ¹² I still have much to say to you, but you cannot bear it now. ¹³ But when he comes, the Spirit of truth, he will lead you into all truth. For he will not speak on his own account but he will speak what he hears, and will declare to you what is to come. ¹⁴ He will glorify me; for he will take from what is mine, and will declare it to you. ¹⁵ All that the Father has is mine; that is why I said: He is taking what is mine and will give it to you.

¹⁶ Yet a little while and you will see me no more, and again a little while

---

121. Cf. Reinhartz, "Grammar of Hate," 420.

122. See the exchange of letters between Pliny the Younger and the emperor Trajan concerning the prosecution of Christians in Pontus in the corpus of the letters of Trajan 10.96f.

123. Cf. Cassidy, *John's Gospel*.

and you will see me. ¹⁷ Then said some of his disciples to one another: What does he mean when he says to us: Yet a little while and you will see me no more, and again a little while and you will see me? And: I am going to the Father? ¹⁸ They said: What does it mean when he says: a little while? We do not know what he is talking about. ¹⁹ Jesus knew that they wanted to ask him, and said to them: You are wondering among yourselves about what I said to you: Yet a little time and you will see me no more, and again a little while and you will see me. ²⁰ Amen, amen, I say to you: You will weep and lament, but the world will rejoice; you will be sorrowful, but your sorrow will be turned into joy. ²¹ When a woman is to give birth, she is troubled because her hour has come; but when the child is born, she thinks no more about her anguish because of her joy that a man has come into the world. ²² So you also have sorrow now, but I shall see you again; then your heart will rejoice, and no one will take your joy away. ²³ On that day, you will no longer ask me for anything. Amen, amen, I say to you: What you ask the Father in my name will be given to you. ²⁴ Until now, you have not asked for anything in my name. Ask, and you will receive so that your joy may be complete.

²⁵ These things I have spoken to you in figures; the hour is coming in which I shall no longer speak to you in images but will tell you plainly about the Father. ²⁶ On that day, you will ask in my name, and I do not tell you that I shall pray the Father for you; ²⁷ for the Father himself loves you, because you have loved me and because you have believed that I have come forth from God. ²⁸ I have come forth from the Father and come into the world; I am leaving the world again and going to the Father. ²⁹ Then his disciples said: Look, now you are speaking plainly and no longer speaking in images. ³⁰ Now we know that you know all things and need to be asked by no one. Therefore, we believe that you have come forth from God. ³¹ Jesus replied: Do you now believe? ³² Look, the hour is coming, and already is, in which you will be scattered, each to his own house, and will leave me alone. But I am not alone, for my Father is with me. ³³ These things I have said to you so that you may have peace in me. In the world you will have tribulation; but take courage: I have overcome the world.

*I*

This marks the beginning of the so-called "third farewell discourse." In it, important themes are taken up from the first discourse in John 13:31–14:31 or, as others would have it, 14:1–31. The starting point is formed by the imminent departure of Jesus from the group of the disciples. The impact on the disciples, their grief, is announced in verses 5–6 and in what follows in verses 7–22 developed in a literary way. Verses 23–24 take up once more the question of intercession in the name of Jesus. With verses 25–33, the chapter comes to a conclusion. Here, new themes come up for discussion: Jesus's speaking in veiled speech or openly and in a way that can be understood; the theme of the "hour"; the future scattering of the disciples; and the support they will find in Jesus in the granting of peace and victory.

## II

### *The Announcement of the Spirit-Paraclete (16:4e–15)*

At the beginning of the discourse, the disciples receive again the promise of the Holy Spirit (cf. John 14:16–17, 26). Verses 8–11 describe the working of the Spirit with regard to the world, verses 12–15, his work with regard to the disciples.

**16:4e–7** The introductory verses link up with the situation of the disciples. They lead from the past through the present into the future. In v. 4e, Jesus speaks in the aorist and in the imperfect. In verses 5–7b, he changes over into the present (or into the perfect with present significance). At the close, Jesus speaks of the future in two different grammatical forms: in main verbs in the future or in subordinate clauses that outline the future. Thus, they prepare for verses 8–11, 12–15, which will speak of the role of the Spirit-Paraclete.

In the introductory words of Jesus "I did not say these things to you from the beginning" (v. 4e), it is not quite clear what is meant by "these things." At first sight, Jesus's announcement of the future expulsion of the disciples from the synagogues and their killing in verses 2–3 could be meant. However, in the following it will be shown that the interest of the narrator shifts from the concrete situation of the disciples after the departure of Jesus to their position in the light of faith: they are separated from Jesus physically. As noticed by K. Haldimann,[124] a temporal distinction is introduced here that was previously lacking. One can distinguish the time in which Jesus is still present among his own, then the moment of his going away, his coming back, and a time in between. Of that, verses 5–6 will speak.

---

124. Cf. Haldimann, *Rekonstruktion*, 287f.

## Jesus Bids Farewell (13:1–17:26)

In v. 5, there occurs a striking contradiction between the words of Jesus that no one is asking him about where he is going and the corresponding questions of the disciples previously recorded (13:36 Peter; 14:5 Thomas). It is possible to explain this contradiction with a literary model that postulates different farewell discourses following one another whereby the final redactor has set no high priority on a composition that is entirely free of contradictions.[125] More satisfactory appears to be the model of *"relecture,"* which explains the contradiction through a new situation among the readers.[126] A version of this is offered by the proposal of Haldimann, who reads the text synchronically but reckons with the fact that it has passed through a process of growth.[127] In chs. 13 and 14, it had dealt with the questions of individual, named disciples. In John 16:5, Jesus addresses himself to possible questions from the whole circle of disciples. On account of their mental state before Jesus's departure, the disciples are not yet in the position to ask the right questions, including the question regarding his destination.

The ignorance of the disciples is linked with grief—despite Jesus's command that they should not let themselves be distressed (cf. 14:1, 27). From the literary point of view, the theme "sorrow, joy" of verses 20–22 is being announced. Theologically, it now becomes clearer that, from John 16:4e on, the time sequence will be worked out more precisely.

As v. 7 shows, in Jesus's view, there is not a moment when the disciples will be left alone. His "departure" (ἀπέρχεσθαι, πορεύεσθαι) is matched by the "coming" (ἔρχεσθαι) of the Spirit-Paraclete. As in John 15:26 it says of the Paraclete that he will be sent from Jesus—a further development from the notion that he will be "given" by the Father (John 14:26), in which there is still an echo of the language of the promise of the Spirit according to Ezek 36:26. One sees how the Old Testament promise is receding more into the background to be replaced by the christological interpretation. The Father has "sent" Jesus (v. 5), and the latter, for his part, sends the Spirit to abide with the disciples.[128]

**16:8–11** The sense of the group of verses that follows is disputed. On the one hand, there is the linguistic question of the meaning of ἐλέγχειν

---

125. This is the reading of Brown, vol. 2, and Schnackenburg, vol. 3.
126. This is the understanding of the text in Dettwiler, *Gegenwart*; Zumstein, 2:127.
127. Cf., again, Haldimann, *Rekonstruktion*.
128. According to Pastorelli, *Paraclet*, 120, the coming of the Paraclete in v. 7 is to be contrasted with his double role with regard to the world and the disciples described in verses 8–11 and 12–15.

and of the triple ὅτι in verses 9–11; on the other hand, a theological question that is connected with the linguistic one: what exactly is the role of the Spirit according to these verses? Is it more didactic or forensic? The verb ἐλέγχειν occurs in John on two other occasions, namely, in John 3:20 and 8:46. In both cases, it clearly has a juridical, forensic meaning. From this, numerous exegetes conclude that a similar sense must be intended in John 16:8. On the other hand, however, the verb has a broader spectrum of meaning such as to "convict," "reprimand," "convince," "explain," "investigate," on the basis of evidence. The translation of the triple ὅτι in verses 9–11 depends partly on the meaning favored. According to some, it has a declarative significance and so means "that"; according to others, it is causal and thus means "because." A survey of the resulting variants in translation and interpretation is given by Barrett,[129] updated in Haldimann.[130] From this survey it emerges that it is advisable to find a solution for ἐλέγχειν which acknowledges both the forensic and the didactic aspects of the verse, and also that a translation be chosen for the ὅτι that allows for both the declarative and causal aspects to be heard (one possibility in English, as in German, would be the colon; the *Einheitsübersetzung*, like the Jerusalem Bible, prefers "that"; our translation chooses "because" like the RSV). This would then lead to something like the following exegesis of verses 8–11.

The Spirit sent by Jesus will show the world what sin, justice, and judgement are and will convict the world of its wrongdoing in its culpability towards Jesus. He will teach the world and convince the world that its sin consists in the denial of faith in Jesus. He will teach the world what righteousness consists of: this justice will happen to Jesus, with the consequence that the disciples will see him no more. He will teach the world and convince it with regard to judgement: the "ruler" of this world is already judged.

That ἐλέγχειν means more than simply "teach" has been well observed by D. A. Carson.[131] He understands the "justice" as that of men. In order to maintain this understanding, though, he must then ascribe an ironic sense to the word. This theory seems improbable despite the typical Johannine device of irony. Moreover, with a glance at the following verses, one can outline the function of the Spirit-Paraclete as "announce

---

129. Cf. Barrett.
130. Cf. Haldimann, *Rekonstruktion*, 303–16.
131. Carson, "Function."

and denounce." This would lead to the establishment of two of the basic principles of the Word theology of the liberation theologians.

**16:12–15** After the description of the function of the Spirit-Paraclete with regard to the world, its function with regard to the disciples is now described. At the beginning in v. 12, there is another reflection on the point in time in which Jesus is speaking to his disciples. While, according to John 14:30, Jesus will not be saying much more to the disciples because the adversary is near, the reason now given is that the disciples are not yet in a position to understand his words. Behind this consideration stands the reflection of the author of this discourse about the times of the presence and absence of Jesus and, in this case, the necessity of the Spirit for understanding the words of Jesus—also in their meaning for the life and welfare of the disciples in this world. "βαστάζειν" means "bear." Thus, the disciples are not yet in a position to be able to understand and accept the repercussion of the words of Jesus on their situation in life.[132]

According to v. 13, as "Spirit of truth," the Spirit will "lead the disciples into all truth." The choice of the preposition ἐν instead of the directional εἰς could be governed by the intention of the author to represent a growth of the disciples in their understanding of the truth rather than a new discovery.[133] The reason for this lies precisely in the fact that the disciples have already known and found the truth in Jesus (cf. John 14:6), and so the Spirit has no role other than to lead the disciples deeper within this truth. In this truth, the disciples will be in a position to understand the past, the present, and the future.

Insofar as the Spirit refers to the words of Jesus, he will glorify Jesus according to v. 14. This expression is well-known to the readers in its employment for the mutual "glorifying" of the Father and the Son (cf., above, 13:31–32). Only in John 21:19 will the verb be used for the glorifying of God through the life or death of a disciple.

The thought that comes to expression in John 16:14 is justified when one considers that everything that Jesus possesses comes from the Father. With this observation, the section closes in v. 15.[134]

In the whole of the present passage, the dimension of time is signifi-

---

132. For the farewell discourses as a whole, see Rahner, "Erinnerung."
133. Early manuscripts read here εἰς instead of ἐν (A B pc), but this might be a simplification. The ἐν is attested, among others, by ℵ² D L W u. a.
134. The verse is missing in a set of ancient manuscripts such as P⁶⁶ ℵ* saᵐˢ boᵐˢˢ. However, this might be put down to homoioteleuton with v. 13.

cant if the situation of the disciples is to be understood. Recently, this has been emphasized above all by Swiss scholars.[135]

As we have already observed, John 16:4e marks the beginning of a section that lasts to the end of the chapter in v. 33 and in which fundamental elements of the kingdom of God are taken up again as they are listed by Paul in Rom 14:17: "For the kingdom of God is not eating and drinking but righteousness, peace and joy in the Holy Spirit."[136] John 16:4e–33 is the single Johannine text in which these four elements are found and in which the concept of "righteousness" also occurs (in vv. 8–10). Generally, this is an issue that has not been taken up in exegesis. John's recourse to the elements of the kingdom in this place would explain also their occurrence together. "Peace" is encountered at the end of the chapter in v. 33; "joy," in the image of the woman who is facing the birth of her child (vv. 21–22), in accordance with an announcement in vv. 6–7; the promise of the "Spirit," in the Paraclete sayings of our passage (vv. 7–15). In the account of the appearance of Jesus to the disciples on the evening of Easter Day in John 20:19–23, "peace," "joy," and the "Holy Spirit" will return as gifts of the Risen One. The promises of John 14:25–27 and 16:4e–33 will be fulfilled.

### From Sorrow to Joy (16:16–24)

The section that begins now contrasts with the preceding one through its christological reflection and its handling of the emotional state of the disciples after Jesus's departure. These disciples hear words of consolation in their sorrow and an encouragement to pray. The expression "these things I have spoken to you in figures" (ταῦτα ἐν παροιμίαις λελάληκα ὑμῖν) in v. 25 marks the beginning of a new and final unit of the text.

The construction of the passage has been worked out by Haldimann,[137] who subdivides it into three main subsections:

I. v. 16
II. vv. 17–18
III. A. v. 19ab; B vv. 19c–e; C vv. 20–22; D vv. 23–24.

---

135. Cf. Zumstein; Weder; Dettwiler, *Gegenwart*.
136. Cf. Beutler, "Synoptic Jesus Tradition."
137. Cf. Haldimann, *Rekonstruktion*, 326f.

# Jesus Bids Farewell (13:1–17:26)

In subsection I, Jesus announces that, after a little while, the disciples will see him no more but will then see him again. In subsection II, the disciples ask one another what these words of Jesus might mean. There is especial focus on Jesus's saying about "a little while" (μικρόν). In subsection III, Jesus speaks in four further subunits:

A. Jesus knows that the disciples would like to ask him something (19a–b) (ἐρωτᾶν)
B. He repeats the words which the disciples have asked among themselves (19c–e)
C. He announces future sorrow and joy for them (20–22)
D. He promises them a time in which they will no longer ask him anything (23–24) (ἐρωτᾶν).

It is clear that this subsection is framed by the concept of "asking, praying." Moreover, the longest subunit within the subsection, verses 20–22, is constructed concentrically with the themes of sorrow and joy. At the beginning stands a saying about sorrow (v. 20); in the middle stands the saying about the woman who is looking forward to the birth of a child and passes from sorrow to joy (v. 21); and the renewed announcement of the joy of the disciples comes at the end without any image (v. 22).

**16:16–19** Jesus's saying in v. 16 that the disciples will not see him any more after a little while but then will see him again after a little while looks like a *relecture* of John 13:33.[138] By contrast with that occasion, however, John 16:16 is not concerned directly with the departure of Jesus but whether his disciples can "see" him, and with this "seeing" a time sequence is introduced. It is possible to distinguish a time before the departure of Jesus, after his departure, and after his appearing again. It is especially for the time in between that the Johannine Jesus will provide instructions and consolation.

Jesus's saying leads to a conversation among the disciples themselves in vv. 17–18.[139] This is constructed chiastically. At the beginning and at the end stands the question: "What does he/it mean?" (τί ἐστιν τοῦτο), refer-

---

138. In v. 16, some manuscripts, like A K N G D 068, the families $f^{1.13}$ as well as the majority text read ὅτι ὑπάγω πρὸς τὸν πατέρα. However, this appears to have been imported from v. 17. The oldest Alexandrian tradition does not support this reading.

139. V. 18a is absent in Codex D, in the Vetus Latina, and in the Syrosinaiticus. However, this could be explained through homoioteleuton with v. 17. The ὃ λέγει in the same verse is textually uncertain.

ring, in the first case, to the whole of the saying of Jesus completed from John 13:33, in the second case only to the expression "Yet a little while" (μικρόν). Thus, the problem appears, above all, as one of the successive phases of the relationship of the disciples to Jesus.

Jesus's answer in v. 19 begins with a direct question to the disciples that shows his knowledge of their conversation among themselves without his being there but also his readiness to help them by overcoming their concern. The following verses serve the latter aim.

**16:20–22** The construction of this group of verses has already been demonstrated. At the beginning, in v. 20, there is another saying about the sorrow of the disciples. They are right to be concerned about the moment when Jesus will no longer be with them. They will be sorry, but the world will rejoice.

The moment will come, however, when their sorrow will be turned into joy. In v. 21, this prospect is clarified with an image, the comparison with the woman who is to bring a child into the world. At first, she feels pain, but then her pain will be turned into joy as soon as the child is born. Kathleen Rushton[140] has emphasized the significance of the process of birth in John, whether here or in the conversation between Jesus and Nicodemus as part of a feminine symbolic world in the Bible and in the New Testament. Just as the woman's pain will be turned into joy, so too, after his return, the sorrow of the disciples left alone by Jesus. In the new situation, the "seeing" of v. 22 now appears in reverse sequence: the text does not say that the disciples will see the Lord but that he will see them. Thus the new relationship between Jesus and the disciples is underlined.

**16:23–24** The connection between verses 19–22 and 23–24 is possibly one of association. To the ἐρωτᾶν ("asking," "praying") of the disciples in v. 19 corresponds the same verb in v. 23. It is not quite clear whether Jesus wishes to say that the disciples will no longer ask him any questions after their new encounter with him or whether he wishes to say that they will no longer have to ask him for anything. Apparently, Jesus's saying moves in the latter direction although the double sense of the verb furnishes a starting point. In this way, the theme of the infallibility of prayer that was already discussed in John 14:13–14; 15:7 is resumed. However, it is added that, until now, the disciples have asked the Father for nothing in the name of Jesus. Once again, there is a revelation of the significance of the end time as a time of infallible prayer in the name of Jesus.

---

140. Cf. Rushton, "Parables"; cf. Hartenstein, "Aus Schmerz wird Freude."

## Jesus Bids Farewell (13:1–17:26)

### The Coming of the Hour (16:25–33)

The third farewell discourse closes with the following verses. The formula "these things I have spoken to you" (ταῦτα ... λελάληκα ὑμῖν) frames the present section (vv. 25 and 33). The theme of the infallibility of prayer in Jesus's name "on that day" is taken up again in vv. 26–27. New themes are added, however, such as Jesus's speaking in veiled language or openly; the theme of the "hour"; the future scattering of the disciples; and the encouragement of peace and victory Jesus bestows on them. With this encouragement, the discourse closes, followed by the prayer of Jesus in John 17 that cannot be counted as part of the farewell discourses in a strict sense.

The narrative structure allows us to discern three sections in the following passage: the continuation of Jesus's discourse (vv. 25–28); the reaction of the disciples (vv. 29–30); and Jesus's closing answer (vv. 31–33). At first glance, the contribution of the disciples appears as an expression of their understanding and their insight in faith. However, it is precisely this insight that is called into question and corrected by Jesus in his final answer.

**16:25–28** The next group of verses follows without any new speech preliminaries. It contrasts with the previous verses through the summary introduction and through the change to a new theme: Jesus's speech in images or without figures.[141] The difference between Jesus's view and that of his disciples lies in the different division of time. Jesus has reached the end of his earthly course and the communication of his message. Thus, the use of the perfect in v. 25 is fully justified. The past is a time for speaking in images (cf. John 10:6). The time, indeed the "hour" will soon come, however, when Jesus will no longer speak in metaphors but proclaim the Father openly. The expression "on that day" characterizes this future revelation as an eschatological message. In this eschatological hour, on that day, the Father will give everything to those who believe in Jesus, even if they have not asked him for it, since the Father loves them and since they have believed in Jesus. Jesus's coming forth from the Father and his return to the Father are the object of the disciples' faith. According to this division of time by Jesus, the moment of his revelation without images is still to come.

---

141. The ἀλλά in this verse, which is attested by numerous manuscripts, underlines this opposition but might be secondary; it is missing in, among others, P$^{svid}$ ℵ B C* D* L W. Instead of ἀπαγγελῶ in the same verse is found also the present ἀπαγγέλλω or ἀναγγελῶ. Nestle-Aland's version is supported by the ancient tradition of P$^{66c}$ A B C* D K L W, among others.

The concept of the "hour," which until now has been used in John for the eschatological hour (John 4:23; 5:25, 28) or for the "hour" of Jesus (John 2:4; 12:23; 13:1; 17:1), is now converted into an "ecclesiological" sense in order to express a new relationship between Jesus and those who believe in him. For Jesus, this "hour" is directly at hand, but it still has to come.

**16:29-30** The disciples take up the theme of the two ways in which Jesus speaks to his own—in images or openly. However, they are mistaken in their assumption that the moment has already come for Jesus to speak openly. It is because of this assumption that they twice employ the temporal adverb "now" (νῦν). Perhaps they think that in this way they can skip over the "hour" of Jesus as the hour of his passion and death before his resurrection.

**16:31-33** It is precisely this view that is disputed by Jesus in what follows. The disciples have not yet reached true faith in him. Much nearer is the "hour" of their scattering when they will be dispersed and leave Jesus on his own—though still in communion with the Father. This warning is accompanied, however, by a word of comfort: Jesus promises his own who will experience tribulation in the world his peace and victory over the world, just as he has already overcome the world.

Two themes of these closing verses merit a tradition-historical explanation: the scattering of the disciples in v. 32 and the promise of peace in v. 33. The imminent scattering of the disciples according to v. 32 finds its precedent in Mark 14:27 par. Matt 26:31. The scriptural basis is Zech 13:7. However, this text knows great differences in its textual transmission. The Masoretic text runs thus: "Rise up, sword, against my shepherd, against the man who is close to me—oracle of the Lord of hosts. Strike the shepherd, then the sheep will be scattered. I will turn my hand against the little ones." The Septuagint presupposes a plural number of shepherds and men who are to be slain. From this point of view, the Synoptics' text is closer to the Masoretic version. In John, the subject is not the shepherd but only the scattering (of the sheep).[142] This was already mentioned in chapter 10 in the shepherd discourse (John 10:12). Jesus is the one who is gathering together the scattered children of God (John 11:52). In John 16:32 also, one can make out a christological dimension in the allusion to Zech 13:7. As soon as Jesus, the shepherd, is struck, the disciples (the sheep) will be scattered. In the end, however, it is he who will gather them together again and make them one. The texts that lie behind this expectation are,

---

142. For the reception of Zech 13:7 in the NT, cf. Hübenthal, *Transformation*, 217–55.

above all, Jeremiah 23 and Ezek 34, texts that were taken up previously in John 10.[143] A further use of Zechariah is found in John 19:37 (Zech 12:10).

The other traditional theme that occurs in our group of verses is that of "peace" (v. 33). In the exegesis of John 14:25–29, we have already indicated the tradition-historical background for this theme in John. According to this, peace belongs to a verbal cluster previously attested in Rom 14:17: "For the kingdom of God is not eating and drinking, but righteousness, peace and joy in the Holy Ghost." In our chapter here, the gift of the Holy Spirit (vv. 7–11, 13–15), righteousness or justice (vv. 8–10) and joy (vv. 20–22) have already been mentioned. The theme of "peace" completes this sequence. In a certain way, this promise of peace anticipates its bestowing by the Risen One on the evening of Easter Day (John 20:19, 21). As long as the disciples still live in this world and experience its opposition, they can summon up hope. Jesus has overcome all the powers that oppose God, the "world" and even death. The disciples can share in this victory (cf. 1 John 4:4; 5:4–5). Thus, they can be confident and full of courage. If they abide in Jesus, like the branches in the vine, they will share in his peace.

## III

What is the message of this third farewell discourse of Jesus in John's Gospel? The answer lies in the main sections of the chapter. Verses 4e–15 are marked by the announcement of the Spirit-Paraclete who will come to the aid of the disciples. In the language of liberation theology, the Spirit, according to our passage, has the double task of "announcing and denouncing." The task of "denouncing," or "accusing," is ascribed to the Spirit in verses 8–11. He will accuse the world on account of its lack of righteousness or justice in a theological and christological sense, but not without repercussions on the keeping of Jesus's commandments, and also, in this sense, on account of its sin. The "denouncing" is matched by the "announcing" of the Gospel (vv. 12–15). In the view of the evangelist, this concerns a task of the Spirit with regard to the disciples, but, in a broader sense, it is possible to discern here the role of the Spirit and the church to announce the future to the world in the light of faith and, in this light, to open up new horizons.

In the middle section of verses 16–24, the subject is especially that

---

143. Cf. Beutler, "Hirtenrede."

of joy which, in a dualistic way, is expressed with a "before" and "after." The time of the disciples' suffering in the world will be followed by a time in which the tears will be wiped from their eyes (cf. Rev 21:4). Perhaps it is precisely the world of the Apocalypse that helps us to understand this passage and put it into practice. Even today, Christians live as strangers in the world, often hated, persecuted, excluded, or even killed. The victory will be theirs, however, just as is declared at the end of the chapter. Their prayers do not remain unheard, and their suffering will be turned into joy. In this hope, Christians can be of good cheer in the joyful expectation of their final encounter with their Lord, who is also the Lord of history.

With that, we have already arrived at the message of the last verses of the chapter, vv. 25–33. The aim of these closing verses seems to be to help the disciples to find their place in the "divine plan." The readers in the Johannine communities are already living in the time after the death and resurrection of Jesus. Thus, there no longer exists for them the danger of wanting to skip over the "hour" of Jesus. In the eschatological fulfillment, there remains the danger of wanting to live without the experience of tribulation (θλῖψις) that Jesus experienced and they too will have to experience. They must embrace this way of Jesus and do so with Jesus, but, in this, they can repose their whole confidence in him.

## 7. The Prayer of the Departing Jesus (17:1–26)

¹ Jesus said these things. Then he lifted his eyes to heaven and said: Father, the hour is come. Glorify your Son, so that the Son may glorify you. ² For you have given him power over all flesh so that he may give eternal life to all whom you have given him. ³ And this is eternal life: that they know you, the only true God, and the one you have sent, Jesus Christ. ⁴ I have glorified you on the earth and finished the work you assigned to me. ⁵ Now, Father, glorify me in your presence with the glory that I had with you before the world existed.

⁶ I have revealed your name to the men whom you have given me out of the world. They belonged to you, and you have given them to me, and they have kept your word. ⁷ Now they have acknowledged that everything you have given me is from you. ⁸ For the words that you gave me, I have given to them, and they have received them. They have known in truth that I have come forth from you, and they have come to the faith that you have sent me. ⁹ I am praying for them; I do not pray for the world but for all those whom you have given me; for they belong to you. ¹⁰ Everything that is mine is yours, and what is yours is mine; I am

glorified in them. ¹¹ I am no longer in the world, but they are in the world, and I am coming to you. Holy Father, keep them in your name, which you have given to me, so that they may be one as we are one. ¹² As long as I was with them, I kept them in your name, which you have given to me. And I have taken care of them and lost none of them, except the son of perdition so that the Scripture may be fulfilled. ¹³ But now I am coming to you, and I am saying these things while still in the world so that they may have my joy to the full. ¹⁴ I have given them your word, and the world has hated them because they are not of the world just as I am not of the world. ¹⁵ I am not praying that you take them out of the world but that you protect them from the Evil One. ¹⁶ They are not of the world just as I am not of the world. ¹⁷ Consecrate them in the truth; your word is truth. ¹⁸ Just as you sent me into the world, so I have also sent them into the world. ¹⁹ And I consecrate myself for them so that they too may be consecrated in the truth.

²⁰ I do not pray only for these ones here but also for all who, through their word, believe in me. ²¹ That they all may be one: as you, Father, are in me and I am in you, that they may also be in us so that the world may believe that you have sent me. ²² And I have given them the glory that you have given to me so that they may be one as we are one, ²³ I in you, and you in me, so that they may become completely one, in order that the world may acknowledge that you have sent me and loved them just as you have loved me.

²⁴ Father, I desire that all those whom you have given me may be with me where I am. Let them see my glory that you have given me because you loved me before the foundation of the world. ²⁵ Righteous Father, the world has not known me, but I have known you, and they have known that you have sent me. ²⁶ I have made your name known to them and will make it known so that the love with which you have loved me may be in them, and I in them.

## I

Jesus closes his words of farewell not with a final exhortation but with a prayer. One can regard it as a continuation of the farewell discourses or as a concluding summary. Be that as it may, the prayer sees the return of central concepts and catchwords from the previous chapters. Moloney has detected a concentric structure in the main sections of the farewell discourses together with the prayer of Jesus in John 17, and this is supported by sound observations.[144] Here, it is presupposed that John 13:1–38 belongs

---

144. Cf. Moloney, 24.

before John 14, John 15:1–16:4d, and John 16:4e–33. The same basic division occurred also in the previous exegesis. The starting point is formed by the correspondences between the first farewell discourse of John 14 and the third in John 16:4e–33, in which the imminent departure of Jesus is in the foreground, linked with the announcement of his coming back. The central section in John 15:1–16:4d is more self-contained and develops the abiding in Jesus with the themes of love and hate. However, the first and last sections, that is, the account of the footwashing and the final prayer of Jesus also show correspondences. For Moloney, what appears central here is that God is to be made known. However, further correspondences can be demonstrated. Thus, according to both sections, Jesus's "hour has come" (John 17:1; cf. 13:1). This hour is the hour of the glorification of the Father by Jesus (17:1, 4; cf. 13:31–32), but also of the glorification of Jesus by the Father (17:1, 5; cf. 17:24; 13:31–32). The prayer of Jesus for the unity of his own in John 17 has its counterpart in the new commandment to love one another in John 13 (vv. 34–35). The "love" of Jesus at the beginning (13:1) is matched by the love of the Father at the end (17:26), as highlighted by Yves Simoens.[145]

The sequence of five sections of farewell discourses does not require that they were composed at the same time. It could also be that later sections take up the earlier ones and complete them (in the sense of *relecture*). The text can still continue to be grasped and understood as a compositional whole.

Broad agreement governs the division of this chapter. At the beginning, Jesus prays for himself in the sense of his glorification by the Father (vv. 1–5); then he prays for the disciples entrusted to him (vv. 6–19, cf. v. 9: "I am praying for them"). Next, he prays for those who will believe in him through the word of the disciples (vv. 20–23, cf. v. 20: "I do not pray only for these ones here"). On the basis of the semantic analysis, it is advisable to regard verses 24–26 as a small concluding section on its own. Here, Jesus is clearly praying with an eye to the two groups mentioned before (after a renewed address in prayer: "Father," v. 24).[146]

It is apparent that no less than six key concepts occur in all four of the sections of the prayer assumed in our discussion of the text: "Father"

---

145. Cf. Simoens, *La gloire*, 55–58; Simoens, *Selon Jean*, 3.719.

146. Ritt, *Gebet*, divides John 17 according to text-linguistic criteria. However, the divisions according to content, which he presents at the outset, thereby retain their validity. Chiefly disputed among scholars is whether verses 6–8 belong to the preceding context or offer an independent section. As argued above, they make sense together with vv. 9–19.

## Jesus Bids Farewell (13:1–17:26)

(πάτερ vv. 1, 5, 11, 21, 24, 25), with which the prayer-address occurs twice (in the first and last sections), clearly as a frame in verses 1–5; "glory, glorify" (δόξα, δοξάζειν, vv. 1, 4, 5, 10, 22, 24); "know" (γινώσκειν, vv. 3, 7, 8, 23, 25); "give" (διδόναι, vv. 2, 4, 6–8, 11–12, 14, 22, 24); "send" (ἀποστέλλειν, vv. 3, 8, 18, 21, 23, 25); "world" (κόσμος, vv. 5–6, 9, 11, 13–16, 18, 21, 23, 24).

The individual sections exhibit their special word fields as will emerge from the detailed analysis. If the first section is, above all, about the proclaiming of the Father by Jesus and thereby his glorification, which is meant to correspond to the glorification of Jesus, then the second is about keeping Jesus's word and the consecration of the disciples, which is made possible by Jesus's "consecration" of himself for them. They are to be consecrated "in truth" (v. 19), whereby a further theme of the second section is mentioned. The unity of the disciples reverberates in the second section (v. 11) and will be developed more comprehensively in the third (vv. 21–23). The disciples' being one has its counterpart in the fourth section in being with Jesus in his glory. Here, there also occurs the theme of the perfection of love with which the farewell discourses began (cf. John 13:1). It is announced at the end of the third section of the prayer (v. 22) and now forms a frame (with John 17:24, 26) for the whole of the farewell discourses.

How are we to explain the prayer of the departing Jesus and its dominant themes here? Some exegetes point to Gnostic or syncretistic texts for a prayer of the revealer before his departure from this world. Thus, Bultmann indicates the *Corpus Hermeticum* and a Manichaean text.[147] Dodd makes a list of correspondences between the *Corpus Hermeticum* and John's Gospel, including John 17 (thus, "Holy Father" and the notion of "consecrating oneself").[148]

There are also examples of prayers in apocalyptic texts. Thus, Carsten Claussen points to the prayers of Ezra (4 Ezra 8:20–36) and of Baruch (2 Baruch 48:2–24).[149] They occur at turning points in the lives of the worshipers and foretell what lies before them. That could also have consequences for the prayer of John 17. Not only does it close the farewell discourses; it also leads into the passion of Jesus.[150]

Nearer to John stands the Gospel of Mark. The second evangelist also

---

147. Cf. Bultmann, 374.
148. Dodd, *Interpretation*, 34.
149. Claussen, "Das Gebet."
150. Further texts for comparison in the intertestamental literature are in Dietzfelbinger, *Abschied*, 256–58, Scholtissek, "Gebet," 199 n. 2.

leaves the scene of the Last Supper to close with the words "When they had sung a hymn, they went out to the Mount of Olives" (καὶ ὑμνήσαντες ἐξῆλθον εἰς τὸ ὄρος τῶν ἐλαιῶν, Mark 14:26). Jeremias sees in this verse a reference to the recitation of the "Great Hallel" at the end of the Jewish Passover feast.[151] It is conceivable that John has personalized this prayer at the end of the Last Supper, indicating that he does not regard Jesus's Last Supper as a Passover meal.

In John 17, there are also elements of Jesus's prayer on the Mount of Olives.[152] Thus, there occur the prayer-address to the Father, "Πάτερ" (John 17:1, among others, Mark 14:36 αββα ὁ πατήρ) as well as the reference to the "hour" (John 17:1), which "is come" (ἐλήλυθεν, John) or "might pass" (παρέλθῃ, Mark 14:35), but then "is come" (ἦλθεν, Mark 14:41).

John gives no account of Jesus's prayer in the Garden of Gethsemane but anticipates the scene in John 12:27–28, as has long been realized.[153] In John 17, the elements of Jesus's prayer in the garden are retained but are found in a new context in a Jesus who is much more sure of himself and concerned only for the welfare of his own.

It has already been demonstrated that the connection between the themes of Jesus's "glorification" and his "hour" as the hour of his death and lifting up has been influenced by the theology of the servant according to Isa 52:13–53:12. With the taking up again of this basic theme of his theology from the beginning of the farewell discourses, the evangelist or final redactor emphasizes the importance of this theme and the coherence of the final text.

The description of Jesus's prayer as a "High Priestly Prayer" relies, above all, on verses 17–19 of the prayer, which speak of the "consecration" of the believers by the Father and the "consecration" of Jesus. The first traces of the designation are in Chytraeus (1530–1600), but it could have older roots. The exegesis will show that the "consecration" of Jesus for his own is to be understood in the sense of his self-offering as revealer.[154]

---

151. Cf. Jeremias, *Abendmahlsworte*, 34; cautious about this, Lührmann, *Das Markusevangelium*, 242.
152. Cf. Beutler, "Synoptic Jesus Tradition," 173.
153. So already Brown, "Incidents"; Beutler, "Psalm 42/43."
154. Cf. Beutler, "Hohepriesterliches Gebet." According to Attridge, "How Priestly," John 17 is, perhaps, answering discussions at the end of the first century CE about the correct understanding of priestly ministry.

*Jesus Bids Farewell (13:1–17:26)*

## II

### *Jesus's Prayer for Himself (17:1–5)*

The first five verses of Jesus's prayer form a self-contained unit. It is marked off by the repetition of the prayer-address "Father" and the theme of the "glorification" of the Son in v. 1 and v. 5. In fact, the introductory five verses display a concentric structure.[155] Just as verses 1 and 5 correspond, so too verses 2 and 4, with their looking back, first to the work of the Father in v. 2, then to that of the Son in v. 4. Both cases are concerned with what the Father has "given" to the Son: power over all flesh to give it eternal life (v. 2) or the "work" that the Father has given to Jesus to finish (v. 4). In the center stands v. 3, which expresses what constitutes the eternal life that Jesus is supposed to be giving from God. It consists in the announcement of the only God and of his Son, Jesus Christ, which may be considered as a central statement that anticipates v. 6 at the beginning of the next section.[156]

At the beginning of the section vv. 1–5, the narrator is creating a transition from the words of Jesus to the disciples in the farewell discourses to his prayer to the Father with which his speech ends. The evangelist has recorded elsewhere prayers of Jesus at decisive points in his life and work, such as before the raising of Lazarus (John 11:41) and in the face of his passion and death in correspondence with the prayer in the garden (John 12:27). In doing this, Jesus "lifts his eyes to heaven," as in John 11:41, but also Mark 6:41 par. at the multiplication of the bread; cf. Mark 7:34. In John 17:1, the reference to "heaven" creates a connection with v. 5 with the mention of the glory that Jesus possessed with the Father before the creation of the world and that he is now supposed to be gaining once more.

The mutual glorification of Father and Son was previously only the object of statements by Jesus, most recently in John 13:31–32. Now, it becomes the object of prayer. This involves the replacement of "God" and "Son of Man" with "Father" and "his Son." The theme of "glorification" is

---

155. Thus, already, Simoens, *La gloire*, 188, who, however, subdivides verses 1–2 and 4–5, each into three units. His concentric structure for the whole of the chapter disregards the linear structure of Jesus's prayer first for himself, then for the disciples, next for those who believe from the word of the disciples before the conclusion.

156. This is the sticking point for the proposal of Becker, 2:615f., with Bultmann, 378, and Schnackenburg, 3:195f., to eliminate the verse as secondary. In fact, the mention of the name "Jesus Christ" occurs only otherwise in John 1:17, but that is in a section that similarly is to be assigned to the late layer in John's Gospel.

yet another echo of the servant of Isa 52:13, but it continues to stand out. Just as the servant fulfilled his commission, so now has Jesus, the Son. Thus, he may hope and pray for the promised glorification (cf., alongside Isa 52:13 LXX, John 12:28 "I have glorified him and will glorify him again").

As in John 13:31–32, we have to distinguish between the coming of Jesus's hour and the moment of his death. In John 17 (as in 13), Jesus sees that the hour has come but he knows that his death is still pending. His "hour" is the moment of the perfect revelation of God in him, the Son sent by the Father, and the gift of "eternal life." That is the subject of v. 2. Mention of the "power" (ἐξουσία) of Jesus recalls his appearance before the commission of the disciples into the world according to Matt 28:18 and may be alluding to that place. Only here it is reformulated in Johannine terms. Jesus has come so that men may have life and have it to the full (John 10:10), i.e., eternal life (cf. John 6:40). When it is the "flesh" that is mentioned here as the receiver of the holy gift of Jesus, then it is man in his creatureliness that is meant, the creatureliness Jesus took on for the sake of men's salvation (cf. John 1:14; 6:51–56) and that needs redemption (cf. John 6:63). The neuter "all" means precisely this human race, which is in need of redemption, considered as a whole.

According to v. 3, "eternal life" consists in knowing the one true God and the Son whom he has sent, Jesus Christ. In the previous course of the Gospel, the promise of "eternal life" has consistently been connected with faith. According to John 5:24, it is faith in the word of Jesus, which is presupposed in the other places (cf. John 3:15, 36; 6:40, 47; 20:31). If "life" on account of "knowledge" perhaps lets one think of Gnostic or Hellenistic parallels, yet knowledge of the "only true God" points to the Scripture of Israel, Deut 6:4. Indeed, this has already been echoed several times in the Fourth Gospel (cf. John 5:44; 8:41–42). Anyway, belief in this only true God does not exclude but includes knowledge of his Son, Jesus Christ, something that, of course, presupposes a Christian perspective.

The theme of knowledge of God also has its roots in the faith tradition of Israel. The promise of a new covenant in Jer 31:31–34 closes with the words: "No one will teach the other any more; no one will say to the other: Know the Lord!, but they will all know me, small and great—an oracle of the Lord" (Jer 31:34). The promises of the first farewell discourse, especially the announcement of a future dwelling of God with his people, already showed the influence of the promises of the new covenant, above all Ezek 36:26. It is seems justifiable to suppose the same tradition in John 17.

Verses 4 and 5 take up again the theme of the mutual glorification

## Jesus Bids Farewell (13:1–17:26)

of Father and Son from v. 1 but in reverse sequence. Thus, the beginning recalls that Jesus has glorified the Father in his earthly work. In v. 1, the glorification of the Father by the Son was seen as a future event. In v. 4, Jesus is already looking back on it. He has finished the "work" the Father assigned to him. Mention of a "work" (ἔργον) of Jesus in the singular is a rare occurrence in John and is found otherwise only in John 4:34. There too, the subject is the "perfection" of this work by Jesus. The crucified Jesus is able to die with the words: "It is finished" (τετέλεσται, John 19:30). He has finished his work. It is this moment Jesus is anticipating in his prayer.

The glorifying of the Father by the Son has its counterpart in that of the Son by the Father. Jesus prays for the latter in v. 5 in words that correspond literally to v. 1. Moreover, there is a return of the prayer-address πάτερ. Now, Jesus's glorification will be described more exactly. Jesus is to regain the glory that he possessed with the Father before the foundation of the world. This notion appears here for the first time in John's Gospel. According to other places, Jesus is to be glorified in the future without that being conceived of as a return to a glory with the Father that was before all time (cf. John 11:41; 13:31–32). However, it is sufficient to think here again of a *"relecture"* of an earlier text through a later one without answering the question of the author. Theological reflection sees in Jesus's glorification at the end of his journey, not the entry into a new form of being but the return to an existence due to him from eternity.[157] Here, the prologue seems to be presupposed, and, in its turn, it could have been attached to the beginning of the Gospel after its initial completion.[158] To the "being with God" (πρὸς τὸν θεόν in John 1:1, 2) corresponds the "with you" (παρὰ σοί), that is, the Father, in John 17:5.

### Jesus's Prayer for His Disciples (17:6–19)

In his prayer for himself, Jesus prays about the culmination of his journey in his future glorification in the presence of the Father. In what follows, Jesus turns his attention to the men who have heard his word in the world

---

157. According to Becker, 2:622, the Johannine view differs here from the (pre-)Pauline one in Phil 2:9–10: "According to Phil 2:9f., the one who is exalted receives his assigned place that surpasses his pre-existent state before his *kenosis*."

158. For the correspondences between the prologue and John 17, cf. O'Grady, "Prologue," who, however, considers both texts as having originated at the same time as the Gospel. Similarly, developing this approach, cf. Lee, "Prologue."

and whom he is now leaving behind. They could be called his disciples but the expression does not occur here. The text contrasts those hearers of Jesus's message who have received his word from him directly with those who have received the proclamation only indirectly. The latter will be the subject of verses 20–22.

The text is divided, first into a historical review in verses 6–8, and then Jesus's speech in the present in which he submits his requests to the Father, in verses 9–19. Before the first imperative, in v. 11d, there is an identification of the disciples for whom he is preparing to pray, in verses 9–11c. After the prayer-address "Holy Father" in v. 11d, a first imperative, "keep them," leads on to the actual prayer of Jesus for his own. The theme of "keeping" is maintained until v. 15, although v. 16 probably still belongs to this context. It is similar to v. 11a–c at the end of the introductory verses 9–11c. The second imperative "consecrate them in the truth" in v. 17 leads on to the concluding verses. This second theme of consecration was already sounded in the prayer-address "Holy Father" in v. 11d and, with its double occurrence in v. 19, rounds off the whole section as well as the closing group of verses, vv. 17–19.

**17:6–8** Jesus's historical review of his work before his prayers in the following verses recalls the "*narratio*" that, in classical rhetoric, preceded the statement of the objective ("*propositio*") and its justification.[159] What has taken place is narrated partly in the aorist, partly in the perfect, partly in the imperfect. At the beginning, in v. 6, stands Jesus's revelation of the divine name, recorded in the aorist. This summarizes his work of revelation in history. Until v. 7, the text then recalls the Father's activity in the past with its continuing effect and thus is in the perfect: from eternity, the Father has determined men for faith in and for belonging to Jesus, and they have kept his word and known that everything that Jesus has comes from the Father. This too is an abiding reality. Equally lasting is the passing on of the words that the Father gave to Jesus to the hearers of the word in v. 8a–c. To this there then corresponds, again in the aorist, in the second part of v. 8, the receiving of the word by those men previously appointed for this and their knowledge in faith that Jesus has been sent by the Father. Again, this takes place in historical time.[160]

---

159. From the point of view of genre criticism, one would be speaking here of an "account report" that precedes the "introduction to the prayer" in vv. 9–11a, the "prayer" in v. 11b and the "justification for the prayer" in vv. 12a–13; cf. Becker, 2:618.

160. Zumstein, "Die verklärte Vergangenheit," correctly points to the different functions of the tenses in John 17: the aorist underlines the historical nature of the sending of

What is meant by the revelation of the Father's "name" by Jesus in v. 6 is not explained at first in any more detail. In any case, we are not dealing here simply with the being of God, with God in himself, but with his relationship with Jesus and with men. Therefore, parallel to the revelation of God's name, our group of verses has the announcing and receiving of the word of God (vv. 6 and 8). This word refers to the sending of Jesus by the Father and his proceeding from the Father, as will become clear in v. 8. Thus, it is the Father of Jesus who is concealed under the name of God.

**17:9-11c** Before the prayer of Jesus after the prayer-address in v. 11d, there is a description of those for whom Jesus is praying. The "I" ('Εγώ) placed first in v. 9 is somewhat surprising. Perhaps it is already preparing for the opposition between the departing Jesus and the disciples who are remaining in the world in v. 11a–c. The role of this group of verses is to clarify, now in the present, for whom Jesus is praying to the Father. Here, there occurs another contrast, the difference between the disciples for whom Jesus is praying, and the world for which he is not interceding. Jesus is praying, therefore, for the disciples or those who believe in him since they belong to him and have been given to him by the Father, just as everything that he has has been transferred to him by the Father; indeed, he possesses everything together with the Father. The text presents the "world" as shorthand for God's creation, as in v. 5 ("before the world existed"), but the "world" also serves as code for the powers opposed to God who are also opposed to Jesus. It is in this sense that Jesus cannot pray for the "world." Here, a greater, unbridgeable gulf is revealed, since even the prayer of Jesus is no longer able to annul the decision against him and the word of God. One can reach the impression of a predestination to unbelief and damnation only by reference to the consistent tendency of John's Gospel to promote the assent of faith (right up to the provisional ending in John 20:30–31). It could be that the dualistic tendency in John 17 is thought to be in need of such correctives.

When it says, at the beginning of v. 11, that Jesus is no longer in the world but that the disciples still are, the dualistic language is abandoned once again. The playing with the several meanings of the "world"-concept belongs to the linguistic difficulties in the exegesis of the Fourth Gospel and also, yet again, of the prayer of Jesus in John 17. Here, what is probably

---

Jesus; the perfect, the abiding result of God's action in Jesus for the believers. Dominating verb here is "giving." The future opens the eschatological dimension.

meant is simply earthly existence, which Jesus is leaving as he now comes to the Father.

**17:11d–16** With the prayer-address "Holy Father" in v. 11d, the text passes over now to the prayer of Jesus for his own in the world. In biblical language, "holy" means belonging to God; it is not actually a moral attribute but an ontological one.[161] God does not belong to the world, and he stands over it as sovereign. God the Father is to keep those belonging to Jesus in his name, that is, remaining united to him, and make them one among themselves. With the second part of the prayer the text anticipates the section in which Jesus will pray for the believers of a later period (see below for vv. 20–23). Probably there is already an echo here of a situation in which it is precisely the correct understanding of Jesus's message that is dividing different groups of disciples or community members. Here, we are not far from the Johannine letters.

The catchword "keep" (τηρεῖν) has already occurred several times in the farewell discourses. Within the framework of covenant theology, it describes, above all, the keeping firm of the commandments of Jesus in love for Jesus (cf. John 14:15, 21, 23–24; 15:10) or keeping his word (John 8:52, 55; 15:20; 17:6). From now on, it will be the role of the Father to keep the disciples (John 17:11, 15), just as Jesus has done during his lifetime (John 17:12). Keeping the disciples or the believers in the Father's name is probably tantamount to keeping them in the possession of the Father. Then, the unity of the believers among themselves belongs to this link to God through Jesus. This thought will be developed in the following section.

Verses 12–13 are marked with a temporal opposition similar to what will be the case again in verses 14–15. According to v. 12, Jesus has kept in the name of the Father those entrusted to him who believe in him. In belonging to the Father, he has protected them effectively except in the case of the "son of perdition," in whom the Scripture is to be fulfilled. Again, Judas is being recalled here as happened already in John 6:70–71; 13:10–11, 18–19.[162] For the "son of perdition," see 2 Thess 2:3. There, the expression is applied to the eschatological adversary ("Antichrist"). The perdition is

---

161. Cf. Balz, "ἅγιος," *EWNT* 1:42f; *EDNT* 1:18.

162. According to Becker, 2:616, a redactor has added a reference to Judas here. Cf., already, Schnackenburg, 3:207, who, however, does not decide. In the consistent characterization of Judas as "betrayer" in John, Wright IV, "Greco-Roman Character Typing," sees the influence of schematic characterization of people through their typical behavior in a way that corresponds to Greco-Roman rhetoric.

## Jesus Bids Farewell (13:1–17:26)

something that goes out from him rather than befalls him as in John. It is not said which passage of Scripture is to be fulfilled in him. From the linguistic formulation, it is possible to think of Prov 24:22a LXX or Isa 57:4 LXX (τέκνα ἀπωλείας). However, the first text is unsuitable since it speaks of the son (υἱός) who observes the word and on that account avoids perdition (ἀπωλείας ἐκτός ἐστιν). The text of Isaiah is closer, describing the lawless as "children of perdition." As a semitism, "son of perdition" probably goes back to Jewish precedents,[163] but the exact text being referred to remains unknown.

The review in v. 12 is followed by the look to the future in v. 13. As previously, in v. 11, Jesus says to the Father, "I am coming to you" (πρὸς σὲ ἔρχομαι). Focus is thus placed again on the disciples, this time not on concern for them but in awareness that Jesus coming to the Father also signifies the reason and occasion for their perfect joy. This is another echo of the theme of the eschatological joy of the disciples, which has occurred repeatedly since chapter 14 (cf. John 14:28 verbally; 15:11; 16:20-22, 24 πεπληρωμένη; similarly, 1 John 1:4). It is the joy of Jesus that the disciples are to share.

Verses 14–15 reveal another time difference, this time between past and future. With an emphasized, preliminary "I" (ἐγώ), Jesus first contrasts his behavior with that of the world. Jesus has imparted his word to the disciples permanently (perfect tense!), but (the καί is adversative) the world has hated them. Once more, this historical experience is conveyed in the aorist. This hatred by the world had already come up in the farewell discourses (John 15:18–25) with a precedent in the great controversies of Jesus in Jerusalem (John 7:7). The reason for the world's hatred of the disciples lies in their origin: like Jesus, they do not hail from the world, understood again here as an area of power opposed to God.[164] Such lines of thought are also familiar to the readers of John's Gospel (cf. John 8:23).

This review of the disciples' experience is followed by the future-oriented prayer for them by Jesus to the Father in v. 15. They are not to be carried away out of this world but only kept from the Evil One. In this way, the prayer of v. 11 is repeated in a negative way. There Jesus asked that the

---

163. Cf. the references in Becker.
164. Here, there is a link to the speech of Pope Benedict XVI in the Concert Hall in Freiburg on 25 September, 2011 (VApS 189) with its call for the "detachment of the church from the world," something that set in motion a debate. Cf. among others, Söding, *In der Welt*.

disciples might be kept in the name of the Father. Keeping from the Evil One probably means—as in the Lord's Prayer in Matt 6:13—the concrete, personal Evil One and not just evil in the abstract.[165] Verse 16 is an almost word for word repetition of v. 14c–d and is absent in some manuscripts but nonetheless claims its place as a transition to verses 17–19. Like Jesus, the disciples too do not come from the world but they are sent into the world.

**17:17-19** The prayer in the imperative in v. 11, "Holy Father, keep them in your name" is followed now by the second request: "Consecrate them in the truth." The motif of holiness was already enshrined and announced in the prayer-address in v. 11. Since there is no such address in v. 17, this strengthens the impression that the two prayers complete and mutually interpret each other. As core of the keeping of the disciples in the name of the Father, it has been emphasized that they are to be kept in God as the Father of Jesus. The disciples know of him through the revelation of Jesus in word and deed. This is an aid to understanding the second prayer, the prayer for the consecration of the disciples in the truth. Thus, v. 17 is concerned, not with cultic consecration but with a consecration through the word of God proclaimed by Jesus (cf. John 15:3), the word of truth, indeed the truth itself. In that way, the thought goes back to John 14:6: "I am the way, the truth and the life." "Consecration" signifies separation from the world and dedication to God. However, this is the way that the disciples too can be sent into the world, as v. 18 maintains. The basis of the consecration of the disciples is Jesus's consecration for them according to v. 19. It takes place through the communication of his word, which is truth. In this way, the small unit beginning in v. 17 is rounded off.[166]

### Jesus's Prayer for the Future Believers (17:20–23)

In the following section, Jesus's prayer opens out to those who will come to believe in him on the word of his disciples. Here, there are two long, complex, and contrasting sentences that also exhibit their own vocabulary:

---

165. How far the whole prayer of Jesus in John 17 is oriented to the Lord's Prayer is, at present, an open question. However, it is increasingly being met with agreement. Cf. Thyen, 678–81 with Thüsing, "Die Bitten"; Schenk, "Die Um-Kodierung."

166. The priestly-cultic aspect of the "consecration" in John 17 is strongly emphasized by Pope Benedict XVI in the second volume of his book *Jesus von Nazareth*, 76–102; cf. the criticism of Theobald, "Das 'hohepriesterliche' Gebet Jesu." Cf. other authors before this debate in Scholtissek, "Gebet," 211–16.

## Jesus Bids Farewell (13:1–17:26)

vv. 20–21 and 22–23. The first part of the group of verses is dominated by the theme of the faith of the future receivers and their fellowship with one another, with God, and with Christ. The second half takes up again the theme of glory, links it with the theme of unity, and leads it on to the theme of love that is introduced afresh here and is leading already to the concluding verses. If in the section of vv. 6–19, verses 6–8 contained, as a preface, the review of the past before the prayer of Jesus, verses 20–23 contain the sequence in reverse: the prayer comes first in vv. 20–21, followed by the review in v. 22.[167]

**17:20–21** At the outset, Jesus makes it clear to whom the following prayer applies: not only for "these," that is, for the disciples alone, who are presupposed in the previous section, but also for future believers. Faith was already the subject in v. 8 without its becoming the dominant theme. In vv. 20–21, it now appears as a key concept that holds together the group of verses by occurring at the beginning and at the end. It encompasses the theme of the unity of the future believers among one another and in the Father as in the Son. The faith of those who will come to know Jesus no longer on account of his own presence but only through the word of proclamation will come up in the narrative of the faith of Thomas in John 20:24–29. There, it will be simply a question of faith in the word of the proclamation. Here, in John 17:20–23, what stands in the foreground is the unity of those who believe in Christ. It is clearly being threatened. Already the commandment of brotherly love among the disciples in John 13:34–35; 15:9–17 intends to address this concern. Here, in John 17, unity is brought directly to the fore. It is grounded in the unity of Jesus with the Father and of the believers in Jesus. According to Scholtissek,[168] what we have here is a *"relecture"* of John 10 where the unity of Jesus and the Father stands in the foreground and has not yet been formulated as the basis of the unity of the believers among one another. According to John 17, the unity of believers is anchored in their indwelling in Jesus who, for his part, dwells in the Father as the Father does in him. We have already come across this vocabulary of immanence in John's Gospel (cf. John 6:56; 10:38; 14:20). It appears to go back to Hellenistic rather than biblical examples.[169]

---

167. Verses 20–21 are again excluded as secondary by Becker, 2:617f., once more with Schnackenburg, 3:214–18, who also refers to the older literary criticism (215 n. 68). Such interventions in the text on the basis of slight thematic and linguistic differences find few champions today.

168. Scholtissek, "Gebet," 206–8.

169. Cf., again, Scholtissek, *In ihm sein*.

Instead of "that they also may be in us," numerous manuscripts affiliated with the majority text have: "that they may be one in us." However, the ancient Egyptian textual tradition has the shorter text,[170] and so the longer version should be understood rather as dittography under the influence of the context.

The unity of the believers is aimed not only at the preservation of the faith community but also has a missionary consequence. It can and should lead to faith in Jesus himself and his sending by the Father. A similar thought had already come up in John 13:35: "By this everyone will know that you are my disciples: if you love one another." It will return in John 17:23 and is significant for the answer to the question whether the Johannine love command is concerned only with the circle of believers or whether it is open to the world that is to receive the message of Jesus and accept it in faith.[171]

**17:22–23** Jesus's prayer is followed by his recollection. It anchors the task in the gift. In doing this, catchwords from the first section of the prayer (17:1–5) are taken up and modified. The glory that Jesus ascribes to the Father and receives from him is now to be bestowed on the believers. This was already anticipated by v. 10. If, there, it was based on the fact that Father and Son have everything in common and let their glory shine on the disciples, so now here it consists of the shining out of the unity that is bestowed on the circle of disciples coming from the Father through Jesus. In this unity, according to v. 23, the disciples are to be perfected, and this marks the occurrence of another Johannine catchword (last mentioned, in v. 13, with the "perfected joy" or "joy to the full"). Through the unity of the believers, the world is to attain faith in the mission of Jesus, as is restated with slight variation in v. 21. There, instead of "faith," it is "knowing" that appears, and this emphasizes the visible nature of the sign of unity.

How can the unity of believers in Jesus act as a sign for the sending of Jesus by the Father? The end of v. 23 gives an indication. The unity of the disciples is an expression of the love that links Father and Son, and that embraces and includes those who believe in Jesus. This is the reason for the occurrence of the catchword appearing in the last three verses of the prayer of Jesus.

**17:24–26** The concluding verses are already separated from the previous context by the renewed prayer-address "Father" (Πάτερ). Apparently,

---

170. Thus $P^{66vid}$ B C* D W it sa ly pbo bo$^{ms}$.
171. Cf. Beutler, "Kirche als Sekte?"

## Jesus Bids Farewell (13:1–17:26)

Jesus is now praying finally for both the two groups previously mentioned. In doing so, he adopts a typical Johannine usage, namely, the neuter: "what you have given me" in the sense of "all those whom you have given me" (cf. John 6:37; 17:2). They are to be where Jesus is and see his glory. In this section, three themes come to the fore: the thought of the future "glory" of Jesus that he will possess before the foundation of the world and the resuming of the theme of "love." To that is added the theme of "knowledge" which like "glory" links this closing section with the opening verses 1–5.

The themes of "glory" and "love" were already linked in v. 24: the believers are to see the glory of Jesus that the Father, in his love, bestowed on him before the foundation of the world.

In v. 25, the third theme is added: that of "knowing." After a repeated but expanded prayer-address, "righteous Father" (Πάτερ δίκαιε), there follows another backward look. The "world," which was mentioned in v. 24, but only as the epitome of creation, now occurs once more as the description of the area that is not open to God's message, and so has not known God. The characterization of the Father as "righteous" allows us to think of the God who acts uprightly. The theme of "righteousness" or "justice" occurs otherwise only in John 16:8, 10, similarly in connection with a failure to assent in faith to Jesus, and there it is linked expressly with judgement. The "world," which has not known the Father as the Father of Jesus, is contrasted with those who have known Jesus in his mission from the Father.

To know the Father and to know Jesus means also to know the "name" of the Father, since he is indeed the Father of Jesus. This is implied in v. 26. Jesus leads to this knowledge. In his life and work until now, he has proclaimed the name of the Father, and he will do this again. This will happen in his "hour." With that there is a further allusion to the beginning of the chapter: "Father, the hour is come" (v. 1). With the theme of "love," the author is going further back still to the beginning of the farewell discourses in John 13:1. If the subject there was the love of Jesus for his own, so now it is the Father's love for Jesus. It is to take up room in future believers, and Jesus himself is to take up residence in them. With that, the theme of indwelling also comes to its close. What was spoken of in John 14:20–23 as promise is now promised once more within the frame of a prayer, the prayer of the departing Jesus that thus comes to its conclusion.

## III

John 17 is a late text. Like a prism, it gathers up in itself all the great themes of the Johannine farewell discourses, indeed, of the whole of John's Gospel: the revelation of the love of God in Jesus Christ; the shining out of the glory of God in him; the sharing of this glory with the disciples; their indwelling in Christ and, ultimately, in God through faith in Jesus; but also the stages on Jesus's journey to his "hour" that, on the one hand, has dawned but, on the other hand, is still pending. As in the coda of a symphony, all these great themes sound together once more.

At the same time, however, John 17 is also an early text. There is probably a threat to the unity of those who believe in Christ, but it is striking what is meant to safeguard this unity and what is not. The disciples will be and remain united through the word of Jesus, which they have received in faith, and through his love, which he has brought to them from the Father. According to John 17, it is not institutions that guarantee the unity of Christians, no office, no authoritative tradition beyond the word that continues to be given. In John 21, Peter is represented as the one commissioned with the care of Jesus's flock, and the beloved disciple is presented as the bearer of the tradition. The Protestant point of view will refer more to John 17 with its care for the unity of Christians, the Catholic more, perhaps, to John 21. Here there remains room for an investigation of the dialectic that marks the Fourth Gospel in its final form.[172]

---

172. Cf. the volume edited by Bienert, *Einheit als Gabe und Verpflichtung*. In recent times, the second volume of Pope Benedict XVI's *Jesus von Nazareth* has led to discussions about the concept of unity represented by the author. Cf. Sattler, "... dass sie alle eins seien"; Koch, "Christliche Ökumene"; Theobald, "Das 'hohepriesterliche' Gebet."

# Jesus's "Hour": Passion, Death, and Resurrection (18:1–20:31)

At the beginning of this section, John 18–20, the basic question arises as to why on earth John the evangelist closes his Gospel with an account of the passion, death, and resurrection of Jesus. Among the commentators, it is Bultmann, above all, who poses this question.[1]

From the beginning John's Gospel is marked by its emphasis on the incarnation in Jesus of Nazareth of the divine Word who took on flesh for the salvation of mankind. In the Bultmannian school, it is discussed whether this incarnation was a full reality or was simply an impression, as Ernst Käsemann asserts.[2] Be that as it may, the coming of Jesus in the flesh constitutes the fundamental salvific reality. The question can then arise as to what additional purpose is to be served by his passion, death, and resurrection. According to Bultmann, it was necessary to reveal the way of the incarnate Word of God right to the end. The conflicts with the Jews are characterized by the war of the light against the darkness. The passion of Jesus "is the victorious conclusion of this war."[3] Jesus announced his passion not as a necessity for him to be killed but as a future "lifting up" and "glorification" (ὑψωθῆναι and δοξασθῆναι).[4] In this passion, Jesus is himself the actor (cf. John 14:31: "I do," ποιῶ). The resurrection of Jesus is "the demonstration of his victory over the world, which has already been achieved (16:33)."[5] The Easter events were

---

1. Cf. Bultmann, 489f.
2. Cf. Käsemann, *Jesu letzter Wille*.
3. Bultmann, 489.
4. Bultmann, 489.
5. Bultmann, 490.

"σημεῖα [signs], just as Jesus's miracles were."[6] They were meant to lead to faith.

> Essentially, after the νῦν ἐδοξάσθη ὁ υἱὸς τοῦ ἀνθρώπου [now is the Son of Man glorified], 13:31, Jesus has already spoken to his own as the one who has been lifted up, the glorified one. His work on earth was thus finished. However, he did not speak the τετέλεσται [it is finished] until he was on the cross, 19:30. For the ὥρα [hour] of his δοξασθῆναι [glorification] (12:23; 17:1), of his μεταβῆναι ἐκ τοῦ κόσμου [going from this world] (13:1) embraces the passion event as a whole, and, in the νῦν [now] 13:31, there is an anticipation of all the following events.[7]

In the part of his commentary devoted to the passion, death, and resurrection of Jesus, Lindars takes up Bultmann's theological approach.[8] According to Lindars, the Fourth Gospel circles around two poles: the incarnation, and the lifting up and glorification of Jesus in his "hour." Bultmann's literary-critical approach has been superseded today, but his attempt at an exegesis of the Fourth Gospel is of abiding significance for the contemporary reader.

All four Gospels conclude with the accounts of the passion and resurrection. With Martin Kähler, one can define the Gospels precisely as "passion narratives with extended introductions."[9] In their basic form, they draw on the ancient confession expressions that have for their content the passion, death, and resurrection of Jesus for the salvation of mankind (cf. 1 Cor 15:3-4; Rom 4:25).

In the Synoptic Gospels, the account of the passion, death, and resurrection of Jesus is prepared in a twofold way. On the one hand, in the second section, Jesus announces three times his coming passion, death, and resurrection (Mark 8:31; 9:31; 10:33-34 par.). On the other hand, there is an early revelation of the opposition against Jesus on the part of the Pharisees because of their different interpretation of the Law. After the story of the healing of the man with the withered hand on the Sabbath, it says in Mark 3:6: "Then the Pharisees went out and conspired with the Herodians to kill Jesus."

6. Bultmann, 491.
7. Bultmann, 489.
8. Lindars, 64.
9. Cf. Kähler, *Der sogenannte historische Jesus*, 60 n. 1 at 59.

## Jesus's "Hour": Passion, Death, and Resurrection (18:1–20:31)

In John, this plan appears in a similar connection. The reason for the intention to kill Jesus lies not only in his infringement of the Law on account of the healing of the paralytic on the Sabbath but, also and especially, in his claim to be one with the Father in his works and ultimately in his being: "Consequently, the Jews persecuted Jesus because he had done this on the Sabbath. Jesus retorted: My Father works until now, and I also work. For this reason, the Jews sought even more to kill him because not only did he break the Sabbath but also called God his Father and so made himself equal with God" (John 5:16–18).

Jesus's announcements of his future passion, death, and resurrection in the Synoptics find no direct correspondence in John. Instead, John has his own peculiar language in which Jesus speaks about it saying that he has to be "lifted up" and "glorified." The first expression is found in the first part of the Fourth Gospel, in John 3:14; 8:28 and 12:32; the latter in John 7:39; 12:23, 28. The commentaries see the significance of these expressions for the inner connection of the two parts of John's Gospel.[10] A further pointer to the future suffering of Jesus is found in the talk of his "going away" (ὑπάγειν) in John 7:33; 8:21, taken up again in 13:33, 36.

A detailed description of the connections between the first and the second parts of John's Gospel is found in the work of Zumstein. First in an article,[11] then in the second volume of his commentary on John,[12] the author makes use of the methods of narrative analysis. With their help, he is able to show how John prepares for the account of the passion, death, and resurrection of Jesus from the very first chapters of the Gospel. This happens in a fourfold way.

First, there are the thematic connections between the two parts of the Gospel. To these belongs the mention of the "Lamb of God who takes away the sin of the world," which occurs already in the witness of the Baptist (John 1:29; cf. 1:36). Jesus is later condemned at the hour in which the Passover lambs are slaughtered. We have already mentioned Jesus's announcements that he will be "lifted up" and "glorified." To this should be added the reference to his "hour," which at first has not yet come (John 2:4; 7:30; 8:20; cf. 7:6 καιρός). It will be the hour of his lifting up on the cross and of his completion (John 12:23, 27; 13:1).

---

10. Cf. Schnackenburg, 3:246 for the "being lifted up"; other authors for the "being glorified": Bultmann, 489; Lindars, 64; Léon-Dufour, 11f.; Moloney, 481f.; Schnelle, 286; Wengst, 195.

11. Cf. Zumstein, "Johanneische Interpretation."

12. Cf. Zumstein, "Johanneische Interpretation," 2:191f.

In the second place, there are the implicit or explicit comments. An explicit reference of this kind is found at the end of the account of the cleansing of the temple in which Jesus announces that he will rebuild the temple when it has been destroyed: "But he meant the temple of his body. When he was raised from the dead, his disciples remembered that he had said this, and they believed the Scripture and the word that Jesus had spoken" (John 2:21-22) Later, the gift of the Spirit is announced for the moment in which Jesus will be glorified (John 7:39). The saying of Caiaphas that it is better that one man die for the people than that the whole nation perishes (John 11:50) is related directly (v. 51) to the imminent salvific death of Jesus. Correspondingly, the narrator interprets Jesus's announcement of his imminent "lifting up" as the manner of his execution (John 12:33). Elsewhere, there are indirect predictions of Jesus's passion either in the sense of "Johannine irony" or of misunderstanding (cf. John 2:19-21; 6:51-53; 7:33-36; 8:21-22; 12:32-34; 14:4-6; 16:16-19).

A third means of connecting the two parts of the Gospel is in the transitional section of John 11-12. On the one hand, it closes the section about Jesus's signs with the last, great sign of the raising of Lazarus in John 11:1-46; on the other hand, with the symbolic power of the raising of Lazarus, together with the ensuing death sentence against Jesus (John 11:47-52) and the anointing of Jesus in Bethany (John 12:1-8), it is already preparing for the passion narrative. So too the coming of the Greeks (John 12:20-36).

Fourth and finally, the depiction of the passion, death, and resurrection in John 13-20 connects with the first part of the Fourth Gospel in that it shows Jesus's superiority even in the hour of his passing away. This is indicated by the footwashing in John 13:1. It is repeated in the scene of the arrest, in the Roman trial of Jesus, and, in fact, in the representation of the crucifixion itself, which depicts Jesus in the middle between two other crucified men and below the inscription that proclaims his royal dignity. Again, the account of Jesus's being taking down from the cross and his burial speaks of the salvation that emanates from his heart, and of his dignity in his burial in the new grave of a wealthy friend.

What is the origin of the Johannine depiction of Jesus's homecoming as his "lifting up" and "glorification"? It has already been suggested that John appears to be taking up the beginning of the Fourth Servant Song of Isa 52:13 in the Septuagint version: "Behold, my servant will understand and will be lifted up and glorified exceedingly" (ἰδοὺ συνήσει ὁ παῖς μου καὶ ὑψωθήσεται καὶ δοξασθήσεται σφόδρα). How strongly Isaiah and the

## Jesus's "Hour": Passion, Death, and Resurrection (18:1–20:31)

notion of the servant has influenced John has already been shown in the exegesis of John 12:20–36. This connection remained hidden for so long only because the fourth evangelist replaced the servant with the title of Son of Man taken from the Synoptics.

How are chapters 18–20 of John constructed? The interpretation of the individual section depends, of course, essentially on its context. As expected, the particular proposals of the exegetes differ from one another. The reason for this lies in the criteria that are adopted for the division of the text. In what follows, this commentary starts out from the criteria of narrative analysis and distinguishes scenes according to the change of time and place, as well as of the people taking part and of the action. Larger sections are observable through the concentric structures that can be observed in John 18–20.

A division of the Johannine passion account according to narrative criteria is found already in Bultmann. He distinguishes four parts of the account: John 18:1–11, the arrest of Jesus; 18:12–27, Jesus before the high priest and the denial of Peter; 18:28–19:16a, Jesus before Pilate; and 19:16b–42, the crucifixion and burial of Jesus.

Already with Schnackenburg, there is a reduction of the four main sections to three which, since then, have been established many times: 18:1–27, the arrest and the Jewish hearing: 18:28–19:16a, the trial before Pilate; and 19:16b–42, the passion: way of the cross, crucifixion, and burial.[13] The present division also follows dramatic criteria.[14] The events of John 18:1–27 play out by night and have two locations: the garden and the palace of the high priest. The events of John 18:28–19:16a take place on the morning of the following day and again have two locations: outside and inside the Praetorium. The events of John 19:16b–42 take place on the afternoon of the same day and again have two locations: Golgotha and the "garden" as the site of Jesus's burial. The change of locations is matched by a change of those taking part.

According to A. Janssens de Varebeke,[15] whom other authors follow,[16] these three main sections of the Johannine passion narrative divide into seven scenes, each with a special emphasis on the middle scenes and corre-

---

13. Cf. Schnackenburg, 3:246–352 (esp. 248); the first and the third main sections are subdivided.
14. Cf. Schenke, 334–39.
15. Janssens de Varebeke, "Structure."
16. Cf. de la Potterie, *Passion*; Mlakuzhyil, *Christocentric Literary Structure*; Schenke (cf. n. 14) for the second and third main sections.

spondences among the other scenes in a concentric arrangement. In a rough association with Janssens de Varebeke (who subdivides John 18:1–4 into 18:1 and 18:2–4), the first main section can be divided in the following way:

18:1–3 The arrival in the Garden of Gethsemane
18:4–9 The encounter of Jesus with the arresting party
18:10–11 Peter's action and his rebuke by Jesus
18:12–14 Jesus is brought to the high priest
18:15–18 Peter's first denial
18:19–24 Jesus is examined by the high priest and brought to Caiaphas
18:25–27 Peter's second and third denials

In the center stands the most important scene: Jesus is brought face to face with Israel's high priest. This is framed by two scenes that depict the lack of understanding or the betrayal of Peter. The second and the penultimate scenes show Jesus in his superiority vis à vis the arresting party and to the high priest. The first and last scenes depict Jesus as betrayed and denied. This division remains hypothetical, but it finds its confirmation in the division of the two following main sections.

The second main section with the Roman trial of Jesus (John 18:28–19:16b) can equally be divided into seven scenes as was already suggested by Schnackenburg[17] (with a precursor in Bultmann[18]). The scenes alternate by means of a change of place between the area in front of the Praetorium and the Praetorium itself. Pilate goes out to the "Jews" who demand the death of Jesus and then back in again to speak with Jesus, of whose innocence he is increasingly convinced. In the center stands the scene of Jesus's crowning with thorns in John 19:1–3.[19] Thus emerges the following structure for the section:

18:28–32 Jesus is led to Pilate. Pilate and the "Jews," scene: outside
18:33–37 inside: Pilate and Jesus (Jesus "King of the Jews")
18:38–40 outside: Pilate and the "Jews"
19:1–3 inside: scourging of Jesus and crowning with thorns
19:4–7 outside: Pilate and the "Jews"
19:8–12 inside: Pilate and Jesus (mention of the "Jews")
19:13–16b outside: Pilate, Jesus, and the "Jews," condemnation of Jesus

17. Schnackenburg, 3:275f.
18. Bultmann, 503–15 knows of six subdivisions.
19. Cf. Brown, 2:859.

## Jesus's "Hour": Passion, Death, and Resurrection (18:1–20:31)

The individual exegesis will demonstrate the correspondences in detail. Worth recording, though, is the mention of the feast of the Passover at the beginning (18:28) and at the end (19:14), with a further mention in the middle (18:39), which is less substantial from a structural point of view. In this section too, the two most important scenes for the self-revelation of Jesus are in the second and penultimate places. The first and the last are partly of a scenic nature in which the last provides a transition to the third main section.

There is also widespread agreement concerning the division of the third and last main section of the Johannine passion narrative in John 19:16c–42. For Janssens de Varebeke, Jesus's death on the cross in John 19:28–30 stands in the central position. He thus connects John 19:16c(17)–19 and 20–22. More recent exegetes find two scenes in these verses but see only a single scene in 19:38–42[20] (two scenes in Janssens de Varebeke). Thus, the following construction emerges:

19:16c–18   The way of the cross and the crucifixion of Jesus
19:19–22   Pilate and the inscription over the cross
19:23–24   The distribution of Jesus's garments
19:25–27   Jesus entrusts his mother to the beloved disciple
19:28–30   Jesus's thirst, the offer of vinegar, Jesus's death
19:31–37   Pilate and the breaking of Jesus's legs, the flow of blood and water
19:38–42   The burial of Jesus by Joseph of Arimathea and Nicodemus; mention of the "garden"

In the center of the composition stands the "legacy" of Jesus in which he entrusts his mother to the beloved disciple. On account of the significance of the beloved disciple for the Johannine (reader-)community, it is tempting to ascribe symbolic power to this scene. Many exegetes also see in this scene a gesture with which Jesus entrusts the community represented by the beloved disciple to his mother.

By contrast with chapters 18–19, there is no agreement among exegetes over the division of chapter 20. All see in John 20 two main sections: the events at the grave on the morning of Easter Day in John 20:1–18 and the encounter of Jesus with the disciples at their meeting place on the evening of the same day in verses 19–29. This is followed by the literary

20. Cf. Schenke, 359.

THE GOSPEL OF JOHN: A COMMENTARY

conclusion of the Gospel in verses 30–31 before the supplement in chapter 21. The subdivision of the two main sections in John 20 is carried out in various ways. Schnackenburg[21] divides verses 1–18 into two scenes: 1–10 and 11–18. Brown supposes only one.[22] Correspondingly, Schnackenburg[23] divides John 20:19–29 into two scenes: vv. 19–23 and 24–28. Brown keeps the section undivided.[24] Schenke finds five scenes in John 20 before the conclusion in verses 30–31: vv. 1–10, 11–17, 18, 19–23, and 24–29.[25] However, it is advisable to differentiate the scenes more exactly corresponding to the information about time, place, people taking part, and action. According to these criteria, the following six scenes emerge for John 20 before the two concluding verses:

20:1–2  Mary Magdalene at the grave; she informs Peter and the beloved disciple
20:3–10  Peter and the beloved disciple at the grave (reference to Scripture)
20:11–18  Mary Magdalene at the grave; she recognizes Jesus
20:19–23  The disciples recognize Jesus: peace, joy, gift of the Spirit
20:24–25  Thomas does not come to faith in Jesus
20:26–29  Thomas comes to faith in Jesus
20:30–31  Conclusion: through faith to life

In the middle of this composition in seven parts stands the scene of the encounter of Jesus with the disciples on Easter evening in which the risen Jesus gives the disciples his eschatological gifts: peace, joy, and the Holy Spirit (cf. Rom 14:17 and John 14:26–28; 16:4e–33). Until v. 18, Jesus is still in the situation of ascending to the Father; from v. 19, he is returning to his own.[26]

---

21. Schnackenburg, 3:355–80.
22. Brown, 2:979–1017.
23. Schnackenburg, 3:380–99.
24. Brown, 2:1018–51.
25. Schenke, 369–71.
26. This basic structure is found in Schneiders in her unpublished dissertation, "The Johannine Resurrection Narrative."

*Jesus's "Hour": Passion, Death, and Resurrection (18:1–20:31)*

## 1. The Arrest of Jesus and the Jewish Trial (18:1–27)

¹ After these words, Jesus went out with his disciples to the other side of the brook Kidron. There was a garden there into which Jesus went with his disciples. ² Judas, who betrayed him, knew the place also, for Jesus often met there with his disciples. ³ Judas brought the soldiers and the officers of the chief priests and Pharisees, and came there with lanterns, torches and weapons. ⁴ Jesus, who knew everything that was going to happen to him, came forward and asked them: Whom do you seek? ⁵ They answered him: Jesus of Nazareth. He said to them: I am he. Judas, who betrayed him, was also standing with them. ⁶ As soon as he said to them: I am he!, they turned back and fell to the ground. ⁷ He asked them again: Whom do you seek? They said: Jesus of Nazareth. ⁸ Jesus answered: I have told you that I am he. So, if you are seeking me, let these men go their way! ⁹ Thus was to be fulfilled the word he had said: of those whom you have given me, I have lost none. ¹⁰ Simon Peter, who had a sword with him, drew it and with it struck the servant of the high priest and cut off his right ear; the servant's name was Malchus. ¹¹ Then Jesus said to Peter: Put back your sword into its scabbard! Am I not to drink of the cup which the Father has given me?

¹² The soldiers, the captain and the officers of the Jews seized Jesus, bound him ¹³ and led him first to Annas; for he was the father-in-law of Caiaphas, who was high priest that year. ¹⁴ It was Caiaphas who had given the Jews the advice: It is better that one man die for the people.

¹⁵ Simon Peter and another disciple followed Jesus. This disciple was known to the high priest and went with Jesus into the high priest's courtyard. ¹⁶ But Peter remained standing outside the door. Then the other disciple came out, the one who was known to the high priest; he spoke to the maid who kept the door and led Peter inside. ¹⁷ Then the maid said to Peter: Are you not also one of this man's disciples? He said: I am not. ¹⁸ The servants and officers had kindled a coal fire and stood beside it to warm themselves; for it was cold. Peter also stood with them and warmed himself.

¹⁹ The high priest asked Jesus about his disciples and about his teaching. ²⁰ Jesus answered him: I have spoken openly before all the world. I have always taught in the synagogues and in the temple where all the Jews gather together. I have spoken nothing in secret. ²¹ Why are you asking me? Ask those who were listening what I have spoken about; look, they know what I have said. ²² When he said this, one of the officers who was standing by struck Jesus in the face and said: Is that the way you answer the high priest? ²³ Jesus replied: If what I said was not right, then show what it was; but if it was right, why strike me? ²⁴ Then Annas sent him bound to the high priest, Caiaphas.

²⁵ But Simon Peter was standing there and warming himself. Then they said to him: Are you not also one of his disciples? He denied it and said: I am not. ²⁶ One of the servants of the high priest, a relation of the one whose ear Peter had cut off, said: Did I not see you in the garden with him? ²⁷ Again, Peter denied it, and, immediately, the cock crowed.

*I*

The Fourth Gospel's account of the passion, death, and resurrection of Jesus begins with the appearance of Jesus before the highest religious and civil authority of the Jews, the Sanhedrin, in John 18:1-27. In accordance with the previously mentioned suggestion, this section is divided into seven scenes. In this way, the arraignment of Jesus before the high priest Annas (vv. 12-14) stands in the middle of the composition. The arrest of Jesus in John 18:1-11 is narrated in three scenes. The scene of the appearance before Annas is followed similarly by three scenes in which Peter and Jesus are protagonists alternately.

The exegesis of the Johannine passion narrative also involves the question of its dependence on sources. If one accepts basic Synoptic influence in John's Gospel, there remain the two models of a direct dependence of the Fourth Gospel on the first three or an indirect dependence by means of a pre-Johannine passion account that was influenced by the Synoptics. The latter is the interpretation of the book by Anton Dauer on John 18:1-19:30.[27] In John 18:4-9, Dauer recognizes the redactional work of the evangelist independent of the tradition, but in the introductory verses 1-3 and in vv. 10-11 he sees the influence of a pre-Johannine source that was influenced by the Synoptics. Maurits Sabbe, one of the most influential representatives of the Louvain school, renders this hypothesis improbable.[28] An argument in his favor lies already in the fact that—and this is also claimed by Dauer—the fourth evangelist would have worked independently of any source in vv. 4-9.[29] If John managed to form the middle part of the section independently, then the question arises whether he was not also able to do it in the other verses, supported by the Synoptics.

27. Dauer, *Passionsgeschichte*.
28. Sabbe, "Arrest."
29. So, too, Williams, *I Am He*.

*Jesus's "Hour": Passion, Death, and Resurrection (18:1–20:31)*

A similar question can be addressed to the attempt by Anderson who supposes for the Johannine passion narrative, first, a Johannine tradition independent of the Synoptics, which would then have been in contact with and influenced by pre-Synoptic and Synoptic traditions.[30]

In dialogue with Dauer, we note in the present section the concrete details in John, such as the brook Kidron in v. 1, the name of Malchus in v. 10, and the mention of Peter in the same verse. As Sabbe demonstrates, the fourth evangelist loves concrete details.[31] This tendency can be shown in the treatment of the Jewish festal cycle in John 5–10. For this reason, it is unnecessary to go back to a non-Synoptic source for the explanation of concrete details. Clearly, John the evangelist had a sufficiently broad vision of the area of the city of Jerusalem in order to depict the way of Jesus and his disciples out of the city as a crossing of the Kidron. The Louvain school also discusses the Johannine character of verses 4–9. As Sabbe notes in an addition to his article,[32] his Louvain colleagues, Neirynck and T. Snoy, reckon here too with Synoptic influence in the motifs of the fulfilling of Scripture and the discharge of the disciples, which changes the Synoptics' flight of the disciples into a dismissal. One can then say, with an *a fortiori* argument, that when Dauer advocates the redactional character of verses 4–9 without recourse to his source, then he must be ready even more to deny the existence of this source in those verses where Synoptic influence can be demonstrated.

## II

### *The Arrival in the Garden of Gethsemane (18:1–3)*

This scene follows the farewell discourses of Jesus. In accordance with the exegesis offered here, the text would have originally followed on from John 14:31. In the present text of the Gospel, the scene of the arrest follows the concluding prayer of Jesus at the end of the farewell discourses. According to John, Jesus does not return to the garden in order to pray but comes from prayer. The introductory scene forms an inclusio both with the last scene of the section as also with the third. Our scene has the theme of the

---

30. Cf. Anderson, "Aspects of Interfluentiality."
31. Cf. Sabbe, "Arrest."
32. Cf. Sabbe, "Arrest," 388.

"garden" in common with John 18:25–27 (cf. the question of the officer of the high priest: "Did I not see you in the garden with him?"). It will occur once again at the end of the passion narrative in John 19:41 and then lead over into the Easter story (John 20:15). With the third scene of John 18:10–12, the three opening verses have the language of weapons in common: just as the soldiers and the officers of the chief priests and Pharisees come with weapons, so, later, Peter draws his sword. In the center stands the self-revelation of Jesus.

**18:1** The first three verses are characterized by the opposition between Jesus and his disciples, on the one hand (v. 1), and Judas with his group, on the other (vv. 2–3). In v. 1, Jesus "goes" "out" from the city; in v. 4, he "comes" "forward" from the garden to which he has returned. The brook Kidron is absent in the Synoptic tradition;[33] in John, there is no mention of Gethsemane. Perhaps the evangelist wanted to avoid a reference to this place. According to John, Jesus was already stricken with the fear of death, but was able to overcome this fear (cf. John 12:27–28). At his entry into his passion, Jesus appears calm and sovereign.

**18:2–3** Only now does the reader experience the fact that night had fallen. Judas appears with his group "with lanterns and torches." At the point when Judas had left the Supper, it was already night (John 13:30), and, viewed symbolically, that probably signified his belonging to the powers of darkness. The group led by Judas is composed of representatives of the Roman occupying force and officers of the Jewish authorities (the σπεῖρα stands for a cohort, in some cases for a maniple, under the command of a captain: χιλίαρχος, v. 12. The cohort was a tenth of a legion, which was made up of approximately of five thousand soldiers). John's account arouses the impression that the whole of the Roman cohort stationed in the Antonia Fortress had sallied forth to arrest Jesus. The whole of the said group comes "with weapons." The single weapon of Jesus will be the power of his word. Judas's task cannot be to command this whole military unit but only to show them the way to the place where Jesus often went.

---

33. According to Karakolis, "Across the Kidron Brook," there could be an allusion to the flight of David over the brook Kidron in 2 Sam 15:23 that is meant to save his kingly dignity. Jesus does not flee but obtains his abiding kingly dignity, even beyond his death.

## Jesus's "Hour": Passion, Death, and Resurrection (18:1–20:31)

### Jesus's Encounter with the Arresting Party (18:4–9)

**18:4** At the beginning of the Johannine account of the passion and death of Jesus, the evangelist recalls that Jesus knew everything that was to come upon him. The statement in v. 4 points back to John 13:1, the beginning of the Last Supper, with the same statement. The superiority of Jesus is demonstrated at further moments of this passion. Before his death, it is again recalled that he knew that now all things had been fulfilled (John 19:28). Jesus entered his passion not only in the full knowledge of what lay before him but also with the resolve not to resist his fate. For this reason, he "comes" "forward" from the garden and asks the military detachment whom they are seeking instead of waiting for them to enquire after his identity and then to lead him away.

**18:5-6** The soldiers' answer implies Christian usage: "Jesus of Nazareth" (Greek Ναζωραῖον). The word chosen allows the resonance of words from Israel's vocabulary (through the roots "Branch" or "dedicated to God"). Jesus's answer is short and clear: "I am he." However, the meaning of these words is debated. In the first place, they certainly signify the identification of Jesus as the person being sought. In addition, however, the formula "I am he" (Ἐγώ εἰμι) appears also to allude to a formula occurring frequently in Deutero-Isaiah with which God makes himself known and vouches for the reliability of his promises (cf. the formula אֲנִי־הוּא Isa 41:4; 43:10, 13, 25; 46:4; 48:12; 51:12; 52:6 as well as Deut 32:39).[34] In the face of the revelation of the divinity, the creature falls to the ground according to the biblical texts. For the New Testament cf. Paul in Acts 9:4; 22:7; 26:14. In John 18:5, 6, 8, there is also the aspect of the superiority of God or of the psalmist over their enemies. The latter "fall to the ground" or "turn back," cf. Ps 26:2; 34:4; 55:10 LXX. The text registers no activity on the part of Judas. He only "was standing with them." For the evangelist, Judas's belonging to the group of Jesus's adversaries is more important than his taking part in the arrest itself (as, perhaps, with the kiss in the Synoptics). Since John 6:64, Jesus has shown himself aware of who it is that will betray him.

**18:7-8** Verse 7 takes up vv. 4 and 5 word for word, and v. 8 recalls the answer of Jesus in v. 5. Now the identification is central: I am the one you are seeking, and, if that is so, let these others go their way. Jesus is sparing his disciples from having to take part in his fate and also from the flight that is recorded by the other evangelists.[35]

---

34. Cf. Williams, *I Am He*.
35. Mardaga, "The Meaning," sees a development in the three Ἐγώ εἰμι sayings of

**18:9** The closing verse of the subsection gives a theological basis for Jesus's answer concerning his disciples with reference to a word that he had spoken previously. According to the Nestle-Aland text, Jesus's statement is referring to John 6:39: "and this is the will of him who sent me, that I let none of those that he has given me perish but that I raise them up at the last day." The same sense is found in a saying of the good shepherd about his sheep in John 10:28: "I give them eternal life. They will never perish, and no one will seize them out of my hand." However, it is also possible to think of the saying of Jesus in the high priestly prayer in John 17:12: "I have lost none of them, except the son of perdition so that the Scripture may be fulfilled." It is difficult to decide among these references.[36] Be that as it may, Jesus can refer to the assurance that he uttered well before the passion that none of his own will perish. In John 18:9, Jesus is showing himself as the good shepherd who protects his own in the moment of danger.

The introductory formula: "Thus was to be fulfilled the word which he had said" is surprising here, since it is otherwise repeated in the passion narrative only for the purpose of introducing a saying of Scripture. The single other example of this kind of thing is found in John 18:32. The question then arises whether the use of this formula to introduce Jesus's words signifies that John is making the word of Jesus into a part of Scripture. With a glance at the role of Scripture in John, it is better to answer this question in the negative. In John, Jesus's word receives an authority that is simply comparable to that of Scripture.

### The Action of Peter and His Rebuke by Jesus (18:10–11)

**18:10** This little scene has the form of a biographical apothegm. An incident leads to a saying of Jesus with which the section ends. Verse 10 depicts an attempt by Peter to defend his master with the sword. With his weapon, Peter is rather like the troop described in vv. 2–3 who had been sent out to arrest Jesus. The mission of Jesus is not to be decided on this level. In his trial before Pilate, Jesus says: "My kingdom is not of this world. If my kingdom were of this world, then would my people fight so

---

John 18:5–8: from identification to theophany and finally to the effort for the disciples thanks to the identification of Jesus. Triple rhythms are not unusual in John. The threefold "I am he" of Jesus is matched by the triple "I am not" of Peter in the denial scenes John 18:17, 25, 27 ("he denied") and the triple restoration in John 21:15–17.

36. Cf. the discussion in Brown, 2:811f.; Schnackenburg, 3:255.

## Jesus's "Hour": Passion, Death, and Resurrection (18:1–20:31)

that I might not be delivered to the Jews. But now is my kingdom not from here." Repeatedly in the Fourth Gospel, Peter is depicted as unreliable and of limited understanding when it comes to faith. This impression will be confirmed in what follows. On the other hand, however, in John 6:68–69, Peter appears as the spokesman who is able to bring the faith in Jesus to expression, and, according to John 21:15–17, he is commissioned by Jesus for this service. At least for the final redaction of John's Gospel, then, Peter does not only appear in a negative light.

**18:11** In his word to Peter, Jesus demands the renunciation of violence. The reason for this lies in the way predetermined for Jesus by the Father. Jesus's saying relates to the Gethsemane scene in the Synoptic tradition (Matt 26:39, 42 par.), in which Jesus prays that the cup might pass from him but submits to the will of God. In John, Jesus shows the same readiness without asking first that the cup might pass from him. Such hesitation was recorded only in the previously mentioned "Gethsemane" scene in John 12:27–28. At the moment of his arrest, Jesus appears as fully master of the situation and ready to accept the will of the Father. In this saying of Jesus, the readers will hear an invitation to trust in the will of the Father in all life's circumstances but also to the renunciation of violence.[37]

### Jesus Is Brought to the High Priest (18:12–14)

This scene stands in the center of the larger section, John 18:1–27, and, in its center, stands Jesus. Readers perhaps wonder why, in this scene, Jesus neither speaks nor acts, but this can be explained by the nature of the situation: from the moment of his arrest, Jesus is subject to the will of others and, on a deeper level, to the will of the Father who has laid down this way for him. The evangelist speaks of Jesus, who is led away by the arresting party (v. 12), but adds two remarks. The first refers to the person of Annas (v. 13), the second to Caiaphas (v. 14). The latter's saying is recalled that it is better that one man die for the people. In this way, the theological significance of the scene is emphasized.

**18:12** John remains faithful to his view that Jesus was arrested by the power of the Roman state in association with the Jewish authorities. There is an added reference to the captain (χιλίαρχος), the commander of the Roman military unit. The officers of the Jewish authorities are identified

---

37. Cf. Scheffler, "Jesus' Non-Violence."

as the "Jews," according to the usual Johannine usage. Jesus is "seized" and "bound." Now, he is given up into the hands of men.

**18:13–14** At the beginning of v. 13, the sentence with which the arrest of Jesus was recorded is brought to its conclusion. Jesus is now "led first to Annas." In a first comment, Annas is introduced. He is the father-in-law of Caiaphas who was high priest that year. In the Synoptic passion narratives, Annas is not mentioned. We find him as the high priest along with Caiaphas at the beginning of the activity of John the Baptist in Luke 3:2, and alongside Caiaphas also in the trial of Peter according to Acts 4:6. According to the passion predictions (Mark 8:31; 10:33 par.), Jesus was condemned not least by "the chief priests." Thus, the existence of a plurality of high priests is presupposed here as well as in Mark 14:55 par. Matt 26:59. John introduces the figure of Annas with a reference to his family relationship with Caiaphas, who was the high priest that year (cf. John 11:49). Probably this expression denotes only that Caiaphas was the one who exercised the office of high priest in the relevant year without intending to say that he exercised it only in this year and that it was changed annually. In v. 14, the connection with the condemnation scene in John 11:47–53 is expressly established.

*Peter's First Denial (18:15–18)*

With this scene, we reach the fifth subunit within John 18:1–27. With a glance at the construction of the whole, we can say that Peter explicitly, or at least implicitly, appears in the first, third, fifth, and seventh scenes while Jesus dominates the second, fourth, and sixth. In the first scene, Peter belongs to the group of disciples who accompany Jesus into the garden. In the third scene, he makes his mark through his "militaristic" action with respect to the servant of the high priest, wishing to defend his master with the sword. He had not understood that the arrest of Jesus was part of the divine plan of salvation that Jesus was allowing to happen to himself. In the fifth and seventh scenes, Peter appears even further distant from his master.[38] With this, he leaves the stage in John and will appear again only in the Easter story.

Already in the Synoptic tradition, the threefold denial of Jesus by Peter takes place in connection with the interrogation of Jesus in the palace of the high priest. According to Mark and the other Synoptics, how-

---

38. Escaffre, "Pierre et Jésus."

ever, the threefold denial follows the hearing. Through the anticipation of the first denial scene, the fourth evangelist creates a contrast between the behavior of Jesus and that of his distinguished disciple. Through the inclusion of the interrogation of Jesus within the denial scenes, it gains a special weight for the readers. The contrast between Jesus and his disciple is thus strengthened.[39]

The figure of the "other disciple" is missing in the Synoptics and so is peculiar to John. Moreover, his acquaintance with the high priest is also proper to John. How far these aspects rest on tradition can no longer be discerned.

**18:15-16a** According to the text, Peter "follows" Jesus on his way to Annas. This expression (ἠκολούθει) appears almost as an example of Johannine irony. In fact, Peter follows his master only physically. He will soon show that he is not behaving as a disciple. At his side appears here "another disciple." It does not say "the other disciple," which would facilitate his identification with the beloved disciple (cf. John 20:2-3). Nevertheless, the evidence for this is his closeness to Peter and the fact that, according to John 18:16, he gains admission for Peter.

**18:16b-d** Thus, the other disciple lets Peter enter the court of the palace of the high priest, Annas. He manages this because he is known to the high priest.

**18:17** The maid at the door appears to recognize Peter and asks him whether he is not a disciple of "this man." Perhaps at this point she actually points her finger at Jesus who is in the same courtyard of the palace.[40] Peter's denial "I am not" weighs all the more heavily. The formula "I am not" (οὐκ εἰμί) is an ironic adopting of the "I am" (ἐγώ εἰμι) of Jesus in the scene of the arrest (vv. 5 and 8) and contrasts with Jesus's repeated "I" (ἐγώ) in the following scene (vv. 20-23). Peter is increasingly on the way to losing his identity.

**18:18** The same impression emerges from v. 18. Here, it says that the servants and the officers had kindled a coal fire and were standing there. The same is then said of Peter. He no longer does or says anything. The coal fire allows us to think of the one that is mentioned in John 21:9. The agreement in vocabulary appears to be deliberate. The same Peter who is warming himself beside the guards has to renew his faithfulness to his Lord who receives him at a coal fire.

---

39. Escaffre, "Pierre et Jésus."
40. Cf. Escaffre, "Pierre et Jésus."

## THE GOSPEL OF JOHN: A COMMENTARY

### Jesus Is Examined by the High Priest and Brought to Caiaphas (18:19–24)

The location of the section which follows led at an early stage to attempts at transposition. According to the text-critical apparatus of Nestle-Aland[28], there are three variants to the most commonly transmitted text: vv. 13, 24, 15, 19–23, 16–18: sys[s]; vv. 13, 24, 14–23, 24: 1195 sy[hmg] Cyr[com]; vv. 13a, 24, 13b, 14–23, 24: 225. All these attempts have in common that they intend to adjust the Johannine account to that of the Synoptics. We have already seen, however, that the arrangement of the text in John can be explained as a result of literary and theological aims. Thus, Jesus now appears before Annas so that he can be asked about his teaching and his disciples.

For the "Jewish trial" of Jesus, there is a remarkable difference between the Synoptics and John that is discussed in all the commentaries. In John, there is no formal Jewish trial. The reason for that is that, according to the fourth evangelist, Jesus has already been condemned to death by the Sanhedrin and, in fact, in the scene referred to in John 18:14, namely John 11:47–53. The individual variations between the Johannine account and that of the Synoptics is explained in the literature in two different ways: either John has used his own source which, for its part, may have leaned on the Synoptics or not, or there was no such source and John composed his account alone on the basis of the Synoptic Gospels.

As before, we are following the proposal of the Louvain school, according to which John composed his passion narrative on the basis of the Synoptic Gospels alone. For the present section, this proposal has been worked out and argued by Sabbe.[41] A similar position is represented by Frank J. Matera who thinks that John wrote his account on the basis of Mark's Gospel alone.[42] This view remains less convincing than that of Sabbe who propounded his contribution five years after Matera whose arguments he discusses.

According to Sabbe, the absence of a Jewish trial of Jesus within the passion narrative is explained by the fact that such a trial has already occurred in John 11:47–53 and that there has already been an account of an investigation concerning the activity and self-understanding of Jesus by the Jewish authorities in John 10:22–39. Already, this investigation led to the attempt of the "Jews" to stone Jesus (John 10:31–32) or arrest him (v. 39).

---

41. Cf. Sabbe, "John 10."
42. Cf. Matera, "Jesus before Annas."

## Jesus's "Hour": Passion, Death, and Resurrection (18:1–20:31)

The interrogation of Jesus by the high priest Annas is explained by the latter's social position and his family relationship to Caiaphas. John exhibits a tendency to give names to people who remain anonymous in the other Gospels. The most recent example occurs in John 18:10, where the name of the disciple who cut off the ear of the high priest's servant is given as that of Peter and where the servant himself is called Malchus. Corresponding to this propensity, John could also have identified the high priest who began the interrogation of Jesus and who remains anonymous in the first three Gospels: it was "Annas." Flavius Josephus provides the information that Annas—high priest from 6 to 15 CE—had five sons who succeeded him in the office of high priest. Since Caiaphas was not a son of Annas, he could have a similar kind of relationship as his son-in-law.

Instead of a Jewish interrogation by Annas, the Synoptics know of a Jewish trial of Jesus by Caiaphas in two stages: a nocturnal setting and one in the hours of the early morning (Mark 14:53–65; 15:1). This trial is concerned with two themes: the activity of Jesus, especially in relation to the temple, and his identity as a messianic claimant and supposed Son of God. These themes were dealt with by John previously. The question of the temple and a saying of Jesus concerning its destruction and restoration in three days was already mentioned in John 2:18–22. The status of Jesus as Messiah and Son of God was dealt with in John 10:22–39. Thus, it was unnecessary to tackle these themes again in John 18. A formal condemnation of Jesus by the Sanhedrin under the high priest (Caiaphas) was already recounted by John in John 11:47–53, as already mentioned.

Only the scene with the slap in the face finds a parallel in the Synoptic Gospels. In Mark (14:65), after the condemnation of Jesus in the night sitting of the Sanhedrin, it says: "And some began to spit on him and to cover his face and to strike him and cried: Show that you are a prophet! The servants also struck him in the face" (cf. Matt 26:67; Luke 22:63–65). In John, Jesus is found alone in the presence of the high priest and some of his servants. Thus, the scene is reduced to the abuse of Jesus by a few people.

What is the construction of the section 18:19–24? At the beginning there is a question of the high priest to Jesus that is rendered in indirect speech (v. 19). Jesus answers in direct speech (vv. 20–21). His answer is followed by a reaction on the part of one of the high priest's servants: he gives Jesus a slap in the face and rebukes him (v. 22). In his answer, Jesus justifies his own conduct and calls in question that of the high priest's servant (v. 23). The high priest does not say a word but sends Jesus bound to his son-in-law, Caiaphas (v. 24).

**18:19** The "high priest" is Annas (cf. Luke 3:2; Acts 4:6). He asks Jesus about his disciples and about his teaching. His question is given in indirect speech, and, for Bernadette Escaffre, this shows clearly his low profile in the Johannine narrative. Within the whole section, Annas does not utter a single word in direct speech.[43] With the question about the disciples, the readers will think of their "dismissal" by Jesus in John 18:8, and of the increasing distancing of Peter that was recounted in the last verses and that had led to the first explicit denial.

**18:20–21** Jesus confines his answer to the second part of the question, that is, the enquiry about his teaching. His answer is given in direct speech, which corresponds to his high profile within the narrative. The language here is Johannine: Jesus has "spoken openly before all the world" and nothing "in secret" (παρρησίᾳ, "openly" occurs nine times in John, in the Synoptics only once: Mark 8:32; λαλεῖν, "speak," and κόσμος, "world," are found throughout in John; ἐν κρυπτῷ, "in secret," occurs again in John 7:4, 10). For Jesus's teaching in the synagogue, the reader will think of John 6:59; for his teaching in the temple, the discourses of chapters 5 and 7–10. Jesus's statement goes back to John 7:25–26 where some Jews say: "Is not that the man they are seeking to kill? And yet he is speaking in complete openness (παρρησίᾳ) and they are letting him do as he pleases. Has the Supreme Council really recognized that he is the Christ?" In the same chapter, Jesus had spoken of his teaching: "My teaching does not stem from me but from the one who sent me" (John 7:16). In his answer to the high priest, Jesus refers to texts like these when he says that he has taught openly, and that his hearers can witness to his teaching.

**18:22** Jesus's answer does not lead to a response from the high priest but to a violent act on the part of one of his servants. The latter slaps Jesus in the face with the rebuke: "Is that the way you answer the high priest?" The highest Jewish authority was not able to grasp the meaning of Jesus's words. Jesus's words sounded like a challenge and a lack of respect in the courtyard of the high priest.

**18:23** Jesus proves to be masterful in his response and equal to the situation. He presents the high priest's servant with a dilemma: either he was not right in what he said, in which case this should be demonstrated, or he was right, in which case the slap in the face was unjustified. The whole scene displays once again the superiority of Jesus that can be observed

---

43. Cf. Escaffre, "Pierre et Jésus," 64.

## Jesus's "Hour": Passion, Death, and Resurrection (18:1–20:31)

from the beginning of the passion narrative in John 18:1. Thus, too, the last direct speech within this scene is reserved for Jesus.

**18:24** The high priest does not react with words but remains silent. He sends Jesus bound to the high priest, Caiaphas. The doubling of the high priests also shows their weakness and their lack of identity.[44] No further investigation on the part of Caiaphas is recorded (cf. v. 28), and so none of the Jewish authorities were able to find any fault in Jesus that would have justified his condemnation.

### Peter's Second and Third Denials (18:25–27)

All three denial scenes are also found in the Synoptics. The chief difference between John's report of the threefold denial of Jesus by Peter and that of the Synoptics consists in the fact that John inserts the scene of the hearing of Jesus before the high priest between the first and second denial scenes. In this way, the contrast between Jesus, who "witnesses," and Peter, who "denies" (cf. John 1:20), is reinforced.

In Mark (14:68), some of the manuscripts record a cock crow after Peter's second denial. This could also contain a warning. John does not take up this textual tradition. A further difference between John and the Synoptics lies in the fact that, according to Mark, the same maid of the high priest who asked Peter whether he was with Jesus of Nazareth, repeats her question and addresses the bystanders. According to John, other men address the question to Peter himself, who denies belonging to Jesus. Thus, the denial becomes more personal and direct.

The biggest differences are found in the third denial. In the Synoptics, there is no element of relationship between the person who asks Peter and Malchus. The group in the courtyard of the high priest assumes a relationship of Peter to Jesus on the ground that he is also a Galilean or that he has a Galilean accent. At this point, in Mark and Matthew, Peter begins to curse and swear that he does not know this man. In Mark (14:72), at this moment, the cock crows for a second time. Here, all three Synoptics record that Peter remembered the word of Jesus that he would deny him before the cock crowed (twice) and went out and wept. In Luke (22:61), there is the additional detail that at this moment Jesus turned to look at Peter, and the latter then wept.

---

44. Cf. Escaffre, "Pierre et Jésus," 58–61.

These elements are absent in John. The figure of Peter shows no feeling, not even regret.[45] The exegesis below will show how far this corresponds to the fourth evangelist's view of Peter.

The construction of the present text unit is easy to determine. Two short scenes follow each other. In v. 25, the second denial of Peter is recorded, in verses 26–27, the third. The words of the people who question Peter are delivered in the historic present, Peter's answers given in the aorist. At the same time, the same verb, "he denied (ἠρνήσατο)," is used twice (cf. John 13:38).

**18:25** This verse picks up the last mention of Peter in John 18:18. In connection with the first denial it had said: "Peter also stood with them and warmed himself." Bernadette Escaffre[46] notes that Peter seems increasingly less active in this scene. He does nothing more, but simply finds himself in a particular place, and that in the presence of those who, as employees of the Jewish authorities who are hostile to Jesus, had arrested Jesus. The same picture is conveyed in John 18:25. Peter's warming stands in contrast to the courage with which Jesus faces up to the Jewish authorities and endures the abuse of one of the high priest's servants.

**18:26–27** The last question addressed to Peter shows him ever more on the defensive. Once more, the form of the question calls for a positive answer. The man who asks Peter is a relation of the Malchus mentioned previously, whose ear Peter had cut off. Thus, he is speaking from personal knowledge. This knowledge is revealed also in the mention of the "garden" as the place where Jesus had been found. For Peter, this could have been a reminder of his belonging to the group of Jesus's disciples up to that moment. But it is this belonging to Jesus which he denies, "again" (πάλιν)," as the text says. His answer is reproduced only in indirect speech. At this point, a cock crows, just as Jesus had foretold in John 13:38. As Escaffre remarks,[47] the only voice which sounds at the end of the section is that of the cock.

In the rest of John's passion narrative, Peter receives no further mention. He appears again in John 20:2 together with the other disciple. Like the other evangelists, the fourth one also assumes that Peter remained in

---

45. At this point in Johann Sebastian Bach's *St. John Passion*, there is added: "and he went out and wept bitterly." However, the librettist has taken this from the Synoptic Gospels (cf. Matt 26:75; Luke 22:62). Apparently, he did not want this detail of the passion narrative to be kept back from the Leipzig audience.

46. Cf. Escaffre, "Pierre et Jésus," 61–63.

47. Cf. Escaffre, "Pierre et Jésus," 57.

the city and was found among the first of those to be granted an appearance of the Risen One. According to John, this happened during the encounter of Jesus with the group of disciples who had remained faithful to him on the evening of Easter Day in John 20:19–23. In chapter 21, Jesus will ask Peter about his loyalty and his love for him before he foretells that he will suffer the fate of his master in a violent death (John 21:15–19). In this way, Peter can serve as a model of identification for the readers just like other men and women who confess their faith in Jesus with courage.[48]

## III

In the literary and theological composition of his account of the arrest of Jesus and of his arraignment before the Jewish authorities, the evangelist allows us to discern his main ideas. In the Johannine account, Jesus appears in his majesty more prominently than in the Synoptics. He knows full well what lies before him, but goes out to meet the arresting party, sovereign and resolute. His "I am he" is a precise echo of his divine self-knowledge. Thus, the officers and soldiers who are supposed to arrest him also fall to the ground at this word. Jesus relies not on earthly power, and so he does not allow Peter to attempt to engage the soldiers with his weapon. At first, he is silent before the high priest, and then he only responds to the question about his teaching, not about his disciples. They are innocent, and so they should be allowed to go their way. The flight of the disciples is turned into a formal dismissal.

Throughout the section, the figure of Peter is contrasted with that of Jesus. We have shown how, in the course of the narrative, the former increasingly loses his identity. If, in the third scene, he shows only lack of understanding where Jesus is concerned, in the fifth and seventh scenes he denies his master three times. He does the same in the moment in which Jesus, fearlessly, if also helplessly, faces the high priest and gives information.

Precisely through this deliberate contrasting of Jesus and Peter by the fourth evangelist, a strong signal goes out to the readers. They should not deny but ought to confess, just as Jesus did. Otherwise, they too, like Peter, are threatened with the loss of their personality. Only after Easter may they hope for a new beginning in the story of their lives.

48. Cf. Beutler, "Faith and Confession."

## 2. The Roman Trial of Jesus (18:28–19:16b)

18 ²⁸ They brought Jesus from Caiaphas to the Praetorium; it was early in the morning. They themselves did not go inside in order that they might not defile themselves but be able to eat the Passover lamb. ²⁹ Pilate, therefore, came out to them and asked: What accusation are you bringing against this man? ³⁰ They answered him: If he were not a criminal, we would not have handed him over to you. ³¹ Pilate said to them: Take him, and judge him according to your Law! The Jews answered him: It is not lawful for us to put any man to death. ³² Thus was the saying of Jesus to be fulfilled, indicating by what death he was to die.

³³ Then Pilate went into the Praetorium again, had Jesus called, and asked him: Are you the King of the Jews? ³⁴ Jesus answered: Are you saying this of your own accord, or have others been telling you about me? ³⁵ Pilate retorted: Am I a Jew? Your people and the high priests have handed you over to me. What have you done? ³⁶ Jesus answered: My kingdom is not of this world. If my kingdom were of this world, then would my people fight so that I might not be delivered to the Jews. But as it is my kingdom is not from here. ³⁷ Then Pilate said to him: Are you a king then? Jesus answered: You say that I am a king. I was born for this and came into the world for this, that I might bear witness to the truth. Everyone that is of the truth hears my voice. ³⁸ Pilate said to him: What is truth?

After he had said this, he went out to the Jews again and said to them: I find no fault in him. ³⁹ But you have a custom that I release someone for you at the Passover. So, would you like me to release the King of the Jews? ⁴⁰ Then they cried out again: Not this man but Barabbas! Now Barabbas was a robber.

19 ¹ Then Pilate took Jesus and had him scourged. ² The soldiers plaited a garland of thorns; then they put it on his head and clothed him in a purple robe. ³ They came up to him and said: Hail, King of the Jews! And they slapped him in the face.

⁴ Pilate went out again and said to them: Look, I am bringing him out to you; you have to know that I find no fault in him. ⁵ Jesus came out; he wore the crown of thorns and the purple robe. Pilate said to them: Behold, the man! ⁶ When the chief priests and the officers saw him, they cried out: Crucify him, crucify him! Pilate said to them: You take him and crucify him! For I find no fault in him. ⁷ The Jews retorted: We have a Law, and by that Law he ought to die, because he made himself the Son of God.

⁸ When Pilate heard this, he feared all the more. ⁹ He went again into the Praetorium and asked Jesus: Where do you come from? But Jesus gave him no answer. ¹⁰ Then Pilate said to him: Are you not speaking to me? Do you not know that I have power to release you and power to crucify you? ¹¹ Jesus answered

## Jesus's "Hour": Passion, Death, and Resurrection (18:1–20:31)

him: You would have no power over me, unless it were given to you from above; therefore, he that delivered me to you has the greater sin. ¹² From that time, Pilate wanted to release him, but the Jews cried out: If you let this man go, you are no friend of Caesar; whoever makes himself a king is rebelling against Caesar.

¹³ At these words, Pilate had Jesus brought out, and sat down on the judgement seat in the place which is called the pavement, and in the Hebrew Gabbatha. ¹⁴ It was the day of preparation for the Passover, at about the sixth hour. Pilate said to the Jews: Behold, your king! ¹⁵ But they cried out: Away, away, crucify him! Pilate said to them: Am I to crucify your king? The chief priests answered: We have no king but Caesar. ¹⁶ Then he handed Jesus over to them to be crucified.

### I

Out of the three parts of the Johannine passion narrative, the central one, John 18:28–19:16b, is the one that is divided most clearly.[49] A subdivision of this part into seven scenes is almost universally accepted. Regarding the beginning, it is debated whether v. 28 belongs to the first scene or is more of a literary introduction corresponding to the concluding comment in John 19:16ab. A reason for John 18:28 being an introduction before the seven scenes could lie in the fact that the following scenes (with the exception of 19:1–3) are characterized by the sequence of Pilate's "going out" and "going in." However, it is better not to regard this verb as the only structural feature separating the scenes from one another. The criteria for the differentiation of the scenes are the information about place, time, persons taking part, and actions, together with some stylistic signals (such as a reference to Scripture or a saying of Jesus, usually at the end of a scene, cf. John 18:32). According to these criteria, it is better to consider John 18:28 as part of the first scene with the spatial datum, "the Praetorium," and the temporal one, "it was early in the morning." As in the narrative introduction of John 18:1–3, John 18:28–32 also has two contrasting groups or representatives of groups. In the case of John 18:28–32, it is the "Jews" and Jesus, who is being led to Pilate.

---

49. Cf., for this section, among others, Blank, "Die Verhandlung vor Pilatus"; Baum-Bodenberger, *Hoheit in Niedrigkeit*; Charbonneau, "'Qu'-as-tu fait?'"; Giblin, "John's Narration"; Diebold-Scheuermann, *Jesus vor Pilatus*; Diebold-Scheuermann, "Jesus vor Pilatus"; de Boer, "The Narrative Function"; Zumstein, "Der Prozess Jesu."

## II

### Jesus Is Led to Pilate. Pilate and the "Jews" (18:28–32)

The first scene in Jesus's Roman trial leans on Mark 15:1 par.; Matt 27:1–2; Luke 23:1. The Synoptic evangelists report the handing over of Jesus to Pilate. According to Mark (15:1), the chief priests, according to Matthew (27:12), the chief priests and the elders accuse Jesus before Pilate. Luke (23:2–3) contains the accusation that Jesus has broken the Jewish and Roman Law with the appeal to sedition and to the refusal to pay taxes as well as the claim to be the Messiah. In John, only the last charge finds an echo.

**18:28** With this verse there begins the last day in the life of Jesus that is described in the sections John 18:28–19:16b (Jesus's Roman trial) and 19:16c–42 (crucifixion, death, and burial of Jesus). The information about time and place helps to distinguish the following scenes from one another. It is now early in the morning. "They" bring Jesus to the Praetorium, the official seat of the Roman procurator, Pontius Pilate. We are not told who "they" are but this can be deduced from the previous scenes: they are the court officials of the Jewish authorities and these authorities themselves. In what follows, the text will speak of the "Jews" (Ἰουδαῖοι) as the Jewish authorities. In John 19:6, "the chief priests and the officers" (οἱ ἀρχιερεῖς καὶ οἱ ὑπηρέται) are named, in 19:15, the "chief priests" (ἀρχιερεῖς). In contrast with the Synoptic Gospels, the Sanhedrin plays no further role in the trial and condemnation of Jesus in John. Already in John 11:47–53 the Sanhedrin has made its decision to kill Jesus, and is mentioned no more.

The Jews avoid entering the Praetorium so as not to defile themselves before the Passover. The commentaries generally see in this detail an example of Johannine irony. The very people who are observing the rules for cultic purity down to the last detail are those who are not hesitating to kill the true Paschal lamb, Jesus Christ. The connection is prompted by the mention of the Passover feast at the end of the Roman trial at the moment of his condemnation to death by crucifixion in John 19:14. The sixth hour mentioned there was the prescribed moment in Jewish tradition for the killing of the Passover lambs.

**18:29–30** In a first exchange, Pilate asks the "Jews," whom he has come out to address, what accusation they are bringing against "this man." The answer of the Jewish group is rather weak. Jesus's guilt is not set out but assumed. They would not have brought him to Pilate if he were not a criminal. At this moment, Pilate appears in a positive light, while Jesus's accusers appear in an unfavorable one as blinded by prejudice.

**18:31** From the beginning, however, Pilate shows the tendency not to become involved in the conflict between Jesus and the Jewish authorities. He therefore suggests that they judge him according to their Law. In their answer, the Jews argue that they do not have the right to execute anyone. Thus, they make use of the power of the Roman state to silence Jesus, their king. The irony continues.

**18:32** In the demand for Jesus to be crucified, the evangelist sees a fulfilling of the saying of Jesus in which he had foretold the manner of his death: his "lifting up" on the cross (cf. John 12:32).

### The First Dialogue between Jesus and Pilate (18:33–38b)

The long stretch of dialogue between Jesus and Pilate agrees with the Synoptic tradition only at the beginning and at the end. The question (or conjecture) of Pilate: "Are you the King of the Jews?" is found word for word in Mark 15:2 par. Matt 27:11 and Luke 23:3. Everything speaks for the fact that John has made use of this traditional element. John also shares with the Synoptics Jesus's answer: "You say that" (cf. the same verse in the Synoptics). The other words of the dialogue between Jesus and Pilate in John 18:34–36, 37f–38a appear either as borrowings from another source or as additions of the evangelist. The latter hypothesis has been established more firmly of late and will be endorsed here.

**18:33–34** In order to form a judgement about the accusations of the Jewish authorities, Pilate enters the Praetorium, has Jesus called, and asks him: "Are you the King of the Jews?" According to the text that has been transmitted, which is also presupposed in the Nestle-Aland[28] edition, Pilate's saying is in the form of a question: "Are you the King of the Jews?" According to another interpretation, which is represented by Martinus de Boer,[50] Pilate's statement would have had the form of a statement: "You are the King of the Jews." According to this author, Pilate never puts in question Jesus's royal dignity provided it is understood in a religious and not a political sense. In his answer, Jesus then understands the saying of Pilate more as a statement than as a question. Thus, Jesus is not putting his kingly dignity in doubt. However, in order to understand it correctly, one

---

50. Cf. de Boer, "The Narrative Function."

must have the right approach to his person. The Jews who have accused him and led him to Pilate do not possess this open and positive approach.

**18:35–36** From the two ways of understanding his question, Pilate chooses the second: others have spoken to him of the royal dignity of Jesus in order to accuse him. It was his people and the chief priests who had accused him of promoting himself out as King of the Jews and who had handed him over. Again, to be King of the Jews signifies no offense to Pilate. So what has Jesus done?

In his answer, Jesus strengthens Pilate's impression that he is not the kind of king that presents any danger to the Romans. His kingdom, says Jesus, is not of this world. The proof of this lies in the fact that otherwise his people would come to his aid. Since—along with John 3:3, 5—John 18:36 is the only text in the Gospel that speaks of the kingdom of God, it is appropriate to demonstrate the connection between the two texts. In conversation with Nicodemus, Jesus explains the conditions for entry into the kingdom of God. In chapter 18, the kingdom of God then appears as the kingdom of Christ.[51] Insofar as the kingdom of Jesus is the present kingdom of God in history, one can say that it is not of this world. This view is also confirmed by the further course of Jesus's conversation with Nicodemus in John 3:13 where Jesus says: "No one has ascended to heaven except the one who has come down from heaven: the Son of Man."

**18:37** In his last contribution to the conversation, Pilate sees his impression that Jesus is a king confirmed, and asks him to confirm this impression further. Jesus's answer is positive, although it also leaves room for an interpretation according to which it is Pilate rather than Jesus himself who sees the latter as a king. In any case, the sense of Jesus's royal dignity has to be clarified. This is the purpose of Jesus's next saying in which he affirms that he is a king and, in fact, does so in order to bear witness to the truth. Elsewhere the Fourth Gospel never speaks of the fact that Jesus was "born" or "conceived"; however, in John, the expression γεννηθῆναι means something more general than a purely physical descent (cf. John 1:13 "from God," ἐκ θεοῦ; 3:3, 7 "from above," ἄνωθεν). Thus, the expression seems to mean the same as the following "came into the world" (cf. John 1:9 and 3:19, of the light, 6:14 of Jesus as a prophet, 9:39; 12:46; 16:28 etc.).

What does it mean that Jesus has come into the world "to bear

---

51. According to Schnackenburg, 3:284 it is better not to conflate the two realities since John 3:3 and 5 concern a heavenly realm whereas John 18:36 actually does not.

witness to the truth"?[52] Everything depends here on the understanding of "truth." In the first half of the twentieth century, the understanding of this Johannine expression in the light of Hellenistic and Gnostic texts prevailed. The "truth" was accordingly the divine reality that makes itself known. Since the discovery of the texts from Qumran, it is clear that the Johannine texts stand closer to biblical and Jewish thinking. The truth is then the divine decree of salvation that is revealed in the end time. In the Qumran texts, there is also mention of the "witnesses of the truth" (1 QS 8.6), applied to the members of the community as bringers of their message. Here, we are close to the Johannine usage. "Witness" retains its forensic sense in John. In the "great trial" between Jesus and the unbelieving world witnesses and testimony are cited on behalf of Jesus. In this, Jesus also bears witness to himself. Just as he "witnesses" to heavenly things (cf. John 3:11, 32), so too he bears "witness to the truth" in the sense of the divine revelation that is being imparted by him.[53] "To bear witness to the truth" thus means more than to testify to it. Jesus takes up his position on behalf of the truth in the great trial between him and the "world," just as John the Baptist before him (cf. John 5:33; in the repetition of the formula in 3 John 3, this forensic background is no longer recognizable).

To grasp the truth to which Jesus bore witness and to make it one's own, one has to be "conceived" or "born" from the truth. Here, the text is recalling John 1:12–13—only those "born from God" become his children—and John 8:47: "Whoever is of God hears the words of God; therefore, you do not hear them because you are not of God." For conception or birth from God, cf., also, 1 John 2:16; 3:10; 4:3.

**18:38a–b** Pilate's answer "What is truth?" has undergone various interpretations. For some (like Bultmann and his school[54]), it is a question of the state's not being responsible for questions of religion and philosophy; for others, Pilate is showing only that he is incapable of understanding the words of Jesus since he is not ready to believe in him. The latter interpretation is to be preferred.

---

52. Cf. for the exegesis of this verse, Beutler, *Martyria*, 318–25.
53. Cf. for this understanding of Johannine truth, de la Potterie, *La vérité*.
54. Cf. Bultmann, 507f.; Schlier, "Jesus und Pilatus."

## Pilate and the "Jews." The Offer of Amnesty (18:38c–40)

After a first meeting with the spokesmen of the "Jews" at the moment of the handing over of Jesus (John 18:28–32) and a first encounter with Jesus (John 18:33–38b), Pilate has formed an initial judgement about Jesus for himself. He is a "King of the Jews" from whom the Roman state has nothing to fear. This understanding lies at the basis of the following scene, which describes a further encounter between Pilate and the representatives of the "Jews."

If one compares this scene in John with the Synoptics (Mark 15:6–14 par.), one can detect that John has clearly abridged it. The "again" (πάλιν) could stem from this tradition (cf. Mark 15:13). Luke has a scene in which Pilate declares Jesus innocent before the chief priests and the leading men of the people (Luke 23:13–16). This text could serve as the basis for John 18:38c–e. According to Luke, Pilate continues to offer the people and their leaders to have Jesus flogged and then released (Luke 23:22). This text could have influenced John 19:1.

**18:38c–f** Pilate now goes out again to the "Jews" who are waiting for him and announces the result of his investigation: he finds no reason to condemn Jesus.

**18:39** As a politician, however, Pilate knows that the Jewish leaders would not be content if he were to let Jesus go without penalty. So he makes them an offer that presents them with a dilemma. He offers to release to them the "King of the Jews" as a Passover amnesty that is here assumed to be an annual custom. Will the "Jews" refuse to let their king be pardoned?

**18:40** However, the Jews cry out: "Not this man but Barabbas,"[55] and the evangelist adds that Barabbas was a robber. Probably this description serves as a contrast with Jesus, the righteous one. In this case, λῃστής is probably thinking of a thief rather than a terrorist. This prompts a comparative glance at John 10:1, 8, 10. The good shepherd comes to the sheep through the door and his concern is their safety; the thief climbs over the

---

55. Literally: "They cry again." The πάλιν causes difficulties here and so early manuscripts already replace it with "all" (πάντες), others with the combination πάλιν πάντες. However, the reading πάλιν recommends itself as the *lectio difficilior*, and also by virtue of its early attestation in P⁶⁰ ℵ B L W 0109 579. So too Nestle-Aland²⁸. Verhelst, "The Johannine Use," discusses different ways of explaining the difficult πάλιν (among others, by borrowing from Mark 15:13), but asks himself in the end, rightly, whether one may be overstating the importance of this favorite Johannine word here.

fence and comes only to steal and to kill. Judas is one such "robber" or "thief," as he is called in the story of the anointing at Bethany (John 12:6).[56]

### The Scourging of Jesus and His Crowning with Thorns (19:1–3)

This scene takes place undoubtedly in the Praetorium. Only the reference to Pilate's "going into" the building is missing. Thus, it is unnecessary to see here a breach in the sequence of scenes characterized by the going out and going in of Pilate.

The same goes for the absence of dialogues in John 19:1–3. Carola Diebold-Scheuermann's suggestion,[57] to see in these verses an "interlude," is not sufficiently substantiated. Moreover, the author also ranks this section among the "scenes." According to the observations of several exegetes following the contribution of A. Janssens de Varebeke,[58] our scene is situated in a seven-scene narrative of which it forms the climax. The attributes of honor ascribed to Jesus here as "King of the Jews" appear at first glance as mockery but on a second look they possess a deeper sense. Jesus is in fact this king.

Once again, John has made free use of the Synoptics. In Mark (15:15) and Matthew (27:26), the scourging of Jesus and his mocking by the soldiers follow Pilate's decision to condemn Jesus. This sequence corresponds to the Roman practice. At the end of their abuse, the soldiers dress Jesus again in his own clothes and lead him out to be crucified. This portrayal does not correspond to the Johannine view, according to which the consequence of the sight of Jesus abused and mocked with the royal robe and bearing the crown of thorns was supposed to move the Jewish leaders to pity. Thus, John prepares for the following scene in which Jesus is led before the "Jews" in a further attempt to move them to clemency.

**19:1** In John, the scourging of Jesus is not part of an offer to the Jewish leaders to release Jesus after chastisement as in Luke 23:16–22. However, the basic thought appears to be the same. A scourged Jesus could lead to compassion for the "King of the Jews" and so also to a pardon from the Jewish authorities. In Roman justice, the scourging generally followed the imposition of the death sentence. John could have reversed the sequence

---

56. Cf. Witetschek, "Ein Räuber."
57. Cf. Diebold-Scheuermann, *Jesus vor Pilatus*, 268–75.
58. See n. 16 above.

in order to give Pilate the opportunity to change the minds of the Jews before a sentence.

**19:2–3** In what follows the abuse of Jesus is described in four elements. The soldiers plait a crown of thorns and put it on Jesus's head; they clothe him in a purple robe; they come up to him and greet him: "Hail, King of the Jews"; and slap him in the face. The first three elements serve to mock Jesus who has claimed to be "King of the Jews." For the readers, this homage towards the "King of the Jews" has a double sense. In the central scene of the Roman trial, Jesus receives the honor of a king, but as a king who reveals himself only to those who believe in him and who are "of the truth" (cf. John 18:37), since "his kingdom is not of this world" (John 18:36).

*Pilate and the "Jews." The Presentation of Their "King" (19:4–7)*

This scene is characterized by three speech contributions of Pilate and two of the chief priests with the officers. Jesus does not utter a word but is led passively out of the Praetorium in order to be presented to the crowd.

The scene of the "Ecce Homo" has no counterpart in the Synoptics. The mocking of Jesus with the purple mantle and the crown of thorns takes place in the courtyard of the Praetorium. In the Synoptics, Jesus is not brought before the crowd in front of the building. Thus, the mocking scene is not connected with Pilate's attempt to get Jesus released (cf. Mark 15:16–20). In the Synoptic tradition, the charge of playing the part of the "King of the Jews" also occurs in connection with the Roman trial of Jesus (cf. Mark 15:2–12 par.). In the Jewish trial before the high priest, Caiaphas (cf. Mark 14:62 par.), Jesus gives a positive answer to the question as to whether he is the Messiah, the Son of the Blessed One. In John, this claim reinforces Pilate's fear at having a man of mysterious origin in his power, and his reluctance on that account to sentence him to death.

**19:4–5** For the third time (after John 18:29 and 18:38c), Pilate leaves the Praetorium in order to meet the group of "Jews." This time, he also has Jesus brought out, wearing the purple robe and the crown of thorns. Pilate's intention to arouse compassion follows from his words: "Look, I am bringing him out to you; you have to know that I find no fault in him." As Jesus appears, Pilate presents him with the words: "Behold the man!" These words of Pilate are as well-known as they are difficult to understand. The simplest meaning could be: "Look here at the human creature in all its wretchedness but also in its innocence." Some exegetes[59] see in Pilate's saying an allusion to Daniel's Son of Man but that would not be a statement of lowliness but of majesty, which does not fit the context.

**19:6–7** The presentation of the suffering and humiliated Jesus does not lead to the pity of the chief priests and officers but rather the opposite. They see again in Jesus a pretended Messiah, if not more, and so they cry: "Crucify him, crucify him!" Pilate undertakes a last attempt to block this wish of the Jews' representatives by passing on to them the responsibility for crucifying Jesus: "Take him and crucify him! For I find no fault in him." This suggestion seems rather an example of Johannine irony since the readers know that the Jewish authorities do not possess the *ius gladii*, the authority to hand out the death penalty and that, in any case, the form of execution for blasphemy is stoning (cf. John 10:31; Acts 7:59). The "Jews" accept Pilate's offer, at least in part, in that they say that, according to their Law, Jesus has to die because he made himself the Son of God. However, at the same time, it is assumed that they do not possess the legal authority to condemn Jesus and execute him.

The statement that Jesus had made himself the Son of God arouses an even greater bewilderment in Pilate and leads to the following scene in verses 8–12.

### Jesus Again Before Pilate (19:8–12)

In the overall composition of John 18:28–19:16b, the following scene stands in the penultimate position. If one is to accept a concentric construction here, then this scene corresponds to the second one with the first dialogue between Jesus and Pilate in John 18:33–38b. This correspondence has been noted by various authors, most recently by de Boer.[60] In these two sections, one can reasonably see the last two "revelation discourses" of Jesus before his death. In the former section, Pilate asks who Jesus is, in the second, where he comes from. In his answers, Jesus also reveals his identity and his origin to the readers. From the Johannine point of view, Jesus's identity is determined by his origin. For this reason, the two sections are complementary.

The demarcation of the section John 19:8–12 has recently been chal-

---

59. So, most recently, Barrett, 520f.; further authors in Schnackenburg, 3:295 n. 66.
60. Cf. de Boer, "The Narrative Function."

lenged by Carola Diebold-Scheuermann.[61] For this author, verse 12 no longer belongs to the dialogue scene but forms the "turning point" of the Roman trial after the last three dialogues. It appears advisable, however, to continue to allocate v. 12 to the dialogue scene. Pilate hears from outside the crying of the "Jews" who put him under pressure but he still remains in the Praetorium. One should not complicate the narrative analysis with its questions about the persons taking part, as well as the details of place and time, with the dramatic analysis that studies the course of the trial of Jesus according to the rules of ancient drama (which actually finds its climax in the "peripety" or turning point).

As a whole, this little scene goes back to the literary and theological work of the evangelist. The exchange over the origin of Jesus is missing in the Synoptic tradition. The only common element in both portrayals lies in the detail that Jesus gives no answer to the question of Pilate (about his guilt in the Synoptics) and that this is a cause of marvel for Pilate (cf. Mark 15:5 par.; Matt 27:12–14).

**19:8–9** The scene is connected with the preceding one through the claim of the "Jews" that Jesus had made himself the "Son of God" (v. 7). The biblical roots of this title in connection with that of "Messiah" or "King of the Jews" remain hidden to the Roman procurator but he knows the title of son of god in its religious dimension from the world of Graeco-Roman culture.

The world of the Greeks and the Romans knew of the "son of god" in the sense of heroes or rulers who were descended directly from the gods, not seldom with a human mother. Since the time of Julius Caesar, the Greek-Oriental mythology had also made its entrance into the Roman religion. So the description of Jesus as "Son of God" could also signify his divine origin. That is why Pilate asks Jesus: "Where do you come from?" Jesus gives no answer to this question. The reason for this lies in the preceding dialogue in John 18:33–38b, in which Jesus had described himself as king in a transcendental sense, as witness to the truth. If Pilate has previously not understood the words of Jesus, then it is scarcely to be hoped that he will comprehend them now.

**19:10–11** Pilate now begins to speak again and asks Jesus why he is giving him no answer. Is Jesus, perhaps, not aware that Pilate has the power to crucify him or release him? With this statement, Pilate remains on the political level. As representative of the Roman state power, Pilate possesses

---

61. Cf. Diebold-Scheuermann, *Jesus vor Pilatus*, 74–81, 173–78.

the judicial power to condemn Jesus or release him. In his answer, Jesus admits the definition of Pilate's power only on the political and human level. Pilate would have no power over Jesus unless it were given him from above. Ultimately, Pilate owes his power to God—that God who is the Father of Jesus Christ. Thus, Pilate's guilt is assessed in accordance with the role that has befallen him in the divine plan of salvation. For this reason, the betrayer's guilt is greater than that of the Roman procurator who is the simple tool of Jesus's enemies and of the disciple who betrayed him.

**19:12** Jesus's answer has reinforced Pilate's fear of condemning this mysterious man. The "omniscient" narrator causes the Jews who are outside in front of the Praetorium to know that Pilate is afraid to give his decision against Jesus, and causes the Jews to cry from outside: "If you let this man go, you are no friend of Caesar; whoever makes himself a king is rebelling against Caesar." In this way, the argument returns to the political level. There is discussion as to whether the title "friend of Caesar" ("friend of the emperor") had a special significance for the Roman procurator, Pontius Pilate. Perhaps he was named as such by Sejanus, co-regent of Tiberius until the year 31 CE. According to Tacitus (*Ann.* 6.8), everyone close to Sejanus could claim the emperor's friendship for himself.[62] With this in mind, one must consider whether Pilate would have made his decision about Jesus before or after Sejanus had fallen into disfavor. In any case, Pilate would have put himself in a difficult position if he had decided in favor of the "King of the Jews." A decision in favor of Jesus could have endangered his position and his political career. This consideration was not lost on Pilate, as is shown in the following scene.

### The Condemnation of Jesus (19:13–16b)

The scene of John 19:13–16b sees the end of the Roman trial according to John 18:28–19:16b. If we regard John 18:28–32 as a first scene (without dividing it into an introduction in v. 28 and a "first scene" in vv. 29–32), then in this first scene we find the same protagonists as in the last one in John 19:13–16b, namely, Pilate, Jesus, and the "Jews."

Again the scene is performed—like the first—in the open, outside the Praetorium. It consists of two exchanges between Pilate and the "Jews," and the commentary of the evangelist.

---

62. Cf. Brown, 2:880.

The exchange between Pilate and the crowd that leads to the repeated cry of "crucify him" appears to go back to the exchange of words regarding the possibility of amnesty (Mark 15:6–15 par.; Matt 27:15–26; Luke 23:17–25). This Synoptic scene also ends with the "handing over" of Jesus to the will of the people. The passive "to be crucified (ἵνα σταυρωθῇ)" is found also in Mark (15:15) and Matthew (27:26), the "handing over to their will" in Luke (23:25).

**19:13** The last scene of the Roman trial takes Jesus out into the open once more. The trigger is the threat by the crowd that Pilate will no longer be a friend of Caesar if he lets Jesus go. So Pilate takes Jesus out of the Praetorium one last time and now takes his seat on the judgement bench. Grammatically, it is possible to understand the expression ἐκάθισεν ἐπὶ βήματος as transitive: "he caused him (Jesus) to take his seat on the judgement bench." In recent times, it is de la Potterie who has strongly favored this interpretation.[63] He finds it, among other places, in the apocryphal Gospel of Peter and in Justin (*1 Apol.* 35.6), gives reasons for this grammatical possibility, and then understands the verse in the sense of Johannine irony: Jesus, the accused, is clearly being mocked but is revealing himself to the readers as the true judge of the world. However, this proposal has not been generally accepted, and, already, Brown marshaled several counter-arguments: in cases of doubt in Greek, when there is a transitive understanding, the personal pronoun in the accusative must stand after ἐκάθισεν.[64] In the Greek Bible, since the Septuagint, ἐκάθισεν is always used intransitively. The Gospel of Peter and the text from Justin are later than John's Gospel and can scarcely be adduced for understanding. Moreover, the Johannine passion narrative is concerned with Jesus's royal dignity and not with his office as judge. The mocking of Jesus is carried out here by the soldiers, not by Pilate, who is always trying to set Jesus free. The detailed reference to the site of the sentence is in accordance with the diligence with which John attends to the exact details of place and time with regard to the scenes of Jesus's passion. Thus, it is better to remain with the traditional understanding.

The Lithostrotos or pavement, Gabbatha in Aramaic, has also led to discussion among exegetes but also archaeologists. For a long time, peo-

---

63. Cf. de la Potterie, "Jésus roi et juge," leaning on older authors going back to Harnack and Loisy.

64. Cf. Brown, *The Death*, vol. 2 (Appendix III.D, 1388–93). The counter-arguments are assembled again by Verheyden, "I. de la Potterie."

ple thought here of a stone pavement that was discovered under the Ecce Homo convent of the Sion sisters in the area of the Antonia Fortress in the North West of the temple mount. However, this pavement appears to go back to the second century CE, that is, to the time after the rebuilding of Jerusalem as Aelia Capitolina. Thus, John's information about the location is better focused on the residence of King Herod, which was used by the Roman procurators especially for their accommodation in Jerusalem for the major feasts. This residence was situated not far from the current Jaffa Gate on the West side of the Old City of Jerusalem.[65]

**19:14ab** The temporal detail has a double sense. On the one hand it provides information about the exact time of Jesus's condemnation, the "hour" of Jesus in its strong Johannine sense. On the other hand, however, the sixth hour of the day of preparation before the feast of the Passover also has a symbolic significance. It was the last moment when all the old leaven had to be removed from the Jewish houses and the time for beginning the slaughter of the Paschal lambs in the temple area. In view of the symbolism of the Paschal lamb for Johannine Christology since John 1:29, 36 ("Behold the Lamb of God"), there is an immediate suggestion that we also recognize in this detail a symbolic meaning.

**19:14c–15** At this point, Pilate seems resolved to condemn Jesus. Otherwise he would not have sat down on the judgement bench. Thus, his words to the Jews: "Behold your king!" appears more of a protestation of his own innocence rather than a last attempt to rescue Jesus (who at this moment was no longer wearing the clothes and symbols of his mocking). Scholars find a similarity between this saying of Pilate in John and his handwashing gesture in Matthew (27:24) with the words: "I am innocent of the blood of this man. It is your affair!" In John 19:15, the Jews answer with the cry: "Away, away, crucify him!" They do not accept Pilate's argument that Jesus is their king. So Pilate makes one last attempt: "Am I to crucify your king?" This idea is not pursued by the crowd. They answer: "We have no king but Caesar." With these words, Jesus's fate is sealed.

At this point, it is clear that the Jewish crowd with their words "We have no king but Caesar" are not only rejecting Jesus as their king but also any king of their own and so all messianic hopes. In order to bring Jesus to the cross, the Jews of John 19 are ready to surrender their dearest and most precious hopes.

**19:16a–b** At the end of this exchange between Pilate and the crowd, the narrator simply remarks tersely: "Then he handed Jesus over to them

---

65. Cf. Schneider, "πραιτώριον," *EWNT* 3:346–48 (esp. 347); *EDNT* 3:145.

to be crucified." Pilate's decision and Jesus's sentence to death on the cross are contained in the expression "handed over." Certainly, the Jewish crowd has no authority to crucify Jesus. Thus, the grammatical form of the word "crucify" is significant. It is used in the passive here. Pilate hands Jesus over to the "Jews" so that he would be crucified by Roman justice and military might.⁶⁶

## III

By contrast with the Synoptics, the actual trial of Jesus within the passion narrative takes place before the Roman forum. The Jewish authorities' decision to kill Jesus has already been recounted previously (John 11:47–53). It is surprising that, at the conclusion of the Roman trial, no actual words of sentence by Pilate are recorded. The reason for that could be that, for John, from the start, it was not Pilate as the judge but Jesus as the king who stood in the center.⁶⁷ Already, in the first interview between Jesus and Pilate in John 18:33–38b, the subject was the kingship of Jesus. In the third scene, in John 18:38c–40, Jesus's royal title remains the dominating theme in the exchange of words between Pilate and the crowd. In the fourth and central scene, again in the Praetorium, the soldiers mock Jesus as King of the Jews (John 19:1–3), in which, even in this travesty, the readers recognize the true king. In the fifth scene, Jesus is led before the crowd in his royal insignia, but they demand his death (John 19:4–7). They make this demand, again from outside, during the last dialogue between Jesus and Pilate in John 19:8–12 with the justification that Jesus had made himself a king. In the last section, John 19:13–16b, Jesus's royal title occurs again three times. This title returns yet again in the inscription over the cross (John 19:19–22), which Pilate causes to be mounted over the head of Jesus and insists on despite the opposition of the Jewish authorities. For the readers, Jesus dies as king just as he has lived as king, and as king will rise again.

The meaning of the royal dignity of Jesus was expressed especially in the first interview between Jesus and Pilate in John 18:33–38b. Jesus's dignity lies in the fact that he is messenger of the message of God, of the

---

66. Devillers, "La croix," sees in the dative "to them" (αὐτοῖς) a dative of interest. Meant are the "Jews," represented by the recently mentioned (v. 15) chief priests.

67. This has now been worked out convincingly by Piper, "The Characterisation."

*Jesus's "Hour": Passion, Death, and Resurrection (18:1–20:31)*

"truth." In the Johannine perspective, the kernel of the message of Jesus is simply this: that Jesus, as the "Son of God" (John 19:7–11), brings news from the heart of God. He does this as "witness to the truth" (John 18:37), even at the cost of his life. The first Christians, for their part, are seen as called to bear witness (cf. Rev 2:13; 11:3; 17:6), just as John the Baptist had already done (John 5:33). This call remains forever a present reality.

## 3. Crucifixion, Death, and Burial of Jesus (19:16c–42)

19 ¹⁶ They took Jesus. ¹⁷ He bore his cross and went out to the place that is called the place of the skull, and in Hebrew Golgotha. ¹⁸ There, they crucified him, and with him two others, one on either side but Jesus in the middle.

¹⁹ Pilate had a plaque made and fastened above the cross; the inscription read: Jesus of Nazareth, the King of the Jews. ²⁰ Many Jews read this plaque, because the place where Jesus was crucified was close to the city. The inscription was composed in Hebrew, Latin and Greek. ²¹ Then the chief priests of the Jews said to Pilate: Do not write King of the Jews, but that he said: I am the King of the Jews. ²² Pilate answered: What I have written, I have written.

²³ After the soldiers had crucified Jesus, they took his clothes and divided them into four, a part for each soldier, and also the tunic. The tunic was without a seam, woven from the top as a single piece. ²⁴ Then they said to one another: We do not want to tear it, but cast lots for it, to discern to whom it is to belong. Thus was the word of Scripture to be fulfilled: They divided my garments among them and cast lots for my robe. This is what the soldiers did.

²⁵ There stood by the cross of Jesus his mother and his mother's sister, Mary, the wife of Clopas, and Mary Magdalene. ²⁶ When Jesus saw his mother and with her the disciple whom he loved, he said to his mother: Woman, behold your son! ²⁷ Then he said to the disciple: Behold your mother! And from that hour, the disciple took care of her.

²⁸ After this, since Jesus knew that all things had now been fulfilled, in order that the Scripture might be fulfilled, he said: I thirst. ²⁹ There was a vessel full of vinegar there. They stuck a sponge full of vinegar on a sprig of hyssop and held it to his mouth. ³⁰ When Jesus had taken the vinegar, he said: It is finished! And he bowed his head, and gave up the spirit.

³¹ Because it was the preparation day and the bodies were not supposed to remain on the cross during the Sabbath – for this Sabbath was a great feast day – the Jews asked Pilate that their legs might be broken and they then be taken down. ³² So the soldiers came and broke the legs of the first, then of the

other who was crucified with him. ³³ When they came to Jesus, however, and saw that he was already dead, they did not break his legs, ³⁴ but one of the soldiers drove a spear into his side, and immediately blood and water flowed out. ³⁵ And the one who saw it has borne witness to it, and his witness is true. And he knows that he is telling the truth so that you too may believe. ³⁶ For that happened so that the Scripture might be fulfilled: Not a bone of his shall be broken. ³⁷ And another Scripture says: They will look on him whom they pierced.

³⁸ Joseph of Arimathea was a disciple of Jesus, but only in secret for fear of the Jews. He asked Pilate if he might take away the body of Jesus, and Pilate gave his permission. So he came and took away the body. ³⁹ Nicodemus came too. On an earlier occasion, he had sought Jesus at night. He brought a mixture of myrrh and aloes, about a hundred pounds. ⁴⁰ They took the body of Jesus and wrapped it in linen cloths together with the fragrant ointments, as is the custom for Jewish burial. ⁴¹ At the place where he had been crucified, there was a garden, and in the garden was a new grave in which no one had yet been buried. ⁴² On account of the preparation day of the Jews and because the grave was close at hand, they laid Jesus there.

*I*

The third and last part of the Johannine account of the passion and death of Jesus begins with the way of the cross and the crucifixion of Jesus. As shown previously, this main section is also divided into seven scenes. The center is occupied not with the account of the death of Jesus but with his legacy: the giving over of his mother to the disciple, but also of the disciple to the mother. Here, the Johannine Gospel tradition is anchored in the beloved disciple.

Regarding the first three scenes, up to the parting of Jesus's garments, there is little recent secondary literature. The research is occupied more with the relationship of the Johannine text to the Synoptic tradition than with the synchronic exegesis of the text.[68] Both aspects are joined together by Culpepper.[69] First, he tackles the differences between the Johannine and Synoptic portrayals: central elements of the Synoptic narrative are totally absent in John. So "there is (1) no mocking at the cross; (2) no penitent thief, (3) no darkness, although John often plays with the

---

68. Cf. among others, Kollmann, *Kreuzigung*.
69. Culpepper, "Theology."

symbolism of light and darkness; (4) no counting of the hours (apart from the notice in 19:14 that it was the sixth hour), though John has spoken repeatedly of Jesus's hour; (5) no rending of the veil, though John tells us of the cleansing of the temple at the beginning of Jesus's ministry; (6) no cry of dereliction; (7) no earthquake; (8) no opening of the graves, though John has spoken earlier of the opening of the graves and reported the raising of Lazarus; and (9) and no confession of the centurion, though John places particular emphasis throughout the Gospel on the recognition of Jesus as "Son of God."[70]

On the other hand, however, Culpepper recognizes in the Johannine account elements that belong to the common tradition:[71] Jesus bears his own cross to a place called Golgotha. He is crucified with two other men. An inscription "King of the Jews" is fastened over his head. His clothes are distributed. Mary Magdalene and other women stand close by. The soldiers offer Jesus vinegar or sour wine to drink. Jesus's last words are reproduced. Witnesses confirm his death. His body is taken from the cross and buried by Joseph of Arimathea. These agreements indicate that John is following a generally accepted tradition about the death of Jesus.

It appears that John has taken over the details relevant for him with the omission of others according to the criteria of his theology. In what follows, Culpepper's observations will remain in sight.

## II

### The Way of the Cross and the Crucifixion of Jesus (19:16c–18)

**19:16c** At the beginning of this scene, a problem of interpretation arises: "They took Jesus" could refer to the persons mentioned in v. 16a, in that case the Jews to whom Pilate had handed over Jesus, or else to the Roman soldiers. With sufficient certainty, we can say that here it is the Roman soldiers, and that for two reasons: (1) The "Jews" possess no authority to carry out a death sentence (cf. John 18:31), and the text of John expressly mentions the Roman soldiers as the body administering the execution (cf. vv. 23–24). (2) In the main details, John is following the portrayal of

---

70. Cf. Culpepper, "Theology," 21.
71. Cf. Culpepper, "Theology," 21.

the Synoptics. According to Mark 15:20 par. Matt 27:31, it is the Roman soldiers who take Jesus out of the city after they have mocked him and abused him. Thus, in all probability, John is thinking of the same actors in this phase of the drama.

**19:17** The way of the cross is described by John as something personal to Jesus: there is no mention of any help from Simon of Cyrene. Jesus appears independent right to the last moment. Luke's scene of the women showing pity is also absent. Jesus is not concerned with religious feelings or things such as sorrow but with the sovereignty of Jesus. The name of the hill to which Jesus is led is given by John in Aramaic and Greek, as happens also in Mark and Matthew. Luke restricts himself to the Greek translation (Luke 23:33).

**19:18** The event of the crucifixion of Jesus is recounted in all the Gospels with a single word, in John, in fact, in a subordinate clause (a relative clause), with a grammatical change of subject (the soldiers instead of Jesus, the grammatical subject in v. 17). Mark and Matthew record that two other men were crucified with Jesus, but only after the scene of the vinegar that is offered and the sharing out of Jesus's clothes. For John, this is something of a special note and is therefore brought forward. Jesus is crucified between the two men. In the Johannine view, this underlines the dignity of Jesus.

### Pilate and the Royal Title of Jesus on the Inscription (19:19–22)

In John, this scene appears to be especially elaborately portrayed and so emphasized. The reason for that might lie in the strong symbolic force of this scene for John. Linguistically, this scene is held together and framed by the word "write." Pilate "wrote" (ἔγραψεν) or "had written" (v. 19), and strongly at the end: "What I have written I have written."

**19:19–20** Only John records that Pilate had the inscription mounted over the cross. Moreover, only in John do we find the full text: "Jesus of Nazareth, King of the Jews." In Mark and Luke, the name of Jesus is missing (but cf. Matt 27:37). In John, the text of the inscription emphasizes the identity of Jesus of Nazareth with the "King of the Jews," a central concept of the Johannine passion narrative. John alone informs us that the text was composed in three languages: Hebrew, Latin, and Greek. With Culpepper, we can regard the reference to the Hebrew as a pointer to the religious world to which Jesus belongs; a reference to the Latin as a pointer to the political world; and a reference to the Greek as a pointer to Jesus's cultural

## Jesus's "Hour": Passion, Death, and Resurrection (18:1–20:31)

environment.[72] The first readers of this inscription are the Jews who come out of the neighboring holy city.

Likewise, with Culpepper, the significance of the different parts of the inscription can be examined.[73] The royal dignity of Jesus had already been proclaimed by one of the first disciples, Nathanael (John 1:49). After the multiplication of loaves, the crowd want to make Jesus king (John 6:15). In John 12:12-15, Jesus enters the holy city as a messianic king, and, in fact, on a donkey according to the prophecy of Zechariah in Zech 9:9. This royal dignity of Jesus remains the dominating theme of the Jewish and Roman trials of Jesus until he is sentenced to death. In John, the theme is linked with the lifting up and glorification of Jesus, both of which are semantically connected with the theology of the servant (cf. Isa 52:13 LXX).

From the beginning, Jesus appears in John's Gospel as "King of Israel." In the prologue, the coming of the Logos to "his own" (John 1:11) is probably not yet meant in the way in which it would come to be developed, as we said in the interpretation of the verse. However, the royal dignity belongs to the theology of the fourth evangelist and is dominant in the twofold trial of Jesus, as has been demonstrated. With hindsight, the Fourth Gospel is intended to lead to the faith that "Jesus is the Christ, the Son of God" and so to life in his name (John 20:31).

An archaeological find could throw further light on the inscription on the cross. According to Maria-Luisa Rigato,[74] a well-preserved and revered little tablet in the Roman basilica of Santa Croce di Gerusalemme contains the text of the inscription on the cross. It is to be found in a chapel behind the apse of the basilica. On the tablet, the middle section of the inscription in Hebrew, Latin, and Greek mentioned by John can be made out. According to Rigato, the tablet depicts a copy of the original, which reached Rome already in the first millennium, before the crusades (with their lack of critical intellectual activity), perhaps in the time of Gregory the Great. If this hypothesis could be corroborated, then this tablet would confirm the Johannine version of the inscription by contrast with the abbreviated form of the Synoptics. The Greek text contains the word "NAZARENOUS," the Latin "NAZARENUS," still easily readable from right to left, written according to the custom that was then acceptable.

**19:21-22** In John—and only John—the title "King of the Jews" is

---

72. Cf. Culpepper, "Theology," 21.
73. Cf. Culpepper, "Theology," 23-26.
74. Rigato, *Il titolo della croce*.

a source of irritation to the "Jews." They turn to Pilate with the request that he have "King of the Jews" altered into the claim of Jesus that he was the King of the Jews. In keeping with the laconic language of the Roman procurator, however, Pilate gives his answer: "What I have written I have written." The impression of de Boer[75] seems to be confirmed that, according to John, in Pilate's eyes, Jesus could actually be the "King of the Jews" so long as this did not affect the interests of the Roman Empire (as king of a "kingdom not of this world" as Jesus had put it). For the readers, Jesus remains King of the Jews, and not only of the Jews, as is also suggested by the inscription in three languages.

### The Sharing of Jesus's Clothes (19:23–24)

In the Synoptics, the sharing out of Jesus's clothes follows on immediately from his crucifixion and is recounted in few words (6–12 words). In John, the scene is inserted after the mention of the inscription and developed much more extensively (67 words). This immediately suggests the significance of the scene for the fourth evangelist. At the beginning and end of the text, the "soldiers" are mentioned as actors. This establishes an inclusio that holds the small unit together.

**19:23a–f** In the Synoptics, the subject of the action is presupposed from the previous context whereas, in John, the soldiers are explicitly named as the actors. This produces a connection with the penultimate scene in which the crucifixion of Jesus was reported. In the Synoptics, the sharing out of Jesus's clothes is narrated using the formula from Ps 22:18. John distinguishes between the narrative and the fulfilling of Scripture at this point. First, he gives an exact description, step by step, of the actions of the soldiers. In this way he is able to distinguish between the top clothes (τὰ ἱμάτια) and the undergarment (χιτών). According to John, four soldiers take part in Jesus's execution. The account states that they first divide Jesus's top clothes into four parts and then that they also deal with the tunic. This distinction does not occur in the Synoptics but probably goes back to the parallelism in Ps 22:18: "They parted my garments among them and cast lots upon my vesture."

**19:23g–24** Jesus's tunic is described in more detail: it is "without seam," "woven from the top as a piece." The expression "from above"

---

75. Cf. de Boer, "Narrative Function."

## Jesus's "Hour": Passion, Death, and Resurrection (18:1–20:31)

(ἄνωθεν) occurs elsewhere in John and usually means origin "from above": cf. the rebirth "from above" in John 3:3, 7 and the origin of the revealer "from above" in John 3:31. Pilate's authority stems "from above" (John 19:11). This wholeness of Jesus's tunic could signify the unity of the body of Jesus himself and of his church. This is how the Church fathers saw it, and this is the view, recently, of Culpepper,[76] who, as a Baptist, could not be suspected of adopting patristic interpretations uncritically. With the decision to cast lots for Jesus's tunic, the soldiers fulfill, literally and in full, v. 18 of Ps 22, the passion psalm.

Other texts are concerned with the theme of unity in John: the announcement of one flock and one shepherd in John 10:16; Jesus's death for the gathering together of the scattered children of God according to John 11:52; Jesus's prayer for the unity of his own in John 17; and the fact that, in the miraculous catch of fish, the net with 153 big fish (which probably stands for the church) is not torn (John 21:11).

### The Legacy of Jesus (19:25–27)

The scene of "the legacy of Jesus" stands in the center of the Johannine account of the passion, death, and burial of Jesus (John 19:16c–42). This results from the fact that the narrative is divided into seven scenes of which the present one, as fourth, stands in the central position.

Few sections in the New Testament in general and in John's Gospel in particular have met with such different interpretations as this one. In the history of the exegesis, a Marian interpretation has been dominant since the time of the fathers. This view is found to the present day especially in Catholic exegesis, not least in francophone research. Here, the emphasis lies either in the fact that Jesus entrusts the beloved disciple as representative of the future community to his mother,[77] or else that he entrusts the mother to the disciple who takes her into his own home, literally, "to his own."[78]

In exegesis outside the Catholic sphere, but also among Catholics in Louvain or Germany, we find a model which prefers to see the beloved disciple in the center of the scene. These authors rely chiefly on the fact

---

76. Cf. Culpepper, "Theology," 27f.
77. de la Potterie, *La parole*.
78. de la Potterie, "Et à partir."

that, at the close of the scene, the disciple takes Jesus's mother into his home and not vice versa. A balanced view in all this is offered in a contribution by Zumstein.[79] The Swiss author does not simply oppose a literal interpretation to the spiritual exegesis of the tradition but discovers in the text a symbolic dimension that does not merely derive from the tradition. According to Zumstein, our section belongs to a series of symbolic texts in which the words have a deeper sense that lies beneath the literal one. In this way, the receiving of the mother by the beloved disciple has a significance for the post-Easter community: the beloved disciple is the reference point not only for the family of Jesus but also for the arising family of believers.

This view is confirmed by the context of John 19:25–27. In all the sections that precede or follow our text, a symbolic dimension can be observed. The crucifixion shows Jesus in between two other crucified men. The inscription stresses his kingly dignity. The rending of his tunic recalls the unity of the community. The thirst of the dying Jesus is, ultimately, his thirst for the salvation of mankind. Blood and water, which flow from his side, point to the post-Easter gift of salvation; his burial in a new tomb is another indication of his majesty and dignity. The wider context too contributes to the understanding of our text in a theological and symbolic manner. The beloved disciple, who lay on Jesus's breast, has immediate access to his master. He knows Jesus's secrets and is the only one to learn who will betray Jesus. He will also accompany Jesus on the way of the cross and be the first disciple to come to Easter faith. It is not by chance, therefore, that he is standing beneath the cross, but in harmony with his role in the overall narrative of John's Gospel. In him, we have a sketch of the future circle of disciples, and in him will this circle also possess its point of reference.

**19:25** This verse introduces a group of women who are standing beneath the cross of Jesus. Here, there are some differences in comparison with the Synoptics (Mark 15:40; Matt 27:55–56; Luke 23:49).[80] John mentions the women's presence before Jesus's death, the Synoptics after it. According to the Synoptics, the women observe Jesus's death from a distance; in John they are standing immediately beneath the cross. In addition, there are differences in the composition of the group. Most recent exegetes see in John four women beneath the cross of Jesus, correspond-

---

79. Zumstein, "Joh 19,25–27."
80. Cf. Sabbe, "Johannine Account."

ing to the four soldiers who divide up Jesus's garments among themselves (v. 23): the mother of Jesus; the sister of his mother; Mary of Clopas; and Mary Magdalene. As already at the marriage in Cana, the mother of Jesus appears alongside a group of disciples. With her, the beloved disciple is also introduced. The presence of Jesus's mother at this moment is of great significance. She is present at the decisive moments in Jesus's life, at the beginning of his public life and at the end. In both cases, she is called "woman" and the subject is the "hour" of Jesus. Thus, her presence frames the whole of Jesus's life.[81]

**19:26–27** The two verses that follow are to be read together. Jesus turns from the cross, first to his mother whom he calls "woman" as in John 2:4, and entrusts the beloved disciple to her as her son. If we only had this verse, then the Marian sense of the scene would be patent. It is followed, however, by an additional verse in which Jesus entrusts his mother to the beloved disciple. After these words, the beloved disciple takes Jesus's mother "to himself/his own." This last expression (εἰς τὰ ἴδια) has led to different interpretations. The meaning of Jesus's words is deduced only from Israelite Law. The mother who loses her last son is no longer in possession of a social network. Thus she needs a person to take care of her, usually another relation. In our text, we see the beloved disciple entrusted with this responsibility.[82]

Naturally, this scene too has its symbolic dimension. The group of disciples and the family of Jesus come together and begin to unite. Here, frequent reference is made to the Synoptic tradition in Mark 3:31–35, in which Jesus's brothers and his mother seek him in order to speak with him. There, Jesus expresses a certain distance with regard to his family and describes those as his mother and his brothers who gather round him and do the will of God. In John's Gospel too, the brothers of Jesus have a secondary significance. At the marriage of Cana, they are simply present (John 2:12) and, before Jesus sets out on the pilgrim journey to the Feast of Tabernacles, they advise him to go up to the feast, in order to reveal himself with signs, something regarded by the evangelist as an indication of their lack of faith (John 7:3–5). Thus, Jesus's family has not yet been integrated into the group of disciples.

---

81. Koperski, "The Mother of Jesus," recognizes a framing between the role of the mother of Jesus at the beginning of the Fourth Gospel (John 2:1–12) and that of Mary Magdalene at the end of the Easter story in John 20:1–2, 11–18.

82. Cf. Neirynck, "Εἰς τὰ ἴδια"; Neirynck, "Short Note."

The scene in John 19:25–27 could be serving to join the two groups to each other. Jesus's family, represented by his mother, is entrusted to the beloved disciple. In Jesus's mother, he will recognize his own mother just as she will recognize her son in the beloved disciple in place of Jesus who is giving up his life in order to be able to bestow it anew.

### The Death of Jesus (19:28–30)

The depiction of Jesus's death follows the Johannine perspective. An initial observation shows that it is not the account of Jesus's death but the legacy of Jesus that stands in the center of the overall composition of John 19:16c–42. In his description of the last moments in the life of Jesus, the evangelist shows the same theological orientation that it has been possible to observe since the beginning of the passion narrative with the scene of Jesus's arrest. Jesus offers himself with complete repose. In John—unlike the Synoptics—he does not die with a cry of complaint that God has forsaken him but with an expression of self-knowledge that he has now "fulfilled all things." The Scripture thus reaches its goal.

**19:28** The text begins with a typical Johannine introductory formula: "After this (μετὰ τοῦτο)," and a reference to the "knowledge" of Jesus about what lay before him, which is also a typical element at the beginning of the sections of the Johannine passion narrative (cf. John 13:1; 18:4). Jesus enters into his passion and also into his last hour in full knowledge of what is coming. In this moment, he knows "that all things have now been fulfilled." The verb occurs only in verses 28 and 30, and signifies in the perfect passive that something "has been brought to fulfillment." Concerning this, there is discussion to what the clause "that the Scripture might be fulfilled" (ἵνα τελειωθῇ ἡ γραφή) refers. Some think that it refers to the following utterance of Jesus: "I thirst." However, it seems better to link this final clause with the previous context. The whole of Scripture speaks about Jesus and announces him. In Jesus, it finds its fulfillment. It is not only this or that detail of the life of Jesus that is foretold in Scripture but Jesus himself and his mission.[83]

The verb τελειόω ("fulfill") occurs four other times in John and expresses the "fulfillment" of the "work" with which Jesus has been commissioned by the Father (John 4:34; 17:4) or of the "work" of the Father

---

83. Cf. Kraus, "Vollendung"; Beutler, "Gebrauch"; Klauck, "Geschrieben."

## Jesus's "Hour": Passion, Death, and Resurrection (18:1–20:31)

(John 5:36). According to John 17:23, the disciples are to be "fulfilled" or "perfected" in unity. In our verse, John 19:28, the perfect passive of τελειόω stands for the fulfillment of Scripture in a preeminent sense.

What is the significance of Jesus's cry: "I thirst"? Here, the Synoptics recount only the physical thirst of Jesus to which there corresponds the offer of vinegar or sour wine. In John, Jesus's thirst has a spiritual and theological dimension. It is the thirst of which he speaks in the conversation with the Samaritan woman with the request: "Give me something to drink" (John 4:7). Just as it is Jesus's food to do the will of his Father and complete his work (John 4:34), the same is true of his thirst. Only so "from deep within him will flow streams of living water" (John 7:38). There is discussion as to which part of Scripture Jesus's saying is referring. Some authors think of Ps 69:21, others, Ps 22:15. A reference to Ps 42:1 would be possible on account of the significance of this psalm in other scenes of the second part of John's Gospel (cf. John 11:33, 38; 12:27; 13:21; 14:1).[84]

**19:29** The soldiers' action originates from the Synoptic tradition (Mark 15:23 par.), which, for its part, depends on Ps 69:21. In this action of the soldiers, one can see a final example of "Johannine irony." In his thirst, all that Jesus receives is vinegar. Moreover, no one understands his true thirst. The sprig of hyssop on which the vinegar is handed to Jesus is certainly not very suitable for this purpose since the shrub is small and has bendy branches. Thus the employment of this plant seems likewise to have a symbolic sense. The hyssop belongs to the feast of the Passover: "Then take a bunch of hyssop, dip it in the blood that is in the basin, and with the blood from the basin touch the lintel and both door-posts!" (Exod 12:22; cf. 12:7). Thus, once again, the death of Jesus is linked to the feast of the Passover and the Paschal lamb.

**19:30** By contrast with the Synoptics (Mark 15:23), Jesus does not disdain to take the vinegar. He wishes to taste the bitterness of suffering to the last drop. With this final gesture, Jesus has completed his work and his mission. He speaks: "It is finished," and with this word he dies.[85] Recently there has been discussion over the language with which Jesus's death is described in John: παρέδωκεν τὸ πνεῦμα. Often this expression is understood in the sense of the words found in the Synoptics: ἐξέπνευσεν (Mark 15:37; Luke 23:46) or ἀφῆκεν τὸ πνεῦμα (Matt 27:50) "he gave up

---

84. Cf. Beutler, "Psalm 42/43."
85. Cf. Bergmeier, "Τετέλεσται."

the ghost/spirit."[86] However, the verb with which John describes Jesus's final moment says something different : παρέδωκεν τὸ πνεῦμα. This verb means "gave over" or "gave away." This is, naturally, the first meaning here.

Once more what we are encountering here is a Johannine *relecture* of the Synoptic tradition. Jesus does not "breathe his spirit out" but "hands over the spirit," probably in the full Johannine sense. Since, in John, Good Friday, Easter, Ascension, and Pentecost ultimately coincide, what we are seeing here is the anticipation of the bestowal of the Spirit on Easter Day (John 20:22) which corresponds to the descent of the Spirit at Pentecost according to Luke's Acts of the Apostles (Acts 2).[87] At the moment of his death, Jesus has come to his "hour." He has been lifted up to the right hand of the Father and can bestow on his own the gift of the Spirit. This is how the evangelist had interpreted Jesus's saying about the streams of living water (John 7:38): "With this he meant the Spirit that all who believe in him were to receive, for the Spirit had not yet been given because Jesus had not yet been glorified" (John 7:39).

### *The Opening of the Side of Jesus (19:31–37)*

The death of Jesus is not described as a cosmic event: the earth does not shake; the veil of the temple is not torn in two; and the dead do not rise from their graves and appear to many in the holy city.[88] Moreover, there is no mention of the confession of the centurion beneath the cross. The events after the death of Jesus are described by John in two scenes and in the center of them there are two groups: the "Jews," Pilate, and the Roman soldiers, on the one hand (vv. 31–37), Joseph of Arimathea and Nicodemus on the other (vv. 38–42). The first scene serves to state the real death of Jesus with its physical and spiritual consequences; the second depicts the honorable burial of Jesus by two of his supporters.

The first scene is, above all, a classic example for literary criticism in the sense of the criticism of sources and redaction. One of the latest repre-

---

86. Thus the *Einheitsübersetzung* of 1980: "He gave up his spirit."
87. Against the pneumatological understanding here, Weidemann, "Der Tod Jesu," 388; Weidemann, "Der Gekreuzigte," 573f., appeals to the Church fathers. However, from the fact that in John πνεῦμα can stand for ψυχή "soul," it does not follow that on this occasion this must be the case. It makes sense to link Jesus's gift of the Spirit in John to his "hour."
88. In the text of Johann Sebastian Bach's *St. John Passion*, the librettist has added this detail from Matthew because the Leipzig public apparently expected it.

## Jesus's "Hour": Passion, Death, and Resurrection (18:1–20:31)

sentatives of this form of exegesis is Becker.[89] In the present narrative, he distinguishes two phases of the revision of the hypothetical pre-Johannine account of the passion, death, and resurrection of Jesus: the hand of the evangelist and that of the "ecclesiastical redaction." In fact, little goes back to the evangelist. The latter follows far more broadly the narrative thread of the pre-Johannine passion narrative. The reference to the eyewitness testimony in John 19:35 goes back to the ecclesiastical redaction, which is interested in the physical death of Jesus, in dispute with the first Gnostic tendencies, and in the testimony of the beloved disciple in the service of the authentic faith of the community (cf. John 21:24). For a series of authors, this verse also has a sacramental meaning that is seen as typical of the ecclesiastical redaction.

In recent years, there has been an increasing tendency to disregard the layers in the text and to treat it in its unity from the final hand. The diachronic aspect comes more to the fore in the form of tradition criticism, especially in the working out of the relationship between the two scriptural quotations in verses 36 and 37 of the Johannine text.

**19:31** Just as in the very beginning of the trial of Jesus (cf. John 18:28), the Jews show themselves to be concerned above all with the keeping of the Law. According to Deut 21:23, the bodies of those who had been hanged were not to remain hanging on a tree or gibbet overnight but had to be taken down and buried before evening. According to the text of John, in the case of Jesus, there was actually a special urgency since the next day was a Sabbath and "a great feast day" to boot (cf. John 7:37). So the Jews ask Pilate to break the legs of Jesus and the other two men who had been crucified in order to hasten their death.

**19:32** Pilate permits the request of the "Jews," and so the soldiers break the legs of the two men crucified with Jesus. The text is operating with a *ritardando* and so heightens the readers' expectation as to what will happen with Jesus. The account turns from those crucified with Jesus to the Crucified One on whom the interest of the readers is focused.

**19:33** The latter, Jesus, is already dead, and so the soldiers do not break his legs. The readers ask themselves again what could possibly happen now to Jesus.

**19:34** The answer follows directly. The soldiers do not break Jesus's legs, but one of them takes his spear and thrusts it into Jesus's side. Immediately, blood and water flow out. Certainly, this event has different levels

---

89. Cf. Becker, 2:704–12.

of significance. Physically, it shows the undeniable death of Jesus. Looked at on a deeper level, the blood and water that flow from the side of Jesus may possess a symbolic sense but, as to just what this symbolic sense is, exegetes are far from agreed.

Some exegetes see in this event a symbolic reference to the sacraments of baptism (water) and the Eucharist (blood). This interpretation is found already in the Church fathers, alongside other interpretations.[90] However, some doubts remain about this interpretation. According to the sequence of the sacraments, one would have expected "water and blood" instead of "blood and water." Moreover, blood is not used as a symbol for the Eucharist elsewhere without the bread. In 1 John 5:6–7, there is mention of three witnesses, "Spirit, water and blood," but more with reference to the coming of Jesus not in water only (his baptism), but also in blood (which he shed on the cross).

On such grounds, Heil reminds the readers of this passage of the role of water in John's Gospel from the baptism of John to that of Jesus, as it was proclaimed by the Baptist, a baptism in the Spirit (John 1:33).[91] The theme returns in the conversation between Jesus and Nicodemus in John 3:1–10 and, in another form, in Jesus's invitation to come to him and drink—an invitation which is interpreted by the evangelist as an announcement of the gift of the Spirit (John 7:37–39). This is matched by the fact that when Jesus dies he does so by "giving over the Spirit" (John 19:30). This Spirit could be finding its physical expression in the water that flowed from the side of Jesus.

A similar consideration can be employed for the blood that came out of Jesus's side. The blood signifies the experience of the victim. Jesus is condmned to death at the moment when the Paschal lambs are slaughtered in memory of the liberation of Israel. Since the saying of the Baptist "Behold, the Lamb of God!" (John 1:29, 36), this conceptual world has been present in John's Gospel, possibly in connection with that of the servant who gives his life for the ransom of many. This view is confirmed by the first scriptural quotation in our text in John 19:36. Scholars are not agreed on the source of this Bible verse. However, a reference to the command not to break the bones of the Paschal lamb according to Exod 12:10, 46 LXX is probable.

**19:35** At this point a witness is introduced. Exegetes are not agreed

---

90. See, among others, Hoskyns, 636–38.
91. Heil, *Blood and Water*.

as to whether this testimony refers to the last event narrated, the flow of blood and water from the side of Jesus, or to the whole scene of the *crurifragium* and the opening of Jesus's side. Worthy of attention is the opinion of Becker,[92] who reckons that the testimony refers to the whole scene. The direct object of the testimony would have been the death of Jesus, the indirect, the flow of blood and water from his side. As shown above, a sacramental understanding of the scene is not certain.

All exegetes point here to John 21:24. However, the similar nature of the two texts does not necessitate a hypothesis of their origin from the same hand. In John 21:24, a church group appears clearly, testifying to the credibility of the witness. In John 19:35, the credibility of the narrator is asserted. It is assured, moreover, that the witness is aware of the credibility of his testimony. His testimony is recorded "so that you too may believe." Also, this turning to the readers does not occur in John 21:24, but rather in John 20:31. Thus there is reason to doubt that John 19:35 originates from the same hand as John 21:24.

**19:36** As often in John's Gospel (cf. 18:9; 19:24), the scene closes with a reference to Scripture, in this case, in fact, a double reference. The source of this quotation has already been suggested. Some authors think of Exod 12:10, 46 LXX and Num 9:12; also of Ps 34:21 where the righteous is promised that his limbs will not be broken.[93] John could have been linking both traditions in order to speak of the fate of Jesus.

**19:37** A further reference to Scripture is added. This text is clearly quoting Zech 12:10. However, the form of this Old Testament text remains uncertain. In the Masoretic text, it is not clear whether the house of David and the inhabitants of Jerusalem are directing their gaze on one who has been pierced or on God whom they have pierced. The Septuagint avoids the problem and reads κατωρχήσαντο "they danced" instead of the correct Hebrew root with the *Vorlage*. Aquila, Symmachus, and Theodotion are closer to the Masoretic text.[94] John and the whole of the primitive Christian tradition read the text attested in John 19:37, which constitutes a *testimonium* of the first Christians. According to Sandra Hübenthal,[95] the text is an "open" one and was "filled" by the reading community of the first Christians. The house of David and the inhabitants of Jerusalem

---

92. Cf. Becker, 2:708.
93. Cf. Menken, *Quotations*, 147–66.
94. Cf. Menken, *Quotations*, 167–85.
95. Hübenthal, *Transformation*, 215.

have looked on the one whom they pierced. Into their place steps the reader's community, which gazes at the Crucified One and finds salvation (cf. John 3:14–15).

### The Burial of Jesus (19:38–42)

The two scenes John 19:31–37 and 19:38–42 have a similar construction:[96] a group of persons or an individual turns to Pilate and asks about the body of Jesus (ἠρώτησα[ε]ν τὸν Πιλᾶτον . . . ἵνα): in the first case, the "Jews"; in the second, Joseph of Arimathea. Subsequently, there are references to the crucifixion (those "crucified" with Jesus, v. 32; the place where Jesus "was crucified," v. 41). At the beginning of the section and at the end (vv. 31, 42), there is a reference to the "day of preparation." The section vv. 38–42 is divided into two subsections: the initiative of Joseph of Arimathea who asks Pilate for the body of Jesus and receives it (v. 38), and the burial of Jesus by Joseph of Arimathea and Nicodemus (vv. 39–42).

**19:38** With the familiar transitional formula "after this" (μετὰ . . . ταῦτα), John passes on to the following scene, and introduces a new person: Joseph of Arimathea. The latter stems from the Synoptic tradition (cf. Mark 15:42–46). According to Mark, Joseph of Arimathea is a respected member of the Sanhedrin; according to Matthew (27:57), a rich man into the bargain and a disciple of Jesus; according to Luke (23:50), a good and righteous man. John adopts Matthew's motif that Joseph was a disciple but modifies it: he was a disciple, but secretly "for fear of the Jews." Such secret disciples of Jesus, even among the members of the Sanhedrin, are also mentioned in other places in John's Gospel (John 12:42–43). At this point, Joseph of Arimathea is displaying courage (cf. Mark 15:43 τολμήσας).

**19:39** At this moment, Nicodemus appears. John introduces him with the same words as he has used for Joseph of Arimathea: "he came" (ἦλθεν οὖν . . . ἦλθεν δέ). From his encounter with Jesus in John 3:1–2, Nicodemus is characterized as the one who "on an earlier occasion had sought Jesus by night."[97] In this cross-reference, one can make out a favorable assessment: the one who had come to Jesus by night for fear of being observed is now coming in broad daylight to help with his burial. Between these two scenes is that in which Nicodemus stands up for Jesus in the

---

96. See Hübenthal, 166.
97. Cf. Auwers, "La nuit"; Dschulnigg, "Nikodemus."

## Jesus's "Hour": Passion, Death, and Resurrection (18:1–20:31)

Sanhedrin and demands that he be treated correctly according to the Law, something that puts him in danger of being regarded as one of these people from Galilee or as a disciple of Jesus (John 7:50–52). Nicodemus can thus be seen as an example for the readers. Just like him, the readers have to reach a faith in Jesus that they confess fearlessly even at risk to themselves.[98]

The theme of the anointing of Jesus seems to have been taken over from the scene of the women who, according to Mark 16:1 par., come to the grave to anoint Jesus. On the other hand, the motif has been prepared already through the scene of the anointing of Jesus in the house of Lazarus (John 12:1–8) or in the house of Simon the leper (Mark 14:3–9; Matt 26:6–13; cf. Luke 7:36–50). The enormous amount of myrrh and aloes (about a hundred pounds) shows the generosity of Nicodemus but also indicates the dignity of Jesus. He is not buried like just another person but as a king who is due the highest honor.

**19:40** According to John, after Jesus's death and before his burial and the sealing of the tomb, Jesus is embalmed. The two men wrap him in linen cloths (ὀθόνια), a motif also found in Luke 24:12 and John 20:6–7 in the scene of the discovery of the empty tomb. The readers will recall the raising of Lazarus, who came forth from the grave tied with bandages. For John, Jesus who is anointed and wrapped in bandages is really dead and, according to human calculations, will not be returning among the living.

**19:41** The place of Jesus's burial is situated in a "garden." Here, the reader will recall the beginning of the passion narrative: Jesus is arrested in a garden. Thus, the garden motif frames the entire passion narrative (John 18:1; 19:41). Some exegetes see here an allusion to the Garden of Eden or to the garden mentioned in the Song of Songs. This conjecture takes on more weight when Mary Magdalene takes Jesus for the "gardener" (κηπουρός, John 20:15).

The fact that Jesus is buried in a new tomb in which no one has yet been interred is yet another indication of his dignity. Only an outstanding personality can be permitted such luxury.

**19:42** The narrative closes with the burial of Jesus as well as details of place and time. These two details are connected: Jesus has to be buried before the beginning of the Sabbath which is a great feast of the Jews, and this is made easier by the fact that the grave is close to the site of the crucifixion. For one last time, the reader is confronted with two ways in which the Law can be interpreted: on the one hand, it is observed by Jesus's

---

98. Cf. Beutler, "Faith and Confession."

disciples; on the other hand, however, it is also brought to fulfillment (cf. John 19:28–30). The account closes with the name of Jesus just as it had begun (cf. John 18:1).

*III*

Right up to the execution of Jesus, his death, and burial, the fourth evangelist conveys to us a picture of his majesty and dignity.[99] On the one hand, he goes on the way of his cross on his own and without help; on the other hand, his enemies like Pilate and the soldiers also contribute to emphasizing his dignity as witnessed by his crucifixion between two others and the inscription over the cross. Jesus dies without a cry of doubt, in loving faithfulness to the last to the work of salvation entrusted to him by the Father. He is anointed and buried as a king. No one can take his dignity from him.

Before Jesus's death, only the four women beneath the cross and the beloved disciple were named. To them is directed the legacy of Jesus, and in it is already indicated a legacy for the community, especially in the entrusting of the mother of Jesus to the disciple who takes her to himself. Other disciples come out of the woodwork only after Jesus's death. Joseph of Arimathea and Nicodemus display courage before the representative of the Roman power. Perhaps they also had a significance for the future: the early Christian community had more to fear from the power of the Romans than from the Jews.[100]

## 4. The Easter Narrative: Jesus's Appearances to the Disciples (20:1–31)

20 ¹ Early in the morning, while it was still dark, on the first day of the week, Mary Magdalene came to the tomb and saw that the stone had been taken away. ² Then she ran swiftly to Simon Peter and the other disciple whom Jesus loved and said to them: They have taken the Lord out of the tomb, and we do not know where they have laid him.

³ Then Peter and the other disciple went out and came to the tomb; ⁴ they

---

99. This aspect is also underlined by Frey, "Edler Tod." Other aspects of the Johannine passion narrative, according to Frey, are the efficacious death, the representative death, and the salvific death. They are contained there with more extensive literature than can be indicated here.

100. Cf. Cassidy, *John's Gospel*.

## Jesus's "Hour": Passion, Death, and Resurrection (18:1–20:31)

ran both together, but because the other disciple outran Peter he reached the tomb first. ⁵ He leaned down and saw the linen cloths lying but did not go inside. ⁶ Then Simon Peter, who was following him, came too and went into the tomb. He saw the linen cloths lying ⁷ and the towel that had lain on the head of Jesus; it was lying not with the linen cloths, however, but rolled up nearby in a place by itself. ⁸ Then the other disciple, who had arrived at the tomb first, went in; he saw and believed. ⁹ For they had not yet understood the Scripture that he must rise from the dead. ¹⁰ Then the disciples returned home.

¹¹ But Mary was standing outside in front of the grave, weeping. While she wept, she leaned down into the tomb. ¹² There she saw two angels sitting, in white robes, where the body of Jesus had lain, one at the head, the other at the feet. ¹³ They said to her: Woman, why are you weeping? She answered them: They have taken away my Lord, and I do not know where they have laid him. ¹⁴ When she had said this, she turned around and saw Jesus standing there but did not know that it was Jesus. ¹⁵ Jesus said to her: Woman, why are you weeping? Whom are you seeking? She thought he was the gardener and said to him: Sir, if you have taken him away, tell me where you have laid him. Then I will fetch him. ¹⁶ Jesus said to her: Mary! Then she turned round and said to him in Hebrew: Rabboni!, which means: Master. ¹⁷ Jesus said to her: Do not hold on to me; for I have not yet ascended to the Father. But go to my brothers and tell them: I am ascending to my Father and your Father, to my God and your God. ¹⁸ Mary Magdalene came to the disciples and declared to them: I have seen the Lord. And she recounted what he had said to her.

¹⁹ On the evening of this first day of the week, when the disciples were together behind closed doors for fear of the Jews, Jesus came, stood among them and said to them: Peace be with you! ²⁰ After these words he showed them his hands and his side. Then the disciples rejoiced when they saw the Lord. ²¹ Jesus said to them once again: Peace be with you! Just as the Father sent me, so I am sending you. ²² After he had said that, he breathed on them and said to them: Receive the Holy Spirit! ²³ Whose sins you forgive, they are forgiven; whose sins you retain, they are retained.

²⁴ Thomas, who was called Didymus, one of the Twelve, was not with them when Jesus came. ²⁵ The other disciples said to him: We have seen the Lord. He retorted: Unless I see the mark of the nails in his hands and put my finger into the mark of the nails and my hand into his side, I will not believe.

²⁶ Eight days later, the disciples were again assembled inside, and Thomas was with them. Then Jesus came through the closed doors, stood in the midst and said: Peace be with you! ²⁷ Then he said to Thomas: Stretch out your finger here and see my hands! Stretch out your hand and put it into my side, and be

not faithless but believing! ²⁸ Thomas answered and said to him: My Lord and my God! ²⁹ Jesus said to him: Because you have seen me, you have come to faith. Blessed are they who have not seen and yet believe.

³⁰ There were many other signs that Jesus did before the eyes of his disciples that are not recorded in this book. ³¹ But these are recorded that you may believe that Jesus is the Christ, the Son of God, and so may have life in his name.

# I

The exegesis of John 20 reveals once again in prism-like fashion the different methods and hermeneutical approaches of Johannine exegesis. In the "classical" Middle European school, the diachronic approach predominated until the second volume of Becker's commentary (1991). Becker distinguishes between a pre-Johannine account of the passion, death, and resurrection of Jesus, revised by the evangelist, and an update by the so-called "ecclesiastical redaction."[101] The greater part of the chapter would go back to the pre-Johannine account of Jesus's passion, death, and resurrection (the women and Mary Magdalene at the empty grave, the visit to the grave by Peter as well as an encounter between Mary Magdalene and Jesus). The figure of the beloved disciple would have been added by the "ecclesiastical redaction." The evangelist is responsible only for some redactional details as well as the scene of John 20:19–23, which leans on the section of the farewell discourses in John 14:15–24.

Other authors investigate the relationship between the text of John and the Synoptic tradition. For the so-called Louvain school, this tradition is sufficient as the basis for the Johannine text.[102] The authenticity of Luke 24:12 (Peter running to the grave) would strengthen this conclusion.[103] In recent times, this opinion has been established more firmly and is more probable than the source-critical model along the lines of J. Becker, not least because here we have documents that are known and do not have to rely on reconstructions.

In the more recent past, scholarly examinations of John 20 have generally preferred a synchronic approach to the text. Zumstein interprets John 20 as a way of faith for the readers.[104] From the narrative point of

---

101. Becker, 2:714–20; the same layers are presupposed in Becker, "Auferstehung," 62–79.
102. Cf. Bieringer, "They Have Taken Away"; Bieringer, "I Am Ascending."
103. Cf. Zeller, "Ostermorgen."
104. Zumstein, "Narratologische Lektüre."

view, it concerns the Easter faith. The actors in the text represent different ways of approaching the resurrection of Jesus. This involves progress from the mere search for Jesus's body to the encounter with him, first only on the basis of a correctly interpreted sign, then on the basis of the understanding of Scripture, and, finally, as an encounter with Jesus face to face. At the end, there is a faith that relies no longer on a visual encounter with Jesus but on the word of proclamation (Thomas). It is in him, above all, that the readers will rediscover themselves.[105]

Martinus de Boer asks about the connection between Jesus's farewell and his death and resurrection.[106] According to de Boer, all the texts in John that speak of Jesus's departure refer to his ascension to the Father and so also to his resurrection. The only exceptions are constituted by those texts that speak of Jesus's "lifting up" and "glorification" and clearly have in view Jesus's "lifting up" on the cross but also his lifting up to the Father. We showed earlier that this usage refers to the Fourth Servant Song (Isa 52:13 LXX). According to de Boer, these texts are not characteristic of Johannine usage and have to be regarded as secondary in comparison with the others that speak of Jesus's departure in the sense of his lifting up to the Father. This suggestion is not entirely convincing since the texts that speak of Jesus's destiny in the sense of the servant appear to be fully integrated into John's Gospel from a literary and theological point of view.

Kelli S. O'Brien reads John 20 in a similar way to that of Zumstein, except that she finds in the beloved disciple an insipid figure who does not occupy much of a position in comparison with Mary Magdalene.[107] In this, she is, perhaps, overlooking the fact that, in our text, the beloved disciple's significance for the Easter faith of the reading community is highlighted and less attention is given to him as an example of lived faith.

How is this chapter constructed? By contrast with chs. 18–19, there is still no general agreement among exegetes about the partition of John 20. All find in this chapter a division into two main sections: the events at the tomb on Easter morning in John 20:1–18 and the encounters of Jesus with the disciples at their meeting place in verses 19–29. This is followed by the first conclusion of the Gospel in verses 30–31 (before the epilogue of John 21). For the subdivision of these two main sections there still exist various opinions. Schnackenburg divides John 20:1–18 into two scenes: vv. 1–10 and

---

105. A similar way of faith is described by Schneiders, "Touching the Risen Jesus."
106. de Boer, "Jesus' Departure."
107. O'Brien, "Written."

11–18.[108] Brown sees only a single scene here with two episodes.[109] Again, Schnackenburg divides John 20:19–29 into two scenes: vv. 19–23 and 24–28; according to Brown the section forms a single scene, again with two episodes. In John 20, Schenke finds five scenes before the conclusion: vv. 1–10, 11–17, 18, 19–23, and 24–29.[110] For the sake of greater clarity, it is advisable to apply to John 20 the grid of narrative analysis with its division according to the criteria of time, place, characters, and action. With these criteria, it is possible to identify six scenes in John 20 before the conclusion:

> 20:1–2 Mary Magdalene at the tomb; she informs Peter and the beloved disciple
> 20:3–10 Peter and the beloved disciple at the tomb (reference to Scripture)
> 20:11–18 Mary Magdalene at the tomb: she recognizes Jesus
> 20:19–23 Jesus's appearance before the disciples on Easter evening
> 20:24–25 Thomas does not come to faith in the Risen One
> 20:26–29 Thomas comes to faith in the Risen One
> 20:30–31 Conclusion: Faith Is the Door to Life

In the center of this seven-part composition stands the scene of the meeting of Jesus with his disciples on the evening of Easter Day, in which the risen Jesus bestows his eschatological gift on the disciples: peace, joy, and the Holy Spirit (cf. Rom 14:17 and John 14:26–28; 16:4e–33). Up to v. 18, Jesus is still on his ascent to the Father; from v. 19, he returns from the Father back to his own.[111]

## II

*Mary Magdalene at the Tomb of Jesus (20:1–2)*

The basis for the Johannine account is found in the Synoptic tradition in the errand of the women to the tomb early on the first day after Passover (Mark 16:1–4; Matt 28:1–3; Luke 24:1–3). In this account, Mary Magdalene

---

108. Schnackenburg, 3:354f.
109. Brown, 2.995.
110. Schenke, 369–71.
111. Cf. Schneiders, "Johannine Resurrection Narrative."

## Jesus's "Hour": Passion, Death, and Resurrection (18:1–20:31)

is named in the first place before a series of other women. The timing for the arrival of the women at the tomb is daybreak in the early morning, a not very suitable detail for the Johannine account. Matthew depicts the process of the resurrection itself, something that is also not suited to the Johannine portrayal. The mistake of Mary Magdalene is captured well by Luke and could have influenced John's description: "Why are you seeking the living among the dead? He is not here" (Luke 24:5).

**20:1** The small scene begins with details of time and place. On the first day of the week, still by night, Mary Magdalene betakes herself to the tomb of Jesus and sees the stone rolled away. One could ask why there is no mention of the previous day, the Sabbath, which was also a great feast.[112] The evangelist wastes no words over this. This is all the more surprising since he carefully calculates the days before Jesus's death and then after his resurrection. In both cases, it is possible to count up a week: from the anointing of Jesus in the house of Lazarus six days before the Passover (John 12:1) to the feast itself, and then the week from the first appearance of Jesus according to John 20:19–23 to the last in John 20:26–28. The narrative flow seems to be completely disturbed here. Along with the narrator, the reader takes no part in the "zero hour" of salvation, the passage from death to life, from darkness to light. So it is not by chance that Mary Magdalene sets out for the tomb during the last hours of the night before the daybreak on Sunday. Her action is described by five verbs in the historic present. The first two verbs describe the arrival of Mary Magdalene at the tomb and the discovery that the stone had been rolled away.

**20:2** The three following verbs describe Mary's reaction. She "runs" and "comes" to Peter and the beloved disciple and "says" to them: "They have taken the Lord out of the tomb, and we do not know where they have laid him." The plural "we" presupposes a group of people who have gone to the tomb, something that could be assumed from the Synoptics by the readers. Here, John's text does not speak of the presence of angels explaining to Mary the fact of the empty tomb. This will follow only later, in verses 11–13. Thus, it is only a confused Mary that we see. The reason for this confusion lies in the fact that she takes the corpse of Jesus for Jesus Christ himself and so is looking for her Lord in the tomb. According to her, it is possible to carry "her Lord" from one place to another. This is her position at the beginning of a path of faith through which she has to pass and on which she can be accompanied by the readers.

---

112. Cf., for this and the following, Stare, "Es ist vollendet."

## Peter and the Beloved Disciple at the Tomb of Jesus (20:3–10)

The textual foundation for this scene seems to lie in Luke 24:12: "But Peter got up and ran to the tomb; stooping and looking in, he saw the linen cloths by themselves; then he went home, amazed at what had happened." The Greek verse of this text is accepted in Nestle-Aland[28] and in the UBS Greek New Testament, even if there with only the lowest level of certainty (D: considerable doubt). The shorter text, without v. 12, belongs to the so-called Western Non-Interpolations which, for a long time, were held to be original. Today, this shorter text, represented chiefly by Codex D Bezae Cantabrigiensis, is considered rather as the result of abbreviations by a scribe of D with the aim of securing a more comprehensible text. The oldest Egyptian text tradition contains the longer text each time, and so also here. The figure of the beloved disciple seems to have been inserted by the evangelist. Here, as also where he appears elsewhere, he seems to be in "competition" with Peter.

**20:3** According to John's portrayal, Peter and the beloved disciple reach the tomb of Jesus together, as is required by the sense (Greek, εἰς τὸ μνημεῖον instead of ἐπὶ τὸ μνημεῖον as already in John 20:1, varying from Mark 16:2).

**20:4** The priority of the beloved disciple corresponds to the Johannine perspective. At the Last Supper, he lies "at Jesus's side" (John 13:23) and is close to Jesus also at the last moment of his life (John 19:26–27). Thus, he also reaches the tomb of Jesus first.

**20:5** According to John, the beloved disciple, as the first one there, sees the linen cloths lying but does not go in out of respect for Peter. The clauses "he leaned down and saw the linen cloths lying" (παρακύψας βλέπει . . . τὰ ὀθόνια) are now said of the beloved disciple and no longer of Peter as in Luke 24:12.

**20:6** Peter "sees the linen cloths lying" as already the beloved disciple before him. Once again, the doubling of the statement can be recognized as recourse to the *Vorlage*.

**20:7** To this is now added reference to the towel that had lain on Jesus's head but which now was lying rolled up in another place. This element is not found in the Synoptic tradition and this has led to discussion concerning its origin and meaning. In John, this appears to possess the meaning of a "sign."

**20:8** This conjecture is strengthened in v. 8: "Then the other disciple, who had arrived at the tomb first, went in; he saw and believed." The

## Jesus's "Hour": Passion, Death, and Resurrection (18:1–20:31)

reader asks how the fact that the towel was rolled up near the linen cloths could lead to Easter faith. From the ordered way in which the towel lay folded up, one could come to the logical conclusion that the action was that of Jesus and not of a hasty grave-robber. Perhaps more convincing is the suggestion of Sandra M. Schneiders[113] to see here an allusion to the cloth that covered the face of Moses when he had spoken with God. When Moses spoke with the Lord, then he took off the cloth (Exod 34:34). This element was taken up in early Christian tradition (cf. 2 Cor 3:7–18). According to Paul, the cloth that covered the glory of the Lord is taken away in Christ. It cannot be excluded that John made use of this image in order to point to the glory of Christ, which Christians can now behold unveiled. The beloved disciple would have come to this faith when he saw Jesus's towel rolled up lying by itself.

**20:9** In the next verse, we have a problem of translation. According to the first possibility, the text is read as follows: "For they had not yet understood the Scripture that he must rise from the dead."[114] This version suggests itself if one starts out from the fact that, at least at the present point in time, the beloved disciple understood the meaning of the Scripture. According to the other possibility, one would translate: "For they did not yet understand the Scripture."[115] Then the beloved disciple would have come to Easter faith for the sole purpose of seeing and correctly interpreting the sign, and the understanding of Scripture would have developed for him subsequently. In that case, however, it would remain open when that was to happen.

**20:10** The return home of the disciples is explained by Luke 24:12. According to this verse, Peter returned back home "amazed at what had happened." According to John, the two disciples return back home. One of them had come to Easter faith; the other, by contrast, not yet. This different situation explains the somewhat banal conclusion of the narrative in John.

In this section, the readers have been led one step further on the way to faith in the Risen One. For the first time, a disciple comes to Easter faith. Not by chance, it is the beloved disciple. Just as he is loved by Jesus, so he too loves his Lord, and has "eyes to see." With his readiness to look for his Lord, he recognizes him also in the unimpressive sign of the towel rolled up and lying by itself. Love opened his eyes for what remained hidden to others, even if they are also pillars of the church.

---

113. Schneiders, "Face Veil."
114. New Jerusalem Bible.
115. *Einheitsübersetzung*, Luther, RSV.

### Mary Magdalene at the Tomb of Jesus (20:11–18)

In the exegesis of the narrative of the encounter between Jesus and Mary Magdalene, there is a mirror once again for the different models of Johannine exegesis. Until after the middle of the twentieth century, historical-critical studies dominated this section of the Fourth Gospel. In the last third of the twentieth century, one can observe a strong feminist interest in this narrative.[116] In the *Feminist Companion to the New Testament*, Harold W. Attridge represents the main features of the contributions about Jesus's saying "Do not hold on to me."[117] Not infrequently, where Mary Magdalene is concerned, the more recent contributions start out from a defective position. She takes no account of Jesus's new mode of being, of the necessity that he has to ascend to the Father or of the limited possibility of access to Jesus for her. Nevertheless, Mary Magdalene appears as an exemplary disciple and herald of Jesus to the other disciples.

Since the turn of the century, there has been a tendency in research to undertake a more basic literary and theological study of the passage. Susanne Ruschmann[118] reads the text from the perspective of *"relecture,"* a viewpoint she has taken over from Zumstein, Dettwiler, and Scholtissek. In the narrative of the encounter of the risen Jesus with Mary Magdalene there are references to the narratives of the call of the first disciples in John 1:35–51 and the farewell discourses, especially John 14:18–20, 21–23. The themes that John 20 and John 14 have in common are "love," "seeing," and "living." For Schneiders, the present passage marks a change in the representation of the body of Jesus.[119] Mary Magdalene is looking for a corpse and has to learn that Jesus is no longer living in the old way. Thus, because of this, she cannot detain him. Jesus is living in a new manner of existence that also includes the body of the nascent community. Of this, the scene in John 20:19–23 will speak. Donald Senior[120] expresses his respect for his Californian colleague but calls for further studies on the mode of existence of believers after their resurrection.

The appearance of Jesus to Mary Magdalene on Easter Day is not attested by any independent tradition in the New Testament. The text which comes nearest to this is the account of a meeting of Jesus with the

---

116. Cf. Perkins, "I Have Seen the Lord"; Beutler, "Frauen und Männer."
117. Attridge, "Don't Be Touching Me."
118. Cf. Ruschmann, *Maria von Magdala*.
119. Schneiders, "Johannine Resurrection Narrative"; cf. Schneiders, "Touching the Risen Jesus."
120. Senior, "Resurrection."

## Jesus's "Hour": Passion, Death, and Resurrection (18:1–20:31)

women who had gone to his tomb according to Matt 28:9–10.[121] This text speaks of two Marys: Mary Magdalene and "the other Mary." The account in Mark 16:9–11 (in the secondary conclusion to Mark) depends on John 20:1–2, 11–18, and the account in Mark 16:12–13 depends on Matt 28:9–10. The account in Matt 28:9–11 is simply added to its literary *Grundlage* Mark 16:1–8, the appearance of Jesus to the women who have gone to the tomb. With Schnackenburg,[122] we can suppose that the accounts are not on the same levels of tradition, and that the report of the appearance of Jesus to the two women is secondary to the discovery of the empty tomb in Mark 16:1–8 (which still filters through in John 20:1–2 and 20:3–10 as well as in Luke 24:1–11, 12). With a comparison of the Gospel accounts, one can observe a development from the appearance of the angels to the women with their message of the resurrection of Jesus to an appearance of Jesus to these women. In the list of the witnesses of Jesus's resurrection in 1 Cor 15:3–8, the women are not included, though that could lie in the fact that the testimony of women was of little weight in the ancient world.

How is the composition constructed? According to the criteria of narrative analysis, John 20:11–18 is divided into three subsections:

- Mary Magdalene at the tomb, and her conversation with the two angels vv. 11–13
- Mary Magdalene meets Jesus vv. 14–16
- Mary Magdalene is sent by Jesus vv. 17–18

In her unpublished dissertation, Schneiders divides the passage according to three stages of the spiritual path of Mary Magdalene, which are each expressed with a participle:[123]

- Mary cries (κλαίουσα, v. 11)
- Mary turns round (στραφεῖσα, v. 16)
- Mary announces (ἀγγέλλουσα, v. 18)

In a first phase, Mary is completely dominated by her grief and incapable of grasping the resurrection of Jesus. In a second phase, she "turns around,"

---

121. For this, more extensively, cf. Bieringer, "I Am Ascending."
122. Cf. Schnackenburg, 3:379f.
123. Schneiders, "Johannine Resurrection Narrative."

not only physically but also spiritually, and is able to recognize Jesus again. In the third phase, she becomes herald to the apostles.

**20:11–13** In v. 11, the narrator takes up the thread again from v. 2. The reader recalls that Mary Magdalene had run into the city to report to Peter and the beloved disciple about the empty tomb. Surprisingly, at the beginning of this passage, she is found once again at Jesus's tomb. This time her frame of mind is also described: she is weeping. At this moment, she discovers two angels in the tomb: one where the head, the other where the feet of the body of Jesus had lain.

In her response to the question as to why she is weeping, Mary repeats the mistake that she had already made in v. 2, interpreting the corpse of Jesus as Jesus himself: "They have taken away my Lord, and I do not know where they have laid him." In comparison with v. 2, two differences can be identified: Mary now speaks of "her" Lord, and so reveals her personal relationship with Jesus, and she no longer speaks in the plural "and we do not know" but in the singular: "and I do not know." The hand of the evangelist can be recognized in both these details.

**20:14–16** Twice in this section, it says that Mary "turned around." On the first occasion, in v. 14, the verb retains its literal sense; on the second, in v. 16, there is, perhaps, a figurative and spiritual meaning in play also. In v. 14, Mary leans down into the tomb and then turns around to the outside where she sees Jesus but without recognizing him. In her is being realized the promise of Jesus in his farewell discourse that those of his own who love him will see him (John 14:19, same Greek verb), but she does not recognize him, that is, she has not "understood" the appearance (cf. John 20:9, where the disciples had not "understood" the meaning of the Scripture). In the following dialogue, Jesus seizes the initiative and asks Mary why she is weeping and for whom she is looking. Maybe the reader will recall the arrest scene in which Jesus had already taken the initiative with the same question: "Whom do you seek?" (John 18:4, 7). An even more vivid memory is that of the scene of the encounter of Jesus with the first two disciples that begins with the same question: "Who are you looking for/what do you want?" (John 1:38). On the basis of this similarity, Ruschmann sees in John 20:11–18 a variation on the theme of discipleship in John's Gospel.[124] In his callings, Jesus does not impose himself but tries to match the inner aspirations of his future disciples. Mary, however, persists in her mistake, takes Jesus for the gardener, and,

---

124. Cf. Ruschmann, *Maria von Magdala*.

## Jesus's "Hour": Passion, Death, and Resurrection (18:1–20:31)

worse still, continues in her error of confusing Jesus with a corpse that could be taken away.

The scene reaches its climax in v. 16. The new recognition of Jesus is described with a short dialogue which is introduced by a new "turning" round by Mary: "Mary!" – "Rabboni! which means Master." The Hebrew or, to be more precise, the Aramaic form of the title of Jesus is to be explained, not by a particularly ancient tradition but by the personal tone of this dialogue. This is the way lovers recognize each other again in the recognition scenes (ἀναγώρισις) of the ancient novels after a long time of separation and seeking.[125] There are biblical echoes here of the Song of Songs in which there is a description of how the lovers seek and eventually find each other (cf. Song 3:1–4). Here too is the motif of the garden,[126] which could be being recalled in the figure of Jesus as the gardener in v. 15.

**20:17-18** The account closes with a double saying of Jesus to Mary. The first part of this is negative. Exegetes are not agreed over the correct translation and meaning of Jesus's command: μή μου ἅπτου. On the basis of the tense, the *Einheitsübersetzung* and the NRSV (with other translations) render it with: "Do not hold on to me."

The reason for this command lies in the following clause: "for I have not yet ascended to the Father." According to this interpretation, it is not a matter of Mary's not being allowed to touch Jesus but rather of not hindering him on his way to the Father. However, with good reasons, Reimund Bieringer[127] suggests reconsidering the translation "do not touch me." The use of the verb in the Septuagint and in the rest of the New Testament suggests this translation. The thought here is of a restraint of Mary before Jesus as the place of the presence of God in analogy with the instructions in the book of Numbers to keep one's distance from the sanctuary.[128] Jesus is thus to ascend (ἀναβαίνειν) to the Father and create access there for the disciples. John's Gospel would thus be interpreting afresh the women's grasping of Jesus's feet on Easter morning according to Matt 28:9.

Some exegetes distinguish between the ascent of Jesus to the Father in the hour of his "lifting up" on the cross and the associated glorification, and his ascension as still outstanding, as is presupposed in his conversation with Mary Magdalene. Basically, it appears to be a question of the same

---

125. The oldest example of this is in the *Odyssey*.
126. Cf. Song 4:12–16; 5:1; 6:2, 11; 8:13.
127. Cf. Bieringer, "I Am Ascending."
128. Cf. Num 3:10; 17:13; in other places, "access" is the subject: 1:51; 3:38; 18:3–4, cf. Bieringer, "I Am Ascending," 231.

movement. Jesus's lifting up on the cross is continued in the Easter event, and Mary Magdalene already becomes a witness to the ascension of Jesus to the Father before the coming again of Jesus to his own is recorded from v. 19 on.

In what follows, Mary is instructed to report to Jesus's "brothers" that he is ascending to his Father and their Father, to his God and their God. The expression "brothers" is employed for the disciples here in John for the first and only time. Insofar as God is the Father of all who believe in Jesus, then one can indeed call Jesus "brother" too. The formula "my Father and your Father" does not create distance but rather gives the reason for God's being the Father of the believers: because he is the Father of the Risen Christ.

Mary Magdalene embraces Jesus's command and takes herself off to the disciples in order to share with them the joyful message of Jesus. The words chosen by the evangelist recall the formulation of the apostolic testimony to the resurrection of Jesus: "I have seen the Lord" (cf. v. 25 and 1 Cor 9:1). Since the time of the Church fathers, this has led to the claim that Mary Magdalene became the "apostle of the apostles." The first church author who speaks in this way is Hippolytus of Rome at the beginning of the third century.[129] Only later, since the time of Gregory the Great has Mary Magdalene been identified with the penitent sinner of Luke 7:36–50, an identification that gave her the ambivalent status that marks her image in Christian preaching and art to the present day. The feminist movement takes John 20:11–18 as the starting point for its demand for a more active role for women in preaching and in ministry in the church.

### Jesus's Appearance to the Disciples on the Evening of Easter (20:19–23)

The division of John 20 into two is broadly accepted. Schneiders makes a helpful observation that the first half (vv. 1–18) contains an ascending movement to the Father, and the second (vv. 19–29) a descending one.[130] A similar observation can be made in John 14: in John 14:1–14, Jesus is leaving the disciples and going to the Father; in John 14:15–24 Jesus "is

---

129. *In Cant.* 67 (edition of Bonwetsch).
130. Cf. Schneiders, "Johannine Resurrection Narrative."

## Jesus's "Hour": Passion, Death, and Resurrection (18:1–20:31)

coming" with his eschatological gifts (cf. John 14:25–29). It will be shown that the scene in John 20:19–23 is well explained against this background. The two following scenes are separated from John 20:19–23 by a period of time. First, there is an account of a meeting of the ten disciples with Thomas, who was not present at the appearance of Jesus on Easter Day; then of an encounter of Jesus with the eleven disciples, including Thomas, after eight days. At the end, we have the (first) literary conclusion of the Gospel in John 20:30–31.

In John 20:19–23, the influence of Luke's Gospel can clearly be discerned and, in fact, of the scene Luke 24:36–49. "(He) stood among them and said to them: Peace be with you (ἔστη εἰς τὸ μέσον καὶ λέγει αὐτοῖς· εἰρήνη ὑμῖν)" is an almost literal version of Luke 24:36 (there, ἔστη ἐν μέσῳ αὐτῶν). In the recognition scene in John, the sign of the hands and feet of Jesus is replaced by the sign of the hands and the side because of the scene in John 19:31–37. Luke also speaks of the disciples' "joy" (24:41) and the gift of the Holy Spirit (24:49). In Luke's view, this gift, the "promise" of the Father, is bestowed at a later time, namely Pentecost (Acts 2).

The authority to forgive sins shows some correspondences to the conferring of the authority to "bind" and to "loose" on earth both on Peter and on the Twelve (Matt 16:19; 18:18).[131] The concern there, however, is with the authority to make binding decisions about teaching.

However, alongside such parallels, the Johannine passage retains its significance within its own context.[132]

The passage can be subdivided into two parallel scenes: vv. 19–20 and 21–23. The first scene is about the recognition of Jesus, the second about his commission.

> Jesus appears among his own and offers them his greeting of peace: v. 19
> A gesture by Jesus: he shows them his hands and his side: v. 20a
> A reaction of the disciples, joy: v. 20b
> Jesus greets his own again with a greeting of peace and a commission formula: v. 21
> A gesture by Jesus: he breathes on them: v. 22a
> A word of commission: vv. 22b–23

---

131. Korting, "Binden und Lösen"; Claudel, "Jean 20,23"; for a Christian-Islamic comparison of the passage, cf. Mohamed and Sorg, "Friede sei mit euch!"
132. Haag, "Aus Angst zur Freude."

**20:19** This long verse gives, first of all, the time, the place, and the circumstances of Jesus's appearance before it speaks of the appearance itself. Here, every element has its theological significance. The temporal detail sets Jesus's appearance on Easter Day itself. Thus, the Spirit is given then and not on Pentecost. "The first day of the week" will be the Christians' holy day in the future. One can also say that Jesus appeared "on Sunday," the day with which the Christians replaced the Sabbath. The place of Jesus's appearance remains inexact. Schneiders has pointed to the fact that Jesus appears precisely in the place "where the disciples were together."[133] This element will find its continuation in the community.[134] The reason why the disciples had assembled behind closed doors may surprise the readers. One could have expected that the disciples would have drawn new hope from the message of Mary Magdalene. This is another sign that the different parts of John 20 follow on each other without any strict logical connection, an observation that can be made again about the sequence of John 20 and John 21.

Jesus's arrival is described with three verbs: he "came," he "stood among them," and he "said." The first verb is unusual for an Easter narrative, indeed unique. The expression chosen is explicable in light of Johannine theology. For John, the "hour" of the lifting up and glorification of Jesus is the "eschatological hour." Thus, ultimately, for John, not only Good Friday, Easter, Ascension, and Pentecost but also the day of the "coming" of Jesus for judgement occur together. "Amen, amen, I tell you: The hour is coming and now is when the dead will hear the voice of the Son of God; and all who hear it will live" (John 5:25). In John, the coming of the Son of Man on the last day and the bestowal of life are marginalized (cf. John 5:28–29; 6:39, 40, 44, 54 in the frame of ch. 6 that could stem from a later hand). Already in the first farewell discourse, in John 14:15–24, Jesus had spoken of his "coming" to his own in the Spirit, personally and together with the Father in the hour of the post-Easter community.[135]

Jesus "stood among them": The expression shows that the assembly of the disciples embodies the preferred place of the revelation of Jesus. Jesus's greeting of peace goes back to John 14:27; 16:33. The peace that was previously promised has now become the Easter gift of Jesus.

---

133. Schneiders, *Johannine Resurrection Narrative*.

134. The liturgical dimension of the Johannine resurrection narrative is emphasized by Weidemann, "Eschatology."

135. See above.

## Jesus's "Hour": Passion, Death, and Resurrection (18:1–20:31)

**20:20** Jesus's unexpected appearance arouses doubt as to his identity among the disciples. So Jesus shows them his hands and his side. The question could be asked why it was not sufficient for them to see the face of Jesus. For the evangelist, the identity between the one who was crucified and the Risen One is of great significance. At the crucifixion, Jesus's hands were pierced; his side was penetrated by the Roman soldier's spear. It is precisely this same one who had been crucified, who died, and who had been taken down from the cross, whom the disciples see in this moment of their Easter meeting. Thus, they are filled with joy, as the departing Jesus had foretold (John 16:20–22).

**20:21** The renewed greeting of peace introduces the second scene. At the same time, John introduces the theme of this scene: the commission that Jesus entrusts to his disciples. This commission consists of a sending. The disciples are sent out by Jesus just as Jesus was sent by the Father. As also elsewhere in John, not only does the relationship between Jesus and the Father correspond to the relationship between Jesus and the disciples, but the one builds upon the other: the sending of Jesus by the Father is the basis of the sending entrusted to the disciples. They are taking part in the sending of the Son.

**20:22** The gesture with which Jesus proves his identity is matched by the gesture that introduces the sending of the disciples. He breathes on them and says: Receive the Holy Spirit! The verb employed recalls two important episodes in salvation history. God "breathes" on Adam and communicates the breath of life to him (Gen 2:7), and the prophet announces a "breathing" of the Spirit over the dry bones of the people of Israel that will bestow new life on them (Ezek 37:9).[136] In both cases, the Septuagint uses the verb ἐμφυσάω, which is also employed in John 20:22. The prophetic text stands between the creation and the new creation in Jesus. The evangelist had already announced the gift of the Spirit for the hour of the glorification of Jesus (John 7:39). Now the hour is come.

For the correct understanding of v. 22, it is important to keep in mind that, according to v. 19, Jesus is standing among the "disciples." It is these disciples on whom Jesus breathes and to whom he imparts his commission. The attempt of William S. Kurz (with the *Catechism of the Catholic Church*) to reduce this circle of disciples to the apostles or the office bearers in the church enjoys no support in the text.[137]

---

136. Cf. Hatina, "John 20,22."
137. Cf. Kurz, "Test Case."

**20:23** The closing verse of the passage receives different interpretations.[138] The problems begin with the correct translation of the Greek text. "Forgiving" sins is comprehensible, but what does "κρατεῖν" mean? In correspondence with Matt 16:19, the *Einheitsübersetzung* of 1980 translates: "refuse forgiveness." However, this rendering is criticized, and rightly so.[139] Thus, here, we prefer the translation: "whose [sins] you retain, they are retained." This is also the version of the revised Luther text.

The verse begins with a positive statement: the disciples are granted authority to forgive sins. This authority is the result of the messianic mission of Jesus, the "Lamb of God who takes away the sin of the world" (John 1:29). Insofar as the eschatological promises are fulfilled in Jesus, the forgiveness of sins will become a reality (cf. Jer 31:34 concerning the new covenant: "For I will forgive their iniquity, and remember their sin no more"). The disciples can proclaim this forgiveness of sins to all who believe in Jesus. The early Fathers of the Church considered baptism as the place where this forgiveness is awarded; other fathers and the magisterium prefer the sacrament of penance or confession. However, Schnackenburg is right to maintain that the question about the institutional locus of the forgiveness of sins is anachronistic and finds no direct answer in the text of John 20:23.[140] The "retaining" of sins probably means simply declaring that someone seems not yet to possess the faith that leads to the forgiveness of sins.

At this point, one can enquire again after the tradition-historical background to the main themes of John 20:19-23. In John, as in Luke (24:36-49), there is a word-cluster consisting of "peace," "joy," and "Holy Spirit." In John 14:25-28, Jesus promises the disciples the gift of the Holy Spirit (v. 26) and his peace (v. 27).[141] He speaks also of the joy that the disciples would experience if, at this moment, they loved his return to the Father (v. 28). In a *"relecture"* of this section, these themes are encountered again, associated with the theme of righteousness, in John 16:4e-33. "Righteousness" occurs only here in John's Gospel (vv. 8-10); the Holy Spirit is promised in verses 7-14; "joy" in verses 20-22, and "peace" in the closing verse 33. It has already been pointed out elsewhere[142] that this word-cluster derives from Rom 14:17, where Paul writes: "For the king-

---

138. See, for this verse, Beutler, "Resurrection."
139. Cf. Weidemann, "Nochmals Joh 20,23."
140. Cf. Schnackenburg, 3:388.
141. See above.
142. Cf. Beutler, *Habt keine Angst*, 90-104; Beutler, *Do Not Be Afraid*, 82-93, 109.

dom of God is not eating and drinking, but righteousness, peace and joy in the Holy Spirit." Paul's definition here is all the more significant in that the kingdom of God is not a characteristic Pauline concept. The apostle is taking it over from tradition. In doing so, he presents us here with the only definition of the kingdom of God in the whole of the Bible. The Old Testament background of these messianic-eschatological promises has already been demonstrated above in the comment on John 14:25–29. It reaches back past the Exilic and post-Exilic prophets to the royal ideology of the Ancient Near East.

### The Meeting of the Disciples with Thomas (20:24–25)

This is a transitional scene not often treated in the commentaries and monographs as a section in its own right. The reason for separating this group of verses from the following lies in the fact that there is a time difference between John 20:24–25 and 26–29, as well as a change of actors and action. It is better, therefore, to interpret each scene individually.

**20:24** This verse reports a fact concerning the first meeting of Jesus with the disciples on Easter Day. At this point, Thomas was not with them. The question as to why this was the case does not seem to concern the evangelist. He is interested in different forms of faith. Other speculations are associated with the name of Thomas. According to Devillers, the second name "Didymus" should be translated with "twin" or with "the double," and would then refer to the twofold (Janus-like) face of Thomas as one who belongs to the group who have seen and believed and at the same time to those who have not seen and yet believe.[143] However, this suggestion remains hypothetical. The second name "Didymus" is found for Thomas also in John 11:16 and 21:2, and appears to signify more a description belonging to the circle of disciples than one given by the post-Easter community.

**20:25** The scene itself consists of a short dialogue. The ten disciples say to Thomas: "We have seen the Lord." Thomas replies with a demand for physical contact with the Risen One. The saying of the ten disciples derives from the words of Mary Magdalene (John 20:18), which are also found in 1 Cor 9:1 and seem to be some kind of "apostolic" formula of testimony to the Risen One. For Thomas, this testimony to the basis of the

---

143. Cf. Devillers, "Thomas."

Easter faith should have been sufficient. However, as with the ten disciples, this testimony finds no response (cf. John 20:19–23 after 20:18). The words with which Thomas demands a physical encounter with Jesus correspond broadly to the gesture with which Jesus shows the disciples his hands and his side. To that is added the place of the nails with which the hands had been pierced. This element matches the Roman practice of nailing the hands of the person crucified, but it could also go back to Ps 22:16.

*Jesus's Appearance before the Disciples together with Thomas (20:26–29)*

The vocabulary of this passage is largely provided by the two previous scenes. This is the case especially for verses 26 and 27. In v. 26, the evangelist goes back to the scene of Jesus's appearance on Easter evening in John 20:19–23; in v. 27, he goes back to the demand of Thomas that was recounted in v. 25. The two final verses are independently formulated and lead to the confession of Thomas and to Jesus's praise of those who do not see but yet believe that concludes the narrative part of John's Gospel in its first version.[144]

**20:26** The scene takes place "after eight days." The exegetes consider this a reference to the Christian assemblies in early Christianity on the first day of the week, Sunday.[145] This temporal detail fits well with the information about place that the disciples were again "inside together." The reference to the closed doors is no more completely comprehensible here. Perhaps it refers rather to the disciples as a closed circle, since fear of the Jews as the reason for the closed doors is no longer mentioned. For the progress of the narrative, it is important that Thomas is now present with the other disciples.

**20:27** After his renewed greeting of peace, Jesus turns directly to Thomas. The "omniscient narrator" recalls exactly the words of Thomas in v. 25 and now puts them into the mouth of Jesus. Jesus commands Thomas to put his finger "here" and his hand into the side of the Lord. The most important command stands at the end: "Be not faithless but believing."

Scholars give different interpretations of this command of Jesus. For

---

144. Cf. Kremer, "Nimm deine Hand."
145. Cf. the reference to this in Moloney, 537, and, again, Weidemann, "Eschatology," 282.

## Jesus's "Hour": Passion, Death, and Resurrection (18:1–20:31)

Rudolf Bultmann,[146] Thomas is the representative of a faith that would like to rely on the actual physical experience of the reality of the Risen One. This kind of faith is contrasted with another that relies on the word of proclamation alone. Recent authors prefer a more dynamic view of Jesus's saying. For the apostolic generation, access to Jesus through a historical, physical encounter was still possible: they could see him, hear him, and touch him. The following generation had to accept the proclamation of the gospel of the resurrection. Thomas represents the transition from the faith of the apostles to the faith of the post-apostolic community. He should have accepted the announcement of the resurrection from the ten disciples and so "been believing" instead of "faithlessly" demanding visible signs of the Risen One.[147]

**20:28** Thomas does not take up the invitation of his Lord but frames a confession of faith with special depth: "My Lord and my God!" The title of Lord is due to the one who had entered into his glory (John reserves it for the risen Jesus). The title "God," applied to Jesus, goes back to its twofold mention in the prologue (John 1:1, 18), and so forms an inclusio that embraces and holds together the whole of John's Gospel.

**20:29** A saying of Jesus brings the small section to a close. The first part of this saying can be understood as a statement or a question. The difference is not significant. Thomas has believed because he has seen. The second half of Jesus's saying blesses those who do not see but yet believe.[148] Roberto Vignolo has studied the form of the macarisms in John 13:17 and 20:29.[149] In John 13:17, those who are blessed are those who do what Jesus has commanded. According to John 20:29, blessed are the ones who have accepted the Easter kerygma without seeing. In both cases, an aspect of human conduct receives the promise of a divine gift as in the other biblical macarisms. The latter of this pair of blessings stands at the end not only of the Johannine account of the passion, death, and resurrection of Jesus but of the whole of the narrative part of this Gospel in its original version (before the supplementary ch. 21). The readers are being led to their situation in life. Like Thomas, their faith depends on the apostolic testimony. Without seeing, they can be blessed and happy because they found their Lord through faith in his word.

---

146. Cf. Bultmann, 539f.
147. Cf., among others, Vanni, "Il crocifisso risorto"; Frey, "Ich habe den Herrn gesehen," 283f.; Bieringer, "They Have Taken Away," 630.
148. Cf., for this verse in comparison with the Gospels, Judge, "A Note."
149. Cf. Vignolo, "Il Quarto Vangelo."

Elaine Pagels[150] has a totally different view of the scene, a view that is contested in a contribution by Peter J. Judge.[151] According to Pagels, John 20:24–29 represents a controversy between Johannine Christianity and the *Gospel of Thomas*. According to *Thomas*, which she places as early as the middle of the first century, true faith consists of a personal encounter with the divine that is possible without belief in the risen Jesus. True redemption comes from within, owing to an authentic self-knowledge. The revealer can, however, assist with the attainment of this self-knowledge. On this reading, John would have been opposing this notion with his own view, according to which confession is part of faith and is instructed by the external word of proclamation. Judge, on the other hand, can base his view (1) on the fact that, according to the opinion of experts, the *Gospel of Thomas* can scarcely be dated before John's Gospel; (2) that, according to John, "salvation" can and must be found not only on the basis of inner experiences but also on that of external connections to Jesus; and (3) that an analysis of the text reveals that Thomas is not portrayed simply as stubborn or faithless but only as one who is asking for a form of access to Jesus that is no longer available. He was justified in believing in Jesus on the basis of a "seeing," and this is precisely what is emphasized once again in John 20:30–31; only the time of this kind of access to Jesus is coming to an end and so Thomas is representing the future generations of believers.

### The First Conclusion of the Gospel (20:30–31)

The last two verses of the chapter no longer belong to the flow of the narrative but lie on another level (the "meta-narrative" level, according to Aletti[152]). These verses close the main part of John's Gospel before the "epilogue" of ch. 21, which is regarded by most exegetes as secondary.[153] Michael Lattke points to the fact that Tertullian appears to presuppose a Gospel that ends with ch. 20.[154] The interpretation of John 20:30–31

---

150. Pagels, *Beyond Belief*, esp. ch. 2 ("Gospels in Conflict: John and Thomas").
151. Cf. Judge, "John 20,24–29."
152. Cf. Aletti, "Les finales."
153. On the comparison of the two conclusions, see among others Roberts, "John 20:30–31"; Markl wonders, "Are John 1:1; 20:30f; 21:24 alluding to the frame of the Pentateuch?"
154. Lattke, "Joh 20,30f."

## Jesus's "Hour": Passion, Death, and Resurrection (18:1–20:31)

depends partly on what interpretation one gives to the concept σημεῖον ("sign") in John 20:30.

**20:30** According to this verse, Jesus performed many other "signs" that are not recorded in this book. The occurrence of the concept "sign" is surprising here. The last time it was used was in a parallel text in John 12:37, where although Jesus had performed so many signs among the Jews, they still did not believe in him. John 20:30 speaks of the "signs" Jesus had performed before the disciples and calls for faith in Jesus. How should we explain the huge gap in the text between the "signs" of John 2–12 and the mention of the "signs" in John 20:30?

According to Bultmann (following Fauré) and his school, John 20:30 is the original conclusion of their hypothetical "signs source."[155] This source is characterized by a theology according to which faith in Jesus is attained precisely by means of his "signs," which are seen and correctly interpreted. The evangelist would have been skeptical of such a theology and corrected it through a theology of faith in Jesus on account of his word. If one adopts this model, the problem remains how the evangelist could conclude with a view that did not correspond to his own. Various suggestions have been made in order to avoid this problem.

According to Hanna Roose,[156] the word σημεῖον in John 20 refers, above all, to the last two signs in John 9 and 11, the healing of the man born blind and the raising of Lazarus. The first text describes the path of a man to faith; in the second, Jesus appears as the bestower of life. Thus, the basic concepts of John 20:30–31 are being prefigured in those texts. An alternative for this suggestion lies in seeing the passion, death, and resurrection of Jesus as his last "signs." For Hans-Christian Kammler,[157] the appearances of the risen Jesus are the "signs" of which John is speaking in John 20:30–31. Gilbert van Belle[158] is sympathetic to this suggestion but would like to see the earlier signs included as well. This is also the view of Thomas Söding.[159] Thus, it is advisable here to have an understanding of the "signs" of Jesus that is not limited to the seven "signs" of John 2–11 but also includes the events of the death, resurrection, and self-revelation of Jesus after Easter.

These "signs" have now been written down in a "book" that stands

---

155. Bultmann, 541.
156. Roose, "Ein (un)passender Schluss?"
157. Kammler, "Die 'Zeichen'; the same suggestion is found in Michaels, 1020ff.
158. van Belle, "The Meaning"; van Belle, "Christology"; van Belle, "L'unité."
159. Söding, "Die Schrift."

as a testimony for Jesus (cf. John 5:39) alongside the Scripture of Israel, though without becoming part of it.

**20:31** The oral witness of the Twelve: "We have seen the Lord" is now replaced by a book. This book is written "that you may believe that Jesus is the Christ, the Son of God, and so may have life in his name." Scholars discuss the original form of the expression for "believe": πιστεύητε or πιστεύσητε. In the first case, it would be in the present subjunctive and mean: "so that you may continue to believe." In the second case, we would have the subjunctive of an ingressive aorist, and the meaning would be: "so that you may come to faith." D. A. Carson[160] defends the aorist and a "missionary" understanding; by contrast, the majority of recent authors, with the oldest Greek manuscripts, prefer the present. Gordon D. Fee does now as well.[161] In that case, the aim of the evangelist would be to encourage the readers to remain in their faith in Jesus and Messiah and Son of God. A further perspective should be added: the courage to proclaim faith in Jesus without fear even in adverse circumstances (like Nicodemus, the man born blind, the apostles, and the women who undertake the proclamation of Jesus).[162]

What is the content of the faith to which John's Gospel would like to lead? According to Carson,[163] it consists of the fact that Jesus is the Messiah and Son of God. Among all the pretenders to the messianic and divine dignity, Jesus is the only man who deserves this title. However, Carson's grammatical argument that the absence of the article should indicate the predicate is not shared by the majority of authors, since proper names often stand without the article without any consequences for their interpretation. Thus, it is advisable to consider the aim of John's Gospel in general and of his resurrection narrative in particular to be faith that Jesus is Messiah/Christ in the sense that has been developed in the course of John's Gospel.[164] This faith has already been applied in the words of Martha at the end of her dialogue with Jesus after the death of her brother, Lazarus: "Yes, Lord, I believe that you are the Christ, the Son of God, who is to come into the world" (John 11:27).

---

160. Carson, "Purpose"; Carson, "Observations."
161. Fee, "Text and Meaning."
162. Cf. Beutler, "Faith and Confession."
163. Carson, "Purpose."
164. So, too, Cardellino, "Testimoni."

# Jesus's "Hour": Passion, Death, and Resurrection (18:1–20:31)

## III

Why does John have a resurrection chapter at all? During his earthly life, Jesus had repeatedly announced that the Son of Man must be "lifted up" and "glorified" once his "hour" had come.

This hour is the hour of his lifting up on the cross. The dying Jesus "hands over the Spirit." What follows then is rather an unfolding of this event in the "hour" of Jesus. The first part of John 20 shows Jesus still on the way to the Father. In the second half of the chapter, Jesus "comes" again to his own so that his second coming reaches into history that is experienced. He does not come with empty hands but brings his eschatological gifts: peace, joy, and the Holy Spirit. With that, even the forgiveness of sins is possible.

The way of Jesus back to his own is matched by the way of the disciples to Jesus in faith. It is not primarily a way that can be traveled on foot. This is also the point: Mary Magdalene goes to the tomb, Peter and the beloved disciple run fast. More important is the inner path to recognition of the Risen One. Mary Magdalene looks for the body of Jesus and thinks that in this way she will find her "Lord." The angel's message is not sufficient to free her from her error. Peter and the beloved disciple also seek Jesus in the tomb and cannot find him. However, the beloved disciple then recognizes the Risen One in the towel that lies rolled up on its own: the veil is taken from the face of Jesus just as it was from Moses. Meanwhile, it is time for Mary Magdalene to see her Lord face to face and recognize the sound of his voice. She is commanded by him to announce to the apostles the joyful news of Jesus's resurrection. They then can also recognize Jesus in their midst. He gives them his gifts of salvation and takes them into his service of reconciliation.

Thomas stands for those Christians who are no longer able to see Jesus face to face. At least at the beginning, he should have come to Easter faith on the basis of the Easter message of the other disciples. Thereby the door is opened for the proclamation of Jesus's resurrection in the course of time. Readers of John's Gospel will feel themselves being addressed. A bridge to the present has been constructed. Thus, they will confess Jesus as living; they will also know themselves to be endowed with his Easter gifts. They will want to pass on the peace of Jesus and his joy in the Holy Spirit.

# Epilogue: Jesus, Peter, and the Beloved Disciple (21:1–25)

¹ After this, Jesus revealed himself to the disciples once again at the Sea of Tiberias, and he revealed himself in the following way. ² Simon Peter, Thomas, called Didymus, Nathanael from Cana in Galilee, the sons of Zebedee and two of his other disciples were together. ³ Simon Peter said to them: I am going fishing. They said to him: We shall also come with you. They went out and got into the boat. But that night they caught nothing. ⁴ When it was morning, Jesus stood on the bank. However, the disciples did not know that it was Jesus. ⁵ Jesus said to them: My children, do you not have any fish to eat? They answered him: No. ⁶ He said to them: Cast the net out on the right side of the boat, and you will find something. They cast out the net and could not draw it in again because it was so full of fish. ⁷ Then the disciple whom Jesus loved said to Peter: It is the Lord! When Simon Peter heard that it was the Lord, he girded himself with his outer garment, because he was naked, and dove into the lake. ⁸ Then the other disciples came with the boat – for they were not far from the shore, only about two hundred cubits from land – and pulled the net with the fish behind them. ⁹ When they got to land, they saw on the ground a fire of coals, and fish and bread lying on it. ¹⁰ Jesus said to them: Bring the fish that you have just caught. ¹¹ Then Simon Peter climbed on to the bank and pulled the net to land. It was filled with 153 fish and, although there were so many, the net did not break. ¹² Jesus said to them: Come and eat! None of the disciples dared to ask him: Who are you? For they knew that it was the Lord. ¹³ Jesus came, took the bread and gave it to them; likewise the fish. ¹⁴ This was now the third time that Jesus revealed himself to the disciples after he had risen from the dead.

¹⁵ When they had eaten, Jesus said to Simon Peter: Simon, son of John, do you love me more than these? He answered him: Yes, Lord, you know that I love you. Jesus said to him: Feed my lambs! ¹⁶ A second time, he asked him: Simon,

## Epilogue: Jesus, Peter, and the Beloved Disciple (21:1–25)

son of John, do you love me? He answered him: Yes, Lord, you know that I love you. Jesus said to him: Feed my sheep! ¹⁷ A third time, he asked him: Simon, son of John, do you love me? Then Peter was grieved because Jesus had asked him for the third time: Do you love me? He answered him: Lord, you know everything; you know that I love you. Jesus said to him: Feed my sheep!

¹⁸ Amen, amen, I say to you: When you were young, you girded yourself and went where you wanted. When you are old, however, you will stretch out your hands, and another will gird you and lead you where you do not want to go. ¹⁹ Jesus said that in order to signify by what death he would glorify God. After these words, he said to him: Follow me!

²⁰ Peter turned around and saw the disciple whom Jesus loved following, the one who had leaned on Jesus's breast at the supper and who had said: Master, who is it that is going to betray you? ²¹ When Peter saw him, he said to Jesus: Lord, what will become of him? ²² Jesus said to him: If I wish that he remain until I come, what is that to you? You follow me! ²³ Then the view spread among the brothers: that disciple will not die. But Jesus did not say to him: He would not die, but: If I will that he remain until I come, what is that to you?

²⁴ This is the disciple who witnessed all this and who has written it down; and we know that his testimony is true. ²⁵ There are many other things that Jesus did. If each one of them were to be written down, I believe that the whole world could not contain the books written.

### I

John's Gospel could have closed with John 20:30–31. Moreover, from a theological point of view, everything has been said already in the Thomas scene in John 20:26–29. The readers have been prepared for their own situation in which they are called to faith without having seen Jesus in physical form. At their commissioning for proclamation, the fledgling community is endowed with the Spirit of Jesus (John 20:19–23). What remains to happen?

Right until the start of modern biblical criticism at the beginning of the Enlightenment, the unity of the Fourth Gospel and its origin from John, the son of Zebedee, were maintained. If another appearance of Jesus and his words to Peter were recorded in John 21, then this had to be a question of additions that seemed important to the evangelist.

The situation altered with the advent of literary criticism, when scholars begain to differentiate between sources and layers of John's

Gospel at the beginning of the twentieth century.[1] It was chiefly two scholars from Göttingen who advanced the new perspective. According to Eduard Schwartz, John's Gospel cannot go back to John, the son of Zebedee since he (as Mark 10:39 lets us suppose) had already suffered martyrdom like his brother James (cf. Acts 12:2). Thus, the Fourth Gospel goes back to a later author so that we have to distinguish between a first draft, later revisions, and supplementary interpolations. It would be to this most recent layer that John 21 would belong, given its identification of the beloved disciple with the apostle and author of the Gospel. Schwartz's Göttingen colleague, Wellhausen, distinguishes in the Fourth Gospel a *Grundschrift* and later revisions that generally build on Johannine passages. Already according to Wellhausen, a great portion of Jesus's discourses appear to be secondary. With the identification of the beloved disciple with the son of Zebedee, John 21 might belong to the most recent layer of John's Gospel. Here, apparently, the Ephesus tradition has been adopted.

The assignment of John 21 to a later layer of John's Gospel also marks most of the critical research of the twentieth century. The commentary by Bultmann became especially decisive here. Within John's Gospel, the Marburg scholar distinguishes among a Gnostic-inspired discourse source, a signs source, a source for the Johannine passion and resurrection narrative, the evangelist, and a so-called "ecclesiastical redaction," which was supposed to make the Gospel—still close to gnosis—acceptable to the great Church. According to Bultmann, John 21 would belong to this final layer. This proposal is also found in the German-speaking authors, Protestant[2] and Catholic,[3] influenced by Bultmann. Recently, though, the talk is more of a "Johannine" or "post-Johannine redaction," so that continuity is stressed alongside discontinuity.

Since the 1970s, there has been a tendency to interpret John's Gospel (like other biblical texts) in its final form, disregarding literary sources or layers or expressly denying such antecedents.[4] In this case, however, it is

---

1. Cf. Beutler, "Der Abschluss," 254–56.
2. Cf., among others, the commentary of Becker.
3. Influential was the work of Richter, *Studien*, which in their literary approach affected the pupils of the editor, Hainz, and so found circulation. In his commentary, Theobald also sees himself as indebted to the literary-critical heritage of Bultmann.
4. van Belle, "L'unité littéraire," advocates expressly the connection of John 21 with the preceding context. The same is true of Hasitschka, "The Significance."

## Epilogue: Jesus, Peter, and the Beloved Disciple (21:1–25)

noticeable that even authors who prefer a synchronic model of exegesis see John 21 as a supplement or epilogue.[5]

Helpful here is Zumstein's suggestion to employ the model of *relecture* for John 21.[6] According to this model, there are texts that can only be understood in such a way that they refer back to another text from which they draw their meaning. This perspective can also be employed for John 21 in its relationship to the previous chapter. In John 21, John's Gospel is being "updated." In this case, it is no longer a matter of who Jesus is but how, in Jesus's view, Peter and the beloved disciple are to be considered. Thus, in John 21, Peter is dominant at first vis à vis the beloved disciple and appears almost exclusively as the conversation partner of Jesus, but, in the course of the chapter, the beloved disciple takes on an increasingly significant profile and is put forward at the end as the decisive bearer of tradition for the reading community. With that, the Gospel can close.

The composition of John 21 can be determined according to the criteria of narrative analysis. The first fourteen verses give an account of a third appearance of Jesus before his disciples after his resurrection. In the center stands the scene of the miraculous catch of fish. A dialogue of Jesus with Peter follows. First, Jesus asks Peter three times about his love for him, to which Peter answers three times (vv. 15–17). Then follows a saying of Jesus with which he predicts the fate of Peter, and at its conclusion he commands him to follow him (vv. 18–19). To Peter's question about what is to happen to the beloved disciple Jesus gives no answer but summons Peter again to follow him (vv. 20–22). Thereupon the narrator interprets Jesus's saying to Peter and preserves it from misunderstanding (v. 23). In v. 24, the narrator identifies the beloved disciple as the author of the preceding Gospel before he concludes his work in v. 25 analogously to the first conclusion in John 20:30–31.

## II

### The Third Appearance of Jesus to the Disciples (21:1–14)

In the interpretation of John 21:1–14, the different methods of approach to John's Gospel show themselves once again. Until the 1990s, the historical-critical contributions were dominant.

---

5. The commentary of Schnelle belongs here.
6. Cf. Zumstein, "Die Endredaktion."

Rudolf Pesch has reconstructed a common tradition lying at the basis of the story of the miraculous catch of fish in Luke 5:1–11 and John 21:1–14.[7] The agreements between the two Gospel texts do not seem sufficient to him to substantiate a dependence of the Johannine text on Luke. Alongside the tradition of the rich catch of fish, the Johannine author would have taken over another tradition narrating an account of Jesus's appearing on the shore of the lake. John would have joined both traditions and added some elements that were important to him. According to Pesch, the author of John 21 would have confined himself to the linking of both traditions without altering them essentially.

Neirynck sees in John 21:1–14 an example that shows how the Johannine text could be understood from recourse to the Synoptic Gospels alone.[8] The alterations to the *Vorlage*, Luke 5:1–11, can be fully explained by the literary and theological perspectives of the author of John 21. The hypothesis (advocated by Pesch) that this author joined two traditions appears less probable to Neirynck since in addition to the narrative of the miraculous catch of fish, little material remains for a story of the appearance of Jesus on the shore of the lake. The theme of the meal to which Jesus invites the disciples could originate from Jesus's question in Luke 24:41: "Have you something to eat here?" The motif of the bread and fish could come from John 6:11. Both the narrative in Luke 5 and that in John 21 focus on the figure of Peter. To Peter's saying: "Depart from me, Lord!" in Luke 5:8 could correspond the statement in John 21:7: "It is the Lord!" This element does not have to be taken back to an additional pre-Johannine source. In the Johannine account, the beloved disciple holds no firm place. He occurs again only in John 21:20. The theme of "following Jesus" could point back to John 1:38 and so be holding the whole Gospel together in the fashion of a bracket.

Fortna is unconvinced by Neirynck's suggestion.[9] He thinks that the Johannine text contains too many elements that cannot be explained from the Synoptic tradition. The vocabulary of both texts is different. John lacks Peter's protest. On the other hand, the Johannine text has elements that are missing in Luke, such as the inability to recognize Jesus; the pulling of the net to land; the 153 large fish; the fact that the net did not break; and the meal of the Risen One with the disciples. This last element could stem

---

7. Pesch, *Fischfang*.
8. Neirynck, "John 21."
9. Fortna, "Reading."

*Epilogue: Jesus, Peter, and the Beloved Disciple (21:1–25)*

from Luke 24. As a result of his investigations, Fortna sees confirmation of his hypothesis of a "signs source" or a "signs Gospel."

Lutz Simon holds a similar view.[10] As in other texts of John's Gospel, he finds in John 21 too a stratification of *Grundschrift* and redaction. The *Grundschrift* would be responsible for the account of the miraculous catch of fish and the appearance of Jesus in John 21:1–14. Here—as elsewhere—the redaction would have added the figure of the beloved disciple. Also, as elsewhere, this figure is contrasted with the figure of Peter. For Lutz Simon, Peter stands for "office," the beloved disciple for "authority." In the correct balance between these two dimensions of the church, John's community and that of the readers can find a secure and reliable basis for their faith. Thus, Simon's diachronic study leads to a synchronic perspective that speaks to the pragmatics of the text.

For his part, Peter Hofrichter[11] remains within the historical paradigm. He subjects John 21:1–14 to a stylistic investigation and, on this basis, identifies two literary layers in the text: the Peter layer (in two stages) and that of the beloved disciple. The Peter layer turns out to be the older and more original, and corresponds to the hypothetical *Grundschrift*; the layer of the beloved disciple is more recent and corresponds to the "redaction" in the sense of the school of Richter to which Hofrichter belongs.

In recent times, such historical-critical schemes have been put in question from the perspective of a stronger synchronic exegesis. For Schneiders in her dissertation, Luke 5:1–11 and John 21:1–14 stem from the same tradition. On the other hand, the narrative of John 21:1–14 is not to be understood merely from the working out of the sources and traditions of the passage. The whole account is "historical," but not "real." Peter and the beloved disciple represent two dimensions of the community: closeness to Jesus in contemplation and in mission. Thus, the last chapter in John is describing the way of faith of those who have not seen and yet have believed. In this sense, John 21 is no foreign body in the Gospel of John.

In his contribution *Erzählte Zeichen*, Christian Welck subjects the historical-critical approaches to John's Gospel to a methodological critique. In his view, the literary approach should be given preference. He thinks[12] that the whole of the Gospel is a coherent text (thus he is in danger of mixing the synchronic approach with a judgement about the text

---

10. Simon, *Petrus*.
11. Hofrichter, "Joh 21."
12. Welck, *Erzählte Zeichen*.

of the Gospel). He sees in John 20:30–21:25 the conclusion of the Gospel. John 21:1–23 is a text about the beloved disciple that serves to legitimate him. Worth heeding are this author's remarks on the beloved disciple as a literary and ideal figure but not necessarily a historical one.

Welck's opinion about the leading role of the beloved disciple in John 21 is not shared by Timothy Wiarda.[13] With good reason, the latter sees a leading role for Peter in John 21:1–23. This is shown by five decisive points that are important for the reader: it is Peter who decides to go fishing (v. 3); he reacts to Jesus's presence and to the miracle (v. 7); he answers Jesus's questions (vv. 15–17); he receives from Jesus a prediction and a command (vv. 18–19); and he also experiences a rebuff by Jesus (vv. 21–22).

Other works in recent years have adduced diachronic and synchronic perspectives. According to G. Blaskovic,[14] John chose Luke 5:1–11 as the basis for his text. However, the author appears not simply as collector and redactor of source texts but also as an author in his own right. Alongside Luke's Gospel, John also employed other texts, even out of his own Gospel, such as John 6 as well as the story of the call of the first disciples in John 1:35–51 and the texts about the beloved disciple. In its final form, the text of John 21 is a recognition story.

Labahn's study remains more strictly along the lines of the Louvain school, which explains the Johannine texts as predominantly from the Synoptics. As also with other Johannine miracle stories, he sees John 21:1–14 as an example of "secondary orality."[15] Luke 5:1–11 remains the principal source, but John's vocabulary diverges so strongly from Luke that one can scarcely imagine Luke's text to be the direct written *Vorlage* of John's text. On the other hand, John takes up some elements that are not connected with the miracle story of the catch of fish as such but are linked to its Lukan version, such as the missionary dimension and the call of the disciples. This reading excludes the Johannine author's recourse to a pre-Lukan form of the tradition. Alongside the intertextual recourse to Luke as a source, Labahn argues similarly for John 1–20 as source, not least the multiplication of loaves and Jesus's walking on the water in John 6:1–22.

Maurizio Marcheselli studies John 21 with the aid of the model of "*relecture.*"[16] The chapter appears as a literary unity but at the same time

---

13. Wiarda, "John 21:1–23."
14. Blaskovic, "Erzählung."
15. Labahn, "Fischen," 135f.; cf. Labahn, "Beim Mahl," 773.
16. Marcheselli, *Avete qualcosa*.

## Epilogue: Jesus, Peter, and the Beloved Disciple (21:1–25)

points to numerous connections with the first twenty chapters of John. The fundamental concepts of John 21:1–14 are the "self-revelation" of Jesus, the "meal," and the "sending." Each of these key concepts is developed. The ecclesiological aspect is also observed by Marcheselli, something to which we shall return.

Before the detailed exegesis, we must glance again at the construction of John 21:1–14. The section can be divided into three scenes: verses 1–3, 4–8, and 9–14. After an introduction (v. 1), there is an account of a first, unsuccessful attempt at fishing by the disciples during the night (vv. 2–3). Jesus appears in v. 4. The scene is played out in the morning and describes a further attempt at fishing that is now crowned with success (vv. 4–8). The third and final scene describes a meal Jesus has prepared and to which he invites the disciples (vv. 9–13). The narrative closes with a comment by the narrator (v. 14). Through the mention of Jesus's "revealing himself" (v. 1, twice, and v. 14) the narrative is rounded off and shows itself to be a self-contained textual unit.

**21:1–3** Verse 1 serves as introduction both for verses 2–14 as well as for the whole section of vv. 2–23. The concept of "revealing himself" holds together not only the passage in vv. 1–14, but also the first verse thanks to its repetition at the end of the verse. It does not occur elsewhere in the narratives of the Easter appearances of Jesus. However, it is found in John's Gospel in a christological sense from ch. 1 on: the Baptist was sent so that Jesus "might be revealed to Israel" (John 1:31). In John 7:4, Jesus's brothers urge him to go up to Jerusalem so that through his spectacular works he might "reveal himself to the world." However, Jesus has to await his "time," which will come with his death and resurrection (v. 6). This moment has arrived in John 21:1. He will reveal himself before the disciples. However, his revelation will not be confined to Israel but will reach the world that is waiting for salvation. The replacement of "coming" (ἔρχεσθαι, John 20:20, 26) with "revealing himself" shows a shift from the christological to the ecclesiological perspective: Jesus is revealing himself to his own.

"After this" (μετὰ ταῦτα), at the beginning of v. 1, is a common formula for the beginning of narratives in John (cf. 6:1; 7:1). Thus, as a formula it is not surprising; what is unexpected is that the account is being continued after the conclusion of John 20:30–31, as if it would be possible to narrate additional resurrection stories without further ado.

The phrase "at the Sea of Tiberias" locates the self-revelation of Jesus. Up to now, John has recounted only appearances of Jesus in Jeruslaem. In this he appears to be related to Luke by contrast with Matthew (and Mark in his secondary conclusion). On the other hand, the Sea of Tiberias is the setting for the miraculous catch of fish in Luke 5:1–11 with which the Johannine account displays many agreements. This lake is called by Mark the "Sea of Galilee" (Mark 1:16), by Luke (5:1) the "Sea of Gennesareth." Clearly the author of John 21 has used the same freedom for himself to call the lake after the requirements and usages of his readers. The same expression "Sea of Tiberias" also appears in John 6:1.

Verse 2 describes the group of disciples who are found at the lake, v. 3, their activity. The expression "they were together" (ἦσαν ὁμοῦ) reminds us of the group of disciples at Jesus's appearance on Easter Day (John 20:19–20) and eight days later (John 20:26). In the present case, however, the disciples are together in order to resume their "lay" job. Their names are taken partly from Johannine tradition, such as "Simon Peter," "Thomas called Didymus" and "Nathanael," partly from the Synoptic tradition according to Luke 5, such as "the sons of Zebedee" and, again, "Peter." The expression "two of his other disciples" creates a lacuna which has to be filled in by the readers. Within a short time, "the disciple whom Jesus loved" will occur in the text (v. 7), and he could belong to the two anonymous disciples or be identified with one of the two sons of Zebedee. The perhaps deliberate blur has been emphasized by Thyen.[17] The author of John's Gospel or of John 21 is deliberately leaving the identity of the beloved disciple in limbo.

The naming of Peter as "Simon Peter" reminds us of John 1:40, of Thomas as "Didymus" of John 11:16, of Nathanael as "from Cana in Galilee" of John 2:1–11. Through the expressions he has chosen, the author of John 21 links this chapter with the body of the Gospel.

The naming of the disciples in v. 2 is followed by a description of their activity in v. 3. At the beginning stands Peter's announcement: "I am going fishing" with the decision of the disciples to go out with him. A reference to their lack of success follows. The readiness and challenge of Peter is surprising for two reasons. The fact that Peter and the first disciples were fishermen together on the Sea of Galilee was not known to the readers until now. Still more astonishing is the fact that Peter had clearly returned to Galilee to the practice of his "lay" job as though Jesus had not sent him out with the other disciples to forgive sins (John 20:21–23). The doubt is reinforced when we hear in what follows that neither Peter nor any other disciple recognizes Jesus on the shore of the lake. This third

---

17. Thyen, "Noch einmal."

## Epilogue: Jesus, Peter, and the Beloved Disciple (21:1–25)

"revelation" of Jesus after his resurrection appears like a first one, something that is not easily explained purely by the methods of synchronic exegesis.

The main difference between the Johannine account and that of Luke consists of the fact that, according to Luke 5:4, Jesus orders Peter to cast out the net while, in John 21:3, Peter himself takes the initiative. This difference seems to have a theological motive. The catch of fish on one's own initiative will fail; the one made at Jesus's invitation will be crowned with success. This is shown a little later in the second attempt at a catch which follows the bidding of Jesus (v. 6). It is noticeable that, in this scene, Peter appears as the undisputed spokesman of the group of disciples whom all the others follow without hesitation. In John's Gospel before John 21, Peter scarcely possesses this authority, apart from his confession of faith in John 6:69, a text that could have been added under the influence of the Synoptic tradition.

Verse 3 goes on to portray the failure of the fishing attempted on their own initiative. For the imagery of John, it might be no accident that the failed attempt at a catch happened "by night" (even if that motif is also found in Luke). In John, the night is a symbol for distance from God. Nicodemus comes to Jesus "by night" (John 3:2). It is necessary to do the works of God as long as it is day; the night is coming in which no one can work any longer (John 9:4). At the moment when Judas leaves the group of disciples in order to betray Jesus, it is night (John 13:30). The fishing will be successful only in the light of morning at the bidding of Jesus (John 21:4–6).[18]

**21:4–8** In the following verses, 4–8, there is an account of the appearance of Jesus on the shore of the lake at dawn. Jesus remains at the center of these verses. In v. 4, we are told that the disciples did not recognize him. In v. 5, Jesus addresses the disciples with the question whether they have anything to eat. The disciples answer in the negative. Thereupon, Jesus seizes the initiative again and tells the disciples to cast out the net. They accept his advice and obtain a rich catch (v. 6). The beloved disciple recognizes Jesus in the miraculous catch, and Peter girds himself and dives into the water in order to meet the Lord (v. 7). Then, the other disciples come too and pull the net to land, full of fish (v. 8).

The temporal detail in v. 4, "in the morning," marks off the following scene from the previous one. During the night, the disciples had

---

18. For this also Labahn, "Beim Mahl," 766f.

caught nothing. In the view of the author, the reason for this lies in the fact that they had tried to fish on their own initiative. They thus found themselves in the dark, and not only in the literal sense. In the light of the morning, Jesus appears, although not recognized by the disciples at first. This is surprising after the two appearances of Jesus in John 20:19–23 and 20:26–29.

Jesus's question in v. 5 is not easily explained as an introduction to the scene of the miraculous catch of fish, but it prepares for the scene of the meal. "My children" (παιδία) is not found elsewhere in John, though probably in 1 John 2:14, 18 as an address to members of the community; cf. τεκνία in John 13:33. The word belongs to sapiential vocabulary. The word προσφάγιον (literally, "side dish," predominantly used of fish) is unusual in the New Testament but matches the word-field of the meal that is taken up again in verses 9–13. In this way, the catch of fish is linked to the ensuing meal, a detail that has been underlined by Marcheselli.[19]

The catch of fish itself is recorded in v. 6 in appropriate vocabulary. The instruction to cast out the net on the right side can be explained by the significance of the right side as the lucky side or even diachronically. On account of the huge number of fish that have been caught, the disciples are not able to haul the net to land. The verb ἑλκύειν corresponds to Johannine usage; cf. John 6:44; 12:32, where it is used metaphorically for God or Jesus who "draw" the believers (to themselves).

In v. 7, there is an unexpected appearance on the part of the beloved disciple who was not mentioned in the tally of the seven disciples in v. 2. As usual, he occurs at the side of Peter. He cries out: "It is the Lord!" This title belongs to Jesus after his resurrection. It is not the beloved disciple but Peter who dives into the water in order to meet Jesus. The scene is similar to the race of the two disciples to the tomb in John 20:3–10. In both cases, the beloved disciple is the first to recognize Jesus or his resurrection while Peter has the priority in access to Jesus. It is not immediately clear why Peter "girds himself." Perhaps Lars Hartman is right in seeing a connection between the "girding himself" of Peter in v. 7 and the "being girded" by others in his old age according to v. 18.[20]

Now, according to v. 8, the other disciples follow in the boat. On account of the multitude of fish, they are scarcely able to haul the net to land. Here, as in verses 6 and 11 the author uses the word ἰχθύς for "fish"

---

19. Marcheselli, *Avete qualcosa*.
20. Hartman, "Attempt."

by contrast with the expression ὀψάριον, which is reserved for the fish prepared for the meal.[21]

**21:9-14** The story of the miraculous catch of fish is followed by that of the breakfast Jesus had prepared for his disciples. This last section of the whole narrative is characterized by frequent changes of subject. In v. 9, it is reported that the disciples found a coal fire on the shore on which fish and bread were already laid. In v. 10, Jesus speaks and tells the disciples to bring the fish they have. This instruction is taken up by Peter in v. 11. There follows, in v. 12, Jesus's invitation to the disciples to partake of the breakfast he has prepared for them, with some uncertainty on the part of the disciples as to who he is. The sharing out of the food by Jesus in v. 13 is described in almost eucharistic terms. Verse 14 confirms that this is the third self-revelation of Jesus after his resurrection.

Before looking at the tradition underlying the text and its guidance of the readers, we shall analyze the individual verses thoroughly once more. In v. 9, the meal prepared by Jesus stands in the center point. Climbing on land, the disciples see the coal fire with the fish and bread prepared by Jesus. The coal fire recalls the one by which Peter warmed himself during the night of his threefold denial of his Lord. In this way, there is already a preparation for the threefold renewal of his loyalty to and love for Jesus (vv. 15–17). The fish prepared by Jesus is now represented, as in verses 10 and 13, by the word ὀψάριον, which is reserved for this passage and for John 6:9, 11 (the scene of the multiplication of loaves).

The whole of verse 10 is stamped with Johannine vocabulary. Again, the prepared fish is called ὀψάριον. The catching of the fish is expressed with a verb that is otherwise employed in John for various attempts to arrest Jesus (cf. John 7:30, 32, 44; 8:20; 10:39; 11:57). In the Synoptics, it occurs only once in another connection (Luke 6:38 πιέζω). Without taking into account the narrative dimension, Jesus's instruction remains incomprehensible since he already has other fish prepared for the disciples.

In v. 11, Jesus's instruction is taken up by Peter, the spokesman for the group of disciples. All have pulled the net (v. 8), but only Peter hauls it on to the land (for ἑλκύω, see above, v. 6), full with 153 big fish. Despite this great number, the net does not break. This last element is interpreted by exegetes as an image of the unity of the community. The 153 remain an enigma. Corrado Marucci distinguishes four solutions:[22]

21. Cf. Pitta, "Ichthys."
22. Marucci, "Significato."

- the "historical model": it is about the precise number of fish that were counted
- the "ichthyological model": according to Jerome, there are 153 different kinds of fish
- the "numeric symbolism model": since Augustine, the number 153 is analyzed for a symbolism which expresses totality (153 = the sum of numbers from 1 to 17 etc.)
- "gematria": the number stands for a sequence of letters (such as "Eneglaim," a place that is mentioned in Ezek 47:10 in connection with the healing of the Dead Sea on account of the spring which, according to Ezek 47:1–11, flowed from the right side [!] of the temple)

With good reason, Marucci remains skeptical of such attempts at interpretation. Perhaps the solution lies in the narrative analysis below.[23]

If one looks for the oldest interpretation of the 153 large fish, it is found in Jerome in his commentary on Ezekiel.[24] In Ezek 47:10–11, the subject is the temple spring that develops into a mighty flood and flows into the Dead Sea, which is thereby revitalized. It is swarming with fish, and these fish cause Jerome to think of John 21:11 with its 153 large fish. For him, they represent the 153 kinds of fish he finds in the Greek author Opianus Cilex (from Cilicia). This is a reference to the variety of the multitudes of peoples gathered in the work of mission. This is a little sly of Jerome, since the text he cites does not yield the number stated. What is important is the connection of John 21:11 with the tradition of the temple spring and the connection with the theme of life and plenty, though without attaching gematrian significance to the place names En-Gedi and En-Eglaim that occur in Ezekiel.[25]

In v. 12, Jesus invites the disciples to breakfast. The verb is confined to the present text (cf., also, v. 15) and to Luke 11:37. The kind of meal is explained by the morning hour and after the catch of fish, but also from the custom of the early Christians to hold their cultic meal on Sunday in the early morning. The tension between the hesitation of the disciples as to who their host is and their knowledge that it is the Lord is not solved easily. An indication towards such a solution is found perhaps in the verb

23. Cf. Nicklas, "153 große Fische."
24. *Comm. Ezech.* 717 (edition of Glorie). Cf. the reference already in Brown, 2:1074, in more detail now in Rastoin, "Encore une fois."
25. This is the case in Rastoin, "Encore une fois." Further gematrian proposals are found in Kiley, "Three More Fish Stories."

## Epilogue: Jesus, Peter, and the Beloved Disciple (21:1–25)

ἐξετάζειν, which means "probe" rather than "ask." The disciples are in danger of seeking, like Thomas, for the identity of the Risen One, but they relinquish the attempt since such indications are ultimately not necessary.

In v. 13, the "coming" of Jesus is the subject for the first time in this text. However, the word ἔρχεσθαι here does not stand for the eschatological coming of the risen Jesus as in John 20:19, 26, but describes only a movement of Jesus towards his disciples in the course of their meeting. The verbs with which the gestures of Jesus are described are familiar to the readers. In fact, they are taken from John 6:11 without the element of "thanksgiving." Even without this word, the vocabulary is eucharistic. The distribution of the fish (with the word ὀψάριον) recalls the same verse.

The closing verse 14 sets the whole incident under the theme of Jesus's "revealing himself." He reveals himself both in the miracle of the fish and in the invitation to the meal. The word τρίτον is employed as an adverb: "for the third time" and does not indicate the presence of a "signs source."[26]

Broad agreement exists among scholars concerning the tradition-historical background of John 21:9–14. On the one hand, the scene of the miraculous catch of fish and the call of Peter in Luke 5:1–11 might have had an influence on the present narrative; on the other hand, it may be influenced by the appearance of Jesus on Easter Day according to Luke 24:36–49. According to common opinion, the contact of the Johannine text with the Synoptics was indirect, but according to the Louvain school it was more direct. In the scene in Luke 24:36–49, Jesus asks the disciples: "Have you anything to eat here?" (ἔχετέ τι βρώσιμον ἐνθάδε; Luke 24:41). After that, Jesus consumes a piece of fish before their eyes. In Luke, the scene has a clear apologetic orientation: the fact that Jesus is eating before the eyes of his disciples is an indication of the true physical nature of his resurrection body (cf. Acts 10:41).

In John, the meal prepared by Jesus for his disciples has another object. Jesus does not partake of the meal, but only offers it. The orientation is not apologetic but ecclesiological. Jesus, who is standing on the bank that the disciples must reach from the sea, has ready for them the life-giving gift of the Eucharist. The disciples contribute to it with the fish that they have caught. To the question whether Jesus also took the fish the disciples had contributed, the readers find no answer. Once more, the text here is displaying a "lacuna" that the readers have to fill.

26. Cf. Neirynck, "Note."

With that is posed already the question concerning the narrative strategy of the text. According to Maurizio Marcheselli, the catch of fish in our passage stands for the missionary work of the group of the Twelve, the meal for the sacrament of the Eucharist.[27] The mixture of both kinds of fish in John 21:4–11—those caught by the disciples and those provided by Jesus, the ὀψάριον—signifies the inner connection of two dimensions of the church: that to the outside, the mission, and that addressed within: the celebration of the worship of the community. Jesus inspires both dimensions and leads them to unity.

The various "lacunae" in the text have to be filled out by the readers. The questions why one man could pull so many fish to land or why the net did not break cannot be answered by the logic of everyday experience but invite the readers to discover dimensions of faith in the narrative. The same goes for the tension between the "knowing" of the disciples of who the man on the shore of the lake is and their desire to ask him. From this point of view, one could also see in the "undecipherable" number of "153 big fish" an invitation to the reflection as to how these have been employed in the course of the history of research. As the last verse of the Gospel will say: "The whole world could not contain the books written."[28]

### The Commission to Peter and His Summons to Follow (21:15–19)

In John 21, there is a special interest in the person of Peter. In the listing of the seven disciples of Jesus who find themselves on the shore of the Sea of Tiberias, he is cited in first place (v. 2). Peter takes the initiative to go fishing (v. 3). On the word of the beloved disciple that the man on the shore is Jesus, he girds himself and dives into the water in order to meet the Lord (v. 7). At the moment in which Jesus commands the disciples to bring the fish they have caught to land, it is Peter who carries out this instruction (v. 11). Thus, from the beginning to the end of the narrative of the miraculous catch of fish, it is Peter who appears as spokesman and protagonist.

The ensuing dialogue takes place between Jesus and Peter. In verses 15–17, Jesus asks Peter three times whether he loves him and commissions him as shepherd of his sheep. In verses 18–19, Jesus predicts Peter's future

---

27. Marcheselli, *Avete qualcosa*.
28. Cf. Nicklas, "153 große Fische."

## Epilogue: Jesus, Peter, and the Beloved Disciple (21:1–25)

and commands him to follow him. In verses 20–22, Jesus replies to a question of Peter about the fate of the beloved disciple. This answer is clarified by the author of John 21 in v. 23.

The beloved disciple enters the foreground increasingly as the chapter progresses. In v. 7, he is introduced as the disciple who is first to recognize the Lord on the shore of the lake and points it out to the other disciples. Thus, the following scenes are already being prepared. In the dialogue between Jesus and Peter in verses 15–23, he appears only as the object. Verses 20–23 serve to clarify a saying of Jesus that the beloved disciple is to "remain." This "remaining" of the beloved disciple is interpreted in the last two verses of the chapter and of the book. In v. 24, he is identified with the one who has written the preceding Gospel (or at least its last part). This book that has been written could not contain all the deeds of Jesus since the whole world would not be sufficient to contain the books which would have to be written.

From the narrative perspective, it is possible to observe a shift in the text from the figure of Peter to that of the beloved disciple. Peter remains the spokesman of the group. At the same time the beloved disciple comes more clearly to the fore as the authority which, on account of its testimony drawn up in a book, stands at the root of the faith of the reading community. Thus, the question remains as to the significance of the commission of Peter as "shepherd" in the dialogue of John 21:15–17.

**21:15–17** This small section is characterized by repetitions with slight variations. Almost all the verbs occur in the present with the exception of ἠρίστησαν (they had eaten) in v. 15 and ἐλυπήθη (he was grieved) in v. 17. The first introduces the scene; the second speaks of Peter's reaction to the triple question of Jesus. In the threefold dialogue, each time the person speaking is not named. This gives rise to a lively account that is further reinforced through the consistent employment of the historic present (six times, λέγει, "he said," literally, "he says"). Through the enumeration "a second time" (δεύτερον) and "a third time" (τρίτον) a rising tension is built up until the end of the dialogue with the appropriate emotion on the part of Peter: "he was grieved" (ἐλυπήθη).

Through the expression "when they had eaten" (ὅτε οὖν ἠρίστησαν) in v. 15, the section is linked to the previous one (cf. v. 12). However, in the first verse of the new scene, the names of the conversation partners are mentioned: "Jesus" and "Simon Peter." When it is resumed in the following verse, the archaic name "Simon, son of John" appears, a name that had not been used since the calling scene in John 1:42 but is attested in the scene at Caesarea Philippi in Matt 16:17. The reference to 1:42 could signify the beginning of a new relationship corresponding to that of the first meeting between Jesus and Peter. The reference to Matt 16:17 recalls the commissioning of Peter in the scene at Caesarea Philippi.

Furthermore, scholars discuss whether the different expressions for "love" (ἀγαπᾶν and φιλεῖν) and "feed" (βόσκειν and ποιμαίνειν) as well as "sheep" (πρόβατα and ἀρνία) constitute only linguistic variations with the same meaning or are the expression of different nuances. McKay[29] has examined the case in great detail and comes to the conclusion that at least for the variants for "feed" and "sheep" there is no difference in content. There is possibly a difference in meaning in the expressions for "love": ἀγαπᾶν and φιλεῖν. The first verb is obtained from the vocabulary of the Septuagint, the second, rather, from Hellenistic usage. Here, too, the difference in meaning is of little significance.

The meaning of Jesus's question in v. 15: "Do you love me more than these?" is disputed. The majority of authors refer Jesus's question to a number of people and then translate as above. Another possible translation would be: "Do you love me more than these things?," with the reference being to Peter's trade.[30] The reference to other persons and not things is justified by the leading role of Peter in John 21.[31] Perhaps Jesus's question is alluding to Peter's self-confidence, exhibited when he promised Jesus that he would never abandon him (John 13:37). Jesus's threefold question could be explained from the triple denial of Peter in John 18:15–18, 25–27. Peter has to renew his relationship of love for and trust in Jesus before he can be entrusted with care for his flock.

Moreover, love of Jesus recalls the chief commandment of love for God from Deut 6:4–5 to which there are references in John 5:41–44 and 8:41–42, cf. 14:15–24. In his confession of his love for Jesus, the Son of God, Peter is conforming to the fundamental commandment of Israel.

The theme of the shepherd who feeds the flock of the people of God is prepared for in the shepherd discourse of John 10:1–18, 26–29. For its part, this discourse is inspired by the theme of the shepherd in the Exilic and post-Exilic prophets (cf. Jer 23 and Ezek 34). Jesus himself is the good shepherd promised by the Father of the people of Israel. He feeds the Lord's flock and is ready to lay down his life for the sheep entrusted

---

29. McKay, "Style."
30. Barbaglia, "Darai la tua vita."
31. Cf. Orsatti, "Mi ami di più."

## Epilogue: Jesus, Peter, and the Beloved Disciple (21:1–25)

to him. In that, Peter is to follow him. The flock entrusted to him remains the flock of the Lord.[32]

The concept of the shepherd is also employed in other texts of the New Testament that speak of the task of the leaders of the Christian community (cf. 1 Pet 5:1–4; Acts 20:28; Eph 4:11). In the First Letter of Peter (5:1), the author calls himself "fellow elder" with the elders of the communities of Asia Minor and exhorts the elders to feed the flock of God in the right way (5:2). In the Letter to the Hebrews, the author calls Jesus "the great shepherd of the sheep" (13:20). This confirms the orientation of the shepherds of the community to Jesus as the source and model of their service.

The relationship of John 21:15–17 to Matt 16:17–18 is not only discussed in Catholic literature.[33] Both texts have in common the commissioning of Peter for service to the community of believers. In Matthew, Peter's commission is formulated in a more strictly legal manner. Despite this, the Catholic exegetical tradition sees a connection between the texts of Matthew and John, for example in the sense of the "promise" and the "bestowal" of the primacy. Since the middle of the twentieth century, it has also been suggested that a tradition about a post-Easter event stands behind the two texts. This soon led to irritation on the part of Rome.[34] Since the Second Vatican Council, Catholic exegesis has also learned to understand the New Testament texts more from their theological content. The text of Matt 16 expresses the conviction of the Syrian church about the primacy of Peter among the apostles. The text of John 21 is not far distant from this conviction. The role of Peter has been studied by various, even ecumenical, groups with consistently closer positions between Catholic and Protestant.[35] A primacy of the bishop of Rome is not derived from Matt 16 and John 21 before the end of the second century. The full teaching of the

---

32. This is also stressed by Öhler, "Der 'Mietling' Petrus." However, it does not follow from this that Peter here and generally in John appears more as a hireling than as a good shepherd. Once he has made good his failure in denial and flight, he can also be appointed shepherd.

33. Cf. Vögtle, "Messiasbekenntnis"; Vögtle, "Ekklesiologische Auftragsworte"; Wilckens, "Joh 21,15–23"; Heckel, *Hirtenamt*.

34. Thus the professor of the Pontifical Biblical Institute, Maximilian Zerwick, SJ, was forbidden to teach by the veto of Pope John XXIII since, in a lecture in Northern Italy, he had echoed the question of Anton Vögtle whether or not the same post-Easter event could lie behind the promise of primacy in Matt 16:18 and the bestowal of primacy in John 21:15–17. The veto was lifted only under Pope Paul VI. Cf. Beutler, "Zerwick, Max."

35. Cf. among others, Brown, Donfried, and Reumann, *Peter in the New Testament*.

jurisdictional primacy of the papacy over the whole church is not found before the time of Popes Innocent III (1199) and Boniface VIII (1303).

**18-19** Jesus's commission to Peter to feed the flock of the Lord is followed now by a command that concerns the relationship of Peter to Jesus. He is to follow him. The small section is introduced with the formula "Amen, amen, I say to you," which is used elsewhere in John to underline Jesus's sayings (cf. John 1:51; 3:3 etc.). This is followed by a saying of Jesus about Peter in two parts, in the indicative throughout (after the three imperatives of verses 15-17). The first saying refers to Peter's past, the second to his future. This double saying displays a semantic tension between youth and old age, girding oneself and being girded as well as between going where one wants and going where one does not want. This is followed by an explanation from the narrator. In conclusion, there is an invitation of Jesus with a present imperative. The tenses used in the passage show a movement from present to past, then to future and finally again to the present. This movement seems to be significant for the pragmatic dimension of the text. Jesus's exhortation to Peter to follow him is taken up again in v. 22.

The introduction of the passage in v. 18 with the formula "Amen, amen, I say to you" lends a high degree of solemnity and reliability to Jesus's saying. The contrasts in the description of the biography of Peter have already been pointed out. The verb "gird oneself" (διεζώσατο) has already been recorded previously in Peter's preparation for diving into the lake (cf. v. 7). Perhaps, in fact, Jesus is deliberately referring to this action. For the future, Jesus predicts to Peter that another will bind his hands. The going where he wants is matched by the going where Peter does not want. The vocabulary and the literary form of Jesus's saying make one think of a proverb. According to Jesus's prophetic word, Peter will suffer the same fate as his Lord, cf. John 18:12-13: "The soldiers, the captain and the officers of the Jews seized (συνέλαβον) Jesus, bound (ἔδησαν) him and led him first to Annas." The vocabulary does not correspond exactly to that of John 21:18 but synonymous verbs are employed. The experience is the same.

At the beginning of v. 19, the narrator explains the metaphors in the previous verse. The prediction that Peter would be led where he did not want to go was a foretelling of his martyrdom. In John's Gospel, the expression "glorify God through his (violent) death" has been employed in connection with Jesus's death on the cross (cf. 12:32). The verb δοξάζω is used for the "glorifying" of Jesus by the Father or the "glorifying" of the Father by the Son (cf., e.g., 13:31–32). A single text that has spoken previously of the fact that God will "glorify" the disciples occurred in John 15:8 in the discourse about the true vine. God will "glorify" the disciples if they bear much fruit. Many recent scholars ascribe the relevant chapter to a later layer than the main stratum of John's Gospel. The use of the verb "glorify" has been heavily "churchified." The same observation can be made in John 21:19: Peter will "glorify" God through his violent death just as his Lord had done before him. This is the explanation for the next command: "Follow me." In the account of Peter's call (John 1:41–42), there was no report of any express commandment of Jesus to Peter to follow him. One could say that Jesus's command in John 21:19 takes up again the call of Peter in John 1:41–42 and completes it so that in this way there is an inclusio between the first and last chapters.

For the origin of the call of Peter to follow in John 21:19, the story of the wonderful catch of fish in John 21:1–14 against the background of Luke 5:1–11 is indicated once more. Luke's account replaces the narratives of Mark (1:16–20) and Matthew (4:18–22), according to whom Jesus commanded the first four disciples (Peter and Andrew, James and John) on the shore of the Sea of Galilee to follow him and in so doing foretold that he would make them "fishers of men." Luke takes up this announcement and applies it to Peter: "From this time on, you will catch men" (Luke 5:10). The Lukan text closes with the statement: "And they brought their boats to land, left all and followed him" (Luke 5:11). The last verb is taken up in John 21:19 and applied to Peter: "Follow me (ἀκολούθει μοι)!"

In the narrative flow of John 21:15–19 it is possible to detect a movement from acting to suffering, something that is also concealing a narrative strategy. Verses 15–17 are still focused on the activity of Peter. Bound in love to his Lord, he has to feed his flock. The first part of v. 18 is still describing the initiative of Peter, who can gird himself and go where he pleases. The turning point is situated in the second part of the comparison: Peter will be girded by another and led where he does not wish to go. The author of John 21 is undoubtedly describing a development in the lived reality of the disciples. Responsibility for the Lord's flock can have consequences for one's own life to the point of having to sacrifice it. The readiness to inspire this has emerged as a consistent aim of John's Gospel.[36]

---

36. Cf. Beutler, "Faith and Confession."

*The Saying about the Beloved Disciple.*
*Second Conclusion of John's Gospel (21:20–25)*

The dialogue between Jesus and Peter about the latter's commission is based on love and his fate (John 21:15–17, 18–19). It is followed by a further one about the beloved disciple (vv. 21–23). Peter's question about this other disciple meets with no answer from Jesus but rather is rebuffed. Instead, there follows a renewed invitation to follow Jesus: σύ με ἀκολούθει, similar to the other in v. 19: ἀκολούθει μοι. In this way, the verb ἀκολουθεῖν frames the group of verses 20–22. Peter sees the beloved disciple "following" Jesus and asks the Lord about the future of this disciple. Jesus does not respond to this question directly; rather, the dialogue ends with the renewed command to Peter: "Follow me!" From this double perspective, v. 23 turns out to be a comment of the author of John 21 that does not belong to the level of the story. The verse explains the true meaning of the saying of Jesus about the beloved disciple and corrects a mistaken interpretation.

The two final verses of the chapter (and of the whole of the Gospel of John) are again focused on the figure of the beloved disciple. This disciple is identified with the authentic witness and author of "these things." The verb γράφειν ("write") leads on from v. 24 to v. 25. The whole world could not contain the books which would have to be written in order to give an exhaustive account of Jesus's deeds. An allusion to John 20:30–31 is seen clearly here.[37] Striking in this connection is the introduction of the first person in the two verses, the first person plural in v. 24 and the first person singular in v. 25: "we know" that the witness of the beloved disciple is true, and "I think" that the whole world could not contain the books that would have to be written in order to describe Jesus's deeds exhaustively. The sense of this double first person will have to be discussed in the detailed exegesis.[38]

**21:20–23** Before plunging into the various historical and literary interpretations of this group of verses, it is a good idea to work out their literal sense. In doing so, we have to maintain the distinction between the dialogue between Peter and Jesus in verses 20–22 and the comment of the narrator in v. 23.

The first two verses (20–21) are linked by the catchword "see." According to v. 20, Peter "sees" (βλέπει) the beloved disciple following (Jesus). An identification of this disciple comes next. In v. 21, a verb of

---

37. Cf., for example, Roberts, "John 20:30–31."
38. Cf., for the following verse again, Beutler, "Der Abschluss."

## Epilogue: Jesus, Peter, and the Beloved Disciple (21:1–25)

"seeing" (ἰδών) occurs again followed by the question about this disciple. The beloved disciple is characterized by a reference to the first scene in which he was introduced by the evangelist, the Last Supper (John 13:23, 25). This serves to connect the main part of the Gospel with ch. 21. Thus a certain superiority of the beloved disciple in comparison with Peter is revealed: he was the disciple who had lain on the breast of Jesus and been able to ask him the question that none of the others was able to ask, precisely because he was "the disciple whom Jesus loved." Peter's question in v. 21 refers to the person and the fate of the beloved disciple. The reason for this could lie in Jesus's command to Peter to follow him in a violent death. The question about the beloved disciple would then be whether this disciple too would suffer the same fate in the future.

According to v. 22, Jesus declines to answer this question and confines himself to a reiterated command to Peter to follow him. Peter should not permit himself any speculation over the fate of the other disciple but take seriously his own calling to follow Jesus to the end.

In his comment in v. 23, the author of John 21 interprets Jesus's answer to Peter. The verb used by Jesus μένειν ("remain, tarry") allows various interpretations. It could be interpreted as an announcement of a physical remaining of the beloved disciple until the day of Jesus's "coming" again, and it could be understood theologically: until Jesus's coming again, the beloved disciple was to "remain" in his character as the closest and truest witness to Jesus and also as a reliable witness in his testimony set down in a book. According to the author of John 21, this is the authentic sense of Jesus's saying.[39]

Until recently, many exegetes have approached the text with historical and biographical questions. In fact, the beloved disciple had died, and the community was asking itself about the meaning of Jesus's saying that he would have to "remain." Jesus had not predicted his remaining in any physical sense but had simply commanded Peter to follow him regardless of whether the beloved disciple had to die or remain alive. Thus, the disciple's death was a possibility despite Jesus's words. This allows for the appearance of the group of disciples who speak in verse 24 and witness to the origin and trustworthiness of the Fourth Gospel as the work of the beloved disciple. Thus, we are standing here at the beginning of the so-called "Johannine school" and the "Ephesian tradition."[40]

---

39. Cf. Winandy, "Le disciple."

40. This view is found, among other places, in the commentaries of Schnackenburg and Brown.

Among contemporary authors, there is an increasing tendency to read the text with the methods of contemporary literary criticism and thus synchronically.[41] The text does not allow itself easily to be employed as a "window" on a world external to the text and lying behind it. The event of the death of the beloved disciple is speculation that cannot be based on the text. The text itself emphasizes Peter's duty to follow Jesus with all the consequences; he is not to be concerned with the fate of the beloved disciple. The true "remaining" of the disciple is fulfilled in the testimony registered in his book.

If one refers Jesus's saying to the immortality of the beloved disciple, this is falsified by that disciple's death. There remains the possibility of understanding the saying differently. For the representatives of the "historical" interpretation of the saying, the evidence is sufficient to indicate that Jesus was not speaking of the exemption of the beloved disciple from death; for the champions of literary and theological exegesis, we should be questioning the meaning of Jesus's saying and indicating in what sense the beloved disciple is "remaining" until Jesus's coming again.

**21:24–25** With that, we have reached the second conclusion of John's Gospel. Verse 24 consists of a nominal clause (ἐστίν, "is") and a verbal one (οἴδαμεν, "we know"), which is followed by a subordinate nominal clause beginning with ὅτι ("because"). The first nominal clause is expanded with two participles, one in the present (μαρτυρῶν, "witnessing"), the other in the aorist (γράψας, "having written"). The introductory demonstrative pronoun οὗτός ("this") is employed anaphorically and clearly refers to the "disciple" (μαθητής) who was named in verses 20 and 23. This disciple is the witness of "these things" (τούτων) and "has written these things" (γράψας ταῦτα). Presumably τούτων ("these things") refers to the same reality as ταῦτα. The meaning is thus: everything that has been written previously, be it the whole Gospel or the last part or the last chapter or the last paragraph. Along the lines of the first conclusion in John 20:30–31, it is better to see the statement as referring to the whole of John's Gospel. As in John 19:35, an unnamed group of disciples in the "we" of the first person plural testifies to the trustworthiness of the beloved disciple. The construction of the verb μαρτυρεῖν ("witness") with the preposition περί ("about") belongs to the typical vocabulary of the Gospel. However, in chs. 1–15, the construction is referred to one person who bears testimony,

---

41. Cf., among others, Hartman, "An Attempt"; Gaventa, "The Archive"; Thyen, "Noch einmal"; Zumstein, "Endredaktion"; Aletti, "Les finales."

## Epilogue: Jesus, Peter, and the Beloved Disciple (21:1-25)

namely, Jesus. Only in the passion and resurrection narrative is περί employed in connection with the events being witnessed: the opened side of Jesus from which blood and water flow (John 19:35), and the deeds of Jesus as a whole (John 21:24).[42]

Verse 25 is missing in the first version of one of the oldest manuscripts of the New Testament, Codex Sinaiticus (fourth century). Nevertheless, its originality is not usually challenged by textual criticism. The construction of the sentence is complicated. An initial, nominal, main clause is followed by a relative clause that is expanded by another relative clause which, for its part, is determined by a conditional clause. The apodosis of this conditional clause contains the verb οἶμαι ("I believe") in the first person singular, which stands in contrast with the first person plural οἴδαμεν ("we know") in v. 24. The sense of v. 25 is similar to that of the first conclusion of the Gospel. The content of the Gospel account is not exhaustive. Jesus did many other things which were not recorded in this book and, if one wanted to write these out, then the whole world could not contain the books in question. This is a way of saying that a materially complete testimony about Jesus is neither possible nor necessary since what has been selected is sufficient to lead to faith in Jesus Christ, the Son of God.

The last two verses of John's Gospel are subject to various interpretations. Those authors who read verses 20-23 from the historical point of view find a historical person in v. 24 and enquire after the "extra-textual" existence of the beloved disciple. In this case, since the days of Irenaeus of Lyon in the second century the answers break down variously as:

- John, the son of Zebedee[43]
- John the Presbyter mentioned by Papias of Hierapolis[44]
- A Jerusalem priest named John mentioned in Acts 4:6[45]

The problem lies in the fact that, at no point in John's Gospel, not even in the closing verses, is there any statement of the name of the beloved disciple. For this reason, the contemporary reader asks himself whether he has to know what the author has kept hidden.

42. Cf. Beutler, "μαρτυρέω," *EWNT* 2:960-62; *EDNT* 2:390f.
43. Thus the tradition since Irenaeus.
44. So following Harnack, especially Hengel, *Frage*.
45. Thus Rigato, "L' 'apostolo'"; Rigato, "La testimonianza di Policrate"; Rigato, "La testimonianza di Papia"; Winandy, "Le disciple."

Difficult too is the identity of the group of the "we" that catches the eye in the οἴδαμεν ("we know"). Those authors who wish to determine the identity of the beloved disciple also think it necessary to do the same for the group of the "we." For the supporters of the "Ephesian hypothesis," according to which the beloved disciple would be John the presbyter mentioned by Papias, what would be standing behind the "we" would be the, hypothetically, emerging Johannine school. Others question the very existence of such a school or community.

A historical-critical reading would also interpret the final verse according to this paradigm. According to authors like Schnackenburg, the statement that the whole world could not contain the books that would have to be written in order to give an exhaustive portrayal of Jesus's deeds is conventional and goes back, rather, to a late redactor.[46] However, his reference to New Wettstein's commentary[47] is not substantiated by the New Wettstein.[48]

Thus the possibility remains of understanding the closing verse of John's Gospel more from the literary point of view and respecting the text's silence on the identity of the beloved disciple. Ahead here is Origen, the first author of a commentary on John (if one excludes that of the Gnostic Heracleon whom Origen cites). According to a series of recent authors, the beloved disciple is an ideal figure who does not necessarily have to correspond to a historical personality.[49] These scholars think that the author of John or its editor makes use of the figure of the beloved disciple to guarantee the trustworthiness of the message of the Fourth Gospel. Just as Jesus rests "in the Father's heart" (John 1:18), so the beloved disciple lies "at Jesus's side" (John 13:23), thus becoming a trustworthy messenger. The οἴδαμεν ("we know") of John 21:24 is not referring to the existence of a Johannine group or community[50] but could be a stylistic device that is meant to secure the acceptance of the testimony by the readers. In this case, it can then be suggested that, in John, "testimony" refers not simply to the external deeds of a life but more to the dimension of revelation expressed in those external deeds. There are relevant examples of this in

---

46. Cf. Cardellino, "Chi rifiuta."

47. Cf. Schnackenburg, 3:448.

48. Cf. Neuer Wettstein, where there is only a quotation from Livy that the whole world could not grasp the military power of the Roman people.

49. Cf. Kragerud, *Lieblingsjünger*; Kügler, *Jünger*; Thyen, who rests firmly on the commentary of Oberbeck.

50. Cf. Bauckham, *Testimony*; Thyen.

## Epilogue: Jesus, Peter, and the Beloved Disciple (21:1–25)

John 1:34 ("this is the Son of God"), 1 John 1:1–4 ("the Word of life"), and 1 John 4:14 ("that the Father has sent the Son as Redeemer of the world").

The identification of the beloved disciple with the author of the Fourth Gospel serves the aim of bestowing on this Gospel an unassailable authority. It was precisely the one who, as the disciple closest to Jesus (especially in the decisive hour of his departure after the cross and resurrection), left behind his testimony in written form, the Fourth Gospel. Far from being a banal ending, even in comparison with the first conclusion of the Gospel in John 20:30–31, this second conclusion actualizes the first in the sense of a *"relecture."* The decisive catchword is that of "writing," which is taken up from v. 24 in v. 25 and there twice repeated. The last words of the Fourth Gospel are γραφόμενα βιβλία, "written books." The Word has become text.

### III

John 21 is not simply an appendix to the previous twenty chapters of the Gospel with a further, third appearance of the risen Jesus to the disciples and words of Jesus to or about these disciples. The chapter can also be understood as a *"relecture"* of all of the preceding part of John's Gospel. Already there has been a decline in the role of Peter in favor of that of the beloved disciple. At the Last Supper, it was not Peter but the beloved disciple who lay at the side of Jesus and learned the identity of the one who was to betray Jesus. Peter promised his Lord to be faithful to him even to death but then fell short, miserably, when he was asked in the courtyard of the high priest whether he belonged to Jesus. Only the beloved disciple stands with the mother of Jesus below the cross. On Easter Day, it is Peter, in fact, who was honored with being first into the empty tomb, but the beloved disciple is the first to recognize the Lord as living. In John 21, this perspective is developed further and concluded.

Peter is the only disciple with whom Jesus converses in John 21. He is honored with the initiative over the fishing, first on his own account and unsuccessfully, then at the bidding of Jesus and with overwhelming success. Jesus asks him about his renewed love for him and thereupon entrusts him with the care of his sheep. He then summons him to follow him, permanently and to the ultimate consequence of a violent death. Thus, if we look back, an altered view of the fourth evangelist regarding the figure of Peter emerges. It might have corresponded to his role and recognition in the nascent Christian community, though it is impossible to derive from this that this was the way for the Gnosticising Gospel of John to become acceptable to the great Church.

The beloved disciple speaks only once in John 21, but there weightily when he recognizes the Lord in the man standing on the shore. In what follows, he gains an additional profile in the words of Jesus and the narrator. First and foremost, these are not speculations about his fate. It is more important that he "remains" until Jesus comes again. It is readily apparent that this "remaining" has nothing to do with his physical existence but means a remaining in his testimony. This testimony has now been set down in the book that he has written, in the Fourth Gospel. In it, he remains present, and, through his witness, so too does the one whose message he brought: the Lord.

Other shifts of perspective can be added to those we have observed. Thus the new "coming" of Jesus after his coming at Easter is now no longer a subject of embarrassment. Added to that is a stronger orientation of the text to the nascent community. As is rightly seen, until John 20, the subject is who Jesus is; now, however, the question is who, according to Jesus's words, some of his disciples are. Here, the "official" commissioning of Peter with the care of Jesus's sheep is significant. An ecclesiastical office is coming into view. It is no longer based on Peter's faith (cf. John 6:69) but it is in his love for Jesus that Israel's chief commandment finds its concrete expression.

To office is added table fellowship. Jesus invites the disciples to breakfast, and this with expressions that recall, at the same time, the miraculous multiplication of bread as well as the celebration of the Eucharist. The location at the Sea of Tiberias also reminds us of John 6 with the narrative of the multiplication of bread and the account of the bread discourse in the synagogue of Capernaum with its eucharistic conclusion. Jesus remains with his own, not only in the office of Peter but also in the gifts that he extends to the celebrating and remembering community and in which he himself is present among them.

Jesus's remaining with his own in his word is not thereby being devalued. Far from it. The Fourth Gospel closes, not with the commissioning of Peter but with a new summons to follow and with the proclamation of the beloved disciple as the true and reliable witness whose book is a valid and secure means of connecting with Jesus. It is in this mutual complement of word, sacrament, and office that the abiding contribution of John 21 for the present and the future of the church may lie.

# Bibliography

## Commentaries

Augustine. *In Iohannis evangelium tractatus CXXIV*. CCSL 36. Turnhout: Brepols, 1954.

———. *Des heiligen Kirchenvaters Aurelius Augustinus ausgewählte Schriften: aus dem Lateinischen übersetzt*. Bibliothek der Kirchenväter. Kempten: Jos. Kösel, 1913–1914.

Barrett, C. K. *Das Evangelium nach Johannes*. KEKSup. Göttingen: Vandenhoeck & Ruprecht, 1990.

Bauer, Walter. *Das Johannesevangelium*. 3rd ed. HNT 6. Tübingen: Mohr Siebeck, 1933.

Beasley-Murray, G. R. *John*. 2nd ed. WBC 36. Nashville: Nelson, 1999.

Becker, Jürgen. *Das Evangelium nach Johannes*. 2 vols. 3rd ed. ÖTK 4.1–2. Gütersloh: G. Mohn; Würzburg: Echter, 1991.

Bernard, J. H. *A Critical and Exegetical Commentary on the Gospel according to St. John*. 2 vols. ICC. Edinburgh: T&T Clark, 1928.

Blank, Josef. *Das Evangelium nach Johannes*. 3 vols. Geistliche Schriftlesung., Erläuterungen zum Neuen Testament für die Geistliche Lesung 4.1–3. Düsseldorf: Patmos, 1977–1981.

Boismard, Marie-Émile, and Arnaud Lamouille. *L'évangile de Jean*. 2nd ed. Synopse des quatre évangiles en français 3. Paris: Cerf, 1987.

Brown, Raymond E. *The Gospel according to John*. 2 vols. AB 29–29A. Garden City, NY: Doubleday, 1966–1970.

Bultmann, Rudolf. *Das Evangelium des Johannes*. KEK 2. 18th ed. Göttingen: Vandenhoeck & Ruprecht, 1964.

Bussche, Henri van den. *Jean. Commentaire de l'évangile spiritual*. 3 vols. Paris: Desclée de Brouwer, 1967.

Cyril. *Sancti Patris Nostri Cyrilli Archiepiscopi Alexandrini in D. Joannis Evangelium*. Edited by Philip E. Pusey. Oxford: Clarendon Press, 1872.

Dietzfelbinger, Christian. *Das Evangelium nach Johannes*. 2 vols. ZBK 4.1–2. Zürich: Theologischer Verlag, 2001.

Haenchen, Ernst. *Das Johannesevangelium. Ein Kommentar*. Edited by Ulrich Busse. Tübingen: Mohr Siebeck, 1980.
Hirsch, Emanuel. *Das vierte Evangelium*. Tübingen: Mohr Siebeck, 1936.
Holtzmann, Heinrich Julius. *Evangelium, Briefe und Offenbarung des Johannes*. 3rd ed. Hand-Commentar zum Neuen Testament 4. Freiburg: Mohr, 1908.
Hoskyns, E. C. *The Fourth Gospel*. Edited by Francis Noel Davey. 2 vols. London: Faber and Faber, 1940.
Keener, Craig S. *The Gospel of John: A Commentary*. 2 vols. Peabody, MA: Hendrickson, 2003.
Kieffer, René. *Johannesevangeliet*. 2 vols. Kommentar till Nya testamentet 4A–B. Uppsala: EFS-förlaget, 1987–1988.
———. "John." Pages 960–1000 in *The Oxford Bible Commentary*. Edited by John Barton and John Muddiman. Oxford: Oxford University Press, 2001.
Kysar, Robert. *John*. ANTC. Minneapolis: Fortress, 1986.
Lagrange, Marie-Joseph. *Évangile selon Saint Jean*. 2nd ed. Études bibliques 4. Paris: Gabalda, 1925.
Léon-Dufour, Xavier. *Lecture de l'Évangile selon Jean*. 4 vols. Paris: Éditions du Seuil, 1988–1996.
Lightfoot, R. H. *St. John's Gospel. A Commentary*. Edited by C. F. Evans. Oxford: Clarendon Press, 1957.
Lindars, Barnabas. *The Gospel of John*. NCB. Grand Rapids, Eerdmans, 1972.
Loisy, Alfred. *Le quatrième évangile. Les épitres dites de Jean*. 2nd ed. Paris: Nourry, 1921.
Marsh, John. *The Gospel of Saint John*. London: Penguin, 1968.
McHugh, John F. *A Critical and Exegetical Commentary on John 1–4*. ICC. London: Continuum, 2009.
Michaels, J. Ramsey. *The Gospel of John*. NICNT 4. Grand Rapids: Eerdmans, 2010.
Mollat, Donatien. "L'Évangile selon Saint Jean." Pages 7–193 in *L'Évangile et les Épitres de Saint Jean*. 2nd ed. Sainte Bible. Paris: Cerf, 1960.
Moloney, Francis J. *The Gospel of John*. SP 4. Collegeville, MN: Liturgical, 1998.
Morris, Leon. *The Gospel according to John*. NICNT 4. Grand Rapids: Eerdmans, 1995.
Neyrey, Jerome H. *The Gospel of John*. The New Cambridge Bible Commentary. Cambridge: Cambridge University Press, 2007.
Origen. *Commentaire sur Saint Jean*. Edited by Cécile Blanc. 5 vols. SC 120, 157, 222, 290, 385. Paris: Cerf, 1966–1992.
———. *Johanneskommentar, Buch I–V*. Edited by Hans Georg Thümmel. STAC 3. Tübingen: Mohr Siebeck, 2011.
Peterson, Erik. *Johannesevangelium und Kanonstudien*. Edited by Barbara Nichtweiss, Kurt Anglet, and Klaus Scholtissek. Würzburg: Echter, 2003.
Rebstock, Bonaventura. *Vom Wort des Lebens. Gedanken zum Johannes-Evangelium im Geist der Heiligen Väter*. 2 vols. Recklinghausen: Paulus, 1949–1950.
Schenke, Ludger. *Johannes. Kommentar*. Düsseldorf: Patmos, 1998.
Schnackenburg, Rudolf. *Das Johannesevangelium*. 4 vols. HThKNT 4.1–4. Freiburg im Breisgau: Herder, 1965–1984.
Schnelle, Udo. *Das Evangelium nach Johannes*. 4th ed. THKNT 4. Leipzig: Evangelische Verlagsanstalt, 2009.

Schulz, Siegfried. *Das Evangelium nach Johannes.* 4th ed. NTD 4. Göttingen: Vandenhoeck & Ruprecht, 1983.
Schwank, Benedikt. *Das Johannesevangelium.* 2 vols. Die Welt der Bibel. Kleinkommentare zur Heiligen Schrift, 7.1-2. Düsseldorf: Patmos, 1966-1968.
Simoens, Yves. *Selon Jean. I (Une traduction), II–III (Une interprétation).* Collection IET 17. Brussels: Institut d'Etudes Théologiques, 1997.
Smith, D. Moody. *John.* ANTC. Nashville: Abingdon, 1999.
Stibbe, Mark W. G. *John.* Readings: A New Biblical Commentary. Sheffield: JSOT Press, 1993.
———. *John's Gospel.* New Testament Readings. London: Routledge, 1994.
Strack, Hermann Leberecht, and Paul Billerbeck. *Kommentar zum Neuen Testament aus Talmud und Midrasch.* 9th ed. Munich: Beck, 1986.
Strathmann, Hermann. *Das Evangelium nach Johannes.* NTD 2. Göttingen: Vandenhoeck & Ruprecht, 1962.
Theobald, Michael. *Das Evangelium nach Johannes: Kapitel 1–12.* Regensburger Neues Testament. Regensburg: Pustet, 2009.
Thyen, Hartwig. *Das Johannesevangelium.* HNT 6. Tübingen: Mohr Siebeck, 2005.
Von Wahlde, Urban C. *The Gospel and Letters of John I–III.* Eerdmans Cricital Commentary. Grand Rapids: Eerdmans, 2010.
Vouga, François, et al. Le quatrième évangile. Lumière et Vie 149. Lyon: Lumière et vie, 1980.
Weiss, Bernhard. *Das Johannesevangelium.* 9th ed. KEK 2. Göttingen: Vandenhoeck and Ruprecht, 1902.
Wengst, Klaus. *Das Johannesevangelium I–II.* Theologischer Kommentar zum Neuen Testament 4.1-2. Stuttgart: Kohlhammer, 2000-2001.
Wikenhauser, Alfred. *Das Evangelium nach Johannes.* 3rd ed. Regensburger Neues Testament 4. Regensburg: Pustet, 1961.
Wilckens, Ulrich. *Das Evangelium nach Johannes.* 17th ed. NTD 4. Göttingen: Vandenhoeck & Ruprecht, 1998.
Zumstein, Jean. *L'évangile selon Saint Jean (13–21).* CNT IVb. Geneva: Labor et Fides, 2007.

## Other Literature

Abramowski, Luise. "Der Apostel von Joh 13,16." *ZNW* 99 (2008): 116-23.
———. "Die Geschichte von der Fußwaschung ( Joh 13)." *ZTK* 102 (2005): 176-203.
Aland, Kurt. "Der Text des Johannesevangeliums im 2. Jahrhundert." Pages 1-10 in *Studien zum Text und zur Ethik des Neuen Testaments.* Edited by Wolfgang Schrage. BZNW 47. Berlin: De Gruyter, 1986.
———. "Eine Untersuchung zu Joh 1,3.4. Über die Bedeutung eines Punktes." *ZNW* 59 (1968): 174-209.
Aland, Kurt, and Barbara Aland. *Der Text des Neuen Testaments. Einführung in die wissenschaftlichen Ausgaben sowie in Theorie und Praxis der modernen Textkritik.* 2nd ed. Stuttgart: Deutsche Bibelgesellschaft, 1989.
Aletti, Jean-Noël. "Les finales des récits évangéliques et le statut du livre et des lecteurs." *RevScRel* 79 (2005): 23-37.

———. "Jn 13—les problèmes de composition et leur importance." *Bib* 87 (2006): 263–72.
Alter, Robert. *The Art of Biblical Narrative*. New York: Basic Books, 1981.
Anderson, Paul N. "Aspects of Interfluentiality between John and the Synoptics: John 18–19 as a Case Study." Pages 711–28 in *The Death of Jesus in the Fourth Gospel*. Edited by Gilbert van Belle. BETL 200. Leuven: Peeters, 2007.
———. *The Christology of the Fourth Gospel: Its Unity and Disunity in the Light of John 6*. WUNT 2.78. Tübingen: Mohr Siebeck, 1996.
———. *The Fourth Gospel and the Quest for Jesus: Modern Foundations Reconsidered*. London: T&T Clark, 2006.
———. *The Riddles of the Fourth Gospel: An Introduction to John*. Minneapolis: Fortress, 2011.
———. "The Sitz im Leben of the Johannine Bread of Life Discourse and Its Evolving Context." Pages 1–59 in *Critical Readings of John 6*. Edited by R. Alan Culpepper. Leiden: Brill, 1997.
Arterbury, Andrew E. "Breaking the Betrothal Bonds: Hospitality in John 4." *CBQ* 72 (2010): 63–83.
Ashton, John. *Studying John: Approaches to the Fourth Gospel*. Oxford: Clarendon Press, 1994.
———. *Understanding the Fourth Gospel*. Oxford: Oxford University Press, 2007.
Asiedu-Peprah, Martin. *Johannine Sabbath Conflicts as Juridical Controversy*. WUNT 2.132. Tübingen: Mohr Siebeck, 2001.
Attridge, Harold W. "'Don't Be Touching Me': Recent Feminist Scholarship on Mary Magdalene." Pages 140–66 in *A Feminist Companion to John II*. Edited by Amy-Jill Levine. Feminist Companion to the New Testament and Early Christian Writings 5. London: Sheffield Academic Press, 2003.
———. "How Priestly Is the 'High Priestly Prayer' of John 17?" *CBQ* 75 (2013): 1–14.
Augenstein, Jörg. *Das Liebesgebot im Johannesevangelium und in den Johannesbriefen*. BWANT 134. Stuttgart: Kohlhammer, 1993.
Aus, Roger D. "The Death of One for All in John 11:45–54 in Light of Judaic Traditions." Pages 29–63 in *Barabbas and Esther and Other Studies in the Judaic Illumination of Earliest Christianity*. Edited by Roger D. Aus. South Florida Studies in the History of Judaism 54. Atlanta: Scholars Press, 1992.
Auwers, Jean-Marie. "La nuit de Nicodème (Jean 3,2; 19,39) ou l'ombre du langage." *RB* 97 (1990): 481–503.
Baarda, Tjitze. "John 8:57b: The Contribution of the Diatessaron of Tatian." *NovT* 38 (1996): 336–43.
Bacinoni, Venance. "L'aveuglement face à la lumière du Christ: révélation, foi et non-foi en Jn 9,1–41." PhD diss. Pontificia Università Gregoriana Rome, 1982.
Back, Frances. *Gott als Vater der Jünger im Johannesevangelium*. WUNT 2.336. Tübingen: Mohr Siebeck, 2012.
Baldensperger, Wilhelm. *Der Prolog des 4. Evangeliums—sein polemisch-apologetischer Zweck*. Freiburg: J. C. B. Mohr, 1898.
Balz, H. "ἅγιος." *EWNT* 1:38–48; *EDNT* 1:16–20.
Bammel, Ernst. "Die Tempelreinigung bei den Synoptikern und im Johannesevange-

lium." Pages 507-13 in *John and the Synoptics*. Edited by Adelbert Denaux. BETL 101. Leuven: Peeters, 1992.

Barbaglia, Silvio. "'Darai la tua vita per me?' Una rilettura della triplice domanda di Gesù a Simone di Giovanni (Gv 21,15-19)." *RivB* 51 (2003): 149-91.

Barnett, Paul W. "The Feeding of the Multitude in Mark 6/John 6." Pages 273-93 in *The Miracles of Jesus*. Edited by David Wenham and Craig Blomberg. Gospel Perspectives 6. Sheffield: Sheffield Academic Press, 1986.

Bassler, Jouette M. "The Galileans: A Neglected Factor in Johannine Community Research." *CBQ* 43 (1981): 243-57.

Bauckham, Richard. *The Testimony of the Beloved Disciple: Narrative, History, and Theology in the Gospel of John*. Grand Rapids: BakerAcademic, 2007.

Bauer, Walter. *Griechisch-deutsches Wörterbuch zu den Schriften des Neuen Testaments und der frühchristlichen Literatur*. 6th ed. Edited by Viktor Reichmann, Kurt Aland, and Barbara Aland. Berlin: De Gruyter, 1988.

Baum-Bodenbender, Rosel. *Hoheit in Niedrigkeit. Johanneische Christologie im Prozess Jesu vor Pilatus (Joh 18,28-19,16a)*. FB 49. Würzburg: Echter, 1984.

Becker, Heinz. *Die Reden des Johannesevangeliums und der Stil der gnostischen Offenbarungsrede*. FRLANT 68. Göttingen: Vandenhoeck & Ruprecht, 1956.

Becker, Jürgen. "Ich bin die Auferstehung und das Leben. Eine Skizze der johanneischen Christologie." *ThZ* 39 (1983): 138-51.

Berger, Klaus. *Exegese des Neuen Testaments: Neue Wege vom Text zur Auslegung*. Uni-Taschenbücher 658. 2nd ed. Heidelberg: Quelle und Meyer, 1984.

―――. *Im Anfang war Johannes: Datierung und Theologie des vierten Evangeliums*. Stuttgart: Quell, 1997.

Bergler, Siegfried. "Jesus, Bar Kochba und das messianische Laubhüttenfest." *JSJ* 29 (1998): 143-91.

―――. *Von Kana in Galiläa nach Jerusalem: Literarkritik und Historie im vierten Evangelium*. Münsteraner judaistische Studien 24. Berlin: Lit, 2009.

Bergmeier, Roland. "Τετέλεσται Joh 19,30." *ZNW* 79 (1988): 282-90.

Betz, Otto. *Der Paraklet: Fürsprecher im häretischen Spätjudentum, im Johannes-Evangelium und in neugefundenen gnostischen Schriften*. AGSU 2. Leiden: Brill, 1963.

Beutler, Johannes. "Der Abschluss des Johannesevangeliums (Joh 21,20-25)." Pages 397-423 in *Biblical Exegesis in Progress: Old and New Testament Essays*. Edited by Jean-Noël Aletti and Jean-Louis Ska. Rome: Editrice Pontificio Istituto Biblico, 2009.

―――. "ἀδελφός." *EWNT* 1:67-72; *EDNT* 1:28-30.

―――. "Der alttestamentlich-jüdische Hintergrund der Hirtenrede in Joh 10." Pages 215-32 in *Studien zu den johanneischen Schriften*. SBAB 25. Stuttgart: Katholisches Bibelwerk, 1998.

―――. "Brüder Jesu." *Neues Bibel-Lexikon* 337.

―――. *Do Not Be Afraid: The First Farewell Discourse in John's Gospel (Jn 14)*. New Testament Studies in Contextual Exegesis 6. Frankfurt am Main: Lang, 2011.

―――. *L'Ebraismo e gli Ebrei nel Vangelo di Giovanni*. Subsidia Biblica 29. Rome: Pontificio Istituto Biblico, 2006.

———. "Die Ehre Gottes und die Ehre der Menschen im Johannesevangelium." *Geist und Leben* 76 (2003): 83-91.

———. "Faith and Confession: The Purpose of John." Pages 19-31 in *Word, Theology, and Community in John*. Edited by John Painter, R. Alan Culpepper, and Fernando F. Segovia. St. Louis: Chalice Press 2002.

———. "Frauen und Männer als Jünger Jesu im Johannesevangelium." Pages 285-93 in *Studien zu den johanneischen Schriften*. SBAB 25. Stuttgart: Katholisches Bibelwerk, 1998.

———. "Der Gebrauch von 'Schrift' im Johannesevangelium." Pages 295-315 in *Studien zu den johanneischen Schriften*. SBAB 25. Stuttgart: Katholisches Bibelwerk, 1998.

———. "Greeks Come to See Jesus (John 12,20f)." *Bib* 71 (1990): 333-47.

———. "Griechen kommen, um Jesus zu sehen (Joh 12,20f)." Pages 175-89 in *Studien zu den johanneischen Schriften*. SBAB 25. Stuttgart: Katholisches Bibelwerk, 1998.

———. *Habt keine Angst. Die erste johanneische Abschiedsrede (Joh 14)*. SBS 116. Stuttgart: Katholisches Bibelwerk, 1984.

———. "Das Hauptgebot im Johannesevangelium." Pages 107-20 in *Studien zu den johanneischen Schriften*. SBAB 25. Stuttgart: Katholisches Bibelwerk, 1998.

———. "Die Heilsbedeutung des Todes Jesu im Johannesevangelium nach Joh 13,1-20." Pages 43-58 in *Studien zu den johanneischen Schriften*. SBAB 25. Stuttgart: Katholisches Bibelwerk, 1998.

———. "Hohepriesterliches Gebet." *LTK* 5:220.

———. "'Ich habe gesagt: Ihr seid Götter.' Zur Argumentation mit Ps 82,6 in Joh 10,34-36." Pages 101-13 in *Hören–Glauben–Denken*. Edited by Gerhard Gäde. Münster: Lit, 2005.

———. "The Identity of the 'Jews' for the Readers of John." Pages 69-77 in *Anti-Judaism and the Fourth Gospel: Papers of the Leuven Colloquium, 2000*. Edited by Reimund Bieringer, Didier Pollefeyt, and Frederique Vandecasteele-Vanneuville. Jewish and Christian Heritage Series 1. Assen, the Netherlands: Royal Van Gorcum, 2001.

———. "Joh 6 als christliche 'relecture' des Pascharahmens im Johannesevangelium." Pages 43-58 in *Damit sie das Leben haben (Joh 10,10)*. Edited by Ruth Scoralick. Zürich: Theologischer Verlag, 2007.

———. *Die Johannesbriefe*. Regensburger Neues Testament. Regensburg: Pustet, 2000.

———. "Der Johannes-Prolog–Ouvertüre des Johannesevangeliums." Pages 77-106 in *Der Johannesprolog*. Edited by Günter Kruck. Darmstadt: WBG, 2009.

———. *Judaism and the Jews in the Gospel of John*. Subsidia Biblica 30. Rome: Pontificio Istituto Biblico, 2006.

———. "Die 'Juden' und der Tod Jesu im Johannesevangelium." Pages 59-76 in *Studien zu den johanneischen Schriften*. SBAB 25. Stuttgart: Katholisches Bibelwerk, 1998.

———. "Kirche als Sekte? Zum Kirchenbild der johanneischen Abschiedsreden." Pages 21-32 in *Studien zu den johanneischen Schriften*. SBAB 25. Stuttgart: Katholisches Bibelwerk, 1998.

———. "'Lasst uns mit ihm gehen, um mit ihm zu sterben' (Joh 11,16)." Pages 327-43 in

*"Perché stessero con lui."* Edited by Lorenzo de Santos, Santi Grasso, and Klemens Stock. AnBib 180. Rome: Gregorian & Biblical Press, 2010.

———. "'Levatevi, partiamo di qui' (Gv 14,31). Un invito ad un itinerario spirituale?" Pages 133–43 in *"Il vostro frutto rimanga" (Gv 16,16): Miscellanea per il LXX compleanno di Giuseppe Ghiberti*. Edited by Anna Passoni Dell'Acqua. Supplementi alla Rivista biblica 46. Bologna: EDB, 2005.

———. "Literarische Gattungen im Johannesevangelium. Ein Forschungsbericht 1919–1980." *ANRW* 25.3.2506–2568. Part 2, *Principat*, 25.3. Edited by H. Temporini and W. Haase. New York: De Gruyter 1989.

———. "μαρτυρέω." *EWNT* 2:958–964; *EDNT* 2:389–91.

———. "μαρτυρία." *EWNT* 2:964–973; *EDNT* 2:391–393.

———. *Martyria. Traditionsgeschichtliche Untersuchungen zum Zeugnisthema bei Johannes*. Frankfurter theologische Studien 10. Frankfurt am Main: Knecht, 1972.

———. *Neue Studien zu den johanneischen Schriften = New Studies on the Johannine Writings*. BBB 167. Göttingen: Vandenhoeck and Ruprecht, 2012.

———. "Psalm 42/43 im Johannesevangelium." Pages 77–106 in *Studien zu den johanneischen Schriften*. SBAB 25. Stuttgart: Katholisches Bibelwerk, 1998.

———. "Resurrection and the Forgiveness of Sins: John 20:23 against Its Traditional Background." Pages 237–51 in *Resurrection of Jesus in the Gospel of John*. Edited by Craig R. Koester and Reimund Bieringer. WUNT 222. Tübingen: Mohr Siebeck, 2008.

———. "5. Sonntag in der Osterzeit (B): Joh 15,1–8." www.perikopen.de

———. "6. Sonntag in der Osterzeit (B): Joh 15,9–17." in: www.perikopen.de

———. "So sehr hat Gott die Welt geliebt (Joh 3,16). Zum Heilsuniversalismus im Johannesevangelium." Pages 263–74 in *Studien zu den johanneischen Schriften*. SBAB 25. Stuttgart: Katholisches Bibelwerk, 1998.

———. *Studien zu den johanneischen Schriften*. SBAB 25. Stuttgart: Katholisches Bibelwerk, 1998.

———. "Synoptic Jesus Tradition in the Johannine Farewell Discourse." Pages 165–73 in *Jesus in Johannine Tradition*. Edited by Robert T. Fortna and Tom Thatcher. Louisville: Westminster John Knox, 2001.

———. "Two Ways of Gathering. The Plot to Kill Jesus in John 11.47–53." *NTS* 40 (1994): 399–406.

———. "Die Überleitung zu den johanneischen Abschiedsreden (Joh 13,31f.). Ein Beispiel der 'relecture.'" Pages 239–50 in *Studien zu Matthäus und Johannes: Festschrift für Jean Zumstein zu seinem 65. Geburtstag = Etudes sur Matthieu et Jean: mélanges offerts à Jean Zumstein pour son 65e anniversaire*. Edited by Andreas Dettwiler and Uta Poplutz. ATANT 97. Zürich: TVZ, 2009.

———. "'Und das Wort ist Fleisch geworden...' Zur Menschwerdung nach dem Johannesprolog." Pages 33–42 in *Studien zu den johanneischen Schriften*. SBAB 25. Stuttgart: Katholisches Bibelwerk, 1998.

———. "'Und die Finsternis hat es nicht ergriffen.' Zur Deutung von Joh 1,5." Pages 29–40 in *Im Geist und in der Wahrheit: Studien zum Johannesevangelium und zur Offenbarung des Johannes sowie andere Beiträge*. Edited by Konrad Huber and Boris Repschinski. NTAbh 52. Münster: Aschendorff, 2008.

## BIBLIOGRAPHY

———. "Unterwegs von der Trauer zur Hoffnung und zum Glauben. Jesu Gespräch mit Marta in Joh 11,20–27." *Gregorianum* 87 (2006): 312–23.
———. "Zerwick, Max." *LTK* 10: 1939f.
———. "Zeuge, Zeugnis, Zeugenschaft. I. Biblisch." *LTK* 10: 1440–42.
———. "Zur Struktur von Joh 6." Pages 247–62 in *Studien zu den johanneischen Schriften*. SBAB 25. Stuttgart: Katholisches Bibelwerk, 1998.
———. "Zwei Weisen der Sammlung. Der Todesbeschluss gegen Jesus in Joh 11,47–53." Pages 275–83 in *Studien zu den johanneischen Schriften*. SBAB 25. Stuttgart: Katholisches Bibelwerk, 1998.
Beutler, Johannes, and Robert T. Fortna, eds. *The Shepherd Discourse of John 10 and Its Context: Studies*. SNTSMS 67. Cambridge: Cambridge University Press, 1991.
Beutler, Johannes, Jean-Daniel Kaestli, Jean-Michael Poffet, and Jean Zumstein, eds. *La communauté johannique et son histoire*. Monde de la Bible. Geneva: Labor et Fides, 1990.
Beutler, Johannes, and A. Meredith. "Johannesevangelium (u. –Briefe)." *RAC* 18 (1998): 646–63.
Bienaimé, Germain. *Moïse et le don de l'eau dans la tradition juive ancienne: Targum et midrash*. AnBib 98. Rome: Biblical Institute Press, 1984.
Bienert, Wolfgang A., ed. *Einheit als Gabe und Verpflichtung. Eine Studie des Deutschen Ökumenischen Studienausschusses (DÖSTA) zu Johannes 17 Vers 21*. Frankfurt am Main: Lembeck, 2002.
Bieringer, Reimund. "I Am Ascending to My Father and Your Father, to My God and Your God (John 20:17): Resurrection and Ascension in the Gospel of John." Pages 209–35 in *Resurrection of Jesus in the Gospel of John*. Edited by Craig R. Koester and Reimund Bieringer. WUNT 222. Tübingen: Mohr Siebeck, 2008.
———. "'They Have Taken Away My Lord.' Text-Immanent Repetitions and Variations in John 20, 1–1." Pages 609–30 in *Repetitions and Variations in the Fourth Gospel: Style, Text, Interpretation*. Edited by Gilbert van Belle, Michael Labahn, and P. Maritz. BETL 223. Leuven: Peeters, 2009.
Bieringer, Reimund, Didier Pollefeyt, and Frederique Vandecasteele-Vanneuville, eds. *Anti-Judaism and the Fourth Gospel: Papers of the Leuven Colloquium, 2000*. Jewish and Christian Heritage Series 1. Assen, the Netherlands: Royal Van Gorcum, 2001.
Bishop, Jonathan. "Encounters in the New Testament." Pages 285–94 in *Literary Interpretations of Biblical Narratives II*. Edited by Kenneth R. R. Gros Louis. Nashville: Abingdon, 1982.
Bjerkelund, Carl J. *Tauta egeneto: Die Präzisierungssätze im Johannesevangelium*. WUNT 40. Tübingen: Mohr Siebeck, 1987.
Blank, Josef. *Krisis: Untersuchungen zur johanneischen Christologie und Eschatologie*. Freiburg im Breisgau: Lambertus-Verlag, 1964.
———. "Die Verhandlung vor Pilatus Joh 18,28–19,16 im Lichte johanneischer Theologie." *BZ* 3 (1959): 60–81.
Blaskovic, Goran. "Die Erzählung vom reichen Fischfang (Lk 5,1–11; Joh 21,1–14). Wie Johannes eine Erzählung aus dem Lukasevangelium für seine Zwecke umschreibt." Pages 103–20 in *Johannes aenigmaticus: Studien zum Johannesevangelium für Herbert Leroy*. Biblische Untersuchungen 29. Regensburg: Pustet, 2000.

Blass, Friedrich, and Albert Debrunner. *Grammatik des neutestamentlichen Griechisch.* 15th ed. Göttingen: Vandenhoeck und Ruprecht, 1979.

Böcher, Otto. *Der johanneische Dualismus im Zusammenhang des nachbiblischen Judentums.* Gütersloh: Verlagshaus Gerd Mohn, 1965.

Böhler, Dieter. "Abraham und seine Kinder im Johannesprolog. Zur Vielgestaltigkeit des alttestamentlichen Textes bei Johannes." Pages 15-29 in *L'Écrit et l'Esprit. Études d'histoire du texte et de théologie biblique en hommage à Adrian Schenker.* Edited by Dieter Böhler, Innocent Himbaza, and Philippe Hugo. OBO 214. Fribourg: Academic Press; Göttingen: Vandenhoeck & Ruprecht, 2005.

Boers, Hendrikus. *Neither on This Mountain Nor in Jerusalem: A Study of John 4.* SBLMS 35. Atlanta: Scholars Press, 1988.

Boismard, Marie-Émile. "L'évolution du thème eschatologique dans les traditions johanniques." *RB* 68 (1961): 507-24.

———. *Le prologue de Saint Jean.* LD 11. Paris: Editions du Cerf, 1963.

Borgen, Peder. *Bread from Heaven: An Exegetical Study of the Concept of Manna in the Gospel of John and the Writings of Philo.* NovTSup 10. Leiden: Brill, 1965.

———. "The Sabbath Controversy in John 5:1-18 and Analogous Controversy Reflected in Philo's Writings." Pages 105-20 in *Early Christianity and Hellenistic Judaism.* Edinburgh: T&T Clark, 1996.

———. "The Scriptures and the Words and Works of Jesus." Pages 39-58 in *What We Have Heard From the Beginning: The Past, Present, and Future of Johannine Studies.* Edited by Tom Thatcher. Waco, TX: Baylor University Press, 2007.

Borig, Rainer. *Der wahre Weinstock. Untersuchungen zu Joh 15,1-10.* SANT 16. Munich: Kösel, 1967.

Boring, M. Eugene. "John 5:19-24." *Int* 45 (1991): 176-81.

Bornhäuser, Karl. *Das Johannesevangelium, eine Missionsschrift für Israel.* BFCT 2.15. Gütersloh: Bertelsmann, 1928.

Bornkamm, Günther. "Zur Interpretation des Johannesevangeliums. Eine Auseinandersetzung mit Ernst Käsemanns Schrift 'Jesu letzter Wille nach Joh 17.'" *EvT* 28 (1968): 8-25.

Botha, J. Eugene. *Jesus and the Samaritan Woman: A Speech Act Reading of John 4:1-42.* NovTSup 65. Leiden: Brill, 1991.

Bowman, John. *Samaritanische Probleme. Studien zum Verhältnis von Samaritanertum, Judentum und Urchristentum.* Stuttgart: Kohlhammer, 1967.

Brant, Jo-Ann, *Dialogue and Drama. Elements of Greek Tragedy in the Fourth Gospel.* Peabody, MA: Hendrickson, 2004.

Brémond, Claude. *Logique du récit.* Paris: Seuil, 1973.

Brodie, Thomas L. "Jesus as the New Elisha: Cracking the Code." *ExpTim* 93 (1981): 39-42.

Brown, Raymond E. *The Death of the Messiah. From Gethesmane to the Grave. A Commentary on the Passion Narratives in the Four Gospels.* 2 vols. New York: Doubleday, 1994.

———. *The Epistles of John. Translated with Introduction, Notes, and Commentary.* AB 30. Garden City, NY: Doubleday, 1982.

———. "Incidents That Are Units in the Synoptic Gospels but Dispersed in St. John." *CBQ* 23 (1961): 143-60.

———. "Die Rolle der Frau im vierten Evangelium." Pages 145–55 in *Ringen um die Gemeinde. Der Weg der Kirche nach den Johanneischen Schriften*. Salzburg: Müller, 1982.
Brown, Raymond E., Karl Donfried, and John H. P. Reumann, eds. *Peter in the New Testament: A Collaborative Assessment by Protestant and Roman Catholic Scholars*. Minneapolis: Fortress, 1973.
Bultmann, Rudolf. "Die Bedeutung der neuerschlossenen mandäischen und manichäischen Quellen für das Verständnis des Johannesevangeliums." *ZNW* 24 (1925): 100–46.
———. *Exegetica. Aufsätze zur Erforschung des Neuen Testaments*. Edited by Erich Dinkler. Tübingen: Mohr Siebeck, 1967.
———. *Die Geschichte der synoptischen Tradition*. FRLANT 29. 6th ed. Göttingen: Vandenhoeck & Ruprecht, 1964.
———. *Theologie des Neuen Testaments*. 5th ed. Tübingen: Mohr Siebeck, 1965.
Busse, Ulrich. "Das Eröffnungszeugnis Joh 1,19–34–Erzählstrategie und -ziel." Pages 33–41 in *ΕΠΙΤΟΑΥΤΟ*. Edited by Jiří Mrázek, Rut Dvořáková, and Štěpán Brodský. Prague: Univerzita Karlova, 1998.
———. "Open Questions on John 10." Pages 6–17 and 135–43 in *The Shepherd Discourse of John 10 and Its Context: Studies*. Edited by Johannes Beutler and Robert T. Fortna. SNTSMS 67. Cambridge: Cambridge University Press, 1991.
Caba, José. *Cristo. Pan de Vida*. Biblioteca de autores cristianos 531. Madrid : Editorial católica, 1993.
Calduch-Benages, Núria. "La fragancia del perfume en Jn 12.3." *EstBib* 48 (1990): 243–65.
Caragounis, Chrys C. "What Did Jesus Mean by τὴν ἀρχὴν in Joh 8:25?" *NovT* 49 (2007): 129–47.
Cardellino, L. "Chi rifiuta la parola di Dio non comprenderebbe neppure se fossero scritte tutte le conversioni (Gv 21,25)." *RivB* 45 (1997): 429–37.
———. "Testimoni che Gesù è il Cristo (Gv 20,31) affinché tutti credano δι' αὐτοῦ (Gv 1,7)." *RivB* 45 (1997): 79–85.
Carson, D. A. "The Function of the Paraclete in John 16:7–11." *JBL* 98 (1979): 547–66.
———. "The Purpose of the Fourth Gospel: John 20:31 Reconsidered." *JBL* 106 (1987): 639–51.
———. "Syntactical and Text-Critical Observations on John 20:30–31: One More Round on the Purpose of the Fourth Gospel." *JBL* 124 (2005): 693–714.
Cassidy, Richard J. *John's Gospel in New Perspective: Christology and the Realities of Roman Power*. Maryknoll, NY: Orbis Books, 1992.
Cazeaux, Jacques. "Concept ou mémoire? La rhétorique de Jean, chap. 8, v. 12–59." Pages 277–308 in *Origine et postérité de l'évangile de Jean. XIII$^e$ Congrès de l'ACFEB Toulouse (1989)*. Edited by Alain Marchadour. Paris: Cerf, 1990.
Ceulemans, Reinhart. "The Name of the Pool in Joh 5,2. A Text-Critical Note concerning 3Q15." *ZNW* 99 (2008): 112–15.
Charbonneau, André. "'Qu'as-tu fait?' et 'D'où es-tu?' Le procès de Jésus chez Jean (18,28–19,16a)." *ScEs* 38 (1986): 203–19, 317–29.
Charlesworth, James H. *The Old Testament Pseudepigrapha*. 2 vols. Garden City, NY: Doubleday. 1983–1985.

Chibici-Revneanu, Nicole. "Variations on Glorification. John 13,31f. and Johannine δόξα-Language." Pages 511–22 in *Repetitions and Variations in the Fourth Gospel: Style, Text, Interpretation*. Edited by Gilbert van Belle, Michael Labahn, and P. Maritz. BETL 223. Leuven: Peeters, 2009.

Claudel, Gérard. "Jean 20,23 et ses parallèles matthéens." *RevScRel* 69 (1995): 71–86.

Claussen, Carsten. "Das Gebet in Joh 17 im Kontext von Gebeten aus zeitgenössischen Pseudepigraphen." Pages 205–32 in *Kontexte des Johannesevangeliums: Das vierte Evangelium in religions- und traditionsgeschichtlicher Perspektive*. Edited by Jörg Frey and Udo Schnelle. WUNT 175. Tübingen: Mohr Siebeck, 2004.

Clivaz, Claire. "D'autres disaient qu'un ange lui avait parlé (Jn 12,29)." Pages 169–85 in *Studien zu Matthäus und Johannes: Festschrift für Jean Zumstein zu seinem 65. Geburtstag = Etudes sur Matthieu et Jean: mélanges offerts à Jean Zumstein pour son 65e anniversaire*. Edited by Andreas Dettwiler and Uta Poplutz. ATANT 97. Zürich: TVZ, 2009.

Coloe, Mary L. *God Dwells with Us. Temple Symbolism in the Fourth Gospel*. Collegeville, MN: Liturgical Press, 2001.

———. "The Missing Feast of Pentecost." SNTSU 34 (2009): 97–114.

———. "Sources in the Shadows: John 13 and the Johannine Community." Pages 69–82 in *New Currents through John: A Global Perspective*. Edited by Francisco Lozada, Jr., and Tom Thatcher. Atlanta: Scholars Press, 2006.

———. "Welcome into the Household of God. The Footwashing in John 13." *CBQ* 66 (2004) 400–415.

Colpe, Carsten. *Die religionsgeschichtliche Schule. Darstellung und Kritik ihres Bildes vom gnostischen Erlösermythus*. FRLANT 78, NF 60. Göttingen: Vandenhoeck & Ruprecht, 1961.

Corley, Jeremy. "The Dishonoured Prophet in John 4,44. John the Baptist Foreshadowing Jesus." Pages 625–34 in *The Death of Jesus in the Fourth Gospel*. Edited by Gilbert van Belle. BETL 200. Leuven: Peeters 2007.

Cortès, Enric. *Los discursos de adios de Gn 49 a Jn 13–17. Pistas para la historia de un género literario en la antigua literatura judía*. Barcelona: Herder, 1976.

Cory, Catherine. "Wisdom's Rescue: A New Reading of the Tabernacles Discourse (John 7:1–8:59)." *JBL* 116 (1997): 95–116.

Cothenet, Edouard. "La nourriture du Christ et sa mission." Pages 181–91 in *Nourriture et repas dans les milieux juifs et chrétiens de l'antiquité: Mélanges offerts au professeur Charles Perrot*. Edited by Michel Quesnel, Yves-Marie Blanchard, and Claude Tassin. Paris: Cerf, 1999.

Culpepper, R. Alan. "Un exemple de commentaire fondé sur la critique narrative: Jean 5,1–18." Pages 135–51 in *La communauté johannique et son histoire*. Edited by Johannes Beutler, Jean-Daniel Kaestli, Jean-Michel Poffet, and Jean Zumstein. Monde de la Bible. Geneva: Labor et Fides, 1990.

———, ed. *Critical Readings of John 6*. Leiden: Brill, 1997.

———. "Current Research in Retrospect." Pages 247–57 in *Critical Readings of John 6*. Edited by R. Alan Culpepper. Leiden: Brill, 1997.

———. "The Theology of the Johannine Passion Narrative: John 19:16–30." *Neot* 31.1 (1997): 21–37.

Daise, Michael A. *Feasts in John: Jewish Festivals and Jesus' "Hour" in the Fourth Gospel.* WUNT 2.229. Tübingen: Mohr Siebeck, 2007.
Danby, Herbert. *The Mishnah.* Oxford: Oxford University Press, 1933.
Danna, Elizabeth. "A Note on John 4:29." *RB* 106 (1999): 219–23.
Daube, David. "Jesus and the Samaritan Woman: The Meaning of συγχράομαι." *JBL* 69 (1950): 137–47.
Dauer, Anton. *Die Passionsgeschichte im Johannesevangelium. Eine traditionsgeschichtliche und theologische Untersuchung zu Joh 18,1–19,30.* SANT 30. Munich: Kosel-Verlag, 1972.
———. "Spuren der (synoptischen) Synedriumsverhandlung im 4. Evangelium." Pages 307–39 in *John and the Synoptics.* Edited by Adelbert Denaux. BETL 101. Leuven: Peeters, 1992.
Dautzenberg, Gerhard. "Freiheit im hellenistischen Kontext." Pages 57–81 in *Der neue Mensch in Christus. Hellenistische Anthropologie und Ethik im Neuen Testament.* Edited by Johannes Beutler. QD 190. Freiburg im Breisgau: Herder, 2001.
De Boer, Martinus C. "Jesus' Departure to the Father in John: Death or Resurrection?" Pages 1–19 in *Theology and Christology in the Fourth Gospel. Essays by Members of the SNTS Johannine Writings Seminar.* Edited by Gilbert van Belle, J. G. van der Watt, and P. Maaritz. BETL 184. Leuven: Peeters, 2005.
———. "The Narrative Function of Pilate in John." Pages 141–58 in *Narrativity in Biblical and Related Texts = La narrativité dans la Bible et les textes apparentés.* Edited by George J. Brooke and Jean-Daniel Kaestli. BETL 149. Leuven: Peeters, 2000.
De La Potterie, Ignace. *La conception et la naissance virginales de Jésus d'après le IV$^e$ évangile.* 2nd ed. EtThéolB 11. Paris: Lumen Gentium, 1981.
———. "Et à partir de cette heure, le Disciple l'accueillit dans son intimité" (Jn 19,27b). Réflexions méthodologiques sur l'interprétation d'un verset johannique." *Marianum* 42 (1980): 84–125.
———. "Jésus roi et juge d'après Jn 19,13 ἐκάθισεν ἐπὶ βήματος." *Bib* 41 (1960): 217–47.
———. "La parole de Jésus 'Voici ta mère' et l'accueil du Disciple (Jn 19,27)." *Marianum* 36 (1974): 1–39.
———. *La passion de Jésus selon l'Évangile de Jean.* Paris: Cerf, 1986.
———. "Structure du Prologue de Saint Jean." *NTS* 30 (1984): 354–81.
———. *La vérité dans Saint Jean.* AnBib 73–74. Rome: Biblical Institute Press, 1977.
Delebecque, Edouard. "Autour du verbe eimi, 'je suis,' dans le quatrième évangile (Note sur Jn VIII,25)." *Revue Thomiste Toulouse* 86 (1986): 83–89.
Dennis, John. "Conflict and Resolution: John 11:47–53 as the Ironic Fulfillment of the Main Plot-Line of the Gospel of John (John 1.1–12)." *SNTSU* 29 (2004): 23–39.
———. *Jesus' Death and the Gathering of True Israel. The Johannine Appropriation of Restoration Theology in the Light of John 11.47–52.* WUNT 2.217. Tübingen: Mohr Siebeck, 2006.
———. "The 'Lifting Up of the Son of Man' and the Dethroning of the 'Ruler of This World.' Jesus' Death as the Defeat of the Devil in John 12,31–32." Pages 677–91 in *The Death of Jesus in the Fourth Gospel.* Edited by Gilbert van Belle. BETL 200. Leuven: Peeters 2007.
———. "Restoration in John 11,47–52: Reading the Key Motifs in the Jewish Context." *ETL* 81 (2005): 57–86.

Derrett, J. Duncan M. "Circumcision and Perfection: a Johannine Equation (John 7:22–23)." *EvQ* 63.3 (1991): 211–24.

———. "Oriental Sources for John 8,32–36?" *BibOr* 43 (2001): 29–32.

Destro, Adriana. and Mauro Pesce. "Kinship, Discipleship, and Movement: An Anthropological Study of John's Gospel." *BibInt* 3 (1995): 266–84.

Dettwiler, Andreas. *Die Gegenwart des Erhöhten. Eine exegetische Studie zu den johanneischen Abschiedsreden (Joh 13,31–16,33) unter besonderer Berücksichtigung ihres Relecture-Charakters*. FRLANT 169. Göttingen: Vandenhoeck & Ruprecht, 1995.

———. "Le prologue johannique (Jean 1,1–18)." Pages 185–203 in *La communauté johannique et son histoire*. Edited by Johannes Beutler, Jean-Daniel Kaestli, Jean-Michel Poffet, and Jean Zumstein. Monde de la Bible. Geneva: Labor et Fides, 1990.

Devillers, Luc. "La croix de Jésus et les Ἰουδαῖοι (Jn 19,16). Crux interpretum ou clé sotériologique?" Pages 384–407 in *The Death of Jesus in the Fourth Gospel*. Edited by Gilbert van Belle. BETL 200. Leuven: Peeters 2007.

———. *La Fête de l'Envoyé. La section johannique de la Fête des Tentes (Jean 7,1–10,21) et la christologie*. Études bibliques NS 49. Paris: Gabalda, 2002.

———. "Une piscine peut cacher une autre. A propos de Jean 5,1–9a." *RB* 106 (1999): 175–205.

———. "Le prologue du quatrième Évangile, clé de voûte de la littérature johannique." *NTS* 58 (2012): 317–30.

———. "Le sein du Père. La finale du prologue de Jean." *RB* 112 (2005): 63–79.

———. "Thomas—appelé Didyme (Jn 11,16; 20,24; 21,2). Pour une nouvelle approche du prétendu jumeau." *RB* 113 (2006): 65–77.

———. "Les trois témoins. Une structure pour le quatrième évangile." *RB* 104 (1997): 40–87.

Dibelius, Martin. *Die Formgeschichte des Evangeliums*. 3rd ed. Tübingen: Mohr Siebeck, 1959.

Diebold-Scheuermann, Carola. *Jesus vor Pilatus. Eine exegetische Untersuchung zum Verhör durch Pilatus (Joh 18,28–19,16a)*. SBB 32. Stuttgart: Verlag Katholisches Bibelwerk, 1996.

———. "Jesus vor Pilatus: Eine Gerichtsszene. Bemerkungen zur joh. Darstellungsweise." *BN* 84 (1996): 64–74.

Dietzfelbinger, Christian. *Der Abschied des Kommenden. Eine Auslegung der johanneischen Abschiedsreden*. WUNT 95. Tübingen: Mohr Siebeck, 1997.

———. "'Die größeren Werke (Joh 14,12f.).'" *NTS* 35 (1989): 27–47.

———. "Die theologische Bewältigung von Tod und Abwesenheit Jesu in den Abschiedsreden des Johannesevangeliums." *Jahrbuch für Biblische Theologie* 19 (2004): 217–41.

Dinechin, Olivier de. "Καθώς: La similitude dans l'évangile selon Saint Jean." *RSR* 58 (1970): 195–236.

Dodd, C. H. *Historical Tradition in the Fourth Gospel*. Cambridge: Cambridge University Press, 1963.

———. *The Interpretation of the Fourth Gospel*. Cambridge: Cambridge University Press, 1953.

―――. "Une parabole cachée dans le quatrième Évangile." *Revue d'Histoire et de Philosophie Religieuses* 42 (1962): 107–15.

Donahue, John R., ed. *Life in Abundance: Studies of John's Gospel in Tribute to Raymond E. Brown*. Collegeville, MN: Liturgical Press, 2005.

Dschulnigg, Peter. "Nikodemus im Johannesevangelium." SNTSU 24 (1999): 103–18.

Dunderberg, Ismo. *Johannes und die Synoptiker: Studien zu Joh 1–9*. Annales Academiae Scientiarum Fennicae, Dissertationes Humanarum Litterarum 69. Helsinki: Suomalainen Tiedeakatemia, 1994.

Duprez, Antoine. *Jésus et les dieux guérisseurs. A propos de Jean*. Cahiers de la Revue Biblique 12. Paris: Gabalda, 1970.

Du Rand, Jan A. Entolē *in die Johannesevangelie en –Briewe*. Nieuwe-Testamentiese Werkgemeenskap van Suid-Afrika. Pretoria: Universiteit van Pretoria, 1981.

―――. *Johannine Perspectives. Introduction to the Johannine Writings*. Pretoria: Orion, 1997.

Earl, Douglas S. "'(Bethany) Beyond the Jordan': The Significance of a Johannine Motif." *NTS* 55 (2009): 279–94.

Egger, Wilhelm. *Methodenlehre zum Neuen Testament*. Freiburg im Breisgau: Herder, 1987.

Eisele, Wilfried. "Jesus und Dionysos. Göttliche Konkurrenz bei der Hochzeit zu Kana (Joh 2,1–11)." *ZNW* 100 (2009): 1–28.

Enders, Markus, and Rolf Kühn. *"Im Anfang war der Logos. . . ." Studien zur Rezeptionsgeschichte des Johannesevangeliums von Antike bis Gegenwart*. Forschungen zur europäischen Geistesgeschichte 11. Freiburg im Breisgau: Herder, 2011.

Ensor, Peter W. "The Glorification of the Son of Man. An Analysis of John 13:31–32." *TynBul* 58 (2007): 229–52.

Escaffre, Bernadette. "Pierre et Jésus dans la cour du grand prêtre (Jn 18,12–27)." *RTL* 31 (2000): 43–67.

Evans, Craig A. "The Function of Isaiah 6:9–10 in Mark and John." *NovT* 24 (1982): 124–38.

―――. "On the Quotation Formulas in the Fourth Gospel." *BZ* 26 (1982): 79–83.

Fauré, Alexander. "Die alttestamentlichen Zitate im 4. Evangelium und die Quellenscheidungshypothese." *ZNW* 21 (1922): 99–121.

Fee, Gordon D. "On the Text and Meaning of John 20,30–31." Pages 2193–2205 in *The Four Gospels, 1992: Festschrift Frans Neirynck*. Edited by Frans van Segbroeck. BETL 100. Leuven: Peeters, 1992.

Felsch, Dorit. *Die Feste im Johannesevangelium. Jüdische Tradition und christologische Deutung*. WUNT 2.308. Tübingen: Mohr Siebeck, 2011.

Fernando, G. Charles A. *The Relationship between Law and Love in the Gospel of John. A Detailed Scientific Research on the Concepts of Law and Love in the Fourth Gospel and Their Relationship to Each Other*. European University Studies, Theology 772. Frankfurt am Main: Lang, 2004.

Fiebig, Paul. *Antike Wundergeschichten zum Studium der Wunder des Neuen Testaments*. Bonn: Marcus & Weber, 1911.

―――. *Jüdische Wundergeschichten des neutestamentlichen Zeitalters unter besonderer Berücksichtigung ihres Verhältnisses zum Neuen Testament bearbeitet*. Tübingen: Mohr Siebeck, 1911.

———. *Rabbinische Wundergeschichten des neutestamentlichen Zeitalters*. 2nd ed. Berlin: De Gruyter, 1933.
Fischer, Günter. *Die himmlischen Wohnungen. Untersuchungen zu Joh 14,2f*. European University Studies, Theology 38. Frankfurt am Main: Lang, 1975.
Fischer, Georg, and Martin Hasitschka. *Sulla tua parola. Vocazione e sequela nella Bibbia*. Rome: AdP, 1998.
Fischer, Joseph A., *Die Apostolischen Väter*. Schriften des Urchristentums 1. Darmstadt: Wissenschaftliche Buchgesellschaft, 1986.
Flink, Timo. "Son and Chosen. A Text-Critical Study of John 1,34." *Filologia Neotestamentaria* 18 (2005); 85–109.
Fortna, Robert T. "Diachronic/Synchronic Reading of John 21 and Luke 5." Pages 387–99 in *John and the Synoptics*. Edited by Adelbert Denaux. BETL 101. Leuven: Peeters, 1992.
———. *The Fourth Gospel and Its Predecessor: From Narrative Source to Present Gospel*. Philadelphia: Fortress, 1988.
———. *The Gospel of Signs*. Cambridge: Cambridge University Press, 1970.
———. "Theological Use of Locale in the Fourth Gospel." Pages 58–95 in *Gospel Studies in Honor of Sherman Elbridge Johnson*. Edited by Massey Hamilton Shepherd and Edward C. Hobbs. Anglican Theological Review, Supplementary Series 3. Evanston, IL: Anglican Theological Review, 1974.
———, and Tom Thatcher. *Jesus in Johannine Tradition*. Louisville: Westminster John Knox, 2001.
Freed, Edwin D. "Jn 1,19–27 in Light of Related Passages in John, the Synoptics, and Acts." Pages 1943–61 in *The Four Gospels, 1992: Festschrift Frans Neirynck*. Edited by Frans van Segbroeck. BETL 100. Leuven: Peeters, 1992.
———. *Old Testament Quotations in the Gospel of John*. NovTSup 11. Leiden: Brill, 1965.
———. "Psalm 42/43 in John's Gospel." *NTS* 29 (1983): 62–73.
Frey, Jörg. "Edler Tod-wirksamer Tod-stellvertretender Tod-heilschaffender Tod. Zur narrativen und theologischen Deutung des Todes Jesu im Johannesevangelium." Pages 65–94 in *The Death of Jesus in the Fourth Gospel*. Edited by Gilbert van Belle. BETL 200. Leuven: Peeters, 2007.
———. "'Ich habe den Herrn gesehen' (Joh 20,18). Entstehung, Inhalt und Vermittlung des Osterglaubens nach Johannes 20." Pages 267–84 in *Studien zu Matthäus und Johannes: Festschrift für Jean Zumstein zu seinem 65. Geburtstag = Etudes sur Matthieu et Jean: mélanges offerts à Jean Zumstein pour son 65e anniversaire*. Edited by Andreas Dettwiler and Uta Poplutz. ATANT 97. Zürich: TVZ, 2009.
———. *Die johanneische Eschatologie I–III*. WUNT 96, 110, 117. Tübingen: Mohr Siebeck, 1997–2000.
Frühwald-König, Johannes. *Tempel und Kult. Ein Beitrag zur Christologie des Johannesevangeliums*. Biblische Untersuchungen 27. Regensburg: Pustet, 1998.
Fuchs, Albert. "Das Verhältnis der synoptischen agreements zur johanneischen Tradition, untersucht anhand der messianischen Perikope Mk 6,32–44 par Mt 14,13–21 par Lk 9,10–17; Joh 6,1–15." SNTSU 27 (2002): 85–115.
Galot, Jean. *Être né de Dieu, Jean 1,13*. AnBib 37. Rome: Biblical Institute Press, 1969.
Gardner-Smith, P. *Saint John and the Synoptic Gospels*. Cambridge: Cambridge University Press, 1938.

Garský, Zbyněk. *Das Wirken Jesu in Galiläa. Eine strukturale Analyse der Intertextualität des vierten Evangeliums mit den Synoptikern*. WUNT 2.325. Tübingen: Mohr Siebeck, 2012.

Gaventa, Beverly V. "The Archive of Excess: John 21 and the Problem of Narrative Closure." Pages 240-52 in *Exploring the Gospel of John: In Honor of D. M. Smith*. Edited by R. Alan Culpepper and C. Clifton Black. Louisville: Westminster John Knox, 1996.

Giblin, Charles H. "John's Narration of the Hearing before Pilate (John 18,28-19,16a)." *Bib* 67 (1986): 221-39.

———. "The Miraculous Crossing of the Sea (Jn 6,16-21)." *NTS* 29 (1983): 96-103.

———. "The Tripartite Narrative Structure of John's Gospel." *Bib* 71 (1990): 449-68.

Girard, Marc. "Cana ou l' 'heure' de la vraie noce (Jean 2,1-12). Structure stilistique et processus de symbolization." Pages 99-109 in *"Il vostro frutto rimanga" (Gv 16,16): Miscellanea per il LXX compleanno di Giuseppe Ghiberti*. Edited by Anna Passoni Dell'Acqua. Supplementi alla Rivista biblica 46. Bologna: EDB, 2005.

———. "Le paradigme de la naissance dans Jn 3,1-21. Critique structurelle et interprétation symbolique." Pages 307-26 in *"Perché stessero con lui."* Edited by Lorenzo de Santos, Santi Grasso, and Klemens Stock. AnBib 180. Rome: Gregorian & Biblical Press, 2010.

Giurisato, Ghiberti. "Il comandamento di Gesù e l'odio del mondo (Gv 15,9-17.18-25)." Pages 145-61 in *"Il vostro frutto rimanga" (Gv 16,16): Miscellanea per il LXX compleanno di Giuseppe Ghiberti*. Edited by Anna Passoni Dell'Acqua. Supplementi alla Rivista biblica 46. Bologna: EDB, 2005.

Gordley, Matthew. "The Johannine Prologue and Jewish Didactic Hymn Traditions: A New Case for Reading the Prologue as a Hymn." *JBL* 128 (2009): 781-802.

Gourges, Michel. "L'aveugle-né (Jn 9). Du miracle au signe: typologie des réactions à l'égard du Fils de l'homme." *NRTh* 104 (1982): 381-95.

———. "Hautē de estin hē krisis (Jn 3,19)." Pages 129-37 in *Le Jugement dans l'un et l'autre Testament*. Edited by Claude Coulot and Denis Fricker. Paris: Cerf, 2004.

Gruber, Margareta. "Die Zumutung der Gegenseitigkeit. Zur johanneischen Deutung des Todes Jesu anhand einer pragmatisch-intertextuellen Lektüre." Pages 647-60 in *The Death of Jesus in the Fourth Gospel*. Edited by Gilbert van Belle. BETL 200. Leuven: Peeters, 2007.

Gundry, Robert H. "The Sense and Syntax of John 3:14-17 with Special Reference to the Use of οὕτως ... ὥστε in John 3:16." *NovT* 41 (1999): 24-39.

Haag, E. "Aus Angst zur Freude, aus Resignation zu Perspektiven, aus Müdigkeit zu Vollmacht (Joh 20,19-23)." *TBei* 27 (1996): 57-60.

Hahn, Ferdinand. "Die Hirtenrede in Joh 10." Pages 185-200 in *Theologia crucis—signum crucis: Festschrift für Erich Dinkler zum 70. Geburtstag*. Edited by Carl Andresen and Günter Klein. Tübingen: Mohr Siebeck, 1979.

Hakola, Raimo. "The Burden of Ambiguity: Nicodemus and the Social Identity of the Johannine Christians." *NTS* 55 (2009): 438-55.

Haldimann, Konrad. *Rekonstruktion und Entfaltung. Exegetische Untersuchungen zu Joh 15 und 16*. BZNW 104. Berlin: De Gruyter, 2000.

Harris, Elizabeth. *Prologue and Gospel. The Theology of the Fourth Evangelist*. JSNTSup 107. Sheffield: Sheffield Academic Press, 1994.

Hartenstein, Judith. "Aus Schmerz wird Freude (Die gebärende Frau). Joh 16,21f." Pages 840–47 in *Kompendium der Gleichnisse Jesu*. Edited by Ruben Zimmermann. Gütersloh: Gütersloher Verlagshaus, 2007.

Hartman, Lars. "An Attempt at a Text-Centered Exegesis of John 21." Pages 69–87 in *Text-Centered New Testament Studies. Text-Theoretical Essays on Early Jewish and Early Christian Literature*. Edited by Lars Hartman and David Hellholm. WUNT 102. Tübingen: Mohr Siebeck, 1997,

Hasitschka, M. "The Significance of the Resurrection Appearance in John 21." Pages 311–28 in *Resurrection of Jesus in the Gospel of John*. Edited by Craig R. Koester and Reimund Bieringer. WUNT 222. Tübingen: Mohr Siebeck, 2008.

Hatina, Thomas R. "John 20,22 in Its Eschatological Context." *Bib* 74 (1993): 196–219.

Heckel, Ulrich. *Hirtenamt und Herrschaftskritik. Die urchristlichen Ämter aus johanneischer Sicht*. Biblisch-theologische Studien 65. Neukirchen-Vluyn: Neukirchener, 2004.

Heekerens, Hans-Peter. *Die Zeichen-Quelle der johanneischen Redaktion. Ein Beitrag zur Entstehungsgeschichte des vierten Evangeliums*. SBS 113. Stuttgart: Katholisches Bibelwerk, 1984.

Heider, George C. "The Gospel according to John: The New Testament's Deutero-Deuteronomy?" *Bib* 93 (2012): 68–85.

Heil, Christoph. "Jesus aus Nazareth oder Betlehem? Historische Tradition und ironischer Stil im Johannesevangelium." Pages 109–30 in *Im Geist und in der Wahrheit: Studien zum Johannesevangelium und zur Offenbarung des Johannes sowie andere Beiträge*. Edited by Konrad Huber and Boris Repschinski. NTAbh 52. Münster: Aschendorff, 2008.

Heil, John Paul. *Blood and Water. The Death and Resurrection of Jesus in John 18–21*. CBQMS 27. Washington, DC: Catholic Biblical Association of America, 1995.

———. *Jesus Walking on the Sea. Meaning and Gospel Functions of Matt 14:22–33, Mark 6:45–52 and John 6:15b–21*. AnBib 87. Rome: Biblical Institute Press, 1981.

Hengel, Martin. "Der 'dionysische' Messias. Zur Auslegung des Weinwunders in Kana (Joh 2,1–11)." Pages 568–600 in *Jesus und die Evangelien. Kleine Schriften V*. WUNT 211. Tübingen: Mohr Siebeck, 2007.

———. *Die Evangelienüberschriften*. Sitzungsberichte der Heidelberger Akademie der Wissenschaften, Philosophisch-Historische Klasse 1984.3. Heidelberg: Winter, 1984.

———. "The Interpretation of the Wine Miracle at Cana. John 2.1–11." Pages 108–12 in *The Glory of Christ in the New Testament. Studies in Memory of G. B. Caird*. Edited by L. D. Hurst and N. T. Wright. Oxford: Oxford University Press, 1987.

———. *Die johanneische Frage. Ein Lösungsversuch*. Contribution on the Apocalypse from Jörg Frey. WUNT 67. Tübingen: Mohr Siebeck, 1993.

Hennecke, Edgar, and Wilhelm Schneemelcher. *Neutestamentliche Apokryphen in deutscher Übersetzung*. 2 vols. Tübingen: Mohr Siebeck, 1964–1968.

Hieronymus. *Commentariorum in Ezechielem Prophetam libri XIV*. Edited by François Glorie. CCSL 75. Turnhout: Brepols, 1964.

Hirsch, Emanuel. *Studien zum vierten Evangelium*. BHT 11. Tübingen: Mohr Siebeck, 1936.

Hoegen-Rohls, Christina. *Der nachösterliche Johannes. Die Abschiedsreden als herme-*

*neutischer Schlüssel zum vierten Evangelium.* WUNT 2.84. Tübingen: Mohr Siebeck, 1996.

Hofius, Otfried. "Das Wunder der Wiedergeburt. Jesu Gespräch mit Nikodemus in Joh 3,1–21." Pages 33–80 in *Johannesstudien. Untersuchungen zur Theologie des vierten Evangeliums.* Edited by Otfried Hofius and Hans-Christian Kammler. WUNT 88. Tübingen: Mohr Siebeck, 1996.

———. "Die Auferweckung des Lazarus. Joh 11,1–44 als Zeugnis narrativer Christologie." Pages 28–45 in *Exegetische Studien.* WUNT 223. Tübingen: Mohr Siebeck, 2008.

Hofrichter, Peter, ed. *Für und wider die Priorität des Johannesevangeliums. Symposion in Salzburg am 10. März 2000.* Theologische Texte und Studien 9. Hildesheim: Olms, 2002.

———. *Im Anfang war der "Johannesprolog." Das urchristliche Logosbekenntnis–die Basis neutestamentlicher und gnostischer Theologie.* Biblische Untersuchungen 17. Regensburg: Pustet, 1986.

———. "Johannes 21 im Makrokontext des Vierten Evangeliums." *TGl* 81 (1991): 302–22.

Holloway, Paul A. "Left Behind: Jesus' Consolation of His Disciples in John 13,31–17,26." *ZNW* 96 (2005): 1–34.

Hübenthal, Sandra. *Transformation und Aktualisierung. Zur Rezeption von Sach 9–14 im Neuen Testament.* SBB 57. Stuttgart: Katholisches Bibelwerk, 2006.

———. "Wie kommen Schafe und Rinder in den Tempel? Die 'Tempelaktion' (Joh 2,13–22) in kanonisch-intertextueller Lektüre." Pages 69–81 in *Intertextualität. Perspektiven auf ein interdisziplinäres Arbeitsfeld.* Edited by Karen Hermann. Aachen: Shaker, 2007.

Hübner, Hans. "ΕΝ ΑΡΧΗΙ ΕΓΩ ΕΙΜΙ." Pages 107–22 in *Israel und seine Heilstraditionen im Johannesevangelium.* Edited by Michael Labahn, Klaus Scholtissek, and Angelika Strotmann. Paderborn: Schöningh, 2004.

Hutton, Jeremy M. "'Bethany Beyond the Jordan' in Text, Tradition and Historical Geography." *Bib* 89 (2008): 305–28.

Janssens de Varebeke, A. "La structure des scènes du récit de la passion en Joh., 18–19. Recherches sur les procédés de composition et de rédaction du Quatrième Évangile." *ETL* 38 (1962): 504–22.

Jeremias, Joachim. *Die Abendmahlsworte Jesu.* 4th ed. Göttingen: Vandenhoeck & Ruprecht, 1964.

———. "ποιμήν." *TWNT* 6:484–501.

Jojko, Bernadeta. *Worshiping the Father in Spirit and Truth. An Exegetical-Theological Study of Jn 4:20–26 in the Light of the Relationship among the Father, the Son and the Holy Spirit.* Tesi Gregoriana, Serie Teologia 194. Rome: Pontificia Università Gregoriana, 2012.

Judge, Peter J. "John 20,24–29. More than Doubt, Beyond Rebuke." Pages 913–30 in *The Death of Jesus in the Fourth Gospel.* Edited by Gilbert van Belle. BETL 200. Leuven: Peeters, 2007.

———. "A Note on John 20,29." Pages 2183–92 in *The Four Gospels, 1992: Festschrift Frans Neirynck.* Edited by Frans van Segbroeck. BETL 100. Leuven: Peeters, 1992.

Jüngling, Hans-Winfried. *Der Tod der Götter. Eine Untersuchung zu Ps 82*. SBS 38. Stuttgart: Katholisches Bibelwerk, 1969.
Kähler, Martin. *Der sogenannte historische Jesus und der geschichtliche, wirkliche Christus*. Munich: A. Deichert, 1892.
Käsemann, Ernst. *Jesu letzter Wille nach Johannes 17*. Tübingen: Mohr Siebeck, 1966.
Kammler, Hans-Christian. *Christologie und Eschatologie. Joh 5,17–30 als Schlüsseltext johanneischer Theologie*. WUNT 126. Tübingen: Mohr Siebeck, 2000.
———. "Jesus Christus und der Geistparaklet. Eine Studie zur johanneischen Verhältnisbestimmung von Pneumatologie und Christologie." Pages 87–190 in *Johannesstudien. Untersuchungen zur Theologie des vierten Evangeliums*. Edited by Otfried Hofius. WUNT 88. Tübingen: Mohr Siebeck, 1996.
———. "Die 'Zeichen' des Auferstandenen. Überlegungen zur Exegese von Joh 20,30+31." Pages 191–211 in *Johannesstudien. Untersuchungen zur Theologie des vierten Evangeliums*. Edited by Otfried Hofius. WUNT 88. Tübingen: Mohr Siebeck, 1996.
Karakolis, Christos. "'Across the Kidron Brook, Where There Was a Garden' (John 18,1). Two Old Testament Allusions and the Theme of the Heavenly King in the Johannine Passion Narrative." Pages 751–60 in *The Death of Jesus in the Fourth Gospel*. Edited by Gilbert van Belle. BETL 200. Leuven: Peeters, 2007.
Karlsen Seim, Turid. "Roles of Women in the Gospel of John." Pages 56–73 in *Aspects on the Johannine Literature. Papers Presented at a Conference of Scandinavian N. T. Exegetes at Uppsala, June 1986*. Edited by Lars Hartman and Birger Olsson. Stockholm: Almqvist & Wiksell, 1986.
Keith, Chris. "The Claim of John 7.15 and the Memory of Jesus' Literacy." *NTS* 56 (2010): 44–63.
———. "The Initial Location of the Pericopa Adulterae in Fourfold Tradition." *NovT* 51 (2009): 209–31.
Kellum, L. Scott. *The Unity of the Farewell Discourse: The Literary Integrity of John 13.31–16.33*. JSNTSup 256. London: T&T Clark, 2004.
Kempter, Mylène. "La signification eschatologique de Jean 3,29." *NTS* 54 (2008): 42–59.
Kiefer, Odo. *Die Hirtenrede. Analyse und Deutungen von Joh 10,1–18*. SBS 23. Stuttgart: Katholisches Bibelwerk, 1967.
Kierspel, Lars. "'Dematerializing' Religion. Reading John 2–4 as a Chiasm." *Bib* 89 (2008): 526–54.
Kiley, Mark. "Three More Fish Stories (John 21:11)." *JBL* 127 (2008): 529–31.
Kimelman, Reuven. "Birkat Ha-Minim and the Lack of Evidence for an Anti-Christian Jewish Prayer." Pages 226–44 in *Jewish and Christian Self-Definition*. Volume 2: *Aspects of Judaism in the Greco-Roman Period*. Edited by E. P. Sanders, A. I. Baumgarten, and Alan Mendelson. London, 1981.
Kirchschläger, Peter G. "'Ich bin der Weg, die Wahrheit und das Leben' (Joh 14,6). Der Wahrheitsanspruch des johanneischen Christus und Wahrheit in anderen Religionen." *BL* 85 (2012): 123–47.
———. *Nur ich bin die Wahrheit. Der Absolutheitsanspruch des johanneischen Christus und das Gespräch zwischen den Religionen*. HBS 63. Freiburg: Herder, 2010.
Klauck, Hans-Josef. "Geschrieben, erfüllt, vollendet: die Schriftzitate in der Johan-

nespassion." Pages 140–57 in *Israel und seine Heilstraditionen im Johannesevangelium*. Edited by Michael Labahn, Klaus Scholtissek, and Angelika Strotmann. Paderborn: Schöningh, 2004.

———. *Judas–ein Jünger des Herrn*. QD 111. Freiburg: Herder, 1987.

Koch, Dietrich-Alex. "Der Täufer als Zeuge des Offenbarers. Das Täuferbild von Joh 1,19–34 auf dem Hintergrund von Mk 1,2–11." Pages 1963–84 in *The Four Gospels, 1992: Festschrift Frans Neirynck*. Edited by Frans van Segbroeck. BETL 100. Leuven: Peeters, 1992.

Koch, Kurt K. "Christliche Ökumene im Licht des Betens Jesu. 'Jesus von Nazareth' und die ökumenische Sendung." Pages 19–36 in *Passion aus Liebe. Das Jesus-Buch des Papstes in der Diskussion*. Edited by Jan Heiner Tück. Ostfildern: Matthias Grünewald Verlag, 2011.

Koester, Helmut. "Gnostic Sayings and Controversy in John 8:12–59." Pages 97–110 in *Nag Hammadi, Gnosticism, and Early Christianity*. Edited by Charles W. Hedrick and Robert Hodgson Jr. Peabody, MA: Hendrickson, 1986.

Kollmann, Hanjo-Christoph. *Die Kreuzigung Jesu nach Joh 19,16–22. Ein Beitrag zur Kreuzestheologie des Johannes im Vergleich mit den Synoptikern*. Europäische Hochschulschriften Theologie 878. Frankfurt am Main: Lang, 2008.

Konings, Johan. "The Dialogue of Jesus, Philip and Andrew in John 6,5–9." Pages 523–34 in *John and the Synoptics*. Edited by Adelbert Denaux. BETL 101. Leuven: Peeters, 1992.

Koperski, Veronica. "The Mother of Jesus and Mary Magdalene. Looking Back and Forward from the Cross in John 19,25–27." Pages 849–58 in *The Death of Jesus in the Fourth Gospel*. Edited by Gilbert van Belle. BETL 200. Leuven: Peeters, 2007.

Korting, Georg. "Binden und Lösen. Zu Verstockungs- und Befreiungstheologie in Mt 16,19; 18,18.21–35 und Joh 15,1–17; 20,23." SNTSU 14 (1989): 39–91.

Körtner, H.-J., and Martin Leutzsch. *Papiasfragmente, Hirt des Hermas*. Schriften des Urchristentums 3. Darmstadt: Wissenschaftliche Buchgesellschaft, 1998.

Kossen, H. B. "Who Were the Greeks of John 12,20?" Pages 91–110 in *Studies in John*. NovTSup 24. Leiden: Brill, 1970.

Kragerud, Alv. *Der Lieblingsjünger im Johannesevangelium. Ein exegetischer Versuch*. Oslo: Osloer Universitätsverlag, 1959.

Kraus, Wolfgang. "Die Vollendung der Schrift nach Joh 19,28. Überlegungen zum Umgang mit der Schrift im Johannesevangelium." Pages 629–39 in *The Scriptures in the Gospels*. Edited by Christopher Tuckett. BETL 131. Leuven: University Press, 1997.

Kreitzer, Larry J., and Deborah Rooke, eds. *Ciphers in the Sand. Interpretations of the Woman Taken in Adultery (John 7:53–8:11)*. The Biblical Seminar 74. Sheffield: Sheffield Academic Press, 2000.

Kremer, Jacob. *Lazarus. Die Geschichte einer Auferstehung. Text, Wirkungsgeschichte und Botschaft von Joh 11,1–46*. Stuttgart: Katholisches Bibelwerk, 1985.

———. "'Nimm deine Hand und lege sie in meine Seite!' Exegetische, hermeneutische und bibeltheologische Überlegungen zu Joh 20,24–29." Pages 2153–81 in *The Four Gospels, 1992: Festschrift Frans Neirynck*. Edited by Frans van Segbroeck. BETL 100. Leuven: Peeters, 1992.

Kubis, Adam. *The Book of Zechariah in the Gospel of John*. EBib 64. Paris: Gabalda, 2012.

Kügler, Joachim. *Der Jünger, den Jesus liebte. Literarische, theologische und historische Untersuchungen zu einer Schlüsselgestalt johanneischer Theologie und Geschichte; mit einem Exkurs über die Brotrede in Joh 6*. SBB 16. Stuttgart: Katholisches Bibelwerk, 1988.

Kuhn, Hans-Jürgen. *Christologie und Wunder. Untersuchungen zu Joh 1,35–51*. Biblische Untersuchungen 18. Regensburg: Pustet, 1988.

Kühschelm, Roman. "Gericht und Rettung. Joh 12,29–33 im Kontext der 'Hellenenrede.'" Pages 131–53 in *Im Geist und in der Wahrheit: Studien zum Johannesevangelium und zur Offenbarung des Johannes sowie andere Beiträge*. Edited by Konrad Huber and Boris Repschinski. NTAbh 52. Münster: Aschendorff, 2008.

———. *Verstockung, Gericht und Heil. Exegetische und bibeltheologische Untersuchung zum sogenannten "Dualismus" und "Determinismus" in Joh 12,35–50*. BBB 76. Frankfurt am Main: Hain, 1990.

Kurz, William S. "Test Case: 'Whose Sins You Shall Forgive' in John 20: Applying Scripture with the Catechism." Pages 237–48 in *The Future of Catholic Biblical Scholarship. A Constructive Conversation*. Edited by Luke Timothy Johnson and William S. Kurz. Grand Rapids: Eerdmans, 2002.

Kysar, Robert. "The Dismantling of Decisional Faith: A Reading of John 6:25–71." Pages 161–81 in *Critical Readings of John 6*. Edited by R. Alan Culpepper. Leiden: Brill, 1997.

———. *The Fourth Evangelist and His Gospel: An Examination of Contemporary Scholarship*. Minneapolis: Augsburg, 1975.

———. *John, the Maverick Gospel*. Louisville: Westminster John Knox Press, 1993.

Labahn, Michael. "Bedeutung und Frucht des Todes Jesu im Spiegel des johanneischen Erzähllaufbaus." Pages 431–56 in *The Death of Jesus in the Fourth Gospel*. Edited by Gilbert van Belle. BETL 200. Leuven: Peeters, 2007.

———. "Beim Mahl am Kohlenfeuer trifft man sich wieder (Die Offenbarung beim wunderbaren Fischfang). Joh 21,1–14." Pages 764–77 in *Kompendium der frühchristlichen Wundererzählungen. Vol 1. Die Wunder Jesu*. Edited by Ruben Zimmermann. Gütersloh: Verlagshaus, 2013.

———. "'Blinded by the Light.' Blindheit, sehen und Licht in Joh 9. Ein Spiel von Variation und Wiederholung durch Erzählung und Metapher." Pages 453–509 in *Repetitions and Variations in the Fourth Gospel: Style, Text, Interpretation*. Edited by Gilbert van Belle, Michael Labahn, and P. Maritz. BETL 223. Leuven: Peeters, 2009.

———. "Bultmanns Konzeption der existentialen Interpretation des neutestamentlichen Kerygmas am Beispiel seiner Exegese des Corpus Iohanneum. Versuch einer Annäherung im Spiegel der neueren Johannesauslegung." Pages 171–207 in *Bultmann und Luther. Lutherrezeption in Exegese und Hermeneutik Rudolf Bultmanns*. Edited by Ulrich H. J. Körtner. Hannover: VELKD, 2010.

———. "Fischen nach Bedeutung—Sinnstiftung im Wandel literarischer Kontexte. Der wunderbare Fischfang in Johannes 21 zwischen Inter- und Intratextualität." SNTSU 32 (2007): 115–40.

———. "'It's Only Love'—Is That All? Limits and Potentials of Johannine 'Ethic'—A Critical Evaluation of Research." Pages 3–43 in *Rethinking the Ethics of John. "Implicit Ethics" in the Johannine Writings*. Edited by Jan Gabriël Van der Watt and Ruben Zimmermann. Contexts and Norms of New Testament Ethics III. WUNT 291. Tübingen: Mohr Siebeck, 2012.

———. *Jesus als Lebensspender. Untersuchungen zu einer Geschichte der johanneischen Tradition anhand ihrer Wundergeschichten*. BZNW 98. Berlin: De Gruyter, 1999.

———. "Jesus und die Autorität der Schrift im Johannesevangelium. Überlegungen zu einem spannungsreichen Verhältnis." Pages 185–206 in *Israel und seine Heilstraditionen im Johannesevangelium*. Edited by Michael Labahn, Klaus Scholtissek, and Angelika Strotmann. Paderborn: Schöningh, 2004.

———. "Living Word(s) and the Bread of Life." Pages 59–62 in *What We Have Heard from the Beginning: The Past, Present, and Future of Johannine Studies*. Edited by Tom Thatcher. Waco, TX: Baylor University Press, 2007.

———. *Offenbarung in Zeichen und Wort. Untersuchungen zur Vorgeschichte von Joh 6,1–25a und seiner Rezeption in der Brotrede*. WUNT 2.117. Tübingen: Mohr Siebeck, 2000.

———. "Eine Spurensuche anhand von Joh 5,1–18. Bemerkungen zu Wachstum und Wandel der Heilung eines Lahmen." *NTS* 44 (1998): 159–79.

———. "Der Weg eines Namenlosen—vom Hilflosen zum Vorbild (Joh 9). Ansätze zu einer narrativen Ethik der sozialen Verantwortung im vierten Evangelium." Pages 63–80 in *Die bleibende Gegenwart des Evangeliums: Festschrift für Otto Merk zum 70. Geburtstag*. Edited by Roland Gebauer and Martin Meiser. MTS 76. Marburg: N. G. Elwert, 2003.

Labahn, Michael, and Manfred Lang. "Johannes und die Synoptiker. Positionen und Impulse seit 1990." Pages 443–515 in *Kontexte des Johannesevangeliums: Das vierte Evangelium in religions- und traditionsgeschichtlicher Perspektive*. Edited by Jörg Frey and Udo Schnelle. WUNT 175. Tübingen: Mohr Siebeck, 2004.

Landis, Stephan. *Das Verhältnis des Johannesevangeliums zu den Synoptikern. Am Beispiel von Mt 8,5–13; Lk 7,1–10; Joh 4,46–54*. BZNW 74. Berlin: De Gruyter, 1994.

Lang, Manfred. "Johanneische Abschiedsreden und Senecas Konsolationsliteratur. Wie konnte ein Römer Joh 13,31–17,26 lesen?" Pages 365–412 in *Kontexte des Johannesevangeliums: Das vierte Evangelium in religions- und traditionsgeschichtlicher Perspektive*. Edited by Jörg Frey and Udo Schnelle. WUNT 175. Tübingen: Mohr Siebeck, 2004.

Langbrandtner, Wolfgang. *Weltferner Gott oder Gott der Liebe? Der Ketzerstreit in der johanneischen Kirche. Eine exegetisch-religionsgeschichtliche Untersuchung mit Berücksichtigung der koptisch-gnostischen Texte aus Nag-Hammadi*. BET 6. Frankfurt am Main: Lang, 1977.

Lattke, Michael. "Joh 20,30f als Buchschluss." *ZNW* 78 (1987): 288–92.

Lausberg, Heinrich. *Der Johannes-Prolog. Rhetorische Befunde zu Form und Sinn des Textes*. Nachrichten der Akademie der Wissenschaften in Göttingen. Göttingen: Vandenhoeck und Ruprecht, 1984.

Lee, Dorothy. "The Prologue and Jesus' Final Prayer." Pages 229–31 in *What We Have Heard from the Beginning: The Past, Present, and Future of Johannine Studies*. Edited by Tom Thatcher. Waco, TX: Baylor University Press, 2007.

Lee, Hye Ja. "*Signore, vogliamo vedere Gesù.*" *La conclusione dell'attività pubblica di*

*Gesù secondo Gv 12,20-36*. Tesi Gregoriana, Serie Teologia, 124. Rome: Pontificia Università Gregoriana, 2005.

Létourneau, Pierre. "'Damit ich keinen Durst mehr habe.' Das Wasser des Lebens im Johannesevangelium." *Concilium* 48 (2012): 514-23.

Lindars, Barnabas. "Capernaum Revisited. Jn 4,46-54 and the Synoptics." Pages 1985-2000 in *The Four Gospels, 1992: Festschrift Frans Neirynck*. Edited by Frans van Segbroeck. BETL 100. Leuven: Peeters, 1992.

―――. "Rebuking the Spirit. A New Analysis of the Lazarus Story of John 11." Pages 542-47 in *John and the Synoptics*. Edited by Adelbert Denaux. BETL 101. Leuven: Peeters, 1992,

Link, Andrea. *"Was redest du mir ihr?" Eine Studie zur Exegese-, Redaktions- und Theologiegeschichte von Joh 4,1-42*. Biblische Untersuchungen 24. Regensburg: Pustet, 1992.

Lohfink, Norbert. *Das Hauptgebot. Eine Untersuchung literarischer Einleitungsfragen zu Dtn 5-11*. AnBib 20. Rome: Pontificio Istituto Biblico, 1963.

―――. "Der Messiaskönig und seine Armen kommen zum Zion. Beobachtungen zu Matt 21,1-17." Pages 179-200 in *Studien zum Matthäusevangelium*. Edited by Ludger Schenke. Stuttgart: Katholisches Bibelwerk, 1988.

Lohse, Eduard, and Annette Steudel, eds. *Die Texte aus Qumran*. 2 vols. Darmstadt: Wissenschaftliche Buchgesellschaft, 2001.

López Rosas, Ricardo. *La señal del templo. Jn 2,13-22. Redefinición Cristológica de lo Sacro*. Colección biblioteca mexicana UPM 12. Mexico: Universidad Pontificia de México, 2001.

Lowe, Malcolm. "Who Were the Ἰουδαῖοι?" *NovT* 18 (1976): 101-30.

Lozada, Francisco, Jr., and Tom Thatcher, eds. *New Currents through John: A Global Perspective*. Leiden: Brill, 2006.

Lührmann, Dieter. *Das Markusevangelium*. HNT 3. Tübingen: Mohr Siebeck, 1987.

Lütgehetmann, Walter. *Die Hochzeit von Kana (Joh 2,1-11). Zu Ursprung und Deutung einer Wunderzählung im Rahmen johanneischer Redaktionsgeschichte*. Biblische Untersuchungen 20. Regensburg: Pustet, 1990.

Luther, Martin. "Vorrede zum Neuen Testament." Pages 29-34 in *Luther Deutsch. Die Werke Martin Luthers in neuer Auswahl für die Gegenwart*. Vol. 5. Edited by Kurt Aland. Göttingen: Vandenhoeck und Ruprecht, 1991.

Luzárraga, Jesus. "El nardo y la Sulamita en la unción de Maryam (Jn 12,1-8)." *Gregorianum* 83 (2002): 679-715.

Mackay, Ian D. *John's Relationship with Mark. An Analysis of John 6 in the Light of Mark 6-8*. WUNT 2.182. Tübingen: Mohr Siebeck, 2004.

MacRae, George W. "Nag Hammadi and the New Testament." Pages 144-57 in *Gnosis: Festschrift fur Hans Jonas*. Edited by Barbara Aland. Gottingen: Vandenhoeck and Ruprecht, 1978.

Madden, Patrick J. *Jesus' Walking on the Sea. An Investigation of the Origin of the Narrative Account*. BZNW 81. Berlin: De Gruyter, 1997.

Maier, Johann. "Das jüdische Verständnis des Psalms 82 und das Zitat aus Psalm 82,6 in Joh 10,34-35." Pages 15-28 in *Im Geist und in der Wahrheit: Studien zum Johannesevangelium und zur Offenbarung des Johannes sowie andere Beiträge*. Edited by Konrad Huber and Boris Repschinski. NTAbh 52. Münster: Aschendorff, 2008.

Malatesta, Edward. *Interiority and Covenant. A Study of εἶναι ἐν and μένειν ἐν in the First Letter of Saint John*. AnBib 69. Rome: Biblical Institute Press, 1978.

Manns, Frédéric. "La fête des Juifs de Jean 5,1." *Antonianum* 70 (1995): 117–24.

Manzi, Franco. "Resa credente o resistenza incredula al segno della risurrezione di Lazzaro." Pages 111–18 in *"Il vostro frutto rimanga" (Gv 16,16): Miscellanea per il LXX compleanno di Giuseppe Ghiberti*. Edited by Anna Passoni Dell'Acqua. Supplementi alla Rivista biblica 46. Bologna: EDB, 2005.

Marcheselli, Maurizio. *"Avete qualcosa da mangiare?" Un pasto, il Risorto, la comunità*. Biblioteca di Teologia dell' evangelizzazione 2. Bologna: EDB, 2006.

Marcus, Joel. "Rivers of Living Water from Jesus' Belly (John 7:38)." *JBL* 117 (1998): 328–30.

Mardaga, Hellen. "The Meaning and the Function of the Threefold Repetition ἐγώ εἰμι in Jn 18.5.6.8. The Fulfilment of Jesus' Protecting Love on the Eve of His Death." Pages 761–68 in *The Death of Jesus in the Fourth Gospel*. Edited by Gilbert van Belle. BETL 200. Leuven: Peeters, 2007.

Marguerat, Daniel. "Le point de vue dans le récit: Matthieu, Jean et les autres." Pages 91–107 in *Studien zu Matthäus und Johannes: Festschrift für Jean Zumstein zu seinem 65. Geburtstag = Etudes sur Matthieu et Jean: mélanges offerts à Jean Zumstein pour son 65e anniversaire*. Edited by Andreas Dettwiler and Uta Poplutz. ATANT 97. Zürich: TVZ, 2009.

Markl, Dominik. "Spielen Joh 1,1; 20,30f; 21,24 auf den Rahmen des Pentateuch an?" Pages 107–19 in *Führe mein Volk heraus : zur innerbiblischen Rezeption der Exodusthematik*. Edited by Simone Paganini. Frankfurt am Main: Lang, 2004.

Markstahler, Uwe. *Der Prolog im Licht der jüdischen Tradition. Der Johannesprolog—ein Schöpfungsbericht*. Bibelstudien 4. Berlin: Lit, 2010.

Martin, Michael W. "Betrothal Journey Narratives." *CBQ* 70 (2008): 505–23.

Martini, Carlo M. *Il problema della recensionalità del codice B alla luce del papiro Bodmer XIV*. AB 26. Rome: Pontificio Istituto Biblico, 1966.

Martyn, J. Louis. *The Gospel of John in Christian History: Essays for Interpreters*. New York: Paulist Press, 1978.

———. *History and Theology in the Fourth Gospel*. New York: Harper & Row, 1968.

Marucci, Corrado. "Il significato del numero 153 in Gv 21,11." *RivB* 52 (2004): 403–40.

März, Claus-Peter. "'Siehe, dein König kommt zu dir. . . .' Der 'Einzug' in Jerusalem." *IKaZ* 38 (2009): 5–13.

Matera, Frank J. "Jesus before Annas: John 18:13–14, 19–24." *ETL* 66 (1990): 38–55.

McCarthy, Dennis J. *Treaty and Covenant. A Study in Form in the Ancient Oriental Documents and in the Old Testament*. AnBib 21. 2nd ed. Rome: Biblical Institute Press, 1981.

McGrath, James F. "Prologue as Legitimation. Christological Controversy and the Interpretation of John 1:1–18." *IBS* 19 (1997): 98–120.

McKay, K. L. "Style and Significance in the Language of John 21:15–17." *NovT* 27 (1985): 319–33.

Meeks, Wayne A. "Equal to God." Pages 91–105 in *Search of the Early Christians: Selected Essays*. Edited by Allen R. Hilton and H. Gregory Snyder. New Haven: Yale University Press, 2002.

———. "Galilee and Judea in the Fourth Gospel." *JBL* 85 (1966): 159–69.

---. *The Prophet-King: Moses Traditions and the Johannine Christology*. NovTSup 14. Leiden: Brill, 1967.
Ménard, J.-E. "Le 'rassemblement' dans le Nouveau Testament et la gnose." Pages 366–71 in *Studia Evangelica VI*. Edited by Elizabeth A. Livingstone. TUGAL 112. Berlin: Akademie-Verlag, 1973.
Menken, Maarten J. J. "'Born of God' or 'Begotten by God'? A Translation Problem in the Johannine Writings." *NovT* 51 (2009): 352–68.
---. "Die Feste im Johannesevangelium." Pages 269–89 in *Israel und seine Heilstraditionen im Johannesevangelium*. Edited by Michael Labahn, Klaus Scholtissek, and Angelika Strotmann. Paderborn: Schöningh, 2004.
---. "John 6:51c–58: Eucharist or Christology?" Pages 183–204 in *Critical Readings of John 6*. Edited by R. Alan Culpepper. Leiden: Brill, 1997.
---. *Old Testament Quotations in the Fourth Gospel: Studies in Textual Form*. CBET 15. Kampen: Kok Pharos, 1996.
---. "'Rivers of Living Water Shall Flow from His Inside' (John 7:38)." Pages 187–203 in *Old Testament Quotations in the Fourth Gospel: Studies in Textual Form*. CBET 15. Kampen: Kok Pharos, 1996.
Merklein, Helmut. "Gott und Welt. Eine exemplarische Interpretation von Joh 2,23–3,21; 12,20–36 zur theologischen Bestimmung des johanneischen Dualismus." Pages 263–81 in *Studien zu Jesus und Paulus II*. WUNT 105. Tübingen: Mohr Siebeck, 1998.
Metzger, Bruce M. *A Textual Commentary on the Greek New Testament. A Companion Volume to the United Bible Societies' Greek New Testament*. 4th rev. ed. Stuttgart: Deutsche Bibelgesellschaft, 1994.
Metzner, Rainer. "Der Geheilte von Johannes 5–Repräsentant des Unglaubens." *ZNW* 90 (1999): 177–93.
Meyer, Annegret. *Kommt und seht. Mystagogie im Johannesevangelium ausgehend von Joh 1,35–51*. FB 103. Würzburg: Echter, 2005.
Migliasso, Secondo. *La presenza dell'Assente. Saggio di analisi letterario-strutturale e di sintesi teologica di Gv 13,31–14,31*. Rome: Pontificia Università Gregoriana, 1979.
Miller, Eddie L. *Salvation-History in the Prologue of John. The Significance of John 1:3/4*. NovTSup 60. Leiden: Brill, 1989.
Mlakuzhyil, George. *Christocentric Literary-Dramatic Structure of John's Gospel*. 2nd ed. AnBib 117. Rome: Gregorian & Biblical Press, 2011.
Moberly, R. W. L. "How Can We Know the Truth? A Study of John 7:14–18." Pages 239–57 in *The Art of Reading Scripture*. Edited by Ellen F. Davis and Richard B. Hays. Grand Rapids: Eerdmans, 2003.
Mohamed, A. F., and T. Sorg. "Friede sei mit euch! (Joh 20,19–23)." *TBei* 26 (1995): 113–17.
Moloney, Francis J. "Can Everyone Be Wrong? A Reading of John 11:1–12:8." *NTS* 49 (2003): 505–27.
---. "The Function of Prolepsis in the Interpretation of John 6." Pages 129–48 in *Critical Readings of John 6*. Edited by R. Alan Culpepper. Leiden: Brill, 1997.
---. *The Johannine Son of Man*. Biblioteca di scienze religiose 14. Rome: LAS, 1976.
---. "Narrative and Discourse at the Feast of Tabernacles John 7:1–8:59." Pages 155–

72 in *Word, Theology, and Community in John.* Edited by John Painter, R. Alan Culpepper, and Fernando F. Segovia. St. Louis: Chalice Press, 2002.

Mörchen, Roland. "Johanneisches 'Jubeln.'" *BZ* 30 (1986): 248–50.

Morgen, Michèle. "Les femmes dans l'évangile de Jean." *Revue de Droit Canonique* 40 (1990): 77–96.

———. "Le festin des Noces de Cana (Jn 2,1–11) et le repas d'adieu (Jn 13,1–30). A l'archè et au telos." Pages 139–54 in *Nourriture et repas dans les milieux juifs et chrétiens de l'antiquité: Mélanges offerts au professeur Charles Perrot.* Edited by Michel Quesnel, Yves-Marie Blanchard, and Claude Tassin. Paris: Cerf, 1999.

———. "Le (fils) monogène dans les écrits johanniques: Évolution des traditions et élaboration rédactionelle." *NTS* 53 (2007): 165–83.

———. "Jean 3 et les évangiles synoptiques." Pages 514–22 in *John and the Synoptics.* Edited by Adelbert Denaux. BETL 101. Leuven: Peeters, 1992.

———. "Le roi d'Israël vient vers la fille de Sion." Pages 334–50 in *Israel und seine Heilstraditionen im Johannesevangelium.* Edited by Michael Labahn, Klaus Scholtissek, and Angelika Strotmann. Paderborn: Schöningh, 2004.

Müller, C. G. "Der Zeuge und das Licht. Joh 1,1–4,3 und das Darstellungsprinzip der σύγκρισις." *Bib* 84 (2003): 479–509.

Müller, Karlheinz. "Joh 9,7 und das jüdische Verständnis des Siloh-Spruches." *BZ* 13 (1969): 251–56.

Neirynck, Frans. "The Anonymous Disciple in John 1." *EThL* 66 (1990): 5–37.

———. "ΕΙΣ ΤΑ ΙΔΙΑ. Jn 19,27 (et 16,32)." Pages 456–64 in *Evangelica I: Collected Essays.* Edited by Frans Neirynck. BETL 60. Leuven: Peeters, 1982.

———. "John 5,1–18 and the Gospel of Mark. A Response to Peder Borgen." Pages 699–711 in *Evangelica II: 1982–1991: Collected Essays.* Edited by Frans van Segbroeck. BETL 99. Leuven: Peeters, 1991.

———. "John 21." *NTS* 36 (1990): 321–36.

———. "Note sur Jn 21,14." *ETL* 64 (1988): 429–32.

———. "Short Note on John 19,26–27." Pages 585–89 in *Evangelica III: 1992–2000: Collected Essays.* Edited by Frans van Segbroeck. BETL 150. Leuven: Peeters, 2001.

*Neues Bibel-Lexikon.* Edited by Manfred Görg, Bernard Lang, Beatrice Rauschenbach, Barbara Fuss, Georg Gafus, and Cornelia Wimmer. 3 vols. Zürich: Benziger, 1991–2001.

*Neuer Wettstein. Texte zum Neuen Testament aus Griechentum und Hellenismus.* Vol. I/2. Texte zum Johannesevangelium. Edited by Udo Schnelle with assistance from Michael Labahn and Manfred Lang, Berlin: De Gruyter, 2001.

Neyrey, Jerome H. "'I Am the Door' (John 10:7,9): Jesus the Broker in the Fourth Gospel." *CBQ* 69 (2007): 271–91.

———. "I Said 'You Are Gods.' Psalm 82,6 and John 10." *JBL* 108 (1989): 647–62.

Nicacci, Alviero. "Logos e sapienza nel prologo di Giovanni." Pages 71–83 in *"Il vostro frutto rimanga" (Gv 16,16): Miscellanea per il LXX compleanno di Giuseppe Ghiberti.* Supplementi alla Rivista biblica 46. Edited by Anna Passoni Dell'Acqua. Bologna: EDB, 2005.

Nicklas, Tobias. "Die johanneische 'Tempelreinigung' (Joh 2,12–22) für Leser der Synoptiker." *TP* 80 (2005): 1–16.

———. "Literarkritik und Leserrezeption. Ein Beitrag zur Methodendiskussion am Beispiel Joh 2,23-4,3." *Bib* 83 (2002): 175-192.

———. "'153 große Fische' (Joh 21,11). Erzählerische Ökumene und 'johanneischer Überstieg.'" *Bib* 84 (2003): 366-387.

Nicol, W. *The Sēmeia in the Fourth Gospel*. NovTSup 32. Leiden: Brill, 1972.

Noetzel, Heinz. *Christus und Dionysos. Bemerkungen zum religionsgeschichtlichen Hintergrund von Joh 2,1-11*. AzTh 1. Stuttgart: Calwer Verlag, 1960.

Nongbri, Brent. "The Use and Abuse of $P^{52}$: Papyrological Pitfalls in the Dating of the Fourth Gospel." *HTR* 98 (2005): 23-48.

Nordheim, Eckhard von. *Die Lehre der Alten I. Das Testament als Literaturgattung im Judentum der hellenistisch-römischen Zeit*. ALGHJ 13. Leiden: Brill, 1980.

Obielosi, Dominic Chukwunonso. *Servant of God in John*. Europäische Hochschulschriften Theologie 878. Frankfurt am Main: Lang, 2008.

O'Brien, Kelli S. "Written That You May Believe: John 20 and Narrative Rhetoric." *CBQ* 67 (2005): 284-302.

O'Day, Gail R. "John 6:15-21: Jesus Walking on Water as Narrative Embodiment of Johannine Christology." Pages 149-59 in *Critical Readings of John 6*. Edited by R. Alan Culpepper. Leiden: Brill, 1997.

———. *Revelation in the Fourth Gospel: Narrative Method and Theological Claim*. Philadelphia: Fortress, 1986.

O'Donnell, Tim. "Complementary Eschatologies in John 5:19-30." *CBQ* 70 (2008): 750-65.

Ognibene, Bruno. "L'ignoranza del presidente del banchetto (Gv 2,9)." *Lateranum* 65 (1999): 123-30.

O'Grady, John F. "The Prologue and Chapter 17 of the Gospel of John." Pages 215-28 in *What We Have Heard from the Beginning: The Past, Present, and Future of Johannine Studies*. Waco, TX: Baylor University Press, 2007.

Öhler, Markus. "Der 'Mietling' Petrus. Beobachtungen zur 'relecture' von Joh 10 in Joh 21." Pages 239-55 in *Im Geist und in der Wahrheit: Studien zum Johannesevangelium und zur Offenbarung des Johannes sowie andere Beiträge*. Edited by Konrad Huber and Boris Repschinski. NTAbh 52. Münster: Aschendorff, 2008.

Okure, Teresa. *The Johannine Approach to Mission. A Contextual Study of John 4:1-42*. WUNT 2.31. Tübingen: Mohr Siebeck, 1988.

O'Loughlin, Thomas. "A Woman's Plight and the Western Fathers." Pages 83-104 in *Ciphers in the Sand. Interpretations of the Woman Taken in Adultery (John 7:53-8:11)*. Edited by Larry J. Kreitzer and Deborah W. Rooke. The Biblical Seminar 74. Sheffield: Sheffield Academic Press, 2000.

Olsson, Birger. "'All My Teaching Was Done in Synagogues. . .'" (John 18,20). Pages 203-24 in *Theology and Christology in the Fourth Gospel. Essays by Members of the SNTS Johannine Writings Seminar*. Edited by Gilbert van Belle, J. G. van der Watt, P. Maaritz. BETL 184. Leuven: Peeters, 2005.

———. *Structure and Meaning in the Fourth Gospel: A Text-Linguistic Analysis of John 2:1-11 and 4:1-42*. ConBNT 6. Lund: Gleerup, 1974.

Orsatti, Mauro. "'Mi ami di più di . . . .' Una proposta per Gv 21,15b." Pages 183-93 in *Generati da una parola di verità (Gc 1,18)*. Edited by Santi Grasso and Ermenegildo Manicardi. Supplementi alla Rivista biblica 47. Bologna: EDB, 2006.

Østenstad, Gunnar. "The Structure of the Fourth Gospel: Can It Be Defined Objectively?" *ST* 45 (1991): 33-55.
Overbeck, Franz. *Das Johannesevangelium. Studien zur Kritik seiner Erforschung. Aus dem Nachlass.* Edited by Carl Albrecht Bernouille. Tübingen: Mohr Siebeck, 1911.
Pagels, Elaine. *Beyond Belief: The Secret Gospel of Thomas.* New York: Random, 2003.
Painter, John. "The Farewell Discourses and the History of Johannine Christianity." *NTS* 27 (1981): 525-43.
———. "Jesus and the Quest for Eternal Life." Pages 61-94 in *Critical Readings of John 6.* Edited by R. Alan Culpepper. Leiden: Brill, 1997.
———. *John: Witness and Theologian.* 3rd ed. Mitcham, Australia: Beacon Hill Books.
———. "John 9 and the Interpretation of the Fourth Gospel." *JSNT* 28 (1986): 31-61.
———. "Quest and Rejection Stories in John." *JSNT* 36 (1989): 17-46.
———. *The Quest for the Messiah. The History, Literature and Theology of the Johannine Community.* 2nd ed. Edinburgh: T&T Clark, 1993.
———. "Sacrifice and Atonement in the Gospel of John." Pages 287-313 in *Israel und seine Heilstraditionen im Johannesevangelium.* Edited by Michael Labahn, Klaus Scholtissek, and Angelika Strotmann. Paderborn: Schöningh, 2004.
Päpstliche Bibelkommission. *Das jüdische Volk und seine Heilige Schrift in der christlichen Bibel.* Verlautbarungen des Apostolischen Stuhls 152. Bonn: Sekretariat der Dt. Bischofskonferenz, 2001.
Parsenios, George L. *Departure and Consolation: The Johannine Farewell Discourse in Light of Greco-Roman Literature.* NovTSup 117. Leiden: Brill, 2005.
———. *Rhetoric and Drama in the Johannine Lawsuit Motif.* WUNT 258. Tübingen: Mohr Siebeck, 2010.
Pastorelli, D. "La formule johannique ταῦτα λελάληκα ὑμῖν (Jn 14,25; 15,11; 16,1.4.6.25.33). Un exemple de parfait transitif." *Filologia Neotestamentaria* 19 (2006): 73-88.
———. *Le Paraclet dans le corpus johannique.* BZNW 142. Berlin, 2006.
Pedersen, Sigfred. "Anti-Judaism in John's Gospel: John 8." Pages 172-93 in *New Readings in John. Literary and Theological Perspectives. Essays from the Scandinavian Conference on the Fourth Gospel.* Edited by Johannes Nissen and Sigfred Pedersen. JSNTSup 182. Sheffield: Sheffield Academic, 1999.
Perkins, Pheme. "'I Have Seen the Lord' (John 20:18). Women Witnesses to the Resurrection." *Int* 46 (1992): 31-41.
Pesch, Rudolf. *Der reiche Fischfang. Lk 5,1-11/Joh 21,1-14. Wundergeschichte, Berufungserzählung, Erscheinungsbericht.* Düsseldorf: Patmos, 1969.
Phillips, Gary A. "'This Is a Hard Saying. Who Can Be Listener to It?' Creating a Reader in John 6." Pages 23-56 in *Narrative and Discourse in Structural Exegesis. John 6 & 1 Thessalonians.* Edited by Daniel Patte. Semeia 26. Chico: Scholars Press, 1983.
Piper, Ronald A. "The Characterisation of Pilate and the Death of Jesus in the Fourth Gospel." Pages 121-61 in *The Death of Jesus in the Fourth Gospel.* Edited by Gilbert van Belle. BETL 200. Leuven: Peeters, 2007.
Pitta, Antonio. "Ichthys ed opsarion in Gv 21,1-14: semplice variazione lessicale o differenza con valore simbolico?" *Bib* 71 (1990): 348-64.

Poirier, John C. "Hanukkah in the Narrative Chronology of the Fourth Gospel." *NTS* 54 (2008): 465–78.

Popkes, Enno E. "The Love of God for the World and the Handing Over ('Dahingabe') of His Son. Comments on the Tradition-Historical Background and the Theological Function of John 3,16 in the Overall Context of Johannine Theology." Pages 609–23 in *The Death of Jesus in the Fourth Gospel*. Edited by Gilbert van Belle. BETL 200. Leuven: Peeters, 2007.

———. *Die Theologie der Liebe Gottes in den johanneischen Schriften. Zur Semantik der Liebe und zum Motivkreis des Dualismus*. WUNT 2.197. Tübingen: Mohr Siebeck, 2005.

Popp, Thomas. "Die konsolatorische Kraft der Wiederholung. Liebe, Trauer und Trost in den johanneischen Abschiedsreden." Pages 523–87 in *Repetitions and Variations in the Fourth Gospel: Style, Text, Interpretation*. Edited by Gilbert van Belle, Michael Labahn, and P. Maritz. BETL 223. Leuven: Peeters, 2009.

———. "Das Kreuz mit den Sakramenten. Ritual und Repetition im Vierten Evangelium." Pages 507–27 in *The Death of Jesus in the Fourth Gospel*. Edited by Gilbert van Belle. BETL 200. Leuven: Peeters, 2007.

Porsch, F. "παράκλητος." *EWNT* 3:64–67; *EDNT* 3:28f.

Porter, Calvin L. "John IX.38,39a: A Liturgical Addition to the Text." *NTS* 13 (1966–1967): 387–94.

———. "Papyrus Bodmer XV (P75) and the Text of Codex Vaticanus." *JBL* 81 (1962): 363–76.

Pryor, John W. "John the Baptist and Jesus: Tradition and Text in Joh 3:25." *JSNT* 66 (1997): 15–26.

———. "John 4:44 and the Patris of Jesus." *CBQ* 49 (1987): 254–63.

Quek, Tze-Ming. "A Text-Critical Study of John 1.34." *NTS* 55 (2009): 22–34.

Rahner, Johanna. "Vergegenwärtigende Erinnerung. Die Abschiedsreden, der Geist-Paraklet und die Retrospektive des Johannesevangeliums." *ZNW* 91 (2000): 72–90.

Rastoin, Marc. "Encore une fois les 153 poissons (Jn 21,11)." *Bib* 90 (2009): 84–92.

Ratzinger, Joseph (Pope Benedict). *Jesus von Nazareth. 2. Vom Einzug in Jerusalem bis zur Auferstehung*. Freiburg im Breisgau: Herder, 2011.

Reim, Günter. "Joh 9—Tradition und zeitgenössische messianische Diskussion." *BZ* 22 (1978): 245–53.

———. "Johannesevangelium und Synagogengottesdienst—eine Beobachtung." *BZ* 27 (1983): 101.

Reinhartz, Adele. "The Grammar of Hate in the Gospel of John. Reading John in the Twenty-First Century." Pages 416–27 in *Israel und seine Heilstraditionen im Johannesevangelium*. Edited by Michael Labahn, Klaus Scholtissek, and Angelika Strotmann. Paderborn: Schöningh, 2004.

Rengstorf, K.-H. "ἀπόστολος." *TWNT* 1:406–46.

Repschinski, B. "Freundschaft mit Jesus: Joh 15,12–17." Pages 155–67 in *Im Geist und in der Wahrheit. Studien zum Johannesevangelium und zur Offenbarung des Johannes sowie andere Beiträge*. Edited by Konrad Huber and Boris Repschinski. NTAbh 52. Münster: Aschendorff, 2008.

Resseguie, J. L. "John 9: A Literary-Critical Analysis." Pages 295–303 in *Literary Inter-*

*pretations of Biblical Narratives II*. Edited by Kenneth R. R. Gros Louis. Nashville: Abingdon, 1982.

Richter, Georg. "Die Fleischwerdung des Logos im Johannesevangelium." *NovT* 13 (1971): 81–126; *NovT* 14 (1972): 257–76.

———. "Die Fußwaschung Joh 13,1–20." *MTZ* 16 (1965): 13–26.

———. *Studien zum Johannesevangelium*. Edited by Joseph Hainz. Biblische Untersuchungen 13. Regensburg: Pustet, 1977.

Riesner, Rainer. "Joh 7,1: Fehlender Wille oder fehlende Vollmacht Jesu." *ZNW* 96 (2005): 259–62.

Rigato, Maria-Luisa. "L' 'apostolo ed evangelista Giovanni,' 'sacerdote' levitico." *RivB* 38 (1990): 451–83.

———. "'Era festa degli Ebrei' (Gv 5,1). Quale?" *RivB* 39 (1991): 25–29.

———. "La sepoltura regale e provvisoria di Gesù secondo Gv 19,38–40." Pages 47–81 in *Atti del VIII Simposio di Efeso su S. Giovanni Apostolo*. Edited by Luigi Padovese. Rome: Istituto Francescano di Spiritualità, Pontificio Ateneo Antoniano, 2001,

———. "La testimonianza di Papia di Gerapoli sul 'secondo' Giovanni e il contesto eusebiano. Riscontri nel Nuovo Testamento." Pages 237–72 in *Atti del VI Simposio di Efeso su S. Giovanni Apostolo*. Edited by Luigi Padovese. Rome: Istituto Francescano di Spririturalità, Pontificio Ateneo Antoniano, 1996.

———. "La testimonianza di Policrate di Efeso su Giovanni evangelista." Pages 108–42 in *Atti del III Simposio di Efeso su S. Giovanni Apostolo*. Edited by Luigi Padovese. Rome: Istituto Francescano di Spririturalità, Pontificio Ateneo Antoniano, 1993.

———. *Il titolo della croce di Gesù. Confronto tra i Vangeli e la Tavoletta-Reliquia della Basilica Eleniana a Roma*. Rome: Pontificia università gregoriana, 2003.

Riniker, Chr. "Jean 6,1–21 et les évangiles synoptiques." Pages 41–67 in *La communauté johannique et son histoire*. Edited by Johannes Beutler, Jean-Daniel Kaestli, Jean-Michel Poffet, and Jean Zumstein. Monde de la Bible. Geneva: Labor et Fides, 1990.

Rissi, Mathias. "Der Aufbau des Vierten Evangeliums." *NTS* 29 (1983): 48–54.

Ritt, Hubert. *Das Gebet zum Vater. Zur Interpretation von Joh 17*. FB 36. Würzburg: Echter Verlag, 1979.

Roberts, Colin. "John 20:30–31 and 21:24–25." *JTS* 38 (1987): 409–10.

Robinson, J. A. T. "The Destination and Purpose of St. John's Gospel." *NTS* 6 (1959–1960): 117–31.

Robinson, James M. *The Nag Hammadi Library in English*. 3rd ed. San Francisco: HarperSanFrancisco, 1990.

Robinson, Maurice A. "Preliminary Observations regarding the Pericope Adulterae Based upon Fresh Collation of Nearly All Continuous-Text Manuscripts and All Lectionary Manuscripts Containing the Passage." *Filologia Neotestamentaria* 13.25–26 (2000): 35–59.

Roose, Hanna. "Joh 20,30f: Ein (un)passender Schluss? Joh 9 und 11 als primäre Verweisstellen der Schlussnotiz des Johannesevangeliums." *Bib* 84 (2003): 326–43.

Roulet, Philippe, and Ulrich Ruegg. "Étude de Jean 6. La narration et l'histoire de la redaction." Pages 231–47 in *La communauté johannique et son histoire*. Edited by

Johannes Beutler, Jean-Daniel Kaestli, Jean-Michel Poffet, and Jean Zumstein. Monde de la Bible. Geneva: Labor et Fides, 1990.

Ruckstuhl, Eugen. *Die literarische Einheit des Johannesevangeliums. Der gegenwärtige Stand der einschlägigen Forschungen*. NTOA 5. Göttingen: Vandenhoeck & Ruprecht; Freiburg, Switzerland: Universitätsverlag, 1987.

———. "Die Speisung des Volkes durch Jesus und die Seeüberfahrt der Jünger nach Joh 6,1–25 im Vergleich zu den synoptischen Parallelen." Pages 2001–19 in *The Four Gospels, 1992: Festschrift Frans Neirynck*. Edited by Frans van Segbroeck. BETL 100. Leuven: Peeters, 1992.

Ruckstuhl, Eugen, and Peter Dschulnigg. *Stilkritik und Verfasserfrage im Johannesevangelium. Die johanneischen Sprachmerkmale auf dem Hintergrund des Neuen Testaments und des zeitgenössischen hellenistischen Schrifttums*. NTOA 17. Göttingen: Vandenhoeck & Ruprecht; Freiburg, Switzerland: Universitätsverlag, 1991.

Rusam, Dietrich. "Das 'Lamm Gottes' (Joh 1,29.36) und die Deutung des Todes Jesu im Johannesevangelium." *BZ* 49 (2005): 60–80.

Ruschmann, Susanne. *Maria von Magdala im Johannesevangelium. Jüngerin–Zeugin–Lebensbotin*. NTAbh 40. Münster: Aschendorff, 2002.

Rushton, Kathleen. "The (Pro)Creative Parables of Labour and Childbirth (John 3.1–10 and 16.21–22)." Pages 206–29 in *The Lost Coin: Parables of Women, Work and Wisdom*. Edited by Mary Ann Beavis. BibSem 86. London: Sheffield Academic Press, 2002.

Sabbe, Maurits. "The Arrest of Jesus in Jn 18,1–11 and Its Relation to the Synoptic Gospels. A Critical Evaluation of A. Dauer's Hypothesis." Pages 355–88 in *Studia Neotestamentica. Collected Essays*. BETL 98. Leuven: Peeters, 1991.

———. "The Johannine Account of the Death of Jesus and Its Synoptic Parallels (Jn 19,16b–42)." *ETL* 70 (1994): 34–63.

———. "John 10 and Its Relationship to the Synoptic Gospels." Pages 75–93, 156–61 in *The Shepherd Discourse of John 10 and Its Context*. Edited by Johannes Beutler and Robert T. Fortna. SNTSMS 67. Cambridge: Cambridge University Press, 1991.

Sabugal, Santos. "La curación del ciego de nacimiento (Jn 9,1–41) ¿Catequesis bautismal o cristológica?" Pages 121–64 in *Segni e sacramenti nel vangelo di Giovanni*. Edited by Pius-Ramon Tragan. Studia Anselmiana philosophica theologica 66. Roma: Editrice Anselmiana, 1977.

Sandnes, Karl O. "Whence and Whither. A Narrative Perspective on Birth ἄνωθεν (John 3,3–8)." *Bib* 86 (2005): 153–73.

Sandt, Huub van de. "The Purpose of Jesus' Death. John 11,51–52 in the Perspective of Did 9,4." Pages 635–45 in *The Death of Jesus in the Fourth Gospel*. Edited by Gilbert van Belle. BETL 200. Leuven: Peeters, 2007.

Sattler, Dorothea. "'... dass sie alle eins seien' (Joh 17,21). Ökumenische Perspektiven von Benedikt XVI. in Aufnahme des Testaments Jesu Christi." Pages 202–21 in *Tod und Auferstehung Jesu: Theologische Antworten auf das Buch des Papstes*. Edited by Thomas Söding. Freiburg: Herder, 2011.

Scheffler, Eben. "Jesus' Non-Violence at His Arrest. The Synoptics and John's Gospel Compared." Pages 739–49 in *The Death of Jesus in the Fourth Gospel*. Edited by Gilbert van Belle. BETL 200. Leuven: Peeters, 2007.

Schenk, Wolfgang. *Evangelium, Evangelien, Evangeliologie: Ein "hermeneutisches" Manifest.* Theologische Existenz 216. Munich: Kaiser, 1983.
———. "Die Um-Kodierung der matthäischen Unser-Vater-Redaktion in Joh 17." Pages 587–607 in *John and the Synoptics*. Edited by Adelbert Denaux. BETL 101. Leuven: Peeters, 1992.
Schenke, Ludger. "Joh 7–10: eine dramatische Szene." *ZNW* 80 (1989): 172–92.
———. *Das Johannesevangelium. Einführung–Text–Dramatische Gestalt.* Kohlhammer Urban-Taschenbücher 446. Stuttgart: Kohlhammer, 1992.
———. "The Johannine Schism and the 'Twelve' (John 6:60–71)." Pages 205–19 in *Critical Readings of John 6*. Edited by R. Alan Culpepper. BibInt 6. Leiden: Brill, 1997.
Schleritt, Frank. *Der vorjohanneische Passionsbericht. Eine historisch-kritische und theologische Untersuchung zu Joh 2,13–22, 11,47–14,31 und 18,1–20,29.* BZNW 154. Berlin: de Gruyter, 2007.
Schlier, Heinrich. "Jesus und Pilatus." Pages 56–74 in *Die Zeit der Kirche. Exegetische Aufsätze und Vorträge.* 3rd ed. Freiburg im Breisgau: Herder, 1962.
Schmidl, Martin. *Jesus und Nikodemus. Gespräch zur johanneischen Christologie. Joh 3 in schichtenspezifischer Sicht.* Biblische Untersuchungen 28. Regensburg: Pustet, 1998.
Schmidt, Ulrich. "Zum Paradox vom 'Verlieren' und 'Finden' des Lebens." *Bib* 89 (2008): 329–51.
Schnackenburg, Rudolf. "Die 'situationsgelösten' Redestücke in Jo 3." *ZNW* 49 (1958): 88–99.
Schneider, G. "πραιτώριον." *EWNT* 3:346–48; *EDNT* 3:144f.
Schneiders, Sandra M. "The Face Veil: a Johannine Sign (John 20:1–10)." *BTB* 13 (1983): 94–97.
———. "The Johannine Resurrection Narrative: An Exegetical and Theological Study of John 20 as a Synthesis of Johannine Spirituality." Diss., Pontificia Università Gregoriana, 1975.
———. "The Resurrection (of the Body) in the Fourth Gospel: A Key to Johannine Spirituality." Pages 168–98 in *Life in Abundance: Studies of John's Gospel in Tribute to Raymond E. Brown.* Edited by John R. Donahue. Collegeville, MN: Liturgical Press, 2005.
———. "Touching the Risen Jesus: Mary Magdalene and Thomas the Twin in John 20." Pages 153–76 in *The Resurrection of Jesus in the Gospel of John*. Edited by Craig R. Koester and Reimund Bieringer. WUNT 222. Tübingen: Mohr Siebeck, 2008.
———. "Women in the Fourth Gospel and the Role of Women in the Contemporary Church." *BTB* 12 (1982): 35–45.
Schnelle, Udo. *Antidoketische Christologie im Johannesevangelium. Eine Untersuchung zur Stellung des vierten Evangeliums in der johanneischen Schule.* FRLANT 137. Göttingen: Vandenhoeck & Ruprecht, 1987.
———. "Die johanneischen Abschiedsreden und das Liebesgebot." Pages 598–608 in *Repetitions and Variations in the Fourth Gospel: Style, Text, Interpretation.* Edited by Gilbert van Belle, Michael Labahn, and P. Maritz. BETL 223. Leuven: Peeters, 2009.
Scholtissek, Klaus. "'Geschrieben in diesem Buch' (Joh 20,30). Beobachtungen zum

kanonischen Anspruch des Johannesevangeliums." Pages 207-26 in *Israel und seine Heilstraditionen im Johannesevangelium*. Edited by Michael Labahn, Klaus Scholtissek, and Angelika Strotmann. Paderborn: Schöningh, 2004.

———. "'Eine größere Liebe als diese hat niemand, als wenn einer sein Leben hingibt für seine Freunde' (Joh 15,13). Die hellenistische Freundschaftsethik und das Johannesevangelium." Pages 413-39 in *Kontexte des Johannesevangeliums: Das vierte Evangelium in religions- und traditionsgeschichtlicher Perspektive*. Edited by Jörg Frey and Udo Schnelle. WUNT 175. Tübingen: Mohr Siebeck, 2004.

———. "Das hohepriesterliche Gebet Jesu. Exegetisch-theologische Beobachtungen zu Joh 17,1-26." *Trierer theologische Zeitschrift* 109 (2000): 199-218.

———. *In ihm sein und bleiben. Die Sprache der Immanenz in den johanneischen Schriften*. Herders biblische Studien 21. Freiburg: Herder, 2000.

———. "Kinder Gottes und Freunde Jesu. Beobachtungen zur johanneischen Ekklesiologie." Pages 184-211 in *Ekklesiologie des Neuen Testaments*. Edited by Rainer Kampling. Freiburg im Breisgau: Herder, 1996.

———. "Mündiger Glaube. Zur Architektur und Pragmatik johanneischer Begegnungsgeschichten: Joh 5 und Joh 9." Pages 75-105 in *Paulus und Johannes: Exegetische Studien zur paulinischen und johanneischen Theologie und Literatur*. Edited by Dieter Sänger. WUNT 198. Tübingen: Mohr Siebeck, 2006.

———. "'Rabbi, wo wohnst du?' (Joh 1,38). Die mystagogische Christologie des Johannesevangeliums (am Beispiel der Jüngerberufungen Joh 1,35-51). Mit Johannes das Evangelium entdecken (3/4)." *BL* 68 (1995): 223-31.

———. "Relecture und réécriture. Neue Paradigmen zu Methode und Inhalt der Johannesauslegung aufgewiesen am Prolog 1,1-18 und der ersten Abschiedsrede 13,31-14,31." *TP* 75 (2000): 1-29.

Schramm, Tim. "ἔρχομαι." *EWNT* 2:138-43; *EDNT* 2:55-57.

Schultheiß, Tanja. *Das Petrusbild im Johannesevangelium*. WUNT 2.329. Tübingen: Mohr Siebeck, 2012.

Schulz, Siegfried. *Komposition und Herkunft der johanneischen Reden*. BWANT 81. Stuttgart: Kohlhammer, 1960.

Schweizer, Eduard. *Ego eimi. Die religionsgeschichtliche Herkunft und theologische Bedeutung der johanneischen Bildreden, zugleich ein Beitrag zur Quellenfrage des 4. Evangeliums*. FRLANT 56. 2nd ed. Göttingen: Vandenhoeck & Ruprecht, 1965.

Schwindt, Rainer. "'Seht das Lamm Gottes, das hinwegnimmt die Sünde der Welt' (Joh 1,29). Zur Frage einer Sühnetheologie im Johannesevangelium." *Trierer theologische Zeitschrift* 119 (2010): 193-216.

Segovia, Fernando F. *The Farewell of the Word. The Johannine Call to Abide*. Minneapolis: Fortress Press, 1991.

———. "The Journeys of Jesus to Jerusalem." Pages 535-41 in *John and the Synoptics*. Edited by Adelbert Denaux. BETL 101. Leuven: Peeters, 1992.

———. "The Journey(s) of the Word of God: A Reading of the Plot of the Fourth Gospel." Pages 23-54 in *The Fourth Gospel from a Literary Perspective*. Edited by R. Alan Culpepper and Fernando F. Segovia. Semeia 53. Atlanta: Society of Biblical Literature, 1991.

———. *Love Relationships in the Johannine Tradition. Agapē/Agapan in I John and the Fourth Gospel*. SBLDS 58. Chico, CA: Scholars Press, 1982.

———. "The Structure, Tendenz and Sitz im Leben of John 13:31–14:31." *JBL* 104 (1985): 471–93.
Seitz, Wendelin Eugen. "Wann werden die Toten auferstehen? Beobachtungen und Gedanken eines Gräzisten zum Johannesevangelium (Kapitel 5, 6 und 11)." *MTZ* 61 (2010): 61–67.
Senior, Donald. "The Resurrection (of the Body) in the Fourth Gospel as a Key to Johannine Spirituality." Pages 199–203 in *Life in Abundance: Studies of John's Gospel in Tribute to Raymond E. Brown*. Collegeville, MN: Liturgical Press, 2005.
Sevrin, Jean Marie. "The Nicodemus Enigma. The Characterization and Function of an Ambiguous Actor of the Fourth Gospel." Pages 357–69 in *Anti-Judaism and the Fourth Gospel: Papers of the Leuven Colloquium, 2000*. Edited by Reimund Bieringer, Didier Pollefeyt, and Frederique Vandecasteele-Vanneuville. Jewish and Christian Heritage Series 1. Assen, the Netherlands: Royal Van Gorcum, 2001.
Siegert, Folker. "Unbekannte Papiaszitate bei armenischen Schriftstellern." *NTS* 27 (1981): 605–14.
Simoens, Yves. *La gloire d'aimer. Structures stilistiques et interprétatives dans le Discours de la Cène (Jn 13–17)*. AnBib 90. Rome: Biblical Institute Press, 1981.
Simon, Lutz. *Petrus und der Lieblingsjünger im Johannesevangelium: Amt und Autorität*. Europäische Hochschulschriften Theologie 498. Frankfurt am Main: Lang, 1994.
Simonis, A. J. *Die Hirtenrede im Johannes-Evangelium. Versuch einer Analyse von Joh 10,1–18 nach Entstehung, Hintergrund und Inhalt*. AnBib 29. Rome: Biblical Institute Press, 1967.
Ska, Jean-Louis. "Jésus et la Samaritaine (Jn 4). Utilité de l'Ancien Testament." *NRTh* 118 (1996): 641–52.
Smith, D. Moody. *The Composition and Order of the Fourth Gospel: Bultmann's Literary Theory*. New Haven: Yale University Press, 1965.
Soares-Prabhu, George M. "Der Blindgeborene. Verständnis eines johanneischen Zeichens im heutigen Indien." Pages 142–56 in *Wir werden bei ihm wohnen: Das Johannesevangelium in indischer Deutung*. Theologie der Dritten Welt 6. Freiburg im Breisgau: Herder, 1984.
Söding, Thomas. "In der Welt, nicht von der Welt. Die Freiburger Rede im Fokus des Neuen Testaments." *Drei Thesen und drei Fragen: Zur Debatte* 42.3 (2012): 11–12.
———. "Die Schrift als Medium des Glaubens. Zur hermeneutischen Bedeutung von Joh 20,30f." Pages 343–71 in *Schrift und Tradition: Festschrift für Josef Ernst zum 70. Geburtstag*. Edited by Knut Backhaus and Franz Georg Untergassmair. Paderborn: Schöningh, 1996.
Staley, Jeff. "The Structure of John's Prologue: Its Implications for the Gospel's Narrative Structure." *CBQ* 48 (1986): 241–64.
Stare, Mira. *Durch ihn leben: Die Lebensthematik in Joh 6*. NTAbh 49. Münster: Aschendorff, 2004.
———. "'Es ist vollendet' (Joh 19,30). Zeitaspekt in der johanneischen Passionsgeschichte." *Protokolle zur Bibel* 15 (2006): 77–92.
———. "'So nämlich liebte Gott die Welt...' (Joh 3,16)." Pages 61–80 in *Im Geist und in der Wahrheit: Studien zum Johannesevangelium und zur Offenbarung des Johannes sowie andere Beiträge*. Edited by Konrad Huber and Boris Repschinski. NTAbh 52. Münster: Aschendorff, 2008.

Stenger, Werner. "Die Auferweckung des Lazarus (Joh 11,1–45). Vorlage und johanneische Redaktion." *Trierer theologische Zeitschrift* 83 (1974): 17–37.
Stibbe, Mark W. G. *John as Storyteller: Narrative Criticism and the Fourth Gospel.* SNTSMS 73. Cambridge: Cambridge University Press, 1992.
Sticher, Claudia. "'Frau Weisheit hat ihr Haus gebaut.' Alttestamentliche Anknüpfungspunkte der Johanneischen Logos-Christologie." Pages 27–47 in *Der Johannesprolog.* Edited by Günter Kruck. Darmstadt: WBG, 2009.
Stimpfle, Alois. *Blinde sehen. Die Eschatologie im traditionsgeschichtlichen Prozess des Johannesevangeliums.* BZNW 57. Berlin: de Gruyter, 1990.
———. "Das 'sinnlose γάρ' in Joh 4,44. Beobachtungen zur Doppeldeutigkeit im Johannesevangelium." *BN* 65 (1992): 86–96.
Story, Cullen I. K. "The Mental Attitude of Jesus at Bethany: John 11.33, 38." *NTS* 37 (1991): 51–66.
Stowasser, Martin. "Die johanneische Tempelaktion (Joh 2,13–17). Ein Beitrag zum Verhältnis von Johannesevangelium und Synoptikern." Pages 41–60 in *Im Geist und in der Wahrheit: Studien zum Johannesevangelium und zur Offenbarung des Johannes sowie andere Beiträge.* Edited by Konrad Huber and Boris Repschinski. NTAbh 52. Münster: Aschendorff, 2008.
Stramare, Tarcisio. "La risposta di Gesù a Maria alle nozze di Cana. Il test della ragionevolezza." *BeO* 44 (2002): 179–92.
Straub, Esther. "Alles ist durch ihn geworden. Die Erschaffung des Lebens in der Sabbatheilung Joh 5,1–18." Pages 157–67 in *Studien zu Matthäus und Johannes: Festschrift für Jean Zumstein zu seinem 65. Geburtstag = Etudes sur Matthieu et Jean: mélanges offerts à Jean Zumstein pour son 65e anniversaire.* Edited by Andreas Dettwiler and Uta Poplutz. ATANT 97. Zürich: TVZ, 2009.
Strotmann, Angelika. "Die göttliche Weisheit als Nahrungsspenderin, Gastgeberin und sich selbst anbietende Speise. Mit einem Ausblick auf Johannes 6." Pages 131–56 in *"Eine gewöhnliche und harmlose Speise"?: Von der Entwicklungen frühchristlicher Abendmahlstraditionen.* Edited by Judith Hartenstein, Silke Petersen, and Angela Standhartinger. Gütersloh: Gütersloher Verlagshaus, 2008.
———. "Relative oder absolute Präexistenz? Zur Diskussion über die Präexistenz der frühjüdischen Weisheitsgestalt im Kontext von Joh 1,1–18." Pages 91–106 in *Israel und seine Heilstraditionen im Johannesevangelium.* Edited by Michael Labahn, Klaus Scholtissek, and Angelika Strotmann. Paderborn: Schöningh, 2004.
Swetnam, James. "The Meaning of πεπιστευκότας in John 8,31." *Bib* 61 (1980) 106–9.
Thatcher, Tom. "The Sabbath Trick: Unstable Irony in the Fourth Gospel." *JSNT* 76 (1999): 53–77.
Theobald, Michael. "Abraham–(Isaak)–Jakob. Israels Väter im Johannesevangelium." Pages 158–83 in *Israel und seine Heilstraditionen im Johannesevangelium.* Edited by Michael Labahn, Klaus Scholtissek, and Angelika Strotmann. Paderborn: Schöningh, 2004.
———. "Der älteste Kommentar zum Johannesevangelium (R. F. Collins)?" Pages 41–75 in *Studien zum Corpus Johanneum.* WUNT 267. Tübingen: Mohr Siebeck, 2010.
———. "'Erinnert euch der Worte, die ich euch gesagt habe...' (Joh 15,20). 'Erin-

nerungsarbeit' im Johannesevangelium." *Jahrbuch für biblische Theologie* 22 (2007): 105–30.

———. "Die Ernte ist da! Überlieferungsgeschichtliche Beobachtungen zu einer johanneischen Bildrede (Joh 4,31–38)." Pages 81–108 in *Im Geist und in der Wahrheit: Studien zum Johannesevangelium und zur Offenbarung des Johannes sowie andere Beiträge*. Edited by Konrad Huber and Boris Repschinski. NTAbh 52. Münster: Aschendorff, 2008.

———. *Die Fleischwerdung des Logos. Studien zum Verhältnis des Johannesprologs zum Corpus des Evangeliums und zu 1 Joh*. NTAbh 20. Münster: Aschendorff, 1988.

———. "Futurische versus präsentische Eschatologie? Ein neuer Versuch zur Standortbestimmung der johanneische Redaktion." Pages 534–73 in *Studien zum Corpus Johanneum*. WUNT 267. Tübingen: Mohr Siebeck, 2010.

———. "Geist- und Inkarnationschristologie. Zur Pragmatik des Johannesprologs." *ZKT* 112 (1990): 129–49.

———. "'Gottes-Gelehrtheit'? (1 Thess 4,9; Joh 6,45)." Pages 249–60 in *Für immer verbündet: Studien zur Bundestheologie der Bibel*. Edited by Christoph Dohmen and Christian Frevel. Stuttgart : Katholisches Bibelwerk, 2007.

———. "Heilige Orte–heilige Zeiten. Die christologische Antwort des Johannesevangeliums." *BK* 59 (2004): 125–30.

———. *Herrenworte im Johannesevangelium*. Herders biblische Studien 34. Freiburg: Herder, 2002.

———. "Das 'hohepriesterliche' Gebet Jesu (Joh 17). Ein Eckpfeiler in der sacerdotalkultischen Wahrnehmung der Passion Jesu durch Joseph Ratzinger." Pages 77–109 in *Passion aus Liebe. Das Jesus-Buch des Papstes in der Diskussion*. Edited by Jan Heiner Tück. Ostfildern: Matthias Grünewald Verlag, 2011.

———. "Im Anfang—das Wort. Zum Johannesprolog." Pages 29–37 in *Herzstücke. Texte, die das Leben verändern*. Edited by Christoph Gellner and Karl-Josef Kuschel. Düsseldorf: Patmos, 2008.

———. "Le prologue johannique (Jean 1,1–18) et ses 'lecteurs implicites.' Remarques sur une question toujours ouverte." *Recherches de science religieuse* 83 (1995): 193–216.

———. *Studien zum Corpus Johanneum*. WUNT 267. Tübingen: Mohr Siebeck, 2010.

———. "Trauer um Lazarus. Womit die Juden Martha und Maria zu trösten suchten (Joh 11,19)." TThSt 114 (2005): 243–56.

———. "'Welt' bei Johannes und bei Paulus." *Communio* 34 (2005): 435–47.

———. "'Wie mich der Vater gesandt hat, so sende ich euch' (Joh 20,21). Missionarische Gestalten im Johannesevangelium." Pages 28–46 in *Zeichen der heilsamen Nähe Gottes. Auf dem Weg zu einer missionarischen Kirche*. Edited by Gebhard Fürst, Johannes Kreidler, Thomas Broch, and Dirk Steinfort. Ostfildern: Schwabenverlag, 2008.

Thüsing, Wilhelm. "Die Bitten des johanneischen Jesus in dem Gebet Joh 17 und die Intentionen Jesu von Nazaret." Pages 265–94 in *Studien zur neutestamentlichen Theologie*. Edited by Thomas Söding. WUNT 82. Tübingen: Mohr Siebeck, 1995.

———. *Die Erhöhung und Verherrlichung Jesu im Johannesevangelium*. 2nd ed. NTAbh 21.1. Münster: Aschendorff, 1970.

Thyen, Hartwig. "Eine ältere Quelle im Hintergrund von Joh 4?" Pages 479–82 in *Studien zum Corpus Iohanneum*. WUNT 214. Tübingen: Mohr Siebeck, 2007.

———. "Entwicklungen innerhalb der johanneischen Theologie und Kirche im Spiegel im Lichte von Joh 21 und der Lieblingsjüngertexte des Johannesevangeliums." Pages 259–99 in *L'évangile de Jean. Sources, rédaction, théologie*. Edited by Martinus de Jonge. BETL 44. Leuven: Peeters, 1987.

———. "Erwägungen zu der Wendung χάριν ἀντὶ χάριτος." Pages 425–28 in *Studien zum Corpus Iohanneum*. WUNT 214. Tübingen: Mohr Siebeck, 2007.

———. "Die Erzählung von den bethanischen Geschwistern (Joh 11,1–12,9) als Palimpsest über synoptischen Texten." Pages 2021–50 in *The Four Gospels, 1992: Festschrift Frans Neirynck*. Edited by Frans van Segbroeck. BETL 100. Leuven: Peeters, 1992.

———. "ὃ γέγονεν: Satzende von 1,3 oder Satzeröffnung von 1,4." Pages 411–17 in *Studien zum Corpus Iohanneum*. WUNT 214. Tübingen: Mohr Siebeck, 2007.

———. "Joh 6,66 und das Schisma unter den Jüngern." Pages 548–53 in *Studien zum Corpus Iohanneum*. WUNT 214. Tübingen: Mohr Siebeck, 2007.

———. "Joh 8,48f: Die Ἰουδαῖοι werfen Jesus vor, er sei ein dämonisch besessener Samaritaner. Indiz für eine besondere Nähe unseres Evangelisten zu samaritanischer Theologie?" Pages 554–60 in *Studien zum Corpus Iohanneum*. WUNT 214. Tübingen: Mohr Siebeck, 2007.

———. "Joh 9,22; 12,42 u. 16,2: ἀποσυνάγωγον ποιεῖν und ἀποσυνάγωγος γενέσθαι." Pages 561–77 in *Studien zum Corpus Iohanneum*. WUNT 214. Tübingen: Mohr Siebeck, 2007.

———. "Johannes 10 im Kontext des vierten Evangeliums." Pages 116–34 and 163–68 in *The Shepherd Discourse of John 10 and Its Context: Studies*. Edited by Johannes Beutler and Robert Tomson Fortna. SNTSMS 67. Cambridge: Cambridge University Press, 1991.

———. "Johannes 13 und die 'kirchliche Redaktion' des vierten Evangeliums." Pages 343–56 in *Tradition und Glaube: das frühe Christentum in seiner Umwelt; Festgabe für Karl Georg Kuhn zum 65. Geburtstag*. Edited by Gert Jeremias. Göttingen: Vandenhoeck & Ruprecht, 1971.

———. "Noch einmal: Johannes 21 und 'der Jünger, den Jesus liebte.'" Pages 147–89 in *Texts and Contexts: Biblical Texts in Their Textual and Situational Contexts. Essays in Honor of Lars Hartman*. Edited by Tord Fornberg and David Hellholm. Oslo: Scandinavian University Press, 1995.

———. *Studien zum Corpus Iohanneum*. WUNT 214. Tübingen: Mohr Siebeck, 2007.

———. "Über die Versuche, die sogenannte 'eucharistische Rede' (Joh 6,51c–58) als redaktionelle Redaktion auszuscheiden." Pages 539–47 in *Studien zum Corpus Iohanneum*. WUNT 214. Tübingen: Mohr Siebeck, 2007.

———. "Zu den zahllosen Versuchen, die vermeintlichen Aporien der Hirtenrede von Joh 10 auf literarkritischen Wegen zu beseitigen." Pages 578–90 in *Studien zum Corpus Iohanneum*. WUNT 214. Tübingen: Mohr Siebeck, 2007.

Tobin, Thomas H. "The Prologue of John and Hellenistic Jewish Speculation." *CBQ* 52 (1990): 252–69.

Traets, C. *Voir Jésus et le Père en lui selon l'évangile de Saint Jean*. Analecta Gregoriana 159. Rome: Libreria editrice dell'Università Gregoriana, 1967.

Tragan, Pius-Ramon. *La parabole du "Pasteur" et ses explications Jean 10,1–18. La genèse, les milieux littéraires*. SA 67. Rome: Editrice Anselmiana, 1980.

Trocmé, Étienne. "Jean et les Synoptiques: L'exemple de Jean 1,15–34." Pages 1935–41 in *The Four Gospels, 1992: Festschrift Frans Neirynck*. Edited by Frans van Segbroeck. BETL 100. Leuven: Peeters, 1992.

———. "Jean 3,29 et le thème de l'époux dans la tradition pré-évangélique." *RevScRel* 69 (1995): 13–18.

Tuñí Vancells, José O. *Jesús y el evangelio en la comunidad juánica*. Biblia y Catequesis 13. Salamanca: Sígueme, 1987.

———. *La verdad os hará libres (Jn 8,31): Liberación y libertad del creyente en el cuarto evangelio*. Barcelona: Herder, 1973.

Turner, John D. "The History of Religions Background of John 10." Pages 33–52 and 147–50 in *The Shepherd Discourse of John 10 and Its Context: Studies*. Edited by Johannes Beutler and Robert Tomson Fortna. SNTSMS 67. Cambridge: Cambridge University Press, 1991.

Ulrichsen, Jarl Henning. "Jesus—der neue Tempel? Ein kritischer Blick auf die Auslegung von Joh 2,13–22." Pages 202–14 in *Neotestamentica et Philonica: Studies in Honor of Peder Borgen*. Edited by Peder Borgen, David Edward Aune, Torrey Seland, and Jarl Henning Ulrichsen. NovTSup 106. Leiden: Peeters, 2003.

Umoh, Camillus. *The Plot to Kill Jesus. A Contextual Study of Joh 11.47–53*. Europäische Hochschulschriften Theologie 696. Frankfurt am Main: Peter Lang, 2000.

———. "The Temple in the Fourth Gospel." Pages 314–33 in *Israel und seine Heilstraditionen im Johannesevangelium*. Edited by Michael Labahn, Klaus Scholtissek, and Angelika Strotmann. Paderborn: Schöningh, 2004.

Van Aarde, A. G. "Narrative Criticism Applied to John 4:43–54." Pages 101–28 in *Text and Interpretation: New Approaches in the Criticism of the New Testament*. Edited by P. J. Hartin and J. H. Petzer. NTTS 15. Leiden: Brill, 1991.

van Belle, Gilbert. "Christology and Soteriology in the Fourth Gospel. The Conclusion to the Gospel of John Revisited." Pages 435–61 in *Theology and Christology in the Fourth Gospel. Essays by the Members of the SNTS Johannine Writings Seminar*. Edited by Gilbert van Belle, J. G. van der Watt, and P. J. Maritz. BETL 184. Leuven: Peeters, 2005.

———, ed. *The Death of Jesus in the Fourth Gospel*. BETL 200. Leuven: Peeters, 2007.

———. "The Faith of the Galileans. The Parenthesis in John 4,44." *ETL* 74 (1998): 27–44.

———. "The Meaning of σημεῖα in John 20,30–31." *ETL* 74 (1998): 300–25.

———. *Les parenthèses dans l'évangile de Jean. Aperçu historique et classification. Texte grec de Jean*. SNTA 11. Leuven: Peeters, 1985.

———. "'Salvation is from the Jews': The Parenthesis in John 4:22b." Pages 370–400 in *Anti-Judaism and the Fourth Gospel: Papers of the Leuven Colloquium, 2000*. Edited by Reimund Bieringer, Didier Pollefeyt, and Frederique Vandecasteele-Vanneuville. Jewish and Christian Heritage Series 1. Assen, the Netherlands: Royal Van Gorcum, 2001.

———. *The Signs Source in the Fourth Gospel. Historical Survey and Critical Evaluation of the Semeia Hypothesis*. BETL 116. Leuven: Peeters, 1994.

———. "L'unité littéraire et les deux finales du quatrième évangile." Pages 297–315 in

*Studien zu Matthäus und Johannes: Festschrift für Jean Zumstein zu seinem 65. Geburtstag = Etudes sur Matthieu et Jean: mélanges offerts à Jean Zumstein pour son 65e anniversaire.* Edited by Andreas Dettwiler and Uta Poplutz. ATANT 97. Zürich: TVZ, 2009.

Vanni, U. "Il crocifisso risorto di Tommaso (Gv 20,24–29). Un'ipotesi di lavoro." *StPatr* 50 (2003): 753–75.

Varghese, Johns. *The Imagery of Love in the Gospel of John.* AnBib 177. Rome: Gregorian & Biblical Press, 2009.

Verhelst, Nele. "The Johannine Use of πάλιν in John 18,40." Pages 795–803 in *The Death of Jesus in the Fourth Gospel.* Edited by Gilbert Van Belle. BETL 200. Leuven: Peeters, 2007.

Verheyden, Joseph. "I. de la Potterie on John 19,13." Pages 817–37 in *The Death of Jesus in the Fourth Gospel.* Edited by Gilbert Van Belle. BETL 200. Leuven: Peeters, 2007.

Vignolo, Roberto. "Il Quarto Vangelo in due parole. In margine ai macarismi giovannei (Gv 13,17; 20,29)." Pages 119–32 in *"Il Vostro Frutto Rimanga" (Gv 16,16): Miscellanea per il LXX Compleanno di Giuseppe Ghiberti.* Edited by Anna Passoni Dell'Acqua. Supplementi alla Rivista biblica 46. Bologna: EDB, 2005.

Vögtle, Anton. "Ekklesiologische Auftragsworte des Auferstandenen." Pages 243–52 in *Das Evangelium und die Evangelien. Beiträge zur Evangelienforschung.* Kommentare und Beiträge zum Neuen Testament. Düsseldorf: Patmos-Verlag, 1971.

———. "Messiasbekenntnis und Petrusverheißung. Zur Komposition Mt 16,13–23." Pages 137–70 in *Das Evangelium und die Evangelien. Beiträge zur Evangelienforschung.* Kommentare und Beiträge zum Neuen Testament. Düsseldorf: Patmos-Verlag, 1971.

Von Wahlde, Urban C. "The Johannine 'Jews.' A Critical Survey." *NTS* 28 (1982): 33–60.

———. "'You Are of Your Father the Devil' in Its Context. Stereotyped Apocalyptic Polemic in John 8:38–47." Pages 418–44 in *Anti-Judaism and the Fourth Gospel: Papers of the Leuven Colloquium, 2000.* Edited by Reimund Bieringer, Didier Pollefeyt, and Frederique Vandecasteele-Vanneuville. Jewish and Christian Heritage Series 1. Assen, the Netherlands: Royal Van Gorcum, 2001.

Wagner, Josef. *Auferstehung und Leben. Joh 11,1–12,19 als Spiegel johanneischer Redaktions- und Theologiegeschichte.* Biblische Untersuchungen 19. Regensburg: Pustet, 1988.

Watson, Alan. "Jesus and the Adulteress." *Bib* 80 (1999): 100–108.

Weder, H. "Das neue Gebot. Eine Überlegung zum Liebesgebot in Johannes 13." Pages 187–205 in *Studien zu Matthäus und Johannes: Festschrift für Jean Zumstein zu seinem 65. Geburtstag = Etudes sur Matthieu et Jean: mélanges offerts à Jean Zumstein pour son 65e anniversaire.* Edited by Andreas Dettwiler and Uta Poplutz. ATANT 97. Zürich: TVZ, 2009.

Weidemann, Hans-Ulrich. "Eschatology as Liturgy: Jesus' Resurrection and Johannine Eschatology." Pages 277–310 in *The Resurrection of Jesus in the Gospel of John.* Edited by Craig Koester and Reimund Bieringer. WUNT 222. Tübingen: Mohr Siebeck, 2008.

———. "Der Gekreuzigte als Quelle des Geistes." Pages 567–79 in *The Death of Jesus in the Fourth Gospel.* Edited by Gilbert van Belle. BETL 200. Leuven: Peeters, 2007.

———. "Nochmals Joh 20,23. Weitere philologische und exegetische Bemerkungen zu einer problematischen Bibelübersetzung." *MTZ* 52 (2001): 121–27.

———. *Der Tod Jesu im Johannesevangelium. Die erste Abschiedsrede als Schlüsseltext für den Passions- und Osterbericht.* BZNW 122. Berlin: de Gruyter, 2004.

Weinreich, Otto. *Antike Heilungswunder. Untersuchungen zum Wunderglauben der Griechen und Römer.* Gießen: Töpelmann, 1909.

Weiss, Wolfgang. *"Eine neue Lehre mit Vollmacht." Die Streit- und Schulgespräche des Markus-Evangeliums.* BZNW 52. Berlin: de Gruyter, 1989.

Welck, Christian. *Erzählte Zeichen. Die Wundergeschichten des Johannesevangeliums literarisch untersucht: Mit einem Ausblick auf Joh 21.* WUNT 2.69. Tübingen: Mohr Siebeck, 1994.

Wellhausen, Julius. *Das Evangelium Johannis.* Berlin: Reimer, 1908.

Wengst, Klaus. *Didache (Apostellehre), Barnabasbrief, Zweiter Klemensbrief, Schrift an Diognet.* Schriften des Urchristentums 2. Darmstadt: Wissenschaftliche Buchgesellschaft, 1984.

Wessel, Friedhelm. "Die fünf Männer der Samariterin. Jesus und die Tora nach Joh 4,16–19." *BN* 68 (1993): 26–34.

Wiarda, Timothy. "John 21.1–23: Narrative Unity and Its Implications." *JSNT* 46 (1992): 53–71.

———. "Scenes and Details in the Gospels: Concrete Reading and Three Alternatives." *NTS* 50 (2004): 167–84.

Wilckens, Ulrich. "Joh 21,15–23 als Grundtext zum Thema 'Petrusdienst.'" Pages 167–83 in *Der Sohn Gottes und seine Gemeinde. Studien zur Theologie der Johanneischen Schriften.* FRLANT 200. Göttingen: Vandenhoeck & Ruprecht, 2003.

Wilkens, W. "Die Erweckung des Lazarus." *TZ* 15 (1959): 22–39.

Willemse, J. "La patrie de Jésus selon Jean IV.44." *NTS* 11 (1964–1965): 349–64.

Williams, Catrin H. *I Am He: The Interpretation of* 'Anî Hû' *in Jewish and Early Christian Literature.* WUNT 2.113. Tübingen: Mohr Siebeck, 2000.

Winandy, J. "Le disciple que Jésus aimait. Pour une vision élargie du problème." *RB* 105 (1998): 70–75.

Witetschek, Stephan. "Ein Räuber: Barabbas im Johannesevangelium." Pages 805–15 in *The Death of Jesus in the Fourth Gospel.* Edited by Gilbert van Belle. BETL 200. Leuven: Peeters, 2007.

Witkamp, L. Th. "The Use of Tradition in John 5,1–8." *JSNT* 25 (1985): 19–47.

Witmer, Stephen. "Overlooked Evidence for Citation and Redaction in John 6,45a." *ZNW* 97 (2006): 134–38.

Wright, William M., IV. "Greco-Roman Character Typing and the Presentation of Judas in the Fourth Gospel." *CBQ* 71 (2009): 544–59.

———. *Rhetoric and Theology: Figural Reading of John 9.* BZNW 165. Berlin: De Gruyter, 2009.

Wucherpfennig, Ansgar. "Gnostische Lektüre des Johannesprologs am Beispiel Herakleons." Pages 107–30 in *Der Johannesprolog.* Edited by Günter Kruck. Darmstadt: WBG, 2009.

———. *Heracleon Philologus: Gnostische Johannesexegese im zweiten Jahrhundert.* WUNT 142. Tübingen: Mohr Siebeck, 2001.

———. "Markus 1,1–3, Johannes 1,1–18 und Herakleons Johanneskommentar im Licht christlicher Kanonentwicklung." Pages 227–44 in *Israel und seine Heilstraditionen im Johannesevangelium.* Edited by Michael Labahn, Klaus Scholtissek, and Angelika Strotmann. Paderborn: Schöningh, 2004.

———. "Das Petrusamt im Johannesevangelium." Pages 72–100 in *Neutestamentliche Ämtermodelle im Kontext.* Edited by Thomas Schmeller, Martin Ebner, and Rudolf Hoppe. QD 239. Freiburg im Breisgau: Herder, 2010.

———. "Tora und Evangelium. Beobachtungen zum Johannesprolog als Versuch einer Antwort auf eine theologische Grundfrage." *StZ* 221 (2003): 486–94.

Wuellner, Wilhelm. "Putting Life Back into the Lazarus Story and Its Reading: The Narrative Rhetoric of John 11 as the Narration of Faith." Pages 113–32 in *The Fourth Gospel from a Literary Perspective.* Edited by R. Alan Culpepper and Fernando F. Segovia. Semeia 53. Atlanta: Society of Biblical Literature, 1991.

Zeller, Dieter. "Der Ostermorgen im 4. Evangelium (Joh 20,1–18)." Pages 145–61 in *Auferstehung Jesu, Auferstehung der Christen: Deutungen des Osterglaubens.* Edited by Lorenz Oberlinner. QD 105. Freiburg im Breisgau: Herder, 1986.

Zerwick, Maximilian. *Analysis philologica Novi Testamenti Graeci.* 2nd ed. Rome: Sumptibus Pontificii Instituti Biblici, 1960.

Zimmermann, Heinrich. "Das absolute Ἐγώ εἰμι als die neutestamentliche Offenbarungsformel." *BZ* 4 (1960): 54–69, 266–276.

Zimmermann, Ruben. *Christologie der Bilder im Johannesevangelium. Die Christopoetik des vierten Evangeliums unter besonderer Berücksichtigung von Joh 10.* WUNT 171. Tübingen: Mohr Siebeck, 2004.

———. "Narrative Ethik im Johannesevangelium am Beispiel der Lazarus-Perikope Joh 11." Pages 133–70 in *Narrativität und Theologie im Johannesevangelium.* Edited by Jörg Frey and Uta Poplutz. Biblisch-theologische Studien 130. Neunkirchen-Vluyn: Neukirchener Verlagsgesellschaft, 2012.

———. "The Narrative Hermeneutics in John 11: Learning with Lazarus How to Understand Death, Life, and Resurrection." Pages 75–101 in *Resurrection of Jesus in the Gospel of John.* Edited by Craig R. Koester and Reimund Bieringer. WUNT 222. Tübingen: Mohr Siebeck, 2008.

Zumstein, Jean. "Bildersprache und Relektüre am Beispiel von Joh 15,1–17." Pages 139–56 in *Imagery in the Gospel of John: Terms, Forms, Themes, and Theology of Johannine Figurative Language.* Edited by Jörg Frey. WUNT 200. Tübingen: Mohr Siebeck, 2006.

———. "Die Endredaktion des Johannesevangeliums (am Beispiel von Joh 21)." Pages 291–315 in *Kreative Erinnerung: Relecture und Auslegung im Johannesevangelium.* 2nd ed. Zürich: Theologischer Verlag Zürich, 2004.

———. "'Ils n'ont pas d'excuse' (Jn 15,18–16,4a)." Pages 165–87 in *Le Jugement dans l'un et l'autre Testament.* Edited by Claude Coulot and Denis Fricker. Paris: Cerf, 2004.

———. "Jesus' Resurrection in the Farewell Discourses." Pages 103–26 in *The Resurrection of Jesus in the Gospel of John.* Edited by Craig R. Koester and Reimund Bieringer. WUNT 222. Tübingen: Mohr Siebeck, 2008.

———. "Die johanneische Interpretation des Todes Jesu." Pages 219–39 in *Kreative Erinnerung: Relecture und Auslegung im Johannesevangelium*. Zürich: Theologischer Verlag Zürich, 2004.

———. "Johannes 19,25–27." Pages 253–75 in *Kreative Erinnerung: Relecture und Auslegung im Johannesevangelium*. Zürich: Theologischer Verlag Zürich, 2004.

———. *Kreative Erinnerung: Relecture und Auslegung im Johannesevangelium*. Zürich: Theologischer Verlag Zürich, 2004.

———. "Die Logien Jesu in der ersten Abschiedsrede und die joh. Schule." Pages 177–87 in *Kreative Erinnerung: Relecture und Auslegung im Johannesevangelium*. Zürich: Theologischer Verlag Zürich, 2004.

———. "Narratologische Lektüre der johanneischen Ostergeschichte." Pages 277–90 in *Kreative Erinnerung: Relecture und Auslegung im Johannesevangelium*. Zürich: Theologischer Verlag Zürich, 2004.

———. "Der Prolog, Schwelle zum vierten Evangelium." Pages 105–26 in *Kreative Erinnerung: Relecture und Auslegung im Johannesevangelium*. Zürich: Theologischer Verlag Zürich, 2004.

———. "Der Prozess Jesu vor Pilatus. Ein Beispiel johanneischer Eschatologie." Pages 241–52 in *Kreative Erinnerung: Relecture und Auslegung im Johannesevangelium*. 2nd ed. Zürich: Theologischer Verlag Zürich, 2004.

———. "Die Schriftrezeption in der Brotrede (Joh 6)." Pages 123–29 in *Israel und seine Heilstraditionen im Johannesevangelium*. Edited by Michael Labahn, Klaus Scholtissek, and Angelika Strotmann. Paderborn: Schöningh, 2004.

———. "Die verklärte Vergangenheit. Geschichte sub specie aeternitatis nach Johannes 17." Pages 207–17 in *Kreative Erinnerung: Relecture und Auslegung im Johannesevangelium*. Zürich: Theologischer Verlag Zürich, 2004.

———. "Wissenskrise und Interpretationskonflikt nach Johannes 9. Ein Beispiel für die Arbeit der johanneischen Schule." Pages 147–60 in *Kreative Erinnerung: Relecture und Auslegung im Johannesevangelium*. Zürich: Theologischer Verlag Zürich, 2004.

# Index of Names

Abramowski, Luise, 356
Aland, Barbara, 24, 25
Aland, Kurt, 21, 22, 24, 25, 37
Aletti, Jean-Noël, 348, 370, 516, 542
Alter, Robert, 114
Anderson, Paul N., 168, 188, 451
Arterbury, Andrew E., 115
Ashton, John, 266
Asiedu-Peprah, Martin, 150
Attridge, Harold W., 428, 504
Augenstein, J., 405–6
Aus, Roger D., 312
Auwers, Jean-Marie, 494

Baarda, Tjitze, 248
Bach, Johann Sebastian, 462, 490
Bacinoni, Venance, 251
Baldensperger, Wilhelm, 9
Balz, H., 434
Bammel, Ernst, 84, 85
Barbaglia, Silvio, 536
Barnett, Paul W., 172
Barrett, C. K., 23, 24, 39, 59, 129, 151, 157, 276, 389, 416, 473
Bassler, Jouett M., 129, 131
Bauckham, Richard, 544
Bauer, Walter, 40, 49, 116, 124, 129, 320
Baum-Bodenberger, Rosel, 465
Beasley-Murray, G. R., 38, 129, 135, 157, 246, 248

Becker, Heinz, 19
Becker, Jürgen, 13, 14, 38, 56, 64, 91, 111, 118, 128, 135, 143, 146, 157, 166, 168, 250, 265–66, 277, 278, 292, 295, 333, 340, 344, 347, 359, 386, 393–94, 429, 431, 432, 434, 435, 437, 491, 493, 498, 522
Berger, Klaus, 15, 269
Bergler, Siegfried, 77, 129, 174, 209
Bergmeier, Roland, 489
Bernard, J. H., 166, 281–82, 347
Beutler, Johannes, ix–xii, 8, 9, 11, 13, 16, 17, 20, 22, 23, 27, 28, 29, 32, 39, 40, 41, 44, 52, 54, 59, 61, 69, 70, 71, 72, 81, 95, 96, 97, 106, 116, 140, 151, 153, 159–61, 167, 171, 189, 191, 209, 226, 235, 242, 244, 247, 277, 278, 282, 284, 285, 300, 302, 303, 305, 310, 311, 312, 313, 322, 336, 337, 338, 344, 354, 356, 364, 370, 374, 381, 382, 383, 385, 386, 389, 396, 400, 402, 404, 407, 408, 409, 418, 423, 428, 438, 463, 469, 488, 489, 495, 504, 512, 518, 537, 539, 540, 543
Bienaimé, Germain, 223
Bienert, Wolfgang A., 440
Bieringer, Reimund, 240, 498, 505, 507, 515
Bishop, Jonathan, 252
Blanc, Cécile, 130
Blank, Josef, 129, 157, 158, 386, 465

589

## INDEX OF NAMES

Blaskovic, G., 526
Blass, Friedrich, 124
Böhler, Dieter, 48
Boers, Hendrikus, 119, 123, 124, 126
Boismard, Marie-Émile, 33, 44, 340, 380
Borgen, Peder, 149, 152, 169, 184–85, 188, 190
Borig, Rainer, 267, 397, 399
Boring, M. Eugene, 155
Bornhäuser, Karl, 9–10
Bornkamm, Günther, 10
Botha, J. Eugene, 112, 113, 118, 119, 121
Bowman, John, 10
Brant, Jo-Ann, 5, 6
Brémond, Claude, 259
Brodie, Thomas L., 253
Brown, Raymond E., 4, 9, 11, 21, 38, 39, 44, 50, 58–59, 75, 79, 99, 129, 143, 157, 216, 219, 237, 238, 250, 258, 276, 282, 321, 334, 348, 389, 415, 428, 446, 448, 454, 475, 476, 500, 532, 537, 541
Bultmann, Rudolf, 4, 5, 13–14, 17, 19, 20, 26, 27, 30, 32, 38, 39, 64, 81, 91, 94, 96, 118, 121, 122, 123, 129, 134, 143, 146, 157, 158, 166, 167, 169, 170, 177–78, 181, 186, 206, 215, 240, 265, 277, 282, 292, 293–94, 340, 347, 353, 356, 374, 375, 377, 397–98, 406, 427, 429, 441–42, 443, 446, 469, 515, 517, 522
Bussche, Henri van den, 135
Busse, U., 56, 271

Calduch-Benages, Núria, 322
Caragounis, Chrys C., 237
Cardellino, L., 518, 544
Carson, D. A., 416–17, 518
Cassidy, Richard J., 12, 412, 496
Cazeaux, Jacques, 233
Ceulemans, Reinhart, 147
Charbonneau, André, 465
Chibici-Revneanu, Nicole, 365
Claudel, Gérard, 509
Claussen, Carsten, 427
Clivaz, Claire, 335
Coloe, Mary L., 348, 358, 370

Colpe, Carsten, 19
Corley, Jeremy, 129
Cortès, Enric, 20, 371–73
Cory, Catherine, 205
Cothenet, Edouard, 123
Culpepper, R. Alan, 145, 150, 170, 181, 192, 480–81, 483, 485

Daise, Michael A., 174
Danna, Elizabeth, 124
Daube, David, 116
Dauer, Anton, 284, 450–51
Dautzenberg, Gerhard, 240
De Boer, Martinus C., 465, 467, 473, 484, 499
De La Potterie, Ignace, 7, 33, 42, 46, 121, 445, 469, 476, 485
Debrunner, Albert, 124
Delebecque, Edouard, 237, 248
Dennis, John, 293, 312, 313, 335
Derrett, J. Duncan M., 216, 239–40
Destro, Adriana, 66, 210
Dettwiler, Andreas, 16, 44, 45, 395, 397–98, 406, 415, 418, 504
Devillers, Luc, 7, 51, 147, 206, 478, 513
Dibelius, Martin, 17
Diebold-Scheuermann, Carola, 465, 471, 474
Dietzfelbinger, Christian, 13, 427
Dinechin, Olivier de, 275
Dodd, C. H., 4, 99, 129, 154, 157, 250, 282, 427
Donfried, Karl, 537
Dschulnigg, Peter, 14, 494
Dunderberg, Ismo, 169
Duprez, Antoine, 147
Du Rand, Jan A., 11

Earl, Douglas S., 57
Egger, Wilhelm, 259
Eisele, Wilfried, 81
Enders, Markus, 51
Escaffre, Bernadette, 456, 457, 460, 461, 462
Evans, Craig A., 342

## Index of Names

Fauré, Alexander, 134, 517
Fee, Gordon D., 518
Felsch, Dorit, 8, 147, 284, 285, 287
Fiebig, Paul, 17
Fischer, Georg, 64, 374
Fischer, Joseph A., 23
Flink, Timo, 61
Fortna, Robert T., 15, 129, 143, 168, 282, 524
Freed, Edwin D., 55, 56
Frey, Jörg, 21, 98, 121, 158, 186, 348, 374, 375-76, 496, 515
Frühwald-König, Johannes, 85
Fuchs, Albert, 172

Galot, Jean, 46
Gardner-Smith, P., 14-15
Garský, Zbyněk, 80, 129
Gaventa, Beverly V., 542
Giblin, Charles H., 8, 179-81, 465
Girard, Marc, 76, 78, 90
Giurisato, Ghiberti, 403
Gordley, Matthew, 40
Gourges, Michel, 98, 251
Gruber, Margareta, 196, 352
Gundry, Robert H., 97

Haag, E., 509
Haenchen, Ernst, 14, 118, 215, 250, 265-66, 271, 340
Hahn, Ferdinand, 265-66, 271, 276, 277
Hainz, Joseph, 347, 522
Hakola, Raimo, 93
Haldimann, K., 398, 414-15, 416, 418-19
Harnack, Adolf von, 476, 543
Harris, Elizabeth, 35
Hartman, Lars, 530, 542
Hasitschka, M., 64, 522
Hatina, Thomas R., 511
Heckel, Ulrich, 267, 537
Heerkerens, Hans-Peter, 88
Heil, Christoph, 129, 224
Heil, John Paul, 178-79, 492
Hengel, Martin, 18, 22, 23, 81, 82, 543
Hirsch, Emanuel, 130
Hoegen-Rohls, Christina, 398

Hofius, Otfried, 91, 93, 94, 95, 96, 97, 99, 293
Hofrichter, Peter, 15, 32, 47, 525
Holloway, Paul A., 371
Holtzmann, Heinrich Julius, 32
Hoskyns, E. C., 129, 282, 390, 492
Hübenthal, Sandra, 87, 326, 422, 493-94
Hübner, Hans, 357
Hutton, Jeremy M., 57

Janssens de Varebeke, A., 445-47, 471
Jeremias, Joachim, 276, 277, 428
Jojko, Bernadeta, 121
Judge, Peter J., 515, 516
Jüngling, Hans-Winfried, 284

Kähler, Martin, 442
Käsemann, Ernst, 10, 441
Kammler, Hans-Christian, 156, 158, 517
Karakolis, Christos, 452
Karlsen Seim, Turid, 322
Keener, Craig S., 38, 129
Keith, Chris, 214, 227
Kempter, Mylène, 105
Kiefer, Odo, 266-67, 270, 397
Kieffer, René, xiii, 7, 8
Kierspel, Lars, 75
Kiley, Mark, 532
Kimelman, Reuven, 260
Kirchschläger, Peter G., 378
Klauck, Hans-Josef, 196, 320, 488
Koch, Dietrich-Alex, 54, 55, 56, 57
Koch, Kurt K., 440
Koester, Helmut, 234, 246
Kollmann, Hanjo-Christoph, 480
Konings, Johan, 172-73, 174
Koperski, Veronica, 487
Korting, Georg, 509
Kossen, H. B., 10
Kragerud, Alv, 544
Kraus, Wolfgang, 488
Kreitzer, Larry J., 229
Kremer, Jacob, 293, 308, 514
Kubis, Adam, 326
Kügler, Joachim, 544

# INDEX OF NAMES

Kühn, Rolf, 51
Kühschelm, Roman, 335, 340, 345
Kuhn, Hans-Jürgen, 64
Kurz, William S., 511
Kysar, Robert, 11, 129, 170, 182

Labahn, Michael, 6, 12, 13, 15–16, 70, 85, 145, 148, 169, 172, 178, 179, 187, 252, 293, 356, 526, 529
Lagrange, Marie-Joseph, 357
Landis, Stephan, 135
Lang, Manfred, 15–16, 85, 371
Langbrandtner, Wolfgang, 13, 265
Lattke, Michael, 516
Lausberg, Heinrich, 32–34
Lee, Dorothy, 431
Lee, Hye Ja, 338
Léon-Dufour, Xavier, 34, 443
Létourneau, Pierre, 117
Lightfoot, R. H., 130, 282
Lindars, Barnabas, xiii, 21, 50, 129, 135, 157, 306, 442, 443
Link, Andrea, 111, 118
Lohfink, Norbert, 324, 381
Loisy, Alfred, 129, 476
López Rosas, Ricardo, 88
Lowe, Malcolm, 104, 244
Lozada, Francisco, Jr., 15
Lührmann, Dieter, 428
Lütgehetmann, Walter, 18, 19, 79, 81
Luther, Martin, 26, 99, 403, 503
Luzarraga, Jesus, 322

Mackay, Ian D., 172, 179, 192, 193–94, 196
MacRae, George W., 20
Madden, Patrick J., 177
März, Claus-Peter, 328
Maier, Johann, 284
Malatesta, Edward, 382
Manns, Frédéric, 146
Manzi, Franco, 293, 307
Marcheselli, Maurizio, 526–27, 530, 534
Marcus, Joel, 223
Mardaga, Hellen, 453
Marguerat, Daniel, 179

Markl, Dominik, 516
Markstahler, Uwe, 34
Marsh, John, 129
Martin, M. W., 114
Martini, Carlo M., 25
Martyn, J. Louis, 5, 12, 68, 225, 259, 260
Marucci, Corrado, 531–32
Matera, Frank J., 458
McGrath, James F., 35
McHugh, John F., 129
McKay, K. L., 536
Meeks, Wayne A., 129, 153, 169
Ménard, J.-E., 314
Menken, Maarten J. J., 46, 69, 170, 185, 188, 189, 190, 222, 223, 326, 493
Meredith, A., 22, 40, 81
Merklein, Helmut, 96
Metzger, Bruce M., 37, 47, 50–51
Metzner, Rainer, 151, 152
Meyer, Annegret, 64
Michaels, J. Ramsey, 517
Migliasso, Secondo, 386
Miller, Eddie L., 39
Mlakuzhyil, George, 7, 445
Moberly, R. W. L., 215
Mörchen, Roland, 248
Mohamed, A. F., 509
Mollat, Donatien, 6, 8, 146, 282
Moloney, Francis J., 38, 75, 129, 157, 170, 189, 204–6, 257, 293, 300, 302, 306, 348, 425–26, 443, 514
Morgen, Michèle, 50, 75, 93, 322, 325
Morris, Leon, 61, 129, 130
Müller, C. G., 113
Müller, K., 255

Neirynck, Frans, xi, xiii, 66, 135, 144, 149, 451, 487, 524, 533
Neyrey, Jerome H., 284
Nicacci, Alviero, 41
Nicklas, Tobias, 85, 102, 112, 113, 532, 534
Nicol, W., 292
Noetzel, Heinz, 80–81
Nongbri, Brent, 24
Nordheim, Eckhard von, 20, 371

# Index of Names

Obielosi, Dominic Chukwunonso, 96, 337
O'Brien, Kelli S., 499
O'Day, Gail R., 118, 119, 121, 122, 170, 179, 180
O'Donnell, Tim, 158
Ognibene, Bruno, 78
O'Grady, John F., 431
Öhler, Markus, 272, 537
Okure, Teresa, 112, 113, 126
O'Loughlin, Thomas, 231
Olsson, Birger, 78, 112, 121, 126, 129, 191
Orsatti, Mauro, 536
Østenstad, Gunnar, 5
Overbeck, Franz, 23

Pagels, Elaine, 516
Painter, John, 11, 65, 68, 169, 181, 186, 250, 325, 394
Parsenios, George L., 5–6, 371
Pastorelli, D., 383, 404, 415
Pedersen, Sigfred, 243
Perkins, Pheme, 504
Pesce, Mauro, 66, 210
Pesch, Rudolf, 524
Philipps, G. A., 171
Piper, Ronald A., 478
Pitta, Antonio, 531
Poirier, John C., 285
Pollefeyt, Didier, 240
Popkes, Enno E., 97, 405
Porsch, F., 383
Porter, Calvin L., 25, 262
Pryor, John W., 101, 130

Quek, Tze-Ming, 61

Rahner, Johanna, 417
Rastoin, Marc, 532
Ratzinger, Joseph (Pope Benedict XVI), 435, 436, 440
Rebstock, Bonaventura, 129
Reim, Günter, 250, 255
Reinhartz, Adele, 411–12
Repschinksi, B., 406
Resseguie, J. L., 252

Reumann, John H. P., 537
Richter, Georg, 14, 49, 118, 157, 295, 340, 347, 359, 522
Riesner, Rainer, 208
Rigato, Maria-Luisa, 23, 146, 322, 483, 543
Riniker, Chr., 172
Rissi, Mathias, 6, 7, 8
Ritt, Hubert, 426
Roberts, Colin, 516, 540
Robinson, J. A. T., 10
Robinson, Maurice A., 226, 227–28
Rooke, Deborah W., 229
Roose, Hanna, 517
Roulet, Philippe, 181
Ruckstuhl, Eugen, 14, 96, 169
Ruegg, Ulrich, 181
Ruschmann, Susanne, 504, 506
Rushton, Kathleen, 420

Sabbe, Maurits, 284, 450–51, 458, 486
Sabugal, Santos, 251
Sandnes, Karl O., 94
Sandt, Huub van de, 313
Sattler, Dorothea, 440
Scheffler, Eben, 455
Schenk, Wolfgang, 436
Schenke, Ludger, 5, 33, 129, 157, 191, 206, 445, 447, 448, 500
Schlier, Heinrich, 469
Schmidl, Martin, 94
Schmidt, Ulrich, 333
Schnackenburg, Rudolf, 9, 28, 44, 46, 50, 72, 91, 96, 124, 129, 143, 146, 157, 166, 168, 177, 179, 236, 237, 241, 250, 266, 273, 276, 282, 334, 340, 348, 386, 397, 415, 429, 434, 437, 443, 445, 446, 448, 454, 468, 473, 499–500, 505, 512, 541, 544
Schneider, G., 477
Schneiders, Sandra M., 321–22, 448, 499, 500, 503, 504, 505, 508, 510, 525
Schnelle, Udo, 10, 16, 129, 135, 143, 157, 250, 354, 389, 443, 523
Scholtissek, Klaus, 16, 64, 152, 190, 252,

## INDEX OF NAMES

275, 287, 379, 384, 386, 397, 400, 406, 427, 436, 437, 504
Schramm, T., 45
Schultheiß, Tanja, 353
Schulz, Siegfried, 20, 118, 234, 377, 386, 398
Schwank, Benedikt, 129, 195
Schwartz, Eduard, 522
Schweizer, Eduard, 19–20, 397, 398
Schwindt, Rainer, 59
Segovia, Fernando F., 7, 8, 394
Seitz, Wendelin Eugen, 186
Senior, Donald, 504
Sevrin, Jean Marie, 93
Siegert, Folker, 22
Simoens, Yves, 364, 426, 429
Simon, Lutz, 525
Simonis, A. J., 267, 273
Ska, Jean-Louis, 112, 114, 119–20
Smith, D. Moody, 13, 129
Snoy, T., 451
Soares-Prabhu, George M., 252
Söding, Thomas, 435, 517
Sorg, T., 509
Staley, Jeff, 6–7, 8
Stare, Mira, 105, 188, 191, 501
Stenger, Werner, 292
Stibbe, Mark W. G., 5
Sticher, Claudia, 40
Stimpfle, Alois, 129, 158
Story, Cullen I. K., 306
Stowasser, Martin, 85
Stramare, Tarcisio, 77
Strathmann, Hermann, 282
Straub, Esther, 152
Strotmann, Angelika, 185
Swetnam, James, 238

Thatcher, Tom, 15, 149–50
Theobald, Michael, 5, 32, 35, 38, 39, 44, 45, 47, 64, 111, 112, 114, 126, 129, 134, 143, 157, 168, 181, 188, 247, 252, 301, 312, 408, 436, 440, 522
Thüsing, Wilhelm, 96, 436
Thyen, Hartwig, 5, 6, 14, 38, 39, 50, 118, 129, 246, 259, 264, 266, 282, 292–93, 294, 297, 357, 436, 528, 542, 544
Tobin, Thomas H., 40, 41
Traets. C., 307
Tragan, Pius-Ramon, 267–68, 276
Trocmé, Étienne, 55, 57–58, 60, 102
Tuñí Vancells, José O., 239
Turner, John D., 277

Ulrichsen, Jarl Henning, 83, 85, 86, 88
Umoh, Camillus, 312

Van Aarde, A. G., 135, 136
Van Belle, Gilbert, 57, 118, 122, 129, 143, 517, 522
Vandecasteele-Vanneuville, Frederique, 240
Vanni, U., 515
Varghese, Johns, 80, 322, 405
Verhelst, Nele, 470
Verheyden, Joseph, 476
Vignolo, Roberto, 356, 515
Vögtle, Anton, 537
Von Wahlde, Urban C., 129, 241, 243, 310
Vouga, François, 169

Wagner, Josef, 292
Watson, Alan, 228–29, 230
Weder, H., 366, 418
Weidemann, Hans-Ulrich, 223, 362, 490, 510, 512, 514
Weinrich, Otto, 17
Weiss, Wolfgang, 129, 404
Welck, Christian, 525–26
Wellhausen, Julius, 32, 41, 522
Wengst, Klaus, 27, 28, 48, 122, 129, 378, 443
Wessel, Friedhelm, 118, 120
Wiarda, Timothy, 92, 526
Wikenhauser, Alfred, 282
Wilckens, Ulrich, 129, 146, 348
Wilkens, W., 292
Willemse, J., 129
Williams, Catrin H., 450, 453
Winandy, J., 541, 543

*Index of Names*

Witetschek, Stephan, 272, 471
Witkamp, L. Th., 144
Witmer, Stephen, 187
Wright, William M. IV, 252, 259, 260, 434
Wucherpfennig, Ansgar, 195
Wuellner, Wilhelm, 293

Zeller, Dieter, 498

Zerwick, Maximilian, 237, 537
Zimmermann, Heinrich, 236
Zimmermann, Ruben, 267, 278, 293, 306
Zumstein, Jean, xi, 16, 33, 35, 105, 184, 185, 187, 252, 362, 365, 395, 399, 409, 415, 418, 432, 443, 465, 486, 498–99, 504, 523, 542

# Index of Primary Sources

## HEBREW BIBLE

### Genesis
| | |
|---|---|
| 1:1 | 37 |
| 1:1 LXX | 31 |
| 1:2–2:4a | 40 |
| 1:20–30 | 40 |
| 2:2–3 | 149, 152 |
| 2:7 | 511 |
| 3 | 242 |
| 4 | 242 |
| 15:1 | 180 |
| 16–21 | 239 |
| 16 | 239 |
| 17:1 | 217 |
| 17:7 | 247 |
| 17:10–12 | 216 |
| 18:22–33 | 380 |
| 21 | 239 |
| 21:8–21 | 239 |
| 22:2 | 49 |
| 24 | 119 |
| 24:10–21 | 114 |
| 24:32 LXX | 114 |
| 28:12 | 72, 324 |
| 29:1–13 | 114, 119 |
| 33:18–19 | 114 |
| 48:4 | 114 |
| 49:10 | 255 |
| 49:10–11 LXX | 326 |
| 49:10–12 | 18 |

### Exodus
| | |
|---|---|
| 2:16–22 | 114, 119 |
| 3:14 | 249 |
| 4:5 | 18 |
| 4:8–9 | 18 |
| 4:28 | 18 |
| 4:30 | 18 |
| 4:31 | 18 |
| 7:9 | 18 |
| 10:1–2 | 18 |
| 11:9–10 | 18 |
| 12:7 | 489 |
| 12:10 | 492, 493 |
| 12:22 | 489 |
| 12:46 LXX | 492, 493 |
| 13:21 | 205 |
| 14 | 18, 178 |
| 14:31 | 162 |
| 16 | 18, 185, 187 |
| 16:2 | 187 |
| 16:4 | 184 |
| 16:15 | 184 |
| 17:1–7 | 116, 223 |
| 19 | 18 |
| 19:16 | 335 |
| 19:19 | 335 |
| 20:6 | 381 |
| 33:20 | 50 |
| 33:23 | 50 |
| 34 | 48, 153 |
| 34:6 LXX | 50 |
| 34:34 | 503 |
| 40 | 48 |

### Leviticus
| | |
|---|---|
| 12:3 | 216 |
| 19:18 | 365, 405, 407 |
| 20:10 | 228, 230 |
| 23:33–43 | 209 |
| 23:40 | 326 |
| 25:8–12 | 248 |
| 26:11 | 385 |

### Numbers
| | |
|---|---|
| 1:51 | 507 |
| 3:10 | 507 |
| 3:38 | 507 |
| 9:9–14 | 174 |
| 9:12 | 493 |
| 11:13 LXX | 174 |
| 14:10–11 | 19 |
| 14:21–22 | 19 |
| 17:13 | 507 |
| 18:3–4 | 507 |
| 20:8–13 | 223 |
| 21:8–9 | 96 |
| 35:30 | 235 |

## Index of Primary Sources

### Deuteronomy
| | |
|---|---:|
| 1:16–17 | 225 |
| 2:14 | 148 |
| 5:10 | 381–82 |
| 5:11 | 381 |
| 6–11 | 404 |
| 6:1–3 | 382 |
| 6:4 | 242, 430 |
| 6:4–5 | 161, 242, 536 |
| 6:46 | 382 |
| 7:8–9 | 108 |
| 7:9 | 382, 404 |
| 7:12 | 404 |
| 7:13 | 108, 384 |
| 10:12–13 | 382 |
| 11:1 | 382 |
| 11:13 | 382 |
| 11:22 | 382 |
| 15:11 | 322 |
| 17:6 | 235 |
| 18:18 | 54, 56, 224 |
| 18:20–22 | 212 |
| 19:15 | 235 |
| 19:19 | 382 |
| 21:23 | 491 |
| 22:22–24 | 230 |
| 30:6 | 382 |
| 30:16 | 382 |
| 30:20 | 382 |
| 32:39 | 453 |

### Joshua
| | |
|---|---:|
| 18:23 | 314 |
| 22:5 | 382 |
| 24:32 | 114 |

### Judges
| | |
|---|---:|
| 11:12 | 77 |
| 13:7 | 194 |
| 16:17 | 194 |

### 1 Samuel
| | |
|---|---:|
| 1:1 | 92 |
| 13:17 | 314 |

### 2 Samuel
| | |
|---|---:|
| 7:12 | 224 |
| 13:23 | 314 |
| 15:23 | 452 |
| 16:10 | 77 |
| 19:22 | 77 |

### 1 Kings
| | |
|---|---:|
| 3:3 | 382 |
| 6:11–13 | 385 |
| 17:1–16 | 80 |
| 17:7–16 | 18 |
| 17:17–24 | 17, 294 |
| 17:18 | 77 |
| 17:23 | 136 |

### 2 Kings
| | |
|---|---:|
| 2:8 | 178 |
| 2:14 | 178 |
| 4:1–7 | 80 |
| 4:18–37 | 17 |
| 4:42 | 175 |
| 4:42–44 | 18, 79–80 |
| 5:10 | 253, 254–55 |
| 17:30–32 | 120 |
| 17:41 | 120 |
| 21:9 | 175 |

### 2 Chronicles
| | |
|---|---:|
| 13:19 | 314 |
| 20:7 | 406 |

### Nehemiah
| | |
|---|---:|
| 1:5 | 382 |

### Job
| | |
|---|---:|
| 9:8 LXX | 178 |

### Psalms
| | |
|---|---:|
| 6:3 | 334 |
| 6:4 | 334 |
| 22 | 485 |
| 22:15 | 489 |
| 22:16 | 514 |
| 22:18 | 484 |
| 26:2 | 453 |
| 27:1 | 234 |
| 34:4 | 453 |
| 34:21 | 493 |
| 35:19 | 408 |
| 40:10 LXX | 356, 361 |
| 41 LXX | 305–6 |
| 41:4 LXX | 306 |
| 41:6 | 374 |
| 41:7 LXX | 305, 334, 360, 374 |
| 41:9 | 356 |
| 41:12 | 374 |
| 42:1 | 489 |
| 42:2 | 379 |
| 42:3 LXX | 376, 379 |
| 42:5 | 305 |
| 42:5 LXX | 374 |
| 42:6 | 334, 360 |
| 42:6 MT | 305 |
| 42:11 | 305, 334, 360 |
| 42/43 | 116, 305, 334, 360, 370, 373, 376, 378–79, 385, 391 |
| 43:3 | 379, 385 |
| 43:5 | 305, 334, 360 |
| 46:5 | 379 |
| 55:10 LXX | 453 |
| 65:5 | 379 |
| 69 | 87 |
| 69:4 | 408 |
| 69:9 | 84, 87 |
| 69:21 | 489 |
| 78:16 | 223 |
| 78:16–20 | 223 |
| 78:20 | 223 |
| 78:24 | 169 |
| 78(77):24 | 184 |
| 78(77):24–25 | 185 |
| 80:8–19 | 397 |
| 80:16 | 401 |
| 81 | 287 |
| 81:6 LXX | 284 |
| 82:6 | 71, 153, 287 |
| 89:3–4 | 224 |
| 93–100 | 389 |
| 105:41 | 116 |

597

# INDEX OF PRIMARY SOURCES

| | | | | | |
|---|---|---|---|---|---|
| 107:23–30 | 178 | 29:18 | 17, 148, 255 | 54:13 | 169, 185, 187 |
| 109:1 LXX | 284 | 35:5–6 | 17, 148, 255 | 56:7 | 84 |
| 113–118 | 205 | 35:10 | 313 | 56:8 | 314 |
| 114:8 | 223 | 40:3 LXX | 55 | 57:4 LXX | 435 |
| 118:20 | 273 | 40:9 | 326 | 60:4 | 313 |
| 118:25–26 | 326 | 40:9–11 | 326 | 60:7 | 313 |
| | | 40:11 | 313 | 60:22 LXX | 313 |
| **Proverbs** | | 41:4 | 236, 453 | 61:1 | 255, 388 |
| 8:22–36 | 40 | 41:8 | 406 | 61:1–2 | 388 |
| 8:31 | 45 | 42–53 | 96 | 61:1–11 | 388 |
| 24:22a LXX | 435 | 42:1 | 61 | 61:3 | 388 |
| | | 42:1 LXX | 61 | 61:5–7 | 388 |
| **Ecclesiastes** | | 43:1 | 180 | 61:7 | 388 |
| 11:5 | 94 | 43:5 | 313 | 61:8 | 388 |
| | | 43:10 | 236, 357, 453 | 61:10 | 388 |
| **Song of Solomon** | | 43:13 | 453 | 61:10–11 | 388 |
| 1:3 | 322 | 43:25 | 180, 236, 453 | 62:4–5 | 80 |
| 1:12 | 322 | 44:2 | 180 | 66:18 | 314 |
| 2:13 | 322 | 44:8 | 180 | | |
| 3:1–4 | 507 | 45:18 | 236 | **Jeremiah** | |
| 4:10–11 | 322 | 45:22 | 236 | 1:1–2 | 215 |
| 4:12 | 322 | 46:4 | 236, 453 | 2:21 | 397 |
| 4:12–16 | 507 | 46:9 | 236 | 3:17 | 314 |
| 4:15 | 322 | 48:12 | 236, 453 | 6:9 | 397 |
| 4:16 | 322 | 49:5 | 313 | 7:11 | 84 |
| 5:1 | 322, 507 | 49:6 | 234 | 17:13 | 231 |
| 6:2 | 322, 507 | 49:18 | 313 | 23 | 270, 423, 536 |
| 6:11 | 507 | 51:12 | 180, 236, 453 | 23:1–2 | 277 |
| 7:8 | 322 | 52 | 338 | 23:1–8 | 277 |
| 7:13 | 322 | 52:6 | 180, 236, 453 | 23:7–8 | 277 |
| 8:13 | 322, 507 | 52:12 LXX | 313 | 23:8 LXX | 313 |
| 8:14 | 322 | 52:13 | 430 | 24:7 | 236 |
| | | 52:13 LXX | 3, 73, 96, 97, 189, 297, 307, 327, 337, 364, 430, 444–45, 483, 499 | 31:31 | 386 |
| **Isaiah** | | | | 31:31–34 | 366, 383, 430 |
| 5:1–7 | 397 | | | 31:33 | 187 |
| 6:9–10 | 343 | | | 31:34 | 430, 512 |
| 6:10 | 341, 343 | 52:13–53:12 | 96, 278, 338, 364, 428 | | |
| 8:6 | 255 | | | **Ezekiel** | |
| 9:1 | 30 | 52:15 | 338 | 6:7 | 236 |
| 11:1–10 | 388 | 52:15 LXX | 338, 342 | 6:13 | 236 |
| 11:12 | 313 | 53:1 | 343 | 11:17 | 313 |
| 12:3 | 223 | 53:1 LXX | 341, 342 | 15:1–8 | 397 |
| 25:6 | 18, 80 | 53:6 | 278 | 16 | 241 |
| 26:19 | 148, 255 | 53:7 | 59, 278 | 17:1–10 | 397 |
| 27:2–4 | 397 | 53:11–12 | 313 | 19:10–14 | 397 |
| 27:12 | 313 | 54:4–8 | 80 | 19:12 | 401 |

598

| | | | | | |
|---|---|---|---|---|---|
| 19:14 | 401 | **Hosea** | | 2:6 | 224 |
| 28:25 | 313 | 1–2 | 241 | 3:1 | 44 |
| 29:13 | 314 | 1:11 | 313 | 3:10–12 | 401 |
| 34 | 270, 277, 278, 536 | 2 | 120 | 3:11 | 58 |
| | | 2:1–3:5 | 80 | 4:14–16 | 30 |
| 34:1–10 | 277 | 10:1 | 397 | 4:18–22 | 539 |
| 34:5 | 277 | | | 5:22 | 401 |
| 34:8 | 277 | **Micah** | | 5:44 | 405 |
| 34:12–13 | 313 | 2:12 | 313 | 6:13 | 436 |
| 34:13 | 277 | 4:6 | 313 | 7:19 | 401 |
| 34:17–22 | 277 | 4:12 | 313 | 8:5–13 | 17, 133 |
| 34:28 | 277 | 5:2 | 224 | 8:11 | 18, 80 |
| 36 | 277 | | | 8:13 | 135 |
| 36:19 | 277 | **Zephaniah** | | 9:6 | 148 |
| 36:25–27 | 94, 99 | 3:15 | 326 | 9:14–15 | 102 |
| 36:26 | 121, 386, 415, 430 | 3:16 | 326 | 9:18–26 | 293 |
| | | 3:19 | 313 | 9:30 | 305 |
| 36:26–27 | 383, 388 | | | 9:34 | 279 |
| 37 | 277 | **Zechariah** | | 9:35–36 | 279 |
| 37:9 | 511 | 1–2 | 335 | 9:37–38 | 125 |
| 37:12 | 277 | 9:9 | 326, 483 | 10:6 | 278 |
| 37:21 | 277, 313 | 10:9 | 277 | 10:17–18 | 409 |
| 37:21–22 | 277 | 10:10 | 277 | 10:22 | 211 |
| 37:24 | 277 | 11 | 277 | 10:24–25 | 355, 408 |
| 37:26 | 278 | 11:4 | 277 | 10:32–33 | 264 |
| 37:27 | 385–86 | 11:7 | 277 | 10:40 | 357 |
| 37:28 | 278 | 11:16 | 277 | 11:2–6 | 255 |
| 38:8 | 313 | 12:10 | 423, 493 | 11:3–5 | 220 |
| 38:12 | 313 | 13 | 277 | 11:4–5 | 148 |
| 39:27 | 313 | 13:7 | 277, 278, 367, 422 | 11:5 | 17, 148 |
| 43:7 | 385 | | | 11:21 | 69 |
| 43:9 | 385 | 13:7 LXX | 278 | 11:25–27 | 155 |
| 47 | 116, 223 | 14 | 205, 209, 229 | 12:24 | 216 |
| 47:1–11 | 532 | 14:6–8 | 205 | 12:24–32 | 279 |
| 47:10 | 532 | 14:8 | 223 | 12:30 | 308 |
| 47:10–11 | 532 | 14:21 | 87 | 12:38–42 | 85 |
| | | | | 12:46–50 | 210 |
| **Daniel** | | **Malachi** | | 13:14–15 | 343 |
| 7:13 | 383 | 3:1 | 55 | 13:30 | 125 |
| 7:13–14 | 156, 189, 364 | | | 13:39 | 125 |
| 7:14 | 96 | | | 13:40 | 401 |
| 7:15–27 | 189 | **NEW TESTAMENT** | | 13:42 | 401 |
| 9:4 | 382 | | | 13:50 | 401 |
| 12:2 | 156 | **Matthew** | | 13:53–58 | 129 |
| | | 1–2 | 209 | 13:55 | 210 |
| | | 2:5 | 219 | 13:57 | 131 |

599

# INDEX OF PRIMARY SOURCES

| | | | | | |
|---|---|---|---|---|---|
| 14:22–33 | 177 | 27:24 | 477 | 4:1–30 | 333 |
| 15:24 | 278 | 27:26 | 471, 476 | 4:11–12 | 343 |
| 16 | 537 | 27:31 | 482 | 4:13–20 | 333 |
| 16:1–2a | 85 | 27:37 | 482 | 4:26–29 | 333 |
| 16:4 | 85 | 27:42 | 71 | 4:29 | 125 |
| 16:16–19 | 64 | 27:50 | 489–90 | 4:35–41 | 179 |
| 16:17 | 219, 536 | 27:53 | 384 | 4:40 | 293 |
| 16:17–18 | 537 | 27:55–56 | 486 | 5:21–24 | 17 |
| 16:17–19 | 67, 440 | 27:57 | 494 | 5:21–43 | 293–94 |
| 16:18 | 537 | 27:62 | 310 | 5:25–34 | 293 |
| 16:19 | 509, 512 | 28:1–3 | 500 | 5:35–43 | 17 |
| 18:3 | 93 | 28:9 | 507 | 5:39 | 308 |
| 18:8–9 | 401 | 28:9–10 | 505 | 5:41 | 293, 308 |
| 18:12–14 | 269 | 28:18 | 430 | 6–8 | 192 |
| 18:18 | 509 | | | 6:1–6 | 129 |
| 18:18–20 | 440 | **Mark** | | 6:3 | 210 |
| 21:1–9 | 324 | 1:2–11 | 55 | 6:4 | 131 |
| 21:5 | 326 | 1:4 | 44 | 6:14–16 | 56 |
| 21:12–13 | 83 | 1:7 | 57, 58 | 6:30–52 | 18 |
| 21:23–27 | 85 | 1:8 | 57 | 6:32–8:33 | 16 |
| 21:33–41 | 397 | 1:11 | 3, 61, 155, 334 | 6:32–44 | 79, 167 |
| 21:45 | 310 | 1:14 | 104 | 6:32–56 | 167 |
| 22:1–10 | 18 | 1:16 | 65, 528 | 6:33–8:33 | xi |
| 22:1–14 | 80 | 1:16–20 | 64, 66, 68, 539 | 6:41 | 429 |
| 23:29 | 130 | 1:19 | 65, 168 | 6:42 | 175 |
| 23:37 | 313 | 1:24 | 194 | 6:45 | 69 |
| 23:39 | 273 | 1:43 | 305 | 6:45–52 | 167, 177, 179 |
| 25:31–46 | 155 | 2:1–3:6 | 144, 149, 153 | 6:53–56 | 167 |
| 26:3 | 310 | 2:1–12 | 17, 143, 151 | 7:1–8:10 | 167 |
| 26:3–5 | 309 | 2:11 | 148 | 7:26–29 | 135 |
| 26:6–13 | 295, 319, 495 | 2:14 | 65, 68 | 7:33 | 254 |
| 26:18 | 211 | 2:18–20 | 102 | 7:34 | 305, 429 |
| 26:21 | 211 | 2:18–22 | 80 | 8 | 56 |
| 26:30–32 | 367 | 2:23–28 | 144 | 8:1–9 | 79 |
| 26:31 | 278, 422 | 2:24 | 144 | 8:11–12 | 135 |
| 26:39 | 455 | 3:1–6 | 144 | 8:11–13 | 167 |
| 26:42 | 455 | 3:5 | 305 | 8:11–33 | 167 |
| 26:45–46 | 389 | 3:6 | 2, 144, 153, 442 | 8:14–21 | 167 |
| 26:59 | 456 | 3:13–14 | 196 | 8:22 | 69 |
| 26:60–61 | 85 | 3:13–19 | 64, 68 | 8:22–26 | 17, 253, 255 |
| 26:67 | 459 | 3:14–15 | 67 | 8:23 | 254 |
| 26:75 | 462 | 3:16 | 67 | 8:27–9:1 | 194 |
| 27:1–2 | 466 | 3:21 | 279 | 8:27 | 194, 195 |
| 27:11 | 467 | 3:22 | 216, 279 | 8:27–30 | 56, 67, 167, 224 |
| 27:12–14 | 474 | 3:30 | 216, 279 | 8:29 | 167, 194, 195 |
| 27:15–26 | 476 | 3:31–35 | 210, 487 | 8:31 | 442, 456 |

# Index of Primary Sources

| | | | | | |
|---|---|---|---|---|---|
| 8:31–32 | 337 | 13:26 | 383 | 15:40 | 486 |
| 8:31–33 | 167, 194 | 13:26–27 | 155 | 15:42–46 | 494 |
| 8:32 | 460 | 14:1 | 310 | 15:43 | 494 |
| 8:33 | 194, 196 | 14:1–2 | 309 | 16:1 | 495 |
| 8:34–9:1 | 195 | 14:3–9 | 294–95, 319, 495 | 16:1–4 | 500 |
| 8:34 | 333 | | | 16:1–8 | 505 |
| 8:35 | 333 | 14:4 | 320 | 16:2 | 502 |
| 9:1 | 93 | 14:18–21 | 359 | 16:9–11 | 505 |
| 9:7 | 3, 155, 334 | 14:20 | 361 | 16:12–13 | 505 |
| 9:18 | 40 | 14:22 | 175 | | |
| 9:19 | 135 | 14:24 | 278, 313 | **Luke** | |
| 9:31 | 337, 442 | 14:25 | 18 | 1–2 | 209 |
| 9:43 | 401 | 14:26 | 428 | 1:30 | 180 |
| 9:48 | 401 | 14:26–28 | 367 | 2:13–22 | 324 |
| 10:12 | 228 | 14:27 | 278, 422 | 2:24 | 87 |
| 10:13–16 | 93 | 14:29–31 | 363 | 2:47 | 214 |
| 10:13–31 | 93 | 14:34 | 305, 334, 360, 374 | 3:2 | 44, 456, 460 |
| 10:15 | 93 | | | 3:7 | 108 |
| 10:17–27 | 93 | 14:35 | 428 | 3:8 | 239 |
| 10:28–31 | 93 | 14:36 | 428 | 3:16 | 58 |
| 10:33 | 456 | 14:41 | 332, 428 | 3:23 | 248 |
| 10:33–34 | 337, 442 | 14:41–42 | 389 | 4:16–30 | 129 |
| 10:39 | 522 | 14:43 | 389 | 4:18–19 | 388 |
| 10:45 | 278 | 14:53–65 | 459 | 4:19 | 248 |
| 10:46–52 | 17, 113, 253 | 14:55 | 456 | 4:24 | 131 |
| 10:47–52 | 255 | 14:57–59 | 85 | 5 | 528 |
| 11:1–10 | 324 | 14:58 | 84 | 5:1 | 528 |
| 11:9–10 | 71 | 14:61 | 3 | 5:1–11 | 64, 67, 68, 168, 524–25, 526, 528, 533, 539 |
| 11:10 | 326 | 14:62 | 472 | | |
| 11:15–17 | 83 | 14:65 | 459 | | |
| 11:16 | 84 | 14:68 | 461 | 5:4 | 529 |
| 11:22–24 | 380 | 14:72 | 461 | 5:8 | 524 |
| 11:27 | 92, 225 | 15:1 | 459, 466 | 5:10 | 539 |
| 11:27–33 | 85 | 15:2 | 467 | 5:11 | 539 |
| 12:1–9 | 397 | 15:2–12 | 472 | 5:24 | 148 |
| 12:10 | 273 | 15:5 | 474 | 6:22–23 | 264 |
| 12:28 | 3 | 15:6–14 | 470 | 6:27 | 405 |
| 12:28–34 | 365, 382 | 15:6–15 | 476 | 6:38 | 531 |
| 12:29–31 | 404 | 15:13 | 470 | 6:40 | 355 |
| 13 | 3, 375 | 15:15 | 471, 476 | 7 | 322 |
| 13:9 | 409, 410 | 15:16–20 | 472 | 7:1–10 | 17, 133 |
| 13:9–13 | 408–9 | 15:20 | 482 | 7:11–17 | 17, 294 |
| 13:11 | 409 | 15:23 | 489 | 7:14 | 308 |
| 13:12 | 410 | 15:32 | 71 | 7:18–23 | 255 |
| 13:13 | 211 | 15:37 | 489 | 7:22 | 17, 148 |
| 13:22 | 135 | 15:39 | 3 | | |

# INDEX OF PRIMARY SOURCES

| | | | | | |
|---|---|---|---|---|---|
| 7:36–50 | 295, 319, 495, 508 | 22:31–34 | 367 | 1:1–18 | xii, 1, 3, 26, 30, 31–52, 138, 311 |
| 8:10 | 343 | 22:43 | 334, 335 | 1:2 | 36, 37, 431 |
| 8:19–21 | 210 | 22:53 | 284 | 1:3 | 22, 36, 37–38, 42, 43, 45, 51, 154 |
| 8:40–56 | 293 | 22:61 | 461 | | |
| 9:10 | 69 | 22:62 | 462 | 1:3a | 38–39 |
| 9:27 | 93 | 22:63–65 | 459 | 1:3a–b | 37 |
| 10:2 | 125 | 22:66–71 | 284 | 1:3b | 38–39 |
| 10:13 | 69 | 22:67 | 284 | 1:3c–4 | 37–38 |
| 10:28 | 356 | 22:70 | 284 | 1:3–5 | 138 |
| 10:37 | 356 | 23:1 | 466 | 1:3c–5 | 37 |
| 10:38–42 | 294–95, 320 | 23:2–3 | 466 | 1:4 | 34, 39, 42, 43, 45, 156 |
| 11:15 | 216 | 23:3 | 467 | | |
| 11:15–23 | 279 | 23:13–16 | 470 | 1:4–5 | 34, 160, 234, 337, 345 |
| 11:16 | 85 | 23:16–22 | 471 | | |
| 11:20 | 3 | 23:17–25 | 476 | 1:5 | 38, 39–40, 42, 43, 44, 45, 106, 337, 345, 361 |
| 11:23 | 308 | 23:22 | 470 | | |
| 11:29–32 | 85 | 23:25 | 476 | | |
| 11:37 | 532 | 23:33 | 482 | 1:6 | 32, 41–42, 43, 44, 106 |
| 11:47 | 130 | 23:46 | 489 | | |
| 12:8–9 | 264 | 23:49 | 486 | 1:6–7 | 33 |
| 12:11–12 | 264 | 23:50 | 494 | 1:6–8 | 30, 32, 33, 34, 40, 42, 43–44, 48, 49, 53, 54, 159, 288 |
| 13:10–17 | 149 | 24:1–3 | 500 | | |
| 13:24 | 273 | 24:1–11 | 505 | | |
| 13:28–29 | 18 | 24:5 | 501 | 1:6–13 | 32–33, 41–47, 51 |
| 13:34 | 313 | 24:12 | 495, 498, 502, 503, 505 | 1:7 | 36, 43, 45, 345 |
| 14:16–24 | 18 | | | 1:7–8 | 44, 409 |
| 15:3–7 | 269 | 24:36 | 509 | 1:8 | 9, 42 |
| 16:19–31 | 294, 308 | 24:36–49 | 509, 512, 533 | 1:9 | 22, 44–45, 59, 160, 234, 302, 336, 337, 345, 399, 410–11, 468 |
| 19:28–40 | 324 | 24:41 | 509, 524, 533 | | |
| 19:38 | 326 | 24:49 | 509 | | |
| 19:45–46 | 83 | 24:53 | 228 | | |
| 19:47 | 214, 284, 309 | | | 1:9–10 | 34, 313 |
| 19:48 | 310 | **John** | | 1:9–11 | 43, 44–45 |
| 20:1–8 | 85 | 1–4 | 31, 133 | 1:9–13 | 43 |
| 20:9–16 | 397 | 1 | 24, 66 | 1:10 | 45, 97, 106 |
| 21:12–13 | 409 | 1:1–11:45 | 24 | 1:10–11 | 58 |
| 21:17 | 211 | 1:1–4:54 | x, 30–138 | 1:10–12 | 34 |
| 21:20–38 | 347 | 1:1–2:11 | 7 | 1:11 | 34, 43, 45, 483 |
| 21:37 | 230 | 1:1 | 3, 22, 31, 32, 33, 36, 47, 138, 286, 431, 515, 516 | 1:12 | 36, 43, 47 |
| 21:38 | 228 | | | 1:12a | 46 |
| 22:1–2 | 309 | | | 1:12a–b | 45–46 |
| 22:2 | 310 | 1:1–2 | 37, 49, 78 | 1:12c | 46 |
| 22:16–18 | 80 | 1:1–4 | 44 | 1:12–13 | 43, 45–47, 106, 138, 244, 337, 469 |
| 22:19 | 188 | 1:1–5 | 32–33, 34, 36–41 | | |
| 22:27 | 350, 352 | 1:1–13 | 34 | | |

602

# Index of Primary Sources

| | | | | | |
|---|---|---|---|---|---|
| 1:12c–13 | 45–46 | 1:26 | 57, 60, 103 | 1:43–45 | 174 |
| 1:13 | 42, 46, 468 | 1:27 | 58, 71, 106 | 1:43–51 | 63, 67–73 |
| 1:13–14 | 42 | 1:28 | 7, 57, 190, 265, | 1:45 | 63, 64, 68, 69, |
| 1:14 | 10, 23, 32–33, | | 287, 297 | | 161, 162, 262 |
| | 34, 42, 48–50, | 1:29 | 53, 58, 59, 63, | 1:45–46 | 69–70, |
| | 51, 65, 66, 78, | | 65, 262, 443, | | 131, 224 |
| | 215, 385, 430 | | 477, 492, 512 | 1:45–51 | 67 |
| 1:14–18 | 33, 34, 47–51 | 1:29–31 | 58–60 | 1:46 | 70, 224 |
| 1:15 | 30, 32, 34, 48, | 1:29–34 | 53, 58–61 | 1:47 | 58, 242 |
| | 49, 53, 59, 106, 159, | 1:30 | 49, 58, 59, 106 | 1:47–48 | 89, 187 |
| | 288, 344, 409 | 1:31 | 60–61, 70, | 1:47–49 | 69, 70–72 |
| 1:16 | 32, 34, 48, | | 254, 527 | 1:47–51 | 69, 70 |
| | 49–50 | 1:31–33 | 107 | 1:48 | 70, 120, 148 |
| 1:16–18 | 33, 48 | 1:32 | 9, 58, 311 | 1:49 | 10, 64, 69, 70, |
| 1:17 | 30, 32, 34, 42, | 1:32–33 | 65 | | 72, 262, 483 |
| | 47, 48, 50, 51, 72, | 1:32–34 | 53, 58, 60–61 | 1:50 | 69, 78 |
| | 429 | 1:33 | 57, 60–61, 99, | 1:50–51 | 70, 72–73, 75 |
| 1:17–18 | 50–51 | | 103, 113, 492 | 1:51 | 63, 64, 67, 69, |
| 1:18 | 3, 33, 48, 50–51, | 1:34 | 9, 54, 55, 58, | | 72–73, 262, |
| | 93, 138, 188, 286, | | 61, 311, 545 | | 324, 538 |
| | 361, 515, 544 | 1:35 | 21, 53, 58, 63, 76 | 2–12 | 4, 30, 75, 517 |
| 1:19–12:36 | 5 | 1:35–36 | 64, 70 | 2–11 | 517 |
| 1:19–10:42 | 7 | 1:35–37 | 65 | 2–4 | 4, 75, 132, 138, |
| 1:19–4:54 | xii, 8 | 1:35–39 | 63 | | 139, 163 |
| 1:19–3:36 | 6, 7 | 1:35–42 | 21, 63–67, 68 | 2 | 210 |
| 1:19–2:12 | 6, 8 | 1:35–50 | 64 | 2:1–12:50 | 7 |
| 1:19 | 9, 53, 54, 55, | 1:35–51 | 14, 30, 62–74, | 2:1 | 53, 67, 69 |
| | 56, 57, 87, 150, | | 75, 262, 340, | 2:1–3a | 76–77 |
| | 186, 311 | | 407, 504, 526 | 2:1–11 | 7, 18, 75, 79–82, |
| 1:19–21 | 71, 224 | 1:36 | 54, 63, 64, 262, | | 88, 89, 137, 145, |
| 1:19–23 | 53–56 | | 443, 477, 492 | | 254, 311, 322, |
| 1:19–28 | 53–58, 64, 281 | 1:37 | 59 | | 370, 528 |
| 1:19–34 | 30, 32, 43, | 1:38 | 63, 64, 65, 74, | 2:1–12 | 30, 74–82, 105, |
| | 52–62, 63, 99, | | 316, 506, 524 | | 132, 160, 208, |
| | 104–5, 159, | 1:38–39 | 65 | | 210, 487 |
| | 288, 409 | 1:39 | 63, 70 | 2:2 | 191 |
| 1:19–51 | 4, 7, 53, 138 | 1:40 | 21, 66, | 2:3–4 | 75, 79 |
| 1:20 | 9, 11, 62, 461 | | 360–61, 528 | 2:3b–4 | 76, 77 |
| 1:20–23 | 105 | 1:40–42 | 63, 66, 174 | 2:4 | 22, 80, 211, 220, |
| 1:22–23 | 55 | 1:41 | 10, 63, 64, 68, | | 332, 422, 443, 487 |
| 1:23 | 54, 378 | | 72, 219, 262 | 2:4–5 | 134 |
| 1:24 | 53 | 1:41–42 | 539 | 2:5 | 76, 77 |
| 1:24–27 | 60 | 1:42 | 21, 63, 67, 535–36 | 2:6 | 76, 104 |
| 1:24–28 | 56–58 | 1:43 | 53, 63, 64, 67–69, | 2:6–8 | 77–78 |
| 1:25 | 71 | | 73, 76, 151 | 2:7 | 76 |
| 1:25–28 | 54 | 1:43–44 | 67, 68–69, 332 | 2:8 | 76 |

## INDEX OF PRIMARY SOURCES

| | | | | | |
|---|---|---|---|---|---|
| 2:9 | 76 | 3:1–2 | 225, 494 | 3:17–18 | 92 |
| 2:9–10 | 78 | 3:1–2b | 91, 92 | 3:17–21 | 108 |
| 2:10 | 76 | 3:1–3 | 92–94, 137 | 3:18 | 51, 98, 108 |
| 2:11 | 2, 18, 19, 73, 75, 76, 78, 86, 88, 131, 137, 254, 332, 342 | 3:1–10 | 492 | 3:18–21 | 92, 98–99 |
| | | 3:1–12 | 91, 93, 95, 100, 107, 270–71 | 3:19 | 98, 234, 361, 468 |
| 2:11–12 | 191 | 3:1–21 | 12, 30, 89–100, 105, 340 | 3:19–20 | 211 |
| 2:12 | 76, 78–79, 136, 209, 487 | | | 3:19–21 | 91, 92, 345 |
| | | 3:1–30 | 105 | 3:20 | 98–99, 416 |
| 2:13–3:21 | 103, 132 | 3:2 | 95, 134, 160, 173, 179, 220, 342, 361, 529 | 3:21–36 | 101 |
| 2:13 | 2, 6, 8, 85, 86, 103, 111, 137, 139, 173, 204, 315 | | | 3:22 | 103, 104, 111, 112, 138, 191 |
| | | 3:2c–3 | 91, 92, 93 | 3:22–24 | 102, 103–4, 112, 113 |
| 2:13–17 | 86–87 | 3:3 | 24, 94, 106, 468, 485, 538 | 3:22–25 | 101 |
| 2:13–22 | 2, 83, 85, 86, 281, 315 | | | 3:22–30 | 54, 101, 102, 108 |
| | | 3:3c | 92 | 3:22–36 | 7, 30, 100–109, 132, 139 |
| 2:13–25 | 30, 83–89 | 3:3–8 | 46 | | |
| 2:14 | 86 | 3:4–8 | 91, 94 | 3:23 | 103, 104 |
| 2:14–15 | 85 | 3:5 | 91, 94, 468 | 3:24 | 102, 104 |
| 2:14–17 | 83, 85 | 3:5b | 92 | 3:25 | 101, 103, 104 |
| 2:14–19 | 85 | 3:7 | 106, 468, 485 | 3:25–26 | 104, 112 |
| 2:15 | 86 | 3:8 | 94 | 3:25–30 | 102, 103, 104–5 |
| 2:16 | 85, 87, 320 | 3:9 | 90, 91, 95 | 3:25–36 | 112 |
| 2:17 | 85, 87, 191 | 3:9–12 | 91, 95 | 3:26 | 9, 43, 44, 101, 287 |
| 2:18 | 86 | 3:9–21 | 91, 105 | | |
| 2:18–22 | 86, 87–88, 324, 459 | 3:10 | 70, 95 | 3:26–30 | 288 |
| | | 3:11 | 92, 95, 106, 469 | 3:27 | 105, 108 |
| 2:19 | 86, 87, 88, 327 | 3:11–12 | 105 | 3:27–30 | 101, 104–5, 105 |
| 2:19–21 | 444 | 3:12 | 91 | 3:28 | 105, 159, 219 |
| 2:19–22 | 288, 319 | 3:12–17 | 92 | 3:29 | 101–2, 105, 159, 211, 270, 322, 404 |
| 2:20 | 86, 87 | 3:13 | 72, 96, 97–98, 184, 189, 468 | | |
| 2:21 | 86, 87, 88 | | | 3:30 | 102, 105 |
| 2:21–22 | 444 | 3:13–17 | 95–98 | 3:31 | 105 |
| 2:22 | 86, 87, 88, 137, 191, 327, 336, 361, 410 | 3:13–21 | 91, 98, 101 | 3:31–32 | 107 |
| | | 3:14 | 72, 96, 96–97, 98, 332, 335, 336, 443 | 3:31–33 | 105–8 |
| 2:23–3:2 | 90 | | | 3:31–36 | 91, 101, 102, 104, 105–9 |
| 2:23 | 18, 86, 88, 90, 160, 173, 192, 220, 342 | 3:14–15 | 97, 494 | | |
| | | 3:14–16 | 97 | 3:32 | 106, 469 |
| 2:23–24 | 86 | 3:15 | 97, 98, 430 | 3:32–33 | 105, 107 |
| 2:23–25 | 85, 86, 88–89, 131, 134, 137, 238 | 3:15–18 | 156 | 3:34 | 105, 106, 107 |
| | | 3:16 | 39, 51, 97, 108, 242, 313, 336 | 3:34–36 | 105–6, 107 |
| 2:24 | 120 | | | 3:35 | 107, 403 |
| 2:24–25 | 187 | 3:16ab | 98 | 3:36 | 39, 44, 106, 108, 156, 430 |
| 2:25 | 148 | 3:16cd | 97, 98 | | |
| 3 | 44, 91 | 3:16–18 | 158 | | |
| 3:1 | 90, 343 | 3:17 | 95, 97–98, 345 | 4–5 | 24 |

604

*Index of Primary Sources*

| | | | | | |
|---|---|---|---|---|---|
| 4 | 111, 114–16, 126, 223, 229 | 4:19–24 | 116, 120–22 | 4:46–54 | 2, 15, 17, 30, 75, 111, 132–38, 139, 145, 146, 160, 173, 311 |
| 4:1–6:71 | 7 | 4:20–26 | 121 | | |
| 4:1–5:47 | 6 | 4:21 | 121, 158, 223 | | |
| 4:1–5:41 | 7 | 4:21–24 | 119, 121 | | |
| 4:1 | 112–13 | 4:22 | 118, 122, 150, 271 | 4:47 | 130, 131 |
| 4:1–2 | 191 | 4:23 | 4, 121, 158, 223, 422 | 4:48 | 131, 218 |
| 4:1–3 | 102, 112–13, 128, 130, 136 | 4:23–24 | 223 | 4:48–49 | 134 |
| | | 4:25 | 219, 271 | 4:48–50 | 134 |
| 4:1–6 | 112–15 | 4:25–26 | 59, 119, 122 | 4:49 | 131, 134 |
| 4:1–26 | 340 | 4:26 | 115, 122, 124, 262 | 4:50 | 131, 134, 138 |
| 4:1–42 | 10, 30, 109–28, 139, 322 | 4:27 | 122, 123, 138, 191 | 4:51 | 138 |
| | | 4:27–30 | 111, 122–24 | 4:51–54 | 136–37 |
| 4:2 | 103, 112–13 | 4:28 | 123 | 4:53 | 131, 134, 136, 138 |
| 4:3 | 101, 130 | 4:28–29 | 122 | 4:54 | 88, 130 |
| 4:4 | 103, 113 | 4:29 | 71, 219 | 5–12 | 30, 224 |
| 4:4–6 | 112, 113–15 | 4:30 | 123, 124 | 5–10 | 4, 31, 133, 155, 163, 214, 451 |
| 4:4–42 | 130, 132 | 4:31 | 124, 191 | | |
| 4:5 | 114 | 4:31–34 | 115, 124–25 | 5 | 2, 116, 139, 140–63, 166–67, 207, 216 |
| 4:6 | 125 | 4:31–38 | 111, 124–26, 138 | | |
| 4:6–7 | 125 | 4:32 | 125, 271 | 5:1–10:42 | x, 7–8, 139–88 |
| 4:6–15 | 174 | 4:33 | 125, 191 | | |
| 4:7 | 111, 115, 124, 126, 489 | 4:34 | 124, 125, 183, 431, 488–89 | 5:1 | x, 2, 6, 8, 30, 86, 103, 142, 147, 173, 204, 207, 208 |
| 4:7–9 | 115, 115–16 | 4:35 | 221 | 5:1–3 | 146–48 |
| 4:7–15 | 111, 115–17 | 4:35–38 | 124, 125–26, 146, 181 | 5:1–4 | 205 |
| 4:7–26 | 111 | | | 5:1–9b | 17 |
| 4:8 | 111, 115, 123, 138, 191 | 4:36 | 125 | 5:1–9c | 142, 145–49, 153 |
| 4:9 | 115, 123 | 4:37 | 125 | 5:1–18 | 144 |
| 4:9c | 111 | 4:38 | 114, 124, 125 | 5:2 | 147 |
| 4:9–10 | 205 | 4:39–40 | 126–27 | 5:2–9c | 143–44 |
| 4:9–15 | 124 | 4:39–42 | 111, 126–27 | 5:3 | 147–48 |
| 4:10 | 117, 271 | 4:40 | 130 | 5:4 | 146, 147, 205 |
| 4:10–12 | 115, 116–17 | 4:41–42 | 126, 127 | 5:5 | 148 |
| 4:12 | 247 | 4:42 | 103, 111, 112, 122, 127, 137, 313, 336 | 5:5–7 | 146, 148 |
| 4:13–15 | 115, 117 | | | 5:5–9a | 150 |
| 4:14 | 185 | 4:43 | 103, 127, 128, 130 | 5:6 | 148, 151 |
| 4:15 | 117, 119, 185 | 4:43–45 | 30, 111, 128–32, 136, 139 | 5:7 | 148 |
| 4:16 | 119, 124 | | | 5:8 | 148 |
| 4:16–18 | 89, 118, 119 | 4:43–54 | 208 | 5:8–9c | 146, 148–49 |
| 4:16–26 | 111, 115, 117, 118–22 | 4:44 | 128–29, 131 | 5:9 | 259 |
| | | 4:45 | 128, 130, 131, 134, 137 | 5:9a–c | 149 |
| 4:18 | 148 | | | 5:9d | 142, 149, 150 |
| 4:18–19 | 187 | 4:46 | 77 | 5:9d–13 | 150–51 |
| 4:19 | 119, 124 | 4:46–47 | 136 | 5:9d–16 | 143 |
| 4:19–20 | 118 | 4:46–50 | 135–36 | 5:9d–18 | 149–53 |

605

## INDEX OF PRIMARY SOURCES

| | | | | | |
|---|---|---|---|---|---|
| 5:10 | 144, 150 | 5:31 | 142, 159, 234 | 6:1–4 | 173–74 |
| 5:10–13 | 150 | 5:31–32 | 159 | 6:1–15 | 19, 79, 167, 168, 171, 172–76, 181, 195 |
| 5:10–18 | 142 | 5:31–39 | 409 | | |
| 5:11–12 | 160 | 5:31–40 | 44, 159–61, 163, 234–35, 311 | | |
| 5:13–21 | 160 | | | 6:1–16 | 7 |
| 5:14 | 150, 151, 254, 261 | 5:32 | 159, 409 | 6:1–21 | 173, 195 |
| 5:15 | 150, 152 | 5:33 | 43, 409, 469, 479 | 6:1–22 | 526 |
| 5:16 | 152, 153 | | | 6:1–25 | 168 |
| 5:16–18 | 150, 152–53, 443 | 5:33–34 | 9 | 6:1–40 | 169, 181 |
| 5:17 | 152 | 5:33–35 | 54, 159–60, 287 | 6:2 | 173, 176, 342 |
| 5:17f. | 143 | 5:34 | 153 | 6:3 | 173, 174 |
| 5:17–30 | 160 | 5:35 | 104, 248 | 6:4 | x, 2, 6, 8, 16, 86, 140, 167, 173–74, 204, 207 |
| 5:18 | 143, 144, 152–53, 166, 207, 216, 219 | 5:36 | 159, 160, 254, 285, 409, 489 | | |
| | | 5:36–37 | 235 | 6:5 | 65, 174 |
| 5:19 | 142, 153, 158, 159, 254 | 5:36–38 | 24 | 6:5–9 | 173, 174–75 |
| | | 5:37 | 50, 409 | 6:6 | 174 |
| 5:19–20 | 154 | 5:37–38 | 159 | 6:7 | 65 |
| 5:19–30 | 142, 153–58, 159, 163, 180, 311 | 5:37–39 | 160–61 | 6:7–8 | 332 |
| | | 5:38 | 44, 401 | 6:8 | 174 |
| 5:19–47 | 143, 150, 153, 163, 172 | 5:39 | 69, 159, 161, 162, 409, 518 | 6:8–9 | 174–75 |
| | | | | 6:8–12 | 24 |
| 5:20 | 403 | 5:39–47 | 147 | 6:9 | 174, 531 |
| 5:21 | 149, 154 | 5:40 | 142, 159, 161 | 6:10–11 | 173, 175 |
| 5:21–23 | 154–55 | 5:41 | 142, 159, 161 | 6:11 | 524, 531, 533 |
| 5:21–28 | 154 | 5:41–44 | 11, 161–62, 211, 215, 311, 344, 536 | 6:12–13 | 173, 175–76 |
| 5:22–23 | 154 | | | 6:13 | 187 |
| 5:22–30 | 159 | 5:41–45 | 142, 163 | 6:14 | 342, 468 |
| 5:23 | 246 | 5:41–47 | 159, 161–63 | 6:14–15 | 169, 173, 176 |
| 5:24 | 430 | 5:42 | 162, 382 | 6:15 | 173, 178, 187, 194, 483 |
| 5:24–25 | 155–56 | 5:42–43 | 161 | | |
| 5:24–27 | 155–56 | 5:42–44 | 163 | 6:16 | 179 |
| 5:24–28 | 154 | 5:43 | 45 | 6:16–18 | 179–80 |
| 5:24–29 | 21, 345 | 5:44 | 161, 215, 382, 430 | 6:16–21 | 167, 168, 170, 171, 176–81 |
| 5:25 | 4, 154, 156–57, 158, 270, 422, 510 | 5:45–47 | 161, 162–63, 172 | | |
| | | | | 6:17 | 78, 179, 180 |
| 5:25–27 | 98 | 5:46 | 69, 162 | 6:17–22 | 24 |
| 5:25–29 | 158 | 5:46–47 | 142 | 6:18 | 179, 187 |
| 5:26 | 156 | 5:47 | 142 | 6:19 | 180, 181, 356 |
| 5:26–27 | 155 | 6–14 | 399 | 6:19–21 | 179, 180–81 |
| 5:26–29 | 24 | 6 | xi, 2, 8, 15, 16, 30, 72, 140, 146, 164–97, 207, 315 | 6:20 | 177, 180 |
| 5:27 | 156 | | | 6:20–40 | 191 |
| 5:28 | 154, 156, 270, 422 | | | 6:21 | 168 |
| 5:28–29 | 98, 143, 153, 154, 156–58, 186, 375, 510 | 6:1–10:42 | 7 | 6:22 | 182, 187 |
| | | 6:1–10:39 | 6 | 6:22–25 | 167, 182, 191 |
| 5:30 | 153, 158 | 6:1 | 103, 208, 527, 528 | 6:22–25a | 182 |

606

## Index of Primary Sources

| | | | | | |
|---|---|---|---|---|---|
| 6:22–27 | 171, 181, 182–83 | 6:41 | 16, 131, 167, 181, 189, 192, 212, 220, 244, 260 | 6:55–57 | 189–90 |
| 6:22–29 | 167 | | | 6:56 | 171, 190, 437 |
| 6:22–40 | 212 | | | 6:57 | 190, 275 |
| 6:22–58 | 180 | 6:41–42 | 184, 186 | 6:58 | 184, 190 |
| 6:22–59 | 171, 181–91 | 6:41–51 | 168, 171, 181, 186–89 | 6:59 | 78, 190–91, 214, 460 |
| 6:22–71 | 194–95 | | | | |
| 6:23 | 183 | 6:41–58 | 181, 192, 193, 212 | 6:60 | 182, 191, 192, 193, 195, 220 |
| 6:24 | 78 | | | | |
| 6:25 | 182, 212 | 6:41–59 | 191 | 6:60–65 | 190 |
| 6:25b | 182 | 6:41–66 | 169 | 6:60–66 | 167, 171, 191–94 |
| 6:25–40 | 168 | 6:42 | 193, 271 | | |
| 6:25–58 | 191 | 6:43 | 189, 192, 212, 220 | 6:60–71 | 192 |
| 6:25–71 | 182 | 6:43–47 | 187 | 6:61 | 189, 192, 220 |
| 6:26 | 88, 316, 342 | 6:43–51 | 186 | 6:61–65 | 192–93 |
| 6:26–27 | 212 | 6:44 | 16, 105, 107, 158, 168, 186, 193, 242, 336, 510, 530 | 6:62 | 72, 78, 96, 184, 192, 194 |
| 6:27 | 16, 107, 170, 171 | | | | |
| 6:27–51c | 168 | | | 6:63 | 94, 193, 195, 224, 430 |
| 6:28–29 | 171, 181, 183–84 | 6:45 | 169, 185, 186 | | |
| | | 6:46 | 50 | 6:64 | 193, 453 |
| 6:29 | 158, 215 | 6:47 | 156, 185, 430 | 6:65 | 193 |
| 6:30 | 88, 182 | 6:48 | 19, 177, 188, 399 | 6:66 | 10, 192, 193–94 |
| 6:30–31 | 167, 184 | 6:48–51 | 187, 188 | 6:67 | 182, 191, 194–95 |
| 6:30–33 | 171, 181, 184–85 | 6:48–58 | 169, 185, 188 | 6:67–69 | 167, 194, 195 |
| | | 6:48–59 | 190 | 6:67–70 | 169 |
| 6:31 | 188 | 6:49 | 190 | 6:67–71 | 171, 174, 176, 194–96 |
| 6:31–47 | 169 | 6:50 | 190 | | |
| 6:31–58 | 172 | 6:50–51 | 184 | 6:68 | 195, 367 |
| 6:32 | 172, 410–11 | 6:51 | 19, 49, 177, 188, 313, 399 | 6:68–69 | 302, 353, 455 |
| 6:32–47 | 185, 188, 190 | | | 6:69 | 171, 195, 529, 546 |
| 6:32–58 | 167 | 6:51c | 188, 278 | 6:70 | 194, 196, 356, 407 |
| 6:34 | 185 | 6:51–52 | 171 | 6:70–71 | 167, 191, 196, 434 |
| 6:34–40 | 171, 181, 185–86 | 6:51–53 | 444 | | |
| 6:35 | 3, 19, 20, 117, 124, 171, 177, 185, 234, 377, 399 | 6:51–56 | 10, 23, 430 | 6:71 | 194, 196 |
| | | 6:51–58 | 170 | 7–10 | 206 |
| | | 6:51c–58 | 16, 170, 174, 181, 350 | 7–8 | 204–6, 211, 229–30 |
| 6:35–51b | 183 | | | 7 | 92, 116, 167, 198–99 |
| 6:36 | 185 | 6:51d–58 | 168 | | |
| 6:36–40 | 185–86 | 6:51–66 | 168 | 7:1–10:42 | 7, 204 |
| 6:37 | 439 | 6:52 | 131, 189, 192, 244 | 7:1–10:39 | 207 |
| 6:38 | 184 | 6:52–58 | 171, 183, 190 | 7:1–10:21 | 139, 198–280 |
| 6:38–40 | 186 | 6:52–59 | 171, 181, 182, 189–91 | 7:1 | 103, 166, 208, 211, 218, 249, 527 |
| 6:39 | 158, 168, 186, 454, 510 | | | | |
| | | 6:53 | 171, 192 | 7:1–2 | 208–9 |
| 6:39–40 | 16 | 6:53–54 | 189 | 7:1–9 | 206, 207–11 |
| 6:40 | 156, 158, 168, 182, 185, 186, 430, 510 | 6:54 | 16, 158, 510 | 7:1–13 | 207–8 |
| | | 6:55 | 171, 190, 411 | | |

607

## INDEX OF PRIMARY SOURCES

| | | | | | |
|---|---|---|---|---|---|
| 7:1–52 | 198–99 | 7:25–29 | 224 | 7:40 | 218 |
| 7:2 | x, 2, 6, 8, 86, 139, 204, 208–9, 218 | 7:25–30 | 217–18 | 7:40–41 | 224 |
| | | 7:25–36 | 213, 217–21, 235, 236 | 7:40–41b | 224 |
| 7:3 | 78, 218, 236, 254, 256 | 7:26 | 71, 218, 225, 443 | 7:40–44 | 213, 220, 221, 222, 224–25, 232 |
| 7:3–4 | 208 | 7:27 | 271 | 7:40–52 | 217 |
| 7:3–5 | 209–10, 487 | 7:27–28 | 270 | 7:41 | 131 |
| 7:4 | 460, 527 | 7:27–29 | 131 | 7:41–42 | 71, 225 |
| 7:5 | 208 | 7:28 | 45, 219, 222, 344 | 7:41c–44 | 224 |
| 7:6 | 211, 527 | 7:28–29 | 217, 219–20, 271 | 7:42 | 219 |
| 7:6–8 | 208, 210 | | | 7:42–43 | 224 |
| 7:6–9 | 210–11 | 7:29 | 219 | 7:43 | 218, 259, 279 |
| 7:7 | 256, 435 | 7:30 | 211, 217, 218, 220, 225, 235, 287, 316, 443, 531 | 7:44 | 220, 224, 287, 316, 531 |
| 7:8 | 211 | | | 7:45–8:20 | 206 |
| 7:9 | 208, 210–11 | | | 7:45 | 92, 218, 225, 230 |
| 7:10–8:59 | 206–207 | 7:30–31 | 213 | 7:45–46 | 218 |
| 7:10 | 211, 249, 460 | 7:31 | 71, 88, 192, 213, 238 | 7:45–49 | 225 |
| 7:10–13 | 208, 211–13 | 7:31–32 | 217, 218, 220 | 7:45–52 | 213, 221, 222, 225–26, 229 |
| 7:10–31 | 206 | 7:31–36 | 217, 218 | | |
| 7:11 | 211–12, 213, 218 | 7:32 | 189, 213, 218, 220, 225, 287, 316, 531 | 7:47–48 | 218 |
| 7:11–12 | 315 | | | 7:48 | 92, 343 |
| 7:12 | 189, 212, 218, 220, 308 | 7:32–44 | 206 | 7:49 | 218 |
| | | 7:33 | 336, 383, 443 | 7:50 | 12, 92, 343 |
| 7:12–13 | 212–13 | 7:33–34 | 217, 220, 365, 366 | 7:50–51 | 12, 93 |
| 7:13 | 218 | | | 7:50–52 | 225, 495 |
| 7:14 | 211, 213–14, 221 | 7:33–36 | 444 | 7:51 | 225 |
| 7:14–15a | 213 | 7:34 | 236, 316 | 7:52 | 131, 227–28 |
| 7:14–18 | 213 | 7:35 | 10, 213, 218, 332 | 7:53–8:11 | 199–200, 221, 226–32, 252 |
| 7:14–19 | 213–14, 216 | 7:35–36 | 217, 220–21 | | |
| 7:14–24 | 166, 213–17 | 7:36 | 221, 228, 316 | 7:53–8:2 | 230 |
| 7:15 | 214, 216, 219 | 7:36–50 | 227 | 7:53–8:1 | 230 |
| 7:15–29 | 213 | 7:37 | 214, 219, 222, 252, 344, 491 | 7:53 | 189 |
| 7:16 | 214–15, 460 | | | 8:1 | 229 |
| 7:17–18 | 215 | 7:37a–b | 222 | 8:3 | 227 |
| 7:18 | 344 | 7:37c | 222 | 8:3–6b | 230–31 |
| 7:19 | 172, 213, 215–16 | 7:37–38 | 116, 205, 221, 223, 226, 229 | 8:3–11 | 228 |
| 7:19–23 | 162 | | | 8:4–5 | 250 |
| 7:19–24 | 229 | 7:37c–38 | 222–23 | 8:6c–8 | 230, 231 |
| 7:20 | 216, 218, 279 | 7:37–39 | 217, 222–24, 232, 492 | 8:9–11 | 230, 231–32 |
| 7:20–24 | 213, 214, 216 | | | 8:12 | 3, 39, 160, 205, 221, 226, 232, 233–34, 242, 252, 279, 285, 345, 361, 377, 399 |
| 7:21 | 214, 216, 254, 256 | 7:37–52 | 221–26 | | |
| 7:21–24 | 149, 216 | 7:38 | 222, 223, 279, 489, 490 | | |
| 7:22–24 | 216 | | | | |
| 7:25 | 213, 218, 219 | 7:39 | 221, 222, 223, 297, 327, 332, 443, 444, 490, 511 | | |
| 7:25–26 | 460 | | | | |
| 7:25–27 | 217, 218–19 | | | | |

608

## Index of Primary Sources

| | | | | | |
|---|---|---|---|---|---|
| 8:12–20 | 44, 159, 229, 232–35 | 8:31–32 | 238–39 | 8:53 | 247 |
| 8:12–30 | 233 | 8:31–36 | 233, 238–40 | 8:54 | 215, 334 |
| 8:12–59 | 200–202, 232–33 | 8:31–58 | 243 | 8:55 | 271, 434 |
| | | 8:31–59 | 233 | 8:56 | 247, 343 |
| 8:13 | 233, 234, 236 | 8:32 | 238, 241 | 8:57 | 233 |
| 8:13–14 | 234–35, 409 | 8:33 | 238, 239, 241 | 8:57–58 | 245 |
| 8:14 | 45, 131, 234, 235, 270, 271 | 8:34 | 256 | 8:57–59 | 248–49 |
| | | 8:34–36 | 239–40 | 8:58 | 247, 248–49 |
| 8:14–22 | 24 | 8:35 | 239 | 8:59 | 211, 214, 221, 233, 245, 252, 337 |
| 8:15 | 235 | 8:36 | 239 | | |
| 8:15–18 | 235 | 8:37 | 241 | 8:59c–d | 253 |
| 8:16 | 235 | 8:37–38 | 241 | 9 | 2, 12, 28, 116, 143, 148, 152, 202–3, 206, 226, 249–50 |
| 8:16–18 | 409 | 8:37–47 | 233, 240–44, 245 | | |
| 8:17–18 | 235 | | | 9:1–10:39 | 206 |
| 8:18 | 409 | 8:38 | 238, 241 | 9:1–10:21 | 206, 250 |
| 8:19 | 271 | 8:39 | 256 | 9:1 | 249, 250, 252–53, 256, 263 |
| 8:19a–b | 235 | 8:39a–c | 241 | | |
| 8:19c–f | 235 | 8:39–41a | 241 | 9:1–3 | 250 |
| 8:19–20 | 235 | 8:39d–41a | 241 | 9:1–5 | 257 |
| 8:20 | 220, 232, 235, 287, 316, 332, 443, 531 | 8:41 | 256 | 9:1–7 | 17, 19, 249–56 |
| | | 8:41–42 | 161, 382, 430, 536 | 9:1–39 | 206 |
| 8:21 | 45, 236, 256, 316, 443 | | | 9:1–41 | 202–3 |
| | | 8:41a | 241 | 9:2 | 151, 252, 253, 264 |
| 8:21–22 | 444 | 8:41b–d | 241 | 9:2–3 | 254, 256, 261, 262 |
| 8:21–24 | 236 | 8:41b–47 | 241–42 | 9:2–5 | 250, 253–54 |
| 8:21–30 | 235–37 | 8:42 | 93 | 9:3 | 253 |
| 8:21–59 | 206 | 8:42–43 | 242 | 9:3a–b | 254 |
| 8:22 | 124, 236 | 8:42–47 | 241 | 9:3–4 | 297 |
| 8:23 | 435 | 8:43 | 242 | 9:3–5 | 252, 253 |
| 8:23–24 | 236 | 8:44 | 27, 240, 242, 245, 247, 411 | 9:3b–5 | 250 |
| 8:24 | 248, 256, 357 | | | 9:3c–5 | 253 |
| 8:25 | 236–37 | 8:44–45 | 242–43 | 9:4 | 253, 256, 314, 361, 529 |
| 8:25a | 237 | 8:45 | 242 | | |
| 8:25b | 237 | 8:46 | 256, 416 | 9:4–5 | 252, 253, 254, 257, 337 |
| 8:25–30 | 236–37 | 8:46–47 | 244 | | |
| 8:26 | 237 | 8:47 | 246, 469 | 9:5 | 19, 39, 160, 206, 234, 242, 251, 253, 256, 279, 345, 399 |
| 8:27 | 237 | 8:48 | 233, 279, 308 | | |
| 8:28 | 72, 158, 207, 248, 332, 335, 336, 345, 443 | 8:48–51 | 245, 245–47 | | |
| | | 8:48–58 | 233 | 9:6 | 252–53 |
| | | 8:48–59 | 245–49 | 9:6–7 | 250, 253, 254–56, 257 |
| 8:28–29 | 237 | 8:49–50 | 246, 247 | | |
| 8:30 | 233, 237, 238 | 8:50 | 215 | 9:7 | 252–53, 253, 255, 263 |
| 8:30–31 | 192, 238 | 8:51 | 246, 247 | | |
| 8:31 | 220, 233, 238, 401, 402 | 8:52 | 233, 245, 246, 308, 434 | 9:8–11 | 250 |
| | | 8:52–56 | 245, 247–48 | 9:8–12 | 251, 257, 259 |

609

## INDEX OF PRIMARY SOURCES

| | | | | | |
|---|---|---|---|---|---|
| 9:8–41 | 250, 256–64 | 10–11 | 24 | 10:11 | 266, 276, 288, 313, 367, 377, 399 |
| 9:9 | 251, 256 | 10 | 153, 249–50 | 10:11–13 | 265 |
| 9:11 | 258, 261 | 10:1 | 249–50, 266, 268–69, 270, 271, 272, 470 | 10:11–15 | 286 |
| 9:12–39 | 250 | | | 10:11–16 | 265 |
| 9:13–17 | 251, 257, 259 | | | 10:11–18 | 270, 271, 273–78, 282 |
| 9:14 | 150, 259, 263 | 10:1–3a | 268 | | |
| 9:16 | 279 | 10:1–5 | 3, 268, 269, 271, 272, 275–76 | 10:12 | 274, 277, 278, 286, 313, 422 |
| 9:17 | 250, 251, 257, 259, 261 | | | | |
| | | 10:1–6 | 265, 266, 268–72, 282 | 10:12–13 | 276 |
| 9:17–22 | 260 | | | 10:13 | 277 |
| 9:18 | 258 | 10:1–10 | 265 | 10:13a | 274 |
| 9:18–23 | 251, 257, 259–60 | 10:1–18 | 207, 222, 250, 265, 266–67, 285–86, 317, 397, 536 | 10:14 | 266, 276, 377, 399 |
| | | | | 10:14–15 | 265, 274–75, 286 |
| 9:21 | 260 | | | | |
| 9:21–30 | 271 | | | 10:14–18 | 265 |
| 9:22 | 12, 71, 212, 219, 244, 258, 260, 263, 344, 410 | 10:1–21 | 203–4, 206, 264–79, 280 | 10:15 | 276, 367, 405 |
| | | 10:2 | 266, 268, 270 | 10:15a | 274 |
| | | 10:2–3a | 269 | 10:16 | 158, 266, 274, 276, 277, 285, 286, 313, 485 |
| 9:22–23 | 258 | 10:2–26 | 265 | | |
| 9:23 | 260 | 10:3 | 270 | | |
| 9:24–25 | 262 | 10:3–4 | 270 | 10:17 | 274, 405 |
| 9:24–34 | 251, 257, 260–61 | 10:3a–4 | 268–69 | 10:17–18 | 274, 276, 278, 288, 313, 367 |
| | | 10:3b–4 | 269 | | |
| 9:27–28 | 264 | 10:3–5 | 270, 286 | 10:18 | 268, 405 |
| 9:29–30 | 270 | 10:3b–5 | 268 | 10:19 | 259, 279 |
| 9:31 | 261 | 10:4 | 270 | 10:19–21 | 213, 220, 222, 250, 278–79, 282, 317 |
| 9:32 | 257 | 10:4–5 | 268 | | |
| 9:33 | 251, 261 | 10:5 | 269, 270 | | |
| 9:34 | 12, 250, 261, 262, 333, 344 | 10:6 | 250, 264, 266, 268, 269, 270, 285, 421 | 10:20 | 216, 279, 288 |
| | | | | 10:21 | 222, 279, 288 |
| 9:34–35 | 258, 410 | 10:7 | 266, 271–72, 377, 399 | 10:22 | x, 2, 6, 8, 139, 206, 207, 214, 222, 264, 285 |
| 9:35–38 | 251, 257, 258, 261–62, 317 | | | | |
| | | 10:7–10 | 265, 271–73, 275–76, 282, 288 | 10:22–23 | 283, 285 |
| 9:35–41 | 251 | | | 10:22–26 | 282 |
| 9:37 | 261, 262 | 10:7–18 | 266 | 10:22–30 | 250, 285 |
| 9:38 | 255 | 10:8 | 271, 272, 470 | 10:22–38 | 317, 324 |
| 9:38–39a | 262 | 10:8b | 271 | 10:22–39 | 206, 280–88, 458–459 |
| 9:39 | 45, 250, 257, 263, 468 | 10:9 | 265, 266, 271, 272, 273, 377, 399 | | |
| | | | | 10:24 | 71, 282, 283, 284 |
| 9:39–41 | 250, 252, 257, 262–64, 317 | 10:9b | 271 | 10:24–25 | 283 |
| | | 10:9–10 | 272, 286 | 10:24–26 | 285 |
| 9:40–10:21 | 206 | 10:10 | 45, 271, 272, 273, 280, 286, 430, 470 | 10:24–30 | 283 |
| 9:40 | 273 | | | 10:25 | 44, 254, 282, 283, 284, 285, 287, 409 |
| 9:40–41 | 250 | | | | |
| 9:41 | 249–50, 254, 261, 267 | 10:10–18 | 281–82 | | |

610

## Index of Primary Sources

| | | | | | |
|---|---|---|---|---|---|
| 10:26 | 282, 285 | 11:1–12:50 | x, 7, 289–346 | 11:21–27 | 292, 295, 300–303, 307 |
| 10:26–29 | 206, 265, 281-82, 283, 536 | 11:1 | 6, 7, 8, 57, 297, 320 | 11:22 | 301–3 |
| 10:27 | 286 | 11:1–3 | 296–97 | 11:22–27 | 292 |
| 10:27–30 | 282, 286 | 11:1–6 | 293, 295–98 | 11:23 | 301, 307 |
| 10:27–39 | 265 | 11:1–44 | 2, 19, 75, 254, 294, 317, 342, 380 | 11:24 | 301–2 |
| 10:28 | 283, 286, 454 | | | 11:25 | 19, 301–2, 377, 399 |
| 10:29 | 282, 286 | | | 11:25–26 | xii, 301 |
| 10:30 | 26, 93, 248, 282, 286, 288 | 11:1–46 | 289, 290–309, 444 | 11:26 | 301–2 |
| 10:31 | 473 | 11:2 | 296–97 | 11:27 | xii, 10, 72, 219, 300–303, 322, 335, 518 |
| 10:31–32 | 283, 286, 458 | 11:3 | 296–97 | | |
| 10:31–39 | 286 | 11:4 | 19, 73, 295, 296, 297, 298, 307, 308, 319 | 11:28 | 303 |
| 10:31–42 | 282 | | | 11:28–29 | 304 |
| 10:33 | 282, 283 | | | 11:28–32 | 293, 304 |
| 10:33–36 | 286–87 | 11:5 | 7, 296, 297, 361 | 11:28–37 | 303–6, 307 |
| 10:33–38 | 283 | 11:6 | 296, 298–99 | 11:30 | 291, 303, 304 |
| 10:34 | 161, 282 | 11:7 | 298–99 | 11:31 | 303, 304 |
| 10:34–36 | 71, 153, 265, 284 | 11:7–15 | 298 | 11:32 | 292, 298, 303–4 |
| | | 11:7–16 | 292–93, 296, 298–300 | 11:33 | 304–5, 333–34, 360, 370, 489 |
| 10:35 | 282 | | | | |
| 10:35–38 | 282, 283 | 11:8 | 299 | 11:33–37 | 293, 304–6 |
| 10:36 | 282, 283, 284, 287 | 11:8–10 | 295 | 11:34 | 304 |
| | | 11:9 | 256 | 11:35 | 305–6 |
| 10:37 | 282 | 11:9–10 | 254, 298–99 | 11:36 | 361 |
| 10:37–38 | 283, 287 | 11:10 | 361 | 11:36–37 | 303–4, 306, 308 |
| 10:38 | 282, 283, 288, 437 | 11:11 | 298–99 | | |
| | | 11:11–13 | 299 | 11:37 | 304 |
| 10:39 | 206, 214, 220, 249, 283, 287, 316, 320, 337, 458, 531 | 11:12 | 298–99 | 11:38 | 305, 307, 489 |
| | | 11:13 | 299 | 11:38a | 306 |
| | | 11:13–15 | 299 | 11:38–39b | 307 |
| 10:40–12:41 | 6 | 11:14 | 298 | 11:38–44 | 293, 307–8 |
| 10:40 | 6, 287, 297 | 11:14–15 | 299 | 11:38–46 | 303, 306–9 |
| 10:40–42 | 7, 53, 54, 57, 206, 207, 265, 280–88, 289, 317 | 11:15 | 296, 298–99 | 11:39–40 | xii, 292, 306 |
| | | 11:16 | 13, 28, 84, 295, 298–300, 333, 367, 410, 513, 528 | 11:39c–40 | 308 |
| | | | | 11:40 | 19, 295, 307, 319 |
| 10:41 | 7 | | | 11:41 | 429, 431 |
| 10:41–42 | 287–88 | 11:17 | 291, 300–301 | 11:41–42 | 306–7, 308 |
| 10:42 | 192, 288 | 11:17–18 | 301, 304 | 11:42 | 335 |
| 10:47–53 | 327 | 11:17–20 | 300–301, 302 | 11:43–44 | 307–8 |
| 11–12 | x, 4, 6, 7, 53, 289–346, 370, 444 | 11:17–27 | 300–303, 304 | 11:45 | 192, 307, 317 |
| | | 11:18 | 7, 300, 320 | 11:45–46 | 220, 293, 303, 304, 306–8, 309 |
| 11 | 8, 140, 148, 149, 230 | 11:19 | 301, 314 | | |
| | | 11:20 | 301, 304 | 11:45–53 | 213 |
| 11:1–21:25 | 7 | 11:21 | 292, 298, 301–3, 304 | 11:46 | 317 |
| 11:1–20:29 | 7 | | | 11:47 | 88, 312 |

611

# INDEX OF PRIMARY SOURCES

| | | | | | |
|---|---|---|---|---|---|
| 11:47–48 | 310–12 | 12:10–11 | 319 | 12:27 | 211, 220, 305, 331, 429, 443, 489 |
| 11:47–52 | 444 | 12:11 | 318 | | |
| 11:47–53 | 317, 342, 456, 458–59, 466, 478 | 12:12 | 323–24, 327 | 12:27–28 | 334, 428, 452, 455 |
| | | 12:12–13 | 325–26 | | |
| | | 12:12–15 | 483 | 12:27–28a | 333–34 |
| 11:47–54 | 289, 309–15 | 12:12–16 | 317, 323, 324 | 12:28 | 297, 319, 331, 332, 363, 430, 443 |
| 11:48 | 312 | 12:12–19 | 289, 323–28, 329, 340 | | |
| 11:49 | 456 | | | 12:28bc | 330 |
| 11:49–50 | 310–11, 312, 316 | 12:13 | 70, 71, 72, 273, 323–24, 325 | 12:28b–29 | 334–35 |
| 11:50 | 312, 444 | | | 12:28b–33 | 330–31, 334–36 |
| 11:50–52 | 312 | 12:13–16 | 324 | | |
| 11:51 | 444 | 12:14–15 | 325–26 | 12:28b–36 | 329 |
| 11:51–52 | 310–11, 312–14 | 12:15 | 323–24, 326 | 12:29 | 330, 335 |
| 11:52 | 311, 312, 314, 422, 485 | 12:16 | 297, 323, 325, 326–27, 332, 336, 361, 410 | 12:30–3:2 | 330 |
| | | | | 12:30–32 | 335–36 |
| 11:53–54 | 314 | | | 12:31 | 287, 330, 336 |
| 11:54 | 310, 314–15, 317 | 12:16–19 | 324 | 12:32 | 176, 242, 319, 330, 331, 332, 443, 467, 530, 538 |
| 11:55–19:42 | 310 | 12:17 | 324, 327 | | |
| 11:55–12:20 | 310 | 12:17–18 | 325, 327 | | |
| 11:55 | 2, 6, 8, 86, 139, 140, 207, 289, 314, 315 | 12:17–19 | 220, 317 | 12:32–34 | 444 |
| | | 12:18 | 324, 342 | 12:33 | 330, 336, 444 |
| | | 12:19 | 324, 325, 327–28, 336 | 12:34 | 71, 319, 330, 331, 332, 335, 336, 341 |
| 11:55–56 | 315–316 | | | | |
| 11:55–57 | 289, 315–16, 317 | 12:20 | 10, 338, 342, 345 | 12:34c | 72 |
| 11:56 | 316 | 12:20–22 | 330, 332 | 12:34–36 | 330–31, 336–39 |
| 11:57 | 220, 310, 316, 531 | 12:20–24 | 221 | 12:35 | 39–40, 220, 299, 330, 331, 361 |
| 12 | 140 | 12:20–28a | 330–34 | | |
| 12:1 | 6, 8, 86, 318, 501 | 12:20–36 | 174, 289, 317, 328–39, 340, 341, 363, 444, 445 | 12:35–36 | 330 |
| 12:1a | 318 | | | 12:36 | 331, 337, 341 |
| 12:1–3 | 319–20 | | | 12:36a–c | 330 |
| 12:1–8 | xii, 294–95, 297, 317, 444, 495 | 12:20–43 | 59, 337, 338 | 12:36d–e | 330 |
| | | 12:21 | 69, 331 | 12:37 | 18, 88, 340–41, 341–42, 517 |
| 12:1–11 | 13, 289, 316–23 | 12:21–36 | 69 | | |
| 12:2 | 318 | 12:22 | 65, 324, 331 | 12:37–38 | 340–43, 345 |
| 12:3–13:10 | 24 | 12:22–24 | 410 | 12:37–41 | 317 |
| 12:3 | 352 | 12:23 | 72, 77, 211, 220, 297, 331, 332, 335, 363, 422, 442, 443 | 12:37–43 | 31, 337–38, 340, 341–44 |
| 12:4 | 318 | | | | |
| 12:4–6 | 319–21 | | | 12:37–50 | 5, 289, 339–46 |
| 12:6 | 196, 272, 318, 471 | 12:23–24 | 332–33 | | |
| 12:7 | 318 | 12:23–28a | 330 | 12:38 | 161, 341, 342–43 |
| 12:7–8 | 319, 320, 321 | 12:23b–28a | 329 | | |
| 12:9 | 318 | 12:24 | 273, 319, 331 | 12:39 | 340–41 |
| 12:9b | 318 | 12:24–26 | 13 | 12:39–40 | 340 |
| 12:10 | 327 | 12:25 | 331, 333 | 12:39–41 | 341, 343 |
| 12:9–11 | 220, 317, 318, 319, 321 | 12:25–26 | 300, 333 | 12:41 | 319, 341, 343 |
| | | 12:26 | 246, 330, 331, 333 | 12:42 | 11, 12, 192, 212, |

612

## Index of Primary Sources

|  |  |
|---|---|
|  | 258, 340–41, 342, 410 |
| 12:42–43 | 220, 260, 317, 343–44, 494 |
| 12:42–44 | 341 |
| 12:43 | 211, 215, 341 |
| 12:44 | 219, 341 |
| 12:44–45 | 344–45 |
| 12:44–50 | 31, 317, 340, 341, 344–45 |
| 12:46 | 39, 160, 234, 242, 302, 361, 399, 468 |
| 12:46–47 | 156 |
| 12:46–48 | 344, 345 |
| 12:47 | 45, 346 |
| 12:49–50 | 344, 345 |
| 12:50 | 345 |
| 13–21 | 53, 75 |
| 13–20 | 4, 444 |
| 13–17 | 4, 190, 391 |
| 13–14 | 348 |
| 13 | 167, 348–49, 363, 398 |
| 13:1 | 8, 86, 211, 220, 332, 347, 348, 350–52, 405, 422, 426, 427, 439, 442, 443, 444, 453, 488 |
| 13:1–20:29 | 5 |
| 13:1–19:42 | 6 |
| 13:1–17:26 | x, xii, 347–40, 390 |
| 13:1–14:31 | 6 |
| 13:1–5 | 348, 351–52 |
| 13:1–17 | 398, 406 |
| 13:1–20 | 347, 348, 349–58 |
| 13:1–30 | 75 |
| 13:1–38 | 348, 425–26 |
| 13:2 | 196, 349, 351, 360 |
| 13:2–3 | 352 |
| 13:2–4 | 352 |
| 13:2–5 | 350 |
| 13:3 | 45, 93, 108 |
| 13:4 | 352 |

|  |  |
|---|---|
| 13:4–5 | 349, 350, 355 |
| 13:5 | 352 |
| 13:6–8 | 352–353 |
| 13:6–10 | 351, 398 |
| 13:6–11 | 348–349, 350, 352–53, 367 |
| 13:6–38 | 348 |
| 13:7 | 354 |
| 13:9–11 | 353 |
| 13:10 | 356, 399 |
| 13:10–11 | 351, 434 |
| 13:11–15 | 348 |
| 13:12 | 354, 354–355 |
| 13:12–17 | 351, 398 |
| 13:12–20 | 347, 349, 350–51, 354–57 |
| 13:13–16 | 352 |
| 13:13–17 | 354, 355–56 |
| 13:15 | 355 |
| 13:15–16 | 347 |
| 13:16 | 355, 357, 406, 408 |
| 13:16–20 | 348 |
| 13:17 | 355, 515 |
| 13:18 | 190, 196, 356, 357, 407 |
| 13:18–19 | 351 |
| 13:18–20 | 354, 356–57 |
| 13:19 | 356–57 |
| 13:20 | 354, 357 |
| 13:21 | 120, 305, 333, 360, 370, 374, 489 |
| 13:21a | 359 |
| 13:21–25 | 359, 360–61 |
| 13:21–30 | 347, 348, 348–49, 350, 353, 356, 358–62 |
| 13:21b–22 | 359 |
| 13:23 | 21, 51, 502, 541, 544 |
| 13:23–25 | 359, 361 |
| 13:25 | 541 |
| 13:26 | 360 |
| 13:26–27 | 356, 359 |
| 13:26–27a | 359, 361 |
| 13:27 | 360 |
| 13:27b–30 | 359, 361 |
| 13:28 | 360 |

|  |  |
|---|---|
| 13:28–29 | 359 |
| 13:30 | 179, 359, 452, 529 |
| 13:31–14:31 | 348, 393, 398, 413 |
| 13:31b–14:31 | 347 |
| 13:31 | 334, 335, 347, 348, 359, 362, 363–64, 365, 369, 402, 442 |
| 13:31a | 347 |
| 13:31–30 | 347 |
| 13:31–32 | 72, 73, 77, 246, 297, 332, 334, 363–65, 369, 417, 426, 429–30, 431, 539 |
| 13:31–35 | 347, 363–66 |
| 13:31–38 | 348–349, 362–67, 370 |
| 13:32 | 363, 402 |
| 13:32a | 364 |
| 13:33 | 220, 316, 336, 365, 366, 369, 372, 376, 383–84, 419–20, 443, 530 |
| 13:34 | 275 |
| 13:34–35 | 347, 348, 364, 365–66, 369, 372, 394, 398, 407, 426, 437 |
| 13:35 | 364, 366, 407, 438 |
| 13:35–38 | 353 |
| 13:36–14:31 | 347 |
| 13:36 | 363, 366, 415, 443 |
| 13:36–37 | 376 |
| 13:36–38 | 348, 365, 366–67, 369–70 |
| 13:37 | 300, 410, 536 |
| 13:37–38 | 363, 366–67 |
| 13:38 | 462 |
| 14–17 | 376 |
| 14 | xi, 348, 363, 368–92, 395–96 |
| 14:1 | 305, 333, 345, 347, 360, 363, 369, |

613

# INDEX OF PRIMARY SOURCES

|  |  |
|---|---|
|  | 373–74, 376, 387, 415, 489 |
| 14:1–3 | 387 |
| 14:1–4 | 373–76 |
| 14:1–14 | 508 |
| 14:1–31 | xi, 348, 368–92, 413 |
| 14:2 | 374, 379 |
| 14:2–3 | 370, 373, 374–76, 378, 385, 387 |
| 14:4 | 373, 376, 377 |
| 14:4–6 | 444 |
| 14:4–24 | 370 |
| 14:5 | 376–377, 415 |
| 14:5–7 | 377–79 |
| 14:5–14 | 370, 376–80, 387 |
| 14:5–24 | 375 |
| 14:6 | 39, 239, 377, 399, 417, 436 |
| 14:7 | 378 |
| 14:7–9 | 379 |
| 14:8–15:10 | 24 |
| 14:8 | 376 |
| 14:8–9 | 65 |
| 14:8–11 | 377, 379–80 |
| 14:9 | 50, 343, 345, 377 |
| 14:10 | 377 |
| 14:10c–d | 379–80 |
| 14:10e | 380 |
| 14:10–11 | 214, 287 |
| 14:10–12 | 387 |
| 14:11 | 254, 377, 380 |
| 14:12 | 377 |
| 14:12–14 | 377, 380 |
| 14:13 | 380, 407 |
| 14:13–14 | 372, 401, 420 |
| 14:14 | 380 |
| 14:15 | 380–382, 384, 387, 434 |
| 14:15–24 | 371, 372, 377, 380–86, 387, 399–400, 403–4, 498, 508–9, 510, 536 |
| 14:16 | 381, 383, 387, 409 |
| 14:16–17 | 370, 371, 372, 381, 382–83, 385, 387, 388, 414 |
| 14:17 | 271, 381, 400, 409 |
| 14:18 | 381, 400 |
| 14:18–19 | 370, 371 |
| 14:18–20 | 504 |
| 14:18–21 | 383–84, 385 |
| 14:19 | 381, 383–84, 506 |
| 14:20 | 384, 400, 437 |
| 14:20–23 | 439 |
| 14:21 | 352, 381, 384, 385, 387, 434 |
| 14:21–23 | 504 |
| 14:22 | 381 |
| 14:22–24 | 384–86 |
| 14:23 | 247, 370, 371, 375, 381, 384–85, 400 |
| 14:23–24 | 387, 434 |
| 14:24 | 381, 385 |
| 14:25 | 386, 389, 404 |
| 14:25–26 | 386, 387 |
| 14:25–27 | 418 |
| 14:25–28 | 396, 512 |
| 14:25–29 | 371, 386–387, 388, 423, 509, 513 |
| 14:25–31 | 371, 377, 386–91 |
| 14:26 | 370, 372, 382, 383, 385, 387, 409, 414, 415, 512 |
| 14:26–28 | 448, 500 |
| 14:27 | 305, 333, 360, 369, 385, 387, 415, 510, 512 |
| 14:27–29 | 387–89 |
| 14:28 | 377, 387, 404, 435, 512 |
| 14:29 | 386, 387, 389 |
| 14:30 | 335, 389, 417 |
| 14:30–31 | 371, 386, 387, 389–91 |
| 14:31 | 16, 345, 347, 348, 364, 369, 387, 389, 390–91, 402, 441, 451 |
| 15–17 | 16, 190, 265, 347, 348, 354, 364, 390–91, 391, 393–394 |
| 15–16 | 347, 394 |
| 15 | 398 |
| 15:1–16:33 | 393–94 |
| 15:1–16:4d | 348, 364, 392–412, 426 |
| 15:1 | 377, 398, 401, 403 |
| 15:1–2 | 398, 398–99 |
| 15:1–8 | 3, 267, 384, 395, 396–402, 407, 410 |
| 15:1–17 | 393–95, 398, 402, 406 |
| 15:2 | 333, 399 |
| 15:3 | 353, 399–400, 401, 436 |
| 15:3–4 | 398, 399–400 |
| 15:3–8 | 398 |
| 15:4 | 400 |
| 15:4–8 | 190 |
| 15:5 | 181 |
| 15:5b–c | 398 |
| 15:5–6 | 398, 400–401 |
| 15:6 | 398, 401 |
| 15:7 | 398, 400, 401, 420 |
| 15:7–8 | 402 |
| 15:8 | 333, 398, 401–2, 539 |
| 15:9 | 400, 402, 403 |
| 15:9–11 | 275, 395, 402–4 |
| 15:9–17 | 395, 398, 402–7, 411, 437 |
| 15:10 | 434 |
| 15:11 | 211, 402, 435 |
| 15:12 | 54, 275, 402, 404–5, 407 |
| 15:12–13 | 367 |
| 15:12–14 | 403 |
| 15:12–17 | 364, 394, 395, 402, 407 |
| 15:13 | 278, 313, 367, 403, 405–6 |
| 15:13–14 | 402 |
| 15:13–15 | 297 |

## Index of Primary Sources

| | | |
|---|---|---|
| 15:13–16 402 | 16:5–6 413–15 | 16:25 266, 285, 421 |
| 15:14 406, 407 | 16:5–7b 414 | 16:25–28 421–22 |
| 15:15 402, 403, 406, 407 | 16:6–7 418 | 16:25–33 414, 421–23, 424 |
| 15:16 196, 333, 356, 401, 402–4, 406–7 | 16:7 383, 415 | 16:26 396 |
| 15:16–17 403 | 16:7–11 423 | 16:26–27 421 |
| 15:17 402–3, 407 | 16:7–14 512 | 16:27–28 93 |
| 15:18–16:15 393 | 16:7–15 396, 418 | 16:28 45, 302, 468 |
| 15:18–16:4d 394–95, 403, 408–10, 411–12 | 16:7–22 414 | 16:29 266, 285 |
| | 16:8 416, 439 | 16:29–30 421, 422 |
| | 16:8–10 388, 396, 418, 423, 512 | 16:30 396 |
| 15:18 395 | 16:8–11 414, 415–17, 423 | 16:31–33 421, 422–423 |
| 15:18–19 211, 403 | 16:9 59 | 16:32 278, 314, 367, 422 |
| 15:18–25 403, 408–9, 435 | 16:9–11 416 | 16:33 347, 388, 396, 404, 418, 421, 422–23, 441, 510, 512 |
| 15:19 408 | 16:10 439 | |
| 15:20 152, 247, 355, 403, 408, 434 | 16:11 335 | |
| | 16:12 417 | 17 108, 125, 190, 347–48, 393, 424–40 |
| 15:21 408, 409 | 16:12–15 88, 414, 417–18, 423 | 17:1 211, 220, 297, 332, 334, 335, 402, 422, 426, 427, 428, 429–31, 442 |
| 15:21–22 403 | | |
| 15:22 380 | 16:12–25 414 | |
| 15:22–24 214, 408 | 16:13 4, 29, 380, 382, 417 | |
| 15:23 211, 395, 408 | | |
| 15:23–25 287, 403 | 16:13–15 423 | 17:1–2 429 |
| 15:24 380, 395 | 16:14 417 | 17:1–5 246, 363, 380, 426–27, 429–31, 438, 439 |
| 15:26 382, 383, 415 | 16:15 417 | |
| 15:26–27 44, 61, 300, 395, 409 | 16:16 396, 418, 419 | |
| | 16:16–19 419–20, 444 | 17:1–26 424–40 |
| 16 24 | 16:16–24 418–20, 423–24 | 17:2 427, 429, 430, 439 |
| 16:1 395 | | 17:3 54, 72, 220, 427, 429, 430 |
| 16:1–3 300 | 16:16–33 393 | |
| 16:1–4d 395, 410 | 16:17–18 418, 419–20 | 17:4 125, 183, 427, 429, 430–31, 488–89 |
| 16:2 12, 258, 260, 344, 410 | 16:19 420 | |
| | 16:19ab 418 | 17:4–5 429 |
| 16:2–3 414 | 16:19a–b 419 | 17:5 297, 335, 402, 426, 427, 429, 430–31, 433 |
| 16:4–33 xi | 16:19c–e 418, 419 | |
| 16:4a 395 | 16:19–22 420 | |
| 16:4b–33 364 | 16:20 419, 420 | 17:5–6 427 |
| 16:4d 395 | 16:20–22 388, 396, 404, 415, 418, 419, 420, 423, 435, 511, 512 | 17:6 247, 254, 429, 432–33, 434 |
| 16:4e 395, 414, 418 | | |
| 16:4e–7 414–15 | | 17:6–8 426, 427, 432–33, 437 |
| 16:4e–15 414–18 | 16:21 419, 420 | |
| 16:4e–33 363, 388, 393–94, 396, 412–24, 426, 448, 500, 512 | 16:21–22 418 | 17:6–19 426, 431–36, 437 |
| | 16:22 419, 420 | |
| | 16:23–24 396, 414, 418, 419, 420 | 17:7 427, 432 |
| | | 17:8 427, 432–33, 437 |
| 16:5 395–96, 415 | 16:24 211, 435 | 17:8a–c 432 |

INDEX OF PRIMARY SOURCES

| | | | | | |
|---|---|---|---|---|---|
| 17:9 | 426, 427, 433 | | 348, 389, 446, 451, | 18:17 | 454, 457 |
| 17:9–11a | 432 | | 452, 461, 495, 496 | 18:18 | 457, 462 |
| 17:9–11c | 432, 433–34 | 18:1–3 | 446, 450, | 18:19 | 459, 460 |
| 17:9–19 | 426, 432 | | 451–52, 465 | 18:19–23 | 458 |
| 17:10 | 427, 438 | 18:1–4 | 446 | 18:19–24 | 446, 458–61 |
| 17:11 | 275, 427, 433–34, | 18:1–11 | 445, 450 | 18:20 | 88, 191, 214, 219 |
| | 435–36 | 18:1–27 | 445, 449–63 | 18:20–21 | 459, 460 |
| 17:11a–c | 432, 433 | 18:2–3 | 452, 454 | 18:20–23 | 457 |
| 17:11–12 | 427 | 18:2–4 | 446 | 18:22 | 459, 460 |
| 17:11d | 432 | 18:3 | 225 | 18:23 | 459, 460–61 |
| 17:11d–16 | 434–36 | 18:4 | 316, 452, 453, | 18:24 | 458, 459, 461 |
| 17:12 | 434, 435, 454 | | 488, 506 | 18:25 | 454, 462 |
| 17:12–13 | 434 | 18:4–9 | 446, 450–51, | 18:25–27 | 446, 452, |
| 17:12a–13 | 432 | | 453–54 | | 461–63, 536 |
| 17:13 | 435, 438 | 18:5 | 224, 453, 457 | 18:26 | 311–12 |
| 17:13–16 | 427 | 18:5–6 | 453 | 18:26–27 | 462–63 |
| 17:14 | 427 | 18:5–8 | 454 | 18:27 | 454 |
| 17:14c–d | 436 | 18:6 | 225, 453 | 18:28–19:16b | 446, |
| 17:14–15 | 434, 435 | 18:7 | 453, 506 | | 464–79 |
| 17:15 | 432, 434, 435 | 18:7–8 | 316, 453 | 18:28–19:16a | 445 |
| 17:16 | 432, 436 | 18:8 | 453, 457, 460 | 18:28 | 447, 461, 465, |
| 17:17 | 432, 436 | 18:9 | 454, 493 | | 466, 475, 491 |
| 17:17–19 | 428, 432, 436 | 18:10 | 451, 454–55, 459 | 18:28–32 | 446, 465–67, |
| 17:18 | 275, 427, 436 | 18:10–11 | 446, 450, | | 470, 475 |
| 17:19 | 427, 432, 436 | | 454–55 | 18:29 | 472 |
| 17:20 | 426 | 18:10–12 | 452 | 18:29–30 | 466–67 |
| 17:20–21 | 437–38 | 18:11 | 455 | 18:29–32 | 475 |
| 17:20–22 | 432 | 18:12 | 316, 452, 455–56 | 18:31 | 467, 481 |
| 17:20–23 | 426, 434, | 18:12–13 | 538 | 18:31–33 | 24 |
| | 436–39 | 18:12–14 | 446, 450, | 18:32 | 454, 465, 467 |
| 17:21 | 26, 275, 366, 384, | | 455–56 | 18:33–34 | 467–68 |
| | 407, 427, 438 | 18:12–27 | 445 | 18:33–37 | 446 |
| 17:21–23 | 427 | 18:13 | 312, 455, 456, 458 | 18:33–38b | 467–69, 470, |
| 17:22 | 427, 437 | 18:13a | 458 | | 473, 474, |
| 17:22–23 | 437, 438 | 18:13b | 458 | | 478–79 |
| 17:23 | 108, 384, 427, | 18:13–14 | 456 | 18:34–36 | 467 |
| | 438, 489 | 18:14 | 455, 456, 458 | 18:35 | 124 |
| 17:24 | 73, 426, 427, 439 | 18:14–23 | 458 | 18:35–36 | 468 |
| 17:24–26 | 426, 438–39 | 18:15 | 66, 130, 458 | 18:36–19:1 | 24 |
| 17:25 | 427, 439 | 18:15–16 | 23 | 18:36 | 468, 472 |
| 17:26 | 108, 426, 427, 439 | 18:15–16a | 457 | 18:36–37 | 94, 178, 215 |
| 18–20 | 441, 445 | 18:15–18 | 446, 456–57, | 18:37 | 45, 270, 302, 378, |
| 18–19 | 499 | | 536 | | 468–69, 472, 479 |
| 18:1–20:31 | x, 6, 441–519 | 18:16 | 457 | 18:37–38 | 24, 239 |
| 18:1–19:30 | 450 | 18:16b–d | 457 | 18:37f–38a | 467 |
| 18:1 | 16, 230, 311–12, | 18:16–18 | 458 | 18:38a–b | 469 |

## Index of Primary Sources

| | | | | | |
|---|---|---|---|---|---|
| 18:38c | 472 | 19:18 | 482, 485 | 19:42 | 494, 495–96 |
| 18:38c–e | 470 | 19:19 | 224, 482 | 20 | 24, 447–48, 496–519 |
| 18:38c–f | 470 | 19:19–20 | 482–83 | 20:1 | 501 |
| 18:38–40 | 446 | 19:19–22 | 447, 478, 482–84 | 20:1–2 | 13, 316, 322, 448, 487, 500–501, 505 |
| 18:38c–40 | 470–71, 478 | 19:20–22 | 447 | | |
| 18:39 | 447, 470 | 19:21–22 | 483–84 | 20:1–10 | 448, 499–500 |
| 18:40 | 470–71 | 19:23 | 420, 487 | 20:1–18 | 447, 499–500, 508 |
| 19–20 | 229 | 19:23a–f | 484 | | |
| 19:1 | 470, 471–72 | 19:23–24 | 447, 484–85 | 20:1–31 | 496–519 |
| 19:1–3 | 446, 465, 471–72, 478 | 19:23g–24 | 484–85 | 20:2 | 21, 462–63, 501, 506 |
| 19:2–3 | 472 | 19:24 | 493 | | |
| 19:2–7 | 24 | 19:25 | 486–87 | 20:2–3 | 457 |
| 19:3–4 | 481 | 19:25–27 | 13, 75, 210, 322, 447, 485–88 | 20:3 | 502 |
| 19:4–5 | 472–73 | | | 20:3–10 | 361, 448, 500, 502–3, 505, 530 |
| 19:4–7 | 446, 472–73, 478 | 19:26 | 21 | | |
| | | 19:26–27 | 487–88, 502 | 20:4 | 502 |
| 19:6 | 466 | 19:28 | 115, 116, 125, 453, 488–89 | 20:5 | 502 |
| 19:6–7 | 473 | | | 20:6 | 502 |
| 19:7 | 474 | 19:28–30 | 447, 488–90, 496 | 20:6–7 | 495 |
| 19:7–11 | 479 | | | 20:7 | 502 |
| 19:8–9 | 474 | 19:29 | 489 | 20:8 | 361, 502–3 |
| 19:8–12 | 446, 473–75, 478 | 19:30 | 431, 442, 488, 489–90, 492 | 20:9 | 70, 503, 506 |
| | | 19:31 | 491, 494 | 20:10 | 503 |
| 19:9 | 80, 270 | 19:31–37 | 447, 490–94, 509 | 20:11 | 505, 506 |
| 19:9–11 | 131 | | | 20:11–13 | 501, 505, 506 |
| 19:10–11 | 474–75 | 19:32 | 491, 494 | 20:11–17 | 448, 500 |
| 19:11 | 105, 485 | 19:33 | 491 | 20:11–18 | 316, 322, 448, 487, 500, 504–8 |
| 19:12 | 72, 474, 475 | 19:34 | 10, 223 | | |
| 19:13 | 476–77 | 19:34–35 | 491 | 20:14 | 506 |
| 19:13–16b | 446, 475–78 | 19:35 | 159, 220, 491, 492–93, 542–43 | 20:14–16 | 505, 506–7 |
| 19:14 | 150, 314, 447, 466, 481 | | | 20:15 | 312, 322, 452, 495, 507 |
| 19:14ab | 477 | 19:36 | 491, 492, 493 | | |
| 19:14c–15 | 477 | 19:37 | 423, 491, 493–94 | 20:16 | 505, 506–7 |
| 19:15 | 466, 477 | 19:38 | 260, 494 | 20:17 | 22, 96, 184 |
| 19:15–19 | 72 | 19:38–39 | 226 | 20:17–18 | 505, 507 |
| 19:16a | 481 | 19:38–40 | 11 | 20:18 | 448, 500, 505, 513–14 |
| 19:16a–b | 465, 477–78 | 19:38–42 | 447, 490, 494–96 | | |
| 19:16b–42 | 445 | | | 20:19 | 22, 212, 383, 388, 423, 448, 509–10, 511, 533 |
| 19:16c | 481–82 | 19:39 | 12, 22, 93, 343, 361, 494–95 | | |
| 19:16c–18 | 447, 481–82 | | | | |
| 19:16c(17)–19 | 447 | 19:39–42 | 494 | 20:19–20 | 509, 528 |
| 19:16c–42 | 447, 466, 479–96 | 19:40 | 495 | 20:19–23 | 388, 418, 448, 463, 498, 500, |
| | | 19:41 | 312, 322, 452, 494, 495 | | |
| 19:17 | 482 | | | | |

617

## INDEX OF PRIMARY SOURCES

| | | | | | |
|---|---|---|---|---|---|
| | 501, 504, 508–13, 514, 521, 530 | 21:1–14 | 3, 177, 361, 523–34, 539 | 21:20 | 21, 524, 540–41, 542 |
| 20:19–29 | 447, 448, 499, 500, 508 | 21:1–15 | 542–43 | 21:20–21 | 540–41 |
| | | 21:1–17 | 67 | 21:20–22 | 523, 535, 540 |
| 20:20 | 388, 404, 511, 527 | 21:1–23 | 526 | 21:20–23 | 535, 540–42, 543 |
| 20:20a | 509 | 21:1–24 | 5 | | |
| 20:20b | 509 | 21:1–25 | x, xi, xii, 7, 520–46 | 21:20–25 | 540–45 |
| 20:21 | 388, 423, 509, 511 | | | 21:21 | 540–41 |
| 20:21–23 | 509, 528 | 21:2 | 513, 528, 534 | 21:21–22 | 526 |
| 20:22 | 490, 511 | 21:2–3 | 527 | 21:21–23 | 540 |
| 20:22a | 509 | 21:2–14 | 527 | 21:22 | 538, 541 |
| 20:22b–23 | 509 | 21:2–23 | 527 | 21:23 | 523, 535, 540, 541, 542 |
| 20:23 | 512 | 21:3 | 526, 528, 529, 534 | | |
| 20:24 | 194, 513 | 21:4 | 88, 527, 529–30 | 21:24 | 21, 23, 61, 159, 361, 362, 491, 493, 516, 523, 535, 540, 541–43, 544, 545 |
| 20:24–25 | 448, 500, 513–14 | 21:4–6 | 529 | | |
| | | 21:4–8 | 527, 529–31 | | |
| 20:24–28 | 448, 500 | 21:4–11 | 534 | | |
| 20:24–29 | 437, 448, 500, 516 | 21:5 | 529–30 | 21:24–25 | 542–45 |
| | | 21:6 | 529, 529–30, 531 | 21:25 | 5, 523, 540, 543, 545 |
| 20:25 | 508, 513–14 | 21:7 | 21, 361, 524, 526, 528, 529–30, 534, 535, 538 | | |
| 20:26 | 383, 388, 514, 527, 528, 533 | | | **Acts** | |
| | | 21:8 | 529–31 | 1:8 | 103 |
| 20:26–28 | 501 | 21:9 | 457, 531 | 1:14 | 210 |
| 20:26–29 | 448, 500, 513, 514–16, 521, 530 | 21:9–13 | 527, 530 | 2 | 490, 509 |
| | | 21:9–14 | 527, 531–34 | 3:6 | 148 |
| 20:27 | 514–15 | 21:10 | 531 | 3:11 | 285 |
| 20:28 | 3, 48, 286, 515 | 21:11 | 485, 531, 532, 534 | 4:6 | 456, 460, 543 |
| 20:29 | 356, 515–16 | 21:12 | 531, 532–33, 535 | 5:12 | 285 |
| 20:30–21:25 | 526 | 21:13 | 531, 533 | 6:1 | 332 |
| 20:30 | 342, 517–18 | 21:14 | 254, 319, 527, 531, 533 | 6:7–8:3 | 412 |
| 20:30f | 516 | | | 6:13–14 | 84 |
| 20:30–31 | 5, 7, 9, 10, 18, 26, 28, 131, 340, 433, 448, 499, 500, 509, 516–18, 521, 523, 527, 540, 542, 545 | 21:15 | 532, 535, 536 | 6:14 | 85 |
| | | 21:15–17 | 21, 162, 195, 196, 272, 454, 455, 523, 526, 531, 534, 535–38, 539, 540 | 7:52 | 130 |
| | | | | 7:59 | 473 |
| | | | | 8:4–8 | 126 |
| | | | | 8:14–17 | 126 |
| | | 21:15–19 | 269, 463, 534–39 | 9:4 | 453 |
| 20:31 | x, 11, 71, 72, 108, 219, 430, 483, 493, 518 | | | 10:2 | 137 |
| | | 21:15–23 | 535 | 10:41 | 533 |
| | | 21:17 | 535 | 11:14 | 137 |
| 21 | x, xi, xii, 3, 7, 16, 35, 48, 195, 440, 520–46 | 21:18 | 13, 538, 539 | 12:1–2 | 412 |
| | | 21:18–19 | 300, 366, 523, 526, 534–35, 538–39, 540 | 12:2 | 522 |
| | | | | 13:25 | 57, 58 |
| 21:1 | 173, 254, 527 | | | 14:3 | 160 |
| 21:1–3 | 527–29 | 21:19 | 417, 538–39, 540 | 14:10 | 148 |

618

## Index of Primary Sources

| | | | | | |
|---|---|---|---|---|---|
| 16:15 | 137 | 13:13 | 155 | **1 Peter** | |
| 16:31 | 137 | | | 5:1 | 537 |
| 16:34 | 137 | **Galatians** | | 5:1–4 | 269, 537 |
| 18:8 | 137 | 1:19 | 210 | 5:2 | 537 |
| 18:24–19:7 | 9 | 4 | 239 | | |
| 19:3–4 | 43 | 4:4 | 26 | **2 Peter** | |
| 20:18–35 | 269 | 5:14 | 404 | 2:19 | 239 |
| 20:28 | 537 | | | | |
| 22:7 | 453 | **Ephesians** | | **1 John** | |
| 26:14 | 453 | 1:10 | 50 | 1:1–4 | 23, 545 |
| 28:26–27 | 343 | 1:23 | 50 | 1:4 | 211, 404, 435 |
| | | 4:11 | 537 | 1:6 | 99 |
| **Romans** | | | | 1:10 | 107 |
| 1:3–4 | 155 | **Philippians** | | 2:1 | 383 |
| 4:25 | 442 | 2:2–11 | 26 | 2:5 | 384 |
| 8:27 | 383 | 2:6–11 | 155 | 2:7 | 366 |
| 8:28 | 382 | 2:9f. | 431 | 2:14 | 530 |
| 8:34 | 383 | 2:9–10 | 431 | 2:15 | 162 |
| 9–11 | 342 | | | 2:16 | 469 |
| 10:16 | 342 | **Colossians** | | 2:18 | 530 |
| 11:8 | 343 | 1:15–18 | 26 | 2:18–19 | 191 |
| 11:16–20 | 122 | 1:16 | 39, 41 | 2:19 | 411 |
| 13:8 | 404–5 | 1:19 | 50 | 2:29–3:10 | 243 |
| 13:9–10 | 405 | | | 3:10 | 469 |
| 14:17 | 388, 396, 418, 423, | **1 Thessalonians** | | 3:11 | 54 |
| | 448, 500, 512–13 | 1:9 | 404 | 3:12–15 | 242 |
| 15:21 | 338 | 2:13 | 215 | 3:16–17 | 162 |
| | | 4:13–18 | 375 | 4:1–3 | 191 |
| **1 Corinthians** | | 5:4 | 40 | 4:1–6 | 243 |
| 2:9 | 382 | 5:12 | 114, 125 | 4:2–3 | 49 |
| 8:6 | 41 | | | 4:3 | 469 |
| 9:1 | 508, 513 | **2 Thessalonians** | | 4:4 | 423 |
| 9:5 | 210 | 2:3 | 434 | 4:7–21 | 162 |
| 10:3 | 224 | | | 4:9 | 51 |
| 10:4 | 224 | **Hebrews** | | 4:12 | 384 |
| 11:17–34 | 358 | 1:1–4 | 155 | 4:14 | 545 |
| 11:23–36 | 175 | 1:3 | 26 | 5:4–5 | 423 |
| 11:24 | 188 | 2:4 | 160 | 5:6 | 382 |
| 15 | 375 | 5:7 | 306 | 5:6–7 | 492 |
| 15:3–4 | 442 | 7:25 | 383 | | |
| 15:3–8 | 505 | 11:37 | 130 | **2 John** | |
| 15:51–52 | 375 | 13:20 | 537 | 5 | 366 |
| 16:16 | 114 | | | 7 | 49 |
| | | **James** | | 12 | 211 |
| **2 Corinthians** | | 2:23 | 406 | | |
| 3:7–18 | 503 | | | | |

619

## 3 John
| | |
|---|---|
| 3 | 469 |
| 9 | 159 |

## Revelation
| | |
|---|---|
| 1:1–2 | 107 |
| 2:13 | 479 |
| 5:12–13 | 365 |
| 7:12 | 365 |
| 11:3 | 479 |
| 12:10 | 364–65 |
| 17:6 | 479 |
| 19:9 | 18 |
| 21:4 | 424 |

# APOCRYPHA AND PSEUDEPIGRAPHA

## Baruch
| | |
|---|---|
| 4:37 | 313 |
| 5:5 | 313 |

## 2 Baruch
| | |
|---|---|
| 48:2–24 | 427 |

## 1 Enoch
| | |
|---|---|
| 83–90 | 267 |
| 89 | 267 |
| 90.38 | 59 |

## 4 Ezra
| | |
|---|---|
| 5:23 | 397 |
| 8:20–36 | 427 |

## Jubilees
| | |
|---|---|
| 16:1ff | 248 |
| 20.7 | 382 |
| 23:10 | 248 |
| 23:11 | 248 |
| 23:15 | 248 |
| 36.5ff. | 382 |

## 1 Maccabees
| | |
|---|---|
| 9:10 | 406 |
| 13:51 | 326 |

## 2 Maccabees
| | |
|---|---|
| 1:9 | 285 |
| 6:28 | 406 |
| 7:9 | 406 |
| 7:37 | 406 |
| 8:21 | 406 |
| 10:7 | 326 |
| 14:37 | 406 |

## Odes of Solomon   13, 19

## Protoevangelium of James
| | |
|---|---|
| 9:2 | 209–10 |
| 17:1–2 | 209–10 |
| 18:1 | 209–10 |

## Sirach
| | |
|---|---|
| 2:15–16 | 382 |
| 24:1–22 | 40 |
| 24:17 | 397 |
| 24:21 | 117, 185 |

## Testament of Benjamin
| | |
|---|---|
| 3.1 | 382 |

## Testament of Joseph
| | |
|---|---|
| 19.8 | 59 |

## Testament of Naphtali
| | |
|---|---|
| 6.1–10 | 179 |

## Testaments of the Twelve Patriarchs   243

## Tobit
| | |
|---|---|
| 13:15 | 313 |

## Wisdom
| | |
|---|---|
| 6:12–16 | 40 |
| 7:13–14 | 406 |
| 7:22–8:1 | 40 |
| 7:27 | 406 |
| 9:1f. | 41 |
| 9:9–10 | 40 |

# CANON DOCUMENTS

("Denzinger-Schönmetzer")
| | |
|---|---|
| DS 180 | 25 |
| DS 186 | 25 |
| DS 1335 | 25 |
| DS 1503 | 25 |
| DS 1504 | 227 |

Muratorian Canon
| | |
|---|---|
| 9 | 21, 25 |

# CODICES

| | |
|---|---|
| Codex 131 | 146 |

Codex Alexandrinus
147, 227, 249

Codex Bezae Cantabrigiensis (D)
38, 227, 249, 321, 419, 502

| | |
|---|---|
| Codex C | 38, 51 |
| Codex L | 286 |

Codex Sinaiticus (Syrosinaiticus)
51, 146, 227, 254, 286, 321, 419, 543

Codex Vaticanus
24–25, 51, 186, 227, 249, 254, 286

Codex Veronensis ("b")
46

Liber Comicus (Lectionary of Toledo)
46

# Index of Primary Sources

## EARLY CHRISTIAN LITERATURE

**Augustine**

*In Evangelium Johannis tractatus*
| | |
|---|---|
| 16.3 | 130 |
| 222 | 389 |

**Cyril of Alexandria**

*In Joannis Evangelium*
| | |
|---|---|
| 531ff. | 390 |

**Didache**
| | |
|---|---|
| 9.4 | 313 |
| 10.9 | 313 |

**Epiphanius**

*Panarion*
| | |
|---|---|
| 33.6 | 22 |

**Epistula Apostolorum** 46

**Eusebius**

*Historia ecclesiastica*
| | |
|---|---|
| 3.31.3 | 21 |
| 3.39.3f. | 22 |
| 6.14.7 | 21 |

**Hippolytus of Rome**

*In Canticum canticorum*
| | |
|---|---|
| 67 | 508 |

*Refutatio omnium haeresium*
| | |
|---|---|
| 7.22.4f. | 22 |
| 7.27.5 | 22 |

**Ignatius of Antioch**

*Epistle to the Ephesians*
| | |
|---|---|
| 20.2 | 313 |

*Epistle to the Philadelphians*
| | |
|---|---|
| 4 | 189 |

*Epistle to the Romans*
| | |
|---|---|
| 7.3 | 189 |

*Epistle to the Smyrnaeans*
| | |
|---|---|
| 7.1 | 189 |

**Irenaeus**

*Adversus haereses*
| | |
|---|---|
| 2.22.5 | 21 |
| 3.1.2 | 23 |

**Jerome**

*Commentariorum in Ezechielem libri XVI*
| | |
|---|---|
| 717 | 532 |

**Justin Martyr**

*Apologia i*
| | |
|---|---|
| 35.6 | 476 |
| 66.2 | 189 |

*Dilogus cum Tryphone*
| | |
|---|---|
| 8.4 | 219 |
| 90.1 | 219 |
| 106.1 | 22 |

**New Testament minuscules**
| | |
|---|---|
| 225 | 221, 227–28 |

**Origen**

*Commentarii in evangelium Joannis*
| | |
|---|---|
| 13.54–55.236–43 | 128, 130 |
| 17.167 | 40 |
| 17.168–70 | 40 |

**Papias**

"Interpretation of the Words of the Lord" 22

**Theophilus of Antioch**

*Ad Autolycum*
| | |
|---|---|
| 2.22 | 22 |

## GREEK AND ROMAN HISTORIANS

**Achilles Tatius**

*Leucippe et Cliptophon*
| | |
|---|---|
| 2.2.1–6 | 82 |

**Aristotle**

*Ethica nicomachea*
| | |
|---|---|
| 1169a | 405–6 |

*Rhetorica*
| | |
|---|---|
| 3.1414b | 35 |

**Corpus Hermeticum** 19, 99–100, 427

**Dio Chrysostom**

*Oration*
| | |
|---|---|
| 3.31 | 178 |

**Diodorus Siculus**
| | |
|---|---|
| 3.66.3 | 81 |
| 4.43 | 178 |

**Euripides**

*Bacchae*
| | |
|---|---|
| 142f | 81 |
| 423f | 81 |
| 651 | 81 |
| 706f | 81 |
| 773f | 81 |

**Homer**

*Hymn to Dionysus*
| | |
|---|---|
| 35–37 | 81 |

# INDEX OF PRIMARY SOURCES

**Lucian**

*Philopseudes*
13 — 178

*Vera historia*
1.7 — 81

**Ovid**

*Metamorphoses*
8.679–83 — 82

**Pausanius**
6.26.1f — 81

**Plato**

*Ion*
534A — 81

**Pliny the Elder**

*Naturalis historia*
2.18.74 — 18
2.231 — 81
5.74 — 82

**Pliny the Younger**

*Epistulae*
10.96f. — 412

**Tacitus**

*Annales*
6.8 — 475

## JEWISH-HELLENISTIC LITERATURE

**Josephus**

*Antiquitates judaicae*
9.288 — 120

*Contra Apionem*
2.53 — 160

**Philo of Alexandria**

*De cherubim*
127 — 41

*Legum allegoriae*
2.55 — 160
3.96 — 41

*De migratione Abrahami*
6 — 41
89–93 — 149

*De vita Mosis*
3.263–81 — 160

*De opificio mundi*
29–35 — 41

*De specialibus legibus*
1.81 — 41

**Pseudo-Philo**

LAB (Liber antiquitatum biblicarum)
12:8 — 397
18:10f. — 397

## NAG HAMMADI TEXTS

Gospel of Thomas — 516
31 — 129, 131
logion 1 — 246
logion 18 — 246
logion 19 — 246
logion 85 — 246

Secret Book of John
NHC II 1 — 20
NHC IV 1 — 20

Three Forms of First Thought
NHC XIII 1 — 20, 41

Thunder: Perfect Mind
NHC VI 2 — 20

## PAPYRUS DOCUMENTS

P5 — 24, 421
P28 — 24
P39 — 24
P45 — 24, 25, 297
P46 — 25
P47 — 25
P52 — 24
P60 — 470
P66 — 22, 24–25, 46–47, 51, 186, 221, 227, 254, 286, 297, 417, 421, 438
P75 — 22, 24–25, 38, 47, 51, 127, 186, 227, 248, 254, 262, 271, 286
P80 — 24
P90 — 24
P95 — 24

Papyrus Egerton
2 — 24

POxy (Oxyrhynchus Papyri)
1.6 — 129, 131

## QUMRAN TEXTS

1QH (Thanksgiving Hymns)
16.7 — 382
16.13 — 382
16.17 — 382

1QM (War Scroll)
1.1–17 — 234
11.7f. — 106–7

## Index of Primary Sources

| | | |
|---|---|---|
| 13.5–16 | 234 | |

**1QS (Rule of the Community)**
| | |
|---|---|
| 3.13–4.26 | 234, 243 |
| 8.1–2 | 99 |
| 8.6 | 469 |

**3Q15.11–12 (Copper Scroll)** 147

**11Q Melch (Melchizedek Document)** 248, 284

**CD (Damascus Document)**
| | |
|---|---|
| 19.1f. | 382 |
| 20.21f. | 382 |

## RABBINIC LITERATURE

**Babylonian Talmud**
| | |
|---|---|
| b.Ber 28b | 260 |

**Mishnah 'Abot**
| | |
|---|---|
| 3.15 | 41 |

**Mishnah Šabb**
| | |
|---|---|
| 7.2 | 151 |
| 10.5 | 151 |

**Mishnah Sukkah**
| | |
|---|---|
| 4:9–10 | 205 |
| 5:1–4 | 205 |
| 5:4 | 205 |

www.ingramcontent.com/pod-product-compliance
Lightning Source LLC
Chambersburg PA
CBHW031538300426
44111CB00006BA/94